Dictionary of Literary Biography

Dictionary of Literary Biography Documentary Series

Dictionary of Literary Biography Yearbooks

1980 edited by Karen L. Rood, Jean W. Ross, and Richard Ziegfeld (1981)

1981 edited by Karen L. Rood, Jean W. Ross, and Richard Ziegfeld (1982)

1982 edited by Richard Ziegfeld; associate editors: Jean W. Ross and Lynne C. Zeigler (1983)

1983 edited by Mary Bruccoli and Jean W. Ross; associate editor Richard Ziegfeld (1984)

1984 edited by Jean W. Ross (1985)

1985 edited by Jean W. Ross (1986)

1986 edited by J. M. Brook (1987)

1987 edited by J. M. Brook (1988)

1988 edited by J. M. Brook (1989)

1989 edited by J. M. Brook (1990)

1990 edited by James W. Hipp (1991)

1991 edited by James W. Hipp (1992)

1992 edited by James W. Hipp (1993)

1993 edited by James W. Hipp, contributing editor George Garrett (1994)

1994 edited by James W. Hipp, contributing editor George Garrett (1995)

1995 edited by James W. Hipp, contributing editor George Garrett (1996)

1996 edited by Samuel W. Bruce and L. Kay Webster, contributing editor George Garrett (1997)

1997 edited by Matthew J. Bruccoli and George Garrett, with the assistance of L. Kay Webster (1998)

1998 edited by Matthew J. Bruccoli, contributing editor George Garrett, with the assistance of D. W. Thomas (1999)

1999 edited by Matthew J. Bruccoli, contributing editor George Garrett, with the assistance of D. W. Thomas (2000)

2000 edited by Matthew J. Bruccoli, contributing editor George Garrett, with the assistance of George Parker Anderson (2001)

2001 edited by Matthew J. Bruccoli, contributing editor George Garrett, with the assistance of George Parker Anderson (2002)

2002 edited by Matthew J. Bruccoli and George Garrett; George Parker Anderson, Assistant Editor (2003)

Concise Series

Concise Dictionary of American Literary Biography, 7 volumes (1988–1999): *The New Consciousness, 1941–1968; Colonization to the American Renaissance, 1640–1865; Realism, Naturalism, and Local Color, 1865–1917; The Twenties, 1917–1929; The Age of Maturity, 1929–1941; Broadening Views, 1968–1988; Supplement: Modern Writers, 1900–1998.*

Concise Dictionary of British Literary Biography, 8 volumes (1991–1992): *Writers of the Middle Ages and Renaissance Before 1660; Writers of the Restoration and Eighteenth Century, 1660–1789; Writers of the Romantic Period, 1789–1832; Victorian Writers, 1832–1890; Late-Victorian and Edwardian Writers, 1890–1914; Modern Writers, 1914–1945; Writers After World War II, 1945–1960; Contemporary Writers, 1960 to Present.*

Concise Dictionary of World Literary Biography, 4 volumes (1999–2000): *Ancient Greek and Roman Writers; German Writers; African, Caribbean, and Latin American Writers; South Slavic and Eastern European Writers.*

Dictionary of Literary Biography® • Volume Three Hundred Eighteen

Sixteenth-Century Spanish Writers

Dictionary of Literary Biography® • Volume Three Hundred Eighteen

Sixteenth-Century Spanish Writers

Edited by
Gregory B. Kaplan
University of Tennessee

A Bruccoli Clark Layman Book

THOMSON
GALE

Detroit • New York • San Francisco • San Diego • New Haven, Conn. • Waterville, Maine • London • Munich

Dictionary of Literary Biography
Volume 318: Sixteenth-Century Spanish Writers
Gregory B. Kaplan

Editorial Directors
Matthew J. Bruccoli and Richard Layman

© 2006 Thomson Gale, a part of The Thomson Corporation.

Thomson and Star Logo are trademarks and Gale is a registered trademark used herein under license.

For more information, contact
Thomson Gale
27500 Drake Rd.
Farmington Hills, MI 48331-3535
Or you can visit our Internet site at
http://www.gale.com

While every effort has been made to ensure the reliability of the information presented in this publication, Thomson Gale does not guarantee the accuracy of the data contained herein. Thomson Gale accepts no payment for listing; and inclusion in the publication of any organization, agency, institution, publication, service, or individual does not imply endorsement of the editors or publisher. Errors brought to the attention of the publisher and verified to the satisfaction of the publisher will be corrected in future editions.

LIBRARY OF CONGRESS CATALOGING-IN-PUBLICATION DATA

Sixteenth-century Spanish writers / edited by Gregory B. Kaplan.
   p. cm. — (Dictionary of literary biography ; v. 318)
  "A Bruccoli Clark Layman book."
  Includes bibliographical references and index.
  ISBN 0–7876–8136–9 (hardcover : alk. paper)
  1. Spanish literature—Classical period, 1500–1700—Bio-bibliography—Dictionaries.
  2. Authors, Spanish—Classical period, 1500–1700 century—Biography—Dictionaries.
  I. Title: 16th-century Spainsh writers. II. Kaplan, Gregory B., 1966- III. Series.
  PQ6064.S59 2005
  860.9'003'03—dc22
                               2005015169

Printed in the United States of America
10 9 8 7 6 5 4 3 2 1

For my wife, Nuria Cruz-Cámara, and our son, Andrew

Contents

Contents

Plan of the Series

. . . Almost the most prodigious asset of a country, and perhaps its most precious possession, is its native literary product— when that product is fine and noble and enduring.

Mark Twain*

The advisory board, the editors, and the publisher of the *Dictionary of Literary Biography* are joined in endorsing Mark Twain's declaration. The literature of a nation provides an inexhaustible resource of permanent worth. Our purpose is to make literature and its creators better understood and more accessible to students and the reading public, while satisfying the needs of teachers and researchers.

To meet these requirements, *literary biography* has been construed in terms of the author's achievement. The most important thing about a writer is his writing. Accordingly, the entries in *DLB* are career biographies, tracing the development of the author's canon and the evolution of his reputation.

The purpose of *DLB* is not only to provide reliable information in a usable format but also to place the figures in the larger perspective of literary history and to offer appraisals of their accomplishments by qualified scholars.

The publication plan for *DLB* resulted from two years of preparation. The project was proposed to Bruccoli Clark by Frederick G. Ruffner, president of the Gale Research Company, in November 1975. After specimen entries were prepared and typeset, an advisory board was formed to refine the entry format and develop the series rationale. In meetings held during 1976, the publisher, series editors, and advisory board approved the scheme for a comprehensive biographical dictionary of persons who contributed to literature. Editorial work on the first volume began in January 1977, and it was published in 1978. In order to make *DLB* more than a dictionary and to compile volumes that individually have claim to status as literary history, it was decided to organize volumes by topic, period, or

From an unpublished section of Mark Twain's autobiography, copyright by the Mark Twain Company

genre. Each of these freestanding volumes provides a biographical-bibliographical guide and overview for a particular area of literature. We are convinced that this organization—as opposed to a single alphabet method—constitutes a valuable innovation in the presentation of reference material. The volume plan necessarily requires many decisions for the placement and treatment of authors. Certain figures will be included in separate volumes, but with different entries emphasizing the aspect of his career appropriate to each volume. Ernest Hemingway, for example, is represented in *American Writers in Paris, 1920–1939* by an entry focusing on his expatriate apprenticeship; he is also in *American Novelists, 1910–1945* with an entry surveying his entire career, as well as in *American Short-Story Writers, 1910–1945, Second Series* with an entry concentrating on his short fiction. Each volume includes a cumulative index of the subject authors and articles.

Between 1981 and 2002 the series was augmented and updated by the *DLB Yearbooks*. There have also been nineteen *DLB Documentary Series* volumes, which provide illustrations, facsimiles, and biographical and critical source materials for figures, works, or groups judged to have particular interest for students. In 1999 the *Documentary Series* was incorporated into the *DLB* volume numbering system beginning with *DLB 210: Ernest Hemingway.*

We define literature as the *intellectual commerce of a nation:* not merely as belles lettres but as that ample and complex process by which ideas are generated, shaped, and transmitted. *DLB* entries are not limited to "creative writers" but extend to other figures who in their time and in their way influenced the mind of a people. Thus the series encompasses historians, journalists, publishers, book collectors, and screenwriters. By this means readers of *DLB* may be aided to perceive literature not as cult scripture in the keeping of intellectual high priests but firmly positioned at the center of a nation's life.

DLB includes the major writers appropriate to each volume and those standing in the ranks behind them. Scholarly and critical counsel has been sought in deciding which minor figures to include and how full their entries should be. Wherever possible, useful references are made to figures who do not warrant separate entries.

Each *DLB* volume has an expert volume editor responsible for planning the volume, selecting the figures for inclusion, and assigning the entries. Volume editors are also responsible for preparing, where appropriate, appendices surveying the major periodicals and literary and intellectual movements for their volumes, as well as lists of further readings. Work on the series as a whole is coordinated at the Bruccoli Clark Layman editorial center in Columbia, South Carolina, where the editorial staff is responsible for accuracy and utility of the published volumes.

One feature that distinguishes *DLB* is the illustration policy—its concern with the iconography of literature. Just as an author is influenced by his surroundings, so is the reader's understanding of the author enhanced by a knowledge of his environment. Therefore *DLB*

volumes include not only drawings, paintings, and photographs of authors, often depicting them at various stages in their careers, but also illustrations of their families and places where they lived. Title pages are regularly reproduced in facsimile along with dust jackets for modern authors. The dust jackets are a special feature of *DLB* because they often document better than anything else the way in which an author's work was perceived in its own time. Specimens of the writers' manuscripts and letters are included when feasible.

Samuel Johnson rightly decreed that "The chief glory of every people arises from its authors." The purpose of the *Dictionary of Literary Biography* is to compile literary history in the surest way available to us—by accurate and comprehensive treatment of the lives and work of those who contributed to it.

The *DLB* Advisory Board

Introduction

During the sixteenth century, Spain found itself at the forefront of European politics and culture. As a powerful component of the Hapsburg Empire, the nation prospered economically as a gateway to the New World, where by the 1520s it controlled territories in North, Central, and South America, the Caribbean, and tracts along the coast of Africa as well as islands in the Pacific. In the arts, and in particular in literature, within Spain there developed one of the leading national schools of the European Renaissance, thus initiating an era known as the Siglos de Oro (Golden Age), which thrived through the seventeenth-century Baroque period. As the 1500s progressed, Spanish Renaissance letters reflected the imprint of foreign influences and developed its own humanistic culture that expressed itself through manifestations of new styles and techniques as well as continuations and rediscoveries of medieval traditions. The trajectory of the Spanish Renaissance was also shaped by an orthodox Catholic religious reform that came to oppose the Protestant Reformation, which ultimately divided the Hapsburg Empire. During the latter half of the sixteenth century, the legacy of this reform became identified with the Counter-Reformation, the Catholic reaction to the rise in Protestantism. The moral police of this movement, the Spanish Inquisition, which was from its inception in late-medieval Spain an institution controlled by the monarchy, systematized cultural repression by censuring works and authors deemed heretical. Spain remained a dominant imperial power as the sixteenth century reached its conclusion, although a toll was in the process of being exacted on the infrastructure of the nation and a loss of naval supremacy threatened its political and commercial hegemony in Europe and America. In spite of an increasingly restrictive social climate, literary activity continued to flourish during the waning decades of the 1500s as Spain entered the second half of its cultural Golden Age.

The death in 1504 of Queen Isabella ended the joint reign of the Catholic Monarchs and began the transition to a Hapsburg dynasty in Spain. Her daughter and heir to the throne, Juana, who was married to Hapsburg heir Philip the Fair, suffered from mental instability—for which she was called "la loca" (the insane woman)—which prevented her from becoming queen. After the death in 1506 of Philip, Ferdinand, still ruler of Aragon and regent of Castile, tended to the administrative affairs of Spain until his own death in 1516. Among Ferdinand's principal concerns were conflicts with the French for control over lands in Italy and the extension of Spanish dominion into Islamic North Africa. While the latter was undertaken in part to capture port cities that served as bases for attacks by pirates on commercial ships in the Mediterranean, it was also one of several endeavors grounded in the ideals that formed the foundation of the Catholic identity that Spain had acquired during the reign of the Catholic Monarchs. In the wake of the capture of Granada and the expulsion of the Spanish Jews in 1492, the monarchy continued to press for the religious unity of Spain in 1502 by ordering the expulsion of all remaining Muslims who did not convert to Catholicism. The descendants of those who converted, collectively known as Moriscos, formed an important sector of the Spanish economy as artisans and experts in agriculture until their own expulsion in the early seventeenth century.

In 1516 the rite of succession fell upon Juana's son, Charles, who was born in Ghent and raised in Flanders. Charles made his first visit to Spain in 1517 in order to claim the Castilian and Aragonese thrones. In 1519, after the death of his grandfather Maximilian I, Charles I of Spain also became Charles V of the Hapsburg Empire and was subsequently elected Holy Roman Emperor. These titles conferred upon him the responsibility for governing lands in central and southern Europe in addition to Spain and its overseas possessions. The ascension to power of a foreign-born king who would be required to spend a considerable amount of time outside the country in order to govern his Continental empire caused widespread popular resentment, especially in Castile. This animus was also fueled by Charles's appointment of foreigners to prominent government posts, his attempts to manipulate the Cortes (Parliament) in order to secure large subsidies for the empire, and his absolutist policies, which also antagonized sectors of the nobility.

The early years of Charles's reign were marked by periods of civil unrest. In 1518 in Valencia, the object of popular discontent was the landed aristocracy, which was forced to flee the city after local guildsmen formed a *germanía* (brotherhood) and took control of the city before being defeated by the Crown in 1523. In 1520, members of the populace who feared a loss of localized authority incited a series of violent uprisings against royal officials in towns throughout Castile. The rebels, whose insurrection is known as the revolt of the *comuneros* (commoners), were initially joined by a group of nobles in opposing the monarchy. After suppressing these revolts, Charles, although an absentee king during more than half of the remainder of his reign, played a more active role in managing affairs in Spain, where he established control over a resentful populace and a debilitated aristocracy.

In order to fortify his authority, Charles continued the policy of promoting national political unity. To this end he respected the federal system of government that had been established by the Catholic Monarchs, whereby *consejos* (councils) oversaw regional affairs and reported to the royal court. On the local level Charles maintained control over Spanish towns by continuing the practice initiated by the Catholic Monarchs of appointing *corregidores* (municipal officials), as well as by heavy taxation, which produced revenue that was needed for the empire.

As Spain entered a period of political stability, the king actively pursued the expansion of his European dominion. Imperial troops became engaged in a series of wars with France caused by a dispute over lands in Italy, which Charles and Francis I, the French monarch, each wanted to control. After the conclusion of the second war, during which imperial forces sacked Rome and imprisoned Pope Clement VII, the situation was temporarily resolved in 1530 when the Pope crowned Charles emperor as well as ruler over most of the Italian Peninsula. Charles was also engaged in several wars with the Ottoman Empire, at the height of its own power, which threatened imperial interests in the Mediterranean and North Africa and which had aligned with France to oppose the Hapsburg Empire on its eastern borders.

Charles also presided over much of the Spanish Age of Discovery, which ran from the voyages of Christopher Columbus during the 1490s through the middle of the 1500s, by which time the nation possessed an overseas empire that included sections of Florida, the modern-day nations of Mexico, Peru, and Chile, as well as islands in the Caribbean. These territories, along with those acquired in the Pacific, provided material wealth and allowed Spain to dominate international trade routes, which it protected with its powerful navy. As a colonial enterprise, Spain established dominance by military conquest, forced conversion to Catholicism, and instituted the use of slave labor, policies that inspired defenses of indigenous peoples by writers such as Bartolomé de Las Casas, a Dominican friar who advocated for peaceful conversions and the personal rights of natives. Spanish dominion in America was maintained with an extensive administrative network with governmental centers in the viceroyalties of New Spain (modern-day Mexico) and Peru.

The spirit of the Reconquista (Reconquest), the medieval crusade to Christianize Islamic Spain, was kept alive during the 1500s in both the effort to convert indigenous peoples of America to Catholicism and a program of national religious reform that was actively pursued by Cardinal Francisco Jiménez de Cisneros, confessor to Queen Isabella, archbishop of Toledo, and a patron of culture who influenced the evolution of the Spanish Renaissance. As the archbishop of Toledo, Cisneros worked from the 1490s until his death in 1517 to instill greater discipline in the Spanish religious orders and improve religious standards among the populace, and his ardent support for Ferdinand's Mediterranean campaigns reflected his vision of extending the Reconquista into Africa. The fruits of the religious reform championed by Cisneros include the fervor that it fomented, which contributed to increased intolerance toward heterodoxy; the foundation of the Jesuit order, which came to play an important role in Spanish missionary efforts abroad; and a surge in spiritual works. The largest corpus of such texts, produced over the course of the 1500s and during the first half of the seventeenth century, consists of ascetic and mystic writings that espouse a panorama of themes, composed by members of a variety of religious orders in addition to nonclerical authors.

Cisneros also dedicated his efforts to reforming the Spanish system of higher education. His plan was to create a university that would incorporate humanistic methods and disciplines in conformity with the ideologies of Catholic orthodoxy, as such laying the foundation for the spiritual character of the Spanish Renaissance. The creation of this university in 1502 at Alcalá de Henares signified that humanism—the ideological foundation of the European Renaissance that began to flourish in Italy during the fifteenth century, when it made its initial inroads in Spanish culture—had evolved into a national phenomenon. Humanism opposed medieval Scholasticism and Aristotelian thought through the primacy it lent to the place of humanity in the cosmos and by seeking inspiration in classical and pagan models. In Spain, humanism influenced both secular and religious literary production, although the tone set at Alcalá reflected the decidedly spiritual nature of the movement. While secular curricula began to take primacy at other European centers of higher education, subjects such as Greek and logic were secondary to theology at Alcalá and were taught as fundamental tools for biblical studies. The emphasis that was placed on humanistic disciplines, and the presence among its faculty of leading Spanish humanists such as Antonio de Nebrija, quickly transformed Alcalá into a center of intellectual activity. The success of the institution was marked in 1517 by the completion by a team of scholars of a multilingual Bible (in Aramaic, Greek, Hebrew, and Latin) known as the *Biblia Políglota Complutense* (Complutensian Polyglot Bible), which reveals in its textual commentaries the ideals of the program of religious reform supported by Cisneros.

Printed editions of the *Biblia Políglota Complutense* were produced at Alcalá, the location of one of many sixteenth-century presses in Spain. Religious and secular books of all types were published, including the works of European humanists and Christian reformers, classical texts, and collections of poetry in both innovative and traditional styles, as well as a variety of genres with novelistic features. One of the most widely disseminated of these genres throughout most of the sixteenth century was the chivalric epic (often referred to as the chivalric novel or chivalric romance), which began to gain favor during the late Middle Ages before undergoing a surge in popularity among Renaissance readers, whose voracious appetite for stories of adventure was satisfied by multiple editions of *Amadís de Gaula* (1508, Amadís of Gaul), the work that initiated the trend, and its sequel, *Las sergas de Esplandián* (1510, The Exploits of Esplandian)—both by Garci Rodríguez de Montalvo—as well as many other series. These escapist tales of fantastic events attracted readers from all social classes, and its impact reverberates in authors ranging from chroniclers of the New World such as Bernal Díaz de Castillo to St. Teresa of Ávila, one of the greatest Spanish mystic writers and one of only a handful of sixteenth-century female authors known to modern scholars.

The pastoral novel, which was born of Italian and classical influences, was in vogue from the late 1500s through the early decades of the seventeenth century. The Spanish pastoral, which perpetuated the bucolic tradition by interweaving prose and verse, was cultivated during the sixteenth century by several renowned writers of the Siglo de Oro, including Jorge de Montemayor, Miguel de Cervantes Saavedra, and Lope de Vega. The Byzantine novel, which was cultivated across Europe, was imitated in Spanish in the mid 1500s and foreshadowed a related narrative form,

the Moorish novel, best exemplified by the anonymous *El Abencerraje y la hermosa Jarifa* (1561, The Abencerraje and the Beautiful Jarifa). Spanish Renaissance readers were also drawn to stories of amorous intrigue, known as sentimental romances (or sentimental novels), and epic depictions of European and American adventures.

The incorporation of Spain into the Hapsburg Empire exposed Spanish culture to influences from abroad. The ideas of the Dutch humanist Desiderius Erasmus found widespread acceptance within intellectual circles, among the clergy, and at the fledgling university founded by Cisneros, although the importance of orthodox Catholic theology at Alcalá may have dissuaded Erasmus from accepting a teaching position at that institution. The rapid rise in popularity of his doctrines during the 1520s may be attributed to several factors, including the presence of a Dutch contingent at the royal court; the appeal of the Erasmian notion of universal Christian peace and political cohesion as a reflection of Charles's imperial goals; the ideological parallels that were considered to exist between the Cisnerian program of spiritual reform and the emphasis placed by Erasmus on inner spirituality; and the printing presses that disseminated translated editions of his works. The Erasmian vision of a harmonious Christian community had a profound influence on some of the most renowned writers and thinkers of the time, including Juan Luis Vives, Alfonso de Valdés, and his brother Juan de Valdés. Some Erasmian views, such as those concerning the corruptness of the Catholic Church and his disdain for religious ceremonies, concepts that formed the foundation of the Protestant Reformation, began to attract the attention of inquisitors by the late 1520s, when its popularity at the royal court began to fade, and the Inquisition eventually identified Erasmism as a conduit to Lutheranism and persecuted its followers.

The spiritual and moral doctrines of Erasmus were especially appealing to *conversos* (converts), that is, descendants of Spanish Jews who converted to Catholicism in order to escape the wave of persecution that culminated with the expulsion of all remaining Jews in 1492. During the fifteenth and sixteenth centuries some *conversos* rose to prominence as royal and municipal administrators and within the church, and intermarriage was common between *conversos* and Old Christians (those Christians who did not possess Jewish ancestries). Owing to political, social, and religious factors, a seamless merger between Old and New Christians failed to occur, and *conversos* were collectively perceived as insincere Christians who adhered to Judaism, a situation that brought the Inquisition into existence. While most *conversos* did not experience firsthand persecution, the procedures of the Inquisition, including the acceptance of incriminating accusations launched by less-than-trustworthy individuals and the practice of concealing the names of accusers, undoubtedly caused consternation and a general fear of denunciation among both sincere and insincere *conversos*.

Conversos were the principal targets of the Spanish Inquisition from its inception through the early decades of the sixteenth century. Persecution also took the form of purity-of-blood statutes, which began to be enacted during the fifteenth century in order to exclude *conversos* from a variety of civil and ecclesiastical offices. Over the course of the 1500s, military orders, universities, and religious orders adopted purity-of-blood statutes, although in practice these restrictions were often circumvented by *conversos*. Prominent figures of Spanish Renaissance letters of *converso* origin include Luis de León, an Augustinian priest who was imprisoned for four years by the Inquisition; Bartolomé de Torres Naharro; and St. Teresa.

The resentment felt by alienated *conversos* is one of the social components said to form the ideological foundation of the picaresque novel, whose parameters were set by *La vida de Lazarillo de Tormes*, which was published anonymously in 1554. Because of its anticlericalism, in particular with regard to the selling of papal indulgences, the Inquisition included the work on its lists of prohibited books. The controversy surrounding its satirical depiction of clerical practices, a theme that surfaces on several occasions in contemporary Spanish literature, did not diminish the appeal of *La vida de Lazarillo de Tormes* as a model for a genre that was frequently cultivated by Spanish writers during the seventeenth century.

Spanish lyric poetry was profoundly shaped by the Italian Renaissance style, in particular by the hendecasyllable (verse of eleven syllables); the Petrarchan sonnet; the revived interest in the works of Horace, Ovid, and Virgil; and Neoplatonism. The latter, a synthesis of Platonic and Christian ideas that exalted the human condition as a reflection of universal harmony, found adherents in Spain among writers of prose and verse, and its presence is felt in both secular and religious works. Close contact between Spain and Italy, much of which was under Hapsburg rule, ensured the transmission of cultural influences.

Although attempts were made during the fifteenth century to compose Petrarchan sonnets in Spanish, the introduction of the Italian lyric style is attributed to a meeting in 1526 between Andrea Navagero, an Italian politician and intellectual, and the Spanish poet Juan Boscán. While the posthumous publication (in 1543) of Boscán's sonnets was instru-

mental in popularizing the hendecasyllable, his greatest contribution may have been involving his friend and fellow poet and courtier, Garcilaso de la Vega. Garcilaso's works, to a greater extent than any other contemporary poet, are informed by the secular classicism of the Spanish Renaissance, and his manipulation of the musical rhythms of the Italian style in pastoral eclogues, Horatian odes, and Petrarchan sonnets left a lasting legacy on the evolution of Spanish lyric verse. The dissemination of Garcilaso's poetry inspired many followers, including those associated with two centers traditionally referred to as the Salamanca school and the Sevillian school, which flourished during the reign of Philip II. León, whose works demonstrate an amalgam of classical themes and Catholic ideologies, best represents the Salamanca school, while Fernando de Herrera, called "el Divino" (the Divine One) by his contemporaries for his erudition and Italianate poetry, reached the zenith of the Sevillian school. The influence of Garcilaso also resonates in religious verse such as that composed by San Juan de la Cruz, a Carmelite priest and humanist whose poetry is informed by mystic themes.

In reaction to the prestige of Italianate poetry, a nationalistic movement developed among poets such as Cristóbal de Castillejo, who advocated the superiority of traditional meters, which had never actually gone out of style. Compilations of late-medieval courtly poetry, known as *cancioneros* (songbooks), were available during the sixteenth century in printed editions that provided poets with models of traditional versification such as the octosyllabic (eight-syllable) and hexasyllabic (six-syllable) lines, as well as cultured verses composed in *arte mayor* (verses of more than eight syllables) and the *conceptismos* (plays on words) and abstract imagery typically found in *cancionero* poetry. One of the most successful of these compilations was the *Cancionero general* (General Songbook), comprising works composed during the second half of the fifteenth century, which was published on nine different occasions after it was first released in 1511. Among the works included in the *Cancionero general* are anonymous *canciones* (songs), *villancicos* (love poems), and *romances* (ballads), which had circulated orally until the fifteenth century, when they gained new prestige among court poets and first appeared in written form. Spanish ballads, like other traditional poetry, were also disseminated individually in printed *pliegos sueltos* (loose sheets of paper). Toward the middle of the sixteenth century many of these ballads were collected in the *Cancionero de romances* (1550?), the first of many published compilations of traditional ballads. Renaissance writers introduced Moorish, mythological, and pastoral themes into their own ballads, which were also published in compilations. These ballads, as well as those composed after the sixteenth century, are collectively referred to as the *romancero nuevo* (new ballads) in order to distinguish them from traditional ballads, which make up the *romancero viejo* (old ballads).

Traditional poetic forms were also incorporated into Spanish drama, which achieved unprecedented popularity and attained its modern form during the sixteenth century. Juan del Encina, who is commonly known as the father of Spanish theater, laid the foundation with his pastoral eclogues, which incorporate both traditional Spanish and Italian motifs, as such providing subsequent dramatists with rustic character types and models of versified theatrical discourse. Encina's techniques were enhanced by several contemporaries, including Gil Vicente, a dramatist at the Portuguese court who composed works in Portuguese and Spanish, and Torres Naharro, the first to establish norms for Spanish theater. The Renaissance *comedia,* a term used at first to allude to the classically inspired dramas described by Torres Naharro but which, by the end of the sixteenth century, could refer to any multiact work, was developed by Lope de Rueda, who also functioned as director and actor in his traveling theater company, as such advancing methods of staging dramas as well as disseminating theater among the higher and lower social classes. Rueda's shorter comic sketches, called *pasos,* prefigured the *entremés,* a genre that found its place between the acts of Baroque *comedias* in order to provide relief from dramatic tension.

Prior to the middle of the sixteenth century, theatrical representations usually took place at the royal court or at the palaces of the high nobility. As a result of the success of professional theater companies, in addition to the existence of greater numbers of dramatic works, a new outlet developed for audiences with the desire, money, and time to attend performances in locales specifically designed for that purpose. Theaters, called *corrales,* began to appear around 1570 in major Spanish cities such as Madrid and Seville, and by the end of the 1500s they could be found in many urban centers. Spaniards rapidly developed the habit of attending the theater on a regular basis and constantly demanded new productions, which permitted dramatists such as Juan de la Cueva to introduce legendary and historical Spanish themes into works written expressly for public performance, thus paving the way for Spanish drama during the Baroque period.

While Spanish culture flourished and its cities experienced growth and commercial prosperity, the long-term economic impact of its involvement in international affairs was rampant inflation and national bankruptcy. Much of the wealth produced by the Spanish colonies was utilized to combat developing pockets of Lutheranism in Charles's German principalities, a movement that evolved into the Protestant Reformation. In order to restore religious unity within his imperial domain, Charles quickly assumed a leading role in opposing the Reformation by calling for the convocation of the Diet of Worms, which condemned Martin Luther's ideas in its edict of 1521. Lutheranism continued to spread during the 1520s, and advocacy by the movement of rebellion against religious tyranny (which was later rebuked by Luther) promoted political dissension in the German principalities, which allied themselves with Denmark, France, and Great Britain in reaction to Charles's attempts to enforce the doctrines of the Edict of Worms. Charles, confronted with the possibility of losing control over northern Germany, a region that provided troops for military campaigns against France and the Ottoman Empire, sought a temporary resolution of the situation, which he achieved in 1532 with an agreement that granted Lutherans freedom to practice their faith until a Catholic Church council could be convened.

The spread of Lutheranism was noticed by the Inquisition, which persecuted the followers of Luther and Erasmus and the Alumbrados (Illuminists), who advocated a mystic spirituality and disdained traditional church ceremonies. While the Inquisition successfully controlled Spanish Illuminism, Protestant communities began to appear around 1550 in Seville and Valladolid. The success of the Reformation and the alliances between Protestants and the enemies of Spain led Charles to petition Pope Paul III for the convocation of a church council. The Pope, concerned with Protestantism within the empire as well as by the foothold gained by Calvinism in Geneva and the Anglican Church in Great Britain, responded by convening the Council of Trent in 1545. Over the next two decades the Council of Trent, which officially ended in 1563, defined the Counter-Reformation by affirming the primacy of traditional church doctrines and institutions and the papacy. The schism between Protestants and Catholics was also cemented by the religious wars conducted in central Europe by Charles (with the support of the papacy) during the 1540s and 1550s, a campaign that ended in 1555 with a treaty that proclaimed religious freedom for Protestants.

While discussions continued at Trent, Charles abdicated the throne in 1556 and divided the Hapsburg Empire. He ceded the title of Hapsburg emperor to his brother, Ferdinand, while giving control of the Netherlands, Spain, and its European and American possessions to his son Philip, who ruled as King Philip II of Spain until his death in 1598. In 1580 Philip was proclaimed king of Portugal, a title he came to possess by birthright as a grandson of King Manuel I of Portugal and through careful negotiations conducted in order to establish supremacy over the five other aspirants who sought the Portuguese crown. Spain and Portugal remained unified politically until 1668.

During the reign of King Philip II, Spain persisted as a European imperial power in spite of a deteriorating national economy and an increasingly repressive society. As he faced two national bankruptcies and a decline in commercial centers such as Burgos and Bilbao, Philip worked to centralize his government by permanently establishing Madrid as his capital in 1561, the same year that construction began on his nearby palace, El Escorial, one of the great monuments of European Renaissance architecture. In order to preserve Spanish hegemony in Europe and promote Catholic unity, Philip continued the policies of his father by conducting military campaigns and forging political alliances.

After establishing control over the Papal States, Philip aligned with the Pope and the Venetian nobility to form a coalition known as the Liga Santa (Holy League), which was successful in combating Turkish forces in the Mediterranean. Philip's attempt to incorporate England into his domain was less fortunate. Political and religious tensions with England, where Protestantism gained a strong foothold, intensified after the death in 1558 of the English queen, Mary Tudor, whose marriage to Philip in 1554 had produced no heir. England came to represent a formidable military threat as well for its attacks on Spanish territories and its support of pirates who raided Spanish commercial vessels. In an effort to depose Mary's successor, Queen Elizabeth I, an ardent supporter of the Reformation, Philip sent the Spanish Armada Invencible (Invincible Navy) to attack the English coast in 1588. The disastrous defeat suffered by the Spanish fleet signified the beginning of a decline in Spanish maritime power and European hegemony and opened overseas trade routes for other nations.

On an ideological plane, the reign of Philip II marked the onset of a period of cultural isolation that reflected the Catholic identity of Counter-Reformation Spain. In order to ensure religious purity, Spanish students were prohibited from studying at foreign institutions of higher education (except for the University of Bologna), and the Inquisition closely monitored intellectual activity and manifestations of heterodoxy. While *conversos* suspected of practicing Judaism in secret continued to appear before tribunals, inquisitorial persecution during the second half of the 1500s focused mainly on the Moriscos and followers of Luther and Erasmus and on censuring objectionable texts. In 1559 the Inquisition produced

its first list of censured books, which included works by Erasmus and Spanish writers who adhered to his ideas, *La vida de Lazarillo de Tormes,* and theatrical pieces that were included for reasons that remain obscure. That same year the first autos-da-fé, public events at which sentences meted out by the Inquisition were pronounced, took place in Seville and Valladolid. In 1568 the Moriscos of Granada reacted to intensified persecution by staging a revolt against the monarchy, which suppressed the insurrection and deported the perpetrators to other regions in Spain. Persecution of Protestants fueled the flames of anti-Spanish sentiment in the Netherlands, which began a conflict with Spain that earned the region its independence in 1648.

The sixteenth century was for Spain a period characterized by territorial expansion, political hegemony, and cultural prosperity in the face of ideological repression. Although the defeat of the Armada Invencible severely debilitated the most potent naval force in Europe, Spain maintained dominion over its vast overseas empire. The struggle to create and preserve Catholic unity, a cause championed by the Catholic Monarchs and continued during the Hapsburg dynasty, ultimately resulted in the loss of European possessions and a closed society that operated according to the norms imposed by the Counter-Reformation. The zeal with which Philip II sought religious conformity, reflected in his military campaigns and support of the Inquisition, enlisted Spain as a symbol of intolerance, a national identity that persisted for centuries and came to be known as La Leyenda Negra (The Black Legend).

While it may have caused authors to be cautious with respect to the incorporation of objectionable themes, censorship by the Inquisition, which produced a list of expurgated books in 1571 and another general one in 1583, did not curb the tide of literary production. With the publication by Mateo Alemán of the *Primera parte de la vida de Guzmán de Alfarache* (1599, First Part of the Life of Guzmán de Alfarache), the picaresque novel continued to evolve. The Spanish passion for the theater increased during the 1600s, when writers such as Lope de Vega and Calderón de la Barca represented the pinnacle of Golden Age drama. As the 1500s concluded, Lope de Vega, Cervantes, and others were already evolving careers that established them as luminaries of the Baroque period. Although plagued by political and religious strife and financial crisis, Spain entered the seventeenth century under King Philip III as a center of artistic activity that continued to flourish as the nation entered the second half of its Golden Age.

—Gregory B. Kaplan

Acknowledgments

This book was produced by Bruccoli Clark Layman, Inc. Charles Brower was the in-house editor.

Production manager is Philip B. Dematteis.

Administrative support was provided by Carol A. Cheschi.

Accountant is Ann-Marie Holland.

Copyediting supervisor is Sally R. Evans. The copyediting staff includes Phyllis A. Avant, Caryl Brown, Melissa D. Hinton, Philip I. Jones, Rebecca Mayo, Nadirah Rahimah Shabazz, and Nancy E. Smith.

Pipeline manager is James F. Tidd Jr.

Editorial associates are Crystal Gleim, Elizabeth Leverton, Joshua Shaw, and Timothy C. Simmons.

In-house vetter is Catherine M. Polit.

Permissions editor is Amber L. Coker.

Layout and graphics supervisor is Janet E. Hill. The graphics staff includes Zoe R. Cook and Sydney E. Hammock.

Office manager is Kathy Lawler Merlette.

Photography editor is Mark J. McEwan. Photography assistant is Dickson Monk.

Digital photographic copy work was performed by Joseph M. Bruccoli.

Systems manager is Donald Kevin Starling.

Typesetting supervisor is Kathleen M. Flanagan. The typesetting staff includes Patricia Marie Flanagan and Pamela D. Norton.

Library research was facilitated by the following librarians at the Thomas Cooper Library of the University of South Carolina: Elizabeth Suddeth and the rare-book department; Jo Cottingham, interlibrary loan department; circulation department head Tucker Taylor; reference department head Virginia W. Weathers; reference department staff Laurel Baker, Marilee Birchfield, Kate Boyd, Paul Cammarata, Joshua Garris, Gary Geer, Tom Marcil, Rose Marshall, and Sharon Verba; interlibrary loan department head Marna Hostetler; and interlibrary loan staff Bill Fetty and Nelson Rivera.

Additional editorial assistance was provided by Kenneth Atwood.

Dictionary of Literary Biography® • Volume Three Hundred Eighteen

Sixteenth-Century Spanish Writers

Dictionary of Literary Biography

José de Acosta
(1540 – 15 February 1600)

Mary Elizabeth Baldridge
Carson-Newman College

BOOKS: *Tercero cathecismo y exposicion de la doctrina christiana, por sermones: Para que los curas y otros ministros prediquen y enseñen a los Yndios y a las demas personas* (Ciudad de los Reyes, Spain: Printed by Antonio Ricardo, 1585);

Confesionario para los curas de Indios: Con la instrucción sobre sus ritos: y exhortacion para ayudar a bien morir: y summa de sus privilegios: y forma de impedimentos del matrimonio (Ciudad de los Reyes, Spain: Printed by Antonio Ricardo, 1585);

De natura Novi Orbis. Libri duo, et De promulgatione Evangelii, apud barbaros, sive De procuranda Indorum salute. Libri sex (Salamanca: Printed by Guillermo Foquel, 1588);

De Christo Revelato, libri novem (Rome: J. Tornerium, 1590);

De Temporibus Novissimis. Libri quattor (Rome: Tornerij, 1590);

Historia natural y moral de las Indias en que se tratan las cosas notables del cielo, y elementos, metales, plantas y animales dellas y los ritos, y ceremonias, leyes y gobierno, y guerras de los Indios (Seville: Printed by Juan de León, 1590); translated by Edward Grimestone as *The Naturall and Morall Historie of the East and West Indies* (London: Printed by Val Sims for Edward Blount & William Aspley, 1604);

Concilium Limanse: Celebratum anno 1583. sub Gregorio XIII. sum. pont. autoritate Sixti Quinti pont. max. approbatum. Iussu catholici regis Hispaniarum, atq[ue] Indiarum (Madrid: Petri Madrigalis, 1591);

Conciones in Quadragessimam: Quarum in singulas ferias numerum & locum index initio præsixus ostendit (Salamanca: Printed by Juan & Andrés Renaut, 1596);

Conciones de Adventu: Id est de omnibus dominicis & festis diebus à dominica vigesimaquarta post pentecosten usque ad

José de Acosta (from Joseph MacDonnell, Jesuit Family Album: Sketches of Chivalry from the Early Society, *1997; University of San Francisco Library)*

quadragesimam (Salamanca: Printed by Juan & Andrés Renaut, 1597);

Conciones ab octava Pasche (Cologne: Printed by Juan & Andrés Renaut, 1600).

Modern Editions: *Historia natural y moral de las Indias, escrita por el p. Joseph de Acosta, de la Compaña de Jesús: Publicada en Sevilla en 1590* (Madrid: Anglés, 1894);

Historia natural y moral de las Indias en que se tratan las cosas notables del cielo, y elementos, metales, plantas y animales dellas y los ritos, y ceremonias, leyes y gobierno, y guerras de los Indios, edited by Edmundo O'Gorman (Mexico City: Fonda de cultura ecónomica, 1940);

De procuranda Indorum salute (Predicación del evangelio en las Indias), translated and edited by Francisco Mateos (Madrid, 1952);

Obras, edited by Mateos (Madrid: Atlas, 1954);

De procuranda Indorum salute: Pacaficacion y colonizacion, 2 volumes, edited by L. Pereña (Madrid: Consejo Superior de Investigaciones Cientificas, 1984);

El tercer concilio limense y la aculturación de los indígenas sudamericanos: Estudio crítico con edición, traducción y comentario de las actas del concilio provincial celebrado en Lima entre 1582 y 1583, edited by Francesco Leonardo Lisi (Salamanca: Universidad de Salamanca, 1990);

Historia natural y moral de las Indias, 2 volumes, edited by Antonio Quilis (Madrid: Ediciones de Cultura Hispánica, 1998).

Editions in English: *The Natural and Moral History of the Indies,* 2 volumes, edited by Clements R. Markham (London: Hakluyt Society, 1880);

De procuranda Indorum salute, 2 volumes, edited and translated by G. Stewart McIntosh (Tayport, Scotland: Mac Research, 1996);

Natural and Moral History of the Indies, translated by Frances M. López-Morillas (Durham, N.C.: Duke University Press, 2002).

Born in Medina del Campo, Spain, in 1540, José de Acosta achieved lasting significance primarily through the works that he wrote about the New World, its inhabitants, and its flora and fauna. A member of the Society of Jesus (the Jesuit order), he had expressed a profound desire to serve in the New World from an early point in his career. As a result, Acosta was sent to Peru on a mission with the Jesuits in 1571, establishing himself for a time in Lima before engaging in extensive travel and service throughout the Peruvian empire. During his stay in Peru, Acosta made a detailed study of the customs, history, and geography of the region and its peoples. In 1586 he began the journey back to Spain, stopping for nearly a year in Mexico, where he studied the native peoples of that region. Upon his return to Spain, Acosta published his *Historia natural y moral de las Indias en que se tratan las cosas notables del cielo, y elementos, metales, plantas y animales dellas y los ritos, y ceremo-*

nias, leyes y gobierno, y guerras de los Indios (1590, Natural and Moral History of the Indians in Which the Remarkable Things Are the Sky, and Elements, Metals, Plants and Their Animals and the Rites, and Ceremonies, Laws and Government, and Wars of the Indians; translated as *The Naturall and Morall Historie of the East and West Indies,* 1604), the book for which he is most remembered. This book, a compendium of ancient, medieval, and Renaissance theories about the New World and Acosta's interpretation of how those theories relate to reality, was published in six different languages within fifteen years of its original publication. Its success might be attributed to the thirst for information about the New World that spread throughout sixteenth-century Europe. Acosta's other books, while not as commercially successful, are nevertheless important for their visions of the rights of the native peoples and their emphasis on the evangelical nature of the conquest of the New World.

Acosta, son of Antonio de Acosta and Ana de Porres, was born into a prosperous merchant family. One of nine children, he knew from an early age that he wanted to enter the Society of Jesus. Acosta likely studied in the Jesuit college at Medina del Campo in 1551, although he did not officially become a Jesuit until 1552. In that year, though he was not yet twelve years old, he ran away from home to join the order in Salamanca. He returned to Medina del Campo later that year to continue his novitiate.

From early in his life as a Jesuit, Acosta expressed a desire to serve God wherever necessary. He felt a particularly keen desire to travel and serve as a missionary in the New World. His travels, however, had to wait until he completed his studies. In 1554 Acosta progressed to the scholasticate of the Jesuit order. He had already begun to write, and before he left Medina del Campo in 1557 he had written several tragedies, most in Latin, which were never published or performed. Between 1557 and 1559 Acosta was posted to several different Jesuit colleges in Castile and Portugal. During these years he both taught and studied in these schools and distinguished himself as a scholar and an outstanding orator. In 1559 Acosta moved to Alcalá de Henares, where he studied philosophy and theology in the university there. As always, he was a dedicated student who mastered all that he studied. In 1567 he finished his studies at Alcalá and was ordained into the presbyterate of the Jesuit order.

The first few years after his ordination, Acosta served in several different places, primarily in small Castilian and Portuguese towns. In 1567 he helped start classes in theology in Ocaña, and he was as successful a professor as he was a preacher and confessor. In 1569 Acosta was moved to Plasencia, where he remained until 1571. After several years of repeated requests, he finally received permission from Rome to go to the New World, and on 8 June 1571 he set sail for the Americas, arriving in Santo Domingo in September and moving on, in stages, to arrive in Lima on 27 April 1572.

Once in Lima, Acosta immediately took up responsibilities similar to those he had exercised in Spain: hearing confessions, teaching theology, and preaching. He soon gained the respect of those with whom he worked. In June 1573 he was sent on a visit to the southern Peruvian empire, which included territories that today form parts of Peru, Bolivia, and Chile. He did not return to Lima until the latter part of 1574. On his journeys Acosta visited many outposts and principal cities of the south, attempting to encourage the Jesuits in those areas to maintain exemplary lives. He also explored the possibilities for new Jesuit foundations and examined the work being carried out among the native peoples. On this trip Acosta gained much of his firsthand knowledge about the native people that he later included in his books, particularly in *De procuranda Indorum salute* (1588, Concerning the Administering of the Salvation of the Indians), which was originally written as a separate book but was first published as a part of *De natura Novi Orbis*. Upon his return to Lima, Acosta began teaching at the Universidad de San Marcos. Much of the content of his lectures from this period was eventually included in *De procuranda Indorum salute* and *De Christo Revelato, libri novem* (1590, Concerning Christ Revealed, Nine Volumes).

During the next few years Acosta became involved in the governance of the Jesuit order in Peru. He was appointed as the consultor of the Inquisition, an office that put him in the position of examining some of the most controversial people and ideas of the day. His duties included judging people whose ideas were deemed heretical. Between the years of 1576 and 1581 Acosta was the provincial (or primary Jesuit authority) of Peru. In this capacity he convened the first Jesuit provincial congregation of Peru, a meeting that was supposed to be held every six years. The purpose of this congregation was to solidify the exact role of the work of the Jesuits among the native peoples.

During this time period, Acosta was working on his first book, *De procuranda Indorum salute*. Written in 1576, the work comprises six books with a total of approximately six hundred pages and deals with one of Acosta's main concerns, the evangelization of the Amerindians. The question of whether the natives in the Americas were capable of understanding the Gospel enough to be evangelized and saved was being hotly debated in both Spain and the New World at that time.

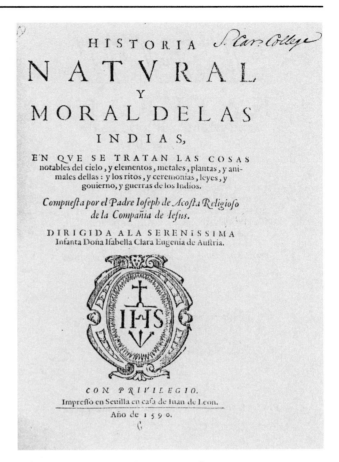

Title page for Acosta's best-known work (Natural and Moral History of the Indians), an attempt at a comprehensive account of the customs, history, and geography of the New World (Special Collections, Thomas Cooper Library, University of South Carolina)

In *De procuranda Indorum salute*, Acosta argues that the Amerindians are capable of being saved and that the evangelization of the Indians is the duty of the Spanish people. Any failure to bring the natives to an acceptance and understanding of God was not, in Acosta's view, a failure on the part of the Amerindians to understand, but a failure on the part of the Spaniards to explain the Gospel message adequately and to live in a manner that was consistent with that message. Acosta includes a section in this book offering practical remedies for common problems (such as political and administrative issues) associated with the spread of Christianity in the New World.

Throughout his years as provincial, Acosta worked hard to improve the efficiency and service of the Jesuits in Peru with the aim of improving the evangelizing services of the Society of Jesus. He was involved in all aspects of the society and its branches in Peru. One of the primary innovations with which

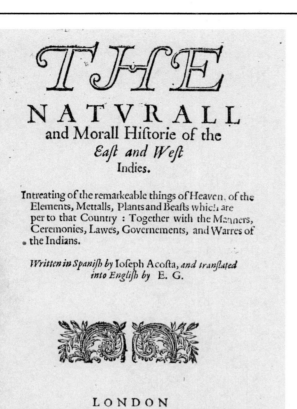

THE
NATVRALL
and Morall Hiſtorie of the
Eaſt and Weſt
Indies.

Intreating of the remarkeable things of Heaven, of the
Elements, Mettalls, Plants and Beaſts which are
per to that Country : Together with the Manners,
Ceremonies, Lawes, Governements, and Warres of
the Indians.

Written in Spaniſh by Ioſeph Acoſta, *and tranſlated
into Engliſh by* E. G.

LONDON
Printed by *Val: Sims* for *Edward Blount* and *William
Aſpley.* 1 6 0 4.

Title page for the first English translation of Acosta's Historia
natural y moral de las Indias *(Special Collections, Thomas
Cooper Library, University of South Carolina)*

Acosta was concerned was learning the native languages in order to preach to the native peoples. He believed that the Amerindians would respond much more positively to the Gospel message if they understood it better. The importance that Acosta placed on the native languages is evident in the work done at Juli, a city largely populated with natives located on the shore of Lake Titicaca. Though many of the native citizens of Juli had been baptized, few understood the catechism completely since it had never been taught in their language. A language school was set up in Juli for the Jesuits who would work among the native people. Among the languages taught were Aymara, Puquina, and Quechua. As a result, according to Claudio M. Burgaleta in his *José De Acosta, S.J. (1540–1600): His Life and Thought* (1999), by the end of Acosta's term as provincial there had been a marked increase in the number of Jesuit brothers who were fluent in various native languages. Though the term expired in 1581, he remained in Peru for six more years, continuing much

of the literary work that he had started and serving as the official theologian of the Third Provincial Council of Lima.

Acosta left Peru in 1586 and stopped for a year in Mexico. There he visited his brother, Bernardino de Acosta, who had also joined the Jesuit ministry in the New World and had been appointed rector of the Jesuit College in Oaxaca. The year that José de Acosta spent in Mexico allowed him to gather information on the Aztecs, which was ultimately included in his *Historia natural y moral de las Indias*. The parts of this book that deal with the Andean regions were originally published in Latin along with *De procuranda Indorum salute* under the title *De Natura Novi Orbis. Libri duo* (1588, Concerning the Nature of the New World. Two Volumes). The first four books of *Historia natural y moral de las Indias* deal with the natural history of Peru and Mexico. They include information about the New World and sometimes offer a refutation of the theories held by classical and patristic authors. For example, in book 1 Acosta notes that the equatorial region does indeed sustain life and is not a "burning zone," uninhabitable because of its proximity to the sun. Aristotle, Pliny, and other classical and patristic authors had previously held the view that no one could survive the heat of the equatorial regions, but Acosta's firsthand experience showed him that this assumption was untrue. Books 5 through 7 of *Historia natural y moral de las Indias* deal with the histories of the Aztecs and Incas, their religions, and their political and social structures (or the "moral history"). This section has been compared to Eusebius of Caesarea's fourth-century *Praeparatio Evangelica* (Preparation for the Gospel), which chronicles the differences and similarities between various religions and how these religions were forerunners of Christianity. Though Acosta clearly did not support or excuse the Amerindian religious practices, he did desire to make them understood in an effort to show that the native religions possessed many practices that seemed to parallel Christian practices. In Acosta's opinion these similarities showed that God had been preparing the New World for evangelization by the Spanish in spite of Satan's corrupting influence in the region.

Acosta's work at evangelizing and training others to evangelize the New World consumed him during his stay there. Sometime before he arrived back in Spain he had already finished two other works: *De Temporibus Novissimis* (1590, Concerning Recent Times) and *De Christo Revelato,* the two of which were written in Latin and published simultaneously in Rome. Both books are collections of patristic and scriptural quotations on apocalyptic and Christological themes.

Upon his arrival back in Spain in 1587, Acosta had two immediate tasks: to seek the publication of his literary works and to recount his vivid descriptions and detailed information about the New World to King Philip II. In 1588 Acosta went to Rome to speak with Pope Sixtus V and the cardinals of the Roman curia. While there he discussed many topics related to the years he spent in Peru and explained why some of the general rules of the Jesuits had been altered to fit more closely the needs of the New World. Upon Acosta's return to Spain, Philip sent him on a series of visitations of the provinces to Andalucía and Aragon. These visitations lasted two years. Subsequent to his return from the visitations, Acosta became directly involved in some of the policies and politics of the Jesuit order and served as the king's agent in a general congregation that was convoked in 1593. As a result of Acosta's position and of the stances that he took in support of the king's agenda, he gained the enmity both of his superior in the Jesuit order, Father General Claudio Aquaviva, and of many of his peers.

The final years of Acosta's life were spent in much the same manner as his earlier years. In 1594 he reassumed the role of rector of the professed house in Valladolid, which he had held prior to his return to Rome in 1592. When his term there was finished, Acosta remained in Valladolid and continued preaching and writing. In 1597 he was transferred to the Jesuit college at Salamanca, where he served as rector. Acosta died in Salamanca on 15 February 1600.

José de Acosta's reputation has varied greatly throughout the years. From being hailed as the "Pliny of the New World" for his descriptions of the culture and the geography of the Americas to being accused of plagiarism, he has alternately been praised and vilified by literary critics. The accusations of plagiarism have, for the most part, been debunked. They began to arise in the late eighteenth century and were common throughout the nineteenth century. Prior to 1780, it was recognized that Acosta did rely on other works, especially for the information about Mexico in his *Historia natural y moral de las Indias*. Indeed, Acosta acknowledged that he had used information given to him by Juan de Tovar, a Mexican Jesuit with whom Acosta had extensive contact. In the sixteenth century, however, it was neither unusual nor prohibited for authors to "recycle" material written by others. Acosta's use of this material was not condemned as plagiarism until the late eigh-

teenth and early nineteenth centuries, when rules governing intellectual property began to gain ground. Because the accusations of plagiarism are rather anachronistic, and because Acosta did give credit to the source of his material, he has been acquitted of wrongdoing by most contemporary critics. He is now considered a pioneer in geophysical sciences, anthropology, ethnography, modern mission theory, biogeography, climatology, and even aeronautical medical research (for his study of altitude sickness in the Andes), and his work is considered among the most advanced of its kind. Though he strives to understand the New World based on Old World ideologies, he stands out from many other Spanish colonial writers in his willingness to refute previously held beliefs if they are not supported by his personal observations.

References:

Don Paul Abbott, *Rhetoric in the New World: Rhetorical Theory and Practice in Colonial Spanish America* (Columbia: University of South Carolina Press, 1996), pp. 60–78;

Claudio M. Burgaleta, *José De Acosta, S.J. (1540–1600): His Life and Thought* (Chicago: Loyola University Press, 1999);

Thayne R. Ford, "Stranger in a Foreign Land: José De Acosta's Scientific Realizations in Sixteenth-Century Peru," *Sixteenth Century Journal,* 29, no. 1 (1998): 19–33;

León Lopetegui, "¿Cómo debe entenderse la labor misional del P. José De Acosta, S.J.?" *Studia Missionalia,* 1 (1943): 115–136;

Lopetegui, "Vocación de Indias Del P. José De Acosta, S.J.," *Revista de Indias,* 1 (1940): 78–91;

Joseph MacDonnell, *Jesuit Family Album: Sketches of Chivalry from the Early Society* (Fairfield, Conn.: Clavius, 1997);

MacDonnell, *José De Acosta, S.J. (1540–1600): Pioneer of the Geophysical Sciences* <http://www.faculty.fairfield.edu/jmac/sj/scientists/acosta.htm> [accessed 29 March 2005];

Gregory J. Shepherd, *An Exposition of José De Acosta's Historia natural y moral de las Indias: The Emergence of an Anthropological Vision of Colonial Latin America* (Lewiston, Pa.: Edwin Mellen Press, 2002).

Francisco de Aldana

(1537 – 4 August 1578)

Laura Trujillo Mejía
University of Tennessee

BOOKS: *Primera parte de las obras, que hasta agora se han podido hallar del Capitán Francisco de Aldana, Alcayde de San Sebastian, el qual murió peleando en la jornada de Africa, adonde murió peleando* (Milan: Pablo Gotardo Poncio, 1589);

Segunda parte de las obras, que hasta agora se han podido hallar del Capitán Francisco de Aldana, Alcayde de San Sebastian, que fue Maestre de Campo General del Rey de Portugal, en la jornada de Africa, adonde murió peleando (Madrid: P. Madrigal, 1591);

Todas las obras que hasta agora se han podido hallar del Capitán Francisco de Aldana, Alcayde de San Sebastián, que fue Maestre de Campo General del Rey de Portugal, en la jornada de Africa, a do murió peleando (Madrid: Luys Sánchez, 1593).

Modern Editions: *Sobre la contemplación de Dios, y los requisitos della: Epístola a Arias Montano* (Madrid: Cruz & Raya, 1934);

Hombre adentro: Epístola de Francisco de Aldana (el Divino) y epístola moral a Fabio (Mexico City: Séneca, 1941);

Epistolario poético completo Francisco de Aldana, edited by Antonio Rodríguez-Moñino (Badajoz, Spain: Diputación Provincial de Badajoz, 1946);

Obras completas, 2 volumes, edited by Manuel Moragón Maestre (Madrid: Consejo Superior de Investigaciones Científicas, 1953);

Poesías, edited by Elías L. Rivers (Madrid: Espasa-Calpe, 1957);

Sonetos, edited by Raúl Ruiz (Madrid: Hiperión, 1983);

Poesías castellanas completas, edited by José Lara Garrido (Madrid: Cátedra, 1985);

Epístola del capitán Francisco de Aldana para Arias Montano (Mexico City: Ediciones del Equilibrista, 1987);

Poesía, edited by Rosa Navarro Durán (Barcelona: Planeta, 1994).

Francisco de Aldana was born in Naples in 1537 to parents who originated from Estremadura. His father, Antonio Villena de Aldana, a captain in the Spanish army, was in charge of the Aquila, Gaeta, and Manfredonia forts. In Parma, Villena de Aldana, married the daughter of Colonel Gonzalo de Aldana, his mother's cousin, a marriage that produced four children: Hernando, Francisco, Cosme, and Porcia. Antonio and his brother Bernardo Villena de Aldana were in the service of the Alvarez de Toledo family. For this reason, in 1539 Antonio was a member of the Castilian and Neapolitan escort that accompanied Leonor de Toledo, the daughter of the viceroy Don Pedro, from Naples to Florence for her marriage to the duke of Florence, Cosimo de' Medici. In 1540 the Villena de Aldana family settled down in Florence. Medici, whose power depended partly on the support of the Spanish troops, put Antonio in charge of the Spanish cavalry, and later of the Liorna and San Miniato fortresses. Francisco de Aldana followed his father and his older brother, Hernando, in his career as a professional soldier and military adviser. He started his military career in 1553, when he was sixteen; at twenty he had his first experience on the battlefield; and at twenty-three he was already captain. The young Aldana possibly participated in the battle of San Quintin. This battle took place in 1557 during the war between Spain and France for the regions of Naples and Lombardy. In 1563 Aldana was appointed lieutenant of the San Miniato fortress.

During the Florentine Renaissance, Aldana and his brother Cosme were raised at the Medici court, where they started writing poetry in Italian and Spanish. Both brothers belonged to the literary circle presided over by the erudite Benedetto Varchi. Varchi translated Seneca and Boecio, made philosophical studies of the poetry of Dante, Petrarch, and Michelangelo, and admired Marsilio Ficino and León Hebreo. Under the influence of Varchi, Francisco wrote courtly Petrarchan sonnets. During this time he wrote several poems dedicated to the Medici family, such as the ones written in 1561 after the death of Lucrecia, daughter of the duke and duchess of Florence. In 1562 he wrote a poem as a reply to a sonnet by Varchi lamenting the death of doña Leonor de Toledo, duchess of Florence.

This poem was the only one of Aldana's published during his lifetime.

Neoplatonism, another major influence in Aldana's poetry, prevailed in sixteenth-century Florentine art, especially in literature, painting, and music. This philosophy was inspired by Plato and was developed by Italian philosophers during the fifteenth century. The philosopher Ficino and Medici founded in Florence a Platonic Academy in 1439. Ficino translated all of Plato's dialogues into Latin, and he synthesized Neoplatonism with Christianity. For those who adhered to Neoplatonism during the Renaissance, all things were a reflection of divine beauty. Man, an imperfect being, was always looking to elevate himself by means of the contemplation of the beautiful, in the form of nature, art, and love for a woman, while Platonic love was dissociated from passion and conceived as intellectual and pure. In his youth Aldana wrote several poems dealing with both Platonic and sexual love, elements that, although they oppose each other, appeared side by side in the poetry of the period.

In 1566 Philip II wrote to the duke of Florence asking for Castilian officers to be sent to the Netherlands. The king had decided to resist the expansion of Calvinism in this region, and to this end he appointed as governor of the Netherlands don Francisco Alvarez de Toledo, Duke of Alba, who began to persecute heretics. Aldana, along with a group of officials, joined the duke in Brussels in 1567 and spent several years under his service in the region. Aldana's first campaign in Flanders was against Count Ludwig de Nassau-Dillenberg, brother of William the Silent, Prince of Orange. In April 1568 the count led an offensive that culminated in the Spanish defeat at Heeiligerlee and the execution of the prisoners. In spite of this defeat, in July the duke of Alba and his army assaulted the enemy lines in Jemminj, resulting in a victory that strengthened Spanish control of the region.

Aldana was unhappy in Flanders, as he expressed in a 1589 epistle to his brother Cosme; he felt nostalgic for his life in Florence, and he disliked the Flemish court and the climate of the region. Nonetheless, Aldana had a good relationship with the duke of Alba and expressed his admiration in his works. Around 1570 Aldana wrote a poem in honor of Anne of Austria, Philip II's fourth wife, and in 1571 he addressed a sonnet to the king in which he alluded to the victory of Lepanto against the fleet of the Ottoman Turks. That same year, Aldana was sent to Spain with a letter of recommendation signed by the duke of Alba for his first visit to that country. The following year he joined as sergeant major the forces of John of Austria, admiral of the Holy League against the Ottoman Empire, victor at Lepanto, and the illegitimate son of Holy Roman

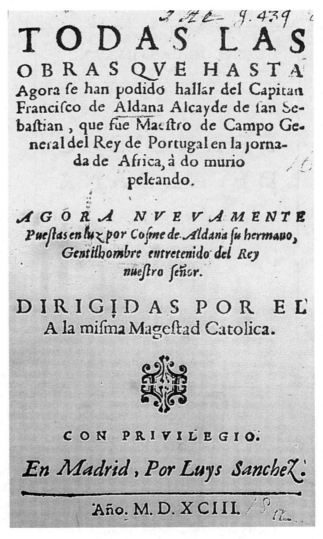

Title page for the first edition of Francisco de Aldana's complete works, published fifteen years after his death in 1578 (Center for Research Libraries, Chicago)

Emperor and Spanish king Charles V, in a campaign against the Turks in the Mediterranean. The troops were assembled in July, but because of some disagreements between the Vatican and the Venetian generals, the expedition only started in September. Finally, on 2 October, the Christian army disembarked in front of the fortress of Modon, but bad weather prevented the assault. John of Austria then decided to postpone the crusade against the infidels.

In December 1572 Aldana was forced to return to the Netherlands because of a new revolt in this region. Dutch rebels had formed a group that combined refugee Calvinists and noblemen, as well as criminals. They found open ports in England and attacked the Spanish positions by sea, and, in 1572, several cities in Holland

CLÁSICOS CASTELLANO

FRANCISCO DE ALDANA

POESÍAS

PQ
6271
.A8
A17
1957

PRÓLOGO, EDICIÓN Y NOTAS DE BLÍAS L. RIVERS

ESPASA-CALPE, S. A.
MADRID

Title page for a modern edition of Aldana's poems, published in 1957 by Espasa-Calpe as part of their Clásicos Castellanos (Castilian Classics) series (Thomas Cooper Library, University of South Carolina)

opened their gates to the rebels. In 1573, under the orders of don Fabrique de Toledo, son of the duke of Alba, Aldana served in conflicts in Haarlem and Alkmaar. The battle of Haarlem ended with a Spanish victory, but it was followed by a rebellion of the troops. For this reason they were forced to take a break in the summer. After two months the army continued on to the city of Alkmaar. The Alkmaar campaign was one of the decisive Flemish victories toward independence from Spain. In the siege of Alkmaar, Aldana was seriously injured, and he was forced to convalesce for the next seven months. During this period he lost the favor of the court after the replacement of the duke of Alba by don Luis de Requesens as governor of the Netherlands. In July 1574 Aldana wrote a letter to the duke, who was already in Spain, informing him of his decision to leave the region. His departure was not possible at the time, however, since he could not obtain the nec-

essary license. In August, Aldana participated in the siege of Leiden, which culminated in the defeat of the Spanish army. In February 1576 the license was finally granted, and Aldana fulfilled his desire of going back to Spain.

The period of almost ten years that Aldana spent in the Netherlands had a significant influence on his poetic work. There he befriended Benito Arias Montano and Bernardino de Mendoza, with whom he exchanged philosophical epistles in verse. Even though Arias Montano participated in the Council of Trent and served as Philip II's chaplain and librarian of the Escorial palace, he ran into trouble with the Inquisition before eventually being acquitted. The same liberal but orthodox Catholicism of Arias Montano and Fray Luis de León can be seen in Aldana's poetry, which he composed during his final years in Flanders. The main topics of his poems during this period are solitude, death, and a mystic desire to separate himself from the world. There is mixed information with regard to the relationship between León and Aldana. Some biographers believe that contact occurred between the two poets, at least through their manuscripts, while others affirm that there is no proof of such contact. In spite of this confusion, there are some parallels in their poetry that can explain the fact that one of Aldana's poems was attributed to León for many years.

Aldana returned to Madrid in 1576, where he again received the protection of the duke of Alba, who had great influence in the Castilian court. Soon after arriving in Madrid, Aldana was named lieutenant of the San Sebastián fortress. Around that time, the king of Portugal requested the aid of his uncle, King Philip II, to carry out an expedition to Africa. In February 1577 Philip II sent Aldana and Diego de Torres to Morocco. The Spanish king wanted to have trustworthy information concerning the power of the Moors after the war of Maluco and Xarife in order to be able to dissuade his nephew from undertaking the campaign. Disguised as merchants, Aldana and de Torres spied on the Moorish military fortifications. They returned to Madrid in June, but the trip had affected Aldana's health, and after some weeks of recovery he traveled to Portugal to present the information about the Muslim fortifications to the Portuguese king Sebastián. Philip II, as well as Aldana, was sure that the report would make the king of Portugal change his opinion. Aldana met Sebastián at the monastery of Belem, where he set forth his findings in Morocco. The Portuguese king was not convinced by Aldana's information of the need to stop the military campaign, and ultimately Aldana decided to accompany him to Africa.

After his return to Madrid, Aldana wrote *Epístola para Arias Montano* (Epistle for Arias Montano) over the course of several years, during which it developed into a longer and more complex poem. It was first published in his *Primera parte de las obras, que hasta agora se han podido hallar del Capitán Francisco de Aldana, Alcayde de San Sebastian, el qual murió peleando en la jornada de Africa, adonde murió peleando* (1589, The First Part of the Works, That Has Recently Been Discovered of Captain Francisco de Aldana, Alcayde de San Sebastian, the One That Died Fighting on the African Expedition, Where He Died Fighting) and has become Aldana's most studied work. In the introduction to *Epístola para Arias Montano* there are some autobiographical elements, including depictions of Aldana's sufferings during his military career and about his decision to abandon the military. As scholars have shown, *Epístola para Arias Montano* is also significant for its mystical humanism and for the same unfulfilled yearning for the divine experience that is found in the poetry of León. Although in *Epístola para Arias Montano* Aldana expresses his wish to retire from the military career and to have a life of contemplation, in his *Otavas al rey don Felipe* (1589, Octaves for the King don Philip in *Primera parte de las obras*), written around the same time as *Epístola para Arias Montano,* he advises the king to attack the enemy in order to consolidate the borders of the empire. Aldana's idea of imperialism was based on the dominant vision in the sixteenth century of Spain as defender of Catholicism.

In September 1577 Aldana petitioned King Philip II to be in charge of the San Sebastián fortress, and he was assigned to the post in November. Before going to San Sebastián, Aldana was in charge of guarding the count of Bura, son of William, Prince of Orange, who was being held as hostage by the king of Spain. In the meantime, King Sebastián insisted on pursuing his campaign to conquer Morocco in order to restore the deposed sultan. In January 1578, he asked his uncle Philip II to send Aldana to Lisbon as his military adviser in Africa. After many rejections of Sebastián's requests, and even though Philip II opposed the plans of his nephew, the Spanish king finally sent Captain Aldana to join the Portuguese monarch, who was already on his way to Morocco. The Portuguese king set out with eight hundred ships and seventy thousand men, hoping to conquer the enemy capital of Fez. Aldana arrived in Arcila in July 1578 accompanied by five hundred Castilian soldiers, but the Portuguese king and his army had already started their march toward the interior of Africa. In Arcila, when Aldana was notified that Sebastián was planning to attack the port of Lareche by land instead of by sea, he informed Pedro de Mezquita, the captain in charge of the fortress, of his intention to return to Spain. Aldana was convinced by the hidalgo Pedro de Marmol to continue with the venture and carried with him the tunic and the helmet used

by Charles V during his victorious entrance in Tunisia as a token of good luck from the Spanish king to his nephew.

Aldana finally joined the Portuguese king and his army near Tres Ribeiros. He found an army devoid of training and experiencing low morale. It is not clear what position was given to Aldana by King Sebastián. Some biographers affirm that he was *maestre de campo general* (general field marshal), the title used by his brother Cosme on the cover of his editions of Aldana's poetry. Others, based on the records from Portuguese historians, state that he was sergeant major. All biographers tend to recognize, however, that he was in charge of the army. On 4 August 1578, there was some disagreement among the members of the council of the Christian army. Some of them wanted to attack the enemy that same day, while others wanted to delay the battle. The ones that were in favor of waiting were counting on the death of the enemy's ailing king, Abdel Malek, to demoralize his army. Although Aldana was never in favor of the African campaign, this time he agreed with King Sebastián that they should go into battle that day. The Portuguese and Castilians were outnumbered five to one by the Moroccans. After experiencing several misfortunes, the infantry was organized under Aldana's orders following the model that the duke of Alba had suggested to the king of Portugal. However, the effects of little preparation on the Portuguese troops were seen when they were decimated by the Moors in the battle of Alcazarquivir, also known as the "Battle of the Three Kings" because the king of Portugal, the king of Fez, and the Moorish pretender to the throne of Fez were killed. Aldana also died, on 4 August 1578, and neither his body nor that of King Sebastián was ever recovered.

Philip II heard about Aldana's death in a report of the battle of Alcazarquivir written by Diego de Torres, the same man that accompanied Aldana on his trip to Africa in 1577 to spy on Moorish fortifications. The Spanish king, not satisfied with the information he received, sent Cristobal de Moura to Lisbon in order to learn more about Aldana's fate. De Moura, the former Portuguese ambassador to Spain, wrote two different messages back to the Spanish king. In the first one he reported that it was commonly believed that Aldana was dead. In the second, he informed Philip II that Aldana was still alive. The most conclusive piece of news related to the death of Aldana is a letter from Juan de Silva, who participated in the battle of Alcazarquivir, to Gabriel de Zayas, a friend of the poet. In this letter, de Silva says that during the battle he talked to Aldana about the loss of the artillery and that he was told by other witnesses that after having a conversation with

Francisco de Aldana

Sonetos

Edición a cargo de Raúl Ruiz

PQ
6271
A8
A6
1984

poesía Hiperión

Cover for a 1983 edition of the sonnets Aldana wrote under the influence of the Italian poet Petrarch (John W. Brister Library, Memphis University)

the Portuguese king, Aldana went back to fight and was killed.

Only one of Francisco de Aldana's poems was printed during his lifetime. After his death, Cosme de Aldana published his work in two volumes. The first one, dedicated to Philip II, was printed in Milan in 1589. The second volume was published in Madrid in 1591. Later, in 1593, the two volumes were printed again in Madrid and appeared as *Todas las obras que hasta agora se han podido hallar del Capitán Francisco de Aldana, Alcayde de San Sebastián, que fue Maestre de Campo General del Rey de Portugal, en la jornada de África, a do murió peleando* (Collection of All the Works by Captain Francisco de Aldana, Lieutenant of San Sebastian, General Field Marshal of the King of Portugal in the Military Expedition to Africa, Where He Died Fighting). In general, Aldana's poetry is the result of the intermingling of the intellectual world of the Renaissance and the violent world of war in which he was an active participant. Aldana certainly had the recognition of the Spanish writers during the sixteenth century, who called him *el*

divino (the divine one). Miguel de Cervantes, for example, mentions Aldana along with contemporary poets Juan Boscán and Garcilaso de la Vega in *La Galatea* (1585, The Galatea) and wrote about Aldana's fame in *Viaje al Parnaso* (1614, Voyage to Parnassus). During the seventeenth century Francisco de Quevedo complained in *Anacreón castellano* (1609, Castilian Anacreontic) about errors that appeared in the two printed volumes of Aldana's poetry and expressed a wish to amend them. In *Laurel de Apolo* (1630, Apollo's Laurel), Lope de Vega praised Aldana's abilities as both a poet and a soldier. Although he is often treated as a secondary author by modern Hispanists, Aldana received acclaim during the Golden Age as one of the most prominent soldier-poets of sixteenth-century Spain.

Biographies:

Antonio R. Rodríguez Moñino, *El capitán Francisco de Aldana: Poeta del siglo XVI (1537–1578)* (Valladolid: Talleres Tipográficos, 1943);

Elías L. Rivers, "New Biographical Data on Francisco de Aldana," *Romanic Review,* 44 (1953): 166–184;

Rivers, *Francisco de Aldana, el divino capitán* (Badajoz: Institución de Servicios Culturales, 1955).

References:

Robert Archer, "The Overreaching Imagination: The Structure and Meaning of Aldana's 'Carta para Arias Montano,'" *Bulletin of Hispanic Studies,* 65 (1988): 237–249;

Carlos X. Ardavin, "Los sonetos amorosos de Francisco de Aldana: Crisis del neoplatonismo y poética del desasosiego," *Confluencia,* 14 (1998): 35–46;

Lydia M. Bernstein, "Francisco de Aldana's Epistle to Galanio: A Poem of Synthesis," *Hispanofila,* 117 (1996): 1–10;

Bernstein, "Tragic Self-Actualization in the Spanish Renaissance: A New Reading of Francisco de Aldana's 'Fabula de Faetonte,'" *Hispanic Journal,* 16 (1995): 109–121;

Luis Cernuda, "Tres poetas metafísicos," *Bulletin of Spanish Studies,* 25 (1948): 109–118;

J. P. W. Crawford, "Francisco de Aldana: A Neglected Poet of the Golden Age in Spain," *Hispanic Review,* 7 (1939): 48–61;

Hernando Cuadrado, *El ciclo amoroso en Francisco de Aldana* (Madrid: Francisco Arellano, 1981);

Lauriane Fallay-d'Este, "Tradition et originalité chez Francisco de Aldana," *Ibérica,* 1 (1977): 119–130;

Juan Ferraté, "Una muestra de poesía extravagante: Las octavas sobre los Efectos de Amor de Francisco de Aldana," in *Dinámica de la poesía: Ensayos de expli-*

cación, 1952–1966, edited by Ferraté (Barcelona: Seix Barral, 1968), pp. 215–243;

Ferraté, "Siete sonetos de Francisco de Aldana," in *Teoría del poema,* edited by Ferraté (Barcelona: Seix Barral, 1957), pp. 69–80;

Lola Gonzalez, "Fonosimbolismo y aliteración: Francisco de Aldana frente a la palabra poética," *Scriptura,* 6–7 (1991): 41–50;

Dolores González Martínez, *La poesía de Francisco de Aldana (1537–1578): Introducción al estudio de la imagen* (Lérida, Spain: Edicions de la Universitat de Lleida, 1995);

Otis H. Green, "On Francisco de Aldana: Observations on Dr. Rivers' Study of El Divino Capitán," *Hispanic Review,* 26 (1958): 117–135;

Green, "A Wedding Introito by Francisco de Aldana (1537–1578)," *Hispanic Review,* 31 (1963): 8–21;

José Lara Garrido, "Las ediciones de Francisco de Aldana: Hipótesis sobre un problema bibliográfico," *Revista de Estudios Extremenos,* 42 (1986): 541–583;

Lara Garrido, "Vision, alegoria y discurso en las 'Octavas a Felipe II' de Francisco de Aldana," *Nueva Revista de Filologia Hispanica,* 36 (1988): 277–301;

Alfredo Lefebvre, *La poesía del Capitán Aldana, 1537–1578* (Concepción, Chile: Universidad de Concepción, 1953);

Julio Neira, *Francisco de Aldana* (Badajoz, Spain: Editora Regional de Extremadura, 1990);

Julián Olivares, "Aldana, Quevedo and la paga del mundo," *Hispanic Journal,* 11 (1990): 57–70;

Elías L. Rivers, "Aldana y Quevedo: Una nota en homenaje a Alfonso Rey," *Edad de Oro,* 18 (1999): 171–175;

Rivers, "A New Manuscript of Poem Hitherto Attributed to Fray Luis de León," *Hispanic Review,* 20 (1952): 153–158;

Carlos Ruíz Silva, *Estudíos sobre Francisco de Aldana* (Valladolid, Spain: Universidad, Secretariado de Publicaciones, 1981);

Ruíz Silva, "Francisco de Aldana, en el cuarto centenario de su muerte," *Revista de Occidente,* 18 (1977): 48–52;

Louise Salstad, "Another Look at Francisco de Aldana's 'Otro aquí no se ve,'" *Romance Notes,* 22 (1982): 335–340;

Salstad, "Francisco de Aldana's Metamorphoses in the Circle," *Modern Language Review,* 74 (1979): 599–606;

Arthur Terry, "Thought and Feeling in Three Golden-Age Sonnets," *Bulletin of Hispanic Studies,* 59 (1982): 237–246;

D. Gareth Walters, "On the Text, Source and Significance of Aldana's Medoro y Angélica," *Forum for Modern Language Studies,* 20 (1984): 17–29;

Walters, *The Poetry of Francisco de Aldana* (London: Tamesis, 1988).

Juan Boscán

(circa 1490 – 21 September 1542)

E. Ernesto Delgado
Bowling Green State University

BOOK: *Las obras de Boscán y algunas de Garcilaso de la Vega repartidas en quatro libros,* 4 volumes, by Boscán and Garcilaso de la Vega (Barcelona: Carlos Amorós, 1543; enlarged edition, Antwerp: Martín Nuncio, 1544; enlarged again, Venice: Gabriel Giolito de Ferraris, 1553; enlarged again, Barcelona: Viuda de Carlos Amorós, 1554).

Modern Editions: *Las obras de Juan Boscán: Repartidas en tres libros,* edited by William I. Knapp (Madrid: Murillo, 1875);

Las treinta of Juan Boscán: An Edition Printed before His Death, edited by Hayward Keniston (New York: Knickerbocker, 1911);

Poemas inéditos de Juan Boscán: Según el manuscito 359 de la Biblioteca Central de la Disputación de Barcelona, edited by Martín de Riquer (Barcelona: Alerta, 1942);

Coplas, sonetos y otras poesías (Barcelona: Montaner & Simón, 1946);

Obras poéticas de Juan Boscan, edited by Riquer, Antonio Comas, and Joaquín Molas (Barcelona: Facultad de Filosofía y Letras, Universidad de Barcelona, 1957);

Las Obras de Juan Boscán, de nuevo puestas al día y repartidas en tres libros, edited, with a preliminary study, by Carlos Clavería Laguerda (Barcelona: Promociones y Publicaciones Universitarias, 1991);

Obra completa, edited by Clavería Laguarda (Madrid: Cátedra, 1999).

OTHER: *Los quatro libros del cortesano, agora nuevamente traducidos en lengua castellana,* translated by Boscán (Barcelona: Pedro Montpezat, 1534).

Juan Boscán is considered one of the key early-modern Spanish poets who introduced the poetry of the Italian Renaissance into Spain. Boscán, along with Garcilaso de la Vega, infused Spanish poetry with new topics and an acute sensibility for sentimental expression of amorous themes that contrasted with traditional medieval *cancionero* (songbook) poetry. Along with Garcilaso, who was the epitome of the well-established noble and court poet of sixteenth-century Spain, Boscán was also *un hombre de armas y letras* (a man of arms and letters), although he never received the military honors given to his more renowned friend.

Born in Barcelona between 1487 and 1492, Boscán (Joan Boschá Almugáver in Catalan) was the son of Juan Valentín Boscán, who was an important judge and shipyard manager of the Generalitat of Catalonia, the most important governmental organization of the region. Boscán's mother was Violante Almugáver, also a longtime patrician citizen of Barcelona. Boscán's grandfather, Joan Francesco Boschá, was a prominent historian and an important ally of the Catholic Monarchs during the succession wars of 1474 and had shown an unconditional loyalty to King Ferdinand's father, Joan II of Aragon, during the turbulent period when the Catalans were fighting for supremacy over the Iberian Peninsula. During these times Boscán's fidelity to King Joan II was especially important, because of the ambitious and threatening influence of Constable Alvaro de Luna, the *valido* (chief minister or favorite) of King Juan II of Castile. Alvaro de Luna was tirelessly facing Aragonese claims over certain Castilian possessions. Years later, Boscán's grandfather also played an important role in the conflict between the kingdom of Aragon and the challenges of the successor of Juan II, King Enrique IV of Castile, who was in the process of taking control of the kingdom of Navarre after the death of its legitimate successor, Charles III, Prince of Viana. Furthermore, Boscán's grandfather became an important supporter of King Joan II when the kingdom of Aragon was about to collapse after two rival factions in Catalonia–the traditional patricians and the newcomers, including professionals and wealthy citizens, artists, and merchants–began an internal revolt in 1461 in an attempt to impose their particular interests. As a consequence of these conflicts, Boscán's family was expelled from Barcelona in 1464 and found refuge in Valencia. After King Joan II of Aragon restored order in 1472 and Boscán's parents returned to Barcelona, they benefited from several royal privileges, many of which were given as a reward by Ferdinand the Catholic. After the death of his father in 1492, Boscán lived with his mother on the annuities granted to her by the city of Barcelona and the Crown of Aragon.

The loyalty that Boscán's family showed to the Aragonese kings' political interests is crucial in understanding the privileges that Boscán enjoyed throughout his life. In a period during which knighthood and chivalric values of the nobility were being slowly replaced by service and financial support to the king, it is no wonder that Boscán found his way into the royal court and reached a privileged position within noble circles. Although details of his life before 1514 scarcely exist, according to documents Boscán was an *alumno* (student) of King Ferdinand and a member of his royal household. He quite possibly left Barcelona between 1507 and 1510 to take up permanent residence at the court of King Ferdinand. By the end of his life King Ferdinand was sixty-four years old, but he still remembered the loyalty that Boscán's grandfather had shown. Before his death the king assured that Boscán was granted important benefits, one of which was the *lezda* de Mediona, a mandatory tax paid by its inhabitants for city trade.

During the same period, Boscán was also under the guidance of Lucas di Marinis (better known as Lucio Marineo Sículo), an important Sicilian courtier and author who wrote the *Epistolarum familiarum* (1514, Family Letters), which includes a correspondence with Boscán in book 12. From this well-versed and cultured man Boscán acquired knowledge of the classics, which allowed him to read and understand the new style used by Italian poets as well as to translate the most representative of Latin and Greek lyrics into Spanish. Boscán states the importance of Marineo's mentorship in a letter written in Latin not later than 1514 (although the exact date of composition is impossible to determine), in which he recognizes how much he has learned from his mentor's guidance: "Tu enim diuturna, ut sic dixerim, vigilantia non solum primis, quod aiunt, litteris meum ingenium exornasti, sed ulterius ad altiora progredi compulisti" (Not only did you enlighten my wits with the first letters, but also encouraged me to go ahead and reach higher level of erudition).

Because the kingdom of Castile and Aragon included important Italian territories such as Sicily, Naples, and the county of Milan, many Italians not surprisingly came to Spain to strengthen the intellectual and artistic contacts that had been established when Alfonso V the Magnanimous, king of Aragon, captured the kingdom of Naples and, fascinated by its sophisticated and refined environment of artists and poets, moved his court there. Important Spanish writers before Boscán, such as Antonio de Nebrija, author of

Title page for an early edition (Salamanca: Pedro Tovans, 1540) of Juan Boscán's 1534 Spanish translation of Il cortegiano *(1527, The Book of the Courtier), by Baldassare Castiglione (from Ramón D. Perés, ed.,* Homenaje a Boscán en el iv centenario de su muerte [1542–1942]: Catálogo de la exposición bibliográfica, *1944; Thomas Cooper Library, University of South Carolina)*

the first *Gramática Castellana* (1492, Castilian Grammar), and the poet and musician Juan del Encina, author of eclogues in the Italian fashion, traveled and spent many years in Italy, returning to Spain with new Renaissance sensitivity. During the same time in Italy, Jacopo Sannazzaro wrote his *Arcadia* (1501), and Virgil's eclogues, translated into Italian by Bernardo Pulci in 1481, began to exert a significant influence on Renaissance culture.

This courtly environment presented Boscán with valuable opportunities to contact important intellectuals and artists who were familiar with new Renaissance ideals from Italy. Perhaps one of the most significant influences for Boscán was the long and unwavering friendship he had with Garcilaso, by then already one of the selected grandees in the court of King Charles V of Spain. It is not certain when and how these two friends met for the first time, but in 1522, during the abortive attempt by the Spanish navy to retake the Isle of Rhodes from Turkish invaders, both Garcilaso and

Boscán participated under the command of the young Fernando Álvarez de Toledo, Duke of Alba, who, although just sixteen years old, was already an experienced man of arms. The relationship established between Álvarez de Toledo and Boscán appears to have been close, and Boscán served as his personal *ayo* (preceptor). The bond between Boscán and Álvarez de Toledo allowed the former to take part in the siege of Florence in 1530, in which Garcilaso also participated. By the time Charles V began to gain support in the Spanish court as the new monarch and emperor of the Holy Roman Empire, Boscán had written most of his *coplas* (short lyric poems) and *canciones* (songs), which make up the first of the four volumes of *Las obras de Boscán y algunas de Garcilaso de la Vega repartidas en quatro libros* (The Works of Boscán and Some by Garcilaso de la Vega Distributed in Four Volumes). The four volumes appeared 20 March 1543, printed by Carlos Amorós in Barcelona. The first three volumes of the set comprise Boscán's works, while volume four comprises Garcilaso's. Although unified by a common concern of love, Boscán's three volumes are different in content and philosophy. They illustrate different stages in Boscán's assimilation of Renaissance ideals and aesthetics. Volume 1 is the result of Boscán's assimilation of medieval poetry, especially that pertaining to courtly love. Volumes 2 and 3 reveal the use of new Renaissance ideals and the incorporation of Italian aesthetics, especially rhyme and verse forms such as sonnets, *liras,* and Horatian epistles.

Volume 1 of *Las obras de Boscán* shows both the significant influence of traditional Castilian poetry with respect to the rhymes, meters, and themes employed by Boscán, and that of the Catalan poet Ausías March, especially in Boscán's use of an abstract tone, his intense melancholy, his scholastic analysis of sadness, and his search for a pure and spiritual love. In contrast to Garcilaso, who explored several genres and themes of the new Italian style, Boscán wrote mostly about love. Volume 1 expresses mainly his still-strong Aristotelian perception of love. While the three most important topics of the late Middle Ages—love, death, and fortune—are present in his poetry, Boscán holds love above the other two. Death is present as a consequence of love, whether resulting from abandonment or because of joyfulness. Fortune is seen as a capricious goddess who changes the fate of love unpredictably. Boscán was committed to expressing the variable moods of love, and, as some scholars have shown, by keeping track of moods shifts in his poems, his poetry can be read as a personal journey into the experience of love.

In his *coplas, canciones,* and *villancicos* (love poems) included in the first book, Boscán is a dexterous versi-fier but still an epigone of the medieval poetry of courtly love. He makes use of the traditional *copla,* which consists of eight-syllable-line verses with consonantal rhyme, and his *canciones* and *villancicos,* also in Spanish octosyllabic meters, are mainly courtly in theme. Boscán's images and expressions in these poems are, like those in many compositions included in the fifteenth-century *cancioneros* (songbooks), components of an intellectual poetry full of the medieval imagery of the troubadours—the castle of love, the allegorical battle of senses, the prisoner of love—and expressions of suffering, pain, anguish, unfulfilled desire, and constant longing to be with the beloved. Book 1 takes also from the troubadour's poetry the Aristotelian-Thomistic theories of the soul. According to these theories, the universe consists of four elements or *calidades:* earth, water, air, and fire. They were, respectively, cold and dry, cold and wet, hot and wet, and hot and dry. Melancholy, phlegm, blood, and choler, the four humors, were produced in the body by a predominance of one of these elements.

The Aristotelian-Thomistic theories of the soul considered three types of souls: a vegetative, a sensitive, and a rational soul. All the natural world—minerals, plants, water—belonged to the first. The second soul existed in the animals and gave them movement and the capacity for procreation. The rational soul was found only in the human being, who received also the angelic nature. Human beings, in order to form rational ideas, pass objects in nature through senses. Four human faculties then filter them: the imaginative faculty, the sensitive memory, the fantasy, and the estimative faculty. Images are then presented to the three highest powers of the soul: *el entendimiento* (understanding), *la memoria* (memory), and *la voluntad* (will). The first decides whether objects are good or bad. If they are considered worthy, they are stored in the memory for safekeeping. The will, considered blind, puts ideas into action when taken from the memory. In addition, passions, different from tangible objects, are separated into irascible and concupiscent appetites and rightly relegated to the sensitive soul. Passions, however, may be so powerful that the rational soul may succumb to them, and they could dictate to the will actions that were deleterious to the human being. Boscán utilizes these ideas in order to depict the spiritual pilgrimage of the soul from the basest elements to the heights of understanding. Before he acknowledges Renaissance ideas of beauty and reason, however, Boscán considers passion as the primary malady of any rational soul. Once passion rules over human will, rational faculties are imprisoned. Then suffering becomes the sole pleasure. In sum, once passion takes control of human will, love is placed a little above animal instinct.

*Title pages for the first four editions of the work collecting Boscán's poems along with those of his friend
Garcilaso de la Vega (from Ramón D. Perés, ed.,* Homenaje a Boscán en el iv centenario
de su muerte [1542–1942]: Catálogo de la exposición bibliográfica, *1944;
Thomas Cooper Library, University of South Carolina)*

Boscán's *coplas, canciones,* and *villancicos,* though traditional in expression and language, reveal an important development toward a personal perception of feelings, which is seen in book 2 of *Las obras de Boscán.* More specifically, scholars have shown how the sequence of poems shown in book 1 brings to light a curious journey into the realm of Boscán's personal life. These works reveal two love affairs experienced by the poet. In *coplas* 1 through 8 Boscán describes the course of his passion, which is ultimately unrequited, for Doña Isabel, whom the poet names in *copla* 2: "señora doña Isabel, / tan cruel / es la vida que consiento, / que me mata mi tormento" (Lady Isabel / life is so cruel / that I consent / that my suffering kills me). In *coplas* 13 through 25 he recounts another adventure in which he drove his feelings to the zenith of suffering. The several *canciones,* which Boscán inserts among the *coplas,* seem to serve as brief interludes that divide the sequences of sentimental adventures into different stages. At the end of book 1 Boscán includes a verse epistle to Admiral Fadrique Enriquez in which he justifies his perception of love. This letter is one of a sequence of six not included in the edition of 1543.

Although Boscán was likely familiar with Petrarch's poetry before or during the writing of his *coplas,* it was not until 1526 that he consciously adopted the style of Italianate poetry and explicitly abandoned the traditional Spanish octosyllabic compositions. The year 1526 was a decisive date for both Castilian poetry and the political stability of the Spanish kingdom. In February 1525 Spanish troops defeated the French in the battle of Pavia, and Francis I, the king of France, was taken to Madrid as prisoner. The next year the French were forced to negotiate and ceded Burgundy in exchange for their king's freedom. The victory in Pavia was an important milestone for Spain: in the coming years Charles V saw his power consolidated both in the Iberian Peninsula and, more importantly, in his European domains. Moreover, the betrothal of the Emperor Charles V to Isabella of Portugal took place in the summer of 1526 in Granada, where the royal court established itself. Since this period was one of negotiations and frequent meetings of foreign delegates, many emissaries joined the royal court in Granada. Also present were important poets such as Diego Hurtado de Mendoza; leading personalities such as the humanist Alfonso de Valdés, recently appointed imperial secretary for Latin letters to the emperor; and Fray Antonio de Guevara, who had successfully completed difficult missionary work among the Valencian Moriscos. In this court Boscán encountered two dignitaries who were decisive for his life and work: Andrea Navaggiero, a prestigious humanist editor of the Aldine Press and the Venetian ambassador to Spain, and Count Baldassare Castiglione, diplomat and humanist author of *Il cortegiano* (1527, The Book of the Courtier) and the papal nuncio of Clement VII in Spain since 1524. When Boscán traveled to Granada with Garcilaso and the duke of Alba as members of the king's court in June 1525, a rich and significant intellectual environment awaited him.

Many scholars such as Carlos Clavería Laguarda and Anne J. Cruz agree that meeting with Navaggiero and Castiglione marked an important turning point in Boscán's poetry. In the introduction to book 2, writing to the duchess of Somma (to whom he also dedicated book 1), Boscán states his renunciation of the traditional Spanish meters and rhymes and confesses that Navaggiero suggested that he write poetry in the style of the Italian writers. From then on Boscán used the Italianate style for his poetry. Although he considered himself to be the first writer to adapt the Italianate style to the Castilian language, many writers before him had attempted to compose verses in the Italianate forms. Among them was Iñigo López de Mendoza, Marqués de Santillana, who wrote forty-two sonnets in the Italian style. Boscán, however, is one of the first, along with Garcilaso, who successfully adapted the rhyme and meter of the sonnet to Spanish verse.

As in Boscán's book 1, the sequence of sonnets in book 2 corresponds to two different points in time, in this instance separated by the poet's discovery of Castiglione's *Il cortegiano* before 1533. Even if it is possible to relate several sonnets to the love affairs expressed in Boscán's *coplas* of book 1, as J. P. Wickersham Crawford suggests in his "Notes on the Chronology of Boscán's Verses" (1927), book 2 also reveals Boscán's changing idea of love, which he came to express according to Neoplatonic ideas. Moreover, while some of Boscán's sonnets express the medieval Aristotelian idea of love, as David H. Darst shows in *Juan Boscán* (1978), and coincidentally utilize the Italian sonnet structure without changing the tone, style, language, and content of the earlier *coplas,* others express a radical change by adopting the Neoplatonic idea of love as a consequence of Boscán's absorption of the philosophy outlined in book 4 of Castiglione's *Il cortegiano.* Presented as Pietro Bembo's ideas, Castiglione's book 4 states that Plato's philosophy of love is based on an ascending transition from the material to the immaterial in which the mind is drawn upward by the love of beauty. Since Neoplatonists give women a more important and more central place with respect to ideal human love, beauty in Platonic ascent is defined specifically as the physical beauty of woman, as it is in and through human love that man can progress from the physical plane through the intellectual plane to the spiritual plane. Woman is no longer seen as the origin of the poet's tormented love. Thus,

Boscán leaves aside the medieval Aristotelian-Thomistic idea that love is a disease of the soul that wastes the flesh of the lover and perturbs the mind in favor of a more rationally oriented perception that involves the use of intellectual faculties. In book 2, for example, in the opening quartet of sonnet 5, Boscán still considers love an agent of endless suffering. Love, as in medieval troubadour poetry, condemns the poet even at an early age to a long life of slavery. Boscán says, "Aún bien no fui salido de la cuna / ni del alma la leche hube dexado, / quando el amor me tuvo condenado / a ser de los que siguen su fortuna" (I had hardly left the crib, / nor had I been weaned from the breast, / when Love had condemned me / to be one of those that follow his banner).

Sonnet 82 of book 2, on the contrary, gives love another function. Here, as stated in Castiglione's *Il cortegiano* in terms of Christian mysticism, Boscán places human love in the context of divine love and gives it a joyful spiritual value. Love is no longer an atavistic force or a hopeless torment; love is rather the "dulce gozar de un dulce sentimiento, / viendo mi cielo estar claro y sereno, / y dulce revolver sobre mi seno, / con firme concluir, que estoy contento" (sweet gratification of a sweet sentiment, / seeing my heaven to be clear and serene, / and sweet remembering in my breast / with firm conclusion that I am content). As stated by Alexander A. Parker in his *The Philosophy of Love in Spanish Literature, 1480–1680* (1985), love of woman is a stage toward, and part of, the love of God; it is a stage that is not left behind but carried up. This philosophy, in effect, idealizes and glorifies human love to the highest possible degree within a religious or theistic view of life.

Whether Boscán read *Il cortegiano* immediately after his encounter with Castiglione in 1526 is unknown. What is certain is the fact that his reading and translation of this book, which was published as *Los quatro libros del cortesano, agora nuevamente traducidos en lengua castellana* (The Four Books of the Courtier, Now Translated in Castilian) in 1534, made a significant impression on Boscán. Because Castiglione died in 1529 and *Il cortegiano* was published in 1528, Boscán quite possibly knew the work before 1533, when Garcilaso sent him a copy and urged him to translate it into Spanish. Book 2 is, therefore, a transitional work, which shows Boscán's interest in assimilating the new Renaissance aesthetics.

Boscán was active in diplomatic matters at this point in his life. He was a member of the party taken by Charles V to Bologna, where the king received the iron crown of the Lombards on 23 February 1530 from the Pope, who crowned him Holy Roman Emperor the following day. Boscán also appears to have accompanied the duke of Alba to Germany in order to deter Turkish forces. According to a letter written by the duke in

1533, Boscán was about to marry Ana Girón de Rebolledo, although the actual marriage document was not signed until 1539. During these years Boscán lived mostly in Barcelona and likely struggled against many detractors who criticized his use of Italian meters. One of the most famous critics was the poet Cristóbal de Castillejo, who lived in Vienna after 1525. He wrote the poem "Reprensión contra los poetas españoles que escriben en verso italiano" (Censure of Spanish Poets Who Write with Italian Meters) shortly after Boscán's death. This poem was published in the Venetian edition (1553) of Boscán's works. In spite of his detractors, Boscán continued to write poems in the Italian style, most of which were included in book 3 of the first edition of his collected works, published in 1543. By this time, many of Boscán's poems were circulating throughout Europe.

Boscán's book 3 includes six long compositions: a 2,793-line poem in hendecasyllabic blank verse, "Leandro y Hero" (The Fable of Leander and Hero); a 385-line epistolary poem, "Capítulo I" (Chapter I); a 347-line courtly letter named "Epístola" (Epistle), like "Capítulo I" in terza rima; a 1,080-line poem in hendecasyllabic royal octaves called "Ottava Rima" (Royal Octave); and the two verse epistles written between Boscán and the poet Diego Hurtado de Mendoza. The two epistles are the 274-line (in terza rima) "Epístola de don Diego de Mendoza a Boscán" (Epistle from Don Diego de Mendoza to Boscán, circa 1539), and the 403-line terza rima poem "Respuesta de Boscán a don Diego de Mendoza" (Response from Boscán to Don Diego de Mendoza). This last poem is one of several in which Boscán openly expresses the new Renaissance ideals and places himself above the material world from where he contemplates the beauties of the natural world and praises their loveliness. The act of contemplation, explains Boscán, is the only means of attaining happiness; the beauty through equilibrium and order gives tranquility to the soul. Similar to Fray Luis de León's late-sixteenth-century odes, Boscán expresses in this poem his *nil admirari* philosophy, the Latin version of the Stoic-Epicurian *ataraxia* (serenity), taken from Horace's *Epistles* I.6: "Nil admirari prope res est una, Numici, / solaque quae possit facere et servare beatum" (For a man not to marvel at anything, seems to me, Numa, / to be something that suffices to give us a tranquil life). In the "Respuesta de Boscán a don Diego de Mendoza," Boscán affirms openly that "el no maravillarse / es propio del jüizio bien compuesto. / Quien sabe y quiere a la virtud llegarse, / pues las cosas verá desde lo alto, / nunca terná de qué pueda alterarse" (I also say that to not marvel / is proper for a well-composed mind. / He who knows and desires to reach virtue, / since he will see everything from on

CÁTEDRA CIUDAD DE BARCELONA
PATROCINADA POR EL EXCMO. AYUNTAMIENTO DE LA CIUDAD
BIBLIOTECA DE AUTORES BARCELONESES

OBRAS POÉTICAS DE JUAN BOSCÁN

Edición crítica por
MARTÍN DE RIQUER
ANTONIO COMAS y JOAQUÍN MOLAS

I

FACULTAD DE FILOSOFÍA Y LETRAS
UNIVERSIDAD DE BARCELONA
1957

*Title page for a scholarly edition of Boscán's poetic works
published by the University of Barcelona (Thomas
Cooper Library, University of South Carolina)*

high, / never will have anything to be disturbed about). Boscán, in saying that to not marvel is an essential trait of a well-composed mind, uses an aesthetic term, since "bien compuesto" means beauty through equilibrium and order. Boscán's "Respuesta de Boscán a don Diego de Mendoza," composed in late 1539 or early 1540, shows the long distance between this new philosophy of contemplation and love and that of his earlier poems.

Except for the "Epístola," the others, especially "Ottava Rima" and "Leandro y Hero," exhibit clear influences from the Neoplatonic ideals in their descriptions of the beloved as an embodiment of all that is good, capable of facilitating the process of the poet's ascent to the realm of ideas. Neither "Leandro y Hero" nor "Ottava Rima" deals with Boscán's personal love experiences; they show great objectivity in a clear narrative style in accordance with the new Renaissance sensibility.

Boscán died on 21 September 1542, after becoming ill at Perpiñán, where he had gone with his friend the duke of Alba. The poet left three daughters, Mariana, Violante, and Beatriz, and a manuscript almost ready for publication. A contract in Catalan dated 27 March 1542 stated that the bookseller Joan Bages had agreed to send to print one thousand copies of Boscán's work for the poet's friends. According to this document, Boscán himself was to control the printed work so that it would not have errors. After Boscán's death, however, his wife, Ana Girón, had to carry out the publication without her husband's revisions. In the preface to the 1543 edition, she details the reasons why she undertook its publication without changing a single word in the poems written by her husband, even if the sequence of the poems may have not reflected Boscán's final decision. She also justifies the inclusion of some of Garcilaso's poems in book 4 as homage to the friendship that the poets shared for many years and the fact that after Garcilaso's death in 1536, Boscán was given his friend's work to edit and dedicate to the duchess of Somma. The haste in publishing Boscán's work is explained in the preface, in which Ana Girón conveys her fear of seeing future unauthorized version of her husband's poems published. By the time Boscán died, many of his poems clearly had been circulating throughout Europe in unauthorized or fragmented editions, apparently with many variants and errors. The editio princeps, published in March 1543, was quickly followed in November by a pirated Lisbon printing with the same title and a reprint in August 1544 produced by Pedro de Castro in Medina del Campo. The reception of *Las obras de Boscán* appears to have been highly favorable. Between 1543 and 1597, twenty-one different editions were printed throughout Europe, some of which included new poems not available to Ana Girón by 1543. In Antwerp in 1544 Martín Nuncio produced an edition that included several new poems: "Conversión de Boscán" (Conversion of Boscán), "Mar de amor" (Sea of Love), and twelve *coplas*. These early editions were followed by many others over the next hundred years. The 1875 edition, *Las obras de Juan Boscán: Repartidas en tres libros* (The Works of Juan Boscán, Arranged in Three Volumes), edited by William I. Knapp, was the first to omit Garcilaso's poems.

Juan Boscán's legacy derives mostly from his role as the first poet who introduced the Italian meters into Spain, not excepting Santillana's sonnets written almost fifty years before. Although he has been overshadowed for centuries by his collaborator and friend Garcilaso, the reception of Boscán's poetry merited modest attention from scholars by the nineteenth century and during the first half of the twentieth century. Notwithstanding this interest, the neglect of Boscán's work among modern scholars may be owing to several factors. As Clavería Laguarda points out in his preliminary study in *Las obras de Juan Boscán, de nuevo puestas al día y repartidas en tres libros* (1991, The Works of Juan Boscán, Newly Updated and Arranged in Three Books), Boscán did not enjoy the prestigious military career of Garcilaso or that of Francisco de Aldana; nor did he arouse burning controversies as did Fernando de Herrera. In addition, Boscán never achieved the prestigious political stature that Diego Hurtado Mendoza did in Spain. Although not as prominent as these contemporaries, Boscán deserves a notable place in Spanish Renaissance poetry. He, along with Garcilaso, brought Renaissance artistry to Spain. The trajectory of his work reveals the evolution of Spanish letters during the transition from the late Middle Ages to the Renaissance and serves as a valuable mirror by which to contemplate the impressive journey of an artist who lived between two periods and experienced the vicissitudes of their changes.

Letter:

Lucius Martineus Siculus, *Epistolarum familiarum libri XVII,* edited by Teresa Jiménez Calvente (Alcalá de Henares: Universidad de Alcalá de Henares, 2001), pp. 624–625.

References:

J. P. Wickersham Crawford, "Notes on the Chronology of Boscán's Verses," *Modern Philology,* 25 (1927): 29–36;

Anne J. Cruz, *Imitación y transformación: Petrarquismo en la poesía de Boscán y Garcilaso de la Vega* (Amsterdam & Philadelphia: Benjamins, 1988);

David H. Darst, *Juan Boscán* (Boston: Twayne, 1978);

Margherita Morreale, *Castiglione y Boscán: El ideal cortesano en el Renacimiento español,* 2 volumes (Madrid: Biblioteca de la Real Academia Española, 1959);

Ignacio Navarrete, *Orphans of Petrarch: Poetry and Theory in the Spanish Renaissance* (Berkeley: University of California Press, 1994), pp. 101–165;

Navarrete, "The Spanish Appropriation of Castiglione," *Yearbook of Comparative and General Literature,* 39 (1990–1991): 35–46;

Alexander A. Parker, *The Philosophy of Love in Spanish Literature, 1480–1680,* edited by Terence O'Reilly (Edinburgh: Edinburgh University Press, 1985), pp. 1–38;

Ramón D. Perés, *Homenaje a Boscán en el iv centenario de su muerte (1542–1942): Catálogo de la exposición bibliográfica* (Barcelona, 1994);

Antonio Prieto, *Andáis tras mis escritos,* volume 1 of *La poesía española del siglo XVI* (Madrid: Cátedra, 1984), pp. 59–92;

Arnold G. Reichenberger, "Boscán's *Epístola a Mendoza,*" *Hispanic Review,* 17 (1949): 1–17;

Martín de Riquer, ed., *Juan Boscán y su cancionero barcelonés* (Barcelona: Archivo Histórico, Casa del Arcediano, 1945);

Elias L. Rivers, "The Horatian Epistle and Its Introduction into Spanish Literature," *Hispanic Review,* 22 (1954): 175–194;

Juan Antonio Vilar Sánchez, *1526: Boda y luna de miel del emperador Carlos V: La visita imperial a Andalucía y el reino de Granada* (Granada: Universidad de Granada, 2000), pp. 63–68.

Cristóbal de Castillejo

(1490? – 12 June 1550)

Anthony J. Cárdenas-Rotunno

BOOKS: *Sermón de amores del maestro buen talante llamado fray Nidel de la orden del Fristel. Agora nuevamente corregido y enmendado* (Medina del Campo?: Pedro de Castro?, 1542);

Diálogo de mugeres. Interlocutores Alethio. Fileno (Venice, 1544);

Diálogo entre dos sabios: el uno llamado Alethio y el otro Fileno de los quales el Fileno habla en fauor de las mugeres: y el Alethio dize mucho mal dellas. Va en metro por el mejor estilo mayores sentencias que sobre el caso hasta oy se a visto (Astorga: Agostín de Paz, 1546);

Diálogo de las condiciones de las mujeres por Cristoval de Castillejo (Toledo: Juan de Ayala, 1546);

Dialogo de mugeres: entre dos sabios: el uno llamado Fileno delos quales el Fileno hablaen fauor dellas: y Alethio defiende va por el mejor estilo y mayores sentencias que hasta oy son vistas (Medina del Campo: Pedro de Castro, 1548);

Diálogo de la condiciones de las mugeres. Son interlocutores Alethio y Fileno (Burgos: Juan de Junta, 1556);

Diálogo que habla de las mugeres. Son interlocutores Alethio que dize mal de mugeres: y Fileno que las defiende. Va nuevamente corregido de algunas cosas mal sonantes; que en otras impresiones solían andar (N.p., 1567);

Las obras de Christoval de Castillejo. Corregidas y emendadas por mandado del consejo de la Santa y General Inquisición, edited by Juan López de Velasco (Madrid: Pierres Cosin, 1573);

Dialogo que habla de las mugeres. Son interlocutores Alethio que dize mal de mugeres: y Fileno que las defiende. Ua nueamente corregido de algunas cosas mal sonantes: que en otras impresiones solian andar (Seville, 1575);

Las obras de Christoval de Castillejo: Corregidas y emendadas, por mandado del Consejo de la sancta y General Inquisicion (Madrid: Francisco Sanchez, 1577);

Diálogo de las condiciones de las mugeres (Valencia, 1600);

Diálogo de las condiciones de las mugeres. Son interlocutores Aleccio y Fileno (Barcelona: Sebastián de Comellas, 1600);

Diálogo entre la Verdad y la Lisonja. En el qual se hallarà como se pueden conocer los aduladores y lisonjeros, que se meten en las casas de los principes, y la prudencia que se deue tener para huyr dellos . . . Con otro tratado de la vida de corte (Alcalá: Andrés Sánchez de Ezpeleta, 1614);

Diálogo de las condiciones de las mugeres en el qual se halla como se han de estimar las nobles, honradas y virtuosas para huyr y aborrecer de las que no los son. Son interlocutores Aletio y Fileno (Alcalá: Andrés Sánchez de Ezpeleta, 1615);

Historia de los dos leales amadores Píramo y Tisbe . . . (Alcalá: Andrés Sánchez de Ezpeleta, 1615).

Modern Editions: *Diálogo de las condiciones de las mugeres,* edited by Francisco Mariano Nipho, *Cajón de sastre literato,* 4 (1781): 109–226;

Obras de Christóbal de Castillejo, secretario del Emperador D. Fernando, 2 volumes, edited by Ramón Fernández (Madrid: Imprenta Real, 1792);

Poesías, in *Poetas líricos de los siglos XVI y XVII,* 2 volumes, edited by Adolfo de Castro, Biblioteca de Autores Españoles, nos. 32, 42 (Madrid: Rivadeneyra, 1854), I: 105–252;

Diálogo entre las mujeres. Sermón de amores, Biblioteca Universal, no. 39 (Madrid: Aribau, 1878);

Farsa de la Constanza, edited by R. Foulché-Delbosc, in "Deux oeuvres de Cristobal de Castillejo," special issue of *Revue hispanique,* 36 (1916): 489–499;

Sermón de amores del maestro buen talante llamado fray Nidel de la orden del Fristel, edited by Foulché-Delbosc, in "Deux oeuvres de Cristobal de Castillejo," *Revue hispanique,* 36 (1916): 499–620;

Diálogo de mugeres, edited by Ludwig Pfandl, *Revue hispanique,* 52 (June–August 1921): 361–429;

Diálogo entre el autor y su pluma, edited by E. Werner, *Revue hispanique,* 71 (1927): 555–585;

Obras, 4 volumes, edited by J. Domínguez Bordona (Madrid: Espasa-Calpe, 1928–1946);

Fábula de Polifemo (Madrid: Cruz & Raya, 1936);

Cancionero de poesías varias: Manuscrito no. 617 de la Biblioteca Real de Madrid, edited by José J. Labrador, C. Ángel Zorita, and Ralph A. DiFranco

(Madrid: El Crotalón, 1986)–includes thirteen poems by Castillejo, pp. 363–366, 391, 476;

"Cinco poemas inéditos de Cristóbal de Castillejo," edited by María Dolores Beccaria Lago, *Boletín de la Real Academia Española,* 67, no. 240 (January–April 1987): 55–75;

Obra completa, edited, with an introduction, by Rogelio Reyes Cano (Madrid: Castro, 1999).

Cristóbal de Castillejo's life span places him in an important transitional period in the history of Spain: the end of the Middle Ages and the beginning of the Renaissance, along with the discovery of the New World, the passing of Spanish royalty from the House of Trastámara to the House of Habsburg, and the Reformation and Counter-Reformation. In the world of letters, specifically poetry, a change from traditional Castilian style, meter, and themes to the new Italianate forms and themes spearheaded by Juan Boscán and perfected by Garcilaso de la Vega took place. Castillejo's poem lambasting this new type of poetry, "Reprehensión contra los poetas españoles que escriven en verso italiano" (Censure against Spanish Poets Who Write in Italian Meter), possibly written in 1543 or 1544, led his first critics to place him at the head of an assumed resistance that opposed this new mode in favor of the more traditional meter. Later critics, however, find him to be in tune with the Renaissance sensibilities of his time in his content and approach while, at the same time, favoring a more traditional meter that was in fact never lost but rather was advantageously employed by many poets who, with feet firmly planted in the Renaissance, have never been considered reactionary.

Little is known of Castillejo's childhood except for conjectures that can be made from his literary legacy. He was born in Ciudad Rodrigo in the province of Salamanca sometime during the last decade of the fifteenth century. Efforts to determine the exact year of his birth have proved futile. At the age of fifteen he began service in the court of the Catholic Monarchs, Ferdinand and Isabella, as a page to their grandson Ferdinand, whose brother was Charles V of Germany and Charles I of Spain. This service translated later into a position as secretary in the Viennese court of Ferdinand, now archduke, who in 1526 became the king of Bohemia and Hungary and in 1531 king of the Romans, finally becoming Holy Roman Emperor six years after the death of Castillejo.

Nevertheless, with the arrival in Spain of Charles in 1517 and all the discontent that the Castilian community was feeling, ostensibly because of what they considered foreign rule–first, after Isabel's death in 1504, at the hand of Ferdinand the Catholic, an Aragonese, and then at that of the Austrian-raised Charles–it seemed

Title page for an early edition (Burgos: Juan de Junta, 1556) of Castillejo's 1544 work, in which two men debate the character and morality of women (from J. Domínguez Bordona, ed., Obras. Prólogo, 1928–1946; Thomas Cooper Library, University of South Carolina)

only prudent for Charles to dissipate any potential threats against himself. Thus, he had Ferdinand, whose kingship was favored by many in the land, sent to Flanders, where he came under the preceptorship of Desiderius Erasmus, later a key point of influence in Castillejo's own literary production as well, though there is no evidence to support the notion that Castillejo accompanied Ferdinand to the Low Lands.

By the time Castillejo was summoned to the court of the Archduke Ferdinand in Vienna, he had entered the order of Cistercian monks in the monastery of San Martín de Valdeiglesias near Toledo. His religious preparation and taking of the cloth occurred between Ferdinand's departure to Flanders in 1518 and his appointing Castillejo as secretary to his court in Vienna in 1525, at the recommendation of Martín de Salinas, Ferdinand's ambassador to his brother's court in Spain and a long-standing friend of Castillejo himself. Once Castillejo found himself in the court of Ferdinand, he never returned to Spain, although records show that he traveled extensively, especially to England and to Italy, the latter country being where he had some of his works published. This detail about his life in court as well as others can be gleaned from a significant epistolary corpus treating various aspects of court life, written by Ferdinand's counselor and chamberlain, Salinas. In Salinas's letters one reads of the high regard in which Castillejo was held in his role as secretary, of Castillejo's constant complaints regarding his poor economic fare in the court, and other bits of information regarding his life. Even here, however, circumspection is required in evaluating their significance. For example, Castillejo's complaints about his economic travails while in the service of Ferdinand may be little more than the poet partaking in a theme much in vogue at the time, the misery and mishaps of life in the court over the peace and bliss of life in the village. How much is fact and how much fiction may never be satisfactorily resolved. Documents make clear that Castillejo maintained an active correspondence with Pietro Aretino, a Venetian contemporary and reputedly one of the most robust and facile writers in the Italian vernacular in the sixteenth century. Castillejo's translations of various classical authors, including Cicero, and his familiarity with texts of other humanist contemporaries—Thomas More and Ulrich von Hütten, for example—make clear that he participated in the cosmopolitan, au courant atmosphere surrounding Ferdinand's court. His involvement in the cultural life of the court suffices to contradict an early evaluation by James Fitzmaurice-Kelly in his introduction to *The Oxford Book of Spanish Verse: XIIIth Century – XXth Century* (1965), in which Castillejo is portrayed as an adamant anti-Italianist traditionalist, an opinion, it appears, based largely on "Reprehensión contra los poetas españoles que escriven en verso italiano" and his use of traditional, predominantly octosyllabic meter in his own poetry, although he uses verses of other lengths as well—including those of four, six, and even twelve syllables.

Regarding his personal life while in Ferdinand's court, Castillejo apparently favored its worldliness over monastic reclusion. Taking his amorous verse into consideration has led some scholars, following the lead of Juan Menéndez Pidal, to believe, perhaps unjustifiably, that Castillejo was a "fraile alegre y mocero, a la manera del Arcipreste de Hita, semejante a él en sus costumbres y en su vena poética, mezcla rara de lubricidad y religión" (a carefree and rakish friar, in the manner of the Archpriest of Hita, similar to him in his habits and in his poetic vein, odd mixture of lechery and religion). This assessment derives from the fact that a large proportion of Castillejo's writing is love poetry and that in these poems he names Anna von Schaumburg, Ana de Aragón, Luisa, Francisca, Inez, Mencia, Gracia, Julia,

Petronilla, a Señora de Lerma, and Angela, as Clara Leonora Nicolay lists in her *The Life and Works of Cristobal de Castillejo, the Last of the Nationalists in Castilian Poetry* (1910). To this list George Irving Dale, in his "The Ladies of Cristóbal de Castillejo's Lyrics" (1952), adds María, Elena, and Ysabel. What Castillejo's relationship with them, if any at all, might have been is difficult to determine, given poetic conventions of the time. On the other hand, letters by Salinas indicate that while Castillejo was not married he was not celibate in the sense of sexual abstention and that he fathered in a stable relationship at least one child.

Castillejo's first two published works also form two of his longer pieces with a love-related theme, respectively consisting of 2,890 and 3,759 lines. The *Sermón de amores del maestro buen talante llamado fray Nidel de la orden del Fristel Agora nuevamente corregido y emendado* (Sermon on Loves of the Good Teacher to Be Called Fray Nidel of the Order of the Fristel: Corrected and Emended Again) was published in 1542 and was followed two years later by the *Diálogo de mugeres. Interlocutores Alethio. Fileno* (Dialogue on Women: Interlocutors, Alethio and Fileno). The *Sermón de amores* is a diatribe against love, whereas the *Diálogo de mugeres* is against women, the agents of love. The *Sermón de amores* consists of two parts. In the first, love, a "mal vezino" (bad neighbor), is said by the renowned, fictional preacher from Florence, Fray Nidel, to rule the entire world. All of nature pursues the dictates of love, and it affects both the clergy and laypeople alike. Castillejo calls it the "poderoso monarca / de nuestra sensibilidad" (powerful monarch / of our sentiments). Two examples of unrequited love are offered: a scholar who pursues a woman named Catalina and an elderly man who pursues a woman named Juana are both rejected and live in torment. The world is governed by a love triangle reflected in the maxim: "Yo por ti, / tú por otro, no por mí" (I for you, / you for another, not me). In the second half, the sermon continues with the notion of mutable fortune: where one wins, one loses; the green field in May becomes the muddy one in winter. While one is loved, nothing can compare to the glory of the feeling, and lovers, male and female, are willing to endure anything that might otherwise be seen as an inconvenience. This part also includes an anecdote about an adulterous man and woman who take advantage of her husband's illness, the result of eating bad grapes, which requires his frequent absence from bed. Each time he rises to take care of his need, the lovers glory in each other until he returns. Finally, the husband cannot escape to the bathroom quickly enough and defecates on the lover, who has been hiding under the bed. Love is compared to war, and the piece ends with the notion that man is sentenced from the cradle to be governed by fortune or love.

The *Diálogo de las mugeres* consists of an anti- and profeminist debate in the mouths of the two protagonists, Alethio and Fileno. Alethio vituperates women in general, then women in the following categories: married women, virgins, nuns, widows, single women (in other words, prostitutes), and women who pander. Alethio's railings adhere to the vices of women standard in antifeminist literature since the fifteenth century. Women are imperfect compared to men; they desire power and have difficult personalities; they are garrulous, cruel, vain, and inconstant. According to Alethio, women in general are inclined toward duplicity. Furthermore, he relates, married women are so evil that a man arrested for polygamy exculpates himself by explaining that his plan was to continue marrying until he found a good woman. Virgins are few and really would prefer not to be virgins. Nuns are given to lust, flirting, and manifest defects in their vocations with superficiality of devotion being given to the pomp of religious ceremony. As Rogelio Reyes Cano indicates in his *Medievalismo y renacentismo en la obra poética de Cristóbal de Castillejo* (1980, The Medieval and Renaissance Essence in Cristóbal de Castillejo's Poetry), the critique of such religious superficiality can be attributed to an Erasmian influence. Widows quickly forget their deceased husbands and just as quickly seek a replacement; single women, prostitutes, are tantamount to animals—wolves, lionesses, birds of prey—and are even worse because they ask for money for their favors. Go-betweens are bothersome and persistent prevaricators.

Fileno's defense of women is significantly less stolid than Alethio's attack and presents the clichés common to this period: women are better than men since at creation they were made from a human rib while men were made from mud; without women life would be distasteful; a man without a woman is a body without a soul, a tree without fruit, and other similar metaphors. He claims married women maintain virtue by preferring to subject themselves to their husbands rather than sin with their lovers. The charms of virgins are compared to nature—they are precious pearls, colorful flowers, and the fullness of the moon, for example. For Fileno, nuns undergo penance voluntarily and their licentiousness is mere hearsay. To defend widows, Fileno accuses Alethio of lacking compassion toward the afflicted and denies Alethio's complaints. As for prostitutes, life demands different professions, and so nature is benefited by variety. Fileno, thus, argues that Alethio speaks from ignorance. Go-betweens do their job well, and men, as thieves and highwaymen, do more evil.

The dialogue ends with Fileno's stating that men are bound to love women and asking Alethio whether he knows of a way to avoid the danger that he sees in them. Alethio confesses he does not, so Fileno proposes speaking about the perfections of his own woman in order to experience consolation. The dialogue ends with Alethio's declining the invitation to listen because he has things to do. Because he wants to please Fileno, though, he suggests that they can continue the dialogue after supper. Rather than contradict Alethio's statements point by point, Fileno more often than not admonishes him to be more charitable and compassionate in his assessments and, rather than refuting the points made, simply denies them. One of the high points of the *Diálogo de las mugeres* is the manner in which Castillejo incorporates popular sayings within his text. As with much of the writing by Castillejo, the humor he presents makes this work palatable.

The remainder of Castillejo's poetic corpus has been divided since the 1573 edition of his works by Juan López de Velasco into three categories: amorous works, works of conversation and past times, and moral writings. The second category includes the *Sermón de amores* and the *Diálogo de las mugeres*.

Reyes Cano, in his introduction to the 1999 edition of Castillejo's *Obra completa* (Complete Works), divides Castillejo's works by genre into poetry, theater, and prose, although some writings—theater, for example—are in fact poetry, and the dialogues included in the poetic categories normally have prose introductions. Poetry constitutes the vast majority, an estimated 96 percent, of Castillejo's total literary output, and the edition by Reyes Cano uses the López Velasco divisions within the poetry. The fragmentary theater piece "Farza de la Constanza" (1522?, Farce about Constance) and Castillejo's prose—principally translations of Cicero's *De senectute* and *De amicitia* and a short piece titled "Carta en latín y romance la cual dizen ser de Castillejo" (Letter in Latin and Spanish Which Is Said to Be Castillejo's)—constitute the remainder of his production. The letter is a bipartite address to Cupid and the Virgin Mary. Castillejo offers a summary of the portion of the address pertaining to Cupid: "Tales penas das, amor, / quales glorias das" (You bestow such affliction, Love, / as you give glory); the latter portion of the address is an invocation to a consolatory Virgin, of whom he requests assistance in obtaining eternal reward. The juxtaposition of erotic love and religion, here almost in the same breath, is commonplace in this period and, according to some critics, attests to a strong rooting in one's faith.

As for Castillejo's love poetry, it ranges from the delicate to the blatantly erotic. A good example of this range might be two oneiric pieces studied by María Dolores Beccaria Lago in her "Dos sueños para una dama: Amor y erotismo en Castillejo" (1989, Two Dreams for One Lady: Love and Eroticism in

LAS OBRAS DE
CHRISTOVAL
De Caftillejo.
Corregidas, y emédadas, por
mandado del Confejo de la
fancta, y General In-
quificion.

IMPRESSAS CON LI-
cencia y priuilegio de fu Mageftad,
para los reynos de Caftilla,
y Aragon.
EN MADRID,
Por Francifco Sanchez. Año de.1577.

*Title page for a 1577 edition of Castillejo's works, with an
explanation that the work had been revised by order of
the Spanish Inquisition (Lilly Library,
Indiana University)*

Castillejo). Each is called "Sueño" (Dream), and in each the dreamer views his beloved. In one, he addresses his lady: "Yo, mi señora, soñaba" (I, my lady, was dreaming). The dreamer dreams that he is in her bedroom and that she is "sin camisa como yo" (without a camisole naked as was I), and after a brief discussion, "con miedo de perder / de gozar de tal muger, deseché los embarazos / y, tomándoos en mis brazos, / di comienzo

a mi plazer" (with fear of losing / the enjoyment of such a woman, I removed impediments / and, taking you in my arms, / I initiated my pleasure). The other "Sueño," which begins "Yo, señora, me soñava / un sueño" / (I, lady, was having / a dream), has the lover viewing his beloved as a *locus amoenus,* or idyllic place. He finds himself along the banks of a river in the month of May, when larks and nightingales sing, and roses and carnations bloom—the dreamer's endless summer. As in the first "Sueño," the lover awakens, and longing for the desired is all that remains. The beginning letter of each stanza in both poems form an acrostic for the name *Ysabel.* The second "Sueño," owing to its allegorical nature, is subject to more than one interpretation, including an erotic one such as the one given to the first "Sueño." Even so, the manner in which the eroticism is veiled in the landscape makes the handling of erotic desire more delicate than in the first.

Castillejo's love poetry views love sometimes as an all-powerful force and sometimes as strife or contradiction, but definitely a force to which all flesh is prone. Otis H. Green, in *Spain and the Western Tradition: The Castilian Mind in Literature from* El Cid *to Calderón* (1968), points out the various elements of courtly love to be found in Castillejo's poetry: *Frauendienst und Vassalität* (service and vassalage to women), making a religion of love, and secrecy. Commenting on Castillejo's amorous poetry in "The Renaissance in Spain: II" (1971), R. O. Jones considers "Fábula de Polifemo" (Story of Polyphemus) "a nicely sensuous poem in its own right. . . . The poem is one of the most enchanting of its time."

In the category of works of conversation and past times, another dialogue, "Diálogo entre el autor y su pluma" (1927, Dialogue between an Author and His Pen), has the narrator pondering what he and his pen have gained in the last thirty years of writing. The voice concludes that what they have gained is defeat, torn clothes, and lost hope. The pen exculpates himself, saying that he writes only what is commanded and that such are the vicissitudes of life. The author berates the pen's lack of compassion but admits he has no one else to turn to. Everyone gains with their tools—the fisherman with his nets, the blacksmith with his hammer—all except the author and his pen. The pen asks for a more-balanced view of matters, saying that something has been gained. After all, it argues, Castillejo has received considerable recognition at court by wielding the pen, even though he is from Ciudad Rodrigo, a city that has never had the honor of having the court reside within its confines. The pen concludes that if Castillejo changes his ways and asks for what he deserves, he might get what he desires. If not, though, at least in exchange for being paid poorly he will be provided with an excellent complaint, which will form part of his literary production. Beccaria Lago sees in this dialogue reminiscences of praise given by More to Bishop Cuthbert Tunstall, an old friend and acquaintance, who after stellar service to the Church and Crown died a prisoner for his faith, one of eleven confessor bishops to do so. A few poems have to do with poets who compose poorly—they make their readers laugh in derision and waste their time reading their scant fare.

The "Reprehensión contra los poetas españoles que escriven en verso italiano" appears in this section as well. This poem begins by stating the analogy that Lutherans are to religion what the Italianists are to poetry. Spanish poets of renown—Juan de Mena and Jorge Manrique, for example—are summoned to defend pure Spanish poetry against those who say that the Castilian meter has no authority to say what can happily be said with Tuscan meter. Based on this poem, Guillermo Díaz-Plaja, following Fitzmaurice-Kelly, writes in his *Historia de la poesía lírica española* (1948, History of Spanish Lyric Poetry) that Castillejo is the leader of a faction, and Emiliano Díez-Echarri and José María Roca Franquesa, in their *Historia de la literatura española e hispanoamericana* (1966, History of Spanish and Hispanic American Literature), identify Castillejo as the leader of the resistance to the Italian influence.

Yet, in the Reyes Cano edition, the poem appearing immediately before the "Reprehensión contra los poetas españoles que escriven en verso italiano," titled "En contradicción de los que escriven siempre o lo más amores" (Against Those Who Always of Most of the Time Write about Love), constitutes another reprimand of sorts to those who waste the elegance of the Castilian language on the triviality of love, sometimes on behalf of others without even knowing the desired love object, often dedicating poems to women who do not even know how to read. Because lovers partake of a surfeit of good and soft bread—that is, because they do not have an accurate frame of reference—they compare their amorous sufferings to a hell. Even the pangs of love pale, however, once syphilis, the "dolor francés" (French disease), results from their amorous activity. Although charges of being retrograde and anti-Italianist are leveled against Castillejo because of the "Reprehensión contra los poetas españoles que escriven en verso italiano," no critic has made Castillejo the leader of an anti-love-poetry movement based on this poem against love. Other poems in this division treat hermaphrodites, Basques seeking *aguinaldos* (Christmas gifts), and young women who enter the convent, and one presents the story of Acteon with the moral: do not make hunting a vice by an immoderate proclivity for it.

The last category for Castillejo's poetry, moral writings, includes his "Diálogo entre Memoria y Olvido" (Dialogue between Memory and Forgetfulness). In it the two characters debate their virtues. Forgetfulness challenges Memory to explain why the world esteems it more than Forgetfulness. Memory says it is responsible for the transmission of arts and sciences, fame, and the glory of positive examples. Forgetfulness counters that Memory is accountable for maintaining infamy, enmity, hatred, battles, and injuries as well; hence, Forgetfulness concludes the poem with "olvidar es lo mejor" (forgetting is best). Castillejo's extensive (2,173 lines) "Diálogo entre la Adulación y la Verdad" (Dialogue between Flattery and Truth) presents Flattery as a dominant force to which everything in the world is subjected. Truth, on the other hand, enters proclaiming its virtues and that it may in fact be mistreated and imprisoned but never conquered. In accordance with the gender of the names, the protagonists are women. Thus, Flattery is referred to as a dangerous, false prostitute; Truth, on the other hand, is a "damsel" and "virgin." A long debate occurs full of examples based on anecdotes and stories to prove their point. In the end, both decide to go to Rome to see which is more sought after. Rome is a place ripe for adulation, and Flattery can pick and choose the best of the crop. Truth concedes that there is strife in Rome as elsewhere but that it has gone well for her. When Flattery questions her about a blow to the eye and tattered clothes received in Rome, however, Truth acquiesces and decides to return to heaven, leaving the world for her antagonist. In this category, too, one poem, "Dies Irae para la noche de Navidad" (Dies Irae for the Night of Christmas), juxtaposes a hymn sung at the mass of the dead with Christmas. Joël Saugnieux, in "El 'Dies Irae para la noche de Navidad,' de Cristóbal de Castillejo" (1974; The "Dies Irae for the Night of Christmas" by Cristóbal de Castillejo), clarifies that the "Dies Irae" was added to the mass of the dead at a much later date so that Castillejo is merely adhering to earlier tradition in which the first coming of Christ at Christmas is connected to the Second Coming, the Final Judgment, and the Day of Wrath.

Another work in this category is "Diálogo llamado aula"—sometimes called "Diálogo de la vida de la Corte" (Dialogue of the Life of the Court)—in which Lucrecio, a young and poor noble, decides to choose a career to earn a living and so reviews eight stations from which he might select one: *oficial* (office holder), *mercader* (trader), *letrado* (lawyer or doctor), *soldado* (soldier), *calongía* (the office of canon or prebendary), *religioso* (religious, as in priest or monk), *grangero* (farmer), and "acogerme a palacio / de algún rey / o príncipe de mi ley" (to seek refuge in the palace / of some king / or prince of my faith), in other words, become a member of some court. He is inclined toward the court but before choosing opts to consult his elder relative Prudencio, a member of the court for forty years. The names are significant: Lucrecio is related to the Latin *lucrum* (profit, gain) and Prudencio to Latin *prudentia* (prudence). Prudencio compares life in the court to the sea full of fish that prey on one another and to a journey at sea billowing with danger: storms, shipwrecks, pirates, and reefs. Lucrecio is not easily deterred, and Prudencio provides anecdotes from firsthand experience that finally dissuade Lucrecio, who decides to seek another profession. The discussion of what that might be is left for another day, thus ending the dialogue.

Little is known about the particulars of Castillejo's demise. Nicolay claims that "his last years are . . . shrouded in oblivion," although his death is known to have occurred on 12 June 1550 in Vienna. He was interred in the burial grounds of the Cistercian monastery in Wiener Neustadt.

Cristóbal de Castillejo had a Janus-like quality about him. Although he did not adopt the Italianate meter of the sonnet form but maintained traditional Castilian meter, the content of his work shows that he too was a product of his times, influenced by Erasmus and More. Lacking the hyperbaton–convoluted word order–for which early Spanish sonnets are notorious, Castillejo's poetry reads easily, allowing the reader to focus on the subtlety of thought without having to expend the additional intellectual effort needed to rearrange syntax. His poetry in many ways continues the style found in early-fifteenth-century *cancionero* poetry. His themes are themes in vogue at the time. His incorporation of popular sayings, anecdotes, and stories and his classical, biblical, and other references place him in a line of sixteenth-century poetry that chose to treat its topics in standard Castilian meter.

References:

María Dolores Beccaria, "Dos sueños para una dama: Amor y erotismo en Castillejo," in *Eros literario: Actas del Coloquio celebrado en la Facultad de Filología de la Universidad Complutense en diciembre de 1988,* edited by Covadonga López Alonso, Juana Martínez Gómez, José Paulino Ayuso, José Marcos Roca, and Carlos Saínz de la Maza (Madrid: Universidad Complutense de Madrid, 1989), pp. 53–65;

Beccaria, "Presencia de la *Utopía* de Tomás Moro en la obra poética de Cristóbal de Castillejo," *Dicenda: Cuadernos de filología,* 1 (1982): 135–141;

J. P. Wickersham Crawford, "Castillejo's Ana," *Hispanic Review,* 2 (1934): 65–68;

Crawford, "The Relationship of Castillejo's *Farsa de la Constanza* and the *Sermón de amores,*" *Hispanic Review,* 4 (1936): 373–375;

George Irving Dale, "The Ladies of Cristóbal de Castillejo's Lyrics," *Modern Language Notes,* 68 (1952): 173–175;

Guillermo Díaz-Plaja, *Historia de la poesía lírica española,* corrected and enlarged edition (Barcelona: Labor, 1948), pp. 111–113;

Emiliano Díez-Echarri and José María Roca Franquesa, *Historia de la literatura española e hispanoamericana,* second edition (Madrid: Aguilar, 1966), pp. 187–189;

James Fitzmaurice-Kelly, introduction, in *The Oxford Book of Spanish Verse: XIIIth Century – XXth Century,* second edition, edited by J. B. Trend (Oxford: Clarendon Press, 1965);

Otis H. Green, *Spain and the Western Tradition: The Castilian Mind in Literature from* El Cid *to Calderón,* 4 volumes (Madison & London: University of Wisconsin Press, 1968), I: 164–167;

Juan Hurtado, J. de la Serna, and Ángel González Palencia, *Historia de la literatura española,* second edition (Madrid, 1925), pp. 318–321;

Victor Infantes, "Postillas por una nueva edición: Los 'accidentes' editoriales del 'Diálogo de Mujeres' de Cristóbal de Castillejo," *Angélica: Revista de literatura,* 3 (1992): 33–65;

R. O. Jones, "The Renaissance in Spain: II," in *The Golden Age: Prose and Poetry. The Sixteenth and Seventeenth Centuries,* volume 2 of *A Literary History of Spain,* edited by Jones (London: Benn / New York: Barnes & Noble, 1971), pp. 28–49;

Begoña López Bueno and Rogelio Reyes Cano, "Garcilaso de la Vega y la poesía en tiempos de Carlos V," in *Siglos de oro, Renacimiento,* edited by Francisco López Estrada, volume 2 of *Historia y crítica de la literatura española,* edited by Francisco Rico (Barcelona: Crítica, 1980), pp. 98–113;

Juan Menéndez Pidal, "Datos para la biografía de Cristóbal de Castillejo," *Boletín de la Real Academia Española,* 2 (1915): 3–20;

Clara Leonora Nicolay, *The Life and Works of Cristobal de Castillejo, the Last of the Nationalists in Castilian Poetry* (Philadelphia: Wickersham, 1910);

Reyes Cano, *Medievalismo y renacentismo en la obra poética de Cristóbal de Castillejo,* Serie universitaria, no. 130 (Madrid: Fundación Juan March, 1980);

Dennis E. Rhodes, "The Printing of the 'Sermón de amores' of Cristóbal de Castillejo," *British Library Journal,* 13, no. 1 (1987): 58–63;

Joël Saugnieux, "El 'Dies Irae para la noche de Navidad,' de Cristóbal de Castillejo," in *Literatura y espiritualidad españolas,* El Soto, no. 24 (Madrid: Prensa Española, 1974), pp. 189–199.

Gutierre de Cetina
(1514/17? – 1556)

J. Ignacio Díez Fernández
Universidad Complutense (Madrid)

BOOK: *Obras de Gutierre de Cetina,* 2 volumes, edited by Joaquín Hazañas y la Rúa (Seville: Díaz, 1895); republished in one volume, with presentation by Margarita Peña (Mexico City: Perrúa, 1977).

Editions and Collections: *Poesías,* edited by Salvador Pérez Valiente (Valencia: Tipografía Moderna, 1942);

Madrigales, sonetos y otras composiciones escogidas, edited by Juan Bautista Solervicens (Barcelona: Montaner & Simón, 1943);

Paradoja: Trata que no solamente no es cosa mala, dañosa ni vergonzosa ser un hombre cornudo mas que los cuernos son buenos y provechosos, introduction by Gonzalo Santonja (Madrid: Clásicos El Arbol, 1981);

Sonetos y madrigales completos, edited by Begoña López Bueno (Madrid: Cátedra, 1981).

The knowledge of Gutierre de Cetina's poetic work has been seriously hindered by the lack of an edition of his poetry. The poet himself (like others of his generation) never published his verse, and his poems were not collected and published during the Golden Age. Cetina's poetry was confined, with few exceptions, to a manuscript circulation that was perhaps not as wide as the circulation of other poets' writings. Not until the end of the nineteenth century was there an edition intended to be complete—*Obras de Gutierre de Cetina* (1895, Works of Gutierre de Cetina), edited by Joaquín Hazañas y la Rúa—although throughout that century several scholars prepared the way for Hazañas y la Rúa's edition, which scholars still use (at least in order to read Cetina's extensive poems). *Sonetos y madrigales completos* (1981, Complete Sonnets and Madrigals), an edition of a significant part of Cetina's poetry including more than 250 poems, was the first published according to modern philological standards.

Another, more subtle element also exerts influence on the dissemination of Cetina's work, that is, the shadow cast by some of this Sevillian's poems on the rest of his repertory. The high esteem accorded to poems such as "Ojos claros, serenos" (Clear and Serene

Gutierre de Cetina (frontispiece of Obras de Gutierre de Cetina; *William T. Young Library, University of Kentucky)*

Eyes), the most famous madrigal in Spanish literature, has relegated other compositions worthy of attention to a secondary status. Cetina's poems include more than two hundred sonnets and the first madrigal composed in Spain. This diversity is also evident in his prose writings, which, while not so abundant, reveal a wider variety of genres than those employed by contemporary writers who have received greater critical attention. Moreover, it is important not to underestimate the significant impact of Cetina's poetic work on the New World, since more of his Petrarchan poems are included in the early New Spain *cancionero* (songbook)

Flores de baria poesía recoxida de varios poetas españoles. Recopilóse en la ciudad de México. Anno del nascimiento de NRO Saluador Ihuchristo de 1577 annos (Flowers of Diverse Poetry Gathered from Various Spanish Poets. Compiled in the City of Mexico. Year of the Birth of Our Savior Jesus Christ of 1577) than any other poet's works. One could in fact consider Cetina to be the introducer and promoter of the new Italian-style poetry in America.

The life of Gutierre de Cetina remains for the most part a mystery. Over a certain period the news about his life comes from a manuscript composed by the painter and writer Francisco de Pacheco, *Libro de descripción de verdaderos retratos de ilustres y memorables varones* (Book of Description of True Portraits of Illustrious and Memorable Men), prepared in Seville and dated 1599. Several aspects of this biography have been modified by archival documentation, however. There is no doubt about his birth in Seville, but it remains unknown exactly what year this occurred, although it can be placed between 1514 and 1517, even if some scholars would put it around 1520. The year of his death is likewise uncertain, although it is clear that Cetina was no longer alive in 1557, according to a judicial document. Cetina belonged to a family of the lower nobility that, according to Álvaro Alonso in his *La poesía italianista* (2002, The Italianist Poetry), "había aumentado su riqueza gracias a sus vínculos con el mundo de la administración y del comercio" (had increased its wealth thanks to its links with the world of administration and trade), and he may have studied humanities before going to the royal court in Valladolid. Nevertheless, "despite the efforts of these scholars, the ancestry of his family remains to be clarified," according to Ruth Pike, who, based on an analysis of the poet's genealogy, argues in her 1990 essay "The Converso Origins of the Sevillian Poet Gutierre de Cetina" against the hidalgo (lower nobility) condition of his family and in favor of the hypothesis that the Cetinas were *conversos* (converts from Judaism to Catholicism). In any event, it does not seem possible to trace features of a *converso* origin in Cetina's work.

Although biographical data has been deduced from texts of some obscure writers, such speculation is generally a risky option when dealing with literary texts, and is even riskier when considering Petrarchan poetry, because this poetry is based, for the most part, on the imitation and re-creation of literary motifs. For this reason, the location of some of Cetina's poems on diverse riverbanks, the variety of poetic names of the loved women, and even the bitter tone of some compositions may not correspond respectively to real locations, real women, or a real sensibility that developed in maturity. Cetina's life seems to coincide with the reign of King Charles I (from 1517 to 1556), whom Cetina served during his stay in Italy from 1538 to 1548, going on several military and diplomatic missions that led him across Europe, North Africa, and America (which he first visited in 1546), where some of his family were established. (His maternal uncle Alonso del Castillo worked as a merchant in America and died in Mexico; all of Cetina's brothers also settled there.) Cetina's stay in Italy, essential as a formative experience for Spanish writers of the time, was initially undertaken for military purposes, typical of the contemporary soldier-poet. From the little that is known about the rest of Cetina's life it is possible to assert that he returned to America, where, in 1554, he was mortally wounded in Puebla while being "envuelto en un lance de amor y celos protagonizado por su amigo Francisco Peralta" (involved in a case of love and jealousy protagonized by his friend Francisco Peralta), as Alonso describes the circumstances. In Mexico, perhaps because of these injuries, Cetina died before 1557.

As a poet Cetina is usually included as a member of the first Petrarchan generation, also called the generation of Garcilaso de la Vega, but owing to the date of his birth (late if compared with other poets of the group), Cetina is considered an epigone. Furthermore, his early death made it impossible for him, unlike other poets of this generation, to know the Spain of the Counter-Reformation. Cetina shares with the poets of his group some typical characteristics: his Italian sojourn, for example; his admiration and imitation of Italian models; his use of the hendecasyllabic line and meters of Italian origin; and his predilection for love as a subject. Like Garcilaso, and unlike others of his generation such as Juan Boscán and Diego Hurtado de Mendoza, Cetina's extant texts exhibit a scarce (previously thought to be nonexistent) devotion to the octosyllabic line, which is evident in ten of his poems. Much more significant, insofar as it is the main part of his production, is Cetina's preference for Italian-style poetry, including imitations of Petrarch and other Italian poets such as Baldassare Castiglione, Luigi Tansillo, Ludovico Ariosto, and Jacopo Sannazaro. Antonio Prieto, in his *La poesía española del siglo XVI* (1984, Spanish Poetry of the Sixteenth Century), explains Cetina's inclination toward Tansillo rather than Petrarch as a matter of temperament, since "la poesía de Tansillo puede ser todos menos introspección interna, intimidad espiritual" (Tansillo's poetry may be anything but personal introspection, inner exploration, spiritual intimacy). About half of the total imitations of other authors' texts are based on poems of the Catalan Ausías March, to whom the other poets of his group (Boscán, Garcilaso, and Hurtado de Mendoza) also looked for inspiration, although Cetina pays more attention to March with almost fifty imitations. Not only is imitation, so characteristic in the Renaissance, an important feature in Cetina but also his skill for Renaissance fusion, for instance, in the union of Tansillo's musicality and March's subjects.

Despite the existence of a couple of works in prose, Cetina is above all a poet. When studying and evaluating his poetic production, it is necessary to take into account several problems concerning attribution, some of them still unsolved. For example, the well-known version of Ovid's *Heroid VII*, "Epístola de Dido a Eneas: Cual suele de Meandro en la ribera" (Epistle from Dido to Aeneas: As It on the Banks of Meandro Is Wont), is attributed to Cetina as well as other poets. Cetina's poetry has been preserved in several manuscripts, with one of these being especially important for the quantity of poems included (more than 250) and also for presumably being a copy of the original just as it says—"sacadas de su propio original que dexo de su mano escrito" (taken from his own original written by his own hand). This sixteenth-century manuscript is titled "Primera parte de las obras en verso de Gutierre de Cetina" (First Part of the Poetic Works of Gutierre de Cetina) and forms part of the Rodríguez Moñino-Brey Collection stored in the Real Academia Española (Royal Spanish Academy). A significant number of Cetina's poems are also included in *Flores de baria poesía*. This manuscript includes more than 80 compositions by Cetina—more than any other poet. The first printed poems of Cetina were published in *Anotaciones* (Annotations), by Fernando de Herrera, in 1580. Afterward, during the eighteenth and nineteenth centuries, other compilations incorporated some of Cetina's poems. Nevertheless, a complete edition of Cetina's poetry, albeit with some problems, was not produced until *Obras de Gutierre de Cetina* in 1895.

As with other members of his generation, at present it is not possible to outline a chronology of Cetina's literary production. Nevertheless, several categories in his poetry may be defined: his introduction and cultivation of the madrigal; his ample use of the sonnet, in which he develops a technique superior to that of other members of his generation; his epistles; his dedication, early in the evolution of Spanish literature, to the Provençal sextine, or sestina; and his attention to other forms (songs, octaves, capitoli, elegies). Among the literary peculiarities of Cetina's poetry, the following stand out: a lack of containment (unlike in Garcilaso's poetry); a preoccupation with descriptions of the female body, particularly the eyes; and a tendency toward certain mannerisms involving witty wordplay. Unlike Garcilaso and other poets of this time period, Cetina did not write eclogues, although pastoral themes are by no means absent from his verse. The main subject of the different poetic genres is love in the

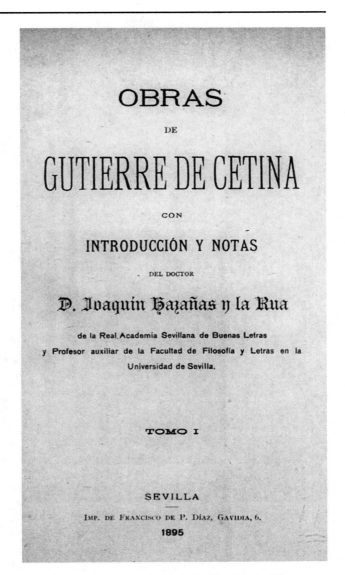

Title page for volume one of Cetina's collected works (Thomas Cooper Library, University of South Carolina)

Petrarchan mode, with its typical features (such as the contrast between past good and present evil or the unattainable lady). Themes related to satire (including critiques of the royal court and city life) and panegyric (in poems dedicated to individuals) are also important.

Among Cetina's poetic compositions, the most famous text is undoubtedly the madrigal "Ojos claros, serenos." In the combination of hendecasyllabic and heptasyllabic lines that this madrigal comprises, Cetina combines elements from Italian and *cancionero* poetry, as such creating an amalgam of Renaissance and traditional Spanish motifs. Cetina's sonnets are characterized by their careful construction and by the importance he placed on technique, a feature that

Cover of the 1981 edition of Cetina's poems edited to modern philological standards (Ekstrom Library, University of Louisville)

brings him closer to the poets of the second half of the sixteenth century. Included among these techniques are Cetina's use of internal rhyme (as in the sonnet "Yo, señora, pensaba antes, creía" [I, Madam, Thought Before, Believed]), and his use of the spreading-gathering enumeration (as in the sonnet "Siendo de vuestro bien, ojos, ausentes" [Eyes, Being Absent from Your Good]), which later enjoyed a preference in the baroque period. Cetina's more-renowned sonnets include "Es lo blanco castísima pureza" (White Is a Most Chaste Purity), which focuses on the symbolism of colors; "Excelso monte do el romano estrago" (Sublime Mount Where the Roman Destruction), an imitation of a sonnet by Castiglione that focuses on the ruin of Carthage, thus anticipating the taste for ruins characteristic of the Spanish baroque; and "Héroes gloriosos, pues el alto cielo" (Glorious Heroes, because the High Heaven), one of the two sonnets dedicated to the heroic Spanish defense

of the fortress of Castilonovo. As for other contemporary poets, the sonnet is for Cetina a form used to exploit many subjects in addition to love.

The majority of Cetina's longer texts are epistles of different sorts that, as the testimony of a devotedness going well beyond that of Boscán and Garcilaso, bring Cetina nearer to the interest in epistle that Hurtado de Mendoza showed, with a much wider corpus in which one can find several epistles and octosyllabic letters. Cetina's epistles employ hendecasyllabic verse and show a preference for Italian terza rima when dealing with love questions (as in his three epistles imitating Ovid) and when developing humorous themes about the royal court and, more specifically, about the stereotype that contrasts life in the village with the complex life in the city (such as in the epistle to Baltasar de León). Several of Cetina's epistles are addressed to real people: "A don Jerónimo de Urrea" (To Don Jerónimo de Urrea), "A la princesa de Molfeta" (To the Princess of Molfeta), "A la príncipe de Ascoli" (To the Prince of Ascoli), "A don Diego Hurtado de Mendoza" (To Don Diego Hurtado de Mendoza), as well as "A Baltasar de León." The epistle dedicated to Hurtado de Mendoza, perhaps the one that most clearly reveals Horatian features, describes events around 1543, which suggests that it was composed close to the birth of the epistolary genre in Spain. The genre originated with Garcilaso's 1534 epistle to Boscán and with an exchange of epistles between Hurtado de Mendoza and Boscán shortly afterward. Several of Cetina's epistles, as in the cases of those by other Spanish authors, reveal a humorous (and satirical) tone quite removed from the more serious tone found in Italian poetic works, especially those by Petrarch.

Despite the recognizable Petrarchism in Cetina's poetry—which is based not only on direct imitations of Petrarch but also on some followers' texts and on the use of motifs proceeding from this dominant trend in sixteenth-century Spanish poetry—it does not seem possible to speak of a Petrarchan *cancionero* in Cetina's case since his poetry does not center on a single beloved individual, one of the most defining features of the poetic compilations that imitate Petrarch. In Cetina's poetry it is easy to detect several feminine names to which the poet sings, usually connected with different geographic locations (such as Dórida in Seville, Amarílida in Valladolid, and Laura in Italy), although it is impossible to identify the real women behind each one of these nicknames.

Critics universally attribute two prose texts to Cetina: "Diálogo entre la cabeza y la gorra" (Dialogue between the Head and the Cap) and "Paradoja en alabanza de los cuernos" (Paradox in Praise of Horns). A manuscript including both of these works (which are explicitly attributed to Cetina) was located in the Fernán Núñez Collection (manuscript 180) at the Bancroft Library, University of California at Berkeley. "Diálogo entre la cabeza y la gorra" seems to be an adaptation of an Italian text, while "Paradoja en alabanza de los cuernos" is a satirical work that belongs to the cultivated genre of the paradoxical encomium. The plays that Cetina is supposed to have written, in Seville and in the New World, are lost.

Despite the fine technique of Cetina's sonnets, despite the esteem that his well-known madrigal "Ojos claros, serenos" attracted, and despite the variety of interests that can be observed in his rich and ample poetry, the significance of Cetina to Spanish Renaissance poetry has not always been recognized. This critical inattention was for centuries in part because of the lack of an edition of his works, which was resolved only at the end of the nineteenth century, and in part because of the disproportionate attention paid to "Ojos claros, serenos." Cetina, unlike Garcilaso and other contemporaries, did not compose a Petrarchan *cancionero*, strictly speaking, although the main subject in his poetry is love. The multiplicity of beloved women, among other features, inevitably hinders the possible arranging of his poetry as a *cancionero*. Furthermore, Cetina's preference for musicality, in addition to his facility for composing verses and his idiosyncratic understanding of poetry, endows his verse with a sense of coldness and lack of intimacy that cannot be compensated for by his notable technical mastery of the sonnet, which likewise distinguishes his poetry from that of his contemporaries. Cetina used several techniques of mannerist influence that were previously unknown in Spain, and features of his work anticipate some of the defining characteristics of Spanish poetry during the second half of the sixteenth century. He successfully introduced in Spain the Italian madrigal, and he cultivated the difficult sextine from Provence. Cetina is the author of a wide collection of epistles that includes Horatian texts, satirical and courtly epistles, love epistles, and also versions of several Ovidian epistles. Finally, there is no doubt whatsoever about the important role of this Renaissance poet in extending the influence of Petrarch throughout Spain and the New World.

References:

Álvaro Alonso, "Gutierre de Cetina," in his *La poesía italianista* (Madrid: Laberinto, 2002), pp. 128–135;

Narciso Alonso Cortés, "Datos para la biografía de Gutierre de Cetina," *Boletín de la Real Academia Española,* 32 (1952): 61–76;

Juan Bautista Avalle-Arce, "Gutierre de Cetina, Gálvez de Montalvo y Lope de Vega," *Nueva Revista de Filología Hispánica,* 5 (1951): 411–414;

Marcel Bataillon, "Gutierre de Cetina en Italia," in *Studia Hispanica in honorem R. Lapesa,* 3 volumes, edited by Eugenio de Bustos and others (Madrid: Cátedra/Seminario Menéndez Pidal, 1972), I: 153–172;

Aubrey Bell, "Cetina's Madrigal," *Modern Languages Review,* 20 (1925): 179–183;

José Manuel Blecua, "Poemas menores de Gutierre de Cetina" and "Otros poemas inéditos de Gutierre de Cetina," in his *Sobre poesía de la edad de Oro: Ensayos y notas eruditas* (Madrid: Gredos, 1970), pp. 44–61, 62–73;

Gregorio Cabello Porras, "La mariposa en cenizas desatada: Una imagen petrarquista en la lírica áurea," in *Ensayos sobre tradición clásica y petrarquismo en el Siglo de Oro* (Almería: Universidad de Almería, 1995), pp. 65–108;

Julio Cejador y Frauca, "El madrigal de Cetina," *Revue Hispanique,* 58 (1923): 108–114;

J. P. Wickersham Crawford, "Notes on the Date of His Birth and the Identity of Dórida," *Studies in Philology,* 28 (1931): 309–314;

Crawford, "Two Spanish Imitations of an Italian Sonnet," *Modern Language Notes,* 31 (1916): 122–123;

José Ignacio Díez Fernández, "Textos literarios españoles en la Fernán Núñez Collection (Bancroft Library, Berkeley)," *Dicenda: Cuadernos de Filología Hispánica,* 15 (1997): 139–182;

Ralph A. DiFranco and J. J. Labrador Herráiz, "El ms. 1578 de la Biblioteca Real de Madrid, con poesías de Cetina, Figueroa, Hurtado de Mendoza, Montemayor y otros," *Boletín de la Biblioteca Menéndez Pelayo,* 69 (1993): 271–305;

María Felisa Fernández Alberté, *Gutierre de Cetina, crítico de la vida cortesana* (Buenos Aires: Eleusis, 1993);

Joseph G. Fucilla, *"Superbi colli" e altere saggi: Notas sobre la boga del tema en España* (Rome: Carucci, 1963);

Herman Iventosch, "The Renaissance Pastoral and the Golden Age: A Translation of a Sonnet of Giraldi Cinthio by Gutierre de Cetina," *Modern Language Notes,* 85 (1970): 240–243;

O. Jimeno Bulnes, "Dos versiones del tratamiento de la temática amorosa en la poesía renacentista: E. Spenser y G. de Cetina," *Bris,* 1 (1992): 159–170;

Rafael Lapesa, "Gutierre de Cetina: Disquisiciones biográficas," in *Estudios Hispánicos: Homenaje a Archer M. Huntington* (Wellesley, Mass.: Wellesley College, 1952), pp. 311–326;

Lapesa, "Más sobre atribuciones a Gutierre de Cetina," in *Homenaje al Excmo. Sr. Dr. D. Emilio Alarcos*

García, volume 2 (Valladolid: University of Valladolid, 1967), pp. 275–280;

Lapesa, "La poesía de Gutierre de Cetina," in *Hommage à Ernest Martinenche: Etudes hispaniques et américaines,* edited by Homero Serís (Paris: Editions d'Artrey, 1939), pp. 248–261;

Lapesa, "Tres sonetos inéditos y una atribución falsa," *Revista de Filología Española,* 24 (1937): 380–383;

Begoña López Bueno, *Gutierre de Cetina, poeta del Renacimiento español* (Seville: Diputación Provincial, 1978);

López Bueno, "La sextina petrarquista en los cancioneros líricos de cuatro poetas sevillanos (Cetina-Herrera-Cueva-Rioja)," *Archivo Hispalense,* 67 (1984): 57–76;

Armando de María y Campos, *La muerte equivocada de Gutierre de Cetina, poeta sevillano del siglo XVI* (Puebla, Mexico: Gobierno del Estado de Puebla, Comisión Puebla V Centenario, 1991);

Ferdinando D. Maurino, "The Theme of the Eyes: Poliziano as a Source of Cetina," *Hispanic Review,* 37 (1969): 362–369;

Donald M. McGrady, "Notas sobre el madrigal 'Ojos claros, serenos' de Cetina," *Hispanic Review,* 65 (1997): 379–389;

Eugenio Mele, "Gutierre de Cetina traduttore di un dialoggo di Pandolfo Collenuccio," *Bulletin Hispanique,* 13 (1911): 348–351;

Mele and Narciso Alonso Cortés, *Sobre los amores de Gutierre de Cetina y su famoso madrigal* (Valladolid: Imprenta Provincial, 1930);

Víctor Montolí Bernadas, *Introducción a la obra de Gutierre de Cetina* (Barcelona: PPU, 1993);

Francisco de Pacheco, "Gutierre de Cetina," in his *Libro de descripción de verdaderos retratos de ilustres y memorables varones,* edited by Pedro M. Piñero and Rogelio Reyes Cano (Seville: Diputación Provincial, 1985), pp. 265–270;

Margarita Peña, "Nuevos datos sobre Gutierre de Cetina y otros poetas españoles en Puebla. Siglo XVI," *Anuario de Letras,* 35 (1997): 509–527;

Ruth Pike, "The Converso Origins of the Sevillian Poet Gutierre de Cetina," *Ibero-Romania,* 32 (1990): 47–54;

Antonio Prieto, "Con un soneto de Gutierre de Cetina," *El Crotalón,* 1 (1984): 283–295;

Prieto, *La poesía española del siglo XVI* (Madrid: Cátedra, 1984), I: 113–122;

José Manuel Rico García, "La epístola de Gutierre de Cetina a don Diego Hurtado de Mendoza," *Philologia Hispanensis,* 4 (1986): 255–274;

Francisco Rodríguez Marín, "Documentos sobre Gutierre de Cetina," *Boletín de la Real Academia Española,* 6 (1919): 54–115;

José Romera Castillo and Antonio Lorente Medina, "Algo más sobre Gutierre de Cetina y México," *Cuadernos de Filosofía y Letras: Letras Hispánicas,* 3 (1985): 33–43;

Lucas de Torre, "Algunas notas para la biografía de Gutierre de Cetina, seguidas de varias composiciones suyas inéditas," *Boletín de la Real Academia Española,* 11 (1924): 388–407, 601–626;

Alfred Miles Whiters, "Further Influences of Auzias March on Gutierre de Cetina," *Modern Language Notes,* 51 (1936): 373–379;

Whiters, *The Sources of the Poetry of Gutierre de Cetina* (Philadelphia: Westbrook, 1923);

Whiters, "Two Additional Borrowings from Petrarch by Gutierre de Cetina," *Hispanic Review,* 2 (1934): 158–161.

Christopher Columbus

(1451 – 20 May 1506)

Millie Gimmel
University of Tennessee

WORKS: *Carta a Luis Santángel* (Barcelona: Pedro Posa, 1493);

"Diario del primer viaje," in *Colección de los Viages y Descubrimientos, que Hicieron por Mar los Españoles desde Fines del Siglo XV: Con varios documentos inéditos concernientes á la historia de la marina castellana y de los establecimientos españoles en Indias,* 5 volumes, edited by Martín Fernández de Navarrete (Madrid: Imprenta Real, 1825–1837); translated by Samuel Kettell as *Personal Narrative of the First Voyage of Columbus to America* (Boston: Wait, 1827);

Libro copiador de Cristóbal Colón: Correspondencia inédita con los Reyes católicos sobre los viajes a América: Estudio historico-critico y edición, 2 volumes, edited by Antonio Rumeu de Armas (Madrid: Testimonio, 1989).

Modern Edition: *Textos y documentos Completos,* second edition, edited by Consuelo Varela and Juan Gil (Madrid: Alianza, 1992).

Editions in English: *Select Documents Illustrating the Four Voyages of Columbus,* 2 volumes, edited and translated by Cecil Jane (London: Hakluyt Society, 1929);

Journals and Other Documents on the Life and Voyages of Christopher Columbus, edited and translated by Samuel Eliot Morison (New York: Heritage, 1963);

The Diario of Christopher Columbus's First Voyage, translated by Oliver Dunn and James E. Kelley Jr. (Norman: University of Oklahoma Press, 1988).

Christopher Columbus (painting by Sebastiano del Piombo, Metropolitan Museum of Art; from Zvi Dor-Ner, Columbus and the Age of Discovery, *1991; Thomas Cooper Library, University of South Carolina)*

Christopher Columbus is remembered for having been the first European to reach the Americas on a deliberate mission. In many ways it is easier to discuss Columbus as an historical figure than as a literary figure; yet, both interpretations of the man and his life are fraught with difficulties. When discussing the life and writings of Columbus, little can be said with any certainty. Columbus himself was given to contradictions and withholding information, and many of his biographers have manipulated facts to present a Columbus in accord with their personal taste. The historical record reveals few facts, and the same problem arises with respect to his works. Few documents of literary merit exist that are indisputably believed to be Columbus's own work. Much of what he wrote was addressed to the Spanish sovereigns with the hope of garnering or reinforcing their continued support for his project of discovery. Few of his works were intended for a broader public, and those that were made available passed through the hands of frequently unknown editors and revisers. Scholars continue to debate the authenticity of the works ascribed to Columbus, and a consensus has yet to be reached on the matter. Further, the translation of Columbus into English has been sporadic since the mid eighteenth century, and many of his letters have yet to be translated. Nonetheless, the impact of the works attributed to Columbus on both his contemporaries and on later writers and scholars cannot be denied. Columbus, or at least the idea of Columbus, and his works have had a tremendous impact on literary production and the popular understanding of the New World from the years immediately following 1492 up to the present. He had the unique opportunity of being, at least symbolically, the first European to experience the New World and respond to it. His response, problematic as it may be, has inspired the imagination of generations of readers and writers.

From Columbus's own reference to his birth, and from contemporary documents, scholars generally agree that Christoforo Colombo was born in the state of Liguria in the northwest corner of Italy sometime around 1451. His parents were Dominico and Susanna Colombo, and he had at least two younger brothers, Bartolomé and Diego, who sailed with him to the New World. Most likely his family lived in or near Genoa and worked in the wool trade. Columbus claims he went to sea when he was eleven and had sailed most of the known world by the time he arrived in Spain with his petition for the Catholic Monarchs, Ferdinand and Isabella. By 1476 Columbus was living in Portugal and sailing for the Portuguese king. He married a Portuguese woman of the lesser nobility, Felipa Perestrello e Moniz, and his first son, Diego, was born in Lisbon in 1480. It appears that he had decided on his plan to reach Asia by sailing west sometime in the 1480s. He approached King João II of Portugal with his plan and was rejected, then shifted his attention to Spain and the recently united kingdoms of Aragon and Castile. Around 1485 he moved to Spain with his son. Many scholars assume the death of his first wife, but there is no concrete proof of this occurrence. It is known that a second son, Fernando, was born to Columbus's mistress, Beatriz Enriquez, in 1488.

At Columbus's first audience with the Spanish regents, in 1486, he was received tepidly. He repeatedly proposed his venture to the Catholic Monarchs and to the king of Portugal, while at the same time his brother Bartolomé offered the same project to the kingdoms of France and England. Finally, in January 1492, just after their completion of the Reconquista (Reconquest) of the Iberian Peninsula from the Moors, Ferdinand and Isabella agreed to finance Columbus's voyage over the Atlantic Ocean. While historical romanticizing insinuates a love affair between Columbus and the queen that led to her financing the voyage by pawning her jewels, this episode is clearly historical fiction. Likewise, the common belief that Columbus wanted to prove that the world was round is also false. By the end of the fifteenth century almost all educated individuals believed that the world was a globe. The only remaining debate concerned its size. Columbus set out to prove that the world was smaller than most of his contemporaries believed.

Columbus seems to have had multiple and conflicting motives for his voyage across the Atlantic. He believed that by sailing west he would discover a route to the Indies that would be much shorter than the current overland road or the newly discovered sea route around the Cape of Good Hope in Africa. His desire to find this shorter route was economic in part. He hoped to get rich off of the spice trade that would open up once the new route was known. He sought gold as well and was confident that he would find the fabled gold-laden land of Ofir. Another part of his mission had an evangelical nature. He believed that the natives of the Far East were eager for news of Christianity and would be willing converts. He also felt that this discovery was merely the first step toward conquering Jerusalem, which was controlled by Muslims. This evangelical zeal becomes more evident in his later life.

On 3 August 1492 Columbus left the Spanish port of Palos with three ships, the *Niña*, the *Pinta*, and the *Santa María*. After stopping for several weeks in the Canary Islands, the small fleet set out on a surprisingly easy voyage west. Apart from some minor unrest among the crew, the trip was generally unmarred by difficulty or obstacle. On 12 October 1492 they made landfall in the Bahamas. From there they moved on to Cuba and Hispaniola. In late December of that same year, the *Santa María* grounded on a reef off the shore of Hispaniola and was used to build a fort to house a group of men left behind when the remaining ships returned to Spain. The settlement, called Navidad, was the first European colony in the Americas. As with most of Columbus's activities, there is no agreement as to whether the scuttling of the *Santa María* was accidental or deliberate, whether Columbus left Spain with the idea of establishing a colony, or whether he was forced by circumstance to leave behind a third of his crew. On 14 January he began his return trip to Spain, stopping in the Azores before arriving in Lisbon on 4 March. The return trip was beset by fierce winter storms, and the *Niña* and the *Pinta* were separated. Columbus was on the first ship to arrive in Seville, and he met with the Spanish monarchs in April 1493. He was greeted with fanfare and pomp, and the Crown awarded him the promised title "Admiral of the Ocean Sea," which he used frequently from that point on. From this first voy-

SEÑOR por que se que aureis plazer dela grand vitoria que nuestro señor me ha dado en mi viaie vos escriuo esta por la ql sabreys como enueinte dias pase a las idias cō la armada q̃ los illustrissimos Rey e Reyna nros señores me dieron dōde yo falle muy muchas Islas pobladas cō gente sin numero: y dellas todas he tomado posesion por sus altezas con pregon y vādera real estendida y non me fue contradicho Ala primera q̃ yo falle puse nonbre sant saluador a comemoracion de su alta magestat el qual maravillosamente todo esto andado los idios la llaman guanabam Ala segūda puse nonbre la isla de santa maria deconcepcion ala tercera ferrandina ala quarta la isla bella ala quinta la Isla Juana e asi a cada vna nonbre nueuo Quando yo llegue ala Juana segui io la costa della al poniente yla falle tan grande q̃ pense que seria tierra firme la prouicia de catayo y como no falle asi villas y luguares enla costa dela mar saluo pequeñas poblaciones con lagente delas q̃les nopodia hauer fabla por q̃ luego fuyan todos: andaua yo adelante por el dicho camino pēsādo deuo errar grādes Ciudades o villas y al cabo de muchas leguas visto q̃ no hauia inouació i que la costa me leuaua alsetētrion de adōde mi voluntad era cōtraria porq̃ el yuierno era ya ēcarnado yo tenia proposito dehazer del al austro y tā bie el vieto medio adelante determine deno aguardar otro tiepo y bolui atras fasta vn señalado puerto de adōde ebie dos hōbres por la tierra para saber si hauia Rey o grādes Ciudades ādoui eron tres iornadas yhallarō ifinitas poblaciōes pequeñas i gēte sin numero mas no cosa de regimiēto por lo qual sebol uierō yo entedia harto de otros idios q̃ ia tenia tomados como cōti nuamēte esta tierra era Isla e asi segui la costa della al oriēte ciento i siete leguas fasta dōde fa zia fin: del qual cabo vi otra Isla al oriēte disticta de esta diez o ocho leguas ala qual luego puse nombre la spañola y fui alli y segui la parte del setentrion asi como dela iuana al oriēte cLxxviii grādes leguas por linia recta del oriēte asi como dela iuana la qual y todas las otras sō fortissimas en demasiado grado y esta enestremo en ella ay muchos puertos enla costa dela mar sin cōparació de otros q̃ yo sepa en cristianos y fartos rrios y buenos y grandes q̃ es maravilla las tierras della sō altas y enella muy muchas sierras y mōtañas altissimas sin cōparació de la isla de cētre frētodas f̃rmosissimas de mil fechuras y todas ādabiles y llenas de arbols de mil maneras i altas i parecen q̃ llegā al cielo i tēgo pordicho q̃ iamas pierde la foia segun lo puede cōphēder q̃ los vi tā verdes i tā hermosos cōmo sō por mayo en spaña i dellos staua flor dos dellos cō fruto i dellos enotraterminno segū es su calidad i cātaua el rui señor i otros pa xaricos demil maneras en el mes denouiēbre por alli dōde io ādaua ay palmas de seis ode ocho maneras q̃ es admiracion verlas por la difformidad fermosa dellas mas asicomo los o otros arboles y frutos e yeruas en ella ay pinares amarauilla eay canpiñas grādissimas eay mi el i de muchas maneras de aues y frutas muy diuersas enlas tierras ay muchas minas deme tales eay gēte istimabile numero La spañola es marauilla las sierras ylas mōtañas y las uegas ilas campiñas y las tierras tan fermosas ygruesas para plantar ysebrar pacuar ganados de to das suertes para edificios de villas elugares los puertos dela mar aqui no hauria chenca sin vista ydelos rios muchos y grandes y buenas aguas los mas delos quales traē oro e los arbo les y frutos e yeruas ay grandes differencias de aquel las dela iuana en esta ay muchas specie rias y grandes minas de oro y de otros metales La gente desta isla y detodas las otras q̃ he fallado y hauido: ni aya hauido noticia andan todos desnudos hōbres y mugeres asi como sus madres los parē haun que algunas mugeres se cobrian vn solo lugar cō vna foia de yer ua: o vna cosa dealgodō quepa ello fazen ellos no tienen fierro ni azero ni armas ni son para ello no por que no sea gente bien dispuesta y de fermosa estatura saluo que sō muy temoroso a marauilla no tiene otras armas saluo las armas delas cañas quando estan cōla simiente al qual ponen al cabo vn palillo agudo eno osan vsar deaquellas que m[...] i[...] vezes m[...] cierto embiar ahora dos o tres hombres alguna villa pa hauer fabla y salir[...]

First page of a letter written by Columbus in 1493 during his return to Spain, in which he tells of the new lands he has found. The letter was widely translated and disseminated, providing Europeans with their first information about the "New World" (New York Public Library; from Mauricio Obregón, The Columbus Papers: The Barcelona Letter of 1493, the Landfall Controversy, and the Indian Tribes, *1991; Thomas Cooper Library, University of South Carolina).*

age resulted two of the most widely read and widely available Columbine texts, *Carta a Luis Santángel* (1493, Letter to Luis Santángel) and the "Diario del primer viaje" (Diary of the First Voyage), which was published in *Colección de los Viages y Descubrimientos, que Hicieron por Mar los Españoles desde Fines del Siglo XV: Con varios documentos inéditos concernientes á la historia de la marina castellana y de los establecimientos españoles en Indias* (1825–1837, Collection of the Maritime Voyages and Discoveries Made by the Spanish since the End of the Fifteenth Century: With Various Unpublished Documents Concerning Castillian Maritime History and the Spanish Colonies in the Indies) and translated as *Personal Narrative of the First Voyage of Columbus to America* in 1827.

Carta a Luis Santángel is also known as the "Carta a Gabriel Sánchez" (Letter to Gabriel Sánchez) and the "Letter to the Sovereigns." Scholars still disagree as to whether they are three distinct letters or three versions of a similar letter. The first two are dated 15 February 1493 and the last is dated 4 March 1493, although many scholars now believe that the March letter was most likely the source of the February letters. In addition to this confusion, the letters to Santángel and Sánchez were most likely revised by someone other than Columbus, and the "Letter to the Sovereigns" remained unpublished until 1989. In spite of its various titles, *Carta a Luis Santángel* is the one work attributed to Columbus that achieved a wide readership during Columbus's lifetime and continues to be excerpted frequently in anthologies.

Carta a Luis Santángel appears to be an adaptation of Columbus's letter to his sovereigns with some of the more technical and commercial content omitted. Likewise the text has been revised to portray both Columbus and his men in a more favorable light. Many scholars feel that this letter was a carefully mediated piece of propaganda. Within a few months of Columbus's return from the Caribbean the Spanish letter had been translated into Latin and Italian and had spread through most of Europe. A German translation appeared in 1497, followed by a second Spanish edition that same year. The letter in Spanish is addressed to Luis Santángel and the Latin versions are addressed to Gabriel Sánchez, perhaps indicating a mistake on the part of the printer or translator or perhaps indicating a different letter, although most of the differences in these two letters can be accounted for by mistakes in translation. The letter purports to be written onboard ship while Columbus was en route to Spain. Columbus records in his diary that he indeed wrote a letter to the Spanish monarchs on 14 February, during a fierce storm in the Atlantic, but that he sealed this letter in a cask and had it thrown overboard. The letter disseminated through Europe was certainly not this letter.

Regardless of its author, editor, or translator, *Carta a Luis Santángel* is the first widely disseminated news of Columbus's successful voyage to the Americas. It informed the opinions of the educated classes of Europe, and its influence can be felt more than five hundred years later. In the letter Columbus describes the islands that he discovered and claimed for Spain, their inhabitants, and their flora and fauna. Throughout the letter Columbus renames the islands that he encounters. Often, but not always, he tells the indigenous name of the land before giving it a European Christian name. The island Guanahaní, the site of the first landfall, was christened San Salvador. The actual location of this island, probably one of the Bahamas, is still uncertain.

Columbus then goes on to describe the geography of these new islands. He tells his readers that the islands are "fertilissimas en demasiado grado" (fertile to an extreme degree) and are full of many kinds of trees and plants. The trees are so huge they rise up to the sky, and everything is as green as it is in May in Spain. Columbus assures his readers that beautiful birds of infinite varieties sing and that there are many mines and excellent fruits. He claims to have found new sources of rhubarb and cinnamon. The land is perfect for sowing crops and raising livestock, as well as for building cities. Natural ports allow easy access to the islands, and the beaches and riverbanks are strewn with gold. The words *maravilla* (marvelous or marvel) and *infinita* (infinite) pepper Columbus's prose. Even a modern reader comes away from the letter with a sense of the awe and astonishment the Spaniards must have felt on finding these tropical islands. One also questions the veracity of such effusive descriptions.

In regard to the inhabitants of the islands, Columbus is equally exuberant in his descriptions. He says that they are without number and comments repeatedly on their nakedness. He almost always uses some variation of "andan desnudos como sus madres los paren" (they go around as naked as their mothers give birth to them) to describe their state of undress. According to Columbus, they are marvelously passive and cowardly while at the same time they are beautiful and hardworking. They are generous to a fault, and Columbus has to order his men not to take advantage of them in unfair trades. They are apparently monogamous and not idolatrous and because of these qualities would make excellent Christians. He goes to great lengths to explain that they appear to be without organized government or religion and implies that they are therefore ripe for exploitation. In his description of the Taino peoples, it is easy to see evidence of Columbus's multiple goals of evangelizing and making money, in this case by exploiting the natives and making them slaves.

The influence of Pliny and other ancient textual authorities is evident in Columbus's descriptions of the Caribes, a fierce tribe known for its practice of cannibalism; the Amazonian women of Matinino (Martinique), who allow men on their island only once a year; the island where all the inhabitants are bald; and Auan, the island whose inhabitants are all born with a tail. By claiming to verify the existence of races described in ancient texts, Columbus inscribes himself in this same tradition and takes on some of the authority granted the ancient authorities. It must also be remembered that for anyone living in late-fifteenth-century Europe, these textual authorities were taken as indisputable fact. In a sense, Columbus felt obligated to find the land and peoples described by Pliny and Marco Polo, among others, since they were what he and all of his contemporaries expected to find. His relationship with the ancients is part of what makes him appealing to modern readers and scholars.

The next important work written by Columbus is his "Diario del primer viaje." Columbus gave this document to the Spanish Crown but retained a copy for himself. Both of these original documents have disappeared. Fernando Columbus, Columbus's illegitimate son and biographer, and Bartolomé de Las Casas, a friend of the family and editor of Columbus's work, both state that he kept a careful diary on all four of his voyages, and both use his diary, often copying passages verbatim, to inform their own works. Only the diary from the first voyage has survived. Unlike *Carta a Luis Santángel,* the diary was unknown to the public until the late eighteenth century, when it was discovered in a private library. This text, like many of the others ascribed to Columbus, is not solely his own work, however, and the diary that survives is Las Casas's personal copy. While many scholars have attempted to discern how much of the existing diary is directly and accurately copied from Columbus's and how much is Las Casas's paraphrase, there is still no clear consensus as to how much or how little of the diary is original. Likewise, it is impossible to know how much was left out or dramatically altered. Some have pointed out that Las Casas's sympathy for the indigenous peoples and his own religious training may have influenced his choice of material from the diary and the way in which he presented the work.

In spite of these issues and the important concerns that they raise, "Diario del primer viaje" is still an invaluable document for understanding the Columbine enterprise. Columbus probably started his journal while he was en route to the Canary Islands, although the first dated entry after the brief introduction is 3 August, the day the small fleet sailed out of the Spanish port of Saltes. The diary ends on 15 March 1493, when

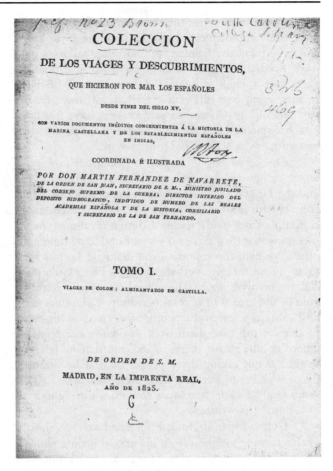

Title page for the first volume of a collection of documents related to the first voyages to the New World (Collection of the Maritime Voyages and Discoveries Made by the Spanish since the End of the Fifteenth Century), compiled by Martín Fernández de Navarrete. Columbus's diary of his first voyage to "New Spain" was originally published in this collection (Thomas Cooper Library, University of South Carolina).

Columbus and his two surviving ships return to Spanish harbors, with a stated plan to sail on to Barcelona to meet the regents there. In terms of content, the diary reiterates many of the same ideas and goals presented in *Carta a Luis Santángel,* and it is also a window into the personality of Columbus and his struggles on the first voyage. A considerable part of the diary is dedicated to nautical descriptions of the route Columbus took and the distance he traveled each day. Much has been made of the fact that he apparently kept one set of records for himself and one set for his crew. Some have taken this deception as proof that Columbus lied to his crew about the distance they had traveled, always telling them that they had gone fewer miles than what he put down in his diary so that they would not panic when they realized how far they were from home. Others have pointed out that he was possibly using two different systems to measure the distance traveled. It would have been impossible to keep the truth from his crew, since the pilot, the helmsman, and other sailors would have needed to be in collusion with their captain to carry out such a wholesale deceit. Even if he were merely using two different standards of measure, the two sets of logs Columbus said he kept have not been clearly explained and are an example of the inconsistencies inherent in "Diario del primer viaje."

One of the best examples of Columbus's inconsistency (or unreliability) in both "Diario del primer viaje" and the *Carta a Luis Santángel* is in his description of his contact with indigenous people. When he describes his communication with them, Columbus almost never mentions that they have no way of understanding each other. Instead, the report of the dialogue he has with them is seemingly verbatim and often, Columbus claims, involves their telling him that there is much gold in the area. On several occasions Columbus actually kidnaps some of the people who come to his boats so that he can take them back to Spain as specimens. There is little in his diary to indicate that he felt any qualms about taking these people or that he doubted his own ability to interpret accurately their words. This same kind of understatement continues throughout all of Columbus's writings.

Columbus undertook his second voyage shortly after returning to Spain from his first, this time with an explicit goal of colonization as well as exploration and discovery. In late September 1493 Columbus set sail for the New World with a fleet of ships and more than one thousand men, as well as a large number of horses and other livestock. From this point forward there was a constant flow of ships and personnel between Spain and the Americas. In late October or early November he arrived in the Caribbean and explored islands in the southeastern Antilles before returning to Hispaniola and the settlement he left at Navidad. He had with him some of the native islanders he had captured on the first voyage and taken to Spain, and these individuals served as his interpreters. When he reached Navidad he found the fort destroyed and all of the men dead. At first he blamed dissent among the men themselves for the failure of this first colony, but he later recanted and blamed the local tribes for the disaster. In spite of this setback, another settlement, Isabela, was created on the island. Like Navidad, this settlement was poorly planned and did not survive for long. Columbus went on to explore the mainland of Hispaniola and the coasts of Cuba and Jamaica, returning to Spain in June 1496. By this time, the Crown had established a bureaucracy in the colonies, and Columbus, controlling and contentious as he was, ran afoul of the colonial government. Several of the members of the second voyage filed complaints against him, which the Catholic Monarchs apparently took to heart. Whether Columbus was forced to return or came back of his own volition is unclear, but it is known that he then spent several years in Spain attempting to regain royal favor.

Little documentation on Columbus's second voyage exists. There is a report of the voyage, but it appears that this text was directed toward the monarchs and did not reach a wider audience. The report was unknown to the public until the discovery of a *libro copiador* (copybook) that includes copies of important documents and which was published under the title *Libro copiador de Cristóbal Colón: Correspondencia inédita con los Reyes católicos sobre los viajes a América: Estudio historico-critico y edición* (Copybook of Cristóbal Colón: Unpublished Correspondence with the Catholic Monarchs on the Voyages to America: Historico-Critical Study and Edition) in 1989. While the document is of historical value and gives insight into Columbus's other works, it is of little interest as a literary document.

After returning to Spain in 1496, Columbus spent the next two years campaigning for and organizing his third trip. He was no longer a court favorite, in large part because the promised wealth from his two prior voyages had yet to materialize and in part because he had proved to be a difficult and unpopular administrator. Apparently, during this period Columbus also refined his knowledge of ancient geography, because references to these texts become more prevalent in his writing from this time on. In May 1498 Columbus set sail with six ships carrying supplies to the colonists on Hispaniola. As the fleet left the Canary Islands, Columbus ordered three of the ships to sail directly to the colony and took the three remaining vessels on a more southerly route via the Cape Verde Islands. After days of boredom, during which time the intense heat spoiled all of the provisions onboard, Columbus finally sighted land in late July of the same year. He spent the next month exploring the new lands he had found. In fact, he had stumbled upon the South American continent. He sailed up the coast of what is now Venezuela and visited the nearby islands as well. The discovery of the mouth of the Orinoco River is one of the most notable aspects of this voyage. Columbus had never encountered a river so large and correctly surmised that it must come out of an immense continent.

After exploring for almost a month, Columbus returned to Hispaniola. There he found the colony in a state of complete disarray. He had left his brothers, Bartolomé and Diego, in charge, and when he returned the colonists were in open revolt against them. Although Columbus was able to quell this revolt as well as a subsequent one, the Crown sent Francisco de Bobadilla in the summer of 1500 to investigate the problems in the

Columbus (foreground) along with his mistress, Beatriz Enriquez, and their son, Fernando; Diego, Columbus's son from his marriage to Felipa Perestrello e Moniz, is pictured at far left (John Carter Brown Library, Brown University; from Zvi Dor-Ner, Columbus and the Age of Discovery, *1991; Thomas Cooper Library, University of South Carolina).*

colonies and Columbus's behavior. Bobadilla ruled against Columbus and his brothers, and they were sent back to Spain in chains. By this point Columbus had come to think of himself as a Job-like figure and refused to allow anyone except the sovereigns themselves to remove his chains. He dramatically appeared in court in shackles and was quickly pardoned.

Columbus's writings about this voyage have come to rival the *Carta a Luis Santángel* in popularity. There are several extant letters from this voyage in the *Libro copiador,* but the work that has had the greatest readership is the "Relación" (Report) of the third voyage. The text is found at the end of Las Casas's transcription of the "Diario del primer viaje" and also appears, with minor variations and additions, in his *Historia de las Indias* (History of the Indies), which was published in Madrid in 1875–1876. This "Relación" was written in August 1498, shortly after Columbus arrived

on Hispaniola after his exploration of the northern coast of South America, two years before his disgraced return to Spain in October 1500.

One of the most interesting features of the "Relación" of the third voyage is that for the first time Columbus's millennialism and religious fervor take precedence over his economic interests, although these interests never disappear entirely. In some ways the "Relación" represents a rhetorical shift in the way that the admiral presents himself and his mission. The letter begins with Columbus's crediting the Holy Trinity with moving the king and queen to support his voyages in order to spread the Catholic faith. He then claims that Isaiah predicted that Spain would discover these new lands and take to them the true faith. Also in this report Columbus begins to present himself as a martyr and unappreciated servant of the Spanish Crown. He makes reference to other great nations, including contemporary Portugal, who generously financed explorers and voyages of discovery, and indirectly asks the Spanish to do as much.

In the "Relación" Columbus puts forth his own view of geography, rejecting that of ancient authorities. Based on variations in his sightings of the North Star, Columbus decided he and his ships were not moving on a level course but were instead moving upward. He then concluded that the world was not round but rather shaped like a pear or a woman's breast, that is, mostly round with a protuberance on one side. He refutes not only Ptolemy but also Aristotle, saying that since they had no knowledge of this part of the world, they could not describe it accurately. After reaching this conclusion, Columbus goes on to claim, based on the magnitude of the rivers he has encountered and on his proof, that this part of the world is more elevated, and that this earthly paradise must be close at hand. Ancient authorities had postulated that the Garden of Eden was perhaps in Africa at the source of the Nile River or at the furthest point of the Orient at the top of an enormous mountain. According to Columbus, Eden, while forbidden to humankind without divine intervention, could be found at the top of the protuberance on the globe of the world.

Columbus also defies the ancients and contradicts himself when he says that the world is bigger than they had surmised and that if the enormous rivers he has encountered are not coming from Eden, they are coming from a vast continent unknown to the ancients. In this letter for the first time, Columbus refers to the lands he has discovered as "otro mundo" (another world). Scholars debate whether he was referring to a world unknown in the ancient world and therefore "new," or if he was referring to a world different from those of Europe, Africa, and Asia but not necessarily unknown to the wise men of antiquity. The report from this voyage places Columbus squarely within the educated debates of his time and simultaneously illustrates his contradictory nature.

After being forcibly returned to Spain in 1500, Columbus waited two and a half years before being granted permission to undertake a fourth and final voyage. On this voyage he took four poorly constructed ships. His brother Bartolomé and young son and later biographer, Fernando, accompanied him as well. The Catholic Monarchs had expressly forbidden his return to Hispaniola, thus hoping to avoid the problems that had occurred the last time Columbus had been on the island. In spite of this prohibition, he went to Hispaniola, where he was denied permission to stay in the harbor, although he knew from his experience on his prior voyages that a huge storm was blowing in. As Columbus and his small group of ships left the harbor, so did a

larger fleet bound for Spain. Most of this fleet was lost at sea, including a ship carrying Columbus's long-standing enemy, Bobadilla. After leaving Hispaniola, Columbus and his ships headed southwest to explore the lands he had discovered on the third voyage and to look in earnest for the strait he believed would connect the lands with the rest of the Asian Indies. For the better part of a year the fleet sailed up and down the Central American coast, hindered by bad weather and leaking, worm-eaten ships. In May 1503 Columbus realized he could not last much longer and attempted to return to the Spanish colonies. By this time he was down to two ships. When he realized he could not make it back to Hispaniola, Columbus attempted to make landfall in Jamaica. Both of his remaining vessels were beached at this time, and the Spaniards could not salvage them. Columbus and the one hundred or so men who had survived were subsequently stranded for almost an entire year. After several attempts by both natives and Spaniards to reach Hispaniola by canoe, one of Columbus's men, Diego de Escobar, arrived in the colony. The colony administrators were in no hurry to come to the aid of Columbus and his men but eventually rescued them in June 1504. Columbus returned to Spain in September of that year.

The report of the fourth voyage, which Columbus wrote in July 1503, was first published in Italian that same year as the "Lettera rarísima" (Remarkable Letter). A copy of the report is also included in the *Libro copiador*. The tone of this letter is remarkably, and understandably, darker than Columbus's other work, in part because it was written while he was stranded on Jamaica. His desperation is evident from the first page of the letter, when he compares himself to Job and the immense trials he underwent. Throughout the voyage his ships are riddled with holes like honeycomb and his own health is in ruins. His descriptions of the storms he encountered are dramatic and clearly exaggerated. He says he battled storms for seventy days and then just a few lines later remarks that the storms lasted eighty-eight days. According to Columbus, the rain was not normal but rather was "otro diluvio" (another biblical flood). He complains that he has no home to call his own in Spain and that he is unable to leave more material wealth to his sons. His suffering is so great that he claims: "non sey si obo otro con mas martirios" (I don't know if there has ever been anyone who suffered more martyrdom than I).

Throughout this letter, Columbus mentions repeatedly the parts of Asia he thinks he is visiting. He claims to be close to Cathay and that the shores of the Caribbean are only a few days' journey from the mouth of the Ganges River. He tells his readers that "el mundo es poco . . . no es tan grande como dicen el vulgo" (the world is small . . . not so large as the masses say). He makes these pronouncements in spite of his admission in the report from the third voyage that he may have found an unknown continent and that the world is much different from what the ancients claimed. Clearly, his rhetorical goals had shifted.

Columbus continues to mention the possibility of gold and textiles and other potential material for trade in this area, although this time he has a more specific reason for wanting to make a profit. After the difficult years on Hispaniola that had followed the composition of the "Relación" of the third voyage, Columbus's spiritual bent had deepened, and during this time he began to focus more and more on the reconquest of Jerusalem, a crusade financed by gains made in the Indies. This goal is made explicit in the "Lettera rarísima" when Columbus cites an unknown prophecy by "el abad Johachin" (the abbot Joaquín) that Spain would liberate the Holy City. At this time he also began to put more emphasis on his own prophetic destiny. From 1493 until his death, Columbus signed his name "Christoferens" (the bearer of Christ), an obvious attempt to focus on the evangelical aspects of his voyages. In this fourth letter he gives a detailed account of a dream in which God spoke to him directly and predicts that in spite of his advanced age he will go on to do great things. In the face of despair and failure, Columbus turned to faith and the approval of God to console him.

When Christopher Columbus returned to Spain for the final time in November 1504, he found that his beloved patron, Queen Isabel, was gravely ill. Columbus himself was suffering from various maladies contracted during or exacerbated by his long years at sea. King Ferdinand proved uninterested in him or his petitions for the restitution he had been promised. During the last year of his life, Columbus worked to gain an audience with the new regents of Spain, Juana and Felipe of Portugal. He was unsuccessful and died on 20 May 1506. He left behind Diego, his legitimate son, and Fernando, his illegitimate son. Columbus had hoped to make his descendants nobility, and in this regard he was successful. Diego married into the Castilian nobility, and Columbus's heirs were all named dukes. In financial matters he was less fortunate and never received the monetary rewards he was promised before and after the first voyage. His reputation suffered even before his death, and Fernando Columbus did his best to rectify it with his biography of his father. Even though Columbus's reputation has waxed and waned with historical and literary fashion, he continues to fascinate and intrigue his readers.

Bibliographies:

Foster Provost, *Columbus: An Annotated Guide to the Scholarship on His Life and Writings, 1750 to 1988* (Detroit: Omnigraphics, 1991);

Moses M. Nagy, *Christopher Columbus in World Literature* (New York: Garland, 1994).

Biographies:

Samuel Eliot Morison, *Admiral of the Ocean Sea: A Life of Christopher Columbus* (Boston: Little, Brown, 1942);

Morison, *Christopher Columbus, Mariner* (Boston: Little, Brown, 1955);

Fernando Colón, *The Life of the Admiral Christopher Columbus by His Son, Ferdinand,* translated by Benjamin Keen (New Brunswick, N.J.: Rutgers University Press, 1959; London: Folio Society, 1959);

Felipe Fernández-Armesto, *Columbus* (Oxford & New York: Oxford University Press, 1991);

Miles H. Davidson, *Columbus Then and Now: A Life Reexamined* (Norman: University of Oklahoma Press, 1997).

References:

Silvio A. Bedini, ed., *The Christopher Columbus Encyclopedia,* 2 volumes (New York: Simon & Schuster, 1992);

Zvi Dor-Ner, *Columbus and the Age of Discovery* (New York: Morrow, 1991);

David Henige, *In Search of Columbus: The Sources for the First Voyage* (Tucson: University of Arizona Press, 1991);

Mauricio Obregón, *The Columbus Papers: The Barcelona Letter of 1493, the Landfall Controversy, and the Indian Tribes: A Facsimile Edition of the Unique Copy in the New York Public Library* (New York: Macmillan, 1991);

José Rabasa, *Inventing America: Spanish Historiography and the Formation of Eurocentrism* (Norman: University of Oklahoma Press, 1993), pp. 49–82;

Margarita Zamora, *Reading Columbus* (Berkeley: University of California Press, 1993).

Juan de la Cueva
(1543 – 1612)

Julio Vélez-Sainz
University of Massachusetts, Amherst

BOOKS: *Obras de Juan de la Cueva, dedicadas al ilustrísimo Señor don Juan Téllez Girón* (Seville: Pescioni, 1582);

Primera parte de las comedias y tragedias de Juan de la Cueva dirigidas a Momo (Seville: Pescioni, 1583);

Coro febeo de romances historiales (Seville: Léon, 1587);

Primera parte de las comedias y tragedias de Juan de la Cueva dirigidas a Momo, second edition (Seville: Léon, 1588);

Comedia del saco de Roma (Barcelona: Cormellas, 1603);

Conquista de la Betica: Poema heroico de Iuan de la Cueua en que se canta la restauracion y libertad de Seuilla por el Santo Rey Don Fernando (Seville: Pérez, 1603);

Segunda parte de las obras de Juan de la Cueva (Seville, 1605).

Modern Editions: *Poèmes inédits, publiés d'après des manuscrits autographes conservés à Séville dans la bibl.,* edited by Fredrik A. Wulff (Lund: Gleerup, 1887);

Historia verdadera del valiente Bernardo del Carpio sacada con toda individualidad de los más insignes historiadores españoles, corrected and augmented edition (Madrid: Hernando, 1893);

Teatro escogido (Madrid: Compañía Ibero-Américana de Publicaciones, 1900);

Comedias y tragedias de Juan de la Cueva, 2 volumes, edited by Francisco A. de Icaza (Madrid: Maestre, 1917);

El infamador, Los siete infantes de Lara, y el Ejemplar poético, edited by Icaza (Madrid: "La Lectura," 1924);

Bernardo del Carpio, edited by Anthony Watson (Exeter, U.K.: University of Exeter, 1974);

Juan de la Cueva's Los inventores de las cosas: A Critical Edition and Study, edited by Beno Weiss and Louis C. Pérez (University Park: Pennsylvania State University Press, 1980);

Fábulas mitológicas y épica burlesca, edited by Jose Cebrián García (Madrid: Editora Nacional, 1984);

Exemplar poético, critical edition by José María Reyes Cano (Seville: Alfar, 1986);

Eglogas completas, edited by Cebrián García (Madrid: Miraguano, 1988);

Juan de la Cueva (drawing by Ruth Pines; from Beno Weiss and Louis C. Pérez, eds., Juan de la Cueva's Los inventores de las cosas: A Critical Edition and Study, 1980; Thomas Cooper Library, University of South Carolina)

Viaje de Sannio, edited by Cebrián García (Madrid: Miraguano, 1990);

La muerte del Rey Don Sancho y reto de Zamora: Comedia del degollado, edited by Juan Matas Caballero (León: Universidad de León, 1997).

Juan de la Cueva is an important literary figure of sixteenth-century Spain. His works consist primarily of drama and poetry, and he also devoted time to translating the classics. Even though Cueva disseminates personal references in all his works, not much is known about his life—only that he visited the Spanish colonies from 1574 to 1577 and that he lived for some time in Portugal after that date.

The Sevillian scholar Santiago Montoto found Cueva's birth certificate in 1932. It states that Cueva was born in the Parroquia de Santa Catalina (Saint Catherine Parish) in Seville: "en miércoles veintre y tres días del mes de octubre, año de mil y quinientos y cuarenta y tres años, batizó francisco fernández de hervas, cura de esta yglesia, a juan, hijo del doctor martín núñez de la cueva y su mujer juana de las cuevas, su mujer legítima" (On Wednesday October twenty-three, 1543, Francisco Fernández de Hervas, father of this church, baptized Juan, son of Doctor Martín López de la Cueva and his legitimate wife Juana de las Cuevas). Juan de la Cueva Garoza was thus the fifth of eight children in a family of noble upbringing in Seville.

Cueva's literary beginnings coincide with his passion for Felipa de la Paz, and he devoted his early lyric compositions to her. Scholar Fredrik A. Wulff asserts that Cueva was introduced to Felipa at the age of seventeen, and his infatuation lasted several years. By 1567 he dedicated several poems to her using the pseudonyms Felice, Felicia, and her own name, Felipa. For instance, in his elegy 2 (fols. 34v–37, vv. 52–57) in *Obras de Juan de la Cueva, dedicados al ilustrísimo Señor don Juan Téilez Girón* (1582, The works of Juan de la Cueva, Dedicated to the Illustrios Señor Don Juan Téilez Girón), he declares:

No era possible ni podia apartarme
de la dulce memoria que aspirava
la FELIce PAsión, que vía forcarme

(It was not possible for me to separate myself
from the sweet memory that exhaled
my FELIcitous PAssion, that was forcing me).

Cueva builds his beloved's name into the compositions in the form of acrostics. These poems may not reveal biographical data about him for, as Richard F. Glenn argues in his *Juan de la Cueva* (1973), his laments of love to Felipa are patterned after the stock images of Iberian Petrarchism and its combination of forbidden love and restrained passion. Garcilaso de la Vega, the Portuguese Luis de Camões, and Cueva's friend Fernando de Herrera provide examples for most of the imagery found in Cueva's poetry. For example, he develops the commonplace jail of the soul in his sonnet 5, the image of the fiery beloved in sonnet 6, and the metaphor of the ship lost in the waves of love in his epistles. He also

composed seven eclogues, 25 elegies, 21 *canciones* (songs), 2 madrigals, and 260 sonnets.

Cueva was also an astute observer of his culture. He is associated with a cultural group called La Escuela de Sevilla (The School of Seville), which he formed along with intellectuals such as Alonso de la Vega, Agustín Ortiz, Diego Girón, and Juan de Mal-Lara and poet Gutierre de Cetina. As was customary at the time, Cueva dedicated poems to each of his fellow academy writers. Cueva also met many contemporary writers in the Sevillian House of Pilatos, owned by the governor, Enríquez de Ribera. It is possible that he made Herrera's acquaintance in that house. They became friends to the point that Cueva allegedly advised him against declaring his fervent love to Leonor de Millán. He did not devote all his youth to love matters (either his own or somebody else's), for Cueva was also an active participant in imperial Spain's national propaganda through his literary group in Seville. At the magnificent reception that the city offered to King Philip II, for example, as poet Mal-Lara depicts in his *Recibimiento que hizo la ciudad de Sevilla al Rey don Phelipe II* (Reception of the City of Seville for the King Philip II), Cueva celebrated Philip's fourth marriage to Anna of Austria. He was also a proud Sevillian, composing testaments to the beauties of his city such as "Bien puedes padre Betis, generoso" (You are capable, generous father Baetis)," in which he praises the Guadalquivir River (also known as the Betis) and mentions that it surpasses in beauty the Po and the Arno.

From this period dates a description of Cueva found in Francisco de Pacheco's *Libro de descripción de verdaderos retratos de ilustres y memorables varones* (Book of the Description of True Portraits of Illustrious and Memorable Men), which remained unpublished until 1599. Pacheco provides a physical and moral semblance of Cueva: "Y solo por su retrato nos consta que fue de buena presencia, robusto de cuerpo, la cabeza abultada y grande, los ojos vivos, la nariz eminente, el cabello crespo, y el semblante rígido. . . . De ellas podremos inferir su carácter circunspecto, su solido juicio, su tesón inflexible por la verdad y por la corrección de los abusos literarios que reynaban en los Escritores y Poetas de su tiempo" (From his portrait we can gather he was good looking: robust, with a large and bulky head, lively eyes, eminent nose, curly hair and rigid semblance. . . . From his works we can infer his judicious character, solid judgment, his firm eagerness for truth and his amendment of the literary abuses that reigned among his contemporary writers and poets). Many of the traits Pacheco describes can be found in Cueva's works. He constantly reflected on his duties as a writer, and he also commented upon the literature of Golden

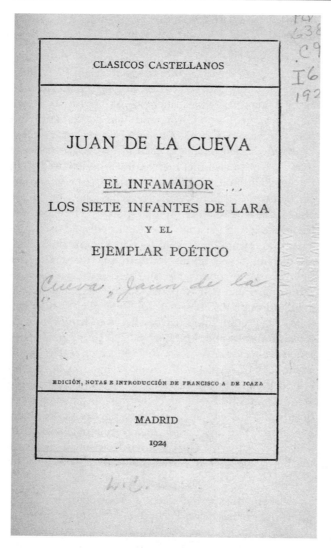

Title page for a 1924 edition that collects two of Cueva's best-known plays, El infamador *(1581, The Defamer) and* Los siete infantes de Lara *(1579, The Seven Princes of Lara), and his 1606 verse treatise on poetry,* El ejemplar poético *(University of Alabama Library)*

from the collection were eventually revised and included in *Obras de Juan de la Cueva, dedicadas al ilustrísimo señor don Juan Téllez Girón. Flores de baria poesía* spread Petrarchism in the New World and contributed to shaping literature in the Spanish colony. Cueva enjoyed Mexico a great deal and devoted poems to the capital of the viceroyalty:

> A toda esta ciudad soi muy propicio,
> i la ciudad a mí,
> . . . Considerais qu'está en una laguna
> México cual Venecia edificada
> sobre la mar, sin diferencia alguna?
> . . . Sin estas hallaréis otras mil cosas
> de que carece España, que son tales
> al gusto, i a la vista deleytosas
>
> (I am pleased by this city,
> and I please her too,
> . . . Have you considered that Mexico is over water,
> with no difference to Venice?
> . . . You will find a thousand more things
> that are lacking in Spain
> that are so delightful to taste and vision).

Mexico offered Cueva marvels that could not be found in Europe. As Jose Cebrián García relates in his *Juan de la Cueva y Nueva España,* however, "en contra de lo que pudiera pensarse ante versos que expresan sin ambages un feliz acomodo, nuestro Cueva, a poco más de un año de residir en la ciudad de México, decide solicitar permiso al Virrey para regresar" (opposite to what one could gather from verses that openly express his adaptation to the place, our Cueva, shortly after one year of residence in Mexico, asks for permission to leave). Cueva was homesick, and in several of his compositions he imagines his beloved hometown across the distance:

> Lugar quieto, dulce i ascondido,
> do Betis suavemente murmurava
> por entre flores i árboles corriendo
>
> (Sweet, hidden and tranquil place
> where Betis softly whispers
> streaming through flowers and trees).

He soon returned to the meadows of the Guadalquivir: by 1577 Cueva was back in Spain and pursuing a literary career, which flowered in the dramatic genre. He wrote prolifically for the stage, though few of his plays are extant. He wrote most of them between the time he returned to Spain and around 1579.

One of Cueva's most important contributions to the development of Spanish theater is his re-creation in his plays of medieval history, which he projected onto contemporary Spain. Plays such as *La Libertad de España*

Age Spain. He was a conscientious writer who attempted to serve imperial Spain by writing of its greatness.

Cueva departed for New Spain in 1574 with his brother, Claudio, who had been appointed by Philip II as *racionero* to the Cathedral of New Spain with a stipend of 500 ducats. While the ambitious Claudio became an active participant in the politics of New Spain, Juan composed several of his poems there. More than thirty of his most celebrated poems are included in the 1577 *cancionero* (songbook) *Flores de baria poesía* (Flowers of Diverse Poetry), along with poems by Cetina, Herrera, Mal-Lara, and Juan de Iranzo. Cueva's poems *por Bernardo del Carpio* (Spain Liberated by Bernardo del Carpio) and *Los siete infantes de Lara* (The Seven Princes from Lara) develop national topics and myths. As a dramatist, Cueva is a transitional figure between Lope de Rueda and Lope de Vega, even though the latter does not mention Cueva. For instance, Cueva limited the number of *jornadas* (acts) from five to four, which Lope de Vega reduced again to three in seventeenth-century *comedias*. Cueva also introduced new metrical forms and incorporated into the plot lyrical elements, both aspects that influenced Lope de Vega.

In 1578 Cueva debuted as dramatist in the newly opened Teatro de las Ataranzas (Theater of the Ataranzas) with his *Comedia de la muerte del rey don Sancho y reto de Zamora* (Comedy of the Death of King Sancho and the Challenge in Zamora). Cueva delved into legends from the *romancero viejo* (traditional ballads) to develop the story of the heirs of the first monarch to rule over Castile and Leon at once, Ferdinand I. Ferdinand divided his kingdom among his sons and his daughter, Doña Urraca. The first act introduces the celebrated figure of El Cid, Ruy Diaz de Vivar, who is commanded by one of Urraca's brothers, King Sancho, to deliver her an official demand for surrender of Zamora, her share of the kingdom. After El Cid reaches Zamora, Urraca and Arias González, a nobleman and Urraca's prime minister, accuse him of having betrayed Ferdinand's wishes. Sancho himself arrives at the walls of Zamora to encounter Vellido Dolfos, who offers to show the monarch a hidden entryway into the city. El Cid attempts to convince Sancho to respect his late father's final testament, but Sancho decides to follow the treacherous Dolfos, who stabs him. In the second act, the fallen king's relatives try to avenge him. Diego Ordóñez de Lara, cousin of Sancho, challenges Arias González, who in turn explains that Dolfos acted on his own behalf. The city sends five champions to defend her accused honor. The third act describes the bloody joust between Diego Ordóñez and Arias's two sons, who are slain. In the fourth act the conflicts among the enraged combatants threaten to erupt into open war. El Cid decides to mediate between Arias and Ordóñez before they kill one another. Zamora is absolved, while Ordóñez is proclaimed winner.

Cueva utilized again the rich medieval chronicle tradition to compose *Los siete infantes de Lara,* which is based on a legend from the *Primera crónica general* (1344, First General Chronicle) compiled by the historical bureau of the king of Castile, Alfonse X. The first part of the legend delves primarily into the princes. When the youngest of them kills a man who insults him, the man's cousins swear vengeance. They send the princes' father, Gonzalo Bustos, to the Moorish king Almanzor with a letter instructing the Moor to keep Bustos there.

Then they capture the princes and execute them, sending their heads to their father. In the second part of the legend Mudarra, the grown son of Bustos and a beautiful Moorish woman of Almanzor's court, wages a vendetta against Ruy Velázquez, the man who murdered his half brothers.

Cueva also wrote nonhistorical dramas, which Glenn labels "novelesque plays." Two of the most notable of these works are *El viejo Enamorado* (The Old Man in Love) and *El infamador* (The Defamer). *El viejo Enamorado* is a rather violent drama that develops the *senex puer* motif, typical in Roman drama, in which a despicable old man courts a young innocent. In the play the old man, Liboso, tries to win Olympia's hand by contriving evidence that Olimpia's other suitor, Arcelo, is already married. In the second act Olimpia rejects Liboso, preferring suicide to marrying the octogenarian. Arcelo challenges Liboso, who sends his necromancer friend Rogerio instead. The magician conjures furies to kidnap Arcelo. In the climactic third act Arcelo is abducted by the furies, while Olimpia attempts to entice Liboso and Rogerio into turning on each other. Liboso stabs the magician, only to be killed himself immediately after by Olimpia. When she is about to stab herself with the knife, an allegorical figure representing Reason offers to take her to her lover's dungeon. The final act tells of Olimpia's dangerous journey to free Arcelo, aided by the god Hymen, who is disguised as a shepherd.

El infamador is one of many Golden Age plays that deal with unrequited love and its consequences. The first act introduces Leucino, a wealthy and vainglorious nobleman who desires the virginal Eliodora. Cueva foreshadows in Leucino the type of libertine that Tirso de Molina afterward immortalized with the character of Don Juan in his *El burlador de Sevilla* (1630, The Seducer of Seville). Leucino sends his pander, Teodora, to her, but Eliodora refuses her requests. When he attempts to rape Eliodora, she invokes the gods to help her, and the allegorical figure Nemesis appears to threaten Leucino with a "fin horrendo" (horrendous ending) if he continues with his wicked plans. In the second act a highly lusty version of Venus, disapproving of Eliodora's chastity, disguises herself as Eliodora's maid to instigate her downfall. The third act opens with a discussion of misogynist authors, including the archpriest of Talavera and Cristóbal de Castillejo, arguably intended to reflect Leucino's highly ungallant attitude. Helped by Teodora and Venus, who try to convince Eliodora that Leucino wants to marry her, the lecherous Leucino and his servant, Ortelio, get access to Eliodora's private room. In the climax, the enraged Eliodora fatally stabs Ortelio in an attempt to save her virginity from Leucino's attacks and is sent to jail. The last act is solely

Juan de la Cueva's Los Inventores de las Cosas

PQ
6388
.C9
C9
1980

A Critical Edition and Study

Beno Weiss

and

Louis C. Pérez

The Pennsylvania State University Press

University Park and London

Title page for the scholarly edition of Cueva's writings on ancient inventors (Inventors and Their Inventions) written around 1606 but unpublished until 1980 (Thomas Cooper Library, University of South Carolina)

from Troy, famously carrying his aged father, Anchises, on his shoulders. The second act shifts to describe Helen's lamenting her misfortune. Ajax Telamon in turn complains that he has not been rewarded for his deeds in the Trojan War. He wishes to be armed with the fallen Achilles' fabulous weapons forged by Vulcan himself. A quarrel over the weapons breaks out between Ajax and Ulysses. Agammenon intercedes between the two contestants. In the third act, a committee of judges formed by Menelaus and Diomedes tries to decide who will be given the magnificent weapons. The wise Nestor is not able to decide either so he invokes the gods for aid and then pronounces in favor of Ulysses. Ajax curses the Greeks and falls on the sword. After his suicide, Ajax is transformed into a flower.

The plot of many of Cueva's dramas is based on the concept of mimetic violence, an aspect that links Cueva with Seneca and the Latin Silver Age writers. In *La Muerte de Ajax Telamón sobre las armas de Aquiles* the contest between Ulysses and Ajax threatens the confraternity of the Greeks, and it can only be solved with Ajax's suicide. In *El infamador* Leucino sexually attacks Eliodora, who in turn kills his servant. In *Los siete infantes de Lara* the youngest prince, Gonzalo González, slays Alvar Sánchez and a messenger, and Sánchez's cousins reciprocate by assassinating the princes. In *El viejo Enamorado* Liboso stabs the magician and is stabbed in turn by Olimpia. In *Comedia de la muerte del rey don Sancho y reto de Zamora* only the calming presence of El Cid prevents a massacre at the gates of Zamora.

Throughout his plays Cueva projects these medieval and classical examples onto contemporary political issues. As John Lihani states in his "La técnica de recapitulación auténtica en el teatro del siglo XVI" (1981, The Technique of Authentic Recapitulation in Sixteenth-Century Theater), "Cueva used historical fact and tradition to encourage political and patriotic action and to make moral and religious statements." For instance, he reflects on the succession to the Portuguese throne in *Comedia de la muerte del rey don Sancho y reto de Zamora*. Clearly preoccupied with the destructive power of hostility, Cueva appears to be arguing through the figure of El Cid that if Spain could be persuaded to lay down her arms, the matter could be discussed reasonably. As Anthony Watson argues in his *Juan de la Cueva and the Portuguese Succession* (1971), Cueva sought to provide a cautionary example of the recurrent pattern of political behavior that had marked medieval Spanish history. His profuse utilization of Spain's historiographical tradition also produced consequences for Renaissance dramatic theory. Following the medieval chronicle tradition Cueva merged myth and reality, which provided a particular sense of mimesis unlike Aristotle's. He devel-

devoted to showing Eliodora's virtue and miraculous salvation. Her own father, following several legendary precedents, attempts to murder her with a poisoned compote that is magically transformed into a bouquet of flowers, and she is sentenced to death, although two wild men keep the court from carrying out the sentence. The goddess Diana appears to force Leucino to repent, and he is condemned to death by drowning. When the river Betis asks Diana not to pollute his waters with Leucino, however, he is buried alive instead. Eliodora is now safe to return home.

The multiple mythological elements in Cueva's plays show that he had an appreciation for classical knowledge. He also utilized ancient history to construct dramas such as *La Muerte de Ajax Telamón sobre las armas de Aquiles* (Death of Ajax Telamon over Achilles' Weapons). The first act deals primarily with Aeneas's flight oped his plots, incidents, and situations with no regard for Aristotle's unities. Arguably Cueva was following the writers of the Latin Silver Age, who were first to forsake Aristotle. Seneca challenged the Aristotelean mode as he makes all the characters, whether high- or low-brow, talk in the same lofty vein. Cueva is not often interested in verisimilitude and thus utilizes unrealistic endings to his plays, such as a murder or some supernatural intervention. He intended to break away from the doctrine of plausibility that dominated *comedia erudita* (erudite drama) in the late fifteenth and early sixteenth centuries.

According to Cebrián García's *Juan de la Cueva y Nueva España,* Cueva finished his long narrative poem *Viaje de Sannio* (Sannio's Journey) on 15 June 1585. Cebrián García argues that Cueva gives qualities of his own in Sannio: "su fidelidad estoica a unos principios éticos y su impenitente e incorregible osadía, revestida de sátira y de burlona mordacidad cuando el caso lo precisa" (his stoic fidelity to ethical principles and his unreflecting and uncorrectable daring sometimes covered by satire and burlesque mordacity). Sannio stems from the figure of the buffoon in ancient Greek and Roman mime, who is cruelly targeted as the butt of all pranks and who undertakes a sojourn through the heavens to the throne of Jupiter to demand recognition for his literary accomplishments. He is rejected, however, and laments:

Veo qu'el siglo tiene en poca estima
al virtuoso pobre i da la mano
al torpe, al inorante, al que se arrima
al rico, qu'el desorden sigue ufano

(I can see that the world does not esteem highly
the virtuous poor and salutes
the inept, the ignorant, and the hustler
with open hand, and disorder remains unaffected).

Cueva wittily censures contemporary Spain for its lack of appreciation of literary value. By 1585, however, Cueva was a highly recognized figure among his fellow writers. Miguel de Cervantes—in his earliest known prose work, the pastoral novel *La Galatea*—praises Cueva: "Dad a Juan de la Cuevas el debido / lugar, cuando se ofrezca en este asiento / pastores, pues lo tiene merecido / su dulce musa y raro entendimiento. / Sé que sus obras del eterno olvido, / a despecho y pesar del violento / curso del tiempo, librarán su nombre, / quedando con un alto claro renombre" (Shepherds! Offer Juan de la Cueva a place amongst you, when he comes to take his chair. His sweet musings and his high knowledge make him worthy of praise. I know that his name will be remembered eternally in spite of the violent course of time and forever he will be renowned).

Cervantes appreciates Cueva for his well-versed compositions and the musicality of his poetry and suggests that he is worthy of eternal fame.

Probably spurred by friendly remarks such as Cervantes's, Cueva undertook one of his most ambitious poems: "Historia y sucesión de la Cueva" (History and Succession of the de la Cueva Family), printed in his *Segunda parte de las obras de Juan de la Cueva* (1605, Second Part of the Works of Juan de la Cueva). In it Cueva provides details about his family and his noble background. He traces his family cachet back to Beltrán de la Cueva, who was granted the duchy of Alburquerque by Henry IV. Beltrán is famous in Spanish history for his popularly acknowledged affair with Queen Juana of Portugal. Queen Juana gave birth to Juana, "la Beltraneja," an illegitimate daughter who contended for the Spanish throne and lost it to Isabella of Castile. After Isabella was crowned in 1467, la Beltráneja as well as Beltrán and their followers were vilified. Cueva intended to restore his family's honor in his poem. Cueva died seven years after *Segunda parte de las obras de Juan de la Cueva,* in 1612.

Juan de la Cueva significantly influenced the development of sixteenth-century drama in both theoretical and practical terms. His dramas introduced gods and mortals to the stage and combined the crude and the sublime while introducing a significant element of political discussion in his plots. He established the four-act structure in Spanish drama and utilized a variety of stanzas in his own plays. He delved into diverse topics from classical antiquity and medieval historiographical and didactic literature. He also challenged Aristotle's *Poetics* by disregarding the unities of place, time, and action. He preferred instead the model set forth by Seneca and the late classic Roman playwrights. For his lyrical compositions Cueva dwelled on the most current model of his time, Petrarchism. He followed Garcilaso and Herrera and dedicated to his beloved Felipa de la Cruz his poems, compositions that foreshadow the baroque obsession with acrostics in poems. Much like his plays, his poems are filled with mythological references that expand their meanings. In both poetry and drama Cueva was a man of his time, a conscientious citizen who used his art to reflect on contemporary issues while fighting for a place in the overpopulated literary system of his period.

References:

David G. Burton, *The Legend of Bernardo del Carpio from Chronicle to Drama* (Potomac, Md.: Scripta Humanistica, 1988);

Burton, "Virtue Triumphant in Cueva's *La libertad de España por Bernardo del Carpio,*" *Bulletin of the Comediantes,* 38, no. 2 (1986): 219–229;

Susan de Carvalho, "The Legend of the *Siete infantes de Lara* and Its Theatrical Representation by Cueva and Later Lope de Vega," *Bulletin of the Comediantes,* 40, no. 1 (1988): 85–102;

Jose Cebrián García, "Juan de la Cueva, traductor de la *Batracomiomaquia,*" *Revista de Literatura,* 47, no. 93 (1985): 23–39;

Cebrián García, *Juan de la Cueva y Nueva España: "Tú encendiste en amor el alma mía"* (Kassel: Reichenberger, 2001);

Teresa Ferrer Valls, *Nobleza y espectáculo teatral, 1535–1622: Estudio y documentos* (Madrid: UNED / Seville: Universidad de Sevilla / Valencia: Universidad de València, 1993);

Richard F. Glenn, *Juan de la Cueva* (New York: Twayne, 1973);

A. Robert Lauer, "The Use and Abuse of History in the Spanish Theater of the Golden Age: The Regicide of Sancho II as Treated by Juan de la Cueva, Guillén de Castro, and Lope de Vega," *Hispanic Review,* 56, no. 1 (1988): 17–37;

John Lihani, "La técnica de recapitulación auténtica en el teatro del siglo XVI," in *Lope de Vega y los orígenes del teatro español: Actas del I Congreso Internacional sobre Lope de Vega,* edited by Manuel Criado de Val (Madrid: EDI-6, 1981), pp. 303–309;

Santiago Montoto, "Juan de la Cueva: Aparece la partida de bautismo del gran dramático," *Blanco y Negro,* 21 February 1932, pp. 89–90;

J. Valentin Núñez Rivera, "'Y vivo solo y casi en un destierro': Juan de la Cueva en sus epístolas poéticas," in *La epístola,* edited by Begoña López Bueno (Seville: Universidad de Sevilla, 2000), pp. 257–294;

Jose María Reyes Cano, *La poesía lírica de Juan de la Cueva* (Seville: Diputación Provincial de Sevilla, 1980);

Jorge A. Silveira y Montes de Oca, "El Romancero y el teatro nacional español: De Juan de la Cueva a Lope de Vega," in *Lope de Vega y los orígenes del teatro español: Actas del I Congreso Internacional sobre Lope de Vega,* edited by Manuel Criado de Val (Madrid: EDI-6, 1981), pp. 73–81;

Anthony Watson, *Juan de la Cueva and the Portuguese Succession* (London: Tamesis, 1971);

Fredrik A. Wulff, "Poèmes inédits de Juan de la Cueva," *Lunds Universitets Arksskrift,* 23 (1887): 1–64.

Papers:

Renaissance editions of Juan de la Cueva's works are rare. The first and only edition of Cueva's *Primera parte de las comedias y tragedias de Juan de la Cueva dirigidas a Momo* is currently housed in the Nationalbibliothek of Vienna (395562-B. CP. ID. 63). The Biblioteca Nacional de Madrid holds one manuscript of the *Exemplar poético* (1585) and one of *Los cuatro libros de los inventores de las cosas* that dates from 1609, even though the title page reads composed in Seville, 1606.

Francisco Delicado

(circa 1475 – circa 1540?)

John Edwards
University of Oxford

BOOKS: *Spechio vulgare per li sacerdoti che administraranno li sacramenti in ciascheduna parrochia* (Rome: Printed by Antonio di Salamanca, 1525);

Retrato de la Loçana andaluza en lengua española muy clarissima, anonymous (Venice, 1528);

El modo de adoperare il legno d'India occidentale: Salutifero remedio a ogni plaga & mal incurabile (Venice: Sumptibus F. Delicati, 1529).

Modern Editions: *Retrato de la Loçana andaluza: En lengua española, muy clarissíma*, facsimile edition, edited by Antonio Pérez Gómez (Valencia: Tipografía Moderna, 1950);

La Lozana andaluza, edited by Bruno M. Damiani (Madrid: Castalia, 1969);

"*El modo di adoperare il legno di India:* A Critical Transcription," edited by Damiani, *Revista Hispánica Moderna*, 36 (1970–1971): 251–271;

Spechio vulgare per li sacerdoti che administraranno li sacramenti in ciascheduna parrochia, in "Nuovi dati intorno alla biografia de Francisco Delicado desunti da una sua sconosciuta operetta (con cinque apendici)," edited by Francisco A. Ugolini, *Annali della Facoltà di Lettere e Filosofia della Università degli Studi de Perugia*, 12 (1974–1975): 443–616;

Retrato de la Loçana andaluza, edited by Damiani and Giovanni Allegra (Madrid: José Porrúa Turanzas, 1975);

Retrato de la Lozana andaluza, edited by Claude Allaigre (Madrid: Cátedra, 1985).

Edition in English: *Portrait of Lozana: The Lusty Andalusian Woman*, translated by Bruno M. Damiani (Potomac, Md.: Scripta Humanistica, 1987).

OTHER: Diego de San Pedro, *Cárcel de amor*, edited by Delicado (Venice: Printed for Juan Batista Pedrezano, 1531);

Fernando de Rojas, *Tragicomedia de Calisto y Melibea*, edited by Delicado (Venice, 1531);

Anonymous, *Amadís de Gaula, Los quatro libros de Amadís de Gaula nuevamente impressos et hystoriados*, edited by Delicado (Venice: Printed for Juan Batista Pedrezano, 1533);

Anonymous, *Primaleón: Los tres libros del muy esforçado cavallero Primaleón et Polendos, su hermano, hijos del Emperador Palmerin de Oliua*, edited by Delicado (Venice: Printed by Juan Antonio de Nicolini de Sabio Alas for Juan Batista Pedrezano, 1534).

Francisco Delicado, or Delgado, was not known as an author, in Spain or elsewhere, until the mid nineteenth century. In 1845, what is now by far his best-known work, the anonymously published *Retrato de la Loçana andaluza en lengua española muy clarissima* (1528, translated as *Portrait of Lozana: The Lusty Andalusian Woman*, 1987) was discovered in Vienna in what is now the Austrian National Library by the Austrian Hispanist Ferdinand Wolf. Wolf immediately published the news, and, in 1857, the Spanish bibliophile and critic Pascual de Gayangos referred to Delicado's 1534 Venice edition of *Primaleón: Los tres libros del muy esforçado cavallero Primaleón et Polendos, su hermano, hijos del Emperador Palmerin de Oliua* (Primaleón: The Three Books of the Very Courageous Knight Primaleón and Polendos, His Brother, Sons of the Emperor Palmerin of Oliua), in which Delicado explicitly claims authorship of *Retrato de la Loçana andaluza*. Since then, this work has been edited on many occasions, and critical studies have partially reconstructed a biography of Delicado as well as an account of his literary output. *Retrato de la Loçana andaluza* continues to be his main claim to fame, however, and is attracting increasing attention as a work of transition from medieval to Golden Age literature, as well as a valuable source for the life of Renaissance Rome and the Spanish role within it, up to the sack of the city in 1527.

Delicado seems to have been born in or near Córdoba, probably at some time between 1475 and the late 1480s. There is no external biographical source for his life, and all that is known about him has to be deduced from texts that he himself wrote or edited. As a child Delicado seems to have lived in Martos, near Jaén. He

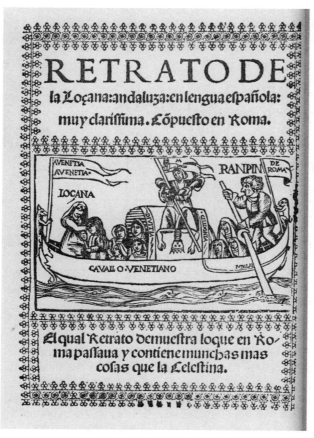

Title page for the first edition of Francisco Delicado's best-known work (1528, Portrait of the Andalusian Lozana in Very Clear Spanish), an account, told mostly in dialogue, of the adventures of Lozana, who becomes a courtesan and procurer in 1510s Rome (from Retrato de la Loçana andaluza, *1975; Thomas Cooper Library, University of South Carolina)*

appears to have been a man of some education and claims, in his introduction to *Primaleón,* to have been a disciple of the distinguished Spanish humanist Antonio de Nebrija. Delicado may have studied at Salamanca University but claims not to have obtained a bachelor's degree. He was probably a *converso,* that is, a Christian of at least partly Jewish origins, and he may have fled from the Inquisition. It is less likely that he departed as a result of Ferdinand and Isabella's edict, dated 31 March 1492, that ordered the Jews in their kingdoms either to convert to Christianity or to leave. In any case, after spending his early years in Spain, he moved to Rome, probably during the reign of Pope Alexander VI (1492–1503). In Rome, apparently, Delicado studied for the priesthood, was ordained priest, and became vicar of Martos, the hometown of his youth. He seems never to have resided in that benefice, though, but to have remained in Rome until 1528, when he departed to Venice. During his Venetian

years he appears to have also been the absentee vicar of Valle de Cabezuela, a village in the Spanish province of Cáceres.

Rome, in the early sixteenth century, was the scene of a rich cosmopolitan life, both within and outside the Papal Court (Curia). The Spanish political and cultural presence in Rome was strong, and Delicado seems to have participated in the educated literary circles there, which included major Spanish writers, such as Juan del Encina and Bartolomé de Torres Naharro. He also frequented, however, the less savory world of pimps and prostitutes, which surrounded, and sometimes appeared to engulf, the Roman Curia, and which had unfortunate personal consequences for him. Delicado's first known work, the *Spechio vulgare per li sacerdoti che administraranno li sacramenti in ciascheduna parrochia* (Vernacular Manual for Priests Who Administer the Sacraments in Any Parish), was thought to be lost before it was edited and published by Francesco A. Ugolini in 1974–1975. This short treatise, which was first published in 1525, was dedicated to Pietro Paolo de Crescentiis, and was intended to provide pastoral advice for parish clergy. It also includes important biographical information about its author, indicating that Delicado was a priest at the parish church of Santa María in Posteruola, in the Urso quarter of Rome. The text states that he wrote this *spechio,* or manual (literally "mirror"), for various priests in the "Sacrosanta Società, o Compagnia dei sacerdoti in Santa Maria in Aquiro" (Most Holy Society or Company of Priests in St. Mary's in Aquiro), including the then-elderly parish priest of Santa María della Pace. Probably in the same year Delicado seems to have published a second short work, *De consolatione infirmorum* (On the Consolation of the Infirm). All that is known of this tract, and its authorship, is to be found in an allusion in the anonymously published *Retrato de la Loçana andaluza.* This allusion indicates both that the work was devoted to describing remedies for syphilis and that its author himself suffered from that disease.

Much more information on this subject is to be found in Delicado's third known work, *El modo de adoperare il legno d'India occidentale: Salutifero remedio a ogni plaga & mal incurabile* (The Method of Applying the West Indian Wood: A Saving Remedy for Every Plague and Incurable Illness). This tract, consisting of fifteen pages in Gothic type, was also published in Rome in 1525 but is now known from a second edition, which appeared in Venice four years later. The work is dedicated to three Italian professors of medicine, Gian Battista Papiense, Domenico Senno, and Giuliano Marciano Rota, for whom Delicado expresses his admiration, thanking them for their support in his battle with syphilis, which had been going on since 1503. He has written in Italian, he says, so that his work will be available beyond the restricted circle of those who understand Latin, and he claims that he is writing, not for his own glorification, but in order to bring the best available medical knowledge to his fellow sufferers. He gives a quite detailed account of the discovery, and the curative powers, of the *leño de guayaco* (guayacum wood). Originally, both native Americans and Spanish colonizers had used the yellowish fruit of this tree, the former to cure elephantiasis and the latter to treat *bubas* (pustules, in this case apparently caused by venereal disease), but attention had soon moved to the wood of the tree itself. Delicado gives a detailed description of the use in treatment of this "wonder drug," which had reached Spain in 1508 and Italy nine years later.

The third part of this short treatise—which Bruno M. Damiani, in his translation of the treatise for the journal *Revista Hispánica Moderna* (1970–1971), describes as "an extremely interesting Renaissance document on medicine, history, and language"—consists of a letter from Delicado's contemporary, the natural historian Gonzalo Fernández de Oviedo, which was brought to Italy by the then Venetian ambassador to Spain, Andrea Navagero, and which corresponds closely to material included in Fernández de Oviedo's major academic work, the *Historia general y natural de las Indias* (1526, General and Natural History of the Indies). The fourth part of Delicado's tract is written in Spanish, in order, he says, to increase the prestige of his native language by using it to discuss this vital cure. In this section he anticipates *Retrato de la Loçana andaluza* by bemoaning, with biblical references to the Psalms and the Book of Revelation, the double plague of warfare and disease in Europe and particularly in contemporary Italy. In the surviving edition of 1529, which appears to have been extended since its first publication, reference is made not only to the French capture of Rapallo in 1488, which was held by many, including Delicado, to have brought syphilis to Italy, but also to the sack of Rome in 1527.

The work concludes with a proclamation by Pope Clement VII, issued on 4 December 1526, granting Delicado a ten-year copyright for his tract and praising his humanitarian zeal in making this efficacious cure for syphilis known to sufferers. The booklet, which continued to be referred to in medical literature until the nineteenth century, has as its frontispiece a woodcut that shows the West Indian guayacum tree, represented as holy wood, that is, as an analogy to the cross of Jesus Christ. The tree is crowned by the Virgin Mary, who holds a pilgrim's staff, and is flanked on the left by the Spanish patron saint, St. James the Greater, and on the right by St. Martha, who holds the palm of honor of a Christian martyr. Martha was the sister of Mary who had entertained Jesus in the Gospel account (Luke 10:38–42) and who, according to medieval tradition, was believed to have had a subsequent life and martyrdom in France. At the foot of the picture, in the posture of a donor in a medi-

eval painting or window, is a cleric, kneeling at the foot of the image of St. James, with the inscription "Francisco Delicado composuit in alma urbe, anno 1525" (Francisco Delicado composed [this] in the Soul City [Rome], in the year 1525). This work seems to be a portrait of Delicado and reveals a fairly short man with a well-trimmed beard, a receding hairline, and an agonized facial expression, whose hands are joined together in an attitude of prayer while also holding a dagger to his chest, as a symbol of his suffering. The presence of St. James is evidently an allusion not only to Delicado's Spanish origins, but also to the Roman Hospital of St. James "of the Spaniards," or "for Incurables," where he seems to have received treatment for his malady.

With or without the help of guayacum wood, Delicado survived the sack of Rome by Spanish, German, and Italian troops, supposedly under the authority of the Holy Roman Emperor Charles V, in May 1527. On 10 February of the following year, he left Rome with many of his Spanish compatriots and headed for the safety of the Republic of Venice, where, soon afterward, he published anonymously the work for which he is mainly known to literature, *Retrato de la Loçana andaluza*. The surviving copy of the work lacks not only its author's name but also any indication of the place and date of its publication or of the name of its printer. It is printed in a mixture of Gothic and humanist type and has a frontispiece that has greatly interested editors and critics. It gives the title of the book and claims that it "contiene munchas más cosas que la *Celestina*" (contains many more things than the *Celestina*). It also includes a complex woodcut, which shows a Venetian gondola, supposedly traveling from Rome to Venice, with Lozana and other ladies on board and her Neapolitan lover, Rampín, acting as gondolier. The core of the book consists of sixty-six *mamotretos* (sketchbooks, notebooks, or tomes), which are enclosed by a dedicatory prologue to an unknown patron, a summary of the argument of the book at the beginning, and a collection of appendices at the end. The appendices consist largely of commentary on what has gone before in the narrative and purport to have been written after Delicado's arrival in Venice. The book is illustrated with woodcuts, most of which appear to have been reused from other works and some of which are used more than once in this text.

Retrato de la Loçana andaluza is a novelistic account of the life of the heroine, Lozana, from her birth in Córdoba, possibly in about 1490; to her retreat from Rome after the 1527 sack; to Venice, according to the frontispiece illustration; and to the Aeolian island of Lipari, according to the text. The book is largely written in dialogue form and includes 125 characters, most of whom make only fleeting appearances and are scarcely identified as individuals. Lozana is named Aldonza at birth; loses

FRANCISCO DELICADO

LA LOZANA ANDALUZA

*Edición,
introducción y notas
de*
BRUNO M. DAMIANI

clásicos *castalia*

Madrid

*Title page for a 1969 edition of Delicado's best-known work,
translated in 1987 as* Portrait of Lozana: The Lusty
Andalusian Woman *(Thomas Cooper Library,
University of South Carolina)*

Inquisition. After a rapid account of her life at this point, there follows a more static description of Lozana's life in Rome, in which she obtains accommodation from a Jewish landlord called Trigo, who swindles her, and soon acquires a new lover, the much younger Rampín, who stays with her for most of her time in the city. Lozana makes her living as a middle-ranking courtesan, as a procurer of younger women for prostitution, and as a supplier of various other services, some of them either dubious or plainly illegal, to women. These services include the sale and application of cosmetics, the sewing up of women who had had sexual intercourse to make them appear to be virgins and hence more marriageable, and the disposal of unwanted babies from bridges over the Tiber River. She also entertains clients of her own, some of whom appear to be minor ecclesiastical and secular officials of the Papal Curia. As in some other Spanish works of the period, Delicado himself, as "Auctor," becomes a character in the book, not only observing the action but also sometimes addressing the characters. In this context, through the mediation of two acquaintances, Silvio and Silvano, he intervenes drastically in Lozana's life toward the end of her time in Rome.

An underlying theme of the book, as María Luisa García-Verdugo observes, is the disastrous physical and moral effect of syphilis, and on these grounds Auctor's friends intervene. Lozana does not immediately heed their warnings of physical and spiritual perdition, but general disillusionment, partly caused by her loss of attractiveness when compared with younger courtesans, eventually brings about a change, and she decides to withdraw from her previous lifestyle. The author states that he finished his text in 1524, but he evidently added further passages, which, as appendices, allude to the sack of 1527. Lozana's ultimate destination is left obscure, though she certainly abandons Rome. Rampín offers her sanctuary in his native Naples, and the text states that she refuses this option, going instead to the volcanic island of Lipari, known in medieval legend as the mouth of hell. In any case, dreams and premonitions, as well as a sense of moral guilt, dominate the latter pages of *Retrato de la Loçana andaluza,* and both Auctor and Lozana appear to be glad to have escaped from the corrupt Rome of Clement VII.

Aside from *Retrato de la Loçana andaluza,* Delicado's publishing seems to have been confined to editions of important literary works by other authors. At that time, Venetian printers and booksellers, some of whom were themselves Spanish, habitually engaged Spaniards to edit, revise, and translate books written in the Castilian language, and Delicado is known to have undertaken such work on at least four occasions. In 1531 he edited two late-fifteenth-century works, Diego de San Pedro's sentimental novel *Cárcel de amor* (1492, Prison of Love) and the text to which he explicitly compared his *Retrato de la Loçana*

her father, as well as her virginity, while still a teenager; and is exiled from Córdoba when her mother loses the legal title to their house there. In Seville she is introduced by an aunt to a merchant from Ravenna called Diomedes. They become lovers and travel the Mediterranean together. At this time Aldonza acquires the name "Lozana" because of her brilliance as a hostess, but things go wrong when Diomedes' father not only forbids them to marry but also lures them to Marseilles and tries to have Lozana killed by drowning at sea. She is spared, though, by the sea captain contracted to do the job and eventually arrives in Rome in March 1513, with no assets but her own body and talents and a smuggled gold ring. She enters the Spanish expatriate community in Rome, consorting with exiled Jews and *converso* refugees from the *andaluza,* Fernando de Rojas's *Tragicomedia de Calisto y Meli-bea* (1502, Tragicomedy of Calisto and Melibea), commonly known as *La Celestina,* which survives in an edition from 1534. After that, he turned his attention to chivalric novels. In 1533 he edited the anonymous *Los quatro libros de Amadís de Gaula nuevamente impressos et hystoriados* (1533; Amadis of Gaul: The Four Books of Amadis of Gaul Newly Printed and Told) and, in the following year, the three books of *Primaleón,* both done for Juan Bautista Pedrezano, a Spanish bookseller in Venice, although printed by Giovanni Antonio de Nicolini. Delicado also included an interesting brief piece, "Introducción que muestra el Delicado a pronunciar la lengua española" (An Introduction by Delicado to the Pronunciation of the Spanish Language) in his editions of *Celestina* and *Primaleón.*

Until the 1950s, *Retrato de la Loçana andaluza* was generally condemned as a salacious work of little or no literary value. The historical content of the work, however, has been traditionally recognized by scholars, and even the most hostile critic, Marcelino Menéndez y Pelayo, writing in his essay "Francisco Delicado y su *Retrato de la Lozana andaluza*" (1961, Francisco Delicado and His *Portrait of the Lusty Andalusian Woman*), considers *Retrato de la Loçana andaluza* to be a valuable source for the social history of Rome in the period between 1523 and 1527. More-recent scholarship has identified the literary dimensions of *Retrato de la Loçana andaluza* and has revealed that the work is informed by Delicado's acute ear for languages—including Catalan, Portuguese, and Italian, as well as Castilian Spanish—and an almost cinematographic sense of realism.

After 1534, nothing more was heard of Francisco Delicado in terms of literary activity, and the circumstances of his death are as obscure as those of his birth. In the study that accompanies his edition of *Spechio vulgare per li sacerdoti che administraranno li sacramenti in ciascheduna parrochia,* Ugolini suggests that Delicado may have returned to Spain in the later 1530s, whereupon he made a pilgrimage to Santiago de Compostela, the shrine of the saint whom, along with guayacum wood, he believed had seen him through his medical problems. The same critic also suggests that he may subsequently have become bishop of the Galician diocese of Lugo, before returning to his childhood home in the modern province of Jaén, where he may have died in 1576. All these suppositions seem improbable, though, given the likely date of Delicado's birth, and do not, in any case, affect the assessment of his literary achievement. Although it may be argued that much of his known output is devoted to "non-literary" purposes, concerned mainly with Christian pastoral work and medicine, Delicado's *Retrato de la Loçana andaluza,* a work that is being increasingly recognized and studied by scholars, establishes him as a sixteenth-century writer of some distinction.

Biography:

Bruno M. Damiani, *Francisco Delicado* (New York: Twayne, 1974).

References:

Tatiana Bubnova, *Francisco Delicado puesto en diálogo: Las claves bajtinianas de* La Lozana andaluza (Mexico City: Universidad Nacional Autónoma de México, 1987);

John Edwards, "Conversion in Córdoba and Rome: Francisco Delicado's *La Lozana andaluza,*" in *Medieval Spain: Culture, Conflict and Coexistence. Studies in Honour of Angus MacKay,* edited by Roger Collins and Anthony Goodman (Basingstoke, U.K.: Palgrave / New York: Macmillan, 2002), pp. 202–224;

Augusta Espantoso de Foley, *Delicado:* La Lozana andaluza (London: Grant & Cutler/Tamesis, 1977);

María Luisa García-Verdugo, La Lozana andaluza *y la literatura del siglo XVI: La sífilis como enfermedad y metáfora* (Madrid: Pliegos, 1994);

Pascual de Gayangos, "Discurso preliminar," in *Libros de caballerías,* edited by Gayangos, Biblioteca de Autores Españoles, no. 40 (Madrid: Hernando, 1925), pp. 3–87;

Angus MacKay, "The Whores of Babylon," in *Prophetic Rome in the High Renaissance Period,* edited by Marjorie Reeves (Oxford: Clarendon Press / New York: Oxford University Press, 1992), pp. 223–232;

Francisco Márquez Villanueva, "El mundo converso de *La Lozana andaluza,*" *Archivo Hispalense,* no. 171 (1973): 87–99;

Marcelino Menéndez y Pelayo, "Francisco Delicado y su *Retrato de la Lozana andaluza,*" in *Orígenes de la novela,* volume 1 of *Obras completas,* edited by Enrique Sánchez Reyes (Madrid: Consejo Superior de Investigaciones Científicas, 1961), pp. 45–65;

Carla Perugini, *I sensi della* Lozana andaluza (Salerno, Italy: Ripostes, 2002);

Ronald E. Surtz, "'Sancta Lozana, ora pro nobis': Hagiography and Parody in Delicado's *Lozana andaluza,*" *Romanisches Jahrbuch,* 33 (1982): 286–292;

Surtz, "Texto e imagen en el *Retrato de la Lozana andaluza,*" *Nueva Revista de Filología Hispánica,* 40, no. 1 (1992): 169–185;

Bruce W. Wardropper, "La novela como retrato: El arte de Francisco Delicado," *Nueva Revista de Filología Española,* 7 (1953): 475–488.

Bernal Díaz del Castillo

(circa 1496 – 3 February 1584)

Claudia Montoya
Midwestern State University

BOOK: *Historia verdadera de la conquista de la Nueva España,* edited by Alonso Remón (Madrid: Imprenta del reyno, 1632); translated by Maurice Keatinge as *The True History of the Conquest of Mexico* (London: Printed for J. Wright by J. Dean, 1800).

Modern Editions: *Historia verdadera de la conquista de la Nueva España,* 2 volumes, edited by Genaro García (Mexico City: Oficina tipográfica de la Secretaría de Fomento, 1904, 1905);

Historia verdadera de la conquista de la Nueva España, edited by Ramón Iglesia (Mexico City: Ediciones Mexicanas, 1950).

Editions in English: *The True History of the Conquest of New Spain,* 5 volumes, translated by A. P. Maudslay (London: Hakluyt Society, 1908–1916);

The Bernal Díaz Chronicles: The True Story of the Conquest of Mexico, translated and edited by Albert Idell (Garden City, N.Y.: Doubleday, 1956);

The Conquest of New Spain, translated and edited by John Michael Cohen (Harmondsworth, U.K. & New York: Penguin, 1963).

Bernal Díaz del Castillo was a soldier, chronicler, and conquistador who wrote only one book for which he is known, *Historia verdadera de la conquista de la Nueva España* (1632; translated as *The True History of the Conquest of Mexico,* 1800). In this work Díaz writes accounts of some of the first Spanish expeditions to the land that became New Spain after the conquest. He also gives a firsthand account of the Spanish attack and defeat of the Aztec Empire. His book belongs under the category of works called literature of the Indies, which includes letters, records, and chronicles. These works embody a wide variety of themes related to the New World, including its discovery and conquest, its geography, and its inhabitants, as well as the customs of these native peoples.

The details of Díaz's life are known through two different sources of information. The first is the author's own *Historia verdadera de la conquista de la Nueva*

Conquistador Hernándo Cortés, who led the conquest of the Aztec Empire in the early 1500s. Bernal Díaz del Castillo accompanied Cortés until 1524 and recounted his experiences in Historia verdadera de la conquista de la Nueva España *(Hospital de Jesus Nazarene, Mexico City; Salvador de Mariaga,* Hernán Cortés: Conqueror of Mexico, *1967; Thomas Cooper Library, University of South Carolina).*

España, in which he narrates passages about his life from the moment he departed from Spain in 1514 up until his last expedition with Hernán Cortés, the most famous captain of the Spanish Conquest of America, in 1524. The second source is a series of documents written by or for Díaz that are, in general, related to his legal disputes with the Spanish monarchy. This second source of information comprises letters written by Díaz, his testimonies in defense of other conquistadors, *probanzas* (proofs) in his favor, *cédulas reales* (royal decrees) he received, and minor documents that mention his name.

There is no record of Díaz's birth since during his time only the birth of noble descendants was registered. It is known, nevertheless, that he was born in Medina del Campo, a prosperous commercial center in the wool trade in the fifteenth century, right in the heart of Castile. His father was Francisco Díaz del Castillo and his mother María Díez Rejón. In his *Historia verdadera de la conquista de la Nueva España,* Díaz claims that he was born in 1492, the year of the discovery of the Americas. As he continues with his narration, however, he gives different dates that contradict the original one. By comparing all the dates he gives with historical events of his time, his biographers have concluded that his birth took place between the years 1495 and 1497. His father was the *regidor* (town councilor) of Medina del Campo, and his family, though poor, had certain prestige in the city because of his father's public duties. Díaz is believed to have taken his father's last name since the tradition during his time allowed for an individual to adopt his father's or mother's last names according to prestige or nobility.

Díaz was around eighteen years old when he left his home in Medina del Campo to join as a volunteer in Pedro Arias de Avila's expedition that departed from Seville for the New World in 1514. During the first three years that he spent in Cuba, Díaz did not do anything of real interest. On 8 February 1517, however, he enlisted in Francisco Hernández de Córdova's expedition, which set sail for the mainland in search of gold. On this trip Díaz visited the territories of Yucatán and Florida. The expedition failed when the Indians refused to be colonized and Hernández de Córdova was mortally wounded and died later in Cuba.

In 1518 Díaz participated in an exploratory voyage, led by Juan de Grijalva, which departed from Cuba. Grijalva and his men reached Yucatán and later sailed along the coast up to what later became Veracruz, whereupon they returned to Cuba. This voyage was a success in spite of the fact that the explorers found themselves in dangerous battles with the natives. Grijalva returned with a modest amount of gold as well as news about the Aztec Empire. Diego de Velázquez, the governor of Cuba, was fascinated by Grijalva's dis-

coveries and sent a new group of explorers to the mainland. In 1519 approximately six hundred soldiers, including Díaz, departed from Cuba on this expedition. Their captain was Cortés, who, by disobeying Velázquez's orders and launching the conquest of Tenochtitlán, became the most famous soldier in Spanish history.

Once in the territory that soon became New Spain, Díaz was both a participant in and a witness to the Spanish Conquest. The soldiers went to Tabasco, where they rescued Jerónimo de Aguilar, a Spaniard who had been caught and imprisoned during a previous expedition. In Tabasco they were also given Malintzi, an indigenous woman who, along with Aguilar, became the translator for the Spaniards. Díaz was a witness to the founding of Veracruz, the most important port in New Spain. He participated in the war against the Tlaxcalans, who became the most powerful indigenous allies of the Spaniards. Díaz gives an account of the Cholula massacre, brought about by Pedro de Alvarado, and also describes the majesty of Tenochtitlán before it was destroyed. In 1521, at the age of twenty-four, Díaz fought against the Aztec army and witnessed their brave resistance and their fall. Although Díaz himself did not stand out in these events, there are nevertheless moments in his life that deserve to be noted, such as when he was assigned as one of the jail keepers of the Aztec emperor Montezuma II.

After the Aztec Empire had been conquered, Díaz asked Cortés for permission to accompany Gonzalo de Sandoval in 1523 on an expedition to the interior of New Spain in search of gold. The expedition reached Coatzacoalcos, where Díaz was given some *encomiendas* (estates granted to Spanish settlers during the colonial era) at the Espíritu Santo province. The indigenous people who had been living on the land were put into the service of their Spanish lords, and in return the lord was supposed to look after the natives' interests and convert them to Christianity. Díaz, however, lost part of this property when he was absent for a while and some other Spanish lords, thinking he was dead, took over the property. Afterward, Díaz accompanied Captain Luis Marín on an expedition to Chiapas with the objective of pacifying the Indians and colonizing the area. In return, he received the village of Chamula as his *encomienda.* Although Díaz now had territory secured in Chiapas, he still tried to find a good *encomienda* where he could make a permanent home, and for this reason he returned to Coatzacoalcos, where he settled in 1524. Díaz, however, had little time to get used to his new life before Cortés arrived to recruit soldiers for a mission to Honduras.

The objective of this expedition was to punish Cristóbal de Olid, an army captain who had rebelled against Cortés's authority in Honduras. For this expedi-

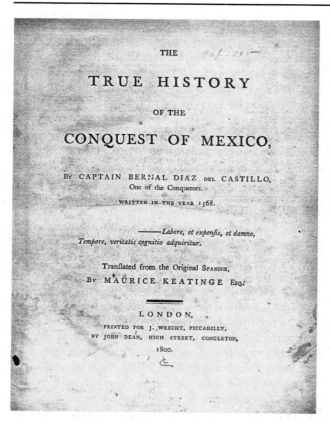

THE

TRUE HISTORY

OF THE

CONQUEST OF MEXICO,

By CAPTAIN BERNAL DIAZ DEL CASTILLO,
One of the Conquerors.

WRITTEN IN THE YEAR 1568.

————Labore, et expensis, et damno,
Tempore, veritatis cognitio adquiritur.

Translated from the Original SPANISH,
By MAURICE KEATINGE ESQ:

LONDON,
PRINTED FOR J. WRIGHT, PICCADILLY,
BY JOHN DEAN, HIGH STREET, CONGLETON,
1800.

Title page for the first English-language edition of Díaz's 1632
Historia verdadera de la conquista de la Nueva España
(Thomas Cooper Library, University of South Carolina)

tion, like the one for the Spanish Conquest, Díaz invested his own fortune, which he put at the service of Cortés. The long and tiring voyage was a failure, even though it was well planned by Cortés. The enemy that defeated them was the vast tropical jungle rather than enemy soldiers. Nevertheless, the expedition left Díaz with a memory that illuminated the rest of his life. Up until that moment he had simply been one of many Spanish soldiers who had arrived in America. For a brief moment, however, Cortés put him in charge of a group, comprised of indigenous people and Spaniards, with a mission to pacify a native revolt. Although this adventure may seem minor, Díaz treasured it as a great event in his life.

When he returned to New Spain, Díaz found out that he had lost his property in Chiapas and that he was about to also lose his property in Coatzacoacos. This situation was reason enough for him to gather documentation that he took to Spain in search of new benefits and *encomiendas*. Like many other conquistadores, Díaz felt he deserved the favors of the Spanish monarchy, not only for having risked his life to defend their interests but also because in many instances he had

risked his own fortune in search of new land for the empire.

What is known about Díaz after the expedition to Honduras is dispersed among different documents. One of these documents serves as proof of his services as a conquistador. It was composed in order to show that the petitioner had served the monarchy in the Spanish conquest and pacification of indigenous territories. Díaz needed to document his participation in order to receive *encomiendas* and public duties. Another document that certified Díaz's participation in the first expeditions to the mainland as well as the conquest and the expedition to Honduras was a letter written by Cortés himself. In this letter Cortés, as the recently named marquis of the Valley of Oaxaca, interceded on behalf of Díaz before the Spanish monarchy. With these documents and others, along with three witnesses who testified that he had indeed taken part in the first expeditions on the mainland as well as in the conquest of the Aztec Empire and the punitive expedition to Honduras, Díaz tried to secure economic prosperity for both himself and his children, both legitimate and illegitimate.

Díaz made his first voyage to Spain in 1538, confident that he would obtain not only recognition for his feats but also material benefits in compensation for so many sacrifices. Nevertheless, the conquistador's wishes did not come true, and the benefits that he did obtain seemed minimal to him. He was named, for example, the general governor of New Spain, but the title only had honorary significance and lacked any real power or benefits. He was also given a royal seal by the Council of the Indies, according to which Pedro de Alvarado–Díaz's old companion in arms and governor of the province of Guatemala–was ordered to give Díaz territory in the form of *encomiendas* in Guatemala. After several setbacks and the death of Alvarado, Díaz finally received three valuable *encomiendas* from the new governor of Guatemala.

In 1541 Díaz moved to Guatemala, where he had a common-law wife, a Guatemalan woman named Angelina. They had a son, whom they named Diego. As an adult Diego also became the lord of *encomiendas*, like his father, and through the Spanish monarchy managed to obtain a coat of arms for the family name Díaz del Castillo. Díaz is known to have had several illegitimate children, but history has lost account of them all except for Diego. In 1544 he married a young Spanish widow, Teresa Becerra, with whom he had nine children. Teresa was the daughter of the conquistador Bartolomé Becerra, who had founded Guatemala.

Díaz made his second voyage to Spain in 1550 with the intention of demanding that the Council of the Indies not comply with a law intended to liberate the indigenous people from the *encomiendas*. Díaz's main interest was to defend the institution of the *encomienda* as a perpetual right of the conquistadores, so that they could pass their lands to their eldest sons. In 1550, before the Council of the Indies in Valladolid, Díaz discussed the issue with, among others, Fray Bartolomé de Las Casas, the most famous contemporary defender of the rights of the indigenous people, and Vasco de Quiroga, an important bishop in Michoacán who was dedicated to the same cause.

On this second trip to Spain, Díaz also presented new demands in the court in exchange for additional privileges, and henceforth he lived without economic worries. Under the *encomienda* system he owned three villages, which provided him with grains, poultry, meat, and dairy products. He had servants for his personal service. He even had special permission to bear arms, a privilege granted by the Spanish monarchy to only highly trusted individuals owing to the rigidity with which the Spanish Empire controlled its colonies. In addition to all these privileges, in 1551 Díaz was named the perpetual *regidor* of the city council of Guatemala, which provided him with a modest pension. By this time he was one of the few remaining Spanish soldiers who had fought in the Conquest. Díaz died on 3 February 1584, at the age of eighty-eight. He was laid to rest in the Cathedral of Antigua Guatemala, where his companion in arms Alvarado was also buried. When he died he was still the *regidor* of the city council, a charge taken over by his son Francisco Díaz del Castillo.

It is believed that Díaz was compelled to begin writing *Historia verdadera de la conquista de la Nueva España* between 1552 and 1557 because of his aspiration to become richer by receiving a larger compensation, which is clearly demonstrated in his constant letters and demands before the Council of the Indies. For Díaz, however, to be compensated and recognized as one of the participants in the Spanish Conquest and pacification of America was no more than a simple act of justice. His true interest lay in giving a more inclusive account of the events. When talking about the conquest, some historians, such as the erudite and aristocratic Francisco López de Gómara, had failed to mention the sacrifices made by hundreds of Spanish soldiers. In his book, after apologizing for not having López de Gómara's rhetorical talent, Díaz comments that he wants to correct the errors and excesses of the other chronicler, since López de Gómara was never in New Spain at the time of the Conquest. Díaz argues that López de Gómara, in his *Conquista de México* (1522, Conquest of Mexico), exaggerates the number of Aztec fighters and, subsequently, the number of Aztec casualties that the Spaniards claimed. As opposed to López de Gómara, Díaz emphasizes that as an eyewitness he can only tell the truth. He is conscious of the fact that the enterprise that he and his companions had undertaken more than thirty years earlier had changed forever the course of history. Therefore, in his work he constantly refers to López de Gómara's text, often pointing out its errors.

Criticism of Díaz's book is divided into two groups. The first group considers it to be a work of pure history and therefore a reliable source of information regarding the conquest. The second group, while not denying the profound historic value of Díaz's work, prefers to classify it as a literary work because of, among other reasons, its autobiographical tone. Because of this tone and the direct and colloquial language that Díaz uses, he is able to manipulate the reader on his behalf. Like many other chroniclers of his time, he was writing his own version of events in the hope of winning recognition and favors from the Spanish Crown.

By refuting López de Gómara's book in *Historia verdadera de la conquista de la Nueva España*, Díaz changed the way in which history is written. For example, he changed the previous historiographic tradition, according to which, in general, there was only one hero of high lineage. By placing himself, a foot soldier, in the middle of the events, Díaz demonstrates that the participation of subordinates is also fundamental in forging history. Díaz thus constantly uses the first person plural, which elevates Cortés's captains and soldiers, along with Díaz himself, to the foreground of the action. This image of the collective hero as a participant in history in the making was completely novel in the sixteenth century. López de Gómara, on the contrary, had presented the completely opposite perspective, which annoyed Díaz since it gave Cortés all the credit without taking into account the contributions of the approximately six hundred soldiers who participated in the conquest.

An outstanding literary quality of *Historia verdadera de la conquista de la Nueva España* is its representation of people and events. A good example is the way Cortés is portrayed in Díaz's text in comparison to López de Gómara's. Cortés is portrayed by López de Gómara as a one-dimensional epic hero, the perfect but predictable protagonist of a classic tragedy. Díaz, on the other hand, portrays a living, dynamic Cortés, who is a more believable and more modern character than López de Gómara's. By depicting Cortés in a more realistic manner, however, he is also able to elevate himself and his fellow soldiers to the category of heroes. Díaz creates a sense of veracity throughout the text by repeating that his is an eyewitness account of the events. Also, he narrates adventures with vivid descriptions, interjects anecdotes in which he recalls the most insignificant details, and creates dialogues that make the reader feel like a true spectator. Díaz re-creates the events in such a detailed manner that the end result is one of total veracity. For example, in describing his comrades, he includes references to their they are the reason why Díaz's work is distinctive for his time. Díaz's book is more literary than historic in another important sense. According to the formula for novels in the Golden Age, these works were presented as true stories without really being so. The elusive quality of the text allows it to be categorized under different genres (historical account, biography, and novel), which brings it closer to contemporary works of fiction.

Another element that creates the effect of authenticity in this work in comparison to other similar works is the manner in which Díaz broaches the theme of religion. If, on the one hand, he admits that his military campaign is successful only with the help of God, on the other hand he avoids falling into the exaggerations committed by writers of his age who, for example, claim to have seen the apostle James the Greater flying above during battles, directing the Spaniards to their triumph. In fact, Díaz shows an ideological openness that was rare among the other chroniclers of the Indies; for him not everything indigenous is satanic, nor everything Spanish divine.

Through *Historia verdadera de la conquista de la Nueva España* it has been possible to ascertain some of Díaz's personality traits. Critics agree that his sensitivity and sense of morality stand out. These two traits are observed when the writer remembers the young emperor Cuauhtémoc, who was hanged by Cortés for treason. In his book Díaz firmly condemns this act, stating that the brave warrior deserved a more dignified death. Moreover, Díaz recognizes the bravery of the Aztec warriors in defending their city, Montezuma's generosity in spite of being a prisoner in his own house, and Malintzi's intelligence, which solved many problems for the Spaniards. *Historia verdadera de la conquista de la Nueva España* has attained acclaim because of its sustained idealism, in that noble acts are praised and cowardly acts criticized, regardless of who committed them. For the manner in which it captures the human facet of the Spanish Conquest, Díaz's book stands out among the works of the Spanish Golden Age.

Díaz finished the first rough draft of *Historia verdadera de la conquista de la Nueva España* in 1568. In 1575, after making many corrections, he sent a clean copy of his manuscript to the king of Spain. This copy, which has since been lost, was the basis for the first edition of the book, which was edited by Friar Alonso Remón of the Order of Mercy and published in 1632. Scholars have determined that the text was altered in this first edition since it is different from other manuscripts that were later found. Nevertheless, the Remón manuscript was accepted as the original version of *Historia verdadera de la conquista de la Nueva España* for many years, and the first translations were based on this version, including the first translation into English, by Maurice Keatinge in 1800. Subsequent editions in German and French were published in 1838 and 1876, respectively.

THE DISCOVERY AND CONQUEST OF MEXICO 1517–1521

by Bernal Díaz del Castillo

Edited from the only exact copy of the original MS (and published in Mexico) by Genaro García. Translated with an Introduction and Notes by A. P. Maudslay. Introduction to the American edition by IRVING A. LEONARD *Published by Farrar, Straus and Cudahy*

F 1230 .D5442 1956 c.2

Title page for a 1956 translation of Díaz's account of the Spanish Conquest, one of several English-language editions of Historia verdadera de la conquista de la Nueva España *published in the twentieth century (Thomas Cooper Library, University of South Carolina)*

names, their titles, their moral character, their places of origin, and even their physical defects, all with prodigious precision. Even though these descriptions may not be true, their presence helps create a sympathetic link between the reader and the characters in the story. With such a detailed narration it is almost impossible for the reader to distrust the narrator. Nevertheless, the text is full of inconsistencies, a clear example being Díaz giving himself titles he never had, such as "captain" and "alférez". Also, he claims to have taken part in the decision-making of the Conquest. The sole purpose of these embellishments is to adjudicate himself some merits that he really never had.

All the techniques used by Díaz to create a sense of authenticity belong to the domain of a literary work, and

The second manuscript of Díaz's work was found in Guatemala and is therefore known as the Guatemala manuscript. This manuscript is considered to be the original one, even though it displays three different types of handwriting. The explanation for this inconsistency is that Díaz revised his work throughout his life, and also possibly employed the assistance of scribes in his later years. Proof of this theory can be found in the prologue, presumably written after all the corrections had been finished, in which Díaz mentions that he is eighty-four years old and that he is almost blind and deaf, which implies that he needed help in finishing up the book. The first edition of the Guatemala manuscript, a textual transcription that preserves the old Spanish spelling, was published in Mexico by Génaro García in 1904–1905. Since then, editors have used García's version as the basis for the publication of Díaz's book. The text of the Guatemala manuscript was also used for the English translation by A. P. Maudslay, which was published in London in 1908–1916, as well as for translations of Díaz's book into French, German, Hungarian, and Danish. A third manuscript of *Historia verdadera de la conquista de la Nueva España* was found in Murcia, Spain in 1797 in the possession of the Alegría family, and has come to be known as the Alegría manuscript. This one is a clean copy of the Guatemala manuscript.

The existence of three manuscripts reveals the difficulty and slow pace at which Díaz's complex text was assembled. With its firsthand narrative, *Historia verdadera de la conquista de la Nueva España* provides a compelling story of the events that led to the Spanish Conquest of the New World. Above all, Bernal Díaz del Castillo introduces a new narrative mode through the use of a collective character, creates a strong effect of veracity through detailed description, and portrays his characters in a realistic and human manner. For the techniques by which he depicts the conquest, Díaz's *Historia verdadera de la conquista de la Nueva España* has become an important work of the Spanish Renaissance and is, after Miguel de Cervantes's *Don Quixote* (1605, 1615), the most translated book in the Spanish language.

References:

Manuel Alvar, *El mundo americano de Bernal Díaz del Castillo* (Santander, Spain: "Publicaciones de la Universidad Menéndez Pelayo," 1968);

Alberto María Carreño, *Bernal Díaz del Castillo: Descubridor, conquistador y cronista de la Nueva España* (Mexico City: Xóchitl, 1946);

Herbert Cerwin, *Bernal Díaz: Historian of the Conquest* (Norman: University of Oklahoma Press, 1963);

Verónica Cortínez, "'Yo Bernal Díaz del Castillo': ¿Soldado de a pie o idiota sin letras?" *Revista Chilena de Literatura,* 41 (1993): 59–69;

R. B. Cunninghame Graham, *Bernal Díaz del Castillo: Semblanza de su personalidad a travéz de su "Historia verdadera de la conquista de Nueva España"* (Buenos Aires: Editora Inter-Americana, 1943);

Manuel Durán, "Bernal Díaz del Castillo: Crónica, historia, mito," *Hispania,* 75, no. 4 (1992): 795–804;

Rolf Eberenz, "Sus ditados y blasones: Las semblanzas de los conquistadores en Bernal Díaz del Castillo," *Versants: Revue Suisse des Litteratures Romanes,* 22 (1992): 5–22;

Luis González y González, "Bernal Díaz del Castillo," in *Obras completas de Luis González y González,* volume 2 (Mexico City: Clío, 1995), pp. 19–50;

Ramón Iglesia, "Semblanza de Bernal Díaz del Castillo," in his *El Hombre Colon y otros ensayos* (Mexico City: El Colegio de México, 1944);

Alfredo León Gómez, *Huellas de España en América: El languaje literario en la "Historia de la Conquista de la Nueva España y el Viaje a las Hibueras" de Bernal Díaz del Castillo* (N.p., 1990);

Salvador de Mariaga, *Hernán Cortés: Conqueror of Mexico* (Coral Gables, Fla.: University of Miami Press, 1967);

Alfonso Mendiola Mejía, *Bernal Díaz del Castillo: Verdad romanesca y verdad historiográfica* (Mexico City: Universidad Iberoamericana, Departamento de Historia, 1991);

Yolanda F. Orquera, *Los castillos decrépitos, o la "Historia verdadera" de Bernal Díaz del Castillo: Una idagación de las relaciones entre cultura popular y cultura letrada* (Tucumán, Argentina: Facultad de Filosofía y Letras, Universidad Nacional de Tucumán, 1996);

Rosa Pellicer, "La organización narrativa de la Historia verdadera de Bernal Díaz del Castillo," *Mester,* 18, no. 2 (1989): 83–93;

Sonia Rose de Fuggle, "El narrador fidedigno: Problemas de acreditación en la obra de Bernal Díaz del Castillo," *Literatura mexicana,* 1, no. 2 (1990): 327–348;

Carmelo Sáenz de Santa María, *Historia de una historia: La crónica de Bernal Díaz del Castillo* (Madrid: Instituto Gonzalo Fernández de Oviedo, 1984);

Sáenz de Santa María, *Introducción crítica a la "Historia verdadera" de Bernal Díaz del Castillo* (Madrid: Instituto Gonzalo Fernández de Oviedo, 1967);

Jesús Támez H., *Tras la huella de Bernal Díaz del Castillo, el soldado cronista* (Mexico City, 1977);

Victor Wolfgang Von Hagen, *Recia guerra: Bernal Díaz del Castillo escribe su historia de la Conquista* (Mexico City: Mortiz, 1993).

Garcilaso de la Vega

(1499 or 1503 – 13 or 14 October 1536)

Bryant Creel

University of Tennessee, Knoxville

BOOKS: *Las obras de Boscán y algunas de Garcilasso de la Vega, repartidas en quatros libros,* by Garcilaso and Juan Boscán (Barcelona: Carlos Amorós, 1543);

Obras del excelente poeta Garcilasso de la Vega: Agores corregidas de muchos errores que en todas las impresiones passadas avia (Salamanca: Matías Gast, 1569);

Obras del excelente poeta Garci Lasso de la Vega, edited by Francisco Sánchez de las Brozas (Salamanca: Lasso, 1574);

Obras del excelente poeta Garci Lasso de la Vega, edited by Fernando de Herrera (Seville: Alonso de Barrera, 1580);

Garcilasso de la Vega, natural de Toledo: Príncipe de los poetas castellanos, edited by Tomás de Tamayo de Vargas (Madrid: Luis Sánchez, 1622);

Obras de Garcilaso de la Vega, príncipe de los poetas castellanos: Cuidadosamente revistas en esta última edición, edited by Luis Brizeño de Córdoba (Lisbon: Pedro Crasbeeck, 1626); translated by J. H. Wiffen as *The Works of Garcilasso de la Vega, surnamed the Prince of Castilian Poets* (London: Hurst, Robinson, 1823);

Obras de Garcilaso de la Vega, with notes by José Nicolás de Azara (Madrid: Imprenta Real de la Gaceta, 1765).

Modern Editions: "Poesías de Garcilaso de la Vega," in *Poetas líricos de los siglos XVI y XVII,* volume 1, edited by Adolfo de Castro, Biblioteca de autores españoles, no. 32 (Madrid: Rivadavia, 1854);

Obras, edited by Tomás Navarro Tomás, Clásicos Castellanos, no. 3 (Madrid: La Lectura, 1911);

Works: A Critical Text with a Bibliography, edited by Hayward Keniston (New York: Hispanic Society of America, 1925);

Garcilaso de la Vega y sus comentaristas: Obras completas del poeta acompañadas de los textos integros de los comentarios de El Brocense, Fernando de Herrera, Tamayo de Vargas y Azara, edited by Antonio Gallego Morell (Granada: Universidad de Granada, 1966);

Garcilaso de la Vega (from Garcilaso de la Vega y sus comentaristas, *1966; Thomas Cooper Library, University of South Carolina)*

Obras completas: Con comentario, edited by Elias L. Rivers (Madrid: Castalia / Columbus: Ohio State University Press, 1974);

Obra poética y textos en prosa, edited by Bienvenido Morros, introduction by Rafael Lapesa (Barcelona: Crítica, 1995).

Edition in English: *The Odes and Sonnets of Garcilaso de la Vega,* translated by James Cleugh (London: Aquila, 1930).

OTHER: Baldassare Castiglione, *Los quatro libros del Cortesano, agora nuevamente traduzidos en lengua castellana por Boscán,* translated by Juan Boscán, prologue by Garcilaso (Barcelona: Pedro Montpezat, 1534).

Authenticity of anguished passion and consummate rhetorical elegance unite with unusual power in the works of the most celebrated of Spanish poets, Garcilaso de la Vega. His elegiac love lyric in the Petrarchan tradition, cast in an urbane and heroic style, earned him an enduring reputation as the greatest lyrical poet of the Spanish Renaissance—"el príncipe de los poetas castellanos" (the prince of Castilian poets), as he is referred to in the title of Tomás de Tamayo de Vargas's 1622 edition of his works. His unusual name, Garcilaso, was a result of the fusion of his given name, García, with his first surname, Laso, a practice common in Spain in the Middle Ages as well as the Golden Age (the sixteenth and seventeenth centuries). A professional soldier, Garcilaso met with an early death in his mid thirties during a military campaign in southern France. Hence, his poetic works are relatively few in number: thirty-eight sonnets, five *canciónes* (songs), two elegies, three eclogues, an epistle, and eight brief compositions in the traditional Castilian style. He also wrote poems in Latin, the surviving three being odes in alcaic verse, in the Horatian tradition.

Garcilaso's artistic innovations are in both the realm of sentiment and the formal realm. On the one hand, his verse generally marks a departure from the tradition immediately preceding him of writing love poetry in a playful style that relied heavily on refined conceptual subtlety and wordplay, as opposed to deep and genuine emotion such as that used in treating the subject of death in the "Coplas por la muerte de su padre" (Stanzas for the Death of His Father), written between November 1476 and 1479 by Jorge Manrique. Garcilaso is the first and foremost Spanish author of truly elegiac—that is, tragic—love poetry. The tasteful solemnity of his treatment of love contrasts with the impression of overrefinement that results from the traditional heavy use of conceptual elements in such poetry. Garcilaso does, however, use elements of conceptual subtlety insofar as they undercut a tendency toward maudlin sentimentality or pompous grandiosity. Part of Garcilaso's genius consists in his ability to achieve sublimity of pathos yet to balance that quality with an attitude of resigned despair and ironic detachment, the modesty of which heightens the heroic pathos of his poems. Bryant Creel has noted in *The Voice of the Phoenix: Metaphors of Death and Rebirth in Classics of the Iberian Renaissance* (2004) that in Garcilaso's verse the tragedy of love is the tragedy of human life itself, which Garcilaso represents as the isolation and defeat of ardent goodwill and vital humanity at the hands of a brutal and pettily mechanical natural order. Yet, the Renaissance appreciation for the beauty of nature also first emerges in Garcilaso's poetry, and such beauty is often a source of torment for the dejected poet-lover, heightening his estrangement. The primary source of the bucolic strain in Garcilaso's verse is the secular interest of Renaissance humanistic culture in the world and in nature, an orientation that emerged with the victory of antidogmatic emphasis of nominalism on subjectivity and the displacement of medieval transcendentalism (God governs from without) by pantheistic immanentism (the universe is pervaded by a divine power working from within). The most influential bucolic poets were Horace and Virgil, who established elements of a conventionally idyllic setting in the classical tradition and, as Rafael Lapesa notes in his introduction to the 1995 collection of Garcilaso's works, *Obra poética y textos en prosa* (Poetic Works and Prose Texts), Jacopo Sannazaro's *Arcadia* (1502) provided Garcilaso with the most-valuable examples of expressing feelings for the enjoyment of natural beauty.

As a formal innovator, Garcilaso helped to introduce the eleven-syllable line used in Italy. Unlike the traditional eight-syllable line, its expansive flow lent itself to an impression of dignity and became preferred for the treatment of noble subjects. With Garcilaso a group of new stanzas became established in Spanish: the *estancia* (eleven- and seven-syllable lines, used in eclogue I), the *lira* (three seven-syllable and two eleven-syllable lines, which was later a verse form preferred by Fray Luis de León and San Juan de la Cruz), and *endecasílabos sueltos* (unrhymed eleven-syllable lines, as used in the "Epístola a Boscán" [1534, Epistle to Boscán]). With Garcilaso the *soneto,* or Petrarchan sonnet, also achieved unprecedented refinement and became the leading stanza in Spanish lyrical poetry from that time on.

Apart from Garcilaso's adaptation to Spanish of Italian verse forms, the naturalness of his language, his humanity, and what has been referred to by Tamayo de Vargas as the "virile beauty" of his verse, much of Garcilaso's fame rests on the innovative Renaissance paganism of his poetry—allusions to classical myth, an absence of religious elements, and his use of traditional Greco-Latin figures such as shepherds and nymphs, who are represented in a Spanish setting. His work marks the adaptation of Renaissance literary influences in Spain, and he is considered by many to exemplify the harmony and clarity of classicist style. The subtlety of Garcilaso's *agudeza* (wit), the manneristic tension between classicism and anticlassicism in his verse, and its elliptical yet suggestive obscurity make him one of

The Castillo de Batres, near Madrid, the ancestral home of Garcilaso's mother, Sancha de Guzmán (from María del Carmen Vaquero Serrano, Garcilaso: Poeta del amor, caballero de la guerra, 2002; Hodges Library, University of Tennessee)

the most intriguingly difficult poets in the Spanish language, even if he can seem to be understood easily. Garcilaso's poetry combines elements of the convoluted syntax and wordplay that were characteristic of lyrics in the fifteenth-century *cancionero* (songbook), or collection of verse; the metaphysical *trobar clus* (closed, enigmatic style) cultivated by the fifteenth-century Valencian poet Ausias March; and thematic motifs of Renaissance classicism. His verse harks back to his poetic predecessors as well as announcing the complex stylistic elements that later characterized great seventeenth-century Baroque poets such as Luis de Góngora y Argote and Francisco de Quevedo.

As a cultural icon, Garcilaso has also come to personify the Spanish Renaissance aristocratic ideal of male character, that of the courtier who paradoxically unites qualities of the warrior with those of the sensitive poet-lover. Attainments in both of those areas had already gained renown in Garcilaso's family line. His parents were descended from prestigious aristocratic families and had ancestors who cultivated both military

and literary pursuits. His father, Garcilaso de la Vega, a younger son of the Suarez de Figueroa and the Mendoza families and a knight of the Order of Santiago, was a soldier in the service of Ferdinand and Isabella in the campaigns against Portugal and Granada, a prominent figure in the political life of the Spanish monarchy, and a grandson of the sister of the famous fifteenth-century poet, soldier, and statesman Iñigo López de Mendoza, Marqués de Santillana. His mother, Sancha de Guzmán, was the granddaughter of the important fifteenth-century poet, author, soldier, and courtier Fernán Pérez de Guzmán. Upon the death of her brother, she became heiress of the estate of Batres, between Toledo and Madrid, and there are unconfirmed claims that she was a second cousin of the queen.

There exists no comprehensive biography of Garcilaso written close enough to the time of his life to be authoritative. The biographical information about him that has been established has been ascertained and pieced together by dint of generations of painstaking scholarly research. He was born, most likely in 1499 or

1503 and certainly before 1504, in Toledo, which at that time was seat of the Spanish throne and the center of the empire. He was the third child and second son of seven children. His father, who died in Burgos in 1512, had been Ferdinand and Isabella's ambassador in Rome from 1494 to 1499. Garcilaso was raised in Toledo by his mother, who had her own estate and, until her death, also retained control of the estate of her husband and hence of the inheritances of all her children. Although Garcilaso's older brother, Pedro, was to be the family's primary heir, Garcilaso received a sizable inheritance from his father, whose name he had been given. In any case, Garcilaso was left without a father sometime between the ages of nine and twelve, although his mother had ample means to care for her children.

Garcilaso grew up in the company of his brothers and sisters. His older sister, Leonor, married in 1511, and Pedro married in 1514. Although the circumstances under which Garcilaso received his education are not known with certainty, he likely studied in Toledo with private teachers employed by his parents. Pedro, a successful student of Latin, may have helped to tutor him as well, but Pedro was increasingly occupied at court, where he served in the retinue of King Ferdinand. Garcilaso's academic training would have been in Latin and based on the new humanistic methods established by Antonio de Nebrija. He must have studied, on the one hand, grammar, rhetoric, and logic and, on the other, classical authors such as Virgil, Ovid, and Horace, whom he was undoubtedly expected to learn by heart. In addition, he would have received the necessary courtier's training in music (he was known to be skilled on the *vihuela,* an early form of the guitar, and the lute), fencing, horsemanship, hunting, and possibly dance and the composition of songs.

The first known episode in Garcilaso's life concerns his participation in 1519 in a civil disturbance related to jurisdiction over a hospital to house mentally disturbed and foundling children. The arrangement made by the founder of the hospital, a high-ranking papal nuncio, was that upon his death (which occurred in 1508) primary control of the hospital would go to cathedral church authorities and would be shared by the town council and a relative of the founder. The exact issue that provoked the disturbance is not known, but it is thought to have been related to the political conflict that ensued in Spain after the death of Ferdinand in 1516. When the new Flemish king, Charles I, arrived in Spain in 1517, the important administrative positions in Castile were peremptorily claimed by his Flemish advisers, and the Castilians lost their traditional power, part of which was vested in local, municipal authority. The notorious royal chancellor William

of Croy was among these advisers, and he arranged for his twenty-year-old nephew, who lived abroad, to fill the lucrative position that had been left vacant when the archbishop of Toledo and former regent of Spain, Cardinal Jiménez de Cisneros, died in 1517. Hence, the church authorities in Toledo, under the influence of the new cardinal, may have been attempting to establish superiority over local civic authority, although in the political division that emerged in the ensuing years new monarchical policies faced both support and opposition from different *regidores* (aldermen) of the town council as well as from different members of the cathedral chapter. In the hospital incident, a group of three armed young nobles entered the hospital with four servants and created a disturbance. The nobles included a great-nephew of the founder of the hospital, a bailiff, and Garcilaso. Criminal charges were brought against the group by the cathedral chapter.

According to documents discovered by María del Carmen Vaquero Serrano and reported in her *Garcilaso: Poeta del amor, caballero de la guerra* (2002, Garcilaso: Poet of Love, Horseman of War), the noble members of the group were exiled from the city for six months and were required to relinquish the arms they had with them during the disturbance and pay court costs; the servants received more-serious punishments, however. The sentences of the three nobles and of the servant of the head of the town council were appealed the same day. The other servants did not appeal, but—since all but the bailiff had fled the city on the day of the disturbance and, like Garcilaso, were absent on the day of sentencing—they may have not been apprehended. Perhaps the primary significance of these events is that they convey a sense of the strained atmosphere that existed in Spain, and especially in Toledo, at a time when absolutism under a new, foreign monarch was meeting with mounting opposition. In 1520 that opposition culminated in the revolt of the Comuneros (the union of autonomous cities).

Vaquero Serrano considers the most important of her archival discoveries concerning Garcilaso's youth to be a notarial document in which a woman identifies herself as the mother of Garcilaso's natural son. The person in question is Doña Guiomar Carrillo, a young noblewoman whose family lived near Garcilaso's family in Toledo. In the document Doña Guiomar states that when she and Garcilaso were both unmarried they had a prolonged love affair that resulted in her giving birth to a baby boy, who was given the name of one of Garcilaso's illustrious ancestors, Lorenzo Suárez de Figueroa. She herself, she says, never married nor took religious vows. Her affair with Garcilaso seems to have lasted at least from 1519 until 1525, the year when he married Doña Elena de Zúñiga, a lady-in-waiting of the

Painting by Juan de la Corte depicting Charles V and Pope Clement VII in Bologna, Italy, in 1530 for Charles's coronation as Holy Roman Emperor. Garcilaso, as a noble in Charles's Spanish court, was likely in attendance (Museo de Santa Cruz, Toledo; from María del Carmen Vaquero Serrano, Garcilaso: Poeta del amor, caballero de la guerra, *2002; Hodges Library, University of Tennessee).*

king's sister. It is not known whether Lorenzo was brought up in Garcilaso's own household or even if the identity of Lorenzo's actual parents was publicly acknowledged, but he seems to have been born about 1521. Before Vaquero Serrano's findings, knowledge of Don Lorenzo's existence was based on a reference to him in an addendum to Garcilaso's will signed in 1529 (but notarized in Toledo by his widow in 1537, after Garcilaso's death), in which he also requests that a non-noble woman in Extremadura, whose virginity he fears he took some time earlier, be given monetary compensation if his suspicions are accurate. The document in which Doña Guiomar explains the parentage of Lorenzo is her testament of 1537, in which she deeds to him the amount of her property that is permitted under such circumstances.

Vaquero Serrano's interest in the new documentation concerns the possibility that there exists a relation between some of the intense love anguish for which Garcilaso's poetry is famous and the circumstance that Garcilaso did not marry Doña Guiomar. The genealo-

gies state that Doña Guiomar's older brother inherited the large family estate that was previously destined to be inherited by her uncle's son; hence, the status of Doña Guiomar's family was comparable to that of Garcilaso's family. Vaquero Serrano believes, however, on the basis of evidence that is rather convincing even if it is not completely conclusive, that Doña Guiomar's older brother, the family heir, was also a supporter of the Comuneros. If such was the case, it is possible either that the king did not approve of the match, that Garcilaso's family did not approve of it, that Doña Guiomar's family did not approve of it, or that there was some combination of those circumstances. In any case, the appeal of the premise that Garcilaso experienced a real, not merely literary, unrequited love that perhaps even lasted his entire life seems to have originated partly in its obviating the need to develop nonbiographical approaches to Garcilaso's poetry, to interpret in broad terms apparently quite personal elements such as the well-known utterance from his eclogue 1: "No me podrán quitar el dolorido / sentir . . ." (They will not be able to take from me my pained / feeling . . .). That Garcilaso's experiences in life contributed to his poetry can hardly be doubted, but that claim does not justify the assumption that the emotion he expresses in his poems was prompted by a desire to refer to any particular, or even real, woman. The anguished subjectivity that, in all its complexity, has come to be an essential feature of modern art first emerged in literature in Garcilaso's day, in the form of tragic love lyricism that drew on the conventional imagery of courtly love.

In 1519 Charles I was elected Charles V, Holy Roman Emperor, and he began to make preparations to go to Belgium, where he would be crowned the following year. The court left Toledo for Santiago de Compostela, Galicia, where the Cortes (Parliament) was to meet before the king set sail from La Coruña. Soon afterward the town council of Toledo sent Pedro Laso to plead in the name of the city to have reparations made for abuses committed by the king's advisers, to object to the special tax increase that was to be levied against municipalities, and to ask the king not to leave Spain. The king was angered by the plea, and Pedro was exiled to Gibraltar, although he instead returned to Toledo to join the Comunero uprising. Shortly afterward, Garcilaso went from Toledo to the court in Santiago in the capacity of *procurador mayor* (municipal representative). He seems to have been given the responsibility of opposing excessive taxation, but the possibility that, unlike his brother, he went to Galicia to represent those in Toledo who supported the king is suggested by the fact that in La Coruña on 16 April 1520, ten days before the revolt of the Comunidades in Toledo (from where the uprising spread), Garcilaso was named a member of the king's Royal Guard. His father had held that position as a youth, and some of his father's old friends, such as the duque de Alba, were still at court. As Vaquero Serrano points out in *Garcilaso: Poeta del amor, caballero de la guerra,* however, Garcilaso had an even more important motive for seeking royal patronage: since he was not the first-born male and heir to the family estate but was a *segundón* (second-born male), he had a need to supplement his income.

In April 1521, a year after Garcilaso had received his appointment to the court, the Comunero army was overcome by heavy rains in Villalar. With its infantry bogged down in the mud, it was defeated by the king's mounted forces, and its leaders were summarily beheaded. It has traditionally been thought that when Garcilaso was named a member of the Royal Guard, he was a firm supporter of the new monarchy and that during the Comunero revolt he and his brother Pedro fought on opposite sides. On the basis of a document that records an event in which Garcilaso was seen leaving Toledo in the company of certain fervent Comuneros, however, and because Pedro Laso was fighting the French with the royal army in May 1521, Vaquero Serrano concludes that both brothers supported the Comuneros from the early stages of the revolt until the defeat at Villalar, after which they both went over to the side of the king. Garcilaso distinguished himself in August 1521 in the Battle of Olías, where he received a wound on the face. Charles V returned to Spain in 1522, after his first crowning as emperor, and he resided first in Palencia and then in Valladolid. He met some of the Comunero demands and allowed more Spaniards to hold positions in government. He placed the rebels on trial and pardoned most of them in exchange for funds that he needed to defray the cost of his election to emperor. Pedro Laso was one of few exceptions to those pardons, and he sought temporary exile in Portugal. Garcilaso went to serve the emperor in Palencia, where he was seen in August 1522.

It is generally thought (on the basis of a single allegation) that in September 1521 Garcilaso joined a Spanish expedition to protect the island of Rhodes from a siege by the Turkish fleet. The Spaniards reached Messina but, shortly after departing for Rhodes from there, were forced by bad weather to turn back and return to Spain; Rhodes fell to the Turks. Vaquero Serrano, in *Garcilaso: Poeta del amor, caballero de la guerra,* suggests two reasons for doubting that Garcilaso sailed for Rhodes. First, he is said to have been at court in Valladolid in October, November, and December 1522. The second reason is that he makes no mention of the expedition in his poems. If Garcilaso did belong to the group bound for Rhodes, it would have placed him at that time in the company of persons whom he in fact did come to know well and who were important to him later in life. One was Don Pedro de Toledo of the House of Alba, whose dukedom was the highest position in the Spanish nobility. Pedro de Toledo later protected him from the wrath of the emperor and, after Garcilaso's second exile, gave him a position at the court of Naples, where he associated with important figures of the literary and intellectual life of the day. The second important contact was the famous poet from Barcelona, Juan Boscán, who became Garcilaso's closest friend and his collaborator in definitively introducing the new, Italianate Renaissance lyric in Spain.

Garcilaso was seen in Pamplona during the period that the court was there between October and December 1523, and there are records to the effect that in November of that year in Pamplona he was made a knight of the distinguished Order of Santiago, an honor bestowed on him by Don Pedro de Toledo. Soon afterward, Garcilaso participated in a military campaign against France, which had taken advantage of the confusion in Spain during the Comunero uprising to

Portrait by Antonio Moro of Fernán de Alvarez de Toledo, the Duke of Alba, who was a friend and patron to Garcilaso in the Spanish royal court (Museo Real de Bruselas; from María del Carmen Vaquero Serrano, Garcilaso: Poeta del amor, caballero de la guerra, *2002; Hodges Library, University of Tennessee)*

March the court moved to Seville and Granada, where the wedding of Charles V and Isabel of Portugal was celebrated for six months.

It is held by some but is inconsistent with the weight of evidence that on the occasion of these celebrations in Seville and Granada Garcilaso met two Italians who had an important impact on Spanish culture. He certainly did meet them at some point. One was Baldassare Castiglione, who had arrived in Spain the year before as papal legate from Rome and who was the author of *Il cortegiano* (The Courtier), the famous Neoplatonist treatise on aristocratic amatory culture and character ideals. That work was published in 1528 and translated in 1534 to Spanish by Boscán at the urging of Garcilaso, who wrote the introduction for the translation. The other Italian was Andrea Navagero, the great humanist and ambassador from Venice who, in a conversation in the Generalife Gardens in Granada, convinced Boscán to adapt to Spanish the twelve-syllable line used in the new Italian lyric. Boscán began his attempts as he returned to Barcelona, and he was soon joined in that project by Garcilaso. Such is the version of these events as Boscán presents it in a letter to the duchess of Soma. He makes no mention of Garcilaso's presence in Granada at that time. Another reason for doubting that Garcilaso was there is that during this period he had responsibilities as alderman of the town council in Toledo, where also his first legitimate son, named Garcilaso de la Vega, was born in the spring of 1526.

It has been traditionally thought that in 1526 or the years immediately following, Garcilaso met, in Granada or Toledo, the woman who inspired many of his poems—Isabel Freire, a Portuguese beauty and member of the retinue of Queen Isabel of Portugal who married a man possibly of *converso* (converted Jewish) descent and later died in childbirth. More-recent scholars have speculated that Garcilaso could have met Isabel Freire earlier, in Portugal during his brother's exile, since one of Pedro Laso's brothers is reported to have been with him in Portugal in 1524. The idea that Garcilaso was passionately in love with Isabel Freire and wrote poems about her is based on a combination of speculation, coincidence, and equivocation. First, in the 1574 edition of Garcilaso's works by Francisco Sánchez de las Brozas, *copla* 2 (stanza 2) is introduced with the words "A doña Isabel Freyre, porque se casó con un hombre fuera de su condición" (To Doña Isabel Freire because she married a man not of her station); it seems less than likely, however, that those words were written by Garcilaso, especially since nothing in the poem is consistent with the theme suggested by that title. Second, in Garcilaso's eclogue 1, two shepherds lament losing the nymphs they love, one of whom married

occupy certain towns near the border. The fact that Garcilaso was present when the Spanish troops took Salvatierra in February 1524 is established by his testament of 1529, in which he arranges to pay back money that he borrowed from a doctor there at the time.

As a novice of the Order of Santiago, Garcilaso was required to devote a year to meditation on his new responsibilities. Where Garcilaso spent that year is not clear, but soon afterward he returned to the service of the emperor, who arranged for him to marry Elena de Zúñiga, a noblewoman at court who had a sizable fortune. The ceremony was in August 1525, and the young couple took up residence in the home of Garcilaso's mother in Toledo, where Garcilaso was an alderman on the town council. In February 1526 an arrangement was reached whereby King Francis I of France, who had been taken prisoner by the Spanish in Pavia in February 1524, would be set free in exchange for, among other things, agreeing to marry the emperor's sister, Leonor of Austria. The wedding took place in Illescas, near Toledo, in February 1526, and in another man and the other of whom (also referred to in eclogue 3) died in childbirth. Early editors of Garcilaso's works have claimed that these two women were both references to Isabel Freire and that both of the shepherds were Garcilaso, in spite of the fact that in the original formulation of those ideas—the version that was their source—the editor, Sánchez de las Brozas, actually states that the second shepherd, Nemoroso, represents Boscán and holds that the nymph whom Nemoroso loves and who died in childbirth was Isabel Freire.

The arbitrary nature of such readings is hard to ignore, especially since suffering in love of the type portrayed in Garcilaso's lyric was a traditional element of literature in the courtly love tradition. Vaquero Serrano suggests in *Garcilaso: Poeta del amor, caballero de la guerra* another theory of the same type, that Garcilaso was platonically in love with his brother Pedro's wife who died in childbirth, a Portuguese woman named Beatriz de Sa. Criticism about Garcilaso has been slow in countering such traditional, biographical perspectives and in favoring views such as that Garcilaso drew on some events from his life to write works that were intended to be primarily fictional and to have far-reaching thematic implications. Nevertheless, it is almost certain that Garcilaso's marriage to Elena de Zúñiga was one of convenience arranged by the emperor, so there is reason to imagine that he may well have had a love life outside of his marriage, possibly with the same Guiomar Carrillo who bore his first child.

In any case, the period between 1526 and 1532 is thought by critics to be when Garcilaso wrote sonnets 1 and 2, works that are famous among scholars but are not among the poet's most popular works because of their elusive semantic multidimensionality. Creel considers the central idea of sonnet 1 to be the poet's recognition of the irony that in the present, when he is experienced enough to assume responsibility for his own actions, his love has caused him to consciously place himself in as much peril as in the past, when he wandered blindly in the labyrinth of immediate experience. The poet's anguish is a result of the fact that he surrendered himself totally to one whose disposition is likely to be no more given to taking his interests into account than he himself is. In a final expression of bitter anguish transparently cloaked with a modern note of almost bemused detachment, he ironically observes that his own self-effacing devotion is indeed shared by his beloved, insofar as his willingness to die of love for her is matched by her willingness to have him do so.

Yo acabaré, que me entregué sin arte
a quien sabrá perderme y acabarme
si quisiere, y aún sabrá querello;

que pues mi voluntad puede matarme,
la suya, que no es tanto de mi parte,
pudiendo, ¿qué hará sino hazello?

(I will end, for I have surrendered artlessly / to one who will find a way to ruin me and destroy me / if that person so wished, / and so it shall be; for since my will can kill me, / that person's, which has less regard for me, / being able to, what will it do but do it?)

In sonnet 2 the poet's strategy of flattery and seduction is hard to identify unless the tone of the poem is regarded as being generally ironic. He rhetorically portrays himself as a defenseless prisoner and the lady as a sadistic military enemy. Although the lady's power can be associated with her beauty, the poet here seems to be trying to shock her by hyperbolically contemplating her heartlessness as resulting in a reversal of roles whereby he has assumed the identity of the submissive female while she that of the domineering male. Yet, the poet's intense need of her as a love object seems also to have resulted in his having developed feelings of angry aggression toward her, whom he ambivalently identifies with the "brutal" intensity of his own unsatisfied longing. The poetic utterance addressed to the lady—words that express an attitude of both protest and appeasing submission—is seen as being addressed to the state of captivity, an oppressively harsh environment where the love he longs for is absent and from which he yearns for release. At the end of the poem, as Creel points out, he bids that the lady, the image of his brutal lack of fulfillment, crush him to death and suppress his helpless libido, of which he has become the image.

En fin a vuestras manos é venido
do sé que é de morir tan apretado
que aun aliviar con quexas mi cuidado
como remedio m'es ya deffendido:
mi vida no sé en qué s'ha sostenido
si no es en aver sido yo guardado
para que sólo en mí fuesse provado
quánto corta una 'spada en un rendido.
Mis lágrimas an sido derramadas
donde la sequedad y el aspereza
dieron mal fruto dellas, y mi suerte:
'basten las que por vos tengo lloradas;
no os venguéys más de mí con mi flaqueza;
allá os vengad, señora, con mi muerte!

(Finally I have come into your hands, / where I know I will die gripped so tightly / that even the remedy of relieving my anguish with complaints is forbidden to me: / I know not on what my life has sustained itself / if it is not on my having been kept / so that on me alone it might be proven how much a sword will cut in one who has surrendered. / My tears have been shed where dryness and harshness / bore poor fruit of them, and my fate: / may those that I have already wept for you

Italian humanist Baldassare Castiglione, an acquaintance of Garcilaso whose guide to courtly life, Il cortegiano *(1528, The Courtier), Garcilaso helped introduce to a Spanish audience (Musée du Louvre, Paris; from María del Carmen Vaquero Serrano,* Garcilaso: Poeta del amor, caballero de la guerra, *2002; Hodges Library, University of Tennessee)*

suffice; / avenge yourself on me no more with my frailty; / avenge yourself, madam, with my death!)

Also thought to have been written between 1526 and 1532 are *canciónes* 1, 2, and 4. Some of Garcilaso's most powerful and interesting love poems, they are similar to sonnets 1 and 2 in that their inspired idealism about love departs from the lover's secret, passive, introverted stance in the Petrarchan tradition and becomes heroically persistent and recklessly fatalistic while it also avoids grandiosity by virtue of its modern, anguished tone. Here a tenacious idealism blindly hurls itself against equally unrelenting obstacles to love (the lady's obduracy, her absence, certain death resulting from unbearable pain) with the lover trusting in nothing but the nobility of his devoted sentiment, producing the sense of a situation that is analogous to a soldier bravely yet painfully advancing in battle while remaining fully cognizant of the likelihood of his own demise.

The conflict of the two unyielding forces gives Garcilaso's poetry a sense of impending doom yet also of triumph in the axiological sphere insofar as the disaffection of the lady takes on the archetypal overtones of a sinister, cold, worldly distrust of altruistic impulses, and the lover's passionate agony and situation as an exile acquire a dignity akin to the martyrdom of the faithful. So it is that the poet, foolish yet dignified and even courageous, persists in his loving solicitude, although he has been brought to a semicrazed state as a result. The first stanza of *canción* 1 exemplifies the extraordinary power of these poems, in which a subtext of urbane wit and gay irony is also not lacking. As Garcilaso, who was familiar with the mental turbulence that accompanies fateful anguish of love, understood, the poet's fantasies of the lady's jeopardy can, as Creel has noted, be regarded as resulting from his having projected his own self-destructive, if noble, desire and suffering on her. The elegantly subtle sweetness of mind of the heartfelt flattery in such tributes to woman have contributed much to the affection with which these poems have been embraced by readers over the centuries. The first stanza of *canción* 1 is particularly suggestive and eloquent:

> Si a la región desierta, inhabitable
> por el hervor del sol demasíado
> y sequedad d'aquella arena ardiente,
> o a la que por el yelo congelado
> y rigurosa nieve es intractable,
> del todo inhabitada de la gente,
> por algún accidente
> o caso de fortuna desastrada
> me fuéssedes llevada,
> y supiesse que allá vuestra dureza
> estava en su crüeza,
> allá os yría a buscar como perdido,
> hasta morir a vuestros pies tendido

(If to the desert region, uninhabitable / because of seething excess of sun / and dryness of burning sand, / or to that which because of freezing cold / and harsh snow is unyielding, / completely uninhabited by people, / by some accident, / or occurrence of miserable fortune, / you were taken from me, / and I knew that your harshness / were there in all its cruelty, / I would go look for you there like one lost, / until dying outstretched at your feet.)

Among the most powerful of all passages in Garcilaso's poetry is *canción* 4, the structure of which critic Rafael Lapesa, in his *Garcilaso: Estudios completos* (1985, Garcilaso: Complete Studies), saw as being deliberately incongruous. It is an intensely introverted allegory on the subject of conflict between thought and feeling and a portrait of the disorienting erosion of ordinary confidence and well-being by the "divine furor" of love. Critics have found the emotional impact of its powerful first stanza in the original Spanish difficult to describe:

> El aspereza de mis males quiero
> que se muestre también en mis razones,
> como ya en los efetos s'ha mostrado;
> lloraré de mi mal las ocasiones;
> sabrá el mundo la causa por que muero,
> y moriré a lo menos confesado,
> pues soy por los cabellos arrastrado
> de un tal desatinado pensamiento,
> que por agudas peñas peligrosas,
> por matas espinosas,
> corre con ligereza más que el viento,
> bañando de mi sangre la carrera

(The severity of my plight I want / to be displayed in my discourse / as it has already been displayed in its effects; / I will lament the causes of my misfortune, / the world will learn the cause of my death, / and I will at least die confessed, / for I am being dragged by my hair / by a thought so senseless / that over perilous, sharp crags / and thorny bushes / it races more lightly than the wind, / bathing the trail with my blood.)

Garcilaso's second and third legitimate sons, Iñigo de Zúñiga (whom he renamed Garcilaso de la Vega after the death of the boy's older brother a few years later) and Pedro de Guzmán, were born in 1527 and 1528 or 1529, respectively. In 1529 the emperor arranged to go to Italy to be crowned by the Pope, and Garcilaso, in order to accompany him, resigned his position as alderman of the town council of Toledo. In April 1529 the emperor arrived in Barcelona and prepared to leave for Italy that summer. He cut his hair short and grew a beard to imitate the appearance of the Roman Caesars, and the nobles at court, including Garcilaso, followed his example. Two days before leaving for Italy, Garcilaso signed his testament, in which he makes his oldest legitimate son the heir of his estate, provides for having his illegitimate son, Lorenzo, pursue a university career, and arranges to have his debts paid, including twenty-seven *ducados* for the peasant girl whom he deprived of her virginity. The first two signatures on the document were those of his friend Boscán, who lived in Barcelona, and of his older brother, Pedro, who went to Italy as well (and, hence, by then must have received the emperor's pardon).

The imperial fleet of some one hundred ships left Barcelona on 28 July 1529 and on 12 August arrived in Genoa with much fanfare. The coronation was planned to take place in Rome, but because of the Turkish invasion of Hungary and the need to lend military assistance, it was decided to schedule the coronation to be held at an earlier date, in Bologna. It took place with splendid pomp and elaborate ceremony on 22 February 1530. Although one must presume that Garcilaso was present at the event, it is noteworthy that there is no evidence that he made mention of it in his poetry. The reason may be that the poet lacked a high degree of patriotic fervor for the new monarchy or that, unlike a poet such as Fernando de Herrera, he was not drawn to heroic and military subjects (he actually expresses on various occasions in his poetry a distaste for war) or affairs of state; but the explanation ultimately is not known. During that trip Garcilaso spent eight months in Italy, and the occasion presumably afforded him a substantial introduction to Italian Renaissance literature and culture. Before the emperor left for Germany in April 1531, he commended Garcilaso in Mantua for his excellent service, granted him a sizable annual stipend, and gave him permission to return to Toledo, a trip Garcilaso undertook a few weeks later and finished before April.

On 14 August of that same year, an event took place that led to Garcilaso's second exile. Although he later claimed that he was there by accident, he was one of four witnesses at the secret marriage in Ávila of his fifteen-year-old nephew and namesake, the oldest son of Pedro Laso, and the eleven-year-old heiress of the duchy of Alburquerque, Isabel de la Cueva. Previously, Garcilaso had given his signature as a witness to an agreement that the marriage would take place. The other witness who signed on Garcilaso's nephew's side was Pedro Laso, and the witnesses on Isabel's side were her mother and her grandmother. Also at that time, negotiations were taking place between Pedro Laso, whose wife had died in childbirth, and Isabel's mother, who had been a widow for ten years. The marriage between Isabel de la Cueva and Pedro's son was opposed by the relatives of Isabel's deceased father, the Alburquerques, who appealed to the king to prevent the union on the grounds that it would jeopardize their lineage. It seems that Pedro still bore a stigma for supporting the Comunero movement. The queen, who was in residence in Ávila, had agreed to the marriage on the condition that her husband give his consent as well. Isabel's mother, however, made prior arrangements to have the marriage administered by a priest and then took Isabel to the cathedral on the pretext of taking her to confession. Approval of the marriage had not yet been received from the king, and, as it happened, Pedro Laso was not present at the marriage nor at the time was he in Ávila.

Shortly before this occasion, Garcilaso had joined a group that accompanied Fernán Alvarez de Toledo, the young duke of Alba, to participate in a campaign against the Turks, who were again invading Germany. At that time the emperor was in Flanders. The queen arranged for Garcilaso, while he was in France, to visit the emperor's sister Leonor, who had recently married the king of France, and for him to both observe the French activities on the border with Spain and consult with the emperor's ambassadors in France. When the emperor's prohibition of the marriage of Pedro's son to Isabel de la Cueva arrived in Spain from Flanders and the queen discovered that Garcilaso had been a witness at the ceremony, Garcilaso, who had departed for Flanders and then Germany, was detained in the Basque town of Tolosa on 3 February 1532 by envoys of the queen and interrogated. At first he evasively stated that since he had learned of the king's displeasure he had not taken part in relations between Isabel and his nephew. Later, however, upon further interrogation, he explained that a page had called him to the cathedral and that when he went there he found that the ceremony was taking place.

Upon confessing, Garcilaso was exiled from the kingdom and forbidden to enter the court, measures that had been prearranged by the queen. The duke of Alba appealed to the queen to suspend Garcilaso's penalty. The queen refused, but when the duke continued his journey he took Garcilaso with him, and the group crossed the Pyrenees in midwinter. The trip is recorded in Garcilaso's eclogue 2, lines 1433–1504. From the border they went to Paris, Utrecht, Cologne, and finally reached the imperial court in Ratisbon, Germany, in late March. In spite of appeals, on 24 March the emperor immediately exiled Garcilaso to an island on the Danube River. Isabel de la Cueva was separated from her mother and grandmother and placed in the custody of the marquise of Lombay, and Pedro Laso's son hid in Portugal, where he was sought by the Spanish authorities. There are definite references to Garcilaso's exile on the Danube in his *canción* 3, which is also considered by scholars such as Tomás Navarro Tomás and Margot Arce de Vázquez to feature, in the beginning stanza, the first conscious appearance in Garcilaso's poetry of enthusiasm for the beauty of nature:

Con un manso rüido
d'água corriente y clara,
cerca el Danubio una isla, que pudiera
ser lugar escogido
para que descansara
quien, como yo estó agora, no estuviera;
do siempre primavera
parece en la verdura
sembrada de las flores;
hacen los ruiseñores
renovar el placer o la tristura
con sus blandas querellas,
que nunca, dia ni noche, cesan dellas.

(With a gentle sound / of clear, running water, / the Danube encircles an island that could / be a place cho-

sen / to give rest / to one who was not in the state I am in now might rest; / where always springtime / appears / in the verdure / sown with flowers; / the nightingales cause / one's pleasure or sadness / to be renewed with their soft plaints, / for they never, day or night, cease from them.)

The poet seeks solace in his knowledge that the temporal afflictions of exile, imprisonment, a destroyed political career, and even the prospect of death are easier to bear than the inner anguish that his soul has already endured because of love. Bienvenido Morros, in his comments on *canción* 3 in *Obra poética y textos en prosa* (1995), believes that Garcilaso's lament of exile on the shores of a river suggests a reference to the Jewish song of exile, Psalm 137, which begins, "By the rivers of Babylon we sat mourning and weeping when we remembered Zion."

Also in early 1532, Garcilaso's daughter was born. She was named Sancha de Guzmán after her maternal grandmother. On approximately 25 June of that year, the emperor's council proposed that upon the completion of the German campaign Garcilaso's place of exile be changed. Of all of the alternatives (a convent, Africa, the fleet, Naples, the upcoming campaign against the Turks in Austria), the final choice was Naples, likely because of the influence of Pedro de Toledo, who was at court at the time and had just been named viceroy of the kingdom of Naples (the Italian Peninsula south of the Papal States). With the Treaty of Blois (1504–1505) Naples had passed from the French to the Spanish, who ruled it through a viceroy until 1707. Whether Garcilaso went to Naples with Pedro de Toledo, who entered the city on 5 September, is not known; but he is known to have been there by November, by a record of his having charged the purchase of a horse to his account as a deputy of the viceroy. Possibly on the occasion of Garcilaso's first arrival in Naples, he visited the grave of his younger brother Fernando de Guzmán, who died in Naples of the plague in 1528 when the city was under siege by the French. The poet's thoughts are recorded in his sonnet 16, an epitaph in which the deceased addresses Naples by its ancient name, Parthenope:

No las francesas armas odïosas,
en contra puestas al airado pecho,
ni en los guardados muros con pertrecho
los tiros y saetas ponzoñosas;
no los escaramuzas peligrosas,
ni aquel fiero rüido contrahecho
d'aquel que para Júpiter fue hecho
Por manos de Vulcano artificiosas,
pudeiron, aunque más yo me ofrecía
a los peligros de la dura guerra,
quitar una hora sola de mi hado;

más infición de aire en solo un día
me quitó al mundo y m'ha en ti sepultado,
Parténope, tan lejos de mi tierra.

(Not hateful French arms / set against the angered breast, / nor venomous shots and arrows / on ramparts guarded with arms; / not dangerous skirmishes, / nor that savage noise / that seems imitated from that one which was made or forged for Jupiter / by the artful hands of Vulcan, / succeeded, as much as I offered myself / to the dangers of cruel war, / in taking a single hour from my fate; / but an infection of the plague in a single day / took me from the world and entombed me in you, / Parthenope, so far from my land.)

The period Garcilaso spent in Naples toward the end of his life is generally thought to have been the most culturally stimulating and artistically productive, although the view that he did not mature stylistically until this period is based on individual preferences of taste and some assumptions about the chronology of his works. Garcilaso's having been designated as the principal representative of Renaissance classicism in Spanish literature has contributed much to the preference that has been shown for his eclogues and certain of his sonnets, particularly sonnets 10, 11, and 23. Because of their relative clarity (which can also invite a facile, biographical reading), idyllic elements, and classical themes, these fine works directly exemplify Renaissance style. A different question is whether these works are Garcilaso's most representative or interesting or are the most appealing to modern taste. More characteristically modern, anguished, and often complex are his *canciónes* 1, 2, and 4 and sonnets 1, 2, 22, 26, and 38, while sonnets 14, 29, and 37 are also works whose appeal remains undiminished over the centuries.

In any case, much of Garcilaso's poetry, including major works such as eclogue 1, is known to have originated in this period. His first stay in Naples lasted more than seven months. While there, he cultivated relations with humanists and poets devoted to studying the classics, composing works in Latin, and reading and discussing the great authors of the Italian Renaissance. He was in close contact with, and likely part of, a group of humanist intellectuals and literati known as the Academia Pontaniana. It had met at the villa of its founder and director, Jacopo Sannazaro, until his death in 1530. It then met at the home of Scipione Capede, who was a lawyer, professor, and poet. He dedicated to Garcilaso his edition of Donatus's commentary on *The Aeneid*, published in 1535.

The members of the Academia Pontaniana included some of the most celebrated Italian cultural figures of the day, such as poet and literary critic Antonio Minturno; Augustinian theologian Girolamo Seripando, the archbishop of Salerno and a cardinal; Antonio Epicuro, author of *Dialogo de tre ciechi* (1525, Dialogue of the Three Blind Men); Bernardino Martirano, the imperial secretary at Naples; and literati such as Placido de Sangro, Gilolamo Borgia, and Catalina and Violante Sanseverino. Among the poets who wrote in Italian, Garcilaso knew especially well Luigi Tansillo, Bernardo Tasso, Giulio Cesare Caraccolo, and Laura Terracina, and through the Academia Pontaniana he met the renowned Pietro Bembo, who years later praised Garcilaso's Latin poems. The influence of Torquato Tasso has been observed in Garcilaso's sonnet 23, a work that has the conventional courtly love pretext of praise and seduction as the persona advances the traditional argument of carpe diem in an attempt to persuade the lady to yield to his love before old age renders her incapable of partaking of life's pleasures.

En tanto que de rosa y d'azucena
se muestra la color en vuestro gesto,
y que vuestro mirar ardiente, honesto,
con clara luz la tempestad serena;
y en tanto que'el cabello, que'n la vena
del oro s'escogió, con vuelo presto
por el hermoso cuello blanco, enhiesto,
el viento mueve, esparce y desordena:
coged de vuestra alegre primavera
el dulce fruto, antes que'l tiempo airado
cubra de nieve la hermosa cumbre.
Marchitará la rosa el viento helado,
todo lo mudará la edad ligera
por no hacer mudanza en su costumbre.

(While the color of the rose and the white lily / is seen in your face, / and while your ardent, chaste eyes / calm the storm with clear light; / and while your hair, selected from vein / of gold, is, in quick flight, / moved, scattered, and disarrayed / by the wind on your white, straight neck: / gather the sweet fruit of your joyful springtime / before time in its anger / covers the lovely mountain peak with snow. / The icy wind will wither the rose / and fleeting time will change everything / so as to make no change in its customs.)

In Naples, Garcilaso also associated with some important Spanish humanists, such as Juan de Valdés (prominent humanist intellectual and Catholic-reformist religious philosopher) and Juan Ginés de Sepúlveda (imperial historian and author, to whom Garcilaso later dedicated a Latin ode). Some scholars have argued that Boscán was in Naples at this time because Tansillo dedicated a laudatory sonnet to him.

In mid April 1533 Garcilaso returned to Spain via Genoa as an ambassador of the viceroy of Naples, carrying letters to the emperor. He arrived in Barcelona on 26 April, three days after the emperor's arrival. During that brief stay in Barcelona, Garcilaso likely helped to

Title page for the first edition of Garcilaso's poetic works, collected along with those of his good friend and fellow poetic innovator Juan Boscán (from Obras completas: Con comentario, *1974; Thomas Cooper Library, University of South Carolina)*

trees, weave rich tapestries depicting painful mythological scenes: Orpheus rescuing Eurydice and losing her again, Apollo's discovery of the death and transformation of Daphne into a laurel tree, and Venus's affliction upon the death of Adonis. The culmination of the poem is a crescendo of pain occasioned by a description of the fourth nymph's embroidery of the death of Elisa and the pain of the shepherd Nemoroso. The impression of distance from emotional pain (unlike in eclogue 1) achieved by the indirect representation of pathos as works within a work is augmented by, at the end of the poem, the nymphs' returning to the river and leaving the scene as peaceful and harmonious as it was at the beginning of the poem.

Before returning to Naples in mid June, Garcilaso briefly visited Toledo, soon after the death of his younger brother Francisco de la Vega in Bologna at the age of approximately twenty-six. On 12 May 1533 Garcilaso and his brother Pedro officially requested that Francisco's testament be opened and read.

Isabel Freire's death in 1533 or 1534 has traditionally been thought (likely erroneously) to have been the occasion on which sonnet 10 was written. Although many critics consider the classicist clarity and structural symmetry of Garcilaso's eclogues 1 and 3 to render them his finest works, his sonnets are unmatched by any poet in the Spanish language. Although they are often more complex and problematic than eclogues 1 and 3, some are exceptional in possessing, on one level, a clarity comparable to that of these two ecologues. In sonnet 10, the pain of present suffering offsets thoughts of past joy in what is, however, ultimately a tribute to treasured ideals that are rekindled by the discovery of certain unspecified effects or relics:

¡Oh dulces prendas por mi mal halladas,
dulces y alegres cuando Dios quería,
juntas estáis en la memoria mía
y con ella en mi muerte conjuradas!
¿Quién me dijera, cuando las pasadas
horas qu'en tanto bien por vos me vía,
que me habíades de ser en algún día
con tan grave dolor representadas?
Pues en una hora junto me llevastes
todo el bien que por términos me distes,
llévame junto el mal que me dejastes;
si no, sospecharé que me pusistes
en tantos bienes porque deseastes
verme morir entre memorias tristes

(Oh sweet objects, discovered to my sorrow, / sweet and happy when God so willed! / Together you are in my memory, / and with it conspire in my death. / Who could have told me, when in time gone by / you brought me so much joy, / that you would some day / be represented to me with so much pain? / Since in one

correct the Spanish translation that Boscán made of Castiglione's *Il cortegiano,* as is explained in the introductory letters written by Garcilaso and Boscán. Garcilaso's letter, addressed to a relative of Boscán named Doña Jerónima Palova de Almogávar, affords interesting insights into Garcilaso's personality. Critics believe that 1534, when Boscán's translation was published, is also the year Garcilaso wrote eclogue 1, with eclogue 3 being written two years later. Eclogue 1 presents the shepherd Salicio's song of complaint at the unfaithfulness of his beloved Galatea. It is immediately followed by the shepherd Nemoroso's elegy for his dead beloved, Elisa. In both cases, the events causing suffering are seen as violations of the normal harmonious order of nature represented by the idyllic pastoral setting. Eclogue 3 (thought by some to have been written in 1536, during the military campaign in which the poet died) opens with some of Garcilaso's most delicate lines in a detailed description of an idealized pastoral setting. Four nymphs then emerge from the Tagus River and, in the shade of willow moment you took from me / all the good that you gave me by degrees, / take from me now the sorrow that you have left me; / if you do not, I will suspect that you placed me among such bounty because you wanted / to see me die amid sad memories).

The popular group of Garcilaso's poems composed of eclogues 1 and 3 and sonnets 10, 11, and 23 have in common a tone of youthful innocence combined with varying degrees of tragic skepticism. That tone is achieved by the portrayal of disenchanted optimism. The poet contemplates an experience of death or loss, but the emphasis is not placed on the virtues or sufferings of the departed loved one but on the pain of the poet or the painful prospect of his having to forfeit a full experience of the richness of life. Since it is optimistic youth that is most vulnerable to disenchantment, the innocent candor of these poems exercises a purifying effect on the reader by presenting an alternative to what might otherwise be an attitude of cynical insensitivity in the face of the brutality of life. Sonnet 11 is an unusually clear example of the manneristic tension between classicism (idyllic repose and harmony) and anticlassicism (the anguish of tragic grief):

Hermosas ninfas, que en el río metidas,
contentas habitáis en las moradas
de relucientes piedras fabricadas
y en columnas de vidrio sostenidas,
. . . .
dejad un rato la labor, alzando
vuestras rubias cabezas a mirarme,
y no os detendréis mucho según ando,
que o no podréis de lástima escucharme,
o convertido en agua aquí llorando,
podréis allá despacio consolarme

(Lovely nymphs bathing in the river / who live happily in mansions / built of shining stones and upheld by crystal columns: / . . . lay aside your work for a moment, raising / your golden heads to look at me, / and you will not pause long, given my sad state; / for either out of pity you will not be able to listen to me, / or, by my being changed into water by weeping up here, / you will be able to console me more at length [when I arrive] down there.)

Nine months passed before Garcilaso left Naples again. On the basis of passages referring to the duke of Alba's return to Toledo and the dating of that event, Garcilaso is thought to have written during this period his longest and most ambitious work, if not the most highly regarded, eclogue 2. More than four times longer than eclogues 1 or 3, eclogue 2 conforms to the general definition of an eclogue by being a dialogue between shepherds, but unlike Garcilaso's other two eclogues it has an overall dramatic instead of a narrative format. It may have been intended to be performed like the dramatic eclogues of Juan del Encina. Although its structure is symmetrical, it is heterogeneous in its components, rather complicated and difficult to interpret, and is thought to be Garcilaso's earliest effort in the pastoral mode. Its primary subject and the focus of the first half is Albanio's narration to Salicio on the subject of the former's experience of sensual impulse and his experience of the madness of unrequited love. Albanio (whom critics have associated with Bernaldino de Toledo, the younger brother of the duke of Alba) loved Camila, but when he made his love known to her she abandoned him. When he finds her again, he tries to retain her by force. She escapes, and losing his sanity from the intensity of pain, he tries to commit suicide but is held and bound by his friends Salicio and Nemoroso. In the second part of the eclogue, Nemoroso narrates his own similar experience and how he was cured by the wise Severo. Nemoroso also narrates at great length the history of the House of Alba and the heroic deeds of the duke of Alba as they were related prophetically to Severo. The thematic relation in this work between the amorous and the heroic motifs and of both to a pastoral setting would seem to be that heroic exploits and military activities are seen as an effective means of overcoming the malignant introversion of despondency in love and of coming in line with idyllic harmony.

Garcilaso's Neapolitan period, from 1532 to 1536, is thought by some critics to be the time when he wrote sonnets 22 and 38, two of his most complex works. On the surface sonnet 22 seems straightforward. The situation represented is that of the poet casually encountering the lady and looking at her breast in order to discover, he explains, whether she is inwardly as beautiful as she is outwardly. The awkwardness of the event, the lady's justifiably defensive reaction to a look that she could believe to be directed at her bosom, the ambiguity of the poet's interest in the woman's breast, and the exact source of the poet's final attitude of despair are, as Creel has noted, some of the issues that must be considered by interpreters of this poem, the images of which may also be translated into allegorical terms.

Con ansia estrema de mirar qué tiene
vuestro pecho escondido allá en su centro
y ver si a lo de fuera lo de dentro
en apariencia y ser igual conviene,
en él puse la vista, mas detiene
de vuestra hermosura el duro encuentro
mis ojos, y no pasan tan adentro
que miren lo qu'el alma en sí contiene.
Y así se quedan tristes en la puerta
hecha, por mi dolor, con essa mano,

que aun a su mismo pecho no perdona;
donde vi claro mi esperanza muerta
y el golpe, que en vos hizo amor en vano,
non esservi passato oltra la gona

(With extreme longing to see what / your breast has
hidden away in its center / and to see if what is within /
matches what is without in appearance and being
equal, / I placed my eyesight on it, but / your beauty's
harsh stroke stops my eyes, / and they do not proceed
inward / so far as to see what your soul contains within
itself. / And so they remain sad at the door / made, to
my sorrow, with that hand / that will not give leave /
even to what is within its own breast; / where I saw
clearly my hope dead / and the blow, which love dealt
you in vain, / not having penetrated beyond your
gown).

Similarly fascinating because of its complexity is sonnet 38. The setting of the poem is a dreary road that
the poet has been traveling in pursuit of a lady. He
stands immobilized by confusion and anguish, unable
either to turn back or continue because each alternative is as painful as the other. At first, this predicament
seems not to present any particular difficulty to the
reader; the poet's affliction seems to be a result of the
lady's refusal to reciprocate, and he seems to be simply expressing the idea that he can neither flee her nor
continue to pursue her. Yet, upon closer examination
several questions arise that a superficial reading of the
poem cannot answer. When the poet says that if he
wants to turn to flee the lady he is unable to do so
because what he sees behind him makes him faint, is
he referring to what is "behind him" before he turns to
flee or afterward? What is it that he sees, and why
does he faint? What is the significance of the high
peak that the persona says he does not dare to climb
because of the many who have attempted to do so but
have fallen? What are the broader implications of the
experience that the poet is having at the moment of
utterance, plunged in a dark abyss and trapped
between two equally undesirable alternatives? Why
has frustration in the situation described had such
severe effects on the poet, producing in him a degree
of anguish that borders on the pathological? Ultimately, an interpretation of this poem must take into
account the relation between the poet's morbid hyper-
sensitivity and his ambivalent attitude toward the
lady, as well as his identification of conflicting parts of
his ego with her different aspects, the result of this latter situation being a debilitating split in his ego and a
conflict vis-à-vis the object that is causing him to oscil-
late between attitudes of yearning and renunciation.
Here again, the vividness of the images invites their
being interpreted allegorically:

Estoy contino en lágrimas bañado,
rompiendo siempre el aire con sospiros,
y más me duele el no osar deziros
que he llegado por vos a tal estado;
que viéndome do estoy y en lo que he andado
por el camino estrecho de seguiros,
si me quiero tornar para hüyros,
desmayo, viendo atrás lo que he dexado;
y si quiero subir a la alta cumbre,
a cada paso espántanme en la vía
exemplos tristes de los que han caydo;
sobre todo, me falta ya la lumbre
de la esperanza, con que andar solía
por la oscura región de vuestro olvido

(I am constantly bathed in tears, / ever rending the air
with sighs, / and it pains me more that I dare not tell
you that I have come to such a state because of you; /
seeing where I am and what has occupied me / on the
narrow road of following you, / if I want to turn to flee
you, / I faint, seeing behind me what I left; / and if I
want to climb to the high peak, / I am frightened at
every step along the way / by sad examples of those
who have fallen; / especially, I now lack the light / of
hope, with which I used to tread / in the dark region of
your forgetfulness).

Garcilaso also likely wrote sonnet 19 and *canción*
5 (which critics have also associated with Bernaldino
de Toledo) in his Neapolitan period, since in the first
he addresses one "Julio," who is thought to be the
famous Neapolitan poet Giulio Cesare Caracciolo,
and the second seems to concern his friend Mario
Galeota's passion for Violante Sanseverino during
Galeota's absence from Naples. *Canción* 5, "Ode ad
florem Gnidi" (named for the neighborhood in
Naples where the lady, compared to a violet, lives),
although classified as a *canción*, actually has the formal
structure and the rhetorical pretext of a Horatian ode.
It is a polished poem written in the stanza known as
the *lira*, a five-line combination of seven- and
eleven-syllable lines named after the first line in the
poem. Instead of concentrating on a subjective experience of the poet, in this work he takes up the cause of
his friend, reminding the lady of the damage that her
cruelty can cause and pleading with her to relieve the
distress of the man who loves her. Of its twenty-two
stanzas the initial passage, in which the poet-persona
wishes that his song had the Orphic power to move
nature and rhetorically admonishes the lady for her
cruelty, is famous:

Si de mi baja lira
tanto pudiese el son, que en un momento
aplacase la ira
del animoso viento
y la furia del mar y el movimiento,

y en ásperas montañas
con el suave canto enterneciese
las fieras alimañas
los árboles moviese
y al son confusamente los trujiese,

no pienses que cantando
sería de mí, hermosa flor de Gnido,
el fiero Marte airado,
. . . .
mas solamente aquella
fuerza de tu beldad sería cantada
. . . .
y cómo por ti sola
. . . .
convertido en vïola,
llora su desventura
el miserable amante en tu figura.

(If the sound of my lowly lyre / had so much power
that in one moment / it could placate the wrath / of the
vigorous wind / and the fury and movement of the sea,
/ and in the rough mountains / with gentle song it could
make tender / the fierce beasts, / move the trees, / and
draw them in confusion toward the sound: / do not
think, beautiful flower of Gnido, / that I would sing / of
fierce and angry Mars . . . , / but only of that / power of
your beauty would I sing . . . , / and of how, because of
you alone . . . / the wretched lover / turned into [con-
sumed by] a violet, / is lamenting in your form / his
misfortune.)

In 1534 Garcilaso was sent to Spain two more
times, once to the court in Toledo in the spring and in
August during the convening of the Cortes in Palencia.
On the second trip he was commissioned to inform the
emperor of the ravages of the western coast of Italy by
the Algerian corsair Barbarossa, who had entered into
an alliance with the Turks, and to carry news of the
counteroffensive that was being organized in Naples.
After a stay of only days, he returned to Naples by land
to avoid Barbarossa's fleet and passed through Barcelona and then Avignon, where his "Epístola a Boscán"
(Epistle to Boscán) suggests he visited the tomb of
Petrarch's Laura.

Garcilaso's status of being legally exiled seems to
have ended when, in October 1534, the emperor
named him the new governor of Reggio on the basis of
the recommendation of the viceroy of Naples, Pedro de
Toledo, who had repeatedly referred to Garcilaso in
glowing terms and asked the emperor to pardon him.
That appointment has been interpreted to mean that
Garcilaso intended at that point in his life to remain in
Naples permanently, since the viceroy mentions his
intention to have Garcilaso's wife move there. Other
events that Garcilaso's biographers have associated
with the final months of 1534 are his finishing his

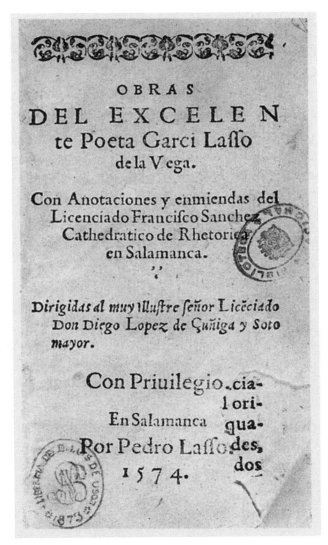

Title page for an early edition of Garcilaso's poetic works, prepared
by Francisco Sánchez de las Brozas, the scholar known as
"El Brocense," or "The Bronze" (from El Siglo de Frai
Luis de León: Salamanca y el Renacimiento,
1991; Thomas Cooper Library, University of
South Carolina)

eclogue 1, which he dedicated to the viceroy of Naples;
the possibility that he was in love with a Neapolitan
lady (a hypothesis advanced by Hayward Keniston on
the basis of arbitrary assumptions as to the dates of
some of Garcilaso's poems but sustained more legitimately by other critics on the basis of elegy 2, especially
lines 38–42); and the birth in Toledo of Garcilaso's last
child—a boy named Francisco, whom he never met.

In the spring of 1535 Garcilaso participated in a
campaign against the Turkish forces in Tunis headed
by Barbarossa, who had established his defenses in a
fortress in Goleta with fifty thousand men. Garcilaso

embarked from Italy with the Neapolitan armada, which joined forces with the emperor's African expedition in Sardinia. In one of the skirmishes around the fortress, Garcilaso received two wounds, a small one on the mouth and a somewhat more serious one on his right arm. Garcilaso refers to those wounds in his sonnet 35, which was written at that time and is addressed to his friend Mario Galeota. In it he attributes responsibility for his wounds to ungrateful Love, which has allied with the enemy to prevent the poet from speaking and writing about him:

> Mario, el ingrato amor, como testigo
> de mi fe pura y de mi gran firmeza
> usando en mí su vil naturaleza,
> teniendo miedo que, si escribo y digo
> su condición, abato su grandeza,
> no bastando su esfuerzo a su crüeza,
> ha esforzado la mano a mi enemigo;
> y ansí, en parte que la diestra mano
> gobierna y en aquella que declara
> los consetos del alma, fui herido.
> Mas yo haré que aquesta ofensa cara
> le cueste al ofensor, ya que estoy sano,
> libre, desesperado y ofendido

(Mario, ungrateful Love, as a witness / to my pure faith and great steadfastness, / treating me in keeping with his vile nature, / which is to offend the most devoted friend, / fearing that if I write and tell about / his disposition I will debunk his greatness, / his courage not being equal to his cruelty, / has strengthened the hand of my enemy; / and thus, in that part which governs my right hand / and in that which states / the concepts of my mind, I was wounded. / But I will make this offense cost / the offender dearly, now that I am healthy, / free, desperate, and offended.)

Garcilaso participated in the victory at Goleta on 14 July and the emperor's triumphant entry into Tunis on 22 July. On the occasion of the conquest of Goleta he wrote his sonnet 33, addressed to Boscán. Again, Garcilaso, as a Renaissance humanist, makes use of the discrepancy between the traditional, in this case ancient, emphasis on martial virtues and the modern preoccupation with subjective emotion to develop rhetorically an a fortiori comparison between the devastations of war and those of love, in that way both qualifying (while exploiting) the human significance of military might and enhancing a regard for the finer sensibilities:

> Boscán, las armas y el furor de Marte,
> que, con su propia fuerza el africano
> suelo regando, hacen que el romano
> imperio reverdezca en esta parte,
> han reducido a la memoria el arte
> y el antiguo valor italiano,

> por cuya fuerza y valerosa mano
> Africa se aterró de parte a parte.
> Aquí donde el romano encendimiento,
> donde el fuego y la llama licenciosa
> solo el nombre dejaron a Cartago,
> vuelve y revuelve amor mi pensamiento,
> hiere y enciende el alma temerosa,
> y en llanto y en ceniza me deshago

(Boscán, the weapons and fury of Mars, / which, irrigating in their own strength the African / soil are making the Roman / Empire come to life again here, / have restored to memory the skill / and courage of ancient Italy, / because of whose strength and courageous hand / Africa was thoroughly terrified. / Here where Roman ardor, / where fire and impetuous flame / left Carthage its name only, / love stirs and disarranges my thought, / and I waste away in tears and ashes.)

A month later, the Neapolitan forces, returning home, stopped at the port of Trapani in Sicily. There a prolonged illness took the life of Bernaldino de Toledo. With expressions of delicate humanity and invocations of stoic fortitude, Garcilaso commemorated the event in his elegy 1, addressed to Don Fernando, Duke of Alba. Garcilaso states at the beginning of the 307-line poem his purpose, to attempt to apply the power of his muse to raise a heart up from a state of being consumed in grief:

> Aunque este grave caso haya tocado
> con tanto sentimiento el alma mía,
> que de consuelo estoy necesitado,
> . . . .
> quise . . . probar si me bastase
> el ingenio a escribirte algún consuelo,
> . . . .
> . . . si las musas
> pueden un corazón alzar del suelo
> y poner fin a las querellas que usas,
> . . . .
> que temo ver deshechas tus entrañas
> en lágrimas, como al lluvioso viento
> se derrite la nieve en las montañas

(Although this grave event has so touched / my soul with so much feeling / that I am in need of consolation . . . , / I wished . . . to test whether my talent would suffice / to provide some comfort to you . . . , / whether the muses / can raise a heart from the depths / and bring an end to the grief that besets you . . . , / for I fear seeing your heart shattered / by sorrow—the way the rainy wind / melts snow in the mountains.)

After a lengthy and powerful evocation of grief, with abundant examples, denunciation of the perennial plight of war in modern times, and comparisons between Don Fernando's suffering and instances from mythology, the second half of the poem becomes ori-

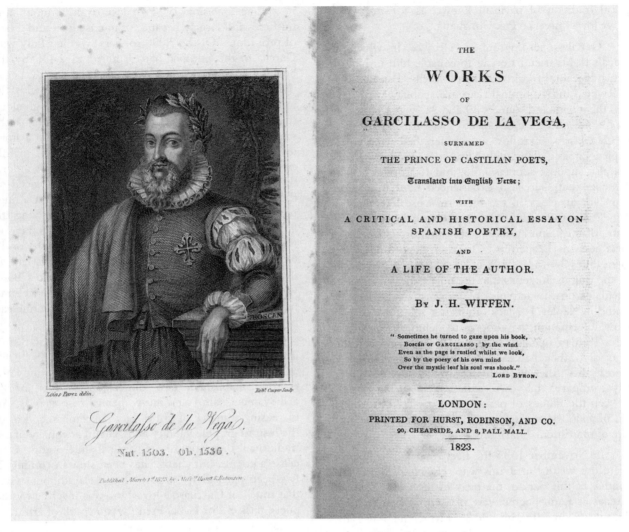

THE

WORKS

OF

GARCILASSO DE LA VEGA,

SURNAMED

THE PRINCE OF CASTILIAN POETS,

Translated into English Verse;

WITH

A CRITICAL AND HISTORICAL ESSAY ON
SPANISH POETRY,

AND

A LIFE OF THE AUTHOR.

By J. H. WIFFEN.

" Sometimes he turned to gaze upon his book,
Boscán or GARCILASSO ; by the wind
Even as the page is rustled whilst we look,
So by the poesy of his own mind
Over the mystic leaf his soul was shook."
LORD BYRON.

LONDON :
PRINTED FOR HURST, ROBINSON, AND CO.
90, CHEAPSIDE, AND 8, PALL MALL.
1823.

Garcilasso de la Vega.
Nat. 1503. Ob. 1536.

*Frontispiece and title page for the first English edition of Garcilaso's collected poems
(Jean and Alexander Heard Library, Vanderbilt University)*

ented toward exhortations of strength, courage, a sense of personal dignity, and expectations of immortality both through fame and the life of the soul. The dislike for war that Garcilaso expresses in lines 76–108 has caused critics to regard him as an interesting instance of a warrior who was also an ardent pacifist:

> ¡Oh miserables hados, oh mezquina
> suerte, la del estado humano, y dura!
> . . . .
> ¿A quién ya de nosotros el ecseso
> de guerras, de peligros y destierro
> no toca y no ha cansado el gran proceso?
> ¿Quién no vio desparcir su sangre al hierro
> del enemigo? ¿Quién no vio su vida
> perder mil veces y escapar por yerro?
> ¿De cuántos queda y quedará perdida
> la casa, la mujer y la memoria,

> y d'otros la hacienda despendida?
> ¿Qué se saca d'aquesto? ¿Alguna gloria?
> ¿Algunos premios? ¿O agradecimientos?

(Oh miserable fate, oh base / and cruel fortune, that of the human state of being! . . . , / Who among us has not felt and been fatigued by the grand course / of wars, dangers, and exile? / Who has not seen his blood spilled by the iron / of the enemy? Who has not seen his life / lost a thousand times and escaped by accident? / How many have lost and will lose / home, wife, and memory, / and others had their property wasted? / What comes of this? Some glory? / Some rewards? Or gratitude?)

In the period when Garcilaso wrote, Desiderius Erasmus wrote his antiwar satire *Querela pacis* (1517, The Complaint of Peace) and spurred a powerful humanistic evangelical tradition of pacifism known as *irenismo,* which strove for a universal Pax Christiana.

Garcilaso also wrote his elegy 2, in which he appeals to his friend Boscán to console him in his torments of jealousy in love, while in Sicily. Lapesa, Elias L. Rivers, and Antonio Prieto are scholars who have seen this poem and sonnets 30 and 31—which, like sonnet 39, are also on the subject of jealousy—as referring to Garcilaso's love for an unidentified woman in Naples. Lapesa, along with Navarro Tomás and Keniston, also suppose sonnets 7, 28, and 19 to refer to love torments that Garcilaso experienced in that relationship. Not an elegy in the modern sense like elegy 1, elegy 2 is in the urbane tradition, delicately tinged with irony, of the Latin epistle or of the amorous elegies of poets such as Propertius. The central portion of this poem (lines 37–144 of 193 lines) is devoted to describing the jealous anxieties that the poet experiences as he speculates on the activities of the mistress he has left behind in Naples. For lack of a better solution and consoling information, he chooses to delude himself and, like a Roman opening his veins in a warm bath, die painlessly rather than capitulate to the fears that would intensify his suffering. In his final reflections he regretfully compares his own situation of being caught between the flames of passion and the cold mortification of jealousy to his friend Boscán's tranquillity in a state of matrimonial harmony.

In November 1535 the fleet returned to Naples, where the victory at Tunis was celebrated for several months. In this period, the peak of his literary career, Garcilaso's Latin poems were praised by Bembo. Garcilaso wrote, in Latin, his ode 3, in which he praises the African Caesar, Charles V, addressing the work to the anti-Erasmian Spanish humanist Ginés de Sepúlveda.

At this time Garcilaso was also at the peak of his military career, a circumstance that led to his death less than a year later. The emperor gave him the command of three thousand Spanish infantry troops to lead in a new imperial campaign, this time to southern France in response to the French invasion of Italy. Garcilaso's new responsibilities made it necessary for him to resign as governor of Reggio in the spring of 1536. He then went to meet his troops, which landed near Genoa in mid May. He divided them into eleven companies, making himself captain of one of them, and joined forces with the emperor before entering France. In mid July from Savigliano, Garcilaso wrote his last letter to a friend, Seripando in Naples. At this time, and/or during a previous military campaign, Garcilaso wrote his eclogue 3, dedicated to María Osorio Pimentel, the wife of his friend and patron Juan de Toledo, Viceroy of Naples.

The invasion of Provence was arduous and unsuccessful, largely because of intense heat and a lack of provisions. Of the 3,000 soldiers who left Italy with Garcilaso, the number had dropped to 2,445 by the beginning of September. The imperial forces began their retreat on 10 September, skirmishing with the inhabitants of the towns that they passed through along the way. On 19 September, four miles from Fréjus, the vanguard of the emperor's infantry came upon a small town, Le Muy, where some 50 Frenchmen, mainly crossbowmen, occupied a tower. Garcilaso was among the first four soldiers who climbed a ladder placed on the side of the tower. From the top of the tower a huge rock was dropped on the group of men, breaking the ladder. Mortally wounded, Garcilaso was taken to Nice, where he died several weeks later, on 13 or 14 October 1536. In his indignation the emperor had all the defenders of the tower hanged. Garcilaso's body was placed in the Dominican monastery of Nice, and two years later it was transferred to the Dominican monastery of San Pedro Mártir in Toledo.

Garcilaso's significance has both a general, historical and a specific, artistic, basis; yet, whereas his historical importance as a personality and a formal innovator is well established, new dimensions of his artistic achievement are constantly being discovered. An increasing number of critics have become skeptical of the historiographic validity and general adequacy of the traditional, biographical approach to interpreting Garcilaso's poems, but change has been slow in coming. It has been particularly argued that the traditional view that much of Garcilaso's love lyric was inspired by the poet's passion for Isabel Freire was a result of arbitrary assumptions. Vaquero Serrano's archival discoveries concerning Garcilaso's early years would seem to bear out suspicions that theories concerning the autobiographical inspirations for Garcilaso's love lyrics were based on incomplete information. Although critics are often tempted to postulate occasions on which Garcilaso wrote poems by matching elements in them with specific events in his life, the archetypal nature of Garcilaso's metaphors makes such speculation highly risky. In fact, out of Garcilaso's fifty-eight poems, only twelve can be definitely matched with specific occasions on or after which he would have had to write them, and of those twelve only seven (*canción* 3, *canción* 5, eclogue 2, the two elegies, and perhaps sonnets 16, 33, and 34) are among Garcilaso's better-known works. The efforts to reorient interpretations of Garcilaso's poetry along more imaginatively metaphorical, nonbiographical lines have not received the active support of all scholars who study him, some of whom are in the field of history; but the view that such efforts are needed continues to gain ground among literary critics, especially as progress is

Sepulchral statues of Garcilaso and his son at their tomb in the Monasterio de San Pedro Mártir in Toledo (from María del Carmen Vaquero Serrano, Garcilaso: Poeta del amor, caballero de la guerra, *2002; Hodges Library, University of Tennessee)*

made in overcoming the difficulties of allegorizing Petrarchist courtly love lyric in broad conceptual terms.

Like Petrarch's influence on authors such as Garcilaso, Garcilaso's impact on Spanish literature was rapid, immense, and lasting. His works were immediately edited and commented on by some of the best minds of the age, including Sánchez de la Brozas (El Brocense) and Fernando de Herrera, and the triumph of Italianism is now seen as marking in Spain the beginning of the Golden Age and of the entire modern epoch. Like the influence of Miguel de Cervantes in prose, there is almost no subsequent important poet who does not show traces of Garcilaso's influence. Spanish poets of note who were contemporaries of Garcilaso and were strongly influenced by the new Italianate verse include Hernando de Acuña, Gutierre de Cetina, Francisco de Figueroa, Francisco de Aldana, Gil Vicente, Gregorio Silvestre, and Francisco Sá de Miranda (who also wrote in Spanish).

The writings of major authors of the period, such as Jorge de Montemayor, Fray Luis de León, San Juan de la Cruz, Cervantes, Lope de Vega, Góngora, Quevedo, and the great Portuguese lyricist Luís de Camões also show Garcilaso's direct influence. Garcilaso's modernity continues to make him an exemplar of poetic inspiration in the present day. It has been said of him that he will live as long as the Castilian language continues to exist. As Rivers writes in *Garcilaso de la Vega: Poems, A Critical Guide* (1980), "of later Spanish authors only Cervantes could approach the European detachment, the Montaignean spirit, of this cosmopolitan aristocrat from Toledo."

Biographies:

Eustaquio Fernández de Navarrete, *Vida del célebre poeta Garcilaso de la Vega* (Madrid: Viuda de Calero, 1850);

Hayward Keniston, *Garcilaso de la Vega: A Critical Study of His Life and Works* (New York: Hispanic Society of America, 1922);

María del Carmen Vaquero Serrano, *Garcilaso: Aportes para una nueva biografía. Los Ribadeneira y Lorenzo Suárez de Figueroa* (Ciudad Real: Oretania, 1999);

Vaquero Serrano, *Garcilaso: Poeta del amor, caballero de la guerra* (Madrid: Espasa Calpe, 2002).

References:

Margot Arce de Vázquez, *Garcilaso de la Vega: Contribución al estudio de la lírica española del siglo XVI,* fourth edition (Rio Piedras: Editorial Universitaria, Universidad de Puerto Rico, 1975);

Bryant Creel, *The Voice of the Phoenix: Metaphors of Death and Rebirth in Classics of the Iberian Renaissance* (Tempe: Arizona Center for Medieval and Renaissance Studies, 2004), pp. 1–174;

Anne J. Cruz, *Imitación y transformación: El petrarquismo en la poesía de Boscán y Garcilaso de la Vega* (Amsterdam & Philadelphia: Benjamins, 1988);

David H. Darst, "Garcilaso's Love for Isabel Freyre: The Creation of a Myth," *Journal of Hispanic Philology,* 3 (1979): 261–268;

Antonio Gargano, *Fonti, miti, topoi: Cinque saggi su Garcilaso* (Naples: Liguori, 1988);

Bernard Gicovate, *Garcilaso de la Vega* (Boston: Twayne, 1975);

Frank Goodwyn, "New Light on the Historical Setting of Garcilaso's Poetry," *Hispanic Review,* 46 (1978): 1–22;

Daniel L. Heiple, *Garcilaso de la Vega and the Italian Renaissance* (University Park: Pennsylvania State University Press, 1994);

Rafael Lapesa, *Garcilaso: Estudios completos,* corrected and enlarged edition (Madrid: ISTMO, 1985);

Ignacio Navarrete, *Orphans of Petrarch: Poetry and Theory in the Spanish Renaissance* (Berkeley: University of California Press, 1994), pp. 73–189;

Antonio Prieto, *Garcilaso de la Vega* (Madrid: Sociedad General Española de Librería, 1975);

Elias L. Rivers, *Garcilaso de la Vega: Poems, A Critical Guide* (London: Grant & Cutler, 1980);

Pamela Waley, "Garcilaso's Isabel, and Elena: The Growth of a Legend," *Bulletin of Hispanic Studies,* 56 (1979): 11–15;

Stanislav Zimic, *Las eglogas de Garcilaso de la Vega: Ensayos de interpretación* (Santander: Sociedad Menéndez Pelayo, 1988).

Inca Garcilaso de la Vega

(1539 – 1616)

Pepa Anastasio
Hofstra University

BOOKS: *La Florida del Ynca. Historia del adelantado Hernando de Soto, gobernador y capitán general del reino de la Florida, y de otros heroicos caballeros españoles e indios, escrita por el Inca Garcilasso de la Vega, capitán de Su Majestad, natural de la gran ciudad de Cuzco, cabeza de los reinos y provincias del Perú* (Lisbon: Pedro Crasbeeck, 1605);

Primera parte de los Comentarios reales que tratan del origen de los Yncas, Reyes que fueron del Perú, de su idolatría, leyes, y gobierno en paz y en guerra: de sus vidas y conquistas, y de todo lo que fue de aquel Imperio y su República, antes que los españoles llegaran a él. Escritos por el Ynca Garcilasso de la Vega, natural de Cuzco, y Capitán de su majestad (Lisbon: Pedro Crasbeeck, 1609);

Historia General de Perú. Trata el descubrimiento del, y como los ganaron los españoles. Las guerras civiles que hubo entre Pizarros, y Almagros, sobre la partija de la tierra. Castigo y levantamiento de tiranos: y otros sucessos particulares que en la historia se contienen. Escrita por el Ynca Garcilasso de la Vega, Capitán de su majestad, etc. (Córdoba: Andrés Barrera, 1616).

Modern Editions: *Obras completas del Inca Garcilaso de la Vega,* 4 volumes, edited by P. Carmelo Sáenz de Santa María (Madrid: Atlas, 1960);

El Inca Garcilaso en sus "Comentarios" (Antología vivida), edited by Juan Bautista Avalle-Arce (Madrid: Gredos, 1964);

Comentarios reales de los Incas, edited by Carlos Araníbar (Lima: FCE, 1991);

Diario del Inca Garcilaso, 1562–1616, edited by Francisco Carrillo Espejo (Lima: Horizonte, 1996);

La Florida del Inca (Las Rozas: Dastin, 2002);

Comentarios reales; La Florida del Inca, edited by Mercedes López-Baralt (Madrid: Espasa-Calpe, 2003);

Comentarios reales de los Incas, edited by César Toro Montalvo (Lima: A.F.A., 2004).

Editions in English: *First Part of the Royal Commentaries of the Yncas,* 2 volumes, translated by Clements R. Markham (London: Hakluyt Society, 1869, 1871);

Inca Garcilaso de la Vega (from Enrique Pupo-Walker,
Historia, creación y profecía en los textos
del Inca Garcilaso de la Vega, *1982;*
Thomas Cooper Library, University
of South Carolina)

The Florida of the Inca: A History of Adelantado, Hernando de Soto, Governor and Captain General of the Kingdom of Florida, and of Other Heroic Spanish and Indian Cavaliers, edited and translated by John Grier Varner and Jeannette Johnson Varner (Austin: University of Texas Press, 1951; London: Thomas Nelson, 1951);

Royal Commentaries of the Incas, and General History of Peru, translated by Harold V. Livermore (Austin: University of Texas Press, 1966).

OTHER: León Hebreo, *La traducción de indio de los tres diálogos de amor de León Hebreo hecha de italiano en español por Garcilaso Inca de la Vega natural de la ciudad de Cuzco, cabeza de los reinos y provincias del Perú. Dirigidos a la sacra Católica Real Majestad del Rey don Felipe Nuestro Señor,* translated by Garcilaso (Madrid: Pedro Madrigal, 1590).

Modern Edition: *Diálogos de amor* (Mexico City: Porrúa, 1985).

Inca Garcilaso de la Vega, also known as Garcilaso Inca de la Vega, is recognized as the first native of the Americas, and the first person of Indian descent, to be published and widely read throughout Europe. He was born Gómez Suárez de Figueroa in Cuzco, Peru, in 1539 to the Incan princess Chimpu Ocllo and the Spanish conquistador Sebastián Garcilaso de la Vega. He traveled to Spain at the age of twenty-one, never to return to Peru. At his death in 1616 he had published four works: a translation from Italian into Spanish of León Hebreo's 1502 Neoplatonic treatise *Dialoghi d'amore* (1590, Dialogues on Love), which was influential in the Spanish Renaissance; *La Florida del Ynca. Historia del adelantado Hernando de Soto, gobernador y capitán general del reino de la Florida, y de otros heroicos caballeros españoles e indios, escrita por el Inca Garcilasso de la Vega, capitán de Su Majestad, natural de la gran ciudad de Cuzco, cabeza de los reinos y provincias del Perú* (1605, The Florida of the Inca. History of the Provincial Governor Hernando de Soto, Governor and Captain General of the Kingdom of Florida, and of Other Heroic Spanish and Indian Cavaliers, Written by the Inca Garcilaso de la Vega, His Majesty's Captain, Native of the Great City of Cuzco, Capital of the Kingdoms and Provinces of Peru), an account of Hernando de Soto's expedition into Florida from 1538 to 1544; and the two volumes of *Los comentarios reales* (Royal Commentaries), the main work for which he is recognized in the history of Hispanic writing. *Los comentarios reales* were published in two parts, the first one appeared in Lisbon in 1609 with the title of *Primera parte de los Comentarios reales que tratan del origen de los Yncas, Reyes que fueron del Perú, de su idolatría, leyes, y gobierno en paz y en guerra: de sus vidas y conquistas, y* de todo lo que fue de aquel Imperio y su República, antes que los españoles llegaran a él. Escritos por el Ynca Garcilasso de la Vega, natural de Cuzco, y Capitan de su majestad. (First Part of the Royal Commentaries, Which Deal with the Origin of the Incas, Former Kings of Peru, with Their Idolatry, Laws, and Government in Peace and in War: With Their Lives and Conquest and with Everything Concerning That Empire and Its Public Affairs before the Coming of the Spaniards. Written by the Inca Garcilaso de la Vega, Native of Cuzco and His Majesty's Captain). The second volume was published posthumously in 1616 under the title *Historia general de Perú. Trata el descubrimiento del, y como los ganaron los españoles. Las guerras civiles que hubo entre Pizarros, y Almagros, sobre la partija de la tierra. Castigo y levantamiento de tiranos: y otros sucesos particulares que en la historia se contienen. Escrita por el Ynca Garcilasso de la Vega, Capitán de su majestad, etc.* (General History of Peru, Dealing with Its Discovery, and How the Spaniards Won It. The Civil Wars That Occurred between the Pizarros and the Almagros, over the Division of Land. Punishment and Revolt of Tyrants: and Other Particular Events That Are Contained in the History. Written by the Inca Garcilaso de la Vega, His Majesty's Captain, etc.). The first volume of *Primera parte de los Comentarios reales de los Incas* describes the history and genealogy of the Incas before the arrival of the Spaniards, and the second relates the Spanish conquest and colonization of Peru during the first decades of the 1500s. Prior to the *Primera parte de los Comentarios reales de los Incas,* several Spanish chroniclers, such as Father Blas Valera, Pedro de Cieza, Francisco de Gómara, and Agustín de Azcárate, had already undertaken the task of describing the Spanish conquest and colonization of the New World, and some of them had focused on Peru and the Incan civilization. Although it is not the only chronicle of these events, Garcilaso's work is particularly significant for several reasons. While the previous chroniclers were of Spanish origin, Garcilaso was of mixed lineage. This ancestry, he often claims in his writing, gives him a vantage point over the other historians (whom Garcilaso, nevertheless, often quotes and comments upon). As a result of his heritage his work incorporates indigenous elements into Western discourse, as such transforming the way Europeans conceived of Incan history and culture.

Whereas on many occasions the life of a particular author offers little information relevant to the understanding of his or her works, in the case of Garcilaso an account of both his life and the early years in the Spanish conquest of Peru is necessary in order to comprehend fully the significance of his writings, especially in light of the fact that he did not publish his works until late in his life. Before the arrival of the Spaniards to Cuzco in 1532, the Incan Empire was divided by a civil war between Atahualpa, the illegitimate son of the Inca Huayna Capac, and Huascar, Huayna Capac's legitimate heir. The Spanish conquistador Francisco Pizarro, who had been given permission by King Charles V of Spain to explore and conquer the territories along the South American western coast, became aware of the dispute between the two Incan leaders and arranged to meet Atahualpa in the town of Cajamarca. Even though the encounter was supposed to be friendly, both parties were ready to attack the other, and Atahualpa was taken prisoner by the Spaniards. Although imprisoned, Atahualpa was still able to arrange the death of Huascar, whereupon he was put on trial by the Spaniards for having murdered his brother. Atahualpa was sentenced to death, and with both Incan leaders dead and the native people demoralized by the collapse of their leadership, the Spaniards marched to the town of Cuzco, the administrative capital of the Incan Empire, and in 1533 took the city and established a government based on the Spanish model. Six years later, in a Cuzco dominated by Spanish rule, Gómez Suárez de Figueroa, later known as Inca Garcilaso de la Vega, was born to a father who was captain of Pizarro's army and a mother who was a cousin of both Huascar and Atahualpa.

Most of the information about Garcilaso's life comes directly from his works and his correspondence. Garcilaso's native language was probably Quechua (the language of the Incas), rather than Spanish (which he also learned at an early age), as he asserts in the prologue to his translation of Hebreo's *Diálogos de amor*. From the many personal references he makes throughout his writings, scholars have concluded that his life as a child in Cuzco was not easy.

Garcilaso's education was the result of his belonging to two different cultures. He received formal training from a variety of tutors. One of his last teachers in Cuzco was Juan de Cuellar, a priest of the cathedral of Cuzco, who had established a school for the sons of the prominent citizens of the city, including those of Spanish, mestizo, and indigenous parentage. The acquaintances made by Garcilaso at this school played a major role in his writings, since they were his direct source of information about Peru after he moved to Spain. Apart from his formal education with Spanish tutors in Cuzco, Garcilaso received a less formal training based not so much in books but in the stories he heard both from his mother's relatives and his father's friends. He often uses precisely this firsthand knowledge as an argument against previous chronicles to claim the authenticity and accuracy of his narration of events. In 1559 Garcilaso's father died in Cuzco, having left him the amount of 4,000 pesos so Garcilaso would study in Spain. A year later, at the age of twenty-one, he left to

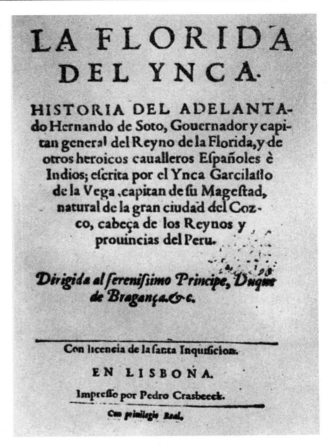

Title page for Garcilaso's first published work (The Florida of the Inca), an account of Hernando de Soto's 1538 New World expedition (from Enrique Pupo-Walker, Historia, creación y profecía en los textos del Inca Garcilaso de la Vega; *Thomas Cooper Library, University of South Carolina)*

pursue his education overseas. After he moved to Spain in 1560, he never again returned to his native Peru.

Other than the biographical information that Garcilaso discloses in a few letters and his work, there are few written documents that present specific information about his life in Spain, the details of which remain mostly a matter of speculation. He is known to have established himself in Montilla, a small town in the southern province of Córdoba, where his father's brother, Alonso de Vargas, was living at the time. As a resident of imperial Spain, Garcilaso was probably confronted with a rigid system of honor that must have created some problems for a person whose social hierarchy and racial profile were not easily defined. Soon after he had arrived in Spain, he went to Madrid to request a reward from the king on behalf of his father's prior services to the Spanish Crown. The Council of Indias, however, ruled against his claims, and Garcilaso decided to go to Seville with the intention of returning to Peru. On 27 June 1563 he applied for the necessary permission for the trip, which never took place because either the permission was denied or Garcilaso reconsidered making the journey. Soon after, on 22 November 1563, there is record that for the first time he signed his name as Garcilaso de la Vega rather than Gómez Suárez de Figueroa. Scholars have suggested that both the impossibility of his going back to Peru and the frustration over his unsuccessful claims in Madrid played an important role in his decision to change his name. Realizing that he would never be able to go back to his native land, Garcilaso must have decided to create a new identity for himself. Convinced that his mestizo origins would never allow him to flourish in a rigid society, he decided to make the most of his intellectual abilities and started to consider a career as a writer, which eventually gained him fame. The possibility of renown might have been one of the reasons behind the choice of the name Garcilaso de la Vega, which had not only been the name of his father and other members of his family but also was the name of the acclaimed poet of the Spanish Renaissance. Garcilaso de la Vega, mestizo from Peru, was thus in the process of creating for himself the identity of a writer. He was not known as the "Inca" until years later.

Garcilaso's first published work was a translation of Hebreo's Neoplatonic dialogues on love, *Dialoghi d'amore,* which was given the Spanish title of *La traducción de indio de los tres diálogos de amor de León Hebreo hecha de italiano en español por Garcilaso Inca de la Vega natural de la ciudad de Cuzco, cabeza de los reinos y provincias del Perú. Dirigidos a la sacra Católica Real Majestad del Rey don Felipe Nuestro Señor* (The Indian's Translation of the Three Dialogues on Love of León Hebreo Done from Italian into Spanish by Garcilaso Inca de la Vega Native of the Great City of Cuzco, Capital of the Kingdoms and Provinces of Peru. Directed to the Sacred Catholic Royal Majesty of King Philip Our Lord). As Garcilaso states in a letter to Maximiliano de Austria, the translation was finished by September 1586, although the work was not published until 1590. In another letter he declares that he started translating for his own entertainment and continued with the task after some friends assured him that the translation would be well received. The *Dialoghi d'amore* was written in Italian around 1502 (and published in 1535) by Judah Abarbanal, better known as León Hebreo (Leon the Hebrew), a Renaissance humanist and Portuguese Jew whose family took refuge in Italy. Hebreo's first dialogue deals with the nature of love, the second with the universality of love, and the final one with its origin. Hebreo's *Dialoghi d'amore* was a popular book, and before the end of the sixteenth century it had gone through ten editions in Italian and had been translated into Latin and into

French. Garcilaso's translation was therefore not the first, but it does seem to be the best in that he succeeded in understanding the spirit of the work he was translating. Some scholars have suggested that Garcilaso identified with Hebreo's experience and philosophy and that he added "Inca" to his name because he was inspired by the example of León "the Hebrew." Having been referred to, often with disdain, as "the Indian," Garcilaso might have decided to accept this adversity and use it as much as possible to his honor and advantage. Whether or not he identified with Hebreo in this way, Hebreo's influence on Garcilaso was profound, and the Neoplatonic view of the universe present in the *Dialoghi d'amore* was influential in all of Garcilaso's subsequent works. The first edition of his translation of the *Dialoghi d'amore* sold out soon after its publication, and before his death Garcilaso applied for permission for a second edition, a plan that was halted by the Inquisition, which included all the editions of Hebreo's work on its *Index Librorum Prohibitorum* (Index of Forbidden Books) of 1612.

Even though the translation of the *Dialoghi d'amore* was Garcilaso's first published work, it was not his first attempt at establishing himself as a writer. On 18 September 1586 he addressed a letter to Maximiliano de Austria, chief abbot of a town near Montilla and member of the royal council of King Philip II, in which he presented him with a draft version of his translation of the *Dialoghi d'amore* in order to ask for his opinion and sponsorship for its publication. Garcilaso closes the letter expressing his hopes that his benefactor would continue to support him with his chronicle of "La Florida," a piece on which he had been working for quite some time before translating the *Dialoghi d'amore.* The work to which he refers is *La Florida del Ynca,* a narrative of the expedition of de Soto, from his departure from Spain in 1538 to the period after his death in 1542. The original draft of *La Florida del Ynca* was completed in 1589, but Garcilaso was not able to arrange for its printing and circulation, in spite of his efforts to procure the sponsorship of the king and become a royal chronicler. Garcilaso found support in Portugal, and *La Florida del Ynca* was published in Lisbon in 1605. This project probably started at least eighteen years before its publication, for in Garcilaso's second letter to Maximiliano, on 12 March 1587, he says that his history of "La Florida" is one-fourth completed and expresses his desire to travel to Las Posadas in order to complete the story. The idea for this work may have occurred to Garcilaso after a meeting with Gonzalo Silvestre, probably before 1570, during Garcilaso's stay in Madrid. Silvestre was a native of Extremadura and was one of many who took part in de Soto's expedition to explore the Florida peninsula. As Garcilaso states in his preface, the story that he narrates is the product of conversations between himself and a friend, whose identity he does not reveal. In the same preface he also maintains that his literary ambition does not soar beyond the point of serving as a scribe for the distinguished hidalgo (gentleman) who is providing him with the accounts.

La Florida del Ynca is divided into six books, one for each year of the expedition. The first book relates the efforts of de Soto to secure permission for his voyage from King Charles V. In the introductory chapters Garcilaso situates the area geographically and reviews other attempts by Ponce de León and Diego Narváez to explore the new land. He then narrates the departure of the expedition and its arrival in Cuba. The second book begins with an account of the arrival of de Soto at the region known today as Tampa Bay and continues with the different expeditions to the regions of Acuera, Ocali, Ochile, and the Apalachee Province. The narrative emphasizes the hardships of this part of the expedition because of the characteristics of the land and the attacks by the native inhabitants. Book 3 relates the march northward from the Apalachee to the region that is now southern Georgia, then toward western South Carolina, and then advancing north and west into Tennessee, and south into Alabama and Mississippi near the end of 1540. Book 4 relates how the search for gold and silver is replaced by the search for salt and describes de Soto's encounter with the Casquin and the Capaha tribes and the arrival of the expedition in Arkansas. The fifth book marks the climax of the work. De Soto, seeing how the hardships of the campaign are weighing on his men both physically and psychologically, is eager to establish a Spanish colony. The party decides to go back to Mississippi, but in June 1542 de Soto falls ill of a fever and appoints Luis de Moscoso Alvarado to succeed him as commander before he dies. The last part of book 5 relates the story of the abandonment of de Soto's project. The expedition party moves westward into unknown land, hoping to meet other Spaniards coming from Mexico, but midway through decides that it would be better to go back to Mississippi. By this time the men are exhausted, and the trip back to the river is much more difficult. Once they arrive, they decide to spend the winter and spring building the boats to take them down the river into the sea. Book 6 recounts the passage of the expedition down the Mississippi, during which there is constant harassment by native attacks, a final battle on the coast, and the party's arrival in Mexico City, where a report to the viceroy is made.

Even though La Florida del Ynca has been considered as a more or less reliable account of de Soto's expedition, it is also read as a work of literature. Critics agree that the work is to a large extent the creation of

the Inca and reflects his tendency toward romance. Others have seen in the work the pervasive influence of novels of chivalry, exemplified by the courtly manners of the natives, the chivalric code of honor observed by some of the chiefs, and the introduction of the sentimental love story of Don Diego Guzmán, who left the expedition to elope with an Indian maiden. La Florida del Ynca is probably Garcilaso's most literary work with respect to the organization of the story (with a beginning, a middle, and an end), the constant shift of the narrative point of view, and the access to the characters' thoughts.

Another interesting aspect of La Florida del Ynca is the purpose that Garcilaso apparently intended for the work. It has been said that one of the main purposes of Garcilaso's work overall and La Florida del Ynca in particular was to educate his contemporaries—the Spanish king, noblemen, lords, the Spaniards in general—with respect to the idea of fundamental equality between the Europeans and the natives of the New World. Insofar as he was aware of the prejudices of the Europeans against the culture and the intelligence of the New World inhabitants, and since he considered himself affected by those prejudices, it became Garcilaso's moral task to provide concrete examples that would include the New World natives within the paradigm of human nature. In his self-assigned role as a historian Garcilaso is trying to propose an exemplary model that promotes equality between the Europeans and the Indians.

When Garcilaso submitted the manuscript for La Florida del Ynca he included the first part of his history of Peru, which became his most famous work. The sponsorship of the Portuguese king granted him the right to add the term comentarios reales (royal commentaries), a right that had previously been denied by the Spanish Crown. The first volume of Los comentarios reales comprises nine books. In the preface to the reader Garcilaso justifies his work as a commentary on previous accounts of the states of the New World carried out by learned Spaniards. He presents his commentary as an extension of and an improvement on such accounts, since, being a native of the New World, he claims to have information that is more accurate. Garcilaso's task in this work is twofold: since the Incan culture had no written document, he wanted to save the legacy of a disappearing civilization and at the same time to correct the existing account of previous, often erroneous accounts written by the Spaniards. One such mistake, he believes, was the conviction that the Incas had a multiplicity of gods. Garcilaso claims that most historians were wrong in that respect because they failed to understand or interpret the Quechua language. Garcilaso is eager to demonstrate that the Incan worship of

HISTORIA
GENERAL DEL
PERV.

TRATA EL DESCVBRIMIENTO DEL,
y como lo ganaron los Españoles. Las guerras ciuiles
que huuo entre Piçarros, y Almagros, sobre la partija
de la tierra. Castigo y leuantamiento de tiranos: y
otros sucessos particulares que en la Historia se contienen.

ESCRITA POR EL YNCA GARCILASO DE
la Vega, Capitan de su Magestad, &c.

DIRIGIDA A LA LIMPISSIMA VIRGEN
Maria Madre de Dios, y Señora nuestra.

Año   1616.

CON PRIVILEGIO REAL.

En Cordoua, Por la viuda de Andres de Barrera

*Title page for the second part of Garcilaso's history of the Spanish
conquest of Peru, which he began in his 1609* Primera parte
de los Comentarios reales que traten del origen de
los Yncas *(First Part of the Royal Commentaries That
Deal with the Origin of the Incas; from Enrique
Pupo-Walker,* Historia, creación y profecía
en los textos del Inca Garcilaso de la
Vega, *1982; Thomas Cooper Library,
University of South Carolina)*

the sun as the one and only god has brought them closer to the Christian concept of God and further away from the multiplicity of gods favored by the pre-Incan culture.

Book 1 of the first part offers, among other things, an introduction to the geographical area of Peru, a review of different theories about the name given to the region, and a brief reflection on what it meant to discover a New World. In this book Garcilaso also writes about the idolatry of the natives and offers various explanations for the creation of the Incan Empire as told to him by his relatives or the common people of Peru. Apart from descriptions of religious ceremonies, there are many other aspects of Incan culture discussed in the work. Most of the second book is dedicated to

Incan accomplishments in different fields: astrology, medicine, geography, mathematics, music, and poetry. More than half of book 4 is dedicated to the life of women in the Incan Empire. In this regard Garcilaso corrects the Spanish chroniclers. It is his understanding that the Spaniards are too ready to interpret what they see or what they hear from the Incas under the light of their own culture and conceptions; Inca Garcilaso, as a member of the Incan community, takes upon himself the task of offering the real significance of the customs. Book 5 describes the system of agriculture, how the Incas dressed, and the Incan system of laws and ordinances. As the work moves on and approaches the arrival of the Spaniards, Garcilaso makes a digression at the end of book 8 to present an inventory of plants and animals present in the territory and the foodstuffs available in the region before the introduction of European products. Book 9 describes the time of Huaina Capac, the rivalry between Huascar and Atahualpa, and the prophecy concerning the arrival of the Spanish.

The first part of the work has been criticized on several fronts, in particular with regard to Garcilaso's sources. Garcilaso claims that his account of both the history and the culture of the Incas is the most authentic and objective because he possesses firsthand information. At the same time, while on many occasions Garcilaso challenges the information given in previous chronicles, he does not hesitate to use these same chronicles as legitimate sources. Moreover, the events that had been related to him by his relatives or by his schoolmates, who were living at a time when the Incan Empire was in decline, may well be the product of the idealization of a glorious past. In any case, even if his commentaries do not present a reliable picture of the Incan culture over the centuries, they do at least compose an invaluable document that describes what the Incas thought of themselves in the 1500s. In this light, Garcilaso is criticized for failing to recognize the existence of native cultures previous to the Incas and for having neglected those aspects of their culture that the Incas might have taken from them. Other critics find in his work an excessively apologetic tone that impelled him constantly to justify and explain his boldness whenever he differed from the most authoritative Spanish historians.

The second part of Garcilaso's *Los comentarios reales,* also a work of considerable length, is divided into eight books. Book 1 presents a brief review of the state of affairs at the end of the first part of his commentaries and a chapter praising the Pizarro family and then moves on to describe the economic situation of the Spanish Crown at the time of the conquest of Peru. After describing Pizarro's earliest explorations and encounters with the Incas, the rest of book 1 focuses on the figure of Atahualpa, his disdain for the Spaniards, his capture, and his execution. Book 2 starts with the arrival of Pedro Alvarado, accompanied by Captain Sebastián de la Vega (Garcilaso's father), to the conquest of Peru, the agreement between Alvarado and Diego de Almagro, and the death of Alvarado.

Book 3 continues with the rivalry between the Spaniards. The younger Almagro kills Pizarro, and Vaca de Castro, who is sent from Spain to investigate the problems in Peru, becomes the governor of Lima, defeats and executes Almagro, and establishes new laws for Peru and Mexico. Book 4 details the arrival of Viceroy Blasco Nuñez Vela, who encounters problems trying to enforce the new laws. Gonzalo Pizarro emerges as the new leader of a rebellion against the viceroy, who is sent to Spain but returns to Peru in order to begin a new war that ends with the death of Nuñez de Vela. Books 5, 6, and 7 narrate additional problems and rebellions confronted by the Spanish government in Peru, and book 8, the last book, depicts the execution of the last native ruler of the Incas, Tupac Amaru, for whom Garcilaso shows great compassion. In general, the second part of the *Comentarios* is more structured than the first, and the chronology is more linear. Garcilaso's sources for this part are varied: the written chronicles, Silvestre's recollections of his time in Peru, Garcilaso's own experience of his early years in Cuzco, and the things he saw and the stories he heard from his father and other Spaniards.

In December 1612, as Garcilaso was making arrangements for his burial in the Cathedral Mosque in Córdoba, he handed the manuscript for the second part of his commentaries to the bishop of Córdoba for his approval before submitting it to the censors of the Inquisition in Madrid, where he also attempted to obtain royal support for his book. The book was not published until a year after Garcilaso's death, however, with a significant difference from the original manuscript. Although he had presented his manuscript as the second part of what he termed *comentarios reales*, the work was published without the term in the title. Scholars have suggested that the Spanish authorities did not want to see that term in the title of Garcilaso's work, perhaps because of the author's mestizo origins. It seems safe to suggest that Garcilaso's ultimate failure to obtain recognition from the Spanish Crown inspired him to address his prologue to mestizos, natives, and Creoles.

Although Inca Garcilaso de la Vega did not receive the attention or respect that he felt he deserved for his accounts of the New World, through his works he has nonetheless achieved his goal of glorifying and preserving his native culture. Because they are instilled with firsthand knowledge and a wealth of information on Peru, the Spanish conquest of that region, and the Incan civilization, Garcilaso's unofficial chronicles and commentaries are now more widely read than many of the other official accounts, if not for their historical value then for the manner by which they preserve the legacy of a disappearing culture that forms part of the foundation of Spanish American society.

References:

José Anadón, ed., *Garcilaso Inca de la Vega: An American Humanist. A Tribute to José Durand* (Notre Dame, Ind.: University of Notre Dame Press, 1998);

Eugenio Asensio, "Dos cartas del Inca Garcilaso," *Nueva Revista de Filología Hispánica,* 7 (1949): 583–593;

Donald G. Castanien, *El Inca Garcilaso de la Vega* (New York: Twayne, 1969);

José Durand, *El Inca Garcilaso, clásico de América* (Mexico City: Secretaría de Educación Pública, 1976);

Aurelio Miró Quesada, *El Inca Garcilaso, y otros estudios garcilasistas* (Madrid: Cultura Hispánica, 1971);

Darío Puccini, "Elementos de narración novelesca en *La Florida* del Inca Garcilaso," *Revista Nacional de Cultura,* 240 (1979): 26–46;

Enrique Pupo-Walker, *Historia, creación y profecía en los textos del Inca Garcilaso de la Vega* (Madrid: Porrúa Turanzas, 1982);

John Grier Varner, *El Inca: The Life and Time of Garcilaso de la Vega* (Austin & London: University of Texas Press, 1968);

Margarita Zamora, *Language, Authority and Indigenous History in the* Comentarios reales de los Incas (Cambridge & New York: Cambridge University Press, 1988).

Alvar Gómez de Ciudad Real
(Alvar Gómez de Guadalajara)
(circa 1488 – 14 July 1538)

Creighton University

BOOKS: *Thalichristia* (Alcalá de Henares, 1522);

Musa Paulina (Alcalá de Henares, 1529);

De Militia Principis Burgundi (Toledo, 1540);

Theológica Descripción de los Misterios Sagrados (Toledo, 1541).

Modern Editions: "Primera parte del triumpho de Amor de m. francisco petrarca traduzido por alvar gómez," in *Cancionero de Juan Fernández de Ixar,* compiled by Juan Fernández de Hijar, edited by José María Azáceta, volume 2 (Madrid: Consejo Superior de Investigaciones Científicas, 1956), pp. 819–862;

"Primera parte del triumpho de Amor de m. francisco petrarca traduzido por alvar gómez," in *El cancionero de Gallardo,* compiled by Bartolomé José Gallardo, edited by Azáceta (Madrid: Consejo Superior de Investigaciones Científicas, 1962), pp. 98–151;

Theológica descripción de los misterios sagrados (Toledo, 1541) (Valencia: Cieza, 1965);

El "Triumpho de Amor" de Petrarca traduzido por Alvar Gómez, edited by Roxana Recio (Barcelona: PPU, 1998).

OTHER: Esteban de Villalobos, *Thesoro de la divina poesía* (Toledo, 1587)—includes satires and verse by Gómez.

In the spirit of the Renaissance, Alvar Gómez de Ciudad Real was a man of both arms and letters. While much of Gómez's life remains a mystery, and he has been underappreciated by modern scholars, his literary career serves as a testimony to the erudition of court intellectuals in Renaissance Spain. While he was an esteemed poet, his fame derives primarily from his work as a translator of Petrarch, which helped to introduce Petrarchan themes into the contemporary Spanish intellectual milieu and, in turn, influenced the literary careers of some of the most renowned Renaissance writers.

Not much is known about the life of Gómez. Based on the date of his death and the indication that he was in his fifties when he died, scholars believe that he was born around 1488, in Guadalajara, although his family was originally from Ciudad Real, the reason for which he is referred to as either Alvar Gómez de Guadalajara or Gómez de Ciudad Real. Critics have at times confused Gómez with Alvar Gómez de Castro, who was from Santa Olalla and from a later time. Alvar Gómez de Ciudad Real was born to Pero Gómez and Catalina Arias, both of whom had close ties to the Spanish monarchy. On his father's side, Gómez's family members had been associated with the kings of Castile since the time of his grandfather, who bore the same name as the writer and was the secretary and accountant to both King Juan II and King Enrique IV during the fifteenth century. On his mother's side, his maternal grandfather, Diego Arias de Ávila, had also been an accountant of Enrique IV. This side of the family was related to the famous fifteenth-century *cancionero* (songbook) poet Rodrigo Cota.

Gómez served King Charles V in Flanders and during this time composed *De Militia Principis Burgundi* (1540, On the Soldiery of the Princes of Burgundy), which was published after his death. Gomez was a soldier who fought in battles in Naples in 1506, Tuscany in 1512, and Pavia in 1525. He was wounded in the last campaign, and from then on he appears to have devoted his time entirely to letters. During the early decades of the sixteenth century he probably participated in the completion of the *Biblia Políglota Complutense* (Polyglot Complutense Bible), a multilingual Bible produced at the Universidad de Alcalá de Henares under the auspices of Cardinal Francisco Jiménez de Cisneros. Gómez is also believed to have attended the crowning of Charles V as Holy Roman Emperor in Bologna in 1530. Gómez was married to Brianda de Mendoza and had at least three children: Pero, Isabel, and María.

At the beginning of the sixteenth century, Gómez entered a debate with respect to the education of young minds, with one side advocating that it should be done through the reading of Christian authors, while the other defended the reading of profane classical authors. Gómez, who enjoyed much prestige, was in favor of the first option and, to support his position, paraphrased David's psalms and St. Paul's epistles. Because of his biblical glosses, Antonio de Nebrija calls Gómez the "Christian Virgil" in the prologue to Gómez's first published work, *Thalichristia* (1522), which comprises 16,400 *hexámetros* (hexameters)—an orthodox Christian text composed in a verse that derives from the Greek and Latin poetic traditions.

Some of Gómez's works were printed after his death through Alejo de Venegas, who was commissioned by Gómez's son, Pero, to examine and publish his writings. Gómez wrote most of his works in Latin, and he acquired a high reputation in his time as a Latin poet. He achieved his greatest renown, however, for a poem in Spanish: "El trihunpho de amor de francisco petrarca traduçido por alvar gomez en guadalajara" (The "Triumph of Love" by Francisco Petrarch Translated by Alvar Gómez in Guadalajara), his translation of one of six triumphs included in Petrarch's fourteenth-century *Trionfo d'amore* (1351–1374, Triumphs of Love). Although several translations of other Italian authors have been attributed to Gómez, there is no evidence to support these attributions. In addition to his translation of Petrarch, Gómez published seven moral satires and some *redondillas* (quatrains) in the anthology *Thesoro de la Divina Poesía* (1587, Treasure of Divine Poetry), which was reprinted at least two times, and three other compositions in *pie quebrado* (short poetic lines) that appear along with his translation of Petrarch in *El cancionero de Gallardo*, a sixteenth-century collection of poems compiled by Bartolomé José Gallardo in the nineteenth century. A few other poems have been attributed to Gómez, in some cases because of the fact that they are inserted into his translation of Petrarch as the text appears on two occasions or in other cases because of the way the works are presented, namely, the fact that they are accompanied by some Italian verses from Petrarch's fourteenth-century *Canzoniere* (Songs), which demonstrates that Gómez knew well Petrarch's work in general. Some of Gómez's letters have also survived, and a few have been published, by Antonio Bonilla in the journal *Revue Hispanique* in 1901.

With respect to the *pie quebrado* poems, Gallardo, in the nineteenth century, calls them "Canción de tormentos" (Song of Torments) because the poet compares his own love torments with those in other creatures; therefore, José María Azáceta considers them to be a single unit, a "love complaint." Francisco Rico,

ALVAR GÓMEZ DE CIUDAD REAL

El "Triumpho de Amor" de Petrarca traduzido por Alvar Gómez

Edición crítica, introducción y notas de
ROXANA RECIO

Prólogo de
VICENÇ BELTRAN

PPU

Barcelona, 1998

Title page of the modern edition of Alvar Gómez de Ciudad Real's best-known work (Triumph of Love), a translation of one of the poems from Francisco Petrarch's fourteenth-century Trionfo d'amore *(Knight Library, University of Oregon)*

reviewing the 1962 edition of *El cancionero de Gallardo* in the *Romanistiches Jahrbuch* for 1964, supported these findings and related these poems with the tradition of authors such as Quirós y Costana.

Nevertheless, during the sixteenth century the most popular work by Gómez was his translation of Petrarch's *Trionfo d'amore*. The translation is the only one of Gómez's works that has been studied by scholars as well as the only one that is available in modern editions. Its popularity can be attested by its presence in three *cancioneros* despite its length, which is close to 1,500 lines, and by its reprint in some *pliegos sueltos* (loose sheets), but mostly by its reprint in several editions of Jorge de Montemayor's *Los siete libros de la Diana* (1558–1559, The Seven Books of Diana), one of the best-selling works of the period. Its influence is even more evident when, a century after its composition, Miguel de Cervantes in *Don Quixote* (1605, 1615) quotes a line from Gómez's translation to show, if ironically, that his hero was following the well-known lines of this poem.

The exact date that Gómez completed his translation of Petrarch's *Trionfo d'amore* is not known, but Rico, in his essay "De Garcilaso y otros petrarquismos" (1978, On Garcilaso and Other Petrarchisms), believes that it was among his early works. While Rico provides no evidence to support his claim, it seems likely for several reasons, including the fact that Gómez wrote his early works while serving as a soldier in Italy and that he devoted the rest of his life to doctrinal works, mostly in Latin. The nature of the project is suitable for a young man who wanted to show his abilities as a poet, and he was likely inspired by the publication in 1512 of the canonical Castilian translation of Petrarch's *Trionfo d'amore,* which enjoyed a high reputation and was reprinted several times. The fact that Gómez's first published work, the *Thalichristia,* was printed in 1522 shows that he combined his activities as a soldier with writing. For that reason, he possibly did likewise during the period from 1506 to 1512, when he was between wars in Naples and Tuscany. In the context of the debate on the education of young people in which Gómez was a part, Petrarch fit perfectly the role of a Christian author because from the fifteenth century on he had been taken as an authority in moral, religious, and historical issues.

Gómez's translation of Petrarch was not published as a separate book until the late twentieth century. Instead, Antonio de Obregón's translation, devoted to all six of Petrarch's triumphs and including the translation of Bernardo Illicino's commentaries, was apparently much better suited as an academic work that would reflect Petrarch's doctrine in the way that it was perceived in his time. Gómez's translation was included in three sixteenth-century *cancioneros: Cancionero de Juan Fernández de Ixar, El cancionero de Gallardo,* and *Cancionero de Lastanosa-Gayangos.*

The *pliego suelto* that bears the title "Triunfo de amor de petrarca sacado y trobado en romance castellano por castillo" (Triumph of Love by Petrarch Rendered in Castilian Romance by Castillo), despite the fact that it credits another translator, is actually a version of the first and third chapters of Gómez's translation and follows the text accompanying the editions of Montemayor's work. The loose attribution to "Castillo," without the full name or any other details, in a marginal and popular form such as the *pliego suelto* does not suggest a serious challenge to Gómez's responsibility for the work. It is impossible to find out who "Castillo"

may have been, although he may have been the person who had the *pliego suelto* edition printed.

Gómez's translation has been generally forgotten since the Renaissance, in part because of the decline in interest in *cancioneros* and *cancionero* poetry. After its initial publication, however, "El trihunpho de amor de francisco petrarca traduçido por alvar gomez en guadalajara" became a successful text. Part of its success derives from the manner by which Gómez in his translation adapts from the Italian original to *cancionero* modes of expression, especially with regard to his depiction of the theme of the youthful soul controlled by love, which was the predominant theme in *cancionero* poetry during the late fifteenth and sixteenth centuries. Although there are also in *cancioneros* satirical, religious, political, moral, and circumstantial compositions, the dominant mode is the love poem. In these love compositions there is always an obstacle between the lover and the loved one, such as rejection by the love object, separation, or the lover himself refusing to pursue his love quest. These obstacles, which are depicted in Petrarch's *Trionfo d'amore,* are related to the courtly-love tradition, according to which the poet presents himself as an unconditional vassal of his lady. Given the centrality of this tradition to *Trionfo d'amore,* it had, not surprisingly, already influenced many fifteenth-century allegories. Spanish authors who embraced this literary conception of love include Íñigo López de Mendoza, Marqués de Santillana; Juan de Flores; and Juan del Encina. Their works anticipated Gómez's translation.

In selecting only one triumph to translate, then, Gómez may have sought to extract from Petrarch's work the closest thing to the popular *cancionero* tradition: its emphasis on love. To accommodate the *cancionero* format he also adapts Petrarch's Italian text to the norms of Castilian poetry by transforming three-line stanzas into octosyllabic stanzas of ten lines and shortening eleven-syllable verses to eight syllables. For a long time critics did not accept Gómez's translation, since the new Italian forms were being embraced by poets such as Garcilaso de la Vega, and use of the eight-syllable verse was considered old-fashioned or thought to reveal a lack of poetic ability. More-recent assessments of the literature of the period, however, advance the notion that there was a confluence of poetic tendencies that continued throughout the sixteenth century and that *cancionero* poetry continued to flourish alongside the new eleven-syllable Italian poems, with most authors employing both forms. Sixteenth-century poetry in Castile thus does not mean necessarily a break with traditional poetry.

"El trihunpho de amor de francisco petrarca traduçido por alvar gomez en guadalajara" played an instrumental role in keeping the late-medieval *cancionero* poetic tradition alive during the sixteenth century as Italianate forms gained in popularity. Moreover, in addition to preserving the octosyllabic verse, he incorporates other late-medieval themes into his treatment of the effects of love in the poet. While Gómez's text follows Petrarch's original stanza by stanza, he makes extensive use of rhetorical figures that are characteristic of *cancionero* love poetry, such as hyperbole, oxymoron, repetition of different forms of the same word, and similes. Gómez also feels free to amplify extensively when dealing with the paradoxical effects of love on the historical characters presented in the work. He departs from the Italian text and uses colloquial language to give more emphasis to themes that are most familiar to the Castilian reader.

Although he underscores some of the negative aspects of love in "El trihunpho de amor de francisco petrarca traduçido por alvar gomez en guadalajara," Gómez's tone is nevertheless a triumphant one insofar as the true lover never regrets his love and always prefers to endure suffering rather than not have loved at all, which is also Petrarch's message. In this regard, while Gómez's translation does not really change Petrarch's ideas, they are given a different expression. Gómez excludes from his translation many of the mythological references that are present in Petrarch's text in deference to the Castilian reader and to adapt it to *cancionero* vocabulary. While Petrarch includes many pagan references in *Trionfo d'amore*, Gómez places more emphasis on the Christian aspects of the poem. This aspect of "El trihunpho de amor de francisco petrarca traduçido por alvar gomez en guadalajara" demonstrates that Gómez was aware that he was writing within a tradition dominated by orthodox Catholic values. Gómez's skill in composing original verses based upon given ideas and adapting them to a new frame is thus similar to the skill he shows in his original poems.

Another important difference between "El trihunpho de amor de francisco petrarca traduçido por alvar gomez en guadalajara" and Petrarch's original is the group of songs inserted into the middle of the translation. The three songs appear in two of the *cancioneros, Cancionero de Juan Fernández de Ixar* and *Cancionero de Lastanosa-Gayangos,* though not in *El cancionero de Gallardo.* As these three love songs have not been found in any other *cancionero,* critics tend to attribute their authorship to Gómez. The first song, "Aunque yo en mis males veo" (Although I See in My Afflictions), is sung by Marcus Aurelius, and the other two, "Salid ya lágrimas mías" (Come out Now, My Tears) and "Pues coraçón no eres mío" (Because, Heart, You Are Not Mine Anymore), are sung consecutively by Achilles. In "Aunque yo en mis males veo," Marcus Aurelius expresses that, in spite of himself, he cannot live without his lady. In "Salid ya lágrimas mías," Achilles declares that he will never be happy again and accepts

Title page for Gómez's work (Theological Description of the Sacred Mysteries), published three years after the author's death in 1538 (from Theológica descripción de los misterios sagrados [Toledo, 1541], 1965; Collection of John Hill, Jean and Alexander Heard Library, Vanderbilt University)

his fate without any hope of being loved, while in "Pues coraçón no eres mío" he confesses that his heart does not belong to him and resigns himself to confront the sorrow caused by love. These three songs help develop the topic of love complaint that is characteristic of "El trihunpho de amor de francisco petrarca traduçido por alvar gomez en guadalajara." Other characteristics of Gómez's translation, such as its accent on pure love or the inclusion of some popular bucolic scenes, make "El trihunpho de amor de francisco petrarca traduçido por alvar gomez en guadalajara" closer to the Neoplatonic current that would be prevalent in the literature of later decades of the sixteenth century. This emphasis on Neoplatonic themes was no doubt the reason for the inclusion of "El trihunpho de amor de francisco petrarca traduçido por alvar gomez en guadalajara" in several editions of Montemayor's *Los siete libros de la Diana.*

The result of all Gómez's alterations is a translation that is much longer than the original. While Petrarch's *Trionfo d'amore* comprises 700 lines, the translation has 1,466. Much of this difference can be attributed to the type of meter selected for the translation, which forces the poet to employ half a stanza (5 lines) for each of Petrarch's tercets. Other alterations are owing to translation techniques during Gómez's time, which evolved during the fifteenth and sixteenth centuries. During the late Middle Ages and early Renaissance, humanist thinkers believed that a word-by-word rendering was the best way to preserve both the message and the style of the authority being translated. These humanists, interested in translations of Latin texts, favored obscure translations that followed the original work closely. This idea began to change during the fifteenth century, however, in the writings of Alfonso de Madrigal, known as "El Tostado" (The Brown One), one of the most esteemed intellectuals of his time. While still paying lip service to word-by-word translation, Madrigal argued that eloquence in the target language was a fundamental criterion to be sought in a translation, and, therefore, the reproduction of the author's eloquence in the original language sometimes needed to be sacrificed for that purpose. Madrigal asserts that a translation is always longer than the original text because, even if one wants to translate word by word, there will be words in the original language with no exact match in the new language, requiring more words to express the same idea. In addition to these linguistic obstacles, another important skill that the translator must have, according to Madrigal, is the lineage of knowledge, that is, expertise in the field and knowledge of how texts are transmitted in different cultures. Madrigal's ideas became accepted norms for translations during the sixteenth century and helped to shape Gómez's version of Petrarch's text. The accepted conventions for translation during Gómez's career permitted him to introduce alterations to the original that made the work more familiar to his readers. The same facet of Gómez's translation, however, was used by later scholars to condemn his version as one that was not literal or complete.

Perhaps the factor that most distinguishes Gómez's work, and that contributed to the immense success of this translation in Europe during the sixteenth century, is his ability to combine narrative and lyrical passages within the same poetic framework. In the centuries that followed, the prejudice against the forms of *cancionero* poetry and against creative translations consigned "El trihunpho de amor de francisco petrarca traduçido por alvar gomez en guadalajara" to oblivion. At the same time, as is demonstrated in sixteenth-century Renaissance Castilian poetry, the Petrarchan

tendencies exhibited by Gómez were eventually embraced. There was no distinction between the Petrarch of *Canzoniere* and that of the *Trionfo d'amore,* as critics have later established; both works were considered part of the same ideological framework and examples of the same poetic fashion. The disregard for this form of development of Petrarchism in Castile gave a partial and limited notion of this movement, as Rico affirms in his "De Garcilaso y otros petrarquismos."

By the time of his death, on 14 July 1538, Alvar Gómez de Ciudad Real had enjoyed an active career in the flourishing culture of the Spanish Renaissance and had acquired esteem as both a poet and a translator and as an expert in Latin, the language of humanism. Nevertheless, aside from Gómez's translation, his other works remain critically unexplored, and the task of discovering his renown during the Renaissance belongs to future scholars who examine his unedited *Thalichristia, Musa Paulina* (1529, The Pauline Muse), and *De Militia Principis Burgundi.* Although "El trihunpho de amor de francisco petrarca traduçido por alvar gomez en guadalajara" overshadows his other compositions and is the only text for which he is known to scholars and readers, Gómez was, like many other intellectual figures of the Spanish Renaissance, a multitalented individual who excelled in more than one language and literary genre.

Letters:

Antonio Bonilla, "Clarorum Hispaniensum Epistolae Inedite," *Revue Hispanique,* 8 (1901): 211–218.

References:

Carlos Alvar, "Alvar Gómez de Guadalajara y la traducción del Triunfo d'amore," in *Medievo y literatura: Actas del V Congreso de la Asociación Hispánica de Literatura Medieval,* edited by Juan Paredes (Granada: Universidad de Granada, 1995), pp. 261–267;

Arturo Farinelli, *Italia e Spagna,* 2 volumes (Torino: Bocca, 1929), I: 65;

Bartolomé José Gallardo, *Ensayo de una biblioteca española de libros raros y curiosos,* volume 1 (Madrid: Gredos, 1968), pp. 618–638;

Juan Catalina García López, *Biblioteca de escritores de la provincia de Guadalajara y bibliografía de la misma hasta el siglo XIX* (Madrid: Sucesores de Rivadeneyra, 1899), pp. 157–166;

Amilcare A. Iannucci and Konrad Eisenbichler, eds., *Petrarch's Triumphs: Allegory and Spectacle* (Ottawa: Dovehouse, 1988), pp. 310–311;

J. M. Laspéras, "La traduction et ses théories en Espagne au XVe et XVIe siècles," *Revue des Littératures Romanes,* 84 (1980): 81–92;

Marcelino Menéndez y Pelayo, *Antología de poetas líricos castellanos,* volume 3 (Madrid: Hernando, 1894), pp. 30–35;

Antonio Prieto, *La poesía española del siglo XVI,* 2 volumes (Madrid: Cátedra, 1984), I: 43;

Roxana Recio, "Alfonso de Madrigal (El Tostado): La traducción como teoría entre lo medieval y lo renacentista," *Corónica,* 19, no. 2 (1991): 112–131;

Recio, "Las canciones intercaladas en la traducción del 'Triunfo de Amor' de Petrarca por Alvar Gómez de Ciudad Real," *Hispanic Journal,* 12, no. 2 (1991): 247–265;

Recio, *Petrarca en la Península Ibérica: El discurso poético en los triunfos* (Barcelona: PPU, 1996);

Recio, *Petrarca y Alvar Gómez: La traducción del "Triunfo de Amor"* (New York: Peter Lang, 1996);

Recio, "La poética petrarquista en los cancioneros: Las composiciones atribuidas a Alvar Gómez," in *"Quién hubiese tal ventura": Medieval Hispanic Studies in Honour of Alan Deyermond,* edited by Andrew M. Beresford (London: Department of Hispanic Stud-ies, Queen Mary and Westfield College, 1997), pp. 309–318;

Francisco Rico, "De Garcilaso y otros petrarquismos," *Revue de Littérature Comparée,* 52 (1978): 325–338;

Rico, "El destierro del verso agudo," in *Homenaje a José Manuel Blecua* (Madrid: Gredos, 1983), pp. 525–551;

Rico, review of *El cancionero de Gallardo,* edited by José María Azáceta, *Romanistiches Jahrbuch,* 15 (1964): 371–376;

Karl Vollmöller, "Der Cancionero Gayangos," *Romanische Studien,* 4 (1879–1880): 197–228.

Papers:

The Biblioteca Nacional in Madrid holds manuscript copies of the three *cancioneros* in which Alvar Gómez de Ciudad Real's translation of Petrarch's *Trionfo d'amore* appears: *El cancionero de Gallardo* (Ms. 3993, fols. 5–16), *Cancionero de Juan Fernández de Ixar* (Ms. 2882, fols. 354–367), and *Cancionero de Lastanosa-Gayangos* (Ms. 17969, fols. 247–296).

Fray Luis de Granada

(1504 – 1588)

Elizabeth Franklin Lewis
Mary Washington College

BOOKS: *Dos meditaciones para antes y después de la sagrada comunión* (Evora, Portugal: Andrés de Burgos, 1554);

Libro de la oración y la meditación (Salamanca: Andrea de Portonaris, 1554; revised, 1566); abridged as *Recopilacion Breue del Libro dela Oracion y Meditacion de L. de Granada, hecha por el mismo autor* (Salamanca: Domingo de Portonaris, 1574); translated by Richard Hopkins as *Of Prayer and Meditation: Wherein Are Conteined Fowertien Devoute Meditations for the Seven Daies of the Weeke, Both for the Morninges and Eueninges: And in Them Is Treyted of the Consideration of the Principall Holie Mysteries of Our Faithe* (Paris: Brumeau, 1582);

Breve tratado de tres principales exercicios (Evora, Portugal: Andrés de Burgos, 1555);

Guía de pecadores, 2 volumes (Lisbon: Ioannes Blavio de Colonia, 1556, 1557; revised edition, Salamanca: Andrea de Portonaris, 1567); translated by Francis Meres as *The Sinners Guyde: A Worke Contayning the Whole Regiment of a Christian Life, Deuided into Two Bookes: Wherein Sinners Are Reclaimed from the By-path of Vice and Destruction, and Brought unto the High-way of Euerlasting Happinesse* (London: Printed by Iames Roberts, 1598);

Manual de diversas oraciones y exercicios espirituales (Lisbon: Ioannes Blavio de Colonia, 1557; revised, 1559);

Compendio de doctrina christiana (Lisbon: Ioannes Blavio de Colonia, 1559);

Treze sermões das tres paschoas do anno e das princhpães festas (Lisbon: Ioannes Blavio de Colonia, 1559);

Tratado de la oración (Lisbon: Ioannes Blavio de Colonia, 1559);

Memorial de lo que debe hacer el cristiano (Lisbon: Ioannes Blavio de Colonia, 1561);

Tratado de algunas muy devotas oraciones para provocar al amor de Dios (Lisbon: Ioannes Blavio de Colonia, 1561);

Vita Christi (Lisbon: Ioannes Blavio de Colonia, 1561);

Concio de officio et moribus episcoporum (Lisbon: Francisco Correa, 1565);

Fray Luis de Granada (from Ramón D. Perés, Historia de la literatura española e hispanoamericana, *1964; Thomas Cooper Library, University of South Carolina)*

Memorial de la vida cristiana, 2 volumes (Lisbon: Francisco Correa, 1565; enlarged edition, Salamanca: Matías Gast, 1574); volume 1 translated by Hopkins as *A Memoriall of a Christian Life: Wherein Are Treated All Such Thinges, as Apperteyne unto a Christian to Doe, from the Beginninge of His Conuersion, until the Ende of His Perfection* (Rouen: George L'oyselet, 1586);

Collectanea moralis philosophiae, 3 volumes (Lisbon: Francisco Correa, 1571);

Primus tomus concionum de tempore (Lisbon: Juan Barrera, 1573);

Segundus tomus concionum de tempore (Lisbon: Juan Barrera, 1574);

Tertius tomus concionum de tempore (Lisbon: Antonio Ribeiro, 1575);

Quinque de poenitentia conciones (Lisbon: Juan Barrera, 1575);

Ecclesiasticae Rhetoricae, sive de ratione concionandi (Lisbon: Antonio Ribeiro, 1576);

Qvartus tomus concionum de tempore (Salamanca: Herederos de M. Gast, 1580);

Conciones de sanctis, 2 volumes (Salamanca: Herederos de M. Gast, 1580);

Index locupletissimus omnium concionum (Salamanca: Herederos de M. Gast, 1581);

Introducción del símbolo de la fe, 4 volumes (Salamanca: Herederos de M. Gast, 1583);

Compendio de la Introducción del símbolo de la fe (Salamanca: Herederos de M. Gast, 1584);

Breve tratado en que se declara de la manera que se podrá proponer la doctrina de nuestra fe y religión cristiana a los nuevos fieles (Salamanca: Herederos de M. Gast, 1584);

Silva locorum qui frequenter in concionibus occurrere solent, 2 volumes (Salamanca: Herederos de M. Gast, 1585);

Doctrina espiritual (Lisbon: Manuel de Lira, 1587);

Vida de P. Maestro Juan de Avila y las partes que ha de tener un predicador del Evangelio (Madrid: Pedro Madrigal, 1588);

Sermón en que se da aviso que en las caídas públicas (Lisbon: Antonio Ribeiro, 1588).

Modern Editions: *Obras,* 14 volumes, edited by Fray Justo Cuervo (Madrid: Fuentenebro, 1906–1908);

Maravilla del mundo, edited, with a prologue, by Pedro Salinas (Mexico City: Séneca, 1940);

Historia de sor María de la Visitación y Sermón de las caídas públicas, edited by Bernardo Velado Graña (Barcelona: J. Flors, 1962);

Obras castellanas completas, 8 volumes, edited by Cristóbal Cuevas (Madrid: Biblioteca Castro, 1994);

Obras completas, 36 volumes to date, edited by Alvaro Huerga (Madrid: Fundación Universitaria Española, 1994–).

Editions in English: *Meditations and Contemplations on the Sacred Passion of Our Lord Jesus Christ and on the Blessed Sacrament: With Instructions on Prayer,* translated by Mary Teresa Austin Carroll (New York: Christian Press Assocation, 1895);

The Sinner's Guide, from the Spanish of the Venerable Father Louis of Granada, revised edition, translated by E. C. McEniry (Columbus, Ohio: Long's College, 1946);

Summa of the Christian Life: Selected Texts from the Writings of Venerable Louis of Granada, O.P., 3 volumes, adapted and translated by Jordan Aumann (Rockford, Ill.: Tan, 1979);

The Sinner's Guide (Rockford, Ill.: Tan, 1985).

OTHER: Diego de Astudillo, *Quaestiones super VIII libros Physicorum, et II De generatione et corruptione,* edited, with a prologue, by Granada (Valladolid: Nicolás Tierry, 1532);

Thomas à Kempis, *Imitación de Cristo,* Spanish translation attributed to Granada (Seville: Juan Cromberger, 1536);

Suma cayetana, edited, with a prologue, by Granada (Lisbon: Ioannes Blavio de Colonia, 1557);

St. John Climacus, *Escala espiritual,* translated by Granada (Lisbon: Ioannes Blavio de Colonia, 1562);

B. de Martyribus, *Stimulus pastorum,* edited by Granada (Lisbon: Francisco Correa, 1565);

Cardinal D. Enrique, *Meditações e homilias,* edited by Granada (Lisbon: Antonio Ribeiro, 1574);

Perla preciosísima, expanded and corrected by Granada (Lisbon: Marcos Borges, 1575);

Martyribus, *Compendium spiritualis doctrinae,* edited, with a prologue, by Granada (Lisbon: Antonio Ribeiro, 1582).

Sixteenth-century Spanish theologian and evangelist Fray Luis de Granada was one of the most popular and well-regarded religious men of his day. A prolific scholar, writer, and preacher, Granada published during his lifetime some forty-five separate texts in three languages (Spanish, Latin, and Portuguese). These texts were original works, editions, and translations of other authors, as well as revisions and additions to his own previously published books. All of his publications are religious in nature, and many of them deal with Granada's special concern with personal spirituality. During his long career as a Dominican priest, Granada proved himself an effective spiritual and political leader. He was a popular preacher, whose renown spread throughout the Iberian Peninsula. He successfully revived ailing convents and helped establish new ones. He was so highly regarded in both religious and political circles that he became a confidant to the kings of Portugal and a liaison between the Portuguese crown and their royal cousins in Spain.

Although admired and influential during his lifetime, in the years since his death Fray Luis de Granada has been largely forgotten and overshadowed by his contemporaries Fray Luis de León, San Juan de la Cruz, and St. Teresa of Ávila. He is now regarded as an example of the importance of Renaissance humanism in sixteenth-century theology. He is also known for his

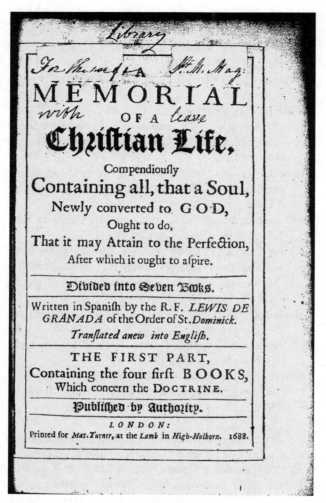

Title page for the English-language edition of Granada's 1565
Memorial de la vida cristiana *(Thomas Cooper Library,*
University of South Carolina)

His mother worked as a washerwoman for the Dominican convent of Santa Cruz in Granada, where her son eventually took his vows as a priest. As a boy he served in the home of the count of Tendilla, where as part of his duties he accompanied the count's children in their studies. Thus, he was exposed to a much better education than was normally afforded a boy of his class. In 1525 Granada took his vows as a Dominican in the convent of Santa Cruz. In 1529 he was chosen by his convent to fill an opening at the Dominican college of San Gregorio in Valladolid. There he studied with some of the most influential and learned theologians of the time, notably Bartolomé Carranza and Melchor Cano, and he was undoubtedly exposed to many of the controversial theological issues of the emerging Spanish Renaissance. At San Gregorio, Granada studied Latin and Greek, ancient philosophy, theology, and the natural sciences through classical authors such as Galen, Pliny, and Ptolemy. In 1532 he demonstrated his talents for scholarship and writing when he published an edition of Diego de Astudillo's *Quaestiones super VIII libros Physicorum, et II De generatione et corruptione* (Questions Concerning the Eight Books of Physics and the Two Books on Generation and Corruption), which was a study of the philosophy of Aristotle. Some modern critics, notably Marcel Bataillon, believe that Granada was also in San Gregorio when he was first exposed to the humanist ideas of Desiderius Erasmus.

The years of study in Valladolid were important to Granada's intellectual formation. The young priest impressed his superiors with his erudition and also with his preaching skills and his ability to work with others. For these reasons he was given the difficult assignment in 1534 of taking over the ailing convent of Escalaceli, near the city of Córdoba. Granada was able to revitalize the convent, its buildings, and grounds and turn it into a vital and active center of religious work. During his time at Escalaceli, Granada's fame as a dynamic orator increased. Alvaro Huerga believes that while at Escalaceli, Granada began work on his *Libro de la oración y la meditación,* which was not to be published until 1554. In 1536, while at Escalaceli, Granada is believed to have published a Spanish translation of *Contemptus Mundi* by Dutch monk and theologian Thomas à Kempis, although this claim has been the subject of debate, since the edition bears no name of the translator. This book, which in Spanish has been translated as *Imitación de Cristo* (Imitation of Christ), presents Christ as a model to the faithful and as an object of prayerful meditation.

After his success at Escalaceli, Granada was sent in 1546 to Badajoz, near the border between Spain and Portugal, to found a new convent. While there he became acquainted with Cardinal Prince Enrique of

close connection and similarity to the Spanish mystics, although his classification as a mystic has been much debated. Of the many texts that Granada left behind, a few stand out for their historical and literary interest: the *Libro de la oración y la meditación* (1554, Book of Prayer and Meditation), *Guía de pecadores* (1556, 1557, Sinner's Guide), and the *Introducción del símbolo de la fe* (1583, Introduction to the Symbol of Faith). All of these works, written in Spanish rather than Latin and directed to a lay audience, demonstrate the humanist's emphasis on the individual, making personal spirituality accessible to the "common" man.

Fray Luis de Granada certainly had common beginnings. He was born Luis de Sarriá to Galician emigrants in the southern Spanish town of Granada in 1504. His parents were commoners, and his father, Francisco de Serriá, died when he was five years old.

Portugal, and in 1551 he moved the short distance across the border to Evora, Portugal, to join his friend at his newly established convent. Granada spent the rest of his life in Portugal, first in Evora and later in Lisbon, although he returned to his native Spain frequently. Granada also became a prominent religious leader in Portugal, where his influence extended from religious matters to politics. In addition to his friendship with the cardinal prince, he was confessor to Portuguese queen Catalina until her death. In 1578, upon the death of his young nephew Sebastian, Cardinal Prince Enrique inherited the Portuguese throne, which created an unusual situation for both Portugal and Spain. Many in Portugal wanted Enrique to renounce his vow of chastity in order to marry and produce an heir, since the king's nephew, Phillip II of Spain, was to be the next king of Portugal if Enrique had no legitimate heir. Granada was caught in the middle of this controversy, and the king of Spain himself sought his support for his bid for Portugal. Yet, despite political pressures from both sides, Granada apparently remained true to his role as a man of God, not a man of politics, and limited his influence on King Enrique, as his confessor, to spiritual matters. Enrique soon died of natural causes, without an heir, and Portugal passed to his nephew Phillip in 1580.

Granada's years in Portugal were his most fruitful, at least in terms of his publications. In 1554 he published his first original works: *Dos meditaciones para antes y después de la sagrada comunión* (Two Meditations for before and after Holy Communion) and *Libro de la oración y la meditación*. These works were followed in 1556 by his *Guía de pecadores*. Both *Libro de la oración y la meditación* and *Guía de pecadores* were placed on the *Index Librorum Prohibitorum* (Index of Prohibited Books) produced by the Inquisition in 1559, for which reason they were revised and republished in 1566 and 1567, respectively. Granada did more than make a few changes to the objectionable elements cited by the Inquisition, however. In both cases he significantly revised and added to each book, amplifying and polishing his ideas.

The *Libro de la oración y la meditación* addresses the question of mental and vocal prayer. Granada advocates mental prayer over vocal prayer, which he finds to be more personal and sincere. The concept of mental prayer was controversial in sixteenth-century Spain. Should a person, especially a person not versed in theology, communicate directly with God, or is the layperson to rely solely on reciting prayers composed for him by the fathers of the church? In his book, Granada clearly shows that he finds mental prayer to be a desirable practice even for the layman, and his book provides instruction in this practice. He explains the purpose and necessary components of prayer and suggests topics for meditation to help a person better communicate with God. He proposes topics for meditation for each day of the week, both morning and night. For example, he instructs the reader on Monday morning to contemplate the Last Supper, including the actual text from the Gospels, followed by some questions for the soul to consider. In the second part of his book Granada also warns of obstacles to the faithful, such as sin, bitterness, worries, and even too much work. He ends his book with a series of sermons arguing the benefits of prayer and meditation and the importance of continuing this practice.

In his next book, *Guía de pecadores,* Granada again aims his teachings at a lay audience, encouraging them to develop the virtues he believes necessary in a faithful Christian. In the prologue he speaks of writing his second book as a response to requests by other priests to help them instruct their congregations. He divides his layman's guide into two parts. The first part, "Primera guía de pecadores" (First Sinner's Guide), begins in a dramatic fashion by warning the reader that his days in this world are numbered and that all will be judged on their good (or bad) works and their faithfulness to God. Granada concludes this part by offering his *Guía de pecadores* to the layperson as a way to turn away from the forces of evil and toward God.

The second part begins with a long list of sins—both mortal and venial—instructing the reader to avoid sin by focusing on Christ. Granada ends this section on a more positive note by listing Christian virtues and how to obtain them. He encourages his reader to take examples from the Bible. The concluding paragraph of *Guía de pecadores* is exemplary of Granada's personal, almost intimate style, which addresses the reader directly in order to encourage him in his faith: "Todo esto sirve para exhortarte a esta noble virtud de fortaleza, para que así seas imitador de aquella santa ánima . . ." (All of this serves to exhort you to follow this noble virtue of fortitude, so that in this way you may be an imitator of that saintly soul . . .). Throughout his life and works, Granada encouraged laymen and -women to develop their own faith and spirituality. His style is simple, direct, and positive. He avoids jargon and heavy or overly negative moralizing and always seeks to provide helpful and practical suggestions for his readers. He has been remembered for this clear and simple prose style, which some feel has been his lasting contribution to Spanish letters.

The first four volumes of Granada's *Introducción del símbolo de la fe* were published in 1583, and a fifth volume, the *Compendio* (Compendium), appeared in 1584. Published when Granada was eighty years old, *Introducción del símbolo de la fe* was his last book and also his longest. It has also been one of his most influential works,

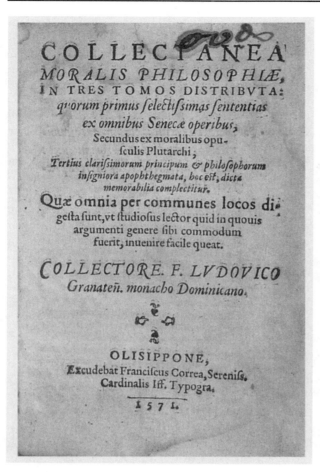

Title page for one of the theological works (Collection of Moral Philosophy) published by Granada during the 1570s (from El siglo de Frai Luis de León: Salamanca y el Renacimiento, 1991; Thomas Cooper Library, University of South Carolina)

inspiring readers far beyond the sixteenth century. The first part, which sings of the "marvels" of nature, combines Granada's scholastic formation with his keen sense of observation of the world around him. Everything in the world, from the earth to the heavens and all the creatures found there, points to the supremacy and goodness of God, says Granada. He sees an orderly and harmonious world, created by God, through which the creator reveals himself. Twentieth-century poet and scholar Pedro Salinas was especially attracted to Granada's uncomplicated understanding of the beauty of nature and to his simple yet poetic prose style in the *Introducción del símbolo de la fe*. Granada seems to depart from his previous work in his last major book, where he becomes more poet than preacher, musing on the glories of creation.

Despite the beauty of this first part, however, it was meant only as an introduction to the rest of the work, which attempts to demonstrate the supremacy of Christianity and explain the mystery of redemption. In the second through fourth parts of the book Granada examines reason and faith. Part 2 compares Christianity to other faiths and philosophies, ending with the stories of faithful and exemplary Christians, accounts of martyrs and miracles that prove the supremacy of Christianity over other religions. Part 3 focuses on the importance of reason in Christianity, explaining the position of the church on the Fall of man and his redemption through the Crucifixion of Christ. This position is, as Granada presents it, both discernable through reason and felt through faith.

Part 4 continues with the same theme, but this time by emphasizing faith over reason. Granada stresses the prophecies of the Old and New Testaments of the Bible, which he maintains reveal God's power. Also in this section, he spends considerable time addressing Jews and the *conversos* (Jewish converts to Christianity). Granada wrote his last book less than one hundred years after the expulsion of the Jews from Spain, which occurred in 1492 after the capture by the Catholic Monarchs of Fray Luis's native city, Granada, and only twelve years before the Dominican priest's own birth. In 1584 Granada was writing this *Introducción del símbolo de la fe* from Portugal, a country to which many of these exiled Jews initially fled. Although he speaks against cruelty to Jews, Granada still attempts through his arguments to inspire a true conversion in those unconverted Jews who might remain in Catholic Spain and Portugal. The final and fifth volume, a compendium, summarizes the arguments in the previous four parts, which enables the final volume to serve as either a shortened version of the longer volumes or as a review of them.

Even after his death in 1588 Granada continued to be revered as an important religious figure. Eighteenth-century prelates saw Granada and other sixteenth-century humanist religious writers as models for their own integration of a "humanistic" approach to spirituality, in contrast to the more ritualistic baroque cult of the seventeenth century. Interest in Granada had been through the years primarily among religious, and especially Dominican, scholars, however, until an author from the Generation of 1898, José Martínez Ruiz (known by his pen name, Azorín), wrote *Los dos Luises y otros ensayos* (The Two Luises and Other Essays) in 1921. In this work Azorín compares Granada with his contemporary León. León, also an important figure in sixteenth-century Spanish humanism, has been more revered and remembered than Granada by literary historians for his profound intellectual writings and especially for his beautiful Renaissance poetry. For Azorín, however, Granada was also admirable, not only for his ideas but also for his simple prose style. Azorín continued to explore Granada's work in another collection of essays, *De Granada a Castelar* (1922, From Granada to Castelar), comparing the Dominican's skill at "forging" prose to that of the old Castilian blacksmiths, who made lovely and delicate shapes out of seemingly unbending iron.

Following Azorín's lead, Generation of 1927 avant-garde poet Salinas also took interest in the prose of Fray Luis de Granada. While in exile after fleeing the aftermath of the Spanish Civil War, Salinas undertook editing the first volume of the *Introducción del símbolo de la fe,* which was published in Mexico as part of a continuing series, *Primavera y flor* (Spring and Flower), begun earlier in Spain. Really a selection from Granada's original, lengthier volume, Salinas called his edition *Maravilla del mundo* (1940, Wonder of the World), a phrase that he took directly from Granada. Salinas, like Azorín before him, was captivated by Granada's simple, yet beautiful prose, and by his keen observation and admiration of the natural world. He compares Granada with other great figures of Spain's Golden Age—notably Cervantes and Velázquez—who are all known and admired for their "realismo descriptivo español" (descriptive Spanish realism). Like these pillars of Spanish culture, Granada too combines realism with artistry: "la realidad temática de la obra se volatiliza al calor poético del estilo y nos deja su esencia poética final. Todo por arte de magia" (the thematic reality of the work vaporizes at the poetic heat of the style and it leaves us its final poetic essence. All by the art of magic). Nonetheless, despite this interest on the part of two important and very influential twentieth-century writers, studies of Granada have paled in comparison to contemporary figures like León or Saint Teresa. Although an influential and popular figure during his day, Granada's lasting significance has been, at least until now, considered to be more religious than literary.

Biographies:

Justo Cuervo, *Biografía de Fr. Luis de Granada, con unos artículos literarios donde se demuestra que el venerable padre y no San Pedro de Alcántara es el verdadero y único autor del Libro de la oración* (Madrid: Librería de Gregorio del Amo, 1895);

Alvaro Huerga, *Fray Luis de Granada: Una vida al servicio de la Iglesia,* Biblioteca de Autores Cristianos, no. 496 (Madrid: Católica, 1988).

References:

Azorín, *De Granada a Castelar* (Madrid: R. Caro Reggio, 1922);

Azorín, *Los dos Luises y otros ensayos* (Buenos Aires: Espasa-Calpe, 1921);

Marcel Bataillon, *Erasmo y España: Estudios sobre la historia espiritual del siglo XVI,* 2 volumes, translated by Antonio Alatorre (Mexico City: Fondo de Cultura Económica, 1950);

Mary Bernarda Brentano, *Nature in the Works of Fray Luis de Granada* (Washington, D.C.: Catholic University of America, 1936);

IV Centenario da morte de Frei Luís de Granada: Actas do colóquio comemorativo (Lisbon: Associação Dos Arqueólogos Portugueses, 1988);

Pedro Laín Entralgo, *La antropología en la obra de Fray Luis de Granada* (Madrid: Consejo Superior de Investigaciones Científicas, 1988);

John A. Moore, *Fray Luis de Granada* (Boston: Twayne, 1977);

Moore, "A Note on Erasmus and Granada," *Romance Notes,* 9, no. 2 (1968): 314–319;

Vicente León Navarro, *Luis de Granada y la tradición erasmista en Valencia (siglo XVIII)* (Alicante: Instituto de Estudios Juan Gil-Albert, 1986);

Ramón D. Perés, *Historia de la literatura española e hispanoamericana* (Barcelona: Sopena, 1964);

Elizabeth Rhodes, "El Libro de la oración de Fray Luis de Granada: Testimonio vivo de la época dorada," in *Fray Luis de Granada: Una visión espiritual y estética de la armonía del universo,* edited by José María Balcells (Barcelona: Anthropos, 1992), pp. 88–98;

Rhodes, "Spain's Misfired Canon: The Case of Fray Luis de Granada's Libro de la oración," *Journal of Hispanic Philology,* 15 (1990): 3–28;

El siglo de Frai Luis de León: Salamanca y el Renacimiento: Colegio del Arzobispo Fonseca, Escueles Menores, Antigua Universidad, Salamanca, octubre-diciembre 1991 (Salamanca & Junta de Castilla y León: Centro Nacional de Exposiciones, Ministerio de Cultura, Dirección General de Bellas Artes y Archivos: Universidad Salamanca, 1991);

Rebecca Switzer, *The Ciceronian Style in Fray Luis de Granada* (New York: Instituto de las Españas en los Estados Unidos, 1927).

Fray Antonio de Guevara

(1480? – 1545)

Emilio Blanco
Universidade da Coruña

BOOKS: *Libro áureo de Marco Aurelio emperador y elocuentísimo orador,* anonymous (Seville: Jacobo Cromberger, 1528); translated by Juan Bourchier, Lord Bernes, as *The Golden Boke of Marcus Aurelius Emperour* (London: Thomas Berthelet, 1534);

Libro llamado Relox de príncipes, en el qual va incorporado el Libro áureo de Marco Aurelio (Valladolid: Nicolás Tierri, 1529); translated by Thomas North as *The Diall of Princes* (London: John Waylande, 1557);

Las obras del illustre señor don Antonio de Guevara obispo de Mondoñedo predicador y chronista y del consejo de su Magestad (Valladolid: Juan de Villaquirán, 1539)—comprises *Una Década de Césares* (translated by Edward Hellowes as *A Chronicle, Conteyning the Liues of Tenne Emperours of Rome: Wherein Are Discouered, Their Beginnings, Proceedings, and Endings, Worthie to Be Read, Marked, and Remembered* [London: Ralphe Newberrie, 1577]); *Aviso de privados y doctrina de cortesanos* (translated as *The Favored Courtier* [London, 1563]); *Menosprecio de corte y alabanza de aldea* (translated by Sir Frances Bryant as *A Dispraise of the Life of a Courtier and a Commendation of the Life of the Labourying Man* [London: Richard Grafton, 1548]); and *Libro de los inventores del arte de marear, y de muchos trabajos que se pasan en las galeras* (translated by Hellowes as *A Book of the Invention to the Art of Navigation, and of the Greate Travelles Whiche They Passe That Saille in Gallies* [London: Ralphe Newberrie, 1578]);

Epístolas familiares (Valladolid: Juan de Villaquirán, 1539); translated by Hellowes as *The Familiar Epistles* (London: Henrie Midleton for Rafe Newbery, 1574);

Segunda parte de las Epístolas familiares (Valladolid: Juan de Villaquirán, 1541);

Libro llamado Oratorio de religiosos y ejercicio de virtuosos (Valladolid: Juan de Villaquirán, 1542);

La primera parte del libro llamado Monte Calvario (Valladolid: Juan de Villaquirán, 1545); translated as *The Mount of Calvarie: Wherein Is Handled All the Mysteries of the Mount of Calvarie, from the Time That Christ*

Fray Antonio de Guevara (from Augustin Redondo, Antonio de Guevara [1480?–1545] et l'Espagne de son temps, *1976; Thomas Cooper Library, University of South Carolina)*

Was Condemned by Pilat, until He Was Put into the Sepulcher, by Joseph and Nichodemus (London: Printed by A. Islip for E. White, 1595);

Menosprecio de corte y alabanza de aldea (Amberes: Martín Nucio, 1546);

La segunda parte del libro llamado Monte Calvario (Valladolid: Sebastián Martínez, 1549); translated as *Mount Calvarie, the Second Part* (London: Printed by A. Islip for E. White, 1597).

Modern Editions: *Prosa escogida,* edited by Martín de Riquer (Barcelona: Miracle, 1943);

Oratorio de religiosos y ejercicio de virtuosos, in *Místicos franciscanos españoles,* volume 2, edited by Juan Bautista Gomis (Madrid: Biblioteca de Autores Cristianos, 1948), pp. 445–760;

Epístolas familiares, edited by José María de Cossío, 2 volumes (Madrid: Aldus, 1950, 1952);

Una Década de Césares, edited by Joseph R. Jones (Chapel Hill: University of North Carolina Press, 1966);

Arte de marear, edited by R. O. Jones (Exeter: University of Exeter, 1972);

Menosprecio de corte y alabanza de aldea. Arte de marear, edited by Asunción Rallo Gruss (Madrid: Cátedra, 1984);

Relox de príncipes, edited by Emilio Blanco (Madrid: Turner, 1994);

Obras completas, 2 volumes to date, edited by Blanco (Madrid: Castro-Turner, 1994–);

Menosprecio de corte y alabanza de aldea, facsimile edition (Santander: Universidad de Cantabria, 1998).

Fray Antonio de Guevara is one of the major prose writers of the first half of the sixteenth century in Spain. In the spirit of the Renaissance, Guevara is the first Spanish author who achieved a classic kind of prose that could be compared with the literature in the ancient world, as Fray Luis de León did during the second half of the century with greater popular success. Guevara's literary style and his peculiar way of re-creating the lives of Greeks and Romans—which often led him to distort or even make up the classic (and contemporary) sources of which he made use—have lessened to a great extent the reputation he had during the sixteenth century. Although in modern times Guevara has not been much studied or read, during his own time, that is, during the Golden Age of Spanish letters, he was one of the most-read prose writers. He was admired by his contemporaneous courtiers, envied (and also silenced) by his humanist colleagues, and imitated and copied by many later authors. His works, which have been translated into many languages (including Latin, the language of culture during the Renaissance, and even into Armenian), have been published in more than six hundred editions and translations. It has been said that, in his time, he was as frequently read as the Bible.

There is little information available on Guevara's life. His exact birthplace is unknown, although he was probably born around 1480 in the Cantabrian village of Treceño to a *converso* family, that is, a family with a Jewish ancestry. Guevara spent his first years there, where he may have learned to read with the local priest, as some of his biographers mention. During the early 1490s, probably in 1492, he left his home village in order to go to the royal court, where he stayed until the mid 1510s. During this time the Guevara family benefited from having supported Philip the Fair, the father of King Charles V. Philip's premature death in 1506 diminished the standing of the Guevara family at the royal court, however. After his possibilities for advancement at the court diminished, and since he did not like the insecurity of voyages across the sea, Guevara chose to enter the church.

Near the end of 1506, or at the beginning of 1507 at the latest, Guevara joined the Franciscan Order. Many theories have been advanced to explain his choice of the Franciscan Order, including a special attraction for its spirituality, familial links with the order, a wish to stand out in literature, and Guevara's *converso* lineage, although none of them seems decisive. Around 1513 or 1514 he must have taken holy orders, and nothing more about him is known, including where he was educated, until 1523. This gap could be important, because information about it might enlighten, at least partially, some of the most controversial facets in his works. During this period the only thing that can be said about Guevara with relative certainty is that his command of the art of preaching must have been noticed by Holy Roman Emperor Charles V, who summoned him in 1521 to serve as preacher in the royal chapel, a post that Guevara began to occupy in 1523.

At this time Guevara began a double career at the royal court, as preacher and representative of the crown. In 1525 he was sent to Valencia as a commissioner of the Inquisition in order to take part in the conversion of the Islamic population, an evangelist mission that he also undertook in 1526 in Granada. Perhaps as a reward for his efforts, Charles V appointed him royal chronicler. For a long time Guevara was thought not to have written even a single line of the chronicle he had been asked for, although Guevara himself insisted on the fact that he wrote it. Modern investigations have Around that time—if what Guevara says may be believed—Charles V borrowed from the author a manuscript of his still-unfinished *Libro áureo de Marco Aurelio emperador y elocuentísimo orador* (1528; translated as *The Golden Boke of Marcus Aurelius Emperour,* 1534) so that he might be entertained while recovering from a bad fever. *Libro áureo de Marco Aurelio emperador y elocuentísimo orador* is presented as a translation (although it is not) and is divided into two clearly differentiated parts: a biography told in novel form about the Roman leader Marcus Aurelius, and an appendix with nineteen letters addressed by Aurelius to various correspondents. According to Guevara, the manuscript was stolen from the royal chamber, copied on several occasions, and finally published in 1528 in Seville anonymously without his authorization. Soon after its initial printing, *Libro áureo de Marco Aurelio emperador y elocuentísimo orador* became one of the most successful works in Europe, and several additional editions were published.

In the summer of 1527 Guevara was chosen to attend a conference in Valladolid at which experts were to share their opinions with regard to a series of proposals on Erasmism. Although Guevara's opinions were not favorable toward Desiderius Erasmus, a position that is understandable in light of Erasmus's criticism of the clergy, his intervention at the conference was moderate in comparison to that of other experts who were present. After returning to the court, where he stayed until 1529, Guevara took time to retire to Valladolid during the last months of 1528 and the beginning of the following year, most likely in order to finish his *Libro llamado Relox de príncipes, en el qual va incorporado el Libro áureo de Marco Aurelio* (1529; translated as *The Diall of Princes,* 1557). This work comprises an enlarged edition of *Libro áureo de Marco Aurelio emperador y elocuentísimo orador* with important differences: what used to be a biography in novel form changes into a treatise on the education of princes; the life of Marcus Aurelius is reorganized into three parts that correspond to the divisions of medieval summae; and the epistles are integrated into the whole narration, which almost disappears to give way to a moral indoctrination. The publication of *Libro llamado Relox de príncipes, en el qual va incorporado el Libro áureo de Marco Aurelio* was a success insofar as six editions were printed during the first four years after its initial printing. The work exerted a significant influence on the trajectory of Guevara's own literary career, during which, in subsequent texts, he employed the same technique of unifying entertainment and moral edification through a particular view of Greek and Roman antiquity.

Near the beginning of 1529 King Charles V selected Guevara for the bishopric of Guadix. Guevara then divided his time between his new pastoral duties and those at the royal court. In 1537 he was appointed bishop of Mondoñedo. Differing opinions exist with regard to why he was appointed to this position. Some scholars believe that the assignment was a punishment to keep Guevara far from the royal court, while others assert that it signified a promotion. In either case, Guevara's position as bishop of Mondoñedo allowed him to serve as the king's counselor after 1529, a post with which he is credited (along with bishop of Mondoñedo, preacher, and chronicler) at the beginning of most of his works. Whether or not he actually served as the king's counselor, which some scholars doubt, his relationship with King Charles V appears to have deteriorated during the 1530s, after which he dedicated his works to other influential individuals such as the king of Portugal or Francisco de los Cobos, King Charles V's chancellor. This tendency is seen, for example, in

Epístolas Familiares (1539; translated as *The Familiar Epistles,* 1574), in which the Spanish monarch is only vaguely mentioned.

After the successes of *Libro áureo de Marco Aurelio emperador y elocuentísimo orador* and *Libro llamado Relox de príncipes, en el qual va incorporado el Libro áureo de Marco Aurelio,* Guevara, surprisingly, did not publish a single book between 1529 and 1539. He was probably working on different projects during those years, because in 1539 he published no less than five books. Four of these works are gathered in a volume with the title *Las obras del illustre señor don Antonio de Guevara obispo de Mondoñedo predicador y chronista y del consejo de su Magestad* (1539, The Works of the Illustrious Mr. Antonio de Guevara Bishop of Modoñedo Preacher and Chronicler and of the Council of His Majesty). The first book in the volume, *Una Década de Césares* (translated as *A Chronicle, Conteyning the Liues of Tenne Emperours of Rome: Wherein Are Discoured, Their Beginnings, Proceedings, and Endings, Worthie to Be Read, Marked, and Remembered*), displays some parallels with his previous two works. Whereas in *Libro áureo de Marco Aurelio emperador y elocuentísimo orador* and *Libro llamado Relox de príncipes, en el qual va incorporado el Libro áureo de Marco Aurelio,* Guevara writes in novel form about Aurelius's life, in *Una Década de Césares* he again follows the historiographic pattern to tell the lives of ten Roman emperors (literally, *década* at that time in Spanish meant "a group of ten"). *Una Década de Césares,* which was popular enough to have five editions, marks the completion of what is known as Guevara's "emperors cycle," and from this point on in the volume his works focus on the court and the life of the courtier. This tendency is exemplified by the next two books included in the volume, *Aviso de privados y doctrina de cortesanos* (translated as *The Favored Courtier,* 1563) and *Menosprecio de corte y alabanza de aldea* (translated as *A Dispraise of the Life of a Courtier and a Commendation of the Life of the Labourying Man,* 1548). These works were not only published together, but they are also intimately related. Both books display an aversion to the royal court, which appears to be more a rhetorical attitude than true sentiment. In *Aviso de privados y doctrina de cortesanos,* which is divided into twenty chapters, Guevara offers some practical pieces of advice to keep the prince's favor and to survive at the court. In *Menosprecio de corte y alabanza de aldea,* which also comprises twenty chapters, a work inspired in the Horatian, Epicurean, and Stoic traditions, Guevara apparently proposes abandoning the court and going to the countryside, but it is not really so, because the good aspects of the countryside are more practical than philosophical. The final book in the volume, *Libro de los inventores del arte de marear, y de muchos trabajos que se pasan en las galeras* (translated as *A Book of the Invention to the Art of Navigation, and of the Greate*

Travelles Whiche They Passe That Saille in Gallies, 1578), includes some pieces of humorous advice concerning voyages across the sea. It is a brief book, and one of Guevara's most humorous, consisting of ten chapters that deal with different aspects of navigation from the passenger's point of view.

During the summer of 1539, Guevara's next work, *Epístolas familiares,* was published in Valladolid. As the title indicates, this work is a compilation of sixty-nine letters, which he usually labels as *letras* (letters) or *razonamientos* (reasonings) rather than *epístolas* (epistles). The letters are addressed either to different people at the court of Charles V or to other individuals who were close to the author. These letters display parallels with those of the great writers of epistles of antiquity, such as Cicero, as well as those of Petrarch and contemporary humanists such as Erasmus. In *Epístolas familiares* Guevara includes humanist debates, sermons, his moral philosophy in his comments on political and ethical issues, and even comments on contemporary topics. These features of *Epístolas familiares,* combined with Guevara's self-confident style, have led several critics to consider these letters as the antecedents to modern essays.

After 1539 Guevara did not feel comfortable in his position as bishop, and he applied in 1540 for a different position in Valladolid, which he did not receive. This disappointment may have changed his character, and perhaps as a result his subsequent works, most of which were written in Mondoñedo, deal with ascetic topics. Such is the case, for example, with *Segunda parte de las Epístolas familiares* (1541, Second Part of Familiar Epistles), in which most of the letters deal with sermons, the presentation of biblical passages, and religious doctrine, although topics related to humanism are still present. In this work Guevara enters a new stage in his literary output, which is normally labeled as the phase of religious works. This phase includes three texts: *Libro llamado Oratorio de religiosos y ejercicio de virtuosos* (1542, Book Called Oratory of the Religious and Exercise of the Virtuous), *La primera parte del libro llamado Monte Calvario* (1545; translated as *The Mount of Calvarie: Wherein Is Handled All the Mysteries of the Mount of Calvarie, from the Time That Christ Was Condemned by Pilat, until He Was Put into the Sepulcher, by Joseph and Nichodemus,* 1595), and *La segunda parte del libro llamado Monte Calvario* (1549; translated as *Mount Calvarie, the Second Part,* 1597). *Libro llamado Oratorio de religiosos y ejercicio de virtuosos* is addressed to the training of religious people as well as to laypeople who want to live decorously. In spite of the topics treated, it includes many adapted subjects from previous books, the same technique that Guevara applies in the other texts that pertain to this phase, which is actually one work divided into two parts: *La primera parte del libro llamado Monte Calvario* and *La segunda*

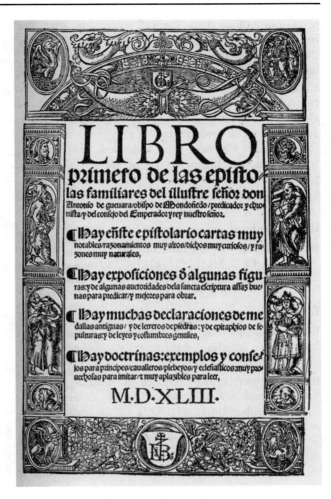

Title page for a 1543 edition of the first volume of Guevara's collected letters, originally published in 1539 (from Epístolas familiares, *volume one, 1950; Thomas Cooper Library, University of South Carolina)*

parte del libro llamado Monte Calvario. The first part deals with the mysteries of Christ's Passion, and the second part concerns the seven words he pronounced on the cross. Both topics were familiar to contemporary readers of ascetic literature.

Fray Antonio de Guevara, who suffered from several illnesses during his lifetime, died on Good Friday in 1545, when he was finishing *La segunda parte del libro llamado Monte Calvario,* which was published posthumously. By the time of his death he had gained international renown, and his books had been published throughout Europe. His linguistic expression reached the epitome of Renaissance style, and his reputation is attested to by the manner in which his work was imitated. Many authors took advantage of the availability of Guevara's works by inserting some of his texts into their own works, something that had occurred since the publication of his first book. During the centuries following his death, however, Guevara's literary style, which seems too elaborate by modern standards, fell out of fashion, and he has become, as the title of Ernest Grey's 1973 study indicates, "a forgotten Renaissance author." At the same time, while his works are no longer as widely read as they were during the Renaissance, Guevara has achieved an enduring renown among scholars for the quality and diversity of his prose, and in particular for his contribution to the birth of the modern essay.

Bibliography:

Emilio Blanco, "Bibliografía de fray Antonio de Guevara, O. F. M. (1480?–1545)," *El Basilisco,* segunda época, 26 (1999): 81–86.

References:

Emilio Blanco, "Las dos redacciones de la vida de Marco Aurelio," *Archivo Ibero-Americano,* 53 (1993): 17–66;

Blanco, "Notas crítico-textuales al *Relox de príncipes,*" *Boletín de la Real Academia Española,* 75 (September–December 1995): 477–522;

Lino G. Canedo, "Las obras de fray Antonio de Guevara," *Archivo Ibero-Americano,* 6 (1946): 441–604;

Pedro Díaz Fernández, ed., *Frai Antonio de Guevara e a cultura do Renacemento en Galicia,* 2 volumes (Lugo, Spain: Servicio Publicacións de la Deputación Provincial, 1993, 1994);

Carlos García Gual, "Ensayando el ensayo. Plutarco como precursor," *Revista de Occidente,* 116 (January 1991): 25–42;

Ernest Grey, *Guevara, a Forgotten Renaissance Author* (The Hague: Nijhoff, 1973);

Francisco Márquez Villanueva, *Menosprecio de corte y alabanza de aldea (Valladolid, 1539) y el tema áulico en la obra de fray Antonio de Guevara,* 2 volumes (Santander: Universidad de Cantabria, 1998);

Asunción Rallo Gruss, *Antonio de Guevara en su contexto renacentista* (Madrid: Cupsa, 1979);

Augustin Redondo, *Antonio de Guevara (1480?–1545) et l'Espagne de son temps: De la carrière officielle aux oeuvres politico-morales* (Geneva: Droz, 1976);

Frida Weber de Kurlat, "El arte de fray Antonio de Guevara en el Menosprecio de corte y alabanza de aldea," in *Studia Iberica: Festschrift für Hans Flasche,* edited by Karl-Hermann Körner and Klaus Rühl (Bern & Munich: Francke, 1973), pp. 669–687.

León Hebreo

(circa 1460 – 1520)

Antonio Cortijo

University of California, Santa Barbara

BOOKS: *Seu orationes, epistolae et epigrammata* (Milan: Signerre, 1496);

Dialoghi d'amore (Rome: Antonio Blado d'Assola, 1535).

Selected Editions: *Dialoghi d'amore composti per Leone Medico, de natione Hebraeo et di poi fatto Christiano* (Venice: Aldo Manuzio, 1541);

Los Diálogos de amor de mestre León Hebreo Abarbanel médico y filósofo excelente (Venice, 1568);

Philographía universal de todo el mundo, de los diálogos de León Hebreo, traducida de italiano en español, corregida y añadida por micer Carlos Montesa (Saragossa: Angelo Tavanno, 1582);

La traduzión del indio de los tres diálogos de amor de León Hebreo hecha de italiano en español por Garcilaso Inca de la Vega, natural de la Ciudad de Cuzco, cabeza de los reinos y provincias del Pirú (Madrid: Pedro Madrigal, 1590).

Modern Editions: *Diálogos de Amor,* edited by Giacinto Manuppella (Lisbon: Instituto de Investigação Científica, 1983);

"Diálogos de Amor" de Leon Hebreo: Traduccion de Garcilaso de la Vega, el Inca, introduction and notes by Miguel de Burgos Nunnez (Seville: Padilla, 1992);

Diálogos de amor, edited by Andrés Soria Olmedo (Madrid: Tecnos/Alianza, 2002).

Edition in English: *The Philosophy of Love,* translated by F. Friedeberg-Seeley and Jean H. Barnes (London: Soncino, 1937).

OTHER: Isaac Abrabanel, *La herencia de los Padres, Haggada, Principio de la fe, Sacrificio de Pascua,* edited by Hebreo (Constantinople: David & Samuel Nahmias, 1505);

Carl Gebhardt, *Dialoghi d'Amore: Hebraeische Gedichte* (Heidelberg: Winters / London: Oxford University Press, 1929).

León or Judas (Yehuda) Abarbanel or Abrabanel, better known as León Hebreo, was one of the outstanding intellectuals of the Spanish Renaissance. Although not much is known about Hebreo's life, his significant contribution to the evolution of Spanish letters and thought, illustrated by the ideas he expresses in the one work for which he is known, is widely recognized by scholars. Hebreo's work represents a synthesis of medieval Jewish rationalism and the Greek philosophical systems of Plato and Aristotle, as well as Muslim, Jewish, and Christian mystical writings. While these influences also shaped the works of Hebreo's contemporaries, what sets Hebreo apart from other Renaissance figures is his concept of the totality of love and its almost pantheistic pervasiveness throughout creation, both in the physical and intellectual spheres.

Hebreo was born in Lisbon sometime around 1460. His father, Isaac Abrabanel, was a famous Jewish scholar and an adviser to the king of Portugal for the Castilian army during the war of Granada. In 1483 Yehuda Abrabanel and his son fled from Portugal to Toledo, Spain, because of accusations that Yehuda had conspired against the monarchy. After the expulsion of the Jews from Spain in 1492, Hebreo's family moved to Italy. In Italy, Hebreo lived in Naples, Barletta, Venice, and probably Florence, where he worked as a doctor and undoubtedly came into contact with Italian Renaissance culture.

During the early 1500s Hebreo composed his most famous work, *Dialoghi d'amore* (1535, Dialogues on Love). Much has been written about Hebreo's reliance in this work upon the philosophy of the Florence Academy, in particular upon the works by Marsilio Ficino and Giovanni Pico della Mirandola. Scholars, such as Carl Gebhardt in an essay accompanying his 1929 German translation of *Dialoghi d'Amore,* have even suggested that Hebreo stayed in Florence and had personal contact with the Italian thinker Pico della Mirandola. There has been a great deal of debate about the original language of the *Dialoghi d'amore.* Although Hebreo's mother tongue was Spanish, some contend that the work was written in Italian, the language in which it was originally published. Others think that it was first

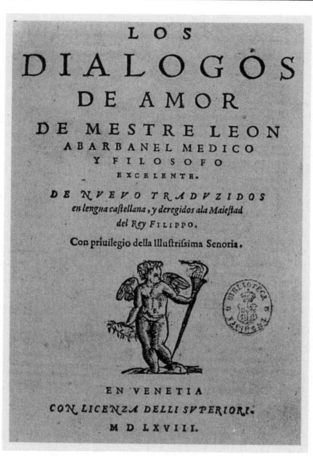

Title page for a 1568 Spanish-language edition of León Hebreo's best-known work (Dialogues on Love), originally published in Italian in 1535 as Dialoghi d'amore *(from Julio Neira, Francisco de Aldana, 1990; Egbert Starr Library, Middlebury College)*

written in Hebrew or *aljamiado,* that is, Spanish in Hebrew characters.

The second and third editions of the *Dialoghi d'amore* (in Italian) were published in Venice by Aldo Manuzio in 1541 and 1545 under the title *Dialoghi d'amore composti per Leone Medico, de natione Hebraeo et di poi fatto Christiano* (Dialogues on Love, Written by Leone, Medical Doctor, Hebrew by Birth, Who Later in Life Converted to Christianity). This title appears to indicate that Hebreo became a *converso* (Jewish convert to Christianity) like many other Jews in fifteenth-century Spain who chose conversion in order to escape mounting persecution. In spite of what the title claims, however, Hebreo apparently never really converted, and the addendum *di poi fatto Christiano* was added to avoid problems with censorship and the Inquisition. In this regard it is also interesting to note that this part of the title did not appear in the fourth and fifth editions of the work. *Dialoghi d'amore* was translated three times into

Spanish during the sixteenth century, first by Rabbi R. Guedalia Ibn Yahia as *Los Diálogos de amor de mestre León Hebreo Abarbanel médico y filósofo excelente* (The Love Dialogues of Master León Hebreo Abarbanel, Excellent Physician and Philosopher), and then by Carlos Montesa, son of Hernando Montesa (who had begun the translation), under the title *Philographía universal de todo el mundo, de los diálogos de León Hebreo, traducida de italiano en español, corregida y añadida por micer Carlos Montesa* (Universal Love-Science, from the Dialogues of León Hebreo, Translated from Italian into Spanish, Corrected and Augmented by Mr. Carlos Montesa). The most famous translation into Spanish is that by Inca Garcilaso de la Vega, *La traduzión del indio de los tres diálogos de amor de León Hebreo hecha de italiano en español por Garcilaso Inca de la Vega, natural de la Ciudad de Cuzco, cabeza de los reinos y provincias del Pirú* (1590, The Translation by the Indian of the Three Love Dialogues by León Hebreo, from Italian into Spanish, by Garcilaso Inca de la Vega, Born in the Great City of Cuzco, Head of the Kingdoms and Provinces of Peru), which was dedicated to Maximiliano de Austria, abbot of Alcalá la Real and member of the council of King Philip II, and to the king himself. The *Dialoghi d'amore* was also translated into Latin and French during the sixteenth century.

Hebreo may have written a second work (as suggested by Gebhardt), *De coeli harmonia* (circa 1500–1510, On Celestial Harmony), which has been lost. It is believed, however, that a summary of this work may be included as part of the second dialogue in *Dialoghi d'amore*. Hebreo was also the editor of his father's works: *La herencia de los Padres* (On Our Father's Inheritance); *Haggada,* a commentary on the Jewish prayer book for Passover; *Principio de la fe* (Principles of Faith); and *Sacrificio de Pascua* (The Sacrifice of Passover), a commentary on the Talmudic work *'Abôt* (Feast of Weeks). These three works were published in 1505 in a single volume in Constantinople and are preceded by some poems written by Hebreo in praise of his father. Hebreo was also the author of some Hebrew poems that have been edited by Gebhardt and published in *Dialoghi d'Amore: Hebraeische Gedichte* (1924, Dialogues on Love: Hebrew Poems).

Hebreo was an outstanding interpreter of Renaissance Neoplatonism. He mixes Platonic ideas on love with other traditions such as Aristotelian realism, Jewish theology, and cabala (Jewish mystical writings). Hebreo has sometimes been confused with medieval thinkers because of his particular conception of the world, which focuses on the idea of hell. Nonetheless, there is an enormous gap between the medieval conception of the world and Hebreo's exaltation of humankind in the vein of Mirandola's praise of human dignity.

For Hebreo, the object of philosophy should be a *philographia* (love science), that is, the description of the universal effects of love, which in fact constitutes a mixture of metaphysics, poetry, science, art, and philosophy. According to this notion, the magnetism of love forms the union of the created world, for love penetrates all the realms of existence, joins them in justice and harmony, and embraces the universe in a totality of both corporeal and incorporeal beings. *Dialoghi d'amore* has been considered a synthesis of philosophical writings deriving from different sources, including the Bible, the Talmud, the Mishná, Aristotle, Averroes, Maimonides, Plotinus, Plato, Hermes Trismegistus, and Pseudo-Dionysius. Many scholars have suggested that Maimonides is particularly important for Hebreo, who follows the former's rationalist and syncretic approach by minimizing the differences between Plato and Aristotle.

The three dialogues that compose the *Dialoghi d'amore* consist of conversations between Filón (the lover) and Sophía, who represents knowledge. The first dialogue deals with love and desire. The second dialogue focuses on the universality of love. According to Hebreo, mundane love is not only common to all things but also necessary, for nobody can be happy without love. The third dialogue analyzes the origin of love. According to Hebreo, love is the principle that dominates all beings, uniting and vivifying reality. Love is the idea of ideas; it has a divine origin. Love is infinite, perfect, and intelligible and represents the final state. Moreover, carnal love, which unites lovers, can be seen as a symbol of spiritual love insofar as lovers become "unum a duobus" (one from two).

Like Aristotle, Hebreo distinguishes three types of love: *delectabilis* (enjoyable), *utilis* (useful), and *honestus* (honest). All of these types assume the existence of the object of desire, for "ninguna cosa se puede amar si primero no existe" (nothing can be loved if it does not exist). *Amor delectabilis* and *amor utilis* exist for the benefit of the body, while *amor honestus* (honest love) exists for the benefit of the soul and the intellect. None of these types of love, however, produces fulfillment in the lover. With regard to the role of wealth, Hebreo states that "las riquezas son instrumento de muchas virtudes morales" (wealth is the instrument through which to attain many moral virtues), although "los bienes útiles nunca hartan a sus poseedores" (useful goods never satisfy their owners). In the same fashion as other authors, Hebreo also includes a psychological characterization of personalities and establishes that seekers of "bona honesta" (honest goods) are known to be happy and rejoicing, while those pursuing "bona utilia" (useful goods) are usually prone to melancholy. An important section of this first dialogue is taken up by the discussion on *honestum* (honesty),

which is defined as "finis hominis" (the goal of man). Hebreo also insists that the love of parents for their children and matrimonial love are composed of *delectabilis, utilis,* and *honestus* love. Several paragraphs on friendship insist on the definition of a true friend as an alter ego, and according to Hebreo, "la buena amistad hace de una persona dos y de dos una" (true friendship makes of one person two and of two people only one). *Amor utilis* is the most perfect of the three types of love and also leads to the most developed form of happiness. This type of love is most perfect when it is the love of God and in God insofar as love is fulfilled in the *bonum* (good) and God is the *bonum honestum* (uttermost goodness).

Hebreo also speaks of the two doctrines that had been used to explain the union between God and his creatures, that is, a union through knowledge (an idea expressed previously by Maimonides and Thomas Aquinas) and a union through love (a concept found in works by Plato, Augustine, and Ficino). Through Sophía, Hebreo asks whether happiness consists of loving God or knowing him. The answer he provides implies both, insofar as happiness is "copulación con Dios" (copulation with God) and involves both an intellectual comprehension and a love experience: "Amamos a Dios con conocimiento y le conocemos con amor" (we love God when we know him and we know him when we love him). The insistence on *beatitudo* (happiness) in this dialogue serves as preparation for the further development of the concept of praise of God in the third part of the work. Throughout this section on *beatitudo* there is a constant echo of the main theme of the Psalms, which is happiness in God's union and glorification.

The second dialogue analyzes the universality of love and draws mainly from Aristotle, Maimonides, and Giovanni Boccaccio. Love binds together heaven and earth as if through a double chain, a chain that expands and contracts itself, a bipolar dynamic that goes from causes to effects and returns from effects to causes. This concept had been expressed during the early thirteenth century by Boncompagno da Signa, in *Rota Veneris* (The Wheel of Love), in which love is defined as a *rota* (wheel) that joins beings and nature together. The main characteristic of this *rota* is its inescapable nature for all beings alike.

Hebreo begins his second dialogue by establishing different types of love among animals and among human beings. He also deals with the reasons for love as established by doctors and astrologers. The former find the origin of love in the conformity of complexions; the latter in the similarity of position of the planets. He then deals with the four elements, the *materia prima* (prime material), generation, and corruption. Hebreo analyzes the basic and inescapable love of the four elements among themselves and indicates that love is more excel-

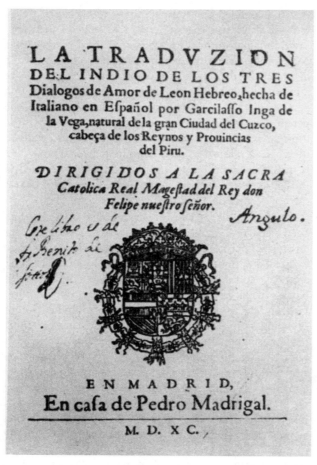

LA TRADVZION
DEL INDIO DE LOS TRES
Dialogos de Amor de Leon Hebreo, hecha de
Italiano en Eſpañol por Garcilaſſo Inga de
la Vega, natural de la gran Ciudad del Cuzco,
cabeça de los Reynos y Prouincias
del Piru.

DIRIGIDOS A LA SACRA
Catolica Real Mageſtad del Rey don
Felipe nueſtro ſeñor.

EN MADRID,
En caſa de Pedro Madrigal.

M. D. X C.

Title page for a Spanish translation of Hebreo's Dialoghi d'amore
*(1590), by the Peruvian-born Inca Garcilaso de la Vega (from
Enrique Pupo-Walker,* Historia, creación y profecía en los
textos del Inca Garcilaso de la Vega, *1982; Thomas
Cooper Library, University of South Carolina)*

lent in the celestial and spiritual bodies than in the inferior ones. For Hebreo, love occupies the totality of
creation in such a way that loving men are able to experience something cosmic within themselves. For this analogy Hebreo utilizes several astrological doctrines known
in the Middle Ages, as well as magical and cabalistic theories.

After a careful revision of the different theories on
the deification of celestial bodies and a review of the symbolic allegories present in Greek mythology, Hebreo
affirms that love, being universal, embraces at the same
time divinity and humankind, human and celestial bodies, and even the *materia prima*. By extension, all of creation is bound in the constantly rotating *rota amoris*
(wheel of love). The strength of this wheel, which is put
in motion by the never-ending circular motion of the
heavens, links all beings to the chain of generation and

corruption. Love engenders with its dynamism a continuous and circular heavenly motion that ties all beings
together. Love is thus the necessary pervasive force of the
universe and its creatures and emanates directly from
God. Further similarities between the concept of the *rota*
and Hebreo's philosophy can be seen in sentences such
as "El amor del hombre es el vínculo del mundo inferior
con la divinidad" (Humankind's love is the chain that
joins together the inferior world with the divinity).
Hebreo reaches this conclusion after having reviewed
several theories by Averroes, Aristotle, and Plato.
Hebreo affirms that "el Amor es causa del ser del
universo" (Love is the reason why the universe exists)
and "no hay ser que no tenga amor" (there is no being
without love). The dialogue ends with an analogy
between love and a magnet, which suggests that there is a
necessary and obligatory attraction among all beings.
Sophía confesses to Philón that she is like Daphnis in
search of her Apollo, a mythological allusion that is commonly employed in works that depict Neoplatonic love.

The third dialogue deals with *amor Dei* (divine love).
For Hebreo, *amor Dei* should not be interpreted as referring to a human being's desire to attain perfection
through the love of God but rather to God's love for Creation. Hebreo begins by analyzing dreams and ecstasis.
Using ideas from Plato, he then deals with the concept of
anima, or soul. He analyzes Plato's ideas, asserting that
"la verdadera luz es la intelectual" (the true light is the
intellectual one), and compares human and divine knowledge. Hebreo also poses five questions on love that can be
read as a summary of the themes discussed in the three
dialogues: Has love been created? When has love been
created? Where has love been engendered? Whence does
love derive? What is the purpose of love? Hebreo's ideas
on love are further revealed in this part of the work in his
definition of love as not different from desire, since it is
"deseo de unión con la cosa amada" (a desire to be joined
to the loved one); his discussion of several terms expressing love in a manner that anticipates subsequent Spanish
authors such as Fray Luis de León; and his summary of
Plato's dialogue *Symposium* and its different characters' definitions of love.

Hebreo conceives of love and divinity as the same
concept, for "todo amado en ser amado participa de la
divinidad" (all loved ones participate in the divinity for
the only reason of their being loved). Since God's love
could not include any imperfection–for God is perfect
and lacks nothing–all things created by God attain their
own perfection through their acts (as humankind can
attain it through virtuous works and knowledge). By
extension, love must include God in order to attain perfection. In this part of *Dialoghi d'amore* Hebreo also reflects
on the ecstatic contemplation of divinity by taking ideas
and images from various mystical traditions (Jewish,

Muslim, and Christian). Hebreo rejects Aristotle's thesis that the world has been created *ab aeterno* (from eternity). He also rejects Plato's concept of chaos as having been created *ab aeterno*. In addition, Hebreo defends both the temporality of creation and of chaos, and drawing from the cabalistic writings, he asserts the principle of the corruption of the inferior world, that is, physical nature and human beings. In contrast to the temporality of worldly things, for Hebreo, God's love is eternal and can be conceived of as God's love for himself as well as for his creations. Divine love is therefore the superior form of love and links humans to God.

When explaining the philosophical view of man as a loving being, Hebreo narrates the myth of Androgynus, according to which man was split in two halves that are condemned to look for each other through their entire lives. Hebreo sees in the myth of Androgynus an allegory of the basic goal of human life, that is, divine contemplation. In this section of the work he also distinguishes three types of human love: *amor intelectualis* (intellectual love), *amor corporalis honestus* (honest carnal love), and *amor corporalis deshonestus* (indecent carnal love). When defining the reasons why the lover longs for a union with the beloved, Hebreo points out that "la unión y fruición de lo hermoso es muy semejante al mismo hermoso" (to unite with the beloved in amorous and joyous union almost equals becoming the beloved himself). He also asserts that procreation, the fruit of an active amorous union, is the desire for immortality.

For Hebreo, the operational principle of knowledge is love. Thus, love and knowledge are united in his philosophy as equivalents of each other: "amare cognoscere est" (loving is knowing). *Cognoscere* (to know) and *apprehendere* (to grasp) imply the concept of *possedere* (to possess), a concept that in turn is implied in amorous desire. In connection with these topics, Hebreo provides a lengthy explanation of the theory of ideas and similarities between Platonic and Aristotelian positions. Having established the agreement between the ideas of Plato and Moses, going so far as to postulate Plato's possible knowledge of the divine Jewish writings, Hebreo develops one of the most memorable metaphors in the *Dialoghi d'amore* when asserting that "la suma sabiduría es nuestra patria, de donde venimos; nuestra felicidad consiste en volver a ella" (knowledge is our true fatherland, whence we come; our happiness consists of returning to this fatherland). Thus, the process of love-knowledge as explained in the Platonic tradition is envisioned by Hebreo as an image of exile derived from Hebrew culture. Hebreo interprets the biblical image of the Babylonian captivity as ignorance and the return to the Promised Land as the process through which the human anima knows and loves his creator. The third dialogue ends by affirming the capability of the human mind and soul to live in a perfect amorous union with the creator.

Hebreo's influence in Europe during the sixteenth century was pervasive. In Italian literature, the impact of the *Dialoghi d'amore* can be seen in such works as Pietro Bembo's *Gli Asolani* (1505, The Asolani) and Baldassare Castiglione's *Il cortegiano* (1528, The Courtier). Moreover, Hebreo influenced a variety of Spanish texts, including poetic and prose works. In Spanish literature and thought, this influence can be seen in *Del amor divino, natural y humano* (On Divine, Natural, and Human Love), by Cristóbal de Acosta; *Tratado de amor en modo platónico* (Treatise on Love in the Platonic Mode), by Francisco de Aldana; and in *Apología en alabanza del amor* (Apology in Praise of Love), by Carlos Montesa. In poetry, Hebreo exerted a strong influence on some of the most renowned writers of the period, including Fray Luis de León. In addition, Hebreo's work had a profound influence on Spanish mystic writers during the sixteenth century, including St. Teresa of Ávila and San Juan de la Cruz, whose central idea was that love is the path to an intimate knowledge of God. Miguel de Cervantes also includes much praise of Hebreo in book 4 of *La Galatea* (1585, Galatea) and pays homage to him as well in the prologue to the first part of *Don Quixote* (1605): "Si tratáredes de amores, con dos onzas que sepáis de la lengua toscana toparéis con León Hebreo, que os hincha las medidas" (If you were to talk about love, just by knowing two ounces of Italian by necessity you will have to stumble upon León Hebreo, who will satisfy you enough).

Inca Garcilaso translated into Spanish the *Dialoghi d'amore,* by far the most widespread and the best of the three Spanish versions of the work. The epilogue of the translation is an index of the most important ideas included in *Dialoghi d'amore* and a summary of the main ideas of the three dialogues. Miguel de Burgos Nunnez, who prepared the edition of Inca Garcilaso's translation for publication in 1992, has noted that Hebreo's work was particularly dear to Inca Garcilaso because "According to Hebreo, love implies a pedagogy of the bonum and the beautiful, that is to say, a pedagogy of civilization; accordingly, to teach this philosophy to the 'hijos del sol' (sons of the god-Sun, to whom Garcilaso's work is tacitly dedicated), that is to say, to the Incas is nothing but a tribute to their civilized culture."

Hebreo's philosophy also influenced the writings of Benedict de Spinoza (also of Spanish-Jewish descent), especially with regard to Spinoza's concept of the soul's love for God. In both authors the soul's intellectual love of God is an *apocatastasis,* that is, the return to God himself of God's love for his creatures. In this context, scholars have found a certain degree of pantheism in Hebreo's theory. Although pantheistic echoes can be perceived throughout the *Dialoghi d'amore,* however, Hebreo never

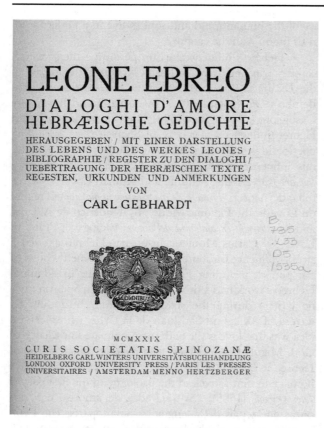

LEONE EBREO
DIALOGHI D'AMORE
HEBRÆISCHE GEDICHTE

HERAUSGEGEBEN / MIT EINER DARSTELLUNG
DES LEBENS UND DES WERKES LEONES /
BIBLIOGRAPHIE / REGISTER ZU DEN DIALOGHI /
UEBERTRAGUNG DER HEBRÆISCHEN TEXTE /
REGESTEN, URKUNDEN UND ANMERKUNGEN
VON
CARL GEBHARDT

MCMXXIX
CURIS SOCIETATIS SPINOZANÆ
HEIDELBERG CARL WINTERS UNIVERSITÄTSBUCHHANDLUNG
LONDON OXFORD UNIVERSITY PRESS / PARIS LES PRESSES
UNIVERSITAIRES / AMSTERDAM MENNO HERTZBERGER

Title page for a German facsimile edition collecting Hebreo's
Dialoghi d'amore, *along with poems he wrote in*
Hebrew (Thomas Cooper Library, University
of South Carolina)

establishes clearly and openly the identity of God and nature, as Spinoza does. José Luis Abellán, in his *Historia crítica del pensamiento español* (1979–1990, Critical History of Spanish Thought), has pointed out that there is a balance in Hebreo's theory between an emanating monism derived from Plato and from Judeo-Christian transcendentalism. Suzanne Damiens, in her *Amour et intelect chez León l'Hebreu* (1971, Love and Intellect in León Hebreo), further distinguishes between Hebreo and Spinoza by defending that in Hebreo there is an independence of the creature from the creator and a constant longing of the creature to secure his or her salvation through an intellectual and amorous effort. This ability of human beings to choose their own destiny, the epitome of human dignity for Renaissance humanists such as Hebreo, occupies a prominent position in *Dialoghi d'amore.*

León Hebreo died in 1520. Although significant aspects of his biography remain a mystery, he has achieved an enduring renown as one of the leading thinkers in Renaissance Spain. His philosophy on love, care-

fully elaborated in *Dialoghi d'amore,* left a significant imprint on the works of subsequent writers. *Dialoghi d'amore,* a compendium of Hebreo's ideas, represents a successful attempt to synthesize several philosophical doctrines dealing with love. Hebreo's work epitomizes Renaissance humanism while preserving God's supreme position in the explanation of the creation of the cosmos, proclaiming and defending human dignity and rationality and seeing man as God's deserving lover. Thus, in spite of the fact that he is for the most part unknown to history, Hebreo's philosophy on love as expressed in his *Dialoghi d'amore* assures his place among the luminaries of the Spanish Renaissance.

References:

José Luis Abellán, *Historia crítica del pensamiento español,* 5 volumes (Madrid: Espasa-Calpe, 1979–1990): III;

José Biedma, "La idea del amor universal en el tiempo de Francisco de los Cobos," *Mágina,* 6 (1996): 8–38;

Suzanne Damiens, *Amour et intelect chez León l'Hebreu* (Toulouse: Privat, 1971);

Sergius Kodera, *Filone und Sofia in Leone Ebreos Dialoghi d'amore: Platonische Liebesphilosophie der Renaissance und Judentum* (Frankfurt am Main & New York: Peter Lang, 1995);

Ulrich Köppen, *Die "Dialoghi d'amore" des Leone Ebreo in ihren französischen Übersetzungen: Buchgeschichte, Übersetzungstheorie und Übersetzungspraxis im 16. Jh.,* Studien zur Literatur- und Sozialgeschichte Spaniens und Lateinamerikas, no. 2 (Bonn: Bouvier, 1979);

Marcelino Menéndez y Pelayo, *Historia de las ideas estéticas en España,* volume 5 (Madrid: Pérez Dubrul, 1883–1891): II;

Julio Neira, *Francisco de Aldana* (Badajoz: Editora Regional de Extremadura, 1990);

Enrique Pupo-Walker, *Historia, creación y profecía en los textos del Inca Garcilaso de la Vega* (Madrid: Porrúa Turanzas, 1982);

Manuel Augusto Rodríguez, *A obra poética de Leão Hebreu* (Coimbra, Portugal: Universidade de Coimbra, Facultad de Letras, 1981);

Isaiah Sonne, *Intorno alla vita di Leone Ebreo,* Quaderni di critica, no. 2 (Florence: Civiltà Moderna, 1934);

Andrés Soria Olmedo, *Los Dialoghi d'amore de León Hebreo: Aspectos literarios y culturales* (Granada: Universidad de Granada, Secretariado de Publicaciones, 1984);

Bernhard Zimmels, *Leo Hebraeus, ein jüdischer Philosoph der Renaissance: Sein Leben, seine Werke und seine Lebren* (Breslau: Koebner, 1886).

Fernando de Herrera
(1534? – 1597)

Louis Imperiale
University of Missouri–Kansas City

BOOKS: *Relacion de la guerra de Chipre y sucesso de la batalla Naual de Lepanto Escrito por Fernando de Herrera, dirigido al ilustrissimo y excelentissimo dõ Alõso Perez de Guzman el Bueno, Duque de Medina Sidonia y Conde de Niebla* (Seville: Printed by Alonso Picardo, 1572)–includes "Cancion en Alabanza de la Diuina Magestad por la vitoria del Señor don Juan";

Algunas obras de Fernando de Herrera al illustriss. S.D. Fernando Enriquez de Ribera Marques de Tarifa (Seville: Printed by Andrea Pescioni, 1582);

Tomás Moro de Fernando de Herrera al ilustrissimo Señor don Rodrigo de Castro Cardenal y Arzobispo de Sevilla (Seville: Printed by Alonso de la Barrera, 1592);

Versos de Fernando de Herrera Emendados y divididos por el en tres libros: A don Gaspar de Guzmán, Conde de Olivares, Gentilhombre de la Cámara del Príncipe nuestro Señor, Alcaide de los Alcazares Reales de Sevilla y Comendador de Bivoras en la Orden de Calatrava (Seville: Printed by Gabriel Ramos Vejarano, 1619);

Rimas de Fernando de Herrera, 2 volumes (Madrid: Imprenta Real, 1786).

Modern Editions: *Poesías*, in *Poetas líricos de los siglos XVI y XVII*, volume 1, edited by Adolfo de Castro (Madrid: Rivadavia, 1854);

Controversia sobre sus anotaciones á las obras de Garcilaso de la Vega: Poesía inédita, edited by José María Asensio (Seville: Geofrin, 1870);

Tomás Moro (Madrid: Sucesores de Rivadeneyra, 1893);

L'hymne sur Lépante, edited by Alfred Morel-Fatio (Paris: Picard, 1893);

Algunas obras de Fernando de Herrera, edited by Adolphe Coster (Paris: Champion, 1908);

Poesías, edited by García de Diego (Madrid: "La Lectura," 1914);

Versos de Fernando de Herrera, edited by Coster (Strasbourg: Heitz & Mündel / New York: Stecher, 1916);

Poesías, edited by García de Diego (Madrid: Espasa-Calpe, 1941);

Fernando de Herrera (from José García López, Historia de la literatura española, *1962; Thomas Cooper Library, University of South Carolina)*

Rimas inéditas, edited by José Manuel Blecua (Madrid: Consejo Superior de Investigaciones Científicas, Instituto Antonio de Nebrija, 1948);

Estudio y edición del Tomás Moro de Fernando de Herrera del Archivo Hispalense, edited by Francisco López Estrada (Seville: Artes Gráficas, 1950);

Poesías, edited by Josep María Espinàs (Madrid: Editorial Barcelona, 1955);

Algunas obras, Sevilla, 1582, edited by Antonio Pérez y Gómez (Cieza, Spain: "La Fonte que Mana y Corre," 1967);

Obra poética, 2 volumes, edited by Blecua (Madrid: Real Academia Española, 1975);

Poesía, edited by Blanca Palacio (Barcelona: Orbis, 1983);

Poesía y poética de Fernando de Herrera, edited by Manuel Angel Vázquez Medel (Madrid: Narcea, 1983);

Poesía, edited by Santiago Fortuño Llorens (Barcelona: Plaza & Janés, 1984);

Poesía castellana original completa, edited by Cristóbal Cuevas García (Madrid: Cátedra, 1985);

Poesía, edited, with introduction and notes, by María Teresa Ruestes (Barcelona: Planeta, 1986);

Fernando de Herrera: Lírica y poética, edited by Ubaldo di Benedetto (Barcelona: Rondas, 1986);

Poesías, edited, with introduction and notes, by Victoriano Roncero López (Madrid: Castalia, 1992);

Algunas obras, edited by Begoña López Bueno (Seville: Fundación Luis Cernuda, 1998);

Anotaciones a la poesía de Garcilaso, edited by Inoria Pepe Sarno and José María Reyes Cano (Madrid: Cátedra, 2001);

Tomás Moro, edited by López Estrada (Seville: Universidad de Sevilla, Secretariado de Publicaciones, 2001).

OTHER: Garcilaso de la Vega, *Obras de Garci Lasso de la Vega con anotaciones de Fernando de Herrera al ilutrissimo i ecelentissimo Señor don Antonio de Guzman, Marques de Ayamonte, Governador del Estado de Milan, i Capitan General de Italia* (Seville: Printed by Alonso de la Barrera, 1580).

Modern Editions: Garcilaso de la Vega, *Las églogas con las anotaciones de Herrera,* annotations by Herrera (Paris & Buenos Aires: Michaud, 1913);

Garcilaso, *Las églogas,* annotations by Herrera (Paris: Bouret, 1939);

Obras de Garcilasso de la Vega con anotaciones de Fernando de Herrera (Madrid: Consejo Superior de Investigaciones Científicas, 1973).

Among the poets most admired by Miguel de Cervantes was Fernando de Herrera, leader of the Seville school and reformer of the Castilian poetic language. It is quite possible that the author of *Don Quixote* (1605, 1615) met him during one of his several trips to the Andalusian capital and that he read Herrera's comments on Garcilaso de la Vega's works. Cervantes knew that Herrera's *Obras de Garci Lasso con anotaciones de Fernando de Herrera al ilustrissimo i ecelentissimo Señor don Antonio de Guzman, Marques de Ayamonte, Governador del Estado de Milan, i Capitan General de Italia* (1580, Works of Garcilaso de la Vega with Comments by Fernando de Herrera to the Most Illustrious and Excellent Don Antonio de Guzman, Marques of

Ayamonte, Governor of the State of Milan, and Captain General of Italy), was not just a mere edition of Garcilaso's poetry but rather an encyclopedia of poetic knowledge, a master course in contemporary poetics, and a digression on a host of topics that the ideal Spanish poet, a man theoretically universal, should master. In his *Viaje al Parnaso* (1614, Journey to Parnassus), Cervantes calls Herrera a *divino espíritu* (divine spirit). He also dedicates to him a moving epitaph, "Soneto a la muerte de Fernando de Herrera" (circa 1597, Sonnet upon the Death of Fernando de Herrera)—published and studied by Adrienne Laskier Martín in her essay "El soneto a la muerte de Fernando de Herrera: Texto y contexto" (1985, The Sonnet on the Death of Fernando de Herrera: Text and Context)—accompanied by a commentary on the love of the Sevillian for Leonor de Gelves. That tribute bears witness to the respect and admiration the author of *Don Quixote* felt toward a man of great artistic sensitivity, vast erudition, and uncommon moral integrity.

Herrera was born in Seville around 1534 to a modest but highly esteemed family. Because of the depiction that Francisco Pacheco offers in his *Libro de descripción de verdaderos retratos de illustres y memorables varones* (1599, Book of the Description of the True Portraits of Illustrious and Memorable Men), it is known that Herrera enjoyed excellent health. Herrera's native city of Seville was, during the poet's lifetime, a point of embarkation for transatlantic voyages and an unrivaled center of world trade. Herrera always lived in Seville and sought refuge from the hustle and bustle of city life in the writing of poetry, composing many ballads, *glosas* (glosses), and *coplas castellanas* (Castilian songs). He is believed to have studied at the school founded in 1551 by Maese Rodrigo de Santaella at the University of Seville, although there is no historical evidence in support of this theory. Herrera was also an avid reader of Italian poetry, the classics, and the Bible, and he translated works by Italian and Latin poets. Of a harsh and recalcitrant disposition, Herrera did not like to ask favors or economic help of any kind and jealously guarded his privacy. Nevertheless, he was subjected to ferocious attacks by the Sevillian intelligentsia, including Rodrigo Caro and Juan Gutiérrez Rufo.

Seeking the solitude and serenity essential for intellectual work, Herrera considered the church the best possible refuge for those who want to enjoy the fullest of freedoms. In 1565 he decided to take minor orders in San Andrés, an out-of-the-way parish, and received a small stipend so that he could devote himself to his bookish pursuits. He turned down a proposal, however, from Rodrigo de Castro, archbishop of Seville, to join his household. Throughout his life he showed a high moral and artistic integrity along with an ill-humored appearance. He respected the honor of others, liked a simple and austere life, jealously defended his independence, did not much care for flattery, and adopted an ascetic attitude with regard to the choice of words and stylistic elaboration in his writings, identifying inspiration with the consciousness of the artist and poetics with poetry. He also had a high regard for historical truth and rejected irony as much as he did mystification.

The poems of Herrera are influenced by the works of illustrious predecessors such as Petrarch, Ausías March, and León Hebreo. Herrera's poetry bears passionate witness to an experience of unrequited love, embodying at the same time the heroic dream of an empire at the point of decline. His eagerness for a linguistic renewal gives his poetry the feeling of participation in a grand project of poetic renovation. In spite of Herrera's isolation, he pays particular attention to contemporary military developments, which he describes in his patriotic *canciones* (songs) by fusing sociopolitical facts, historical developments, religious precepts, a latinizing Castilian, and an absolute conception of beauty without any contact with prosaic reality. In his "Canción al señor don Juan de Austria vencedor de los moriscos en las Alpujarras" (1571, Ode to Don Juan de Austria, Conqueror of the Moors in the Alpujarras) the poet praises the courage and tenacity of King Philip II's brother, who quelled a Muslim revolt between 1568 and 1571; in "Canción por la victoria del Señor Don Juan" (1572, Ode to the Victory of Don Juan) he proudly celebrates the role of the Spanish navy at the victory of Lepanto in 1571; and in "Canción por la pérdida del Rei don Sebastián" (1579, Ode to the Defeat of King Sebastian), Herrera commemorates the death in 1578 of the Portuguese king at the "Battle of the Three Kings" in El Ksar el Kebir, Morocco.

The human and artistic drama of Herrera takes place between poetry and history on the one hand and the remembrance and glorification of Spanish deeds and the voluptuousness of erotic suffering on the other. In Spain, the national pride in imperial power reached its highest point precisely during Herrera's time. Herrera's epic turn is a product of his fondness for national history and his interest in contemporary developments. Rhetorical decorum and Hispanic pride, rather than melodramatic sentimentality, are found in his patriotic verses, which reflect the influence of the solemn tone of the Bible and echo a messianic imperial mission. Herrera was a meticulous poet who subjected many of his works to several revisions. Sometimes the difference between versions

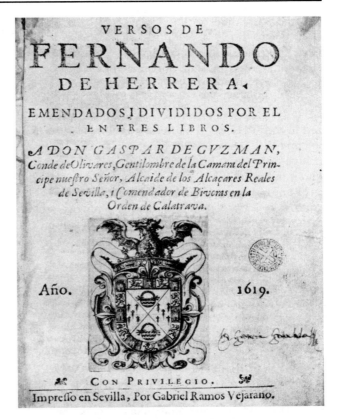

Title page for the first posthumous collection of Herrera's verse (*from* Obra poética, *volume two, edited by José Manuel Blecua, 1975; Thomas Cooper Library, University of South Carolina*)

affected not only the structure of a particular line but also the syntax of the poem.

In the elegy "Canción por la pérdida del Rei don Sebastián" the poet bemoans the death of the young Portuguese sovereign, presenting a glittering, ever-changing world that is far away from the nostalgic simplicity that informs Garcilaso's poetry. This work is one of several poems, including Herrera's sonnets with an urban setting and those that he dedicated to people who more or less embodied the poet's ideals, that may be considered together thematically. Other works in this group are the occasional poems he dedicated to Philip II and to the city of Seville and elegies such as "Tú, que en tierna flor de edad luciente" (You, in the Tender Flower of Your Shining Age), which approximates the lexical paroxysm of the Baroque.

Herrera's love for Leonor de Gelves took the poet from a deep spirituality to a tortured sensuality and made him forget for many years the heroic world of the epic. There are two well-defined periods in his love poetry: the first is that of the "Rimas juveniles" (Youthful Rimes), which are full of ardor and charm, as if the possession of the beloved had been real. In these poems flows a platonic attitude toward love. The poet, transformed by the joyous vision of the beloved, arrives at a state of painlessness and resignation before the unreachable dream. The second period in Herrera's love poetry is represented by the metaphysical ideal of an intellectual love, immortalized in the "Poesías" (Poems), a corpus of poetry that he amplified in successive editions. Herrera's concept of love becomes subtly Petrarchan, and the beloved, who is light, sun, star, and fire, escapes from reality in a continuous stream of ingenious metaphors. These features of Herrera's poem identify him as a pre-Baroque poet who set standards for that whole future school.

Herrera composed poems in which he evokes his platonic love for Doña Leonor de Milán de Córdoba y Aragón, wife of Don Álvaro Colón y Portugal, Count of Gelves. In 1559 Don Álvaro, a Sevillian aristocrat and patron of poets, left the court for the bucolic peace of his Gelves palace. Given his eloquence and vast knowledge, Herrrera was frequently invited to attend the *tertulia* (literary salon) sponsored by the count. Herrera occupied an important place within the literary circle led by the humanist Juan de Mal Lara, and he cultivated many friendships with local poets, men of letters, painters, and artists. In this social milieu Herrera composed his works, which are characterized by the mastery of technique, the love of formal beauty, the faithfulness to classical models, and the purity of poetic language. In Herrera's poetry, the reader senses echoes of Horacian Epicureanism as well as Seneca's Stoicism. Nevertheless, Herrera was never able to attain the sweetness, the subtlety, and the gracefulness of Garcilaso's verse nor the creative emotion found in Luis de Góngora's works.

Herrera came to the realization that a modern sensibility was born in Spain with Garcilaso, as such reflecting a progressive triumph of Italian models as they appear in Baldassare Castiglione, Giovanni Della Casa, and Pietro Bembo. A new lyricism and a new concept of love had been expressed by Garcilaso in Castilian, a poetic language that previously had not differentiated much from the language of day-to-day communication. Herrera, concerned with the parameters of a strictly poetic language in Castilian and sensing the need to define this language with absolute precision as something apart from the language of communication, set himself a goal, the starting point of which was Garcilaso. As an expression of his obsession with reorganizing poetic structures in Spanish, Herrera composed his *Obras de Garci Lasso de la Vega con anotaciones de Fernando de Herrera*.

Herrera considered Garcilaso to have been the author who had succeeded in taking Spanish poetry to its highest level, as Petrarch had done in Italy. For Herrera, Garcilaso had been a poet of vast erudition, whose daring adoption of Italianate forms made him a model for other Spanish poets.

Herrera undertakes two different tasks in his *Obras de Garci Lasso de la Vega:* the first oriented toward aesthetics, and the second consisting of commentaries. Given the process of transmission of Garcilaso's work, and in particular because of the existence of several manuscripts of different origins with controversial interpretations, Herrera realized the need to compare existing texts of Garcilaso's poems, a task that he carries out with the rigor of a scientist and the sensitivity of a poet. What occupies Herrera is the aesthetic value of Garcilaso's poetry: he constructs his own version of the poet's verse without in any way writing a parallel text or one alien to the textual tradition of Garcilaso's production. Following stylistic criteria, his commentaries pay particular attention to the rhythm, the choice and order of words, the general coherence of the poem, and particularly to meter or to purely phonic value. Herrera also deals with the problem of the defense of Spanish not only against Latin, but even vis-à-vis Italian.

With Garcilaso, the classics, and the Italians as his models, in his commentaries Herrera endows the Castilian language with all the riches that humanistic culture could provide. He employs profuse sources having to do with the topics with which he deals—medicine, history, modern inventions, and literary theory. While these sources compose the foundation for his commentaries, Herrera ultimately expresses his own viewpoint, be it in reference to Petrarch or to his Italian followers. He deals with the different poetic genres, an analysis in which the pages devoted to the study of the sonnet overshadow those he dedicates to *canciones* (songs), elegies, eclogues, or epistles. (Herrera's aim of writing an "arte poetica" appears repeatedly in the *Obras de Garci Lasso de la Vega con anotaciones de Fernando de Herrera* without there being any evidence that the project was ever carried out.) As a result of this extended and intellectual exploration, Herrera succeeded in creating a new poetic canon.

Several years before the publication of the *Obras de Garci Lasso de la Vega con anotaciones de Fernando de Herrera,* Garcilaso had already gained renown after the publication of several different editions of his poems. His works were edited by his friend Juan Boscán as an appendage to his own poetry in an edition published in 1543, and the well-known humanist Sánchez de las Brozas (known as El Brocense) published editions of Garcilaso's poetry in 1574 and

1578. The commentaries by El Brocense are similar to those put forth by other humanists and grammarians of the period, whose ultimate objective was to determine the sources for Garcilaso's poems. Herrera's commentaries demonstrate innovative methods of analytical study and pave the way for modern stylistic studies of poetry.

Herrera presents his impressions of Garcilaso's poems in the *Obras de Garci Lasso de la Vega* and transforms Garcilaso into a classic by bestowing upon him the title of foremost representative of the new poetic sensibility originating in Italy known as Petrarchism. Although Herrera's readings of Garcilaso's poems are in some ways similar to those of El Brocense, Herrera constructs his interpretations in order to deal with the problem that truly interests him, that of poetic language. Basing himself in the editio princeps and other manuscripts, Herrera corrected previous printer's errors, fixed the text of Garcilaso's poems, and added many explanatory notes. His goal was to explain how Garcilaso became the writer who had taken Spanish to its highest peak. Herrera's task is similar to that undertaken by Pietro Bembo in regard to Petrarch's poetry. By commenting on Petrarch, Bembo created a poetic language of his own that succeeding poets adopted as a point of departure. Herrera thought it necessary to point out both Garcilaso's successes as well as his mistakes in order to inaugurate a new literary language. He thus felt compelled to study the different genres and poetic forms—particularly, the sonnet—as well as the different stylistic resources and rhetorical devices, lending special attention to phonic elements and to neologisms. This critical apparatus presupposes a poetics whose main tenet is the existence of a new poetic expression. In his readings of Garcilaso's works, Herrera established that a poem does not become a work of art only by means of wit but also by erudition and mastery of the craft. Such an approach makes Herrera a truly modern European poet, as he has been recognized by modern scholars. Elias L. Rivers, in his "Herrera's *Odes*" (1995), considers Herrera's preoccupation with the creation of a poetic language to be the central topic of the *Obras de Garci Lasso de la Vega con anotaciones de Fernando de Herrera* and grounds his argument in Herrera's analyses. In their 2001 edition, *Anotaciones a la poesía de Garcilaso,* Inoria Pepe Sarno and José María Reyes Cano emphasize the importance of Herrera's intervention in fixing the text of Garcilaso's poetic corpus.

In spite of the ardor of his love, which appears clearly in his poems, Herrera was never able to conquer the chastity of his muse, the countess Leonor. Sighs, requests, and plaints had no effect upon her

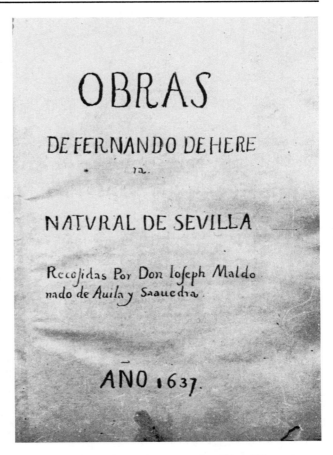

Hand-drawn title page for a manuscript edition of Herrera's collected poetry (from Obra poética, *volume two, edited by José Manuel Blecua, 1975; Thomas Cooper Library, University of South Carolina*)

firmness. Fully conscious of his unhappiness, the poet expresses his unrequited love and bewails Leonor's unwillingness to respond, as he blesses the yoke, both hard and sweet, under which he labors. This silent love—*luz sin luz* (light without light)—of Herrera is the counterpart to Garcilaso's for Isabel Freyre, another woman to whom access was forbidden. The names that Herrera uses to refer to Leonor—Luz, Eliodora, Aglaya, Lumbre, Estrella, Lucero, Sirena, Aurora, Delia, Esperanza, Clearista, Leucotea, and Egle—constitute variations of *luz* (light), which symbolizes the luminous ether that animated the poet during more than twenty years.

As a testimony to the contemporary renown he achieved, Fernando de Herrera earned the name "el Divino" (the divine one) among those who appreciated his mastery of poetic discourse. In addition to Cervantes, Francisco de Quevedo praises the prolific genius of the Andalusian poet, and Lope de Vega esteems Herrera's ability, which he considers to be greater than that of any other poet, to celebrate in

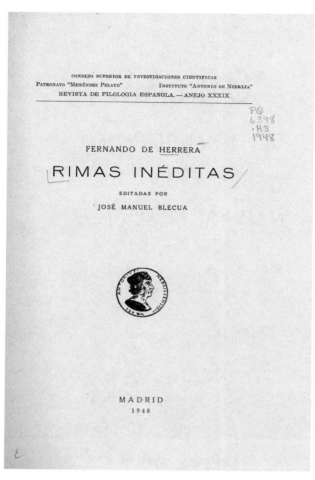

CONSEJO SUPERIOR DE INVESTIGACIONES CIENTIFICAS
PATRONATO "MENÉNDEZ PELAYO"　　　INSTITUTO "ANTONIO DE NEBRIJA"
REVISTA DE FILOLOGIA ESPAÑOLA. — ANEJO XXXIX

FERNANDO DE HERRERA

RIMAS INÉDITAS

EDITADAS POR
JOSÉ MANUEL BLECUA

MADRID
1948

*Title page for a twentieth-century collection of Herrera's
previously unpublished verse (Thomas Cooper Library,
University of South Carolina)*

verse the Spanish naval victory at Lepanto. Modern scholars continue to see Herrera as one of the great linguistic innovators in Castilian. His commentaries on Garcilaso's poems also establish his significance as a scholar of literature who impacted future schools of literary analysis. Herrera remained a productive writer until the end of his lifetime despite losing two of the major influences on his literary career. In 1581 Leonor died, leaving the poet in despair. The following year the count of Gelves died, which deprived the Sevillian poet of the privilege of attending literary meetings at the palace. From that moment on, Herrera dedicated himself to completing an ambitious project: a history of the world up to the death of Charles V. He finished his *Tomás Moro* (Thomas More) and published it two years later. Herrera was still working on poems to be sent to the printer when he died suddenly in 1597, at age sixty-three.

References:

José Almeida, *La crítica literaria de Fernando de Herrera* (Madrid: Gredos, 1976);

Fredo Arias de la Canal, *El protoidioma en la poesia de Fernando de Herrera* (Mexico City: Frente de Afirmación Hispanista, 1997);

Andreina Bianchini, "Fernando de Herrera's *Anotaciones:* A New Look at His Sources and the Significance of His Poetics," *Romanische Forschungen,* 88 (1976): 27–42;

Bianchini, "Herrera: Questions and Contradictions in the Critical Tradition," *Caliope,* 1, nos. 1–2 (1995): 58–71;

Bianchini, "Herrera and Prete Jacopin: The Consequences of the Controversy," *Hispanic Review,* 46 (1978): 221–234;

José María Blecua, "De nuevo sobre los textos poéticos de Herrera," *Boletín de la Real Academia Española,* 38 (1958): 377–408;

José Cebrián, "Cuatro poesías inéditas de Fernando de Herrera," *Bulletin of Hispanic Studies,* 69, no. 3 (July 1992): 263–268;

Gaetano Chiappini, *Fernando de Herrera y la escuela sevillana* (Madrid: Taurus, 1985);

Miguel Cruz Giráldez, "Fernando de Herrera: ¿Poeta épico frustrado?" *Archivo Hispalense,* second series 69 (1986): 7–14;

Ubaldo di Benedetto, "Fernando de Herrera: Fuentes italianas y clásicas de sus principales teorías sobre el lenguaje poético," *Norte: Revista Hispano-Americana,* 394 (November–December 1996): 33–63;

William Ferguson, *La versificación imitativa en Fernando de Herrera* (London: Tamesis, 1981);

Joseph Fucilla, *Estudios sobre el petrarquismo en España* (Madrid: Consejo Superior de Investigaciones Científicas, 1960);

Mario García, *Humanidad y humanismo de Fernando de Herrera, el Divino* (Montevideo: Corporación Gráfica, 1955);

José García López, *Historia de la literatura española,* seventh edition (Barcelona: Vicens-Vives, 1962);

Jorge Guillén, "The Poetical Life of Herrera," *Boston Public Library Quarterly,* 3 (1951): 102;

Rafael Herrera Montero, *La lírica de Horacio en Fernando de Herrera* (Seville: Universidad de Sevilla, 1998);

José María Irizar, "La naturaleza en Herrera," *Revista de Literatura,* 7 (1955): 82–98;

Peter M. Komanecky, "Quevedo's Notes on Herrera: The Involvement of Francisco de la Torre in the Controversy over Gongora," *Bulletin of Hispanic Studies,* 52 (1975): 123–133;

Aron David Kossoff, "Another Herrera Autograph: Two Variant Sonnets," *Hispanic Review,* 33 (1965): 318–325;

Kossoff, "Herrera, editor de un poema," in *Homenaje a Rodríguez-Moñino: Estudios de erudición que le ofrecen sus amigos o discípulos hispanistas norteamericanos* (Madrid: Castalia, 1966);

Kossoff, *Vocabulario de la obra poética de Herrera* (Madrid: Real Academia Española, 1966);

Adrienne Laskier Martín, "El soneto a la muerte de Fernando de Herrera: Texto y contexto," *Anales Cervantinos,* 23 (1985): 213–220;

Fernando Lázaro Carreter, "Dos notas sobre la poética del soneto en los Comentarios de Herrera," *Anales de Literatura Española,* 5 (1980): 315–321;

Begoña López Bueno, *La poética cultista de Herrera a Góngora: Estudios sobre la poesía barroca andaluza* (Seville: Alfar, 1987);

Nadine Ly, "Tradicion, memoria, literalidad: El caso de Gongora," *Bulletin Hispanique,* 97, no. 1 (July–December 1995): 347–359;

Jeremy Medina, "A Note on Theme and Structure in Herrera's 'Cancion a la batalla de Lepanto,'" *Romance Notes,* 13 (1972): 507–510;

José María Micó, "Norma y creatividad en la rima idéntica: A propósito de Herrera," *Bulletin Hispanique,* 86, nos. 3–4 (July–December 1984): 257–308;

Juan Montero, "Castelvetro, Aristóteles y Herrera en la respuesta al Prete Jacopín (y va de plagios)," *Archivo Hispalense,* second series 69 (1986): 15–26;

Montero, *La Controversia sobre las anotaciones herrerianas* (Seville: Ayuntamiento de Seville, 1987);

Montero, "Otro ataque contra las anotaciones herrerianas: La epistola 'A Cristobal de Sayas de Alfaro' de Juan de la Cueva," *Revista de Literatura,* 48, no. 95 (January–June 1986): 19–33;

Bienvenido Morros Mestres, *Las polémicas literarias en la España del siglo XVI: A propósito de Fernando de Herrera y Garcilaso de la Vega* (Barcelona: Quaderns Crema, 1998);

Ignacio Navarrete, "Decentering Garcilaso: Herrera's Attack on the Canon," *PMLA,* 106, no. 1 (January 1991): 21–33;

Emilio Orozco Díaz, "Realidad y espíritu en la lírica de Fernando de Herrera," *Boletín de la Universidad de Granada,* 23 (1951): 3–35;

Francisco Pacheco, *Libro de descripción de verdaderos retratos de illustres y memorables varones* (Seville, 1599);

Ricardo Padrón, "Exile and Empire: The Spaces of the Subject in Fernando de Herrera," *Hispanic Review,* 70 (Autumn 2002): 497–520;

Inoria Pepe Sarno, "Bianco il ghiaccio, non il velo: Ritocchi e metamorfosi in un sonetto di Herrera," *Strumenti Critici,* 15 (October 1981): 458–471;

R. M. Price, "Herrera's Sonnet 'Aquel sagrado ardor que resplandece,'" in *Readings in Spanish and Portuguese Poetry for Geoffrey Connell,* edited by Nicholas G. Round and D. Gareth Walters (Glasgow: University of Glasgow, Department of Hispanic Studies, 1985), pp. 178–189;

Mary Gaylord Randel, *The Historical Prose of Fernando de Herrera* (London: Tamesis, 1971);

Elias L. Rivers, "Herrera's *Odes,*" *Caliope,* 1, nos. 1–2 (1995): 46–57;

Francisco Ródriguez Marín, "El divino Herrera y la condesa de Gelves," in his *Miscelánea de Andalucía* (Madrid: Páez, 1927), pp. 155–202;

María Teresa Ruestes Sisó, *Las églogas de Fernando de Herrera: Fuentes y temas* (Barcelona: Promociones y Publicaciones Universitarias, 1989);

Paul Julian Smith, "The Rhetoric of Presence in Poets and Critics of Golden Age Lyric: Garcilaso, Herrera, Gongora," *Modern Language Notes,* 100, no. 2 (March 1985): 223–246;

Stanko B. Vanich, "Criticos, critiquillos y criticones: Herrera el Sevillano frente a Sevilla," *Papeles de Son Armadans,* 92 (1979): 29–55;

Michael Woods, "Herrera's Voices," in *Mediaeval and Renaissance Studies on Spain and Portugal in Honour of P. E. Russell,* edited by F. W. Hodcroft (Oxford: Society for the Study of Mediaeval Languages and Literature, 1981), pp. 121–132.

San Juan de la Cruz

(24 June 1542 – 12 December 1591)

Marilyn Stone
New York University

BOOKS: *Subida del monte Carmelo y Noche oscura del alma* (Jaén, 1578);

Llama de amor viva (Alcalá de Henares, 1618);

Obras espirituales que encaminan a una alma a la mas perfecta union con Dios en transformacion de amor (Alcalá de Henares: Andres Sanchez, 1618);

Obras espirituales que encaminan una alma a la perfecta union con Dios por el Venerable PF Iuan de la Cruz, primer descalzo de la reforma de N. Senora del Carmen, Coadjutor de la Bienauenturada Virgen S. Teresa de Iesus Fundado ra de Iamisma reforma . . . (Barcelona: Sebastian de Cormellas, 1619);

Cantique d'amour divin entre Jésus-Christ et l'âme dévoté (Paris, 1622);

Declaracion de las Canciones que tratan del Exercicio de Amor entre el alma y el Esposo Cristo (Brussels: Godofredo Schoevarts, 1627);

Opere Spirituali che conduocono l'anima alla perfetta unione con Dio, composte dal Ven. P.F. Giouanni della Croce (Rome: Francesco Corbelletti, 1627);

Obras del venerable i mistico dotor F. Joan de la Cruz (Madrid: La Viuda de Madrigal, 1630).

Modern Editions: *El Cántico espiritual: Según el manuscrito de las Madres carmelitas de Jaén,* edited, with notes, by Matias Martinez de Burgos (Madrid: "La Lectura," 1924);

Cántico espiritual y poesías de San Juan de la Cruz, según el códice de Sanlúcar de Barrameda, edited, with notes, by P. Silverio de Santa Teresa, C.D. (Burgos: Monte Carmelo, 1928);

Poesias completas y comentarios en prosa a los poemas mayores, edited by Dámaso Alonso and Eulalia Galvarriato de Alonso (Madrid: Aguilar, 1963);

Obras, introduction, prologue, and notes by Jose Luis L. Aranguren (Barcelona: Vergara, 1968);

El Cántico espiritual segun el Manuscrito de las Madres Carmelitas de Jaén, edited by de Burgos (Madrid: Espasa-Calpe, 1969);

Poesías, edited by Paola Elia (Madrid: Castalia, 1990);

Obras completas, sixth edition, edited by Eulogio Pacho (Burgos: Monte Carmelo, 1998);

San Juan de la Cruz (Museo Provincial, Granada; from Emilio Orozco Díaz, Poesía y mística: Introducción a la lírica de san Juan de la Cruz, *1959; Thomas Cooper Library, University of South Carolina)*

Poesia, twelfth edition, edited by Domingo Ynduráin (Madrid: Cátedra, 2002).

Editions in English: *The Complete Works of St. John of the Cross of the Order of Our Lady of Mount Carmel,* translated by David Lewis, edited by the Oblate Fathers of Saint Charles (London: Longman, Green, Longman, Roberts & Green, 1864);

Ascent of Mount Carmel, third revised edition, translated
and edited, with a general introduction, by E.
Allison Peers (Garden City, N.Y.: Image, 1962);

The Collected Works of St. John of the Cross, translated by
Kieran Kavanaugh and Otilio Rodriguez (Garden
City, N.Y.: Doubleday, 1964);

The Poems of Saint John of the Cross, translated, with an
introduction, by Willis Barnstone (Bloomington:
Indiana University Press, 1968);

The Poems of St. John of the Cross, translated by John Frederick Nims, third edition (Chicago: University of
Chicago Press, 1979);

John of the Cross: Selected Writings, edited, with an introduction, by Kavanaugh (New York: Paulist,
1987).

The Spanish writer San Juan de la Cruz, who
attended a school for poor children in his early life, rose
to become a mystic, a doctor of the Catholic Church,
and the author of world-renowned lyric poetry. He was
a devout man who lived and wrote in Spain during a
time when religious issues were an important concern
in all of Europe. Together with St. Teresa of Ávila, he
was one of the organizers of a new religious order, the
Discalced Carmelites, which exerted an important influence on the changes that were taking place in the Catholic Church at the time. Juan wrote his best-known
work, *Cántico espiritual* (1627, Spiritual Canticle), in a
prison cell in 1578. The well-known Spanish critic and
scholar Marcelino Menendez y Pelayo called *Cántico
espiritual* celestial, divine, and ineffable, and the American author Willis Barnstone asserted that Juan was "a
poet unsurpassed in the Spanish language, a companion
in quality to Sappho." From written accounts, he never
seemed to have become discouraged or embittered, in
spite of persecution and imprisonment by members of
his own order. He also wrote works of mystic theology,
and he left a profound mark on church history.

During the lifetimes of Juan and Teresa, the mystic experience was thought to be the union of the intellect with a divine force. In the sixteenth century that
mystic experience was felt by many members of religious orders, who believed that they could reach a state
of ecstasy that might provide them with insights and
help them to overcome doubts about faith. Many sixteenth-
century Spanish mystics considered this process an
internal journey, a quest for a union with the spirit of
God. That quest was informed by intense personal
prayer and the desire for a simpler, reformed, religious
way of life. The difficulties and the suffering experienced by Juan during the "dark night" of his life are
especially poignant when they are compared to the
exquisite poetry he composed. Although he lived
through torturous moments, he was able to express ide-

als of love and beauty with intense passion and simplicity. The first edition of his works was published in
Alcalá de Henares in 1618. He was beatified by Clement X in 1675, canonized by Benedict XIII in 1726, and
named "Mystic Doctor of the Church" by Pius XI in
1926. Juan was named the patron saint of Spanish poets
in 1952.

Juan de Yepes was born on 24 June 1542 in Fontiveros, a small town in Ávila in the area of Castile
known for its waterfalls, fountains, and abundant vege-
tation. He may have been born into a family of *conversos,* that is, Jews who had converted to Christianity
during the fifteenth century in order to escape persecution. In a nearby town, Torrijos, exists the record of the
marriage of a couple named Gonzalo Yepes and Elvira
Gonzalez, who are believed to be Juan's grandparents.
The son of Gonzalo and Elvira, also named Gonzalo,
had many opportunities to make an advantageous marriage, but he fell in love with a housemaid, Catalina
Alvarez from Torrijos. His father objected to that marriage and threatened to disinherit his son. A kindly
businessman from Fontiveros is said to have provided
Catalina with a job in his silk factory so that she could
support herself. Gonzalo and Catalina married, despite
his family's disapproval, and the young couple settled
in Fontiveros and had three sons, Francisco, Luis, and
Juan. There are still many controversies concerning the
details of Juan's early life and his ancestors, many of
whom are addressed in the essays in Dámaso Chicharro's *De San Juan de la Cruz a los Machado: Jaén en la
literatura espanola* (1997, From St. John of the Cross to the
Machado Brothers: Jaén in Spanish Literature).

The Yepes family disowned Gonzalo because of
his marriage to Catalina, and the young family lived in
poverty. Gonzalo suffered from ill health and died
when Juan was six years old. Catalina struggled to support her sons, and eventually they moved to Medina
del Campo, where she made her living as a weaver, as
did her eldest son, Francisco. Life was difficult for Catalina and her family during these years; her second son,
Luis, died during childhood. From an early age Juan
helped his mother obtain the barest necessities to enable
the family to survive. He was enrolled in the Colegio de
los Ninos de la Doctrina (School for Orphaned Children), a public school for orphaned children who were
taught the skills of woodworking, painting, and carpen-
try from local craftsmen. He also had some interest in
art: as a youth he skillfully drew an image of Jesus'
Crucifixion that the Spanish artist Salvador Dalí later
made famous. Don Alonso Álvarez de Toledo, the
director of the hospital in Medina del Campo, hired
Juan to work at the Hospital de las Bubas; a philanthro-
pist, Álvarez de Toledo hoped that Juan might eventually train for holy orders. In the Hospital de las Bubas,

Drawing of the Crucifixion by Juan de la Cruz as a boy. It is preserved at the Convento de la Encarnación in Ávila, where his partner in founding the Discalced Carmelite order, Santa Teresa de Jesús, lived for more than thirty years (from Emilio Orozco Díaz, Poesía y mística: Introducción a la lírica de san Juan de la Cruz, *1959; Thomas Cooper Library, University of South Carolina).*

patients suffered from epilepsy, leprosy, tuberculosis, and other terminal illnesses. In spite of these conditions, Juan never fled from the suffering of the patients there or from the fevers, hallucinations, and pain he witnessed. He eventually gained a reputation as an adept caregiver during the six years he spent in the service of the sick and the poor. While Juan was working at the hospital he met a young doctor named Gomez Pereira, who made systematic, accurate, objective descriptions of the symptoms of each of the diseases experienced by the people there. Juan, then young and impressionable, observed this physician and his technique.

The director of the hospital allowed Juan to attend a local Jesuit College provided that he would not overlook his hospital duties. As a boy he had learned to read in only a few days, and when he studied humanities with the Jesuits in Medina del Campo, from 1559 to 1563, he absorbed many subjects quickly, including

Latin and Greek, and gained the rhetorical skills that he later refined in his works. He entered the Carmelite order at the age of twenty-one and donned that habit in 1563, assuming the name of Juan de Santo Matia. When he studied at the University of Salamanca he probably lived at the Carmelite College, where masters of the order taught classes. He is known to have spent four years there, because his name appears in the university records from 1564 to 1568. He may have followed the courses for students who were preparing to become priests, since his name is listed in the prescribed curriculum as *teólogo* (theologian) at a later date. In 1569 he began to study theology at the University of Salamanca. Juan even taught at that university while he was still a student. At Salamanca he was likely exposed to the classes and theories of Fray Luis de León. The latter was a well-known poet and teacher who was then engaged in a dynamic struggle. He believed that the mysteries of religion should be expressed in the language of the people, and as an expression of this belief he translated into Spanish the biblical Song of Songs, one of the most influential texts for mystic writers such as Juan and Teresa. Although the subjects that Juan studied and the acquaintances he made at Salamanca are not documented, his works reveal a deep familiarity with the Bible, and he frequently cites passages from it in his writings. In addition, many critics have noted the influence of the writings of León on Juan's works.

After leaving Salamanca, Juan returned to Medina del Campo, where he was ordained a priest in 1567 and said his first mass in the presence of his mother. After his ordination the Jesuits of Medina del Campo introduced Juan to Teresa de Jesús, a nun of the Carmelite order. He was twenty-five, and she was fifty-two. In spite of the disparity in their ages and the plans that Juan had made to join the strict Carthusian order in Segovia, Teresa convinced him to work with her to spread the Carmelite reform she had begun. Her idea was to found new communities of friars and nuns in order to extend the influence of the Carmelite notion of the contemplative existence, which consisted of a life of enclosure and prayer. In 1567 the director of the Carmelite order visited Teresa's Discalced Convent at Ávila and granted her permission to found other houses and to create two priories for friars. On 20 November 1568 Juan took the vows of the new order and joined Antonio de Heredia and Jose de Cristo in helping to establish its first monastery in a simple house that had been given to Teresa as a gift. Juan was novice master of this first monastery of Discalced Carmelites, at Duruelo. There he took the name of Juan de la Cruz (John of the Cross). Teresa, impressed with Juan's abilities, appointed him subprior of the convent, the first of the male communities to return to the primitive rule.

This rule would combine the contemplative and the active parts of life. Thus, in the monasteries and convents there would be scheduled hours of prayer every day, fasting, total abstinence from meat, and a life of poverty and of going barefoot (the meaning of *discalced*). They openly welcomed a life of physical hardship with the goal of enhancing the life of the spirit.

Juan and Teresa lived during a time of conflict for Spain, when issues of religion and the desire for political power led to conflicts with Muslims, Jews, and *conversos*. Of particular relevance with respect to mystics such as Juan and Teresa was the socioreligious climate of fear and mistrust generated by the Spanish Inquisition—which was controlled by the monarchy since its inception in 1480 during the time of the Catholic Monarchs—an institution that viewed mysticism in a skeptical light. Tribunals could imprison anyone judged to possess beliefs that were not in accord with those of orthodox Catholicism. During the second half of the sixteenth century, the strong support for the Inquisition by the Spanish monarchy was exemplified by Philip II, an austere and ascetic ruler who saw himself (and by extension Spain) as the defender of Catholicism. Over the course of his reign, religious persecution increased as the Spanish Inquisition intensified its activities. The king also wished to reform the religious orders, and he encouraged Teresa to return to the austerity of the original Carmelite order of the thirteenth century. The early Carmelites practiced poverty, fasting, long silences, and discipline. The active part of their program was preaching, hearing confession, and counseling. Their activities of reform spread and attracted university students, and a house of studies was opened at Alcalá de Henares, where Juan became the rector.

When Teresa came back to Ávila to direct her convent, Juan joined her to work on the process of changing the order. At Duruelo the symptoms of an illness that had followed Juan throughout his life reappeared. Little is known about its exact nature, but he suffered from fevers and swellings in his limbs from his youth until his death. Juan, Antonio de Jesús, and José de Cristo drew the attention of people in Duruelo and the surrounding countryside. Their work consisted of preaching, offering spiritual advice, teaching, and caring for the sick. A gentleman in a neighboring village had a church built for them to house their growing community. Convents for the Discalced Carmelites were also established in Toledo and Pastrana. The attempts of these pioneering Carmelites to create a new order and to renovate and popularize an older form of spiritual life met with dissent, however; King Philip II challenged their authority. They were censured by the general chapter, and Teresa was humiliated even though she had founded the first house of Discalced

Carmelites in Ávila in 1562. By her death in 1582 she had established fourteen priories and sixteen convents. The reforms of Teresa and Juan incurred disputes and jealousies, and in 1577 the hostility of the unreformed Carmelites led them to denounce Juan to the Inquisition.

As a result of these difficulties Juan was kidnapped and dragged to Toledo, where he was imprisoned by friars who locked him in a small, dark room. Once a week he was taken to eat and to get flogged, which left his body covered with sores. After six months of this harsh treatment Juan was given a new jailer, who furnished him with paper, pen, and ink. At that time he began to write *Cántico espiritual*, a commentary on the poem he had composed with the same name. After he had been jailed for eight months he decided to flee, and he escaped from his prison at night by letting himself down with a rope he had made of twisted cloth. He had only a small notebook with him as he wandered through the streets until he reached the house of Discalced nuns, who took him in and hid him. He was rescued by Don Pedro Mendoza, canon of the Toledo Cathedral, who brought him to his own house in the darkness. On the night of his escape Juan has been said to have dictated the verses he had thought about while he was in jail.

After his imprisonment Juan was protected by the Order of the Discalced Fathers. He was appointed rector of the Carmelite College in Baeza. He acted as prior in Granada and Segovia and was vicar general of the Discalced order, for which he founded male communities in Córdoba, Jaén, and Murcia. In 1591, because of opposition to Juan's role, there were attempts to expel him from the order. Subsequently, Juan was not elected to any office, and a pension was given to him at the age of forty-nine. He was sent to a formerly deserted hermitage of La Penuela in the Sierra Morena Mountains; there his ulcerated foot, which had never been treated, worsened, and he fell seriously ill. Voluntarily, Juan went to the priory in Ubeda, where he knew that the prior had a grudge against him. He died there on 12 December at the age of forty-nine.

Juan (like Teresa) wrote about orthodox mysticism, and his writings ultimately reached Portugal, France, and Italy, where they were read by persons of every social class. Some scholars have noted that many versions of his works were copied down by the friars and nuns of the Discalced order, and many other persons were able to make or obtain copies of their manuscripts. No manuscripts in Juan's own hand have survived. It is not known, therefore, when he composed his works, although it is generally thought that he did most of his writing while serving as prior in Granada during the late 1570s and 1580s. Probably during this

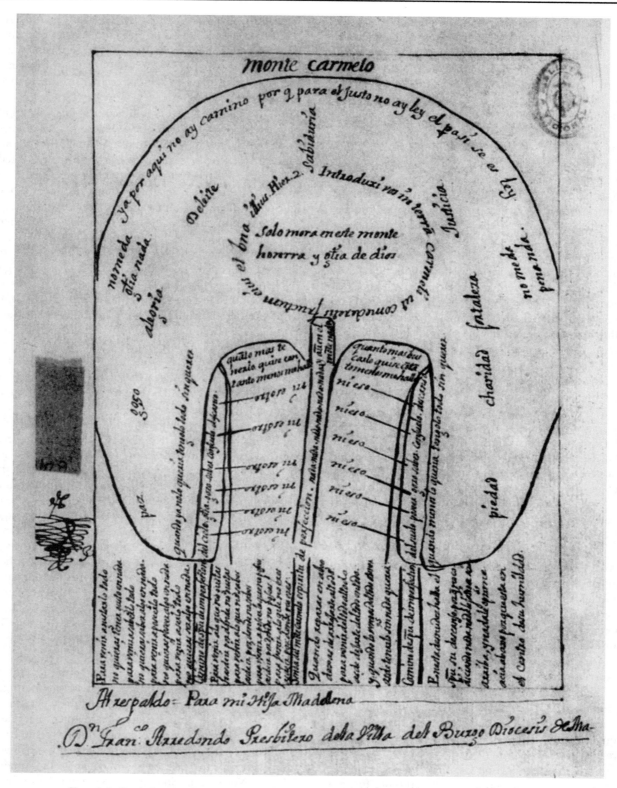

Juan de la Cruz's drawing illustrating the teachings of his 1578 work Subida del monte Carmelo *(Ascent of Mount Carmel; Biblioteca Nacional, Madrid; from Emilio Orozco Díaz,* Poesía y mística: Introducción a la lírica de San Juan de la Cruz, *1959; Thomas Cooper Library, University of South Carolina)*

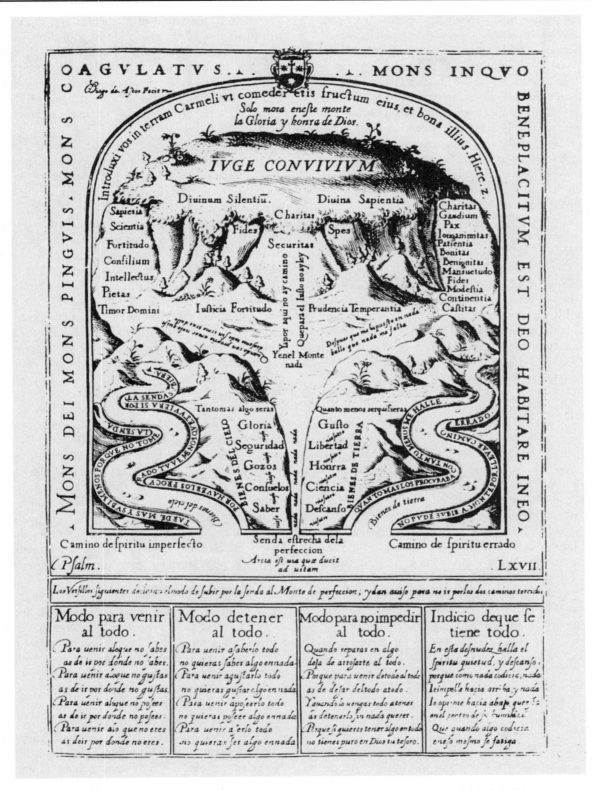

Another version of Juan de la Cruz's diagram from Subida del monte Carmelo, *included in the 1619 edition of his collected works (from Gerald Brenan,* St. John of the Cross: His Life and Poetry, *1973; Thomas Cooper Library, University of South Carolina)*

time Juan composed his four major poems with commentaries: *Subida del monte Carmelo* (translated as *Ascent of Mount Carmel*, 1962) and *Noche oscura del alma* (Dark Night of the Soul), which were published together in 1578; *Llama de amor viva* (1618, Living Flame of Love); and *Cántico espiritual*. Although written several years before his death, these poems did not become well known until the early seventeenth century. *Cántico espiritual* appeared for the first time in European literature in a French translation made directly from manuscripts in 1621 in the court of Louis XIII of France, several years before it was published in Spanish in 1627. The first complete edition of Juan's works was published in Madrid in 1630. The number of translations of his works is enormous; among the best known are those in Latin, Italian, English, German, French, Portuguese, Flemish, Polish, Hungarian, Czech, and Japanese.

Around 1578 Juan composed *Subida del monte Carmelo,* a work of three volumes that deals with suffering endured by the soul and how perfection is sought through faith and charity. *Subida del monte Carmelo* includes a commentary on the first stanzas of *Noche oscura del alma*. This poem, like Juan's other works, includes imagery that may be interpreted in two ways, that is, in both mystic and profane manners. Depending on the reader's comprehension of mysticism, the poem expresses what may be seen as the evolution of a mystic or an erotic relationship. An example of this dual meaning appears in the verses "oh noche, que juntaste / Amado con amada, / amada en el Amado transformada" (oh night, who joined / the Lover with the beloved, / the beloved transformed into the Lover), verses that can be understood in either sense. In *Subida del monte Carmelo,* Juan focuses on the difficult path that the soul must take to perfect itself eventually as it overcomes the worldly desires imposed on it. As such, *Subida del monte Carmelo,* along with *Noche oscura del alma, Llama de amor viva,* and *Cántico espiritual,* are all works that function as extended commentaries on the author's poems.

Although many of Juan's works have attained popularity, he is arguably best known for *Cántico espiritual,* whose original title, *Declaracion de las Canciones que tratan del Exercicio de Amor entre el alma y el Esposo Cristo* (The Explanation of the songs which deal with the expression of love between the soul and Christ the husband), was shortened in 1630 by Jerónimo de San José. The work (a commentary in prose to the poem of the same name) was written at the suggestion of Ana de Jesús, the prioress of the convent in Granada. In the *Cántico espiritual* Juan describes how he visualized the different stages of mystic ascension and explains systematically how the soul searches for divinity. Stanzas 1 through 12 deal with what he calls the "vía purgativa" (purgative path), consisting of discipline and distancing oneself from the world of the senses and the material world; stanzas 13 through 21 deal with the "vía iluminativa" (illuminative path) of contemplation, meditation, and concentration of the soul on God; stanzas 22a to the last one explain the "vía unitiva" (unitive path), that is, that after a dark night of struggle of the soul there is a kind of matrimony or spiritual union with God.

From a literary and aesthetic point of view, the reader can understand *Cántico espiritual* simply as a beautiful, dramatic love poem and can appreciate its metaphors, style, poetic techniques, and the musicality of the words. At the same time, it is difficult for the reader to understand many of the images described by the poet, and some scholars have suggested that the internal crisis that Juan calls the love of God can never be compared to any ordinary erotic experience. The biblical source for *Cántico espiritual* is the Song of Songs. The author of that work, according to tradition the biblical King Solomon, takes the reader, metaphorically, into the fresh air, the vineyards, the villages, and the mountains where one can almost smell the air of springtime. For many centuries the Hebraic tradition has interpreted this text—in particular the relationship between the lover and his beloved—as an allegory of the relationship between God and Israel, that is, a love song for some distant messianic age. In the *Cántico espiritual* the *esposo* (bridegroom) represents God, and the *esposa* (bride) is the soul. In both the *Cántico espiritual* and the Song of Songs there are metaphors of the flaming arrows of love that wound the heart and of the clear fountain from which torrents of fresh water spring forth. At times the poetic metaphors used by Juan come directly from the Bible, while at other times they are merely evocations of bucolic scenes of mountains and vineyards populated by goats, deer, turtledoves, and pigeons.

The literary environment of the Renaissance also plays an important role in understanding the structure and meaning of *Cántico espiritual*. The work is written in a form called the *lira,* of Italian origin and frequently employed in sixteenth-century Spanish poetry, it comprises stanzas of seven and eleven syllables. The *lira* received its name because of the first lines of a poem written by Garcilaso de la Vega. That multiple editions of Garcilaso's works appeared in *Medina del Campo* and at the University of Salamanca in the sixteenth century is further suggestion of his influence on Juan. Many of the metaphors used by Garcilaso, such as "el agua pura de la fuente" (the clear water of the fountain), "prado de verduras" (the green meadow), and "rebaño de paz" (the peaceful flock), also appear in Juan's verses.

Scholars and writers have recognized on several occasions that some of the images are reminiscent of the verses of León, another renowned Spanish Renaissance poet. Francisco García Lorca, one of the best-known twentieth-century Spanish scholars in his *De fray Luis a San Juan: La escondida senda* (1972, From Fray Luis to San Juan: The Hidden Path), points out the definite presence of León in *Noche oscura del alma, Llama de amor viva,* and *Cántico espiritual.* García Lorca notes similarities in the metric form and in the overall plan in the verses of the two poets. He has also identified more than thirty stanzas in poems written by Juan that have a direct relationship to the poems of León. García Lorca even suggests that when Juan wrote the *Cántico espiritual* while in jail, he might have been recalling the similar fate of León, who was also imprisoned.

Some modern scholars have found sources and similarities between the works of Juan and the works of Hebrew and Arabic authors. For example, Catherine Swietlicki, in "Entre las culturas españolas: San Juan de la Cruz y la cábala cristiana popular" (Between the Spanish Cultures: San Juan de la Cruz and the Popular Christian Cabala), a paper presented at a 1991 international conference on the poet, describes the intricate knowledge of the Hebrew Bible demonstrated by Juan in his writings. She notices a connection between his writings and some cabalistic ideas derived from the significant and influential work of Jewish mysticism, the *Sefer ha-Zohar* (The Book of Enlightenment) from the late thirteenth century. In particular, Swietlicki finds influences on Juan in the idea of the "dark night" of the Exodus (especially the dark night of the flight of the Israelites from Egypt), the metaphorical night of the wanderings of the Jews in the desert, and their desperate yearnings to meet with God in the promised land. Luce López-Baralt, in several studies she has published on Juan's works, connects the idea of "a dark night of the soul" with Sufi mysticism.

Although his life was characterized by poverty and poor health, and he was ultimately faced with fighting expulsion from his order, San Juan de la Cruz's enduring legacy is that of one of the greatest Spanish mystics and one of the most gifted composers of Spanish Renaissance verse. In his works Juan expresses feelings of divine love by describing the elements of human love in his portrayal of the creatures and the natural settings of this world. His poetry and commentaries reflect his erudition by evoking many biblical images and his literary style expresses the aesthetic theories and values of the Spanish Renaissance. At the same time, his writings are distinctive for the manner in which they are informed by mystic themes that seem to depict experiences he himself lived through. To describe those experiences he used some precedents found in the imagery of the Song of Songs, and, like that work, Juan's works have been understood in both mystical and profane

Title page for the first edition of Juan de la Cruz's collected spiritual writings (from Poesías, 1990; Thomas Cooper Library, University of South Carolina)

senses. Juan's poetry and prose continue to be read by modern readers and studied by scholars from a variety of disciplines, and he has gained fame as a poet, a philosopher, a theologian, and an experienced mystic. In his works he attempts to put the exaltation and rapture he felt during his mystical experiences into words, and as a result he continues to attract readers and inspire critics centuries after his death.

Bibliography:
Manuel Diego Sánchez, *San Juan de la Cruz: Bibliografía del IV centenario de su muerte* (Rome: Teresianum, 1993).

Biographies:
Bruno de Jesús-Marie, *Saint John of the Cross,* edited by Benedict Zimmerman (New York & London: Sheed & Ward, 1932);

Jesús Sacramentado, *The Life of St. John of the Cross,* translated by Kathleen Pond (London & New York: Longmans, Green, 1958).

References:

Actas del Congresi Internacional Sanjuanista: Ávila, 23–28 de septiembre de 1991, 3 volumes (Ávila: Junta de Castilla y León, Consejería de Cultura y Turismo, 1993);

Alfonso Baldeón Santiago, "Educar en la libertad: Releyendo las cautelas de San Juan de la Cruz," *San Juan de la Cruz,* 27, no. 1 (2001): 5–31;

Jean Baruzi, *Saint Jean de la Croix et le problème de l'expérience mystique* (Paris: Alcan, 1924);

José María Bermeo, "La poesía de San Juan de la Cruz," *Vida Nueva,* 2258 (2000): 38–39;

Gerald Brenan, *St. John of the Cross: His Life and Poetry* (Cambridge: Cambridge University Press, 1973);

David Centner, "Christian Freedom and the Nights of St. John of the Cross," *Carmelite Studies,* 2 (1982): 3–80;

Dámaso Chicharro, *De San Juan de la Cruz a los Machado: Jaén en la literatura española* (Jaén: Universidad de Jaén, 1997);

Ross Collings, "Accepting the Spirit as Guide: St. John of the Cross and Unpredictable Prayer," *Mount Carmel,* 48, no. 3 (2000): 34–37;

R. P. Crisógono de Jesús, O.C.D., *Vida y obras de San Juan de la Cruz, Doctor de la Iglesia Universal* (Madrid: Biblioteca de Autores Cristianos, 1950);

Rómulo Cuartas Londoño, "San Juan de la Cruz, pastor, maestro, profeta," *San Juan de la Cruz,* 27, no. 1 (2001): 33–60;

Denis Edward, "Experience of God and Explicit Faith: A Comparison of John of the Cross and Karl Rahner," *Thomist,* 46 (1982): 33–74;

Francisco García Lorca, *De fray Luis a San Juan: La escondida senda* (Madrid: Castalia, 1972);

Bernard Gicovate, *San Juan de la Cruz* (New York: Twayne, 1971);

Robert A. Herrera, *St. John of the Cross: Introductory Studies* (Madrid: Espiritualidad, 1968);

John Paul II, *Faith According to St. John of the Cross,* translated by Jordan Aumann (San Francisco: Ignatius, 1981);

Luce López-Baralt, *Asedios a lo indecible: San Juan de la Cruz canta al éxtasis transformante* (Madrid: Trotta, 1998);

López-Baralt, "El *Cántico Espiritual* o el júbilo de la unión transformante," *ACIS* (1996): 163–204;

López-Baralt, *San Juan de la Cruz y el Islam: Estudio sobre las filiaciones semíticas de su literatura mística* (Mexico City: Colegio de México, Centro de Estudios Lingüísticos y Literarios, 1985);

José C. Nieto, *Mystic, Rebel, Saint: A Study of St. John of the Cross* (Geneva: Droz, 1979);

Miguel Norbert-Ubarri, "Paralelismos entre el canzioniere de Petrarca y los poemas de San Juan de la Cruz: Celosía de una vitalidad amorosa 'a lo divino,'" *San Juan de la Cruz,* 27, no. 1 (2001): 81–92;

Emilio Orozco Díaz, *Poesía y mística: Introducción a la lírica de san Juan de la Cruz* (Madrid: Guadarrama, 1959);

Eulogio Pacho, "Beatificación y canonización de San Juan de la Cruz: Otros procesos olvidados," *Monte Carmelo,* 109 (2001): 107–123;

E. Allison Peers, *Handbook to the Life and Times of St. Teresa and St. John of the Cross* (London: Burns, Oates, 1954);

Bernard Sesé, "San Juan de la Cruz y la cuestion de lo femenino," *Revista de espiritualidad,* 239, no. 60 (2001): 245–258;

Catherine Swietlicki, "Entre las culturas españolas: San Juan de la Cruz y la cábala cristiana popular," *Actas del Congresi Internacional Sanjuanista: Ávila, 23–28 de septiembre de 1991,* volume 1 (Ávila: Junta de Castilla y León, Consejería de Cultura y Turismo, 1993), pp. 259–267;

José Angel Valente and José Lara Garrido, eds., *Hermenéutica y mística: San Juan de la Cruz* (Madrid: Tecnos, 1995).

Fray Bartolomé de Las Casas

(1474 – 31 July 1566)

Luis C. Cano
University of Tennessee, Knoxville

BOOKS: *Aqui se contiene unos avisos y reglas para los confessores que oyeren confessiones delos españoles que son o han sido en cargo a los indios delas Indias del mar Océano* (Seville: Sebastián Trugillo, 1552);

Brevissima relación de la destruycion de las Indias (Seville: Sebastián Trugillo, 1552); translated as *A Briefe Narration of the Destruction of the Indies by the Spaniards* (London, 1625);

Aqui se contiene una disputa, o controversia, entre el Obispo fray Bartolomé de Las Casas y el doctor Ginés de Sepúlveda (Seville: Sebastián Trugillo, 1552);

Entre los remedios que don fray Bartolomé de las Casas . . . refirió por mandado del Emperador . . . : en los ayuntamientos que mando hacer su magestad de perlados y letrados y personas grandes en Valladolid el año de mil a quinientos y quarenta y dos para reformación de los Indias . . . (Seville: Jacome Cromberger, 1552);

Este es un tratado q el obispo dela ciudad real de Chiapa dõ Fray Bartholomé de las Casas o Casaus compuso por commission del Consejo Real delas Indias: Sobre la materia delos yndios que se han hecho en ellas esclavos (Seville: Sebastián Trugillo, 1552);

Aqui se cõtiene treynta proposiciones muy jurídicas en las quales sumaria y succintamente se tocã muchas cosas pertenecientes al derecho q la yglesia y los principes christianos tienen o puede tener sobre los infieles de qual quier especie que sean (Seville: Sebastián Trugillo, 1552);

Tratado cõprobatorio del imperio soberano y principado universal que los Reyes de Castilla y León tienen sobre las Indias (Seville: Sebastián Trugillo, 1553);

Historia de las Indias, 5 volumes, edited by Feliciano Ramírez de Arellano, Marqués de la Fuensanta del Valle, and José León Sancho Rayón (Madrid: Ginesta, 1875–1876); translated by Andrée Collard as *History of the Indies* (New York: Harper & Row, 1971);

De las antiguas gentes del Perú, edited by Marcos Jiménez de la Espada (Madrid: Hernández, 1892);

Apologética historia de las Indias, edited by Manuel Serrano y Sanz (Madrid: Bailly, Bailliere, 1909);

Fray Bartolomé de Las Casas (frontispiece for Retratos de los españoles ilustres *[Madrid, 1795]; from Ramón Menéndez Pidal,* El Padre Las Casas: Su doble personalidad, *1963; Thomas Cooper Library, University of South Carolina)*

Del único modo de atraer a todos los pueblos a la verdadera religión, edited by Agustín Millares Carlo (Mexico City: Fondo de Cultura Económica, 1942); translated by Francis Patrick Sullivan as *The Only Way,* edited by Helen Rand Parish (New York: Paulist Press, 1992);

Los tesoros del Perú, edited and translated by Ángel Losada (Madrid: Consejo Superior de Investigaciones Científicas, Institutos Gonzalo de Oviedo y Francisco de Victoria, 1958);

De regia potestate; o Derecho de autodeterminación, edited by Luciano Pereña (Madrid: Consejo Superior de Investigaciones Científicas, 1969).

Modern Editions: *Obra indigenista,* edited by José Alcina Franch (Madrid: Alianza, 1985);

Historia de las Indias, 3 volumes, edited by André Saint-Lu (Caracas: Ayacucho, 1986);

Obras completas, 14 volumes, edited by Paulino Castañeda Delgado (Madrid: Alianza, 1988–1998).

Editions in English: *The Tears of the Indians: Being an Historical and True Account of the Cruel Massacres and Slaughters of Above Twenty Million Innocent People, Committed by the Spaniards in the Islands of Hispaniola, Cuba, Jamaica, &c.: As Also in the Continent of Peru, & Other Places of the West-Indies, to the Total Destruction of Those Countries,* translated by John Phillips (London: Printed by J.C. for Nath. Brook, 1656);

Bartolomé de Las Casas: A Selection of His Writings, edited and translated by George Sanderlin (New York: Knopf, 1971);

The Devastation of the Indies: A Brief Account, translated by Herma Briffault (New York: Seabury Press, 1974);

A Short Account of the Destruction of the Indies, translated by Nigel Griffin (New York: Penguin, 1992).

OTHER: *Personal Narrative of the First Voyage of Columbus to America,* edited by Las Casas, translated by Samuel Kettell (Boston: Wait, 1827); Spanish version published as *Relación del primer viaje de D. Cristobal Colón* (Buenos Aires: Emecé, 1942).

A missionary, historian, and human-rights activist, Fray Bartolomé de Las Casas was the first European advocate of the indigenous people of America and the first to expose the atrocities that the aborigines endured during the Conquest of the New World. Controversy has been intimately attached to Fray Bartolomé's name, however. While many scholars distinguish him as "Protector de los Indios" (Protector of the Indians), a title that the Spanish Crown conferred onto him, others take a more cautious view of his achievements, and still others think he was even partially responsible for the beginning of the institution of slavery in the Americas. A vigorous critic of the Spanish administration and its involvement in the mission of bringing the Gospel to the New World, Las Casas did not promote revolt against the Spanish Crown, whose legitimacy to rule in South America he always accepted. In his books he not only provides a record of the brutality of colonization, but he also argues against the concept of the Indians as an inferior race. Las Casas maintained that they were fully rational beings with a culture that, while certainly primitive in its technology and in many of its practices, was equal to anything the Old World had produced.

Bartolomé de Las Casas was born in Seville in 1474. His ancestors, the Casaus, originally from France, had been established in Spain for more than two hundred years. In that period, the name Casaus lost the French spelling and acquired the Spanish form, Las Casas. His father, Pedro de Casaus, a minor businessman, accompanied Christopher Columbus on his second expedition in 1493. Pedro acquired enough wealth in the New World to provide Bartolomé with an excellent education, which gave him the opportunity to attend both the Cathedral Academy in Seville and the prestigious University of Salamanca. In Salamanca he obtained a degree in law in 1498 after studying both law and theology. There is no indication that he ever practiced law, and he did not take religious orders until he arrived in the Americas. Although there is no real evidence, some biographers believe that the young Bartolomé could have traveled with his father when he sailed with Columbus on his third voyage in 1498.

In 1502 Las Casas accompanied the Spanish conqueror Gonzalo Fernández de Oviedo to the New World, and during the following years he participated in several expeditions. He helped to control indigenous uprisings and was rewarded with several privileges from his superiors. In 1510, when he was thirty-six years old, Las Casas was ordained a Roman Catholic priest in the city of Santo Domingo, capital of Hispaniola. He is believed to be the first priest ever to be consecrated in the colonies. He participated as a chaplain in the conquest of Cuba, and for this service he was awarded with an *encomienda,* a legal system of tributary labor that included not only an estate but also the services of the natives living on it. In return for being the beneficiary of the forced labor in fields and mines, the *encomendero* (the owner of an *encomienda*) was responsible for instructing the natives in the Christian doctrine.

As an *encomendero,* the new priest witnessed some extreme examples of misery and of unjust and cruel practices against the natives. This firsthand experience of the mistreatment of the indigenous peoples of America motivated him to give up his *encomienda* and denounce the Spanish exploitation of these peoples. It must be said, however, that Las Casas's campaign was not aimed to target slavery itself. His initial purpose was to encourage the practice of conversion and direction of the Indians by peaceful means, not by violence and cruelty. Las Casas was convinced that the rapidly disappearing native population of America could not physically endure the hard labor imposed by the Spanish and recommended the importation of African slaves, who he believed were more fit for hard labor than the Indians. These instances of proposing black slavery have been the issue most widely criticized in the life and work of Las Casas. He was not the first one, however, to come up with the idea of developing a plan of slavery. By the sixteenth century, slavery was a common practice in Portugal and Spain. Both countries had a well-established system of forced importation and trade of an almost exclusively black African workforce, first to the Iberian Peninsula, then to the African Atlantic islands, and finally to the Americas.

Determined to procure improved conditions for the Indians, Las Casas set sail to Spain in 1515 to present his complaint before the king. After a conference, during which Las Casas described the abusive treatment of the subjected native population by the Spanish settlers, a sympathetic Ferdinand the Catholic promised a second interview. This royal audience never occurred, because Ferdinand died in January 1516. At that time, his grandson and successor, King Charles I, resided in Flanders. Firmly determined to present his case on behalf of the Indians, Las Casas resolved to travel to Flanders to get an audience with the new king. On his way to the Flemish court, he stopped in Madrid, where he met the regent cardinal Francisco Jiménez y Cisneros. Informed by Las Casas of the cruelties and oppression of which the Indians were victims, Jiménez named him "Protector de los Indios" and in 1520 authorized him to found a model colony in Cumaná, Venezuela.

Las Casas devised a plan to convert the native peoples of Central and South America to Catholicism and to establish a Christian administration similar to the successful *misiones* (missions) developed by the Jesuits two centuries later. His plan consisted of the development of communities in which both the Indians and the Spaniards would share the administrative responsibilities. The main goals were to protect the natives from extermination and to provide a pacifistic approach to evangelization without sacrificing the profits of the Crown. The king approved the plan in 1520, and the northeastern coast of Venezuela was selected as the location for the project. After establishing the first settlement there in Cumaná, Las Casas departed for Santo Domingo in an attempt to give an

Title page for Las Casas's best-known work, translated in 1625 as A Briefe Narration of the Destruction of the Indies by the Spaniards, *a graphic account of Spanish atrocities that contributed to the spread of "La Leyenda Negra" (The Black Legend) (from Rodolpho Barón Castro,* La Población de El Salvador, *1942; Thomas Cooper Library, University of South Carolina)*

account of his work and to get the Spanish administration more involved in the protection of the Indians. Soon after his departure, the colony was destroyed by a native revolt that Las Casas blamed on his own countrymen, accusing them of having instigated the catastrophe out of ill will toward himself and his projects.

In 1522, profoundly saddened by the failure of his project and blaming himself for the death of those who fell in Cumaná, Las Casas became a member of the Dominican order on the island of Santo Domingo. Little is known of his life during the following four years, except that he spent most of his time studying religious sciences, especially theology. During these years Las Casas resolved to report the events that he had witnessed since the discovery of America and started writing both *Historia de las Indias* (translated as

History of the Indies, 1971) and *Apologética historia de las Indias* (Apologetic History of the Indies), which were unpublished until 1875–1876 and 1909, respectively.

By 1530 Hernán Cortés had taken possession of Moctezuma's empire in Mexico, and Francisco Pizarro had been granted the title of viceroy of the Peruvian territory in South America. Having observed the events that threatened the extinction of the Indians, Las Casas decided to take the necessary steps to prevent the development in Peru of the *repartimientos,* grants of land that virtually awarded to the grantee the right to seize a specified number of natives and compel them to produce gold and silver for nothing. With the consent of his Dominican superiors, Las Casas traveled to Spain and obtained the necessary legislation from the king to prevent the natives of Peru from sharing the same fate of those of New Spain and Mexico.

Between 1536 and 1538 Las Casas launched a missionary campaign in northeastern Guatemala. During this period he completed his first important work, *Del único modo de atraer a todos los pueblos a la verdadera religión* (first published in 1942; translated as *The Only Way,* 1992), his own version of how the conquest should take place. The main thesis of this long text is that the only viable way to influence and promote the conversion of a human being is through peaceful and persuasive means, which rejects once again the violent ways adopted by many of the Spanish settlers. Las Casas fervently believed that the Indians should understand the new faith before embracing it, and he made it clear that war was wrong as a method of spreading religious beliefs. His campaign in favor of the Indians received strong support from the bull *Sublimis Deus* (Sublime God)–promulgated by Pope Paul III in 1537–which defined the indigenous Americans as rational beings with souls, proclaimed their right to receive the Christian faith, and called for protection of their lives and property.

Three years later Las Casas was granted permission from his Dominican superiors to return to the Spanish court with the purpose of inducing the Council of the Indies to enact the necessary legislation against the *encomienda* system and the slavery of Indians. The king responded to the recommendations of the council by proclaiming the Leyes de Indias (New Laws of the Indies) in November 1542. These laws prohibited all future enslavement of Indians, implemented humane treatment of those already enslaved, and attempted to put an end to the *encomienda* institution by limiting ownership of slaves to a single generation.

It is a consensus among scholars of Las Casas that his most influential and best-known work, *Brevis-*

sima relación de la destruycion de las Indias (1552; translated as *A Briefe Narration of the Destruction of the Indies by the Spaniards,* 1625), was the principal factor that convinced the Council of the Indies as well as the king to adopt the radical new legislation. Written during the years 1541 and 1542, *Brevissima relación de la destruycion de las Indias* is a graphic description of all the massacres, brutal expeditions, cruelties, and thefts committed by the Spanish settlers against the Indians. For example, in one of the many passages in which the author expresses his horror for the violent action of his countrymen, Las Casas writes: "Y otra cosa no han hecho de cuarenta años a esta parte . . . sino despedazallas, matallas, angustiallas, afligillas, atormentallas y destruillas por las estrañas y nuevas y varias y nunca oytras tales vistas ni leídas ni oídas maneras de crueldad" (For forty years they have done nothing . . . but mutilate, murder, harass, afflict torment, and destroy them with extraordinary, incredible, innovative, and previously unheard cruelty). Las Casas, however, never accused the Spanish government of being guilty of the atrocities he described in his manuscript. Instead, he admits that the monarchy, including Ferdinand, Isabella, Charles, and King Philip II, did everything possible to ameliorate the conditions of the Indians and to protect them from the rapacity of the Spanish conquerors.

Before its publication, *Brevissima relación de la destruycion de las Indias* was submitted to the king and his ministers. The work was not printed until ten years later, whereupon it was rapidly translated into several European languages and met with extraordinary success. The graphic depiction of the horror and abuses committed by Las Casas's countrymen provoked a strong reaction against the Spanish colonial system in America and was the main source of information used by other European maritime powers to promote nationalistic sentiments against Spanish hegemony. The perpetuation of this anti-Spanish sentiment, which was also fomented by religious conflicts and national interests, contributed to the development of what has been called La Leyenda Negra (The Black Legend). From the perspective of this legend, all the Spanish conquerors were no more than brutes, interested only in gold, pillage, and rape, who left a trail of savage destruction wherever they went. La Leyenda Negra provided powerful ideological sanction for the involvement of Great Britain in the New World and gave the Dutch, French, Germans, and Italians strong arguments against the territorial control held by King Philip II.

While *Brevissima relación de la destruycion de las Indias* became the best known of Las Casas's writings, it was not the only work that he wrote during this trip to Spain. In 1542, at the king's command, he also wrote a treatise consisting of a series of recommendations, or *remedios* (remedies), for the reform of the administration of the Indies. A decade later a part of the treatise was reprinted as *Entre los remedios que don fray Bartolomé de las Casas . . . refirió por mandado del Emperador . . . : En los ayuntamientos que mando hacer su magestad de perlados y letrados y personas grandes en Valladolid el año de mil a quinientos y quarenta y dos para reformación de los Indias* (Some of the Remedies That, at the Emperor's Suggestion, Don Bartolomé de Las Casas Proposed . . . : In the Councils of Priests and Scholars and Influential People of Valladolid Summoned by His Majesty in the Year 1542 for the Reformation of the Indies), in which Las Casas presents twenty legal, moral, and practical reasons to prove that the Indians should not be given to the Spaniards in *encomienda,* in vassalage, or in any other manner.

After copies of the Leyes de Indias were sent to the viceroys, governors, and *audiencias* (legislative and administrative institutions that represented the authority of the Spanish king) in the Americas, Las Casas traveled to Barcelona to express his gratitude to the king and, while there, was surprised by his appointment as the new bishop of Cuzco, Peru. In an effort to be consistent with his plea that his labor in favor of the Indians was not moved by private interest, Las Casas did not accept the honor bestowed upon him and left Barcelona to escape possible pressure. He did not, however, escape being elevated to the episcopate. Ciudad Real de Chiapa had been recently constituted into a diocese, and the first bishop who had been appointed died on his way to Guatemala. Las Casas was subsequently nominated bishop of Chiapa in 1543, and this time he could not elude the royal decision. He received his official consecration in 1544, and, armed with the Leyes de Indias, he set sail to his new bishopric in July. Upon arrival, Las Casas experienced hostility from settlers and officials who rejected the sections of the laws that abolished slavery and disinherited the families of the *encomenderos.* Las Casas did not weaken his radical beliefs. Instead, during the Easter season he announced that any Spaniard who was guilty of inhumane practices against the Indians or refused to release his Indians as mandated by the Leyes de Indias was to be denied absolution. This extreme measure provoked a hostile reaction, and even some of the members of his clergy resisted the bishop's decision.

The Council of the Indies was showered by a torrent of protests that were filed against Las Casas. The bishop resolved to answer these accusations with his own complaint against his defiant parishioners and demanded the enforcement of the Leyes de Indias

Title page for a 1620 Dutch edition of Las Casas's Brevissima relación de la destruycion de las Indias *(Rare Books and Special Collections, Thomas Cooper Library, University of South Carolina)*

before the *oidores* (auditors) of the royal *audiencia.* Although the auditors' reception to Las Casas's plea was not what the bishop had in mind, he managed to convince them to send to Ciudad Real an auditor who would see to the execution of the new laws. Tense encounters took place between the settlers and the prelate, and as a result a riot nearly broke out in Ciudad Real and almost everyone turned against Las Casas. Peace was restored after diplomatic conversations, but the animosity between the spirited bishop and his angry congregation did not subside.

In November 1545 King Charles, in response to the arguments and petitions of the colonists' representatives, revoked the law of inheritance, and in April 1546 he authorized the granting of *encomiendas* so as to afford the necessary protection of the natives without injuring the interests of the settlers too much. Meanwhile, Las Casas planned a trip to Mexico City in order to attend an assembly of all of the bishops and the most prominent ecclesiastics of New Spain, called together by the special royal commissioner, Francisco Tello de Sandoval, the president of the royal *audiencia* in Mexico. The synod approved some important articles with the aim of improving the living conditions of the Indians, but it failed to address the issue of slavery, the main objective of Las Casas's agenda. The request was well received by the viceroy of New Spain, Antonio de Mendoza, and by Tello de Sandoval. Mendoza, however, feeling apprehensive that the doctrine of restitution would bring even more hostile reactions from the Spanish colonists, elected to withhold the application of the proposal.

Las Casas did not return from Mexico City to Ciudad Real. Instead, he decided to go to Spain in order to present his case to the king. Upon arrival he found himself under fire. At court his opponents presented formal denunciations against the bishop for his actions in Ciudad Real. Among his detractors was Juan Ginés de Sepúlveda. A distinguished scholar of Aristotle, Sepúlveda was the official historian of the Spanish Crown. In 1547 he wrote *Democrates Secundus, de Justis Belli Causis Apud Indios* (The Second Democrates, or The Just Causes for Waging War against the Indians) to defend the Spanish Conquest of the Americas. Basing his views on Aristotle's concept of "slaves by nature," Sepúlveda believed that the Indians were biologically and culturally inferior and that they were therefore condemned to be dominated by a more cultured society. According to this perspective, Spain was required to fulfill its role in civilizing the Indians and for that purpose was permitted to resort to force if the natives should resist.

Sepúlveda presented four reasons to explain why the Indians should have been forcibly converted. According to him, the natives were barbarous, committed crimes against natural law, and killed and oppressed innocent people, and he argues as well that war may be waged against the infidels in order to prepare the way for preaching the faith. King Charles convoked a meeting of theologians and scholars in 1550 in Valladolid to decide whether or not war for conquest might be undertaken against the Indians, and Las Casas and Sepúlveda were summoned to appear before the assembly. Las Casas rebutted the royal historian's propositions, presenting four answers to Sepúlveda's four reasons. With respect to the first allegation that the indigenous people had a barbarous nature, Las Casas pointed out that the Spaniards were displaying more savage and thus more barbarous behavior than the Indians. He attempted to invalidate the second of Sepúlveda's reasons by saying that punishments themselves reflect jurisdiction over other people, but the Spaniards had none over the Indians. With regard to Sepúlveda's third reason, Las Casas argued that even if the Indians did sacrifice humans to their gods or ate them, such practices should be accepted, because it is better to tolerate the deaths of a few innocent victims than to start a war against a large group of people that would result in the death of many human beings. Finally, to refute the fourth argument, Las Casas contended that the Gospel did not include any argument in favor of proclaiming the forgiveness of sins by subjecting a nation to an armed militia and pursuing repentance with force. The outcome of the Valladolid meeting was not clear. Both Las Casas and Sepúlveda claimed victory, but no formal decision was handed down. While Las Casas seemed to have received official approval from the theologians who presided over the debate, his victory was a fruitless one; in the end, the advocates of the *encomienda* system eventually triumphed. The debate was published as *Aqui se contiene una disputa, o controversia, entre el Obispo fray Bartolomé de Las Casas y el doctor Ginés de Sepúlveda* (Dispute between Bishop fray Bartolomé de las Casas and doctor Ginés de Sepúlveda) in 1552.

After the debate Las Casas resolved to stay in Spain. This decision did not come as a surprise. Most of Las Casas's biographers concur that from the moment he left Mexico he planned to surrender his post in Ciudad Real. This decision was made effective in 1550, but it did not diminish the intensity of his crusade in favor of the Indians. He continued his work to obtain supplementary provisions in order to improve the conditions of life of the people of the New World and to provide more missionaries for the Indies. Between 1551 and 1552 Las Casas traveled throughout Spain recruiting friars and workers and collecting funds for the missions in Guatemala and Chiapa. He also kept busy by preparing some of his manuscripts for publication. Between 1552 and 1553 he published eight works, among them a revised version of *Brevissima relación de la destruycion de las Indias;* the treatise *Este es un tratado q el obispo dela ciudad real de Chiapa dō Fray Bartholome de las Casas o Casaus compuso por commission del Consejo Real delas Indias: Sobre la materia delos yndios que se han hecho en ellas esclavos* (1552, This is a treatise that Don Fray Bartolomé de las Casas o Casaus, Bishop of the royal city of Chiapa, wrote by commission of the Royal Council of the Indies on the subject of the Indians who have been enslaved), which had been requested by the Council of Valladolid in 1542; *Aqui se cōtiene treynta proposiciones muy jurídicas en las quales sumaria y succintamente se tocā muchas cosas pertenecientes al derecho q la yglesia y los principes christianos tienen o puede tener sobre los infieles de qual quier especie que sean* (1552, Treatise confirming the Sovereign Empire and Universal Princedom that the Kings of Castile and Leon possess over the Indies); and *Tratado cōprobatorio del imperio soberano y principado universal que los Reyes*

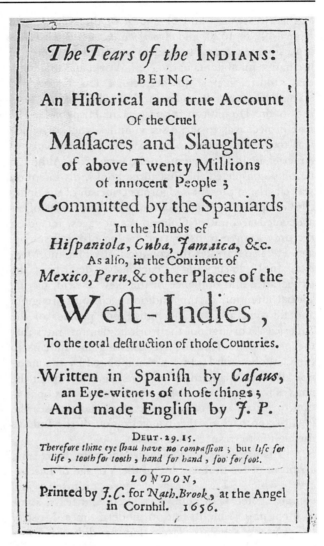

Frontispiece and title page for a 1656 translation of Las Casas's exposé of the bruality of the Spanish conquistadores (Thomas Cooper Library, University of South Carolina)

de Castilla y León tienen sobre las Indias (1553, Comprobatory Treatise on the Imperial Sovereignty and Universal Jurisdiction That the Kings of Castile and León Have over the Indies), all of them concerning Las Casas's dominant preoccupation: the defense of the Indians.

By 1555 a strong activist movement was evolving among the Spanish colonists in America in order to request the establishment of the *encomienda* system in perpetuity. Meanwhile, the economic situation in Spain was deteriorating, and the nation was on the brink of bankruptcy. Representatives of New World settlers offered a significant amount of money to the king as a matter of compensation for granting perpetuity to the *encomienda* system. The colonists' proposition was highly attractive to King Philip, who ascended the throne after Charles abdicated in 1556. Aware of the potential dangers of this agreement for the Indians, Las Casas wrote a letter to the king's confessor, Bartolomé Carranza de Miranda, urging him to persist in opposing what, according to Las Casas, would result in the imminent destruction of the natives of the Indies. Las Casas begged him to use his influence to persuade the monarch not to make any decision during Philip's absence from Spain. His strategy was successful, and the royal ruling, made after the king returned from England, was unfavorable toward making the *encomiendas* perpetual.

From then on Las Casas lived in Valladolid, where he served as an adviser on American affairs and finished the final drafts of two of his most important works: *Historia de las Indias,* a lengthy account of the

Spanish discovery and Conquest of the New World from 1492 to 1520, and *Apologética historia de las Indias,* a passionate attempt to present a systematic report of the native inhabitants in the New World and to defend that culture against its detractors. Las Casas had started *Historia de las Indias* in 1527 while he was staying in the Dominican monastery in Hispaniola. His first project was to write six volumes, each of which was to give a detailed account from the discovery of America in 1492 to events in the year 1550. Although he only completed the first three books, his intention was clearly to present a vigorous criticism of the Spanish Conquest. In *Historia de las Indias,* Las Casas offers a detailed account of Columbus's voyages, including the only known transcript of the log of his first voyage. He also narrates the conquest of Cuba and Mexico until 1520 and generously describes the exuberance and opulence of the New World, paying special attention to the traditions, customs, religion, and idiosyncrasies of the indigenous peoples of the Americas. Throughout the work he demonstrates that the original motivation of converting the Indians to the Catholic faith had been manipulated by the ambition of some Spaniards who were eager to exploit the natives for profit. Las Casas also expresses his opposition to forced and mass conversions and stresses the idea of approaching the evangelization of the Indians through faith, respect, and reason.

Historia de las Indias includes the only direct transcription of Columbus's log of the Voyage of Discovery, which Las Casas copied himself and complemented with abundant letters and texts, some of them impossible to find in modern times. Most of Las Casas's scholars agree that he did not know Columbus, but that he was well acquainted with his sons, Diego and Fernando, from whom he obtained documents written by Columbus. Las Casas had asked that *Historia de las Indias* be withheld from publication for forty years after his death, and it remained unedited until 1875–1876, when it was published in Spain.

The main purpose of *Apologética historia de las Indias* is to prove Indian competence by Aristotelian principles and comparisons with other cultures from the past. Las Casas wanted to change the perception of the Indians as inferior, irrational beings and to show their potential through the description of the different components of their culture, among them their religion, myths, political life, art, and literary productions.

By 1564 Las Casas was ninety years old. That year he wrote a treatise in defense of the Peruvian people that appears to be his last work. Originally written in Latin as "Thesauris qui Reperiuntur in Sep-

ulchris Indorum" (About the Treasures That Are Found in the Tombs of the Indians), this work was published four centuries later under the title *Los tesoros del Perú* (1958, The Treasures of Peru). The style and arguments of this work are quite similar to those found in his other writings. Convinced that his death was near, Las Casas wrote and signed his testament in 1564. He fell ill and soon thereafter died, on 31 July 1566, in the convent of Our Lady of Atocha in Madrid.

Ambiguity seems to be the operative word to describe the historical perception of Fray Bartolomé de Las Casas. His lifelong struggle against the intolerance, ambition, and cruelty of the Spanish settlers in the New World makes him deserving of the title of "Protector de los Indios" and one of the precursors of the modern movement in defense of human rights. On the other hand, he has been blamed for the beginning of the slavery system in America and for helping to create a stereotypical image of the Indians. Furthermore, some scholars have questioned Las Casas's accuracy in his descriptions of the Spanish Conquest. Despite such qualifications, though, he is universally recognized for his importance as a writer of literature and history.

Letters:

Carta de amonestaciõ del obpo de Chiapa don Fray Bartolomé de Las Casas a los muy M. Señores preside[n]te y oydores de la real audiencia (London: Whittingham, 1854);

Carta de don fray Bartolomé de Las Casas, Obispo de Chiapa a los Muy Rev. y Charissimos Padres del capitulo provincial de Guatimala (London: Whittingham, 1854);

Carta del señor don frey Bartolome de Las Casas al Illustre y Muy Magnifico señor don Mercurino Arborio de Gattinara (London: Whittingham, 1854);

Cartas y memoriales, edited by Paulino Castañeda Delgado (Madrid: Alianza, 1995).

Biographies:

Arthur Helps, *The Life of Las Casas, the Apostle of the Indies* (London: Bell & Daldy, 1868);

L. A. Dutto, *The Life of Bartolomé de Las Casas and the First Leaves of American Ecclesiastical History* (St. Louis: Herder, 1902);

Francis Augustus MacNutt, *Bartholomew de Las Casas, His Life, Apostolate, and Writings* (Cleveland: Clark, 1909);

Manuel Giménez Fernández, *Bartolomé de Las Casas: Delegado de Cisneros para la reformación de las Indias: 1516–1517,* 2 volumes (Seville: Escuela de Estudios Hispano Americanos, 1953);

Ramón Menéndez Pidal, *El Padre Las Casas: Su doble personalidad* (Madrid: Espasa-Calpe, 1963);

Henry Raup Wagner and Helen Rand Parish, *The Life and Writings of Bartolomé de Las Casas* (Albuquerque: University of New Mexico Press, 1967);

Giménez Fernández, "Fray Bartolomé de Las Casas: A Biographical Sketch," in Juan Friede and Benjamin Keen, eds., *Bartolomé de Las Casas in History: Toward an Understanding of the Man and His Work* (DeKalb: Northern Illinois University Press, 1971), pp. 67–125.

References:

Rodolfo Barón Castro, *La población de El Salvador: Estudio acerca de su desenvolvimiento desde la época prehispánica hasta nuestros días* (Madrid: Consejo Superior de Investigaciones Científicas, Instituto Gonzalo Fernández de Oviedo, 1942);

Marcel Bataillon, *Estudios sobre Bartolomé de Las Casas,* translated by J. Coderch and J. A. Martínez Schrem (Barcelona: Península, 1976);

Mauricio Beuchot, *Los fundamentos de los derechos humanos en Bartolomé de Las Casas* (Barcelona: Anthropos, 1994);

Pedro Borges, *Quién era Bartolomé de Las Casas* (Madrid: Rialp, 1990);

Leslie Crawford, *Las Casas, hombre de los siglos: Contemporaneidad de sus ideas antropológicas* (Washington, D.C.: Secretaría General, Organización de los Estados Americanos, 1978);

Enrique Díaz Araujo, *Las Casas, visto de costado: Crítica bibliográfica sobre la leyenda negra* (Madrid: Fundación Francisco Elías de Tejada y Erasmo Pèrcopo, 1995);

Juan Friede and Benjamin Keen, eds., *Bartolomé de Las Casas in History: Toward an Understanding of the Man and His Work* (DeKalb: Northern Illinois University Press, 1971);

Lewis Hanke, *All Mankind Is One: A Study of the Disputation between Bartolomé de Las Casas and Juan Ginés de Sepúlveda in 1550 on the Intellectual and Religious Capacity of the American Indians* (DeKalb: Northern Illinois University Press, 1974);

Hanke, *Bartolomé de Las Casas: An Interpretation of His Life and Writings* (The Hague: Nijhoff, 1951);

Hubert J. Miller, *Bartolomé de Las Casas: Protector of the Indians* (Edinburg, Tex.: New Santander, 1972);

André Saint-Lu and others, *Estudios sobre Fray Bartolomé de Las Casas* (Seville: Universidad de Sevilla, 1974).

Fray Luis de León

(1527 – 23 August 1591)

Dana C. Bultman
University of Georgia

BOOKS: *In Cantica Canticorum Salomonis explanatio* (Salamanca: Lucas a Junta, 1580); revised and enlarged as *F. Luysii Legionensis Augustiniani diuinorum librorum primi apud Salmanticenses interpretis explanationum in eosdem* (Salamanca: Guillermo Foquel, 1589);

In Psalmum vigesimum sextum explanatio (Salamanca: Lucas a Junta, 1580);

De utriusque agni typici, atque veri inmolationis legitimo tempore (Salamanca: Lucas a Junta, 1582);

De los nombres de Christo (2 volumes, Salamanca: Juan Fernández, 1583; revised and enlarged edition, 3 volumes, Salamanca: Herederos de Mathias Gast, 1585); translated by Edward J. Schuster as *The Names of Christ* (St. Louis: Herder, 1955);

La perfecta casada (Salamanca: Juan Fernández, 1583); translated by Alice Philena Hubbard as *The Perfect Wife* (Denton, Tex.: College Press, 1943);

Exposición del Psalmo Miserere mei (Salamanca: Antonio Ramírez, 1607);

Obras propias, y traducciones latinas, griegas y Italianas: Con la parafrasi de algunos Psalmos, y Capitulos de Iob, edited by Francisco de Quevedo (Madrid: Imprenta del Reyno, 1631); original poems translated by Henry Phillips Jr. in *Poems from the Spanish of Fray Luis Ponce de León* (Philadelphia: Privately printed, 1883);

Exposición del Libro de Job, edited by Diego Tadeo González (Madrid: Pedro Marín, 1779);

Traducción literal y declaración del Libro de los Cantares de Salomón (Salamanca: Francisco de Toxar, 1798);

Obras del M. Fr. Luis de León, de la Orden de San Augustín, reconocidas y cotejadas con varios manuscritos auténticos, 6 volumes, edited by Fray Antolín Merino (Madrid: Viuda de Ibarra, 1804–1816);

Opera nunc primum ex mss. ejusdem omnibus P. Augustiniensium studio edita, 7 volumes, edited by Marcelino Gutiérrez (Salamanca: Episcopali Calatravae Collegio, 1891–1895);

Fray Luis de León (from Aubrey F. G. Bell, Luis de León: Un estudio del renacimiento español, *1927; Thomas Cooper Library, University of South Carolina)*

De Legibus o Tratado de las Leyes, edited and translated by Luciano Pereña Vicente (Madrid: Consejo Superior de Investigaciones Científicas, 1963);

Quaestiones variae, edited by José Rodríguez Díez (Madrid: Escurialenses, 1992);

In Epistolam ad Romanos Expositio, edited by Gonzalo Díaz García (Madrid: Escurialenses, 1993).

Modern Editions: *Obras del P. Mtro. Fr. Luis de León,* 4 volumes, edited by Antolin Merino (Madrid: Reino, 1885);

Cantar de los Cantares, con introducción y preparación de Jorge Guillén (Salamanca: Sígueme, 1980);

De los nombres de Cristo, edited by Cristóbal Cuevas, fifth edition (Madrid: Cátedra, 1986);

Obra mística de Fray Luis de León, translated into Spanish by José María Becerra Hiraldo (Granada: University of Granada, 1986);

La perfecta casada, edited by Mercedes Etreros (Madrid: Taurus, 1987);

Poesía completa, edited by José Manuel Blecua (Madrid: Gredos, 1990);

Obras completas castellanas, 2 volumes, fifth edition, introduction and notes by Félix García, revised by Rafael Lazcano (Madrid: Editorial Católica, 1991);

Cantar de los cantares. Interpretaciones: Literal, espiritual, profética, translated into Spanish by Becerra Hiraldo (Madrid: Escurialenses, 1992);

Exposición del libro de Job, edited by Javier San José Lera (Salamanca: University of Salamanca, 1992);

Poesía original, edited by Esteban Gutiérrez Díaz-Bernardo (Madrid: Castalia, 1995);

Reportata theologica, edited by José Rodríguez Díez (Madrid: Escurialenses, 1996);

Poesías completas: Obras propias en castellano y latín y traducciones e imitaciones latinas, griegas, bíblicos-hebreas y romances, edited by Cuevas (Madrid: Castalia, 1998);

Escritos sobre América, edited and translated by Andrés Moreno Mengíbar and Juan Martos Fernández (Madrid: Tecnos, 1999).

Editions in English: *Lyrics of Fray Luis de León,* with English renderings by Aubrey F. G. Bell (London: Vates & Washbourne, 1928);

The Unknown Light: The Poems of Fray Luis de León, translated by Willis Barnstone (Albany: State University of New York Press, 1979);

The Names of Christ, translated, with an introduction, by Manuel Durán and William Kluback, preface by José Ferrater Mora (New York: Ramsey / Toronto: Paulist Press, 1984);

A Bilingual Edition of Fray Luis de León's La perfecta casada: *The Role of the Married Woman in Sixteenth-Century Spain,* edited and translated by John A. Jones and Javier San José Lera (Lewiston, N.Y.: Edwin Mellen Press, 1999).

OTHER: *Traducciones de Horacio,* in *Obras del excelente Poeta Garci Lasso de la Vega. Con anotaciones y enmien-das del Maestro Francisco Sánchez* (Salamanca: Pedro Lasso, 1574), pp. 91, 94, 97, 114;

"Canción a nuestra Señora, 'Virgen que el sol más pura,'" in Juan López de Ubeda, *Vergel de flores divinas* (Alcalá de Henares, 1582);

Los libros de la Madre Teresa de Jesús, edited by León (Salamanca: Guillermo Foquel, 1588);

Apología de los libros de la Madre Teresa de Jesús y de su impresión en lengua vulgar, in Fray Tomás de Jesús, *Compendio de los grados de Oración* (Madrid: Luis Sánchez, 1615), pp. 17–20;

Orationes tres ex codice manuscripto, in Fray Juan de la Cruz, *Declaración de los mandamientos de la ley, artículos de la fe, sacramentos, y ceremonias de la iglesia, en treinta y dos sermones, sacados de latín en romance. Añádense al fin tres sermones latinos del maestro fray Luis de León hasta ahora inéditos* (Madrid: Benito Cano, 1792);

"Vida de Santa Teresa. (Ms. inédito)," *Revista Augustiniana,* 5 (1883): 61–66, 95–102, 195–203;

"Expositio in Genesim," edited by Hipólito Navarro, *Ciudad de Dios,* 203 (1990): 200–225.

Fray Luis de León was a Catholic theologian deeply dedicated to an accurate and detailed interpretation of the Bible and the formulation of a rigorous moral philosophy. Adept in Greek, Hebrew, and Latin, León was an Augustinian monk and a well-known professor of theology and law at the University of Salamanca. His use of language is considered a model of lucidity and depth of content. He was an excellent poet but did not seek to publish his poetry during his lifetime. This decision was motivated in part by the perceived triviality of poetry in comparison to theology, according to conservative sixteenth-century values, and to León's own sense of decorum concerning his most personal writings. Manuel Durán, in his *Luis de León* (1971), writes of León: "He exemplified perhaps better than any other Spaniard of his time the complexities and inner contradictions of the Spanish Renaissance." As a public figure León elicited great loyalty as well as fierce opposition among his fellow professors at Salamanca. As a writer he blended biblical interpretation, which was rooted in his exceptional linguistic expertise, with an enthusiasm for classical Greek and Roman poetry and an admiration for contemporaneous Spanish mysticism.

León became a champion of the humanist ambition to disseminate a thorough knowledge of Scripture in the vernacular to those readers without the ability to understand Latin or who were prohibited by the church from reading the Bible. His writings are characterized by the conviction that Scripture, rather than the chivalric and sentimental tales of secular literature he considered dangerously immoral, had the power to lead readers to virtue. Although he praised the idealized life of simple retreat that he inherited from Stoicism, he was an active public figure.

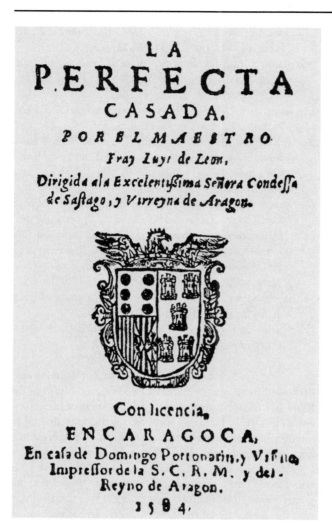

LA
P.ERFECTA
CASADA.
POR EL MAESTRO
Fray Luys de Leon,
Dirigida ala Excelentiſsima Señora Condeſſa
de Saſtago, y Virreyna de Aragon.

Con licencia,
EN CARAGOCA,
En caſa de Domingo Portonariis, y Viſua
Impreſſor de la S. C. R. M. y del.
Reyno de Aragon.
1584,

Title page for an early edition of León's 1583 guide to morals
for married women (The Perfect Wife; from Alberto
Barasoain, Fray Luis de León, *1973; Thomas*
Cooper Library, University of South Carolina)

During his lifetime he achieved his desire to provide a wider audience with access to the benefits of Scripture. His intricate commentaries explicating portions of the Bible in Spanish were highly popular with his contemporaries. As a scholar he sought the most accurate interpretations even when they diverged from tradition and made him vulnerable to harsh critique. León defended the importance of establishing a biblical text free from errors through textual criticism, as well as the value of comparing versions of the original texts. Accused of questioning the authority of the Vulgate, St. Jerome's Latin translation of the Bible, and of translating the Song of Songs into Spanish, although the church had prohibited such translation explicitly since the Council of Trent, León spent nearly five years, from 1572 to 1576, imprisoned by the Inquisition. He was eventually absolved of all wrongdoing, and his exemplary courage to

maintain his principles after his release was highly celebrated. Since then his moral triumph has been regarded as a bright point in Spanish intellectual history. His writings include many translations of biblical and classical texts into Spanish, some twenty-three original poems in Spanish, and several major biblical treatises and commentaries in both Spanish and Latin, many of which he composed during his imprisonment.

León was born in 1527 in Belmonte, Cuenca, to Lope de León and Inés de Varela. He was the first of six children. In 1534 the family moved to Madrid, where his father worked as a lawyer. In 1541 León's father became a judge in Granada, and Luis was sent to Salamanca to study canon law under the tutelage of his uncle Francisco. There he became an Augustinian novitiate in the convent of San Pedro in 1543, taking the habit on 29 January 1544. The first record of León as a student of theology dates from 1546 to 1547, the year of the earliest copy of a matriculation book preserved by the University of Salamanca. León's teachers included the renowned thinkers Melchor Cano and Domingo de Soto.

Both León's father and mother had Jewish ancestry, a fact that his enemies exploited in their portrayal of him as a heretical Catholic who favored Jewish traditions. Scholars accept that although he was silent about it, Luis was conscious of his social vulnerability as a descendent of *conversos* (as Jewish or Muslim converts to Christianity were known), because in 1548 the *sambenitos* (penitential inquisitorial garments) of Leonor de Villanueva, León's great-grandmother, and her sister Juana Rodríguez were hung in the Collegiate Church of Belmonte as a reminder of their religious transgressions. The two women had been reconciled for continuing to practice Judaism in Cuenca in 1512, and their garments were first hung there in the cathedral. A decree in 1529 ordered the garments moved to Belmonte, where León's family had to bear the dishonor of such a public reminder in their hometown.

The extent to which León identified with and was influenced by his Jewish heritage continues to be an issue for debate among scholars, and opinions are wide-ranging. Many studies on León have focused on the Augustinian and Neoplatonic traditions within Christianity that shaped his work, without exploring non-Christian sources. Other scholars, such as A. Habib Arkin and Karl A. Kottman, have argued that Jewish, cabalistic, and Arabic traditions in the Iberian Peninsula informed his work and resulted in his characteristic exegetic techniques. While Colin P. Thompson, in his *The Strife of Tongues: Fray Luis de León and the Golden Age of Spain* (1988), favors exploring the influence of these traditions on León's work, he doubts the value of attributing a *converso* identity to an individual who was several generations removed from conversion. According to Thompson, while León wanted Christians to understand the Old Testament fully, his relationship to

Jewish sources and the cabala (Jewish mysticism) were characteristic of "the world of sixteenth-century scholarship, which loved to probe difficult texts for hidden meanings, and which found in extra-canonical Jewish literature an endlessly fascinating source for this."

In 1552 León graduated with a bachelor's degree in theology from the University of Toledo, after which he traveled between Salamanca, Toledo, Soria, and Alcalá de Henares, meeting and witnessing the activities of major humanists of the day. In 1554 the eminent director of the Polyglot Bible, Benito Arias Montano, showed León his commentary on the Song of Songs, eventually giving him a copy in 1561. Arias Montano's commentary may have influenced León's own translation of the same biblical text several years later; it was among León's papers seized by the Inquisition. In 1556 León attended the University of Alcalá de Henares as a student of Hebrew and biblical exegesis with Cipriano de la Huerga, an important fact in his later defense of the value of reading Old Testament texts in Hebrew.

León returned to Salamanca in 1559, during a time in Spain when interest in humanism and enthusiasm for philology were offset by an intense fear of Protestantism. That year there was a decree forbidding Spaniards to study at most foreign universities, and autos-da-fé were held in Valladolid and Seville to repress Protestant circles. León made his transition from student to teacher in the midst of these historical realities. In 1560 he graduated as a licentiate and master of theology at Salamanca but failed at his first attempt at winning a chair, that of biblical exegesis. The winner was his friend and fellow Hebraist Gaspar de Grajal. Eventually, in 1561 León won the minor chair of St. Thomas against six opponents.

Also in 1561, León undertook his first major translation of a biblical text, at the request of his cousin Isabel Osorio, a nun in the convent of Sancti Spiritus. Because she could not read the Latin version of the Song of Songs, León translated the text into Spanish for her and wrote an accompanying commentary. The biblical text was considered difficult to interpret and potentially dangerous owing to its vivid and sensual evocation of passionate love. Intended for her private use, the manuscript was copied and circulated. According to León in later testimony in his defense, a young monk named Diego de León entered his cell and made the first unauthorized copy of the document for which he was denounced some eleven years later to the Inquisition.

Perhaps owing to its controversial nature, the manuscript itself circulated unpublished in a large number of copies for more than two hundred years before it appeared in 1798 as *Traducción literal y declaración del Libro de los Cantares de Salomón* (A Literal Translation and Explanation of the Book of the Songs of Solomon). This first major work was written during his "polemical period," as

Félix García (in his 1991 edition of León's complete works) refers to his years as a young professor. Although this text is one of León's earliest, in his description of the Song of Songs the independence and maturity of his opinions are evident. Since the allegorical interpretation regarding Christ and the church is well known, León reasons, he intends to focus only upon a profound interpretation of divine love. He is dedicated to evoking the sound, meaning, and context of the original work, which he considers a fictional, literary piece of writing: "Porque se ha de entender que este Libro en su primer origen se escribió en metro, y es todo él una égloga pastoril, donde con palabras y lenguaje de pastores, hablan Salomón y su Esposa, y algunas veces sus compañeros, como si todos fuesen gente de aldea" (Because it should be understood that this Book in its original form was written in verse, and as a whole is a pastoral eclogue, in which Solomon and his Wife, and sometimes their companions, speak with the words and language of shepherds, as if they were all villagers). To view the Song of Songs in this modern manner was highly unusual for his time. León is not prudish about his translation; instead he relishes the aesthetic beauty of the original and wishes to communicate it well by systematically summarizing and translating each chapter of the book. He comments line by line upon the text, offering up analyses of individual Hebrew words and comparing them to the translations found in the Latin Bible, upon which he clearly wishes to improve. León's extraordinary attention to Hebrew in this work, written initially for one female reader, reveals a writer who wrote in the context of teaching, wished to disseminate his deep understanding, and viewed language as both a sensual and conceptual vehicle toward knowledge of the divine. Literature and Scripture for León came together in their use of multifaceted words and layers of meaning.

In 1565 León won the chair of Durando, an event that was accompanied by an escalation of the rivalries between the Augustinians and the Dominicans at the University of Salamanca. Around this time he took part in a commission to recommend reprinting an edition of the Bible based upon the edition of Robert Estienne, the French printer and humanist, with annotations attributed to the noted French Hebraist and Hellenist François Vatable. León, along with other Hebraists from Salamanca, Grajal and Martín Martínez Cantalapiedra, found themselves in strong opposition to the views of the Dominicans and Jeronomites led by León de Castro, an event that played a key role in his trial. This period in León's life was also marked by heightened administrative responsibilities and frequent illnesses. In 1566 he was named administrator of the Augustinian College of San Guillermo in Salamanca, and in 1567 he took on the position of vice rector of the university. As a professor, León taught a course called "De fide" (On Faith) in 1567–1568, arguing at length in favor of the controversial notion that the Hebrew text of the Bible had not become corrupt, as had been traditionally agreed, but at times offered, along with the Greek text, more reliable readings than did the Latin.

In 1570 León traveled to Córdoba and Madrid. A member of the committee from the University of Salamanca in charge of salary raises for minor chairs, he was responsible for presenting the raise proposal to King Philip II and was eventually successful in procuring the proposed raise. In addition, he began significant friendships during this time with the noted musician Francisco Salinas and the prominent scholar Francisco Sánchez de las Brozas, known as "El Brocense." Elias L. Rivers, in *Fray Luis de León: The Original Poems* (1983), affirms that León must have been engaged in translating Horace's odes at this time as well, since his translations are included anonymously in the commentaries of the scholarly edition of Garcilaso de la Vega's poems by El Brocense. The volume was published in 1574 when León was imprisoned. In it he is referred to only as "un docto de estos reinos" (a scholar of these kingdoms), an example of his underground identity as a poet that developed in the absence of a published edition of his poetry during his lifetime. León's interest in poetry is sometimes viewed as contradictory to his strict morality and theological focus. Although a Catholic theologian, he respected the cultural differences of the classical works that he translated by such writers as Horace, Virgil, and Pindar and did not attempt to mold them to his views. David J. Hildner, in his *Poetry and Truth in the Spanish Works of Fray Luis de León* (1992), states, "In his translations from the classics, he rests content with the original poetic images and fictions, leaving them practically untouched, although they often contradict the Judaeo-Christian theology, ethics, of the natural 'science' of his day."

The unity in León's work can be found in his understanding of language as a medium for divine communication. His poetic style is characterized by a studied naturalness, lucidity, and elegance. His imitation of classical forms, mythological allusions, and Latinate vocabulary link him aesthetically to Garcilaso and Luis de Góngora. The majority of his original poems seem to have been composed between 1569 and 1584. Nearly all are difficult to date with certainty, and the dates given to single poems by individual scholars can vary by more than ten years.

The composition of one of his best-known odes, "Profecía del Tajo" (1631; translated by Barnstone as "The Tagus River Prophecy" in *The Unknown Light: The Poems of Fray Luis de León,* 1979) is dated 1569 by Esteban Gutiérrez Díaz-Bernardo because it is in part an imitation of Horace's "The Prophecy of Nereus" and thus was probably written during the same period as his translations of Horace. The ode begins with the sin of lust, the legendary cause of the invasion of the Iberian Peninsula by the Moors in 711. In his verses León projects vivid images of rushing armies brandishing swords and the bloody fall of Visigoth Spain. According to legend, King Rodrigo's rape or seduction of a young noblewoman provoked her father, Count Julián, to avenge himself by allowing Arab and Berber Muslims to enter the peninsula through Ceuta. León personifies the Tagus as a stern river god who prophesies to Rodrigo the violent repercussions of his unjust actions: "En mal punto te goces, / injusto forzador; que ya el sonido / y las amargas voces, / y ya siento el bramido / de Marte, de furor y ardor ceñido" (May your pleasures be damned, / lawless ravisher; I already hear the sounds / and bitter voices, / and hear the roar / of Mars girt with fury and passion).

Like Helen's abduction by Paris that sparked the Trojan War, la Cava's downfall marks the end of the Visigoth dominance. The moral overtone, according to Gutiérrez Díaz-Bernardo, is a warning to just men against indulging in amorous passion. This general moral warning is set in the context of the particularities of Spanish history. Rivers views the poem as an expression of sixteenth-century Spanish nationalism and León's "love for his country." Catherine Swietlicki, writing in *Spanish Christian Cabala: The Works of Luis de León, Santa Teresa de Jesús, and San Juan de la Cruz* (1986), makes similar remarks with regard to León's view of Spain's destiny: "The friar felt that Spain—and perhaps the Spanish conversos in particular—would play a major part in the tumultuous times prior to the Second Coming." Such comments suggest that while León incorporated myths of past classical Greek and Roman literature into his poetry, he was less tolerant of coexisting cultures, such as those of Islam, that posed political and economic challenges to Spain.

By October 1570 León had returned from the court in Madrid and was back in Salamanca. Although St. Teresa of Avila, whose works León edited after her death, was visiting the city at that time, they are not believed to have ever met. León has been frequently studied together with the mystics St. Teresa and St. Juan de la Cruz, and some scholars have viewed León's poetry as mystical. While León displayed a deep interest in the works of mystics, however, he did not claim to have mystical knowledge. Thompson suggests his mystic tendencies derive more from "his thorough reading of the spiritual classics" than from personal experience. If one defines mysticism as an ineffable union with the divine, León's ode "Noche serena" (1631; translated as "Serene Night" in *The Unknown Light*), probably composed in 1570, suggests a desire for mystic union rather than a realization of that desire. In "Noche serena" León expresses his frustration with worldly life and his inability to bridge his separation from the transcendent ideal he sees in the starry night skies: "¡Morada de grandeza, / templo de claridad y hermosura! / Mi alma que a tu alteza / nació" (Where grandeur has its home, / temple of beauty and of clarity! / My soul for your high dome / was born). Further on, the poet asks who could see the beauty of the stars and planets at night and not be filled with a wish to give up earthly existence and join heavenly perfection. León's mysticism is not of a visionary or experiential nature. In poems such as "Noche serena" he exhibits a strong desire to exceed the limitations of human imperfection and earthly squalor. He is different from St. Teresa and St. Juan de la Cruz in that he does not stress the importance of transcending the intellect and thus reaching higher knowledge.

The end to this active period in León's life came in July 1571 when the Dominican professors Bartolomé de Medina and Castro presented the Inquisition with seventeen propositions detailing the supposedly heretical opinions held by León. The most serious charges against him were based upon his translation and commentary of the Song of Songs. He was accused of translating a biblical text, following the original Hebrew instead of the Latin of the Vulgate, and of strengthening the literal meaning of the Song of Songs, thus weakening the prevailing scholastic allegorical interpretation. Other Hebraists were also accused, and that autumn, while awaiting the decision of the Holy Office, León fell ill. On 25 March 1572, Grajal, Martínez Cantalapiedra, and León were arrested. Two days later they were imprisoned by the Inquisition in Valladolid. The fact that all were of Jewish descent has led scholars to conclude that their accusers were motivated out of bigotry in addition to the intense personal rivalry between the two groups of men. In León's own written defense he emphatically states that Medina and Castro falsely accused him out of a desire for personal advancement.

During the years León spent in his prison cell, under adverse conditions that contributed to his ill health, he is thought to have written *In Psalmum vigesimum sextum explanatio* (1580, Commentary on the Twenty-Sixth Psalm), several of his odes, and the majority of his *Exposición del Libro de Job* (1779, Commentary on the Book of Job) and to have initiated work on *De los nombres de Christo* (1583; translated as *The Names of Christ,* 1955). León describes his determination to write while in prison to the nobleman Pedro Portocarrero in the dedication of *De los nombres de Christo:* "no me parece que debo perder la occasion de este ocio" (I do not believe I should waste the opportunity of this leisure). His previous responsibilities had left him no time to act upon his desire to make the depth of scriptural teachings accessible to readers of Spanish; now León believed God had provided him with a chance to do so in prison.

León was active in complaining about the lack of speed regarding his case. His friend Grajal died in the same Valladolid prison in 1575 awaiting a verdict, and León worried about suffering the same fate. Finally, in September 1576 the tribunal initiated a verdict. Two mem-

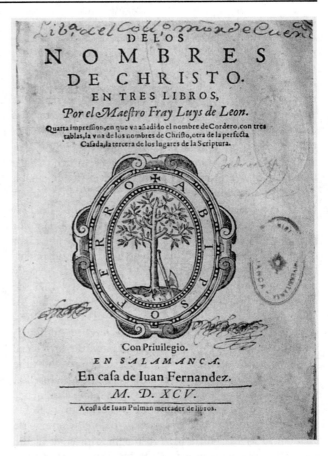

Title page for an early edition of León's 1583 work (translated as The Names of Christ, *1955), a dialogue in which three characters expound on the different names for Jesus Christ used in the Bible (from* El siglo de frai Luis de León: Salamanca y el Renacimiento, *1991; Thomas Cooper Library, University of South Carolina)*

bers recommended that León be privately reprimanded and made to recant publicly. They thought that he should be obligated to explain before an audience of his students and colleagues the offensive propositions in his work for which he had been arrested, and they recommended he be prohibited from teaching for the remainder of his life. Four other members of the tribunal recommended torture, although they agreed that his guilt had not been completely proven. According to historian Angel Alcalá in *Proceso Inquisitorial de Fray Luis de León: Edición paleografica, anotada y crítica* (1991, Inquisitorial Trial of Fray Luis de León: Paleographic, Critical, and Annotated Edition), torture was an infrequent recourse in Inquisition trials and notable in this case since it put the prisoner's life at risk. On 7 December León's final sentence was announced: he was completely absolved. This narrow escape from the earlier determination of the tribunal was probably because of the intervention of the newly appointed inquisitor, Cardinal Quiroga. The Inquisition limited itself to reproaching him for having taken up dangerous topics and confiscated León's manuscript of his translation and commentary of the Song of Songs. In addition, he was advised to practice moderation and caution, a recommendation he subsequently disregarded. Martínez Cantalapiedra was also absolved soon after, and Grajal was acquitted posthumously.

Freed on 11 December 1576, León returned to Salamanca on 30 December in triumph, wearing a white habit as a sign of his innocence. His poem "Al salir de la cárcel" (1631; translated as "Upon Leaving Prison" in *The Unknown Light*) expresses his sentiments and desire for peaceful solitude. León renounced his claim on the chair of Durando in favor of the man who had held it during his imprisonment and was named to a chair of theology instead. According to legend, on 29 January 1577 he appeared in his lecture hall and began by addressing his students in the manner he always had—"Dicebamus hesterna die . . ." (As we were saying yesterday . . .)—although almost five years had passed. Pedro Suárez, the provincial father of the Augustinian order, ordered León at this time to begin publishing his works. León now found himself at the height of his abilities and with considerable influence among those who had supported him during his trial. He held the chair of moral philosophy before winning the chair of Holy Scripture—the most significant chair at the University of Salamanca—in 1579. He also earned a master of arts degree from the University of Sahagún and during this time probably composed his most famous ode, "La vida retirada" (1631; translated as "Secluded Life" in *The Unknown Light*), in which he praises the virtues of seclusion, simplicity, nature, and wisdom. The most noteworthy feature of the poem is León's evocation of the divine harmony found in creation and the poet's relationship to it in contrast to the suffering and chaos experienced by others in their worldly ambitions. Durán explains that the ode, like much of León's writing, charts a movement from the general to the particular and personal, with a self-portrait at the end that "offers us a Luis de León transformed into classical allegory: the happy man, the perfect serene philosopher, the eternal poet crowned with ivy and laurel."

In 1580 León's first published works appeared: two Latin texts, *In Cantica Canticorum Salomonis explanatio* (Commentary on the Song of Solomon), which built upon his earlier Spanish commentary and which he revised and amplified in a 1589 edition, and *In Psalmum vigesimum sextum explanation*. In 1582 León had a second brief encounter with the Inquisition after participating in a public discussion of predestination, but he was only lightly reprimanded by the Inquisitor Cardinal Quiroga. That same year Juan López de Ubeda included in his *Vergel de flores*

divinas (Garden of Divine Flowers) the only one of León's odes to be published during his lifetime, "A Nuestra Señora" (translated as "To Our Lady" in *The Unknown Light*). In this long poem León praises the Virgin Mary as a beacon of light and hope. He creates a detailed portrait of her scriptural significance, rather than simply her beauty, alternating descriptions of her attributes with requests for her powerful intercession in alleviating the poet's suffering.

León's two most influential texts in Spanish, *De los nombres de Christo* and *La perfecta casada* (translated as *The Perfect Wife*, 1943), were first published together in 1583. Both texts challenge conservative opposition by translating Scripture, and they prove Spanish a suitable medium for elevated subjects. After being revised and published in a definitive 1585 edition, *De los nombres de Christo* became a popular work; seven editions were printed by 1605. A dialogue with characteristics of a treatise, the text begins in a country setting with three characters: Marcelo, Juliano, and Sabino. Marcelo, a figure identifiable with León because of his weariness with academic life, is cajoled by his companions into expounding upon the meanings of some of the multiple names of Christ found within Scripture. The playfulness of the characters while engaged in discourse is balanced by the depth of biblical analysis in the text. Hildner has identified this duality as an underlying structure in León's works—"on the one hand, a constant contextualization of speech (in time, space, and specific personalities); on the other hand, a decontextualization of speech out of the particular and figurative into the universal and abstract." Marcelo agrees hesitantly to explain just a few of the many names of Christ, and in each chapter León offers a thorough and lucid discussion of one name, never, according to Marcelo, exhausting all the interpretive possibilities each name suggests. In León's understanding of language, words are intimately connected to truth and to Marcelo's discussion of the divine names. In the first chapter, on the name "Pimpollo" (Bud of the Lord), Marcelo explains that God's purpose in creating the universe was to communicate himself to his creatures, and thus this particular name points to the fact that the fruit of all God's creative effort was the perfect communication of himself that took place in the incarnation.

La perfecta casada was also highly popular, appearing in six editions by 1632. A moral guide to married life for women, León dedicated the work to a young relative of his, María Varela Osorno. Of all his texts, this one may have had the greatest influence upon popular culture since it became a customary gift for young brides. Following a structure similar to that of his translation and commentary on the Song of Songs, León bases his treatise on the ideal wife upon a line-by-line translation of Prov. 31:10–31, paying close attention to the Hebrew original. The overall intention is to provide a guide to virtue in order to help women merit esteem from their husbands and honorable reputations. If one takes into consideration that monastic life was respected as a higher spiritual ideal than matrimony, the work can be read as a defense of the importance of a married woman's social role, which León defines in terms of overseeing the household economy and embodying frugality, diligence, modesty, and confidence in one's husband. Ample evidence of sixteenth-century misogyny is interspersed with intimate passages revealing León's own domestic character. His perfect wife possesses masculine attributes, and the text abounds with Platonic associations of the feminine with the monstrous and the irrational. Nevertheless, he also encourages independent decision making and economic activity.

León threads through *La perfecta casada* a critique of the ill treatment of those of lower rank and the corruption of the nobility. Advising gentleness toward servants and reminding the reader that in succeeding generations the roles of servant and master could be reversed, he writes that all human beings are made by God of the same material: "hay tan vanas algunas, que casi desconocen su carne, y piensan que la suya es carne de ángeles, y las de sus sirvientas de perros, y quieren ser adoradas dellas, y no acordarse dellas si son nascidas" (there are some [women] so vain who do not seem to know their own bodies and think that their own flesh is that of angels whilst that of their maidservants is that of dogs, and they want to be adored by their servants but they do not give a thought to whether they are alive or not). Passages such as this one suggest that, on an allegorical level, the text may be interpreted as a critique of Spain's ruling class.

León remained active during his final years. He had two audiences with King Philip II, in 1586 and 1587, representing the interests of the University of Salamanca. In 1588 he published *Los libros de la Madre Teresa de Jesús* (The Books of the Mother Teresa of Jesus), his edition of the works of St. Teresa. In 1589, under the general title *F. Luysii Legionensis Augustiniani diuinorum librorum primi apud Salmanticenses interpretis explanationum in eosdem* (Fray Luis de León Professor of Theology and First in Holy Scripture Salamancan Commentator of Interpretation There of the Same), he published four Latin works. In March 1591, just a few months before his death, León finished his *Exposición del Libro de Job,* although the text was not published until almost two centuries later, in 1779. Before his imprisonment he had initiated this work at the request of Ana de Jesús, a Carmelite nun and close friend of St. Teresa, and he dedicated it to her with the wish that she identify her own suffering with that of the Old Testament figure who endured great calamity without losing his faith in God. The work is considered to be his greatest biblical commentary and reflective of the culmination of his style. León exhibits a profound engagement with justice, basing his

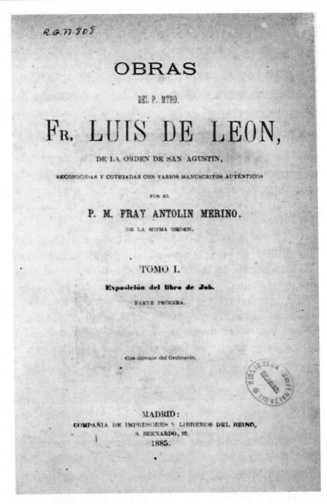

Title page for the first volume of a four-volume edition of León's collected works (from El siglo de frai Luis de León: Salamanca y el Renacimiento, *1991; Thomas Cooper Library, University of South Carolina)*

belief in its existence upon a demonstration of the logic of God. He describes the Book of Job as a text that offers multiple insights into history, doctrine, and prophecy. His painstakingly detailed original interpretation is analogous, according to Thompson, to the sort of enrichment of the English language found in the King James Bible. Thompson asserts that León's desire to disseminate his "incarnational view" of the language of Scripture motivated his biblical commentaries; yet, his exposition of Job "is nevertheless as scholarly and as complex as if it had been intended for a Latin readership of professional theologians." León was among those authors of his age who had high expectations of his readers.

At the age of sixty-four, León died in Madrigal de las Altas Torres, Ávila, on 23 August 1591 and was buried in Salamanca in the convent of San Augustín. At the time he was writing a biography of St. Teresa, which he left unfinished. Although much of his poetry circulated in manuscript form for many years, not until 1631 was it published in a modest volume edited by Francisco de Quevedo, *Obras propias, y traducciones latinas, griegas y Italianas: Con la parafrasi de algunos Psalmos, y Capitulos de Iob* (Original Poetry, and Latin, Greek, and Italian Translations: With the Paraphrases of Some Psalms, and Chapters of Job). Quevedo considered León's verse to be a superlative model of the use of the Spanish language: "son en nuestro idioma el singular ornamento y el mejor blasón de la habla Castellana" (in our language they are the most exceptional ornament and greatest emblem of Castilian speech).

Fray Luis de León was a remarkable individual and one of the major intellectuals of the Spanish Renaissance. His works have been acclaimed by readers and scholars and have exerted diverse cultural and literary influences. The publication of many studies, useful facsimile editions, and Spanish translations of his Latin works in the latter part of the twentieth century demonstrates a continued interest in his theological insights and literary legacy.

Letters:

"Cartas," in *Epistolario español*, volume 2, edited by Eugenio de Ochoa y Ronna, Biblioteca de Autores Españoles, no. 62 (Madrid: Rivadeneyra, 1870), pp. 49–57.

Bibliography:

Rafael Lazcano González, *Fray Luis de León: Bibliografía*, second edition (Madrid: Revista Augustiniana, 1994).

Biographies:

Aubrey F. G. Bell, *Luis de León: Un estudio del renacimiento español*, translated by Celso García (Barcelona: Araluce, 1927);

Rafael Lazcano González, "Fray Luis de León: An Extraordinary Man," translated by M. J. O'Connell, *Augustinian Heritage*, 39, no. 1 (1993): 35–77.

References:

Angel Alcalá, ed., *Proceso Inquisitorial de Fray Luis de León: Edición paleografica, anotada y crítica* (Junta de Castilla y León: Consejería de Cultura y Turismo, 1991);

José Ramón Alcántara Mejía, *La escondida senda: Poética y hermenéutica en la obra castellana de fray Luis de León* (Salamanca: Ediciones Universidad de Salamanca, 2002);

Dámaso Alonso, "Notas sobre Fray Luis de León y la poesía renacentista," in his *Obras completas*, volume 2 (Madrid: Gredos, 1973), pp. 769–788;

A. Habib Arkin, *La influencia de la exégesis hebrea en los comentarios bíblicos de Fray Luis de León* (Madrid: Consejo Superior de Investigaciones Científicas, Instituto "Benito Arias Montano," 1966);

Alberto Barasoain, *Fray Luis de León* (Madrid: Júcar, 1973);

Victor García de la Concha, ed., *Fray Luis de León*, Academia Literaria Renacentista (Salamanca: Universidad de Salamanca, 1981);

Cristóbal Cuevas, "Fray Luis de León," in *Historia y crítica de la literatura española*, volume 2, edited by Francisco Rico and Francisco López Estrada (Barcelona: Crítica, 1980), pp. 382–425;

Manuel Durán, *Luis de León* (New York: Twayne, 1971);

Helen Dill Goode, *La prosa retórica de Fray Luis de León en "De los nombres de Cristo": Aportación al estudio de un estillista del Renacimiento español* (Madrid: Gredos, 1969);

David J. Hildner, *Poetry and Truth in the Spanish Works of Fray Luis de León* (London: Tamesis, 1992);

Karl A. Kottman, *Law and Apocalypse: The Moral Thought of Luis de León* (The Hague: Nijhoff, 1972);

Rafael Lapesa, "El cultismo en la poesía de Fray Luis de León," in his *Poetas y prosistas de ayer y de hoy: Veinte estudios de historia y crítica literarias* (Madrid: Gredos, 1977), pp. 110–145;

Francisco Rico, *El pequeño mundo del hombre: Varia fortuna de una idea en las letras españolas* (Madrid: Castalia, 1970);

Elias L. Rivers, *Fray Luis de León: The Original Poems* (London: Grant & Cutler, 1983);

Ricardo Senabre, *Tres estudios sobre Fray Luis de León* (Salamanca: Universidad de Salamanca, 1978);

El siglo de frai Luis de León: Salamanca y el Renacimiento: Colegio del Arzobispo Fonseca, Escuelas Menores, Antigua Universidad, Salamanca, octubre–diciembre 1991 (Salamanca & Junta de Castilla y León: Centro Nacional de Exposiciones, Ministerio de Cultura, Dirección General de Bellas Artes y Archivos, Universidad de Salamanca, 1991);

Catherine Swietlicki, *Spanish Christian Cabala: The Works of Luis de León, Santa Teresa de Jesús, and San Juan de la Cruz* (Columbia: University of Missouri Press, 1986);

Colin P. Thompson, *The Strife of Tongues: Fray Luis de León and the Golden Age of Spain* (Cambridge & New York: Cambridge University Press, 1988);

Karl Vossler, *Fray Luis de León*, third edition (Madrid: Espasa-Calpe, 1969).

Lope de Rueda

(1510? – 1565?)

Denise M. DiPuccio
University of North Carolina, Wilmington

BOOKS: *Compendio llamado El Deleitoso, en el cual se contienen muchos pasos graciosos del excellente poeta y gracioso representante Lope de Rueda para poner en principios y entremedias de colloquios y comedias,* edited by Juan de Timoneda (Valencia: Juan de Timoneda, 1567);

Las segundas dos Comedias del excellente poeta, y representante Lope de rueda, edited by Timoneda (Valencia: Juan de Timoneda, 1567);

Registro de representantes, a do van registrados por Juan de Timoneda muchos y graciosos passos de Lope de Rueda y otros diversos autores, edited by Timoneda (Valencia: Juan de Timoneda, 1570);

Las quatro comedias y dos coloquios pastoriles del excellente poeta y gracioso representante Lope de Rueda, edited by Timoneda (Valencia: Juan de Timoneda, 1576).

Modern Editions: *Obras,* 2 volumes, edited by marqués de la Fuensanta del Valle (Madrid: Perales & Martínez, 1895, 1896);

Obras de Lope de Rueda, 2 volumes, edited by Emilio Cotarelo y Mori (Madrid: Real Academia Española, 1908);

Registro de representantes, edited by Adolfo Bonilla y San Martín (Madrid: Ruiz, 1917);

Teatro, edited by J. Moreno Villa (Madrid: La Lectura, 1924);

Pasos completos, edited by F. Sáinz de Robles (Madrid: Aguilar, 1944);

Pasos, edited by Salvador Novo and Mercedes López (Mexico City: Secretaría de Educación Pública, 1946);

Pasos, edited by J. M. Blecua (Saragossa: Clásicos Ebro, 1950);

Pasos completos de Lope de Rueda, edited by F. García Pavón (Madrid: Taurus, 1966);

Eufemia. Armelina, edited by Fernando González Ollé (Salamanca: Anaya, 1967);

Los engañados. Medora, edited, with introduction and notes, by González Ollé (Madrid: Espasa-Calpe, 1973);

Lope de Rueda (frontispiece for Pasos, *1950; Thomas Cooper Library, University of South Carolina)*

Pasos, edited by González Ollé (Madrid: Cátedra, 1981);

Las cuatro comedias, edited, with introduction and notes, by Alfredo Hermenegildo (Madrid: Taurus, 1985);

Coloquio de Timbria, in *Antología del teatro español del siglo XVI,* edited by Hermenegildo (Madrid: Biblioteca nueva, 1998), pp. 227–263.

Edition in English: *The Interludes,* translated by Randall W. Listerman (Ottawa: Dovehouse, 1988).

Lope de Rueda made two significant contributions to the development of secular theater in Spain. First, he was a professional dramatist, manager, and actor; people paid to see works he wrote, probably directed, and acted in, accompanied by a cast of actors from his own company. Lope and his theatrical troupe traveled from town to town performing his own and other dramatists' works. Other anonymous men may have exercised all three of these trades before Lope; nevertheless, Lope is the first for whom historical documents attest to the fact that he earned a living by establishing his own company and writing and acting in plays. Second, Lope did not create but certainly perfected a dramatic genre known as the *paso,* a short comic interlude often placed between acts of a more serious play. Although Lope wrote several full-length plays, he found his true creative outlet in the *paso.* Moreover, the *paso* later influenced the evolution of comic theater in Spain and the *teatro menor,* a term that literally means "minor theater" but is used to refer to short plays, usually of one act.

Virtually nothing is known about Lope's childhood, his formal education, how he became interested in the theater, how he discovered that he had a talent for writing or acting, or how he decided to give up his lucrative career as a goldsmith and enter the world of performance. He was probably born in Seville around 1510. Perhaps he learned his trade from an Italian acting company, of which he may have been a member, operating in Spain in the late 1530s. A second possible venue for early exposure to theater was the Catholic Church. Religious *autos,* short plays that reenacted the Eucharist or other religious phenomena, were performed on holidays, such as Corpus Christi.

Historical artifacts provide useful information regarding not only the life of an itinerant professional actor but the somewhat rudimentary staging techniques in the theater of early-modern Spain. During a twenty-five-year period spanning 1540–1565, Lope traveled all over the Iberian Peninsula giving performances at court, in patios of neighborhood houses, and in *corrales* (open-air public theaters) in towns along the way. Lope apparently garnered considerable success and fame in the secular and religious arenas. For example, in 1551 he participated in a theater festival in honor of Felipe II's visit to Valladolid. In 1554 he staged another spectacle for Felipe II and the heir apparent, Prince Don Carlos, in the city of Benavente. Felipe was most likely en route to England to wed the princess Mary, Elizabeth I's half sister. A chronicler from the period noted that the king enjoyed this *auto,* which dealt with the sacred Scripture. A contract from the period shows that on 8 May 1552 the city council of Valladolid put Lope in charge of public representations and offered him an annual salary. Lope even received an award for best performance in the Corpus Christi festival in 1559.

Contracts from the mid 1550s provide a glimpse into some of the day-to-day realities of managing a theatrical troupe. Guilds played a significant role in the development of theater in Spain by hiring people to write plays for special occasions. Many of the religious pieces written and performed by Lope and his cohorts were commissioned by the guilds of various tradesmen and artisans, including wine merchants and silk dealers. A document signed by Lope in 1543, the first concrete evidence of his life as a professional, shows that he was hired for the second year in a row by the laborers' guild to perform for Corpus Christi in Seville an *auto* called *Asunción de Nuestra Señora* (The Assumption of Our Lady). The document also specifies a salary and lists some props, including two carts, that were necessary for the performance. Lope's mode of travel seems to have doubled as a stage. A second document from the same year, also signed by Lope, refers specifically to a bed with a curtain, both of which were needed for another commissioned piece. These contracts also show that he was responsible for several aspects of a performance. In addition to writing the play and setting up the performance space, Lope furnished the costumes and hired actors, singers, and dancers. Some of the contracts actually stipulated how many performers were involved and how much Lope was earning. For eight golden ducats, Lope wrote and performed an *auto* titled *Seno de Abrahán* (Abraham's Bosom), which called for eight actors to play the roles of Abraham, Lázaro, and six spirits.

Like most other types of peninsular theater, the *paso* originates in Italian theater, more specifically in the commedia dell'arte (comedy of the guild in the art of performance). Typically, a company of traveling players performed (for a paying audience) humorous improvisational skits with stock characters. Lope may have been a member of a troupe owned by an Italian named Mutio or Muzio, who was in Seville in 1538. The *paso* occupies an unusual position in the repertoire of Spanish theater, particularly in its relationship to the full-length *comedia* (three-act plays composed and performed in the sixteenth and seventeenth centuries). Once again, the practices of Italian theater paved the way for Lope de Rueda. Italian playwrights placed humorous interludes, called *intermedii,* between the acts of their plays. Later, these comic scenes were incorporated, first as one-line jokes, then as whole scenes, into the main action of the play. Most often, the short piece was related to the main plot. Finally, humorous scenes, only tangentially related to the main action, were interspersed throughout the full-length play. The *paso* follows this same pattern of independence, dependence, and independence with regard to the *comedia*. Some of Lope de Rueda's *pasos* were actually parts of full-length plays; the minor characters of the *comedia* become protagonists of the *paso*. Other *pasos* always stood on their own. Nevertheless, even the *pasos* that formed part of a larger play could have been, and in all likelihood were, performed as discrete units.

The *paso* served multiple artistic and practical functions. Entertaining a demanding and, in this case, paying audience was perhaps the most obvious aesthetic function. The *paso* also offered comic relief from the serious events of the main play and created suspense by protracting the resolution of the problems from one scene to the next. The *paso* also served some practical purposes, such as giving the actors time to change costumes or create the illusion of a greater length of time elapsing between scenes. At times, the *paso* had the power to decide the commercial appeal of a play. Even a bad play could be a success if the *pasos* were entertaining enough.

From these aesthetic and practical considerations the *paso* developed into a dramatic genre with its own set of themes, characterization, language, and structure. The *paso* often deals humorously with serious themes. Against the backdrop of Catholic Spain, characterized as defender of the faith responsible for saving the world from the heretical Protestants and other religious deviants, the *paso* stages comical anecdotes about the Inquisition, witchcraft, theft, and adultery. It also deals with social ills, including poverty, hunger, and unemployment. Given that its protagonists are often from the lower classes, food and hunger are recurring motifs. Worried about where his next meal will come from, the protagonist often tries to dupe another character into sharing special treats, steals food from local merchants, or refuses to share his own meager horde with others. This aspect of the *pasos* has invited conjecture on the theory that Lope is the author of the anonymous *La vida de Lazarillo de Tormes* (1554, The Life of Lazarillo de Tormes), the eponymous protagonist of which gets hungrier and hungrier with each new master he serves.

Unlike the mainstream *comedia*, which stages an idealized aristocratic world, the *paso* portrays a realistic demimonde. Stock characters, none of which rises above the negative stereotypes associated with his or her social or racial lot, abound. For example, many *pasos* depict the *simple*, an uneducated simpleton, who unsuccessfully tries to better some small detail of his world. A second staple of the *paso* is the misnamed *listo* (clever one), who, although not quite as dull-witted as the *simple*, is intellectually and ethically challenged. He thinks he is clever and often urges the *simple* into action, with disastrous results. As with all comedy, the spectator can laugh when the foibles of the characters are exposed because he or she feels superior to them. Other caricatures introduced in Lope's *pasos* are the cowardly bully, the scoundrel student, the quack doctor, the prostitute, the unfaithful wife, the clever thief, the impoverished scholar, and the lazy servant. Finally, other groups marginalized by society, such as blacks, gypsies, Moors, and slaves, are often portrayed with particular racial or ethnic traits that would be considered stereotypes by modern standards. Sometimes actors played the stock character for many years and even became known by the name of the character. Such was the case with an actor named Cosme Pérez, who played the simpleton Juan Rana in more than forty pieces. Actor and character led parallel lives, and their names were often interchanged even in some legal documents.

While the characters of the *paso* are derivative and predictable, the language is innovative and lively. Unlike the overly stylized verse of the full-length *comedia*, the realistic prose of the short *paso* captures the idiomatic expressions, dialects, and slang spoken by different social and racial groups on the streets of Madrid in the mid sixteenth century. Furthermore, the humor of the piece often depends on the misuse of language by one or more of the characters. The *simple* frequently mispronounces words, displaces letters, follows instructions to an exaggerated extreme, takes figurative meanings literally, uses malapropisms, and jumbles syntax to form illogical utterances. For these reasons, the language of the *paso* presents the contemporary reader with a special set of challenges and is often even harder to read and understand than many other literary texts of the period. Unlike the courtly language of the *comedia*, the street language of the *paso* often does not appear in standard dictionaries. The reader is often left to intuit meaning through context, rely on heavily glossed texts, or consult research done by historical linguists.

In terms of structure, the *paso* involves straightforward episodic plotlines. There are no secondary threads to weave into the story. The plot often revolves around a joke played on the *simple* or a quarrel between two or more of the stock characters. The protagonists do not confront life-changing decisions or circumstances. These stories are small, involving stakes that seem trivial to the spectator, albeit not to the character. In a few instances, like "El convidado" (The Guest), the plot may be based on a real event.

Were it not for the efforts of his friend Juan de Timoneda, Lope's works would not be available today. During a nine-year period, from 1567 to 1576, Timoneda published Lope's *comedias* and *pasos*. By his own admission, Timoneda freely edited the works. Because Lope himself wrote his plays to be performed, not published, the definitive written texts and the dates of composition remain elusive. Some critics believe that

Las ſegundas dos
Comedias del excellẽte poeta, y re-
preſentante Lope de Rueda, a-
gora nueuamente ſacadas
a luz por Ioã Timo
neda.

Comedia llamada   Comedia llamada
de los engañados.   Medora

LOPE DE RVEDA.

Impreſſas en Valencia, en caſa de Ioã Mey
a la plaça de la yerua. Año. 1567.

Vendenſe en caſa de Ioan Timoneda:

*Title page for one of the editions of Lope's works (The Second
Two Comedies of the Excellent and Representative Poet Lope
de Rueda) published by his friend Juan de Timoneda
between 1567 and 1576 (from Los engañados.
Medora, 1973; Thomas Cooper Library,
University of South Carolina)*

the pastoral colloquia and *comedias* predated the *paso*. An examination of these earlier pieces gives the reader a glimpse of the dominant dramatic forms of the day and shows a possible evolution of the *paso*. Nevertheless, assertions regarding a stylistic maturity will always remain tentative owing to the fact that the *paso*, in all likelihood, began as a comic scene within a full-length play and finally became a completely separate text. The *paso* could well have been written and performed simultaneously with the colloquies and *comedias*.

If Lope's dramatic output had been limited to the pastoral colloquies, he would not occupy a place of eminence in the history of Peninsular theater. Nevertheless, despite the fact that *Coloquio de Camila* (Camila's Colloquy) and *Coloquio de Timbria* (Timbria's Colloquy) have little literary or theatrical merit, they do mark an impor-

tant step in the development of theater, namely, the movement of the performance from the palace to the *corral*. While most of his predecessors composed plays for the aristocrats, Lope aimed for the masses. Both colloquies deal with a group of shepherds or goatherds living in seclusion in the mountains. In both plays, one or more characters are hiding their true identity, do not know their own true identity, or have been transformed beyond recognition. This confusion has often been caused by scorned lovers, jealous stepparents, or greedy siblings. Furthermore, both plays rely on the dramatic technique of having an outsider reveal to the audience information about events that occurred before the beginning of the play. This information leads to the denouement. Both plays also include outlandish events, such as kidnappings by Turks and visits from supernatural beings.

A love triangle sets the events in *Coloquio de Timbria* in motion. Isacaro loves Timbria, but she loves Troico. After twists and turns in the plot, it is revealed that Troico is really Urbana, Isacaro's long-lost sister, who was disguised as a man and hidden in the woods to protect her from an evil stepmother. In the final scene of the play, Timbria readily assures Urbana that since she cannot love her as a boyfriend, she will love her as a sister. Moreover, Timbria recognizes another shepherd, Asobrio, as her brother and learns that her real name is Toscana. Engagements are arranged. Asobrio will marry Urbana/Troico; Isacaro, Timbria/Toscana.

Interspersed into the flat characterization, stilted language, and unbelievable plot of *Coloquio de Timbria* are five *pasos*: "La mantecada" (The Sweet Roll), "La negra liviana" (The Fickle Black Woman), "El olvidado de sí mismo" (Forgotten by Himself), "El empajado" (Hidden in a Haystack), and "El ratón manso" (The Tame Rat). Four of these *pasos* involve the simpleton Leno. In "La mantecada," Leno confesses to Troico that he ate the puff pastries that Timbria prepared for Troico. The comedy resides principally in Leno's circumlocutions in confessing his crime. "El olvidado de sí mismo" offers a comic take on unknown identities, which are integral to the main play. In a setting where no one is who he or she seems to be, Leno also struggles with his own humorous identity crises. He went for kindling, fell asleep, and woke up with a sack over his head. Not only has he forgotten his name, he also thinks he has died or at least entered another world. He asks an old hag, Mesiflua, to call him "Leno," the name he had when he was alive, to see if he can remember his name. Miraculously enough, Leno remembers his name when Mesiflua calls him by it. "El empajado" is really a continuation of "El olvidado de sí mismo." Leno asks Troico if his ass has returned to the stables and asks her to go find out from the animal what happened (as if the ass could talk). In order to avoid a possible encounter with his angry master, Leno decides to hide in the hay. "El ratón manso" concludes Leno's adventures. Sulco, his master, asks Leno where he has been. He sent him for kindling some time ago. Leno, covered in straw, claims that he is not Leno but a huge rat from a land of giants, where men have fifty-two joints in their fingers and measure fifteen by twenty-two leagues.

Racial prejudices of the time are evident in the remaining *paso*, "La negra liviana." Violeta, a shepherdess, insults Fulgencia, a black maid, with an array of derogatory names: *galga* (greyhound), *mirla* (blackbird), *perra* (bitch), *simia* (ape), *urraca* (magpie), *lechuza* (owl), and *cuerva* (raven). To prevent an argument, Isacaro asks Fulgencia to sing a song. He then asks her for a hug before he leaves to tend his flocks. Fulgencia feigns insult to her honor but gives in to Isacaro, thereby reinforcing her reputation of a woman of easy virtue. Her language also captures the essence of some cultural stereotypes. For example, she responds to a question with the sentence "Si, por ciertoz, siñor; fablamo y servimo a buena fe" (Yes, of course, sir, we speak and serve in good faith). Fulgencia's Spanish, however, is not grammatically or phonetically correct, and a more accurate translation of her response might be "Yeah, sure, mista, we talk and serve ya good."

Lope's second pastoral comedy, *Coloquio de Camila,* also entails the unknown identities of two lovers. Although Camila and Quiral love each other, they may not openly declare their affections because Socrato, Camila's guardian, has arranged a marriage between his beautiful ward and a wealthy but doltish barber named Alonso. The young lovers eventually marry, but not before divine intervention puts them through a tortuous plot. The desperate Camila, about to commit suicide, meets Fortune, who informs Camila that she is Galatea, daughter of Alonso and the deceased Sofronia. Fortune also reveals that Socrato's real name is Anastasio and that he was separated from a son, Selvagio, some years ago. By the final scene of the play all identities are revealed, fathers are reunited with their offspring, and the nuptials between Camila and Quiral (who, it turns out, is Selvagio) are announced. The mortals acknowledge that their fates have been controlled by the heavens, for even the tiniest shaking of the leaves forms part of a greater cosmic symphony of movement.

Two *pasos*, "Los linajes" (Lineages) and "La fiesta del Corpus Christi" (The Feast of Corpus Christi), provide comic relief to the main play and focus on the domestic affairs of two minor characters from *Coloquio de Camila*. In "Los linajes" two spouses argue about lin-

eages. Ginesa claims that she is the daughter of a respectable councilman; her husband, Pablos, says that Ginesa's father was an olive-oil vendor who was whipped for being a thief. The banter exchanged between the spouses offers a comic counterpoint to the serious tone surrounding the characters' true identities in *Coloquio de Camila*. "La fiesta de Corpus Cristi" features the same pair of spouses. Pablos comes home complaining because he fell off his mule and into a ditch during one of the Corpus Christi processions. The real comedy resides in Pablos's linguistic deformations. For example, one of the parades tells the story of "el Hijo Pródigo" (the Prodigal Son), but Pablos first calls him "el Hijo Prólogo" (the Prologue Son) and then "el Hijo Hipócrito" (the Hypocritical Son). Later, when referring to the character of King Herod (Herodes), he calls him "Adora," which can be translated as "he adores."

Lope's four *comedias,* possibly representing the next stage of his dramatic career, are derived from earlier Italian plays. Once again, each play is accompanied by several comic interludes. Believed to be Lope's first *comedia, Medora* deals with look-alike twins, Angélica and Medoro. Years before the opening of the play, a gypsy kidnapped Medoro and substituted her deathly ill child in his crib. Much to the surprise of the parents, their healthy "son" (the gypsy's ill baby) soon died. Now, years later, the gypsy returns to town with Medoro, who is disguised as a woman so that no one will recognize him. Medoro's disguise greatly confuses the young nobleman Casandro, who is in love with Angélica and understandably takes Medoro for his sister. After a series of scenes in which characters mistake one another for someone else, the gypsy reveals Medoro's true identity and asks for forgiveness for having kidnapped him years ago. Angélica also reveals that she and Casandro are betrothed. Pardons are granted and nuptials are announced.

Three *pasos* are included as parts of scenes of *Medora.* "El valentón" (The Braggart) features Gargullo, who swears that he will avenge a dishonor caused him by one Peñalba. The confrontation between the two men, however, proves Gargullo's cowardice. In "Tantico pan" (A Little Bit of Bread), the simpleton Ortega convinces Perico to give him a small piece of bread to sop up the juices of a delicious stew that he has waiting at home. Said stew does not exist, but Ortega does get his morsel of bread. A gypsy dupes Gargullo into giving her his gold chain, some coins, and cloak in "La gitana ladrona" (The Thieving Gypsy). Throughout the *paso* Gargullo thinks that he is outwitting an unsuspecting victim. With the intent of stealing it, Gargullo promises to guard over a sack of jewels while the gypsy goes in search of food. In her absence, Gargullo opens the sack only to discover that it is filled with coal, not jewels. Not only does he lose the opportunity to steal her goods, he has forfeited his own possessions. "La gitana ladrona" may also have utilized a technique intended to involve the audience. The gypsy mentions several streets in Valencia. Some scholars believe that references, such as the names of streets, characters, or taverns, may have changed from town to town in order to make the performance more immediate for an audience comprising locals.

Similar to *Medora*, *Los engañados* (The Deceived), probably published in the late 1530s, revolves around look-alike twins and involves disguise. *Los engañados* takes place in Módena in 1537 some ten years after the second sack of Rome. Verginio is the father of extraordinarily similar-looking twins, Fabricio and Lelia. The former was lost in the sack; the latter currently resides in a convent. Lelia dons male attire, calls herself Fabio, and inserts herself as a page in the house of a young noblewoman, Clavela. These shenanigans are part of Lelia's attempts to win back Lauro, a suitor whose affection has shifted to Clavela. She hopes to make Clavela fall for Fabio and abandon Lauro so that he will return to his first love. Ultimately, Lelia's ruse works, but not before her cross-gendered identity causes a great deal of confusion for all concerned. Complications are compounded by the fact that Fabricio, who is alive and well and living in Rome, chooses to return to Módena during this time. In several scenes, Verginio and several servants mistake Fabricio for Lelia and vice versa. In the final scenes of the play, when all true identities are revealed, Verginio rejoices that his son is still alive and approves his children's betrothals. Lelia will marry Lauro, and Fabricio will wed Clavela. At least two scenes of *Los engañados* serve no other purpose than to showcase the comic language and silly actions of some rather dim-witted servants. Scene 3 centers on the squabbles between two domestic servants, the slave Guiomar and the maid Julieta. Scene 5 deals with a simpleton servant, Pajares, who has trouble donning his cloak and following his master's instructions. Although these scenes have not been labeled *pasos* per se, they share the same dramatic functions with those *pasos* connected to *Medora*.

Eufemia, probably published in the early 1540s, alternates between two spheres of action in unnamed cities. At the beginning of the play, two siblings, Eufemia and Leonardo, live in one city. Despite his sister's misgivings, Leonardo departs for an unknown location and becomes the secretary of a wealthy noble named Valiano, who, as coincidence would have it, wants to marry Eufemia and asks Leonardo about his sister's character. Leonardo assures his master that Eufemia is a virtuous woman. Shortly thereafter, a man named Paulo denigrates Eufemia's character by telling

Valiano that he slept with her and that he can describe her body in detail, including the fact that she has a mole on her right shoulder. Valiano vows to make Leonardo pay for lying to him. Eufemia then learns that Leonardo will be beheaded in twenty days if he cannot clear his name. Cristina, the maid, confesses that she gave a full description of Eufemia to a stranger and even gave him a strand of hair from the aforementioned mole while Eufemia was asleep. Eufemia vows to clear up the situation.

Eufemia goes to the city where Leonardo is being held captive. Taking advantage of the fact that she is a stranger in town whom no one will recognize, Eufemia asks for Valiano's assistance on a matter of grave injustice. The nobleman vows to help and assures her that he will be impartial. Eufemia publicly accuses Paulo of stealing a jewel from her the last time they slept together. Paulo repeatedly announces in front of several witnesses that he has never seen this woman before in his life, let alone slept with her. Eufemia then reveals her true identity, and everyone knows that Paulo lied about having dishonored her. Valiano marries Eufemia, pardons Leonardo, and condemns Paulo.

Two intercalated *pasos* actually overpower the main plot of *Eufemia*. "El matón cobarde" (The Cowardly Bully) deals with another braggart who finds an excuse to avoid confrontation. "La novia negra" (The Black Bride) depicts a courting scene by members of the lower classes. At first, the greedy Eulalla plays hard to get but then succumbs to Polo's advances and agrees to marry him if he will give her a parrot and a monkey. Similar to the earlier "La negra liviana," this *paso* includes many examples of linguistic deformation by Eulalla, especially with proverbs. In fact, Polo often serves as interpreter between Eulalla and the audience. This *paso* also presents the reader with an example of how the *pasos* may have segued to and from the larger *comedia*. "La negra liviana" begins and ends with references to the action of *Eufemia*. Polo remarks that he is en route to Leonardo's trial. Although the later *pasos* eventually become completely independent from the *comedia*, these pieces are still tangentially connected to it.

Lope's last *comedia*, *Armelina*, shares with the pastoral colloquies the theme of unknown identities and supernatural intervention in the affairs of mortals. No scholars have made conjectures about date of composition. Pascual, the blacksmith, has arranged a marriage for his adopted daughter, Armelina, to the insensitive dolt Diego de Córdoba. The audience witnesses a comic scene in which Diego proves himself an unworthy suitor. Wooing Armelina on her balcony, Diego clumsily compares her beauty to the tools of his shoemaking trade. Later, Justo, a tourist newly arrived to the city, sees Armelina and instantly falls in love with her, despite the fact that she appears to be the daughter of a lowly blacksmith. Viana, Justo's tutor and adoptive father and, as the audience is about to learn, Armelina's real father, came to this city about five months ago on a mission. Many years ago, his four-year-old daughter, Florentina, was abducted. Via several magical communications, including a conversation with Medea from the underworld, Viana learns that it is urgent that he find Armelina before disaster strikes.

Meanwhile, Armelina, desperately seeking a way to escape her arranged marriage, is about to commit suicide when Neptune intervenes. The god of the sea tells Armelina that her real name is Florentina and that she is Viana's daughter. Neptune accompanies Armelina home and reveals everyone's true identity. In addition to disclosing that Armelina is Florentina, he states that Justo is Pascual's long-lost son. The play ends with the announcement of the marriages of Armelina/Florentina to Justo, and Mencieta the maid to Beltranico the page. Neptune returns to the sea. *Armelina* has one *paso,* "El ensalmo" (The Cure), which enacts the proverb "the cure is worse than the disease." Guadalupe, a simpleton, complains that he cannot open his eyes. Mencieta puts a plaster of hen fat and yeast on his back in order to cure Guadalupe of his sleepy eyes. At the end of the *paso,* the simpleton goes off in search of a cure for the cure.

In *Compendio llamado El Deleitoso, en el cual se contienen muchos pasos graciosos del excellente poeta y gracioso representante Lope de Rueda para poner en principios y entremedias de colloquios y comedias* (1567, Compendium Called Delightful in Which Are Contained Many Amusing Interludes by the Excellent Poet and Amusing Actor Lope de Rueda to Include at the Beginnings and during Intermissions of Colloquia and Plays) and *Registro de representantes, a do van registrados por Juan de Timoneda muchos y graciosos passos de Lope de Rueda y otros diversos autores* (1570, Registry of Actors in Which Are Registered by Juan de Timoneda Many Amusing Pasos by Lope de Rueda and Other Authors) Juan de Timoneda compiled what is acknowledged by all critics to be the highlight of Lope's dramatic compositions. Timoneda states that Lope wrote these pieces to be included at the beginning of, or between acts of, full-lengths plays. He numbered, but did not title, the *pasos.* It is, however, less confusing to refer to the different pieces by the titles added by subsequent editors of Lope's work. *Compendio llamado El Deleitoso* includes seven *pasos.* "Los criados" (The Servants) and "La carátula" (The Mask) involve the same characters, thereby suggesting that, at one time, these two *pasos* were part of a larger *comedia.* In "Los criados" Alameda and Luquitas cannot resist the temptations of a doughnut shop and end up spending their master's money to buy some tasty treats. Luquitas plans to tell their master, Salcedo, that there was a huge rush of people at the cheese and onion stalls and that he had to call the bailiff because one of the merchants cheated him of his change. The simpleton Alameda, however, in his attempts to corroborate, gets confused and says some nonsense phrases. He claims that there were "tantas cebollas en la prisa" (so many onions in the rush) and "tantas cebollas en el queso" (so many onions in the cheese). Salcedo does not believe their stories and warns them both that they will be punished when they get home. In "La carátula" Salcedo turns the tables by telling his servant an outlandish story, which the gullible Alameda believes. Salcedo convinces Alameda that a carnival mask is really the scalped skull of a murdered grave keeper, Diego Sánchez. Salcedo then pretends to be Sánchez's ghost, confronts Alameda, and convinces him that he must find his corpse in the river, bring it to the graveyard, and cry out "Sánchez," or Alameda will be buried alive with other bodies in the cistern. Alameda agrees, and the audience is left to imagine the next scene in which the simpleton causes a ruckus in the cemetery.

As suggested by the title, "Cornudo y contento" (Cuckold and Content) deals with adultery from a humorous perspective. To get her husband, Martín, out of the house so that she can have a rendezvous with Jerónimo, her student boyfriend, Bárbara feigns illness and sends Martín to the doctor for medicine. On this particular trip to the doctor's office, Martín explains that he, not his wife, drank the purgative prescribed by the doctor the previous day. The learned student, Jerónimo, told him that since Bárbara was too sick to drink the medicine, Martín should take it on her behalf. Given that theirs is a marriage of spirit and flesh, this sacrifice would ensure Bárbara's recovery. To make matters worse, the two lovers convinced the cuckold that if he shared their meal of roast chicken, his wife's health would suffer even more. The queasy and hungry Martín asks the doctor for a remedy. By the end of the *paso,* Bárbara not only has Martín begging forgiveness but promising to fast for nine days while she makes a novena in a remote place. The adulterous couple leaves, and, no doubt, Martín will be the brunt of future ruses that will make him suffer more indignities in the name of his wife's good physical or spiritual health.

"El convidado" (The Guest) suggests that not only the uneducated are duped by their acquaintances. Despite the fact that he has no money, the lawyer Zaquima creates the illusion of prosperity. Only his servant, Brazuelos, knows that Zaquima's academic robes serve as a blanket in the evening. Zaquima unthinkingly invites a student traveler to his house for dinner and then realizes that he has no money for food. Brazuelos comes up with a plan that will allow Zaquima to

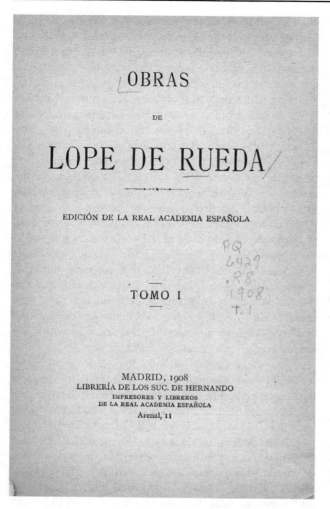

OBRAS

DE

LOPE DE RUEDA

EDICIÓN DE LA REAL ACADEMIA ESPAÑOLA

TOMO I

MADRID, 1908
LIBRERÍA DE LOS SUC. DE HERNANDO
IMPRESORES Y LIBREROS
DE LA REAL ACADEMIA ESPAÑOLA
Arenal, 11

*Title page for the first volume of the 1908 edition of Lope's
collected works (Thomas Cooper Library,
University of South Carolina)*

save face and not renege on his invitation. Brazuelos promises to tell the guest that his master was called away on urgent business. Nevertheless, instead of going through with the planned scheme, Brazuelos exposes his master's lies and poverty. The angry traveler sends both servant and lawyer to the devil.

Zaquima's language is often as deceiving as his clothes. For example, when he asks Brazuelos a favor, one has trouble identifying exactly what Zaquima is saying: "querría suplicar á vuesa merced me hiciese merced de me hacer merced, pues estas mercedes se juntan con esotras mercedes que vuesa merced suele hacer, me hiciese merced de prestarme dos reales" (I would like to beg your grace to do me the graciousness of the gracious favor of graciously lending me two dollars, for this graciousness will be added on to other graciousnesses that your grace usually performs). Linguistic obfuscation, then, is not limited to ignorant sim-

pletons. Zaquima has learned to use language to cover up the meaning of his words.

In the next *paso,* "La tierra de Jauja" (The Land of Joy), two thieves, Honzigera and Panarizo, regale the simpleton Mendrugo with tales of the land of joy, where rivers flow with milk and honey, fountains spout cream cakes, and trees grow trunks of succulent bacon and leaves of delicious donuts. While Mendrugo listens to this mouthwatering tale, the thieves eat the contents of his casserole. Once the simpleton realizes what Honzigera and Panarizo have done, he vows to call for the authorities, but they have escaped. In addition to the constant theme of food and hunger, this *paso* introduces a cultural reference to the Spanish Inquisition. When the thieves meet Mendrugo, he is carrying a meal to his imprisoned wife. The simpleton mentions that everything is going to turn out okay because his wife is going to be made a bishop. People accused of a wide range of offenses, including witchcraft and prostitution, were often punished by having to wear a conical cap, which resembled a bishop's miter. Mendrugo, however, thinks his wife is being honored and looks forward to the day when he too shall wear a similar crown. "La tierra de Jauja," then, is an example of how the *paso* could deal humorously with a serious, even deadly, reality of Golden Age Spain.

"Pagar y no pagar" (Pay and Nonpayment) focuses on a dolt who misunderstands instructions. A nobleman, Brezano, sends his servant, Cebadón, to pay overdue rent. En route, the slow-witted Cebadón meets up with the crafty Samadel, who convinces the servant that he is the landlord. Cebadón hands over the rent to the thief, who promptly scampers off, leaving Cebadón to face an angry master. Brezano had told Cebadón that the landlord wears an eyepatch and walks with a limp. He also told the servant to get a receipt from the landlord. The humor of this *paso* results from the ways that Cebadón manages to ignore or misinterpret every instruction given by his master.

Lope's most famous *paso,* "Las aceitunas" (The Olives), is often included in anthologies as representative of the tradition of the *teatro menor* in Spain. Of all of his works, "Las aceitunas" has received the most critical attention, despite the fact that, in terms of language, theme, and characterization, it is the least representative of Lope's *pasos.* No simpleton freely deforms language; no greedy servant dupes an unsuspecting master. Toruvio and his wife, Agueda, argue about the price that they will charge once some newly planted olives are ripe for market. Agueda quotes one price; Toruvio, another. The spouses' bickering soon escalates into a shouting match. Aloxa, a neighbor, overhears the arguments and tries to intervene by offering to buy the olives. He assures everyone that he will pay a fair price.

Nevertheless, when Aloxa asks to see the goods, even Toruvio sees how ridiculous it is to be arguing over the price of seeds.

All three *pasos* by Lope de Rueda from *Registro de representantes* deal with theft. In the first, "Los lacayos ladrones" (Lackey Thieves), Madrigalejo and Molina present a thieves' code of honor. They ask how one can present a respectable persona to the world, when, for example, in the case of the cuckold, one does not know he has been offended or, in the case of the thief, one cannot avoid a public lashing because his hands are tied. A sheriff enters in pursuit of Madrigalejo, who answers all of the sheriff's questions with evasive double meanings and then unwittingly hands over self-incriminating evidence. Despite his cleverness, he gets caught.

"El rufián cobarde" (The Coward Bully) deals with another case of distorted honor. Sebastiana reveals that Estepa's girlfriend has been spreading vicious rumors around town about Siguenza. For example, she claims that Siguenza's ears were cut off because he is a convicted thief. Siguenza gets angry and concocts an outlandish story about how he valiantly cut off his own ears to use as weapons against a legion of soldiers. He then briefly acknowledges that he did spend some time rowing on the king's galleys. Impressions of Siguenza's bravery quickly fade when his enemy, Estepa, appears onstage. When Siguenza sees his enemy approaching, he hands over his sword to Sebastiana so that he will not have to fight. Estepa wants to avenge his honor because Siguenza has been spreading rumors that he was whipped for being a thief. Under pressure, Siguenza quickly capitulates, and by the end of the *paso* the braggart has lost his sword, his girlfriend, and his honor to Estepa. Siguenza's humorous sense of honor plays havoc with more serious portrayal of the honor code in the mainstream *comedia*.

"La paliza" (The Generous Beating) depicts a reversal of the usual pattern, in which the servant is always ready to connive his way into a meal or treat. Dalagón, the master, wants to know who ate his nougat. He accuses and then beats each of his four servants. Finally, Guillemillo reminds his master that he stored the candy in his desk. An apologetic Dalagón wants to make up for his mistake and abuse by dividing the remaining sweets among the servants. As it turns out, none of them like nougat and, therefore, take more pleasure in pelting their master with the candy rather than eating it.

Several of Lope's contemporaries and immediate successors praise his dramatic writing, applaud his acting ability, and acknowledge his place in the evolution of Spanish drama. The most famous of these accolades comes from Miguel de Cervantes, the author of *Don Quixote* (1605, 1615). In the prologue to one of the first editions of his own plays, published in 1615, Cervantes summarizes the cherished occasion on which, as an adolescent, he first saw a play performed by Lope. Other authors of the period, including Juan de la Cueva, Lope de Vega, Agustín de Rojas, and Baltasar Gracián, praise Lope de Rueda's works and/or comment on the influence he has had on their works. One can easily see the *simple* as a forerunner of the *gracioso* (buffoon), one of the staples of the Golden Age *comedia*. Moreover, the *paso* continued to reinvent itself, as a comic one-act play, throughout the history of Spanish theater. The *sainete* (humorous one-act play) in the eighteenth century, the *género chico* (one-act theater) in the nineteenth century, and even some of the socially committed theater of the mid twentieth century can find their roots in the *paso*.

Bibliographies:

Fred Abrams, "Lope de Rueda: Una bibliografía analítica en el cuarto centenario de su muerte (1565–1965)," *Duquesne Hispanic Review*, 19, no. 4 (1965): 39–55;

Vicente Tuscón, *Lope de Rueda: Bibliografía crítica* (Madrid: Consejo Superior de Investigaciones Científicas, 1965);

References:

Fred Abrams, "The Date of Composition of Lope de Rueda's *Comedia Eufemia*," *Modern Language Notes*, 76 (1961): 766–770;

Othón Arróniz, *La influencia italiana en el nacimiento de la comedia española* (Madrid: Gredos, 1969), pp. 51–62, 73–134;

Eugenio Asensio, *Itinerario del entremés desde Lope de Rueda a Quiñones de Benavente* (Madrid: Gredos, 1965);

Manuel V. Diago, "Lope de Rueda y los orígenes del teatro profesional," *Criticón*, 50 (1990): 41–65;

Randall W. Listerman, "Some Material Contributions of the 'Commedia dell'arte' to the Spanish Theater," *Romance Notes*, 57, no. 2 (Winter 1976): 194–198;

Carolyn Nadeau, "Sweetmeats and Preserves: Food Imagery in Lope de Rueda's *Pasos*," in *Texto y Espectáculo: Selected Proceedings of the Fifteenth International Golden Age Spanish Theatre Symposium (March 8–11, 1995), at the University of Texas, El Paso*, edited by José Suárez García (York, S.C.: Spanish Literature Publications, 1996), pp. 86–94;

Hugo Albert Rennert, *The Spanish Stage in the Time of Lope de Vega* (New York: Hispanic Society of America, 1909);

Sharon D. Voros, "Lope de Rueda," in *Spanish Dramatists of the Golden Age: A Bio-Bibliographical Sourcebook*, edited by Mary Parker (Westport, Conn.: Greenwood Press, 1998), pp. 188–204.

Juan de Mariana

(1535 or 1536 – 16 February 1624)

Robert A. Gorman
University of Tennessee

BOOKS: *Historiae de rebus Hispaniae* (Toledo: Petri Roderici, 1592);

De ponderibus et mensuris (Toledo: Thomas Gusmanium, 1599);

De rege et regis institutione (Toledo: Petrum Rodericum, 1599); translated by George Albert Moore as *The King and the Education of the King* (Washington, D.C.: Country Dollar, 1948);

Historia general de España: Compuesta primero en Latín, despues buelta en Castellano, 2 volumes (Toledo: Pedro Rodriguez, 1601); translated by John Stevens as *The General History of Spain: From the First Peopling of It by Tubal, till the Death of King Ferdinand, Who United the Crowns of Castile and Aragon, with a Continuation to the Death of King Philip III* (London: Richard Sare, 1699);

Tractatus VII (Cologne: Sumptibus Antonij Hierati, 1609);

Discurso de las enfermedades de la compañia el p. Juan de Mariana: Con una disertación sobre el autor y la legitimidad de la obra, y un apéndice de varios testimonios de Jesuitas españoles que concuerdan con Mariana (Madrid: D. Gabriel Ramírez, 1768);

Obras del Juan de Mariana, 2 volumes, edited by Francisco Pí y Margall (Madrid: Rivadeneyra, 1854).

Modern Editions: *Historia general de España,* 10 volumes (Barcelona: J. Francisco Oliva, 1839–1840);

El rey y de la institución real, translated by Crelion Acivaro (Barcelona: Literario-Editorial, 1880).

Juan de Mariana (frontispiece from Georges Cirot, Etudes sur l'historiographie espagnole: Mariana, historien, *1904; from Alan Soons,* Juan de Mariana, *1982; Thomas Cooper Library, University of South Carolina)*

Father Juan de Mariana's legacy is clearly more interesting than either his behavior or his published work. Like others before him, the Jesuit Mariana was doggedly opposed to secular and religious decision makers who were corrupt, vainglorious, stupid, or faithless. This opposition, say some scholars, conferred on him a reputation for decency in what was a dishonest time. Like others before him as well, Mariana accused tyrants of violating both the public trust and God's will and suggested that tyrannicide, carefully planned and performed, was justifiable in extreme circumstances. This suggestion, others argue, caused the death of legitimate monarchs and disrupted God's hierarchically ordered universe. From this viewpoint, Mariana was a rebel and libertine. Finally, also like others before him, Mariana wanted the Society of Jesus to heed the advice of its own distinguished members before acting in their name. Thenceforth, for many Catholics, Mariana became one of the most maligned members of the Jesuit order.

In fact, Mariana's lifework is essentially conventional, and even his ardent supporters acknowledge that it is rarely read. He was a monarchist and a stubborn

Jesuit frustrated primarily by process rather than substance. Prescient enough to recognize certain features of what others later called the Enlightenment, Mariana applied them to strengthening the medieval church and state. He lacked the foresight and courage to condemn policies that others both in and out of the church soon repudiated. In short, while he may have inadvertently helped inspire the constitutional tradition of the seventeenth century, he did so while tolerating activities modernists would condemn as immoral and unjust.

Juan de Mariana was born in 1535 or 1536 in the small town of Talavera in Castile, apparently the illegitimate son of the clergyman Juan Martinez de Mariana and a woman named Bernadina Rodriguez. A brother died early. A sister later became a nun. Rumors that the Marianas were *conversos* (converts from Judaism to Christianity) have never been verified. In fact, little is known of Mariana until he entered the Society of Jesus in January 1554. The official Catholic position on these early years, according to the 1910 edition of the *Catholic Encyclopedia*, merely states: "He joined the order 1 January 1554. Nothing more is known of his parentage or his family history."

After completing his novitiate, Mariana studied philosophy and theology at the University of Alcalá. He was a superior student and in 1561 was chosen to teach at the Roman College of the Society of Jesus. He was ordained the same year. In 1565 Mariana went to teach in Sicily and, later, in Messina and Palermo. Four years later he joined the faculty of the Jesuit College in Paris. While there, Mariana earned a doctor of theology degree at the Sorbonne. As a student in Paris he likely read works by Francis Hotman and Theodore Beza, Reformation thinkers who favored limiting, and in extreme cases resisting, the rule of tyrants.

Mariana returned to his native Spain in 1574, thirteen years after leaving, and settled in Toledo. There he wrote and studied, at least until his growing scholarly reputation brought him into public service. He was appointed synodial examiner and counsel of the Spanish Inquisition and, later, censor of all scriptural works. In this capacity he was assigned to examine the Polyglot Bible of Arias Montano, which some Spanish theologians had denounced. He decided in favor of Montano, thereby disappointing many Jesuits and likely establishing Mariana's reputation in the order for insubordination. Mariana also helped compile a list of prohibited books that appeared in 1584, a project that was supervised by the inquisitor general, Gaspar Quiroga. Although Mariana was somewhat uncomfortable with the rigid procedures of the Inquisition, he nonetheless supported its work and its intolerance of religious diversity. Jews and heterodox Christians, in fact, affronted Mariana. Jews in particular, he wrote, were faithless as well as low and base people who deserved their horrid

fates. Sympathetic scholars intimate that Mariana was a merciful priest during indecent times, but this humane Jesuit advocated death for heretics.

Mariana published his most popular work, *Historiae de rebus Hispaniae* (The General History of Spain), in 1592. Like all of Mariana's published writings, *Historiae de rebus Hispaniae* was written in Latin. He later wrote a Spanish translation of this work titled *Historia general de España: Compuesta primero en Latín, despues buelta en Castellano* (1601; translated as *The General History of Spain: From the First Peopling of It by Tubal till the Death of King Ferdinand, Who United the Crowns of Castile and Aragon, with a Continuation to the Death of King Philip III*, 1699), in which he added five books to the original, extending the analysis of Spain from 1428 to the death of King Ferdinand the Catholic in 1516. Later still, Mariana wrote two new supplements chronicling the history of Spain through 1621. After his death, other scholars undertook to keep the long narrative up-to-date.

Historiae de rebus Hispaniae appealed to Spanish intellectuals primarily because of its grand scope and elegant writing. Both the Latin and Spanish editions are considered among the finest examples of writing ever produced in Spain. With its series of posthumous continuations, *Historiae de rebus Hispaniae* became the accepted historical record. Its actual content is more problematic. Professional historians have noted Mariana's lack of rigor and his penchant for synthesizing the judgments of others rather than plowing through primary sources and announcing original interpretations. *Historiae de rebus Hispaniae* is essentially an eclectic compilation of secondary material, not a creative analysis of Spanish history. Perhaps this quality has contributed to its wide appeal.

Mariana published his most significant political work, *De rege et regis institutione* (translated as *The King and the Education of the King*, 1948), in 1599. This controversial book, about the origin, nature, and mechanics of just governments, shaped Mariana's legacy more than any other single project. Written to help educate Prince Philip, *De rege et regis institutione* is unsystematic and occasionally contradictory, reinforcing the received scholarly opinion that Mariana is neither an accurate historian nor a systematic political philosopher. Because of a series of unrelated events and Mariana's own ambiguity, however, the book generated unwarranted notoriety that transformed his life and muddied his reputation among those royalists and Catholics that he ostensibly represented.

De rege et regis institutione consists of three separate sections: Mariana describes the origin and nature of just governments first, followed by narratives on royal education and statecraft. Even in the late sixteenth century, treatises concerned with educating princes had a long history. Part 2 of *De rege et regis institutione* is a particularly ordinary example of this type of literature. In the tradition of Desiderius Erasmus, it endorses a royal curricu-

First page of book 14 from Mariana's general history of Spain, published in Latin in 1592 and in Spanish as Historia general de España *in 1601 (courtesy of The Lilly Library, Indiana University)*

lum based on both humanism and Catholicism. Similarly, Mariana's discussion of statecraft in part 3 adheres to the ideas of Niccolò Machiavelli. The significance of *De rege et regis institutione* in the history of ideas is based solely on Mariana's political theory, which is found in part 1 of the work.

Mariana proffers a tantalizing interpretation of the origins of human society and government that is cobbled from so many diverse ideas and thinkers that informed readers are easily overwhelmed and occasionally confused. Without ever referring directly to the biblical version of Eden and the Fall, Mariana describes primitive man as fragile, weak, and helpless. God somehow imprints desire and reason onto the human psyche. Faced with external threats from animals, nature, and acquisitive warriors, men are forced to socialize for protection and to live decently. This period in history is the "Golden Age," marked by fraternity, equality, and peace as people organize into families and a primitive civil society. Strong, selfish people eventually threaten the weak

and innocent. In response, common people yield to one perceived as wise and virtuous, who will rule others to assure human survival. This single leader will formulate written laws inspired by God, nature, and the expectations of those who acknowledge his rule. Monarchy is therefore the most natural and best form of government. It is more efficacious than divided forms of government and reinforces the natural, divine order of things by ensuring that superior people who know God's word control the ignorant mobs. Monarchs who inherit their power, moreover, are likely wiser and more capable than those gaining power by force or appointment. Kings, however, are also lawgivers obligated to obey natural, divine, and human forces.

Modernists accent Mariana's suggestion that humans willfully establish civil society and government to satisfy their needs. Medievalists see only Mariana's disdain for common people and his hierarchic, Christocentric worldview, while classicists hear echoes of Greek and Roman social theory. Here, in short, is a distinctive, if perplexing, mixture of Aristotelian notions of human reason and sociability, Seneca's state of nature, doctrines of original sin and divine right of kings, social-contract theory, Roman and medieval legal concepts, Thomism, Scholasticism, and artistic license.

Mariana's preference for monarchy in *De rege et regis institutione* is eventually qualified by the assertion that kings need the consent of subjects, expressed indirectly through an elective assembly of those suited to serve. Monarchs are wise and virtuous but also human. History has shown that greed and passion often push good kings over the edge into lawlessness. Indeed, Mariana agrees with the conciliarists that even popes can fall into illegitimacy, and hence they too need the advice of a learned council. An aristocratic check on royal power, such as the Cortes in Spain (an assembly convoked by the king and attended by landed aristocrats from the estates of the different kingdoms then composing the nation), can guarantee that kings obey natural and divine law as well as the customs of their citizens. Mariana calls this division of power "mixed constitutionalism." He uncompromisingly rejects the direct rule of citizens. Mariana is frightened of what he calls the common man and advises that the institutional check on monarchs be composed only of wealthy, educated, aristocratic Catholics who approve the king's preferences when levying taxes and, when necessary, change the order of succession. Executive and military powers are reserved solely for the monarch.

Mariana now poses an important question: what would happen if a king were selfishly to ignore his people's needs and become a tyrant? Mariana's answer is that the authority of the commonwealth is greater than that of kings, who originally emerged from the needs and wishes of the people. Tyranny, for Mariana, is thus the most evil of governments because it ignores God, nature, and citizens. The question of how to eliminate a tyrant takes up two entire chapters of *De rege et regis institutione*.

Mariana scans history in order to learn how to recognize and deal with tyrants. Referring to instances primarily in Spain and France in which tyrants were violently deposed, Mariana concludes that a leader who forcefully takes power, illegally and without public approval, may be killed by anyone and by any means. On the other hand, if a tyrant begins legitimately the issue is fuzzier, because legitimate rulers should be tolerated unless their crimes include ignoring the law, depriving the commonwealth of needed resources, or disrespecting Catholicism and the church. When these heinous activities commence, public meetings—presumably a meeting of the Cortes—should warn the king to repent or, if necessary, formulate plans to drive him from power. If all else fails, or if public meetings are forbidden, Mariana advises that some brave and honorable individual must slay the king. This hero first must be certain the public approves, and he must also accept the guidance of learned, serious, and holy men. Poison is a favored means, but only if placed on a garment or saddle. Mariana feels it indecent to secretly mix poison into a tyrant's drink, perhaps because he fears that the act of tyrannicide might then resemble the act of involuntary suicide. Contact with a poisoned surface, apparently, is less ambiguous. In any case, Mariana presumes that the mere threat of tyrannicide will stop its appearance.

No Jesuit, Mariana included, ever encouraged Christians to accept regicide as an acceptable political tactic. Many, however, had already advocated tyrannicide, not regicide, when oppression became unbearable. Moreover, Mariana's ideas echo what many Protestants of the time were saying, and to some extent what John of Salisbury, St. Thomas Aquinas, and other Scholastics—in Spain and elsewhere—had openly advocated or implied. Mariana, in short, was neither the originator of the concept of tyrannicide nor its most articulate or well-known spokesman.

Historians disagree about whether Mariana implied that Jesuits alone are qualified to depose a tyrant, or if some kind of emergency public body must be convened. Mariana is vague and inconclusive on this issue. As in so many other areas, his understanding of church-state relations is both conventional and confusing. *De rege et regis institutione* supports the doctrine of the two swords, or two powers, popularized by Pope Gelasius at the end of the fifth century. This doctrine grants church and state separate identities and functions under God's law. It never assigns secular powers to the papacy. Mariana also suggests, however, like John Calvin, that spiritual leaders should serve in public assemblies to reinforce Christian

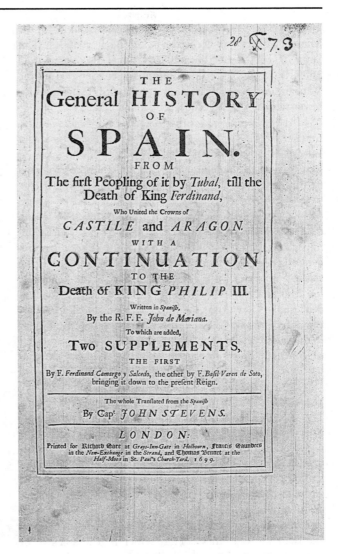

Title page for the first English translation (1699) of Mariana's Historia general de España *(Thomas Cooper Library, University of South Carolina)*

morality and repress heretics. Modernists emphasize the insistence of the work on separating church and state. Traditionalists feel Mariana is subtly advocating theocracy in *De rege et regis institutione*.

The Society of Jesus was founded by St. Ignatius de Loyola and received its constitution in 1540. With its leader, or general, appointed for life and with its principle of unquestioning obedience and hierarchic organization, the Jesuits resembled a military body as much as a religious order. For a time even the Vatican felt threatened. It disbanded the Jesuits in 1773, only to have the order restored in 1814. Mariana entered the society in 1554 and remained until his death. Some Jesuits have denied that Mariana ever wrote about the order. Most historians, however, agree that Mariana wrote his notorious

Discurso de las enfermedades de la Compañía (Discourse on the Matters in Need of Remedy in the Society of Jesus) in 1605 or 1606, even though it was not discovered until 1609. It was published posthumously, condemned by the Vatican, and never translated into English. Mariana also never retracted the allegations he made in it.

The *Discurso de las enfermedades de la Compañía* illustrates how the doctrines of *De rege et regis institutione* might be applied to the order. Mariana accuses the Society of Jesus of abusing its mandate and argues that the problems in the order were caused by centralizing power in the office of the general, who had become a kind of tyrant. Mariana's remedy is to assign greater authority to the opinions of the oldest members of the society, including himself. In particular, Mariana wants the general congregation of the order to advise the general, creating an ecclesiastical version of a mixed constitution. Some historians feel Mariana wanted to decentralize the Vatican as well as the Jesuits. They argue that this conciliarism enhanced his reputation as a reformer, despite his steadfast commitment to the order. In the short run, however, Mariana managed to infuriate both the order and the Vatican simultaneously.

Aside from minor essays that were later anthologized, Mariana's last significant published work, *Tractatus VII* (Seven Treatises), was published in Cologne, Germany, in 1609 and consists of seven small, previously written discourses. Most deal with Mariana's thoughts on history, certain events of significance to Spain, and the author's personal tastes. Many have never been translated, and church authorities censured some. Two of the essays are noteworthy: "De morte et immortalitate" (On Death and Immortality) and "De monetae mutatione" (Of Alterations in the Currency). The former is Mariana's most personal writing, a humanistic dialogue enlivened by characterization, humor, and learning. It reveals Mariana's growing interest in sports and games, his idiosyncratic advice to grieving Catholics, and some thoughts about his own turbulent life. The latter is a factual analysis of monarchs, some in Spain, who tried to enrich themselves immorally and without consulting their constituent assemblies. He focuses on kings who conspired to raise the value of currency even as their silver content declined and then flooded their countries with worthless currency. Mariana concludes that fiscal policy is better left to the people's deputies than to kings alone. As a precaution, kings should declare their personal assets before taking office.

Mariana was arrested within months of publishing *Tractatus VII*. The Spanish monarch was irritated by the antiroyalist economic critique of "De monetae mutatione." Shortly after, a chance sequence of events dramatically altered the remainder of Mariana's life. In 1610 Francois Ravaillac murdered Henry IV in Paris. Records of the assassination were lost in a fire eight years later, so there is no conclusive evidence of Ravaillac's motives. He apparently acted alone. Immediately after the murder, however, *De rege et regis institutione* and its author received the blame and were accused of advocating regicide. Mariana's works were ceremonially burned in front of the Notre-Dame Cathedral and later in London as well. Pope Paul V and Jesuit General Claudio Acquaviva both disowned the book and condemned regicide, although *De rege et regis institutione* continued to enjoy royal favor in Spain. At about the same time, the Jesuit Robert Bellarmine published a treatise advocating pontifical deposition and outlawry of heretical monarchs, something Mariana would have never even suggested. Bellarmine too was the focus of royalist rage in France. Mariana—vainly objecting that critics had confused regicide and tyrannicide and had not read his book—was tried and sentenced to lifelong imprisonment in a Franciscan convent in Madrid.

Juan de Mariana's final years are somewhat obscure. Church officials claim that a contrite Mariana was belatedly freed shortly before his death. Many historians, however, feel he was probably released in 1611, after promising to correct offensive passages in *Tractatus VII*. Mariana died on 16 February 1624, in his house in Toledo. Predictably, some contemporaries praised Mariana for his courage, learning, and foresight. Others ridiculed both his scholarship and his well-known stubborn, abstemious personality. For many years after his death, Catholics, especially in France, tied Mariana to the hated theory of regicide and accused the Jesuits of subversion.

References:

J. W. Allen, *A History of Political Thought in the Sixteenth Century* (London: Methuen, 1928);

Rodolfo Barón Castro, *La población de El Salvador: Estudio acerca de su desenvolvimiento desde la época prehispánica hasta nuestros días* (Madrid: Consejo Superior de Investigaciones Científicas, Instituto Gonzalo Fernández de Oviedo, 1942);

Georges Cirot, *Etudes sur l'historiographie espagnole: Mariana, historien* (Bordeaux: Feret / Paris: Fontemoing, 1904);

Cirot, "La famille de Juan de Mariana," *Bulletin Hispanique*, 6 (1904): 309–331;

Cirot, "Mariana Jesuite: La jeunesse," *Bulletin Hispanique*, 38 (1936): 295–352;

Oscar Jászi and John D. Lewis, *Against the Tyrant: The Tradition and Theory of Tyrannicide* (Glencoe, Ill.: Free Press, 1957);

Guenter Lewy, *Constitutionalism and Statecraft during the Golden Age of Spain: A Study of the Political Philosophy of Juan de Mariana, S.J.* (Geneva: Droz, 1960);

George H. Sabine, *A History of Political Theory*, revised edition (New York: Holt, 1950), p. 362;

Alan Soons, *Juan de Mariana* (Boston: Twayne, 1982).

Pedro Mejía

(1497 – 17 January 1551)

Jacqueline Ferreras
Université de Paris X-Nanterre

BOOKS: *Silva de varia lección* (Seville: Dominico de Robertis, 1540; enlarged edition, Valladolid: Juan de Villaquirán, 1550–1551); translated by Thomas Milles as *The Treasuries of Ancient and Modern Times* (London: W. Jaggard, 1613–1619);

Historia imperial y cesárea, en la cual se contienen las vidas y hechos de todos los Césares, desde Julio César hasta el emperador Maximiliano (Seville: Juan de León, 1545);

Coloquios (Seville: Dominico de Robertis, 1547);

Historia de Carlos V, edited by Raymond Foulché Delbosc, *Revue Hispanique,* 44, (1918): 1–556;

Relación de las Comunidades de Castilla, edited by Muñoz Moya y Montraveta (Barcelona: Cerdanyola del Vallés, 1985).

Modern Editions: *Historia del emperador Carlos Quinto,* edited by Juan de Mata Carriazo, Crónicas Españolas, no. 7 (Madrid: Espasa-Calpe, 1945);

Coloquios del docto y magnífico caballero Pero Mexía (Seville: Bibliófilos Sevillanos, 1947);

Silva de varia lección, 2 volumes, edited by Antonio Castro (Madrid: Cátedra, 1989, 1990);

Diálogos (Seville: Libano, 1999).

Edition in English: *Diálogos o Coloquios of Pedro Mejía,* translated, with introduction and notes, by Margaret L. Mulroney (Iowa City: The University, 1930).

OTHER: Isocrates de Apolonia, *Parénesis o exhortación a la virtud,* translated by Mejía (Seville: Dominico de Robertis, 1548);

Parénesis, in *Elogio de la locura,* by Desiderius Erasmus (Madrid: Sáez Hermanos, 1936), pp. 463–476.

Pedro Mejía (portrait by Francisco Pacheco; from Historia del emperador Carlos Quinto, *1945; Thomas Cooper Library, University of South Carolina)*

In the first half of the sixteenth century, Pedro Mejía was an emblematic figure among Sevillian humanists. Several literary portraits left eloquent testimonies of his fame: Alonso Morgado, in his *Historia de Sevilla* (1587, History of Seville), characterized him as: "El muy docto y muy magnífico Cavallero Pedro Mexía, cuya opinión en todo género de buenas letras es de mucha autoridad, y la puede prestar a qualquiera cathólica escriptura" (The very erudite and distinguished gentleman Pedro Mejía, whose opinion regarding any kind of good literature commands much authority, and could be applied to any Catholic scripture). Francisco Pacheco recalled him as well in his *Libro de descripción de verdaderos retratos de ilustres y memorables varones* (1599, Book of Description of Real Portraits of Famous and Memorable Gentlemen) as an erudite man with a delicate constitution. According to Pacheco, Mejía was entirely devoted to his studies, once he had

161

accomplished his daily chores: "Sólo se hallaba con fuerzas para estudiar y escribir . . . . la mañana asistía a la iglesia, y lo que le sobraba el día gastaba en los ministerios que tenía a su cargo. Las noches eran todas de los libros" (He only had strength to study and write . . . . In the morning he would go to church, and the rest of the day, he would spend it in the ministries of which he was in charge. His nights belonged to the books). Pacheco underlined Mejía's talent for mathematics and astrology, "en que era conocidamente el más aventajado, pues por excelencia fue llamado el Astrólogo como Aristóteles el Filósofo" (in which he was famous for being the most knowledgeable, and his excellences earned him the title of Astrologist, just as Aristotle the Philosopher). Mejía's works were remarkably successful, if one is to judge by the abundance of the Spanish editions, as well as by the Italian, German, French, and Dutch translations of his books. Mejía was a fascinated witness of his time, the center of which was Seville. As the gateway to the New World during the first half of the sixteenth century, Seville became the main subject and source of inspiration of his "chronicals."

Seville's location, ninety kilometers away from the sea on the Guadalquivir River, preserved its port from all types of dangers. It benefited as well from nearby agricultural and mining riches—namely olive trees, grapevines, wheat, and the mercury from the Almaden's mines—and from its industrial tradition of silk manufacturing since the last third of the fifteenth century. The city was well placed to respond to the growing demand for goods from the American colonies, on which it held a monopoly. As a business center, Seville developed itself in the great turmoil that characterizes the Renaissance. The Casa de Contratación (Contracting House) played a major role in its development toward modernity. Created in 1504, this institution centralized all nautical activities in the Iberian Peninsula: not only did it enforce state control upon all exchanges with America (passengers, merchandise, precious metals), but it was also a center of applied sciences and professional training. The discovery of the Pacific Ocean in 1513 (by Vasco Nuñez de Balboa) and the first trip around the world started by Ferdinand Magellan (from which only Juan Sebastián El Cano came back in 1522) made Seville the most important center of cartography in Europe: Diego Ribero's world map, which is considered the first scientific map in the world, appeared in Seville in 1529.

Throughout the sixteenth century, and impelled by the printing press, an intense intellectual activity left fervent accounts of the turmoil generated by all the maritime discoveries. The first *academias* of the peninsula were created in Seville, and the most distinguished minds of the time used to gather in such circles as the

Academia de Hernán Cortés. Seville offered a highly diversified social spectrum. It was dominated by the great nobility, such as the Gúzman family, which absorbed other titles of nobility and relied on other families of *converso* businessmen (Christians of Jewish descent), whom they protected in exchange for their services. Seville was, indeed, a place where the opposition between Old and New Christians was exceptionally harsh.

Mejía was born in Seville in 1497 and resided there most of his life, until his death in 1551. He was bound to this energizing cultural center by family ties and professional activities. He descended from an ancient line that originated in the northern Spanish region of Galicia and spread throughout the entire province of Andalusia, particularly in the areas of Seville and Córdoba around the middle of the thirteenth century. Juan de Mata Carriazo, in his introduction to the 1945 edition of Mejía's *Historia del emperador Carlos Quinto* (History of the Emperor Charles V), traced Mejía's genealogy to the existence of an Alonso Fernández Mejía in 1368. His father, Rodrigo Mejía, was mayor of Niebla, a town near Seville, in 1508, and his mother, Juana de Valderrama, came from an Hidalgo family from the town of Ecija. His paternal grandfather, Pedro Mejía, belonged to the city council of Seville as a *veinticuatro* ("twenty-four": a member of the nobility with a seat at the municipal council) from 1476 to 1487, and his great-grandfather Rodrigo Mejía was *jurado* (member of the municipal council) of Seville in 1450. Mejía inherited the pride of his ancestors and a conservative brand of Catholicism, opposed to any type of reformist openness.

Mejía received the typical education of a son belonging to the middle nobility at the beginning of the sixteenth century. He was taught skill with a sword as well as with a quill pen. He learned Latin and a little Greek, and he was in Salamanca between 1516 and 1526, studying canonical and civilian law. Although it has not been proven that he obtained his diploma, he is known never to have practiced law. There are no records left of his life between 1526 and 1530, but according to Carriazo, Mejía, despite his young age, was already famous for his knowledge of mathematics in 1526. He was called by Fernando Columbus, Christopher Columbus's son, to establish a world map and a navigation chart to be used as a reference for the Casa de Contratación.

As soon as 1531, Mejía participated in poetry contests. His name appeared along with those of other authors in the 1535 Seville edition of the *Cancionero General del Castillo* (General Songbook of Castile), first published in 1511. He might also have been the author of poems signed under the pseudonym of "Caballero

Cesáreo." He maintained epistolary exchanges with the great Spanish thinker Juan Luis Vives, living in Bruges, and with Juan Ginés de Sepúlveda. Among his correspondence two letters were found addressed to Desiderius Erasmus, dated 1530 and 1533.

Through his professional activities, Mejía held an emblematic position in Seville: in 1537, he was named royal cosmographer at the Casa de Contratación, with a salary of 30,000 *maravédis* per year, a midlevel salary for this type of position, according to a document from the *Archivo de Indias* (Archive of the Indies) cited by Carriazo. The cosmographer's duties at the Casa de Contratación consisted in assisting the *piloto mayor* (chief pilot) to administer the tests to the future boat pilots, in correcting and completing the navigation maps, in meeting every Monday from 2:00 P.M to 5:00 P.M. at the Casa de Contratación, and in stamping diverse instruments that were meant to be sold, such as quadrants and astrolabes. Mejía was thus in contact with the most advanced maritime and geographical knowledge of his time, which he strove to vulgarize in two of his works: *Silva de varia lección* (1540; translated as *The Treasuries of Ancient and Modern Times,* 1613–1619) and *Coloquios* (1547, Colloquia). In 1538 he became alcalde of the Santa Hermandad, the examining judge in charge of prosecuting delinquents, judging them, and overseeing the application of the sentence. His position as a *veinticuatro* also made him a powerful man in Seville.

He had been the royal cosmographer for three years and alcalde of the Santa Hermandad for two when he published his first masterpiece, *Silva de varia lección*. He achieved such overwhelming success that in December of the same year, the Sevillian editor Juan Cromberger published another edition, with ten additional chapters. The ninth edition, published in Valladolid in 1550–1551, represents the complete work, with an added fourth part and twenty-two new chapters. In a little more than a century, *Silva de varia lección* was published thirty-two times in Castilian and seventy-five times in other languages: thirty in Italian, thirty-one in French, five in English, five in Dutch, and four in German. It was successfully imitated by the Italians Francesco Sansovino and Gieronimo Giglio, as well as by the French Antoine du Verdier and Louis Guyon, whose works were published several times along with their translation of the *Silva de varia lección*. The English translations were pillaged to produce other compilations. It was, according to José María López Piñero, the best-known work of scientific diffusion in Europe throughout the sixteenth century. It was then eventually forgotten in the second half of the seventeenth century, to be known and evaluated only by a few specialists, whose opinions regarding its value were varied.

Title page for a posthumously published collection of humanist dialogues by Mejía (from Ramón D. Perés, Historia de la literatura española e hispanoamericana, *1964; Thomas Cooper Library, University of South Carolina)*

Mejía was well aware of the fact that *Silva de varia lección* inaugurated a new genre, the *miscelánea* (miscellaneous). This genre, one of the most read and in demand throughout the sixteenth and seventeenth centuries, characterized the didactic concern of Humanists to collect all knowledge, including the geographical information that came with the discovery of the New World. The spread of the printing press (starting in 1472 in Spain), particularly, popularized the genre, allowing for the dissemination of knowledge in the vernacular language. Mejía justified the title and the genre of *Silva de varia lección* in the prologue: "Lo que aquí escrivo, es tomado de muy grandes y aprobados auctores, como el que corta planta de muy buenos árboles para su huerta o jardín. . . . Escogí, assí, esta manera de escrevir por capítulos sin orden y sin perseverar en un propósito, a imitación de grandes auctores antiguos que escrivieron libros desta manera. . . . y por esto, le puse por nombre Silva, porque en las selvas y bosques están las plantas y árboles sin orden ni regla" (What I am writing here is taken from great and approved authors, just as one takes the plants from very good trees for his orchard or his garden. . . . I chose, thus, this way of writing chapters without any order and without persevering in only one endeavor, just like the great ancient writers who composed books in this manner. . . . This is the reason why I named it *Silva* [Forest] because in the forests and in the woods, plants and trees do not follow any given order nor rules). The author is inspired by both ancient and modern writers and by his own professional experience. His innovation lies in the way he selected his sources and in the art he brought to writing the text, following a technique that Fernando Lázaro Carreter described as *imitación compuesta* (composed imitation)—in other words, that of an imitation rethought according to the sociohistorical context and didactic intentions of the author. The work could be read both as an entertaining selection of different stories and anecdotes and as a collection of information and reflections regarding moral and scientific questions. A good part of *Silva de varia lección* is dedicated to subjects related to natural science, which was a subject of utmost importance during the Renaissance. Astronomy is one of its main topics and is treated with exceptional didactic talent, as entire chapters are devoted to the phenomena of the heat wave, the age of the world, the calculation of the calendar, the celestial wonders, the birth and death of Jesus Christ, and the measure of the diameter of Earth. Another chapter is dedicated to the formation of winds. Several chapters discuss astrology, an essential science at the time and one of Mejía's specialties. As a devout Catholic, he considered that the stars were in some way the instruments of divine will, the second cause for the phenomena for which mankind had no explanation, and he discusses therefore the influence of the stars upon human abilities and relationships. Another important part of *Silva de varia lección* is dedicated to historical erudition in all its forms. Mejía rigorously quotes his sources, a scrupulousness remarkable for his time. As a Christian, he attributes a decisive role to providence in the making of history. He evokes past empires, such as the Byzantine and Roman. He tells of events and anecdotes regarding religious history, such as the stories of the popes or that of the Knights Templar. Following a trend of his time, Mejía is also interested in the biographies and feats of well-known figures such as Muhammad and the Greek philosophers Diogenes, Heraclitus, and Democritus, as well as accounts of extraordinary and marvelous events. He also echoes the social and political concerns of his epoch and reflects upon love and marriage, the education of children, the value of work, the ills of alco-

hol, moral examples provided by the animal kingdom, the qualities of a good government, royal power, and tyranny.

Mejía's *Historia imperial y cesárea, en la cual se contienen las vidas y hechos de todos los Césares, desde Julio César hasta el emperador Maximiliano* (Imperial and Caesarean History, in Which Are Contained the Lives and Deeds of All the Caesars, from Julius Caesar until the Emperor Maximilian) was published in 1545. This considerable work is organized chronologically and includes the biographies of all ancient Roman and medieval emperors, from Julius Caesar to Maximilian I of Austria, the grandfather of Charles V, presenting the great figures of each of these emperors' reigns and the biographies of all the popes. The author provides an accurate list of references. Antonio Castro Díaz, in his *Los "Coloquios" de Pedro Mexía* (1977, The "Colloquia" of Pedro Mejía), underlines the rigor of Mejía, who used Latin, Spanish, Italian, and French sources faithfully. The book is a masterwork for two main reasons: Mejía's talent for summarizing his sources, and the care he takes to locate each emperor's life in the context of the popes and the great men of his time. Mejía addressed it to the future Philip II, who answered, expressing the satisfaction he had derived from reading it: "tendremos memoria dello para favoreceros" (we shall remember it well to favor you). The work was successful and was translated into Latin, Italian, German, and Dutch, published more than thirty times altogether. It is both an intelligent and useful compilation.

Historia imperial y cesárea was intended to support the hegemonic endeavor of Charles V to make Spain the modern heir of the Roman Empire. It is the first work of its kind to be written in Castilian; its conception is a testimony to the modernity of its author, who strove to illustrate his narrations with irrefutable examples in order to support his arguments and convince his readers. Mejía wrote that "aviendo yo determinado, y aun alguna vez prometido, prosiguiendo mi propósito ya començado de escribir alguna cosa para publico provecho de mi Patria y Nación. . . . ningún género de escritura me pareció que convenía más, ni a mí me agradó ni satisfizo tanto, como tratar alguna grande y verdadera historia" (having determined and even sometimes promised to pursue the endeavor that I had already begun, that is, to write something of benefit for my Country and Nation . . . no other genre of writing seemed to be more convenient, neither pleased nor satisfied me as much as speaking of some great and true history). This prologue may constitute one of the most beautiful praises of history ever written in Castilian, according to Carriazo, for Mejía placed the historical discipline above any other discipline. This book clearly

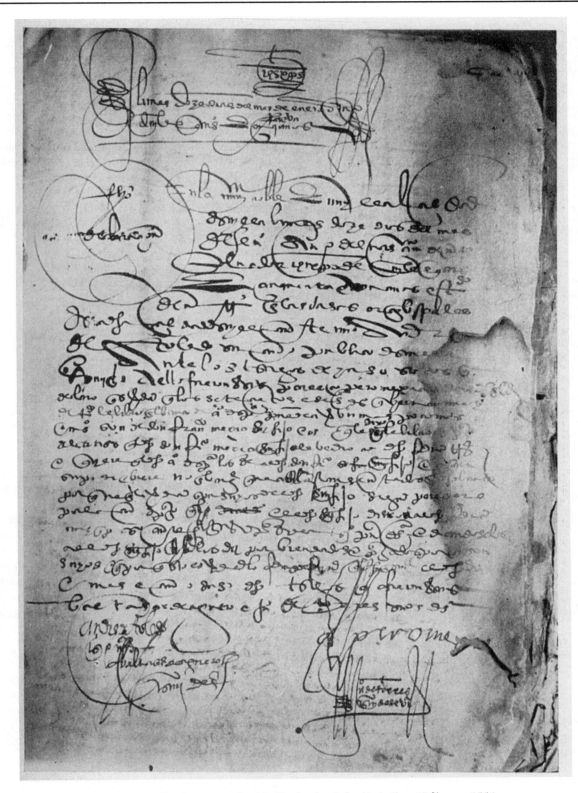

Mejía's last will and testament, signed by him five days before his death on 17 January 1551
(Archivo de Protocolos de Sevilla; from Historia del emperador Carlos Quinto, *1945;*
Thomas Cooper Library, University of South Carolina)

*Mejía's tombstone in Seville, placed on his grave in 1586,
thirty-five years after his death (from* Historia del
emperador Carlos Quinto, *1945; Thomas
Cooper Library, University of South Carolina)*

announces the great work that will follow, the *Historia
del emperador Carlos Quinto.*

During the winter of 1546–1547, Mejía had written the *Coloquios,* a characteristic example of the most
successful genre in the sixteenth century, the humanist
dialogue. The humanistic dialogue is modeled for the
most part after the philosophical dialogues of Plato,
Aristotle, and Cicero but also after Lucian, who was
first imitated by Italian humanists from the fifteenth

century such as Giovanni Pontano, and after Erasmus's
Colloquia (1518, Colloquies), which became famous in
Spain circa 1525. Mejía's *Coloquios* comprises conversations in vernacular language on a variety of topics. It
was immediately quite successful and was published
more than ten times before the end of the century, as
well as translated into French, Italian, and English. The
first dialogue is written in two parts. It is a discussion
on physicians and the two manners of practicing medicine, through theoretical knowledge or out of empirical
experience. The next two dialogues, "Coloquio del convite" (The Banquet Colloquy) deal with banquets and
diets, another controversial theme at the time because
of the emperor's taste for the rich Bourguignon cuisine,
which contrasted with traditional Castilian sobriety.
Three other dialogues, which feature the same characters as the first two, disseminate the new astronomical,
maritime, and meteorological discoveries. "Coloquio
del sol" (Sun Colloquy) comments on natural phenomena such as eclipses; the roundness of Earth and its
dimensions in comparison with the sun and the moon;
the antipode; the density of the body; and universal
gravity. "Diálogo de la tierra" (Dialogue of the Earth)
deals with the atmosphere, the four elements, and the
disposition of the land and the seas on Earth. "Coloquio Natural" (Natural Colloquy) is dedicated to
diverse meteorological phenomena, such as thunder,
lightning, rain, hail, snow, frost, and dew. Placed after
"Coloquio del sol," the "Coloquio del porfiado" (Colloquy of the Obstinate) raises, under the appearances of a
friendly chat, serious questions about the importance of
dialogue in the quest for truth and about the relativity
of human knowledge, since the truth is experienced by
individual minds. The character known as Porfiado systematically contradicts his interlocutor regarding good
and evil, what is true or false, and what is fair or not.
The second part of this dialogue praises the donkey as
a model of humility and usefulness according to the
Greek and Christian traditions. It demonstrates also the
importance of the formal appearance of things and of
the oratory art in order to be convincing.

The conversations take place either in the streets
of Seville, through which the protagonists are riding
their horses, on the steps of the Iglesia Mayor (main
church), or in their homes, as in the second part of the
"Coloquio del convite." The rides give rise to comments upon the current events of the city. As they go to
visit one of their friends, the two characters of the
"Diálogo de los médicos" (Dialogue of the Doctors)
comment upon the progress of the construction of the
new houses: "en grande manera se ha enmendado en
Sevilla, porque todos labran ya a la calle y de diez años
a esta parte se han hecho más ventanas y rejas a ella
que en los treinta de antes" (Seville has been improved

in a great way, for they are all now working on the street, and more windows and bars have been built in the last ten years than in the past three decades). In the "Coloquio del sol," one of the characters briefly recounts Ferdinand Magellan's travels in order to prove the roundness of Earth, and the other, stunned, answers, "¡Santa María! ¿Eso pasa así?" (Holy Mary! Is it really the way it works?).

In July 1548 Charles V named Mejía imperial chronicler. The other court historiographers were Juan de Sepúlveda, Florián de Ocampo, and Bernabé del Busto. The new position was rewarded with a yearly salary of 80,000 *maravédis,* and Charles V allowed Mejía not to follow the court displacements for health reasons, as is shown in documents signed in Augsburg in 1548. Mejía therefore did not live near the emperor, but he might have had all the necessary documents to be an historiographer, particularly the letters Charles V received from his generals, if one is to judge by the exactitude and precision with which the war events are related. At such a remove Mejía could reflect upon the events he described.

Historia del emperador Carlos Quinto can be considered Pedro Mejía's masterpiece. Although interrupted by the author's death, it continues up to the events of 1530. According to Pacheco, "atendiendo a su nuevo cargo comenzó a escribir con tanta verdad y con tan copioso y elegante aparato de elocuencia que si acabara esta Historia, fuera sin duda una de las mejores que jamás se compusieron" (in fulfillment of his new charge, he set off to write with such truth and with such copious and elegant eloquence that if he were to finish that History, it doubtlessly would have been one of the best that was ever composed). It remained unpublished until the twentieth century, when it was resurrected by René Costes's research; Costes, however, died in 1917 during World War I, and the critical edition that he prepared remained unpublished. The first editor is Carriazo, who based his edition on the best available manuscript. The work began to circulate in manuscript shortly after Mejía's death, and it was used without any scruples by Fray Prudencio de Sandoval for his *Historia de la vida y hechos del emperador Carlos V* (1604–1606, History of the Life and Facts of the Emperor Charles V). Marco Guazzo's *Historie di Tutte le Cose Degne di Memoria* (1540) was one of the sources that Mejía used specifically to relate the ceremonies organized for the coronation of Charles V. According to Carriazo's study in his edition of *Historia del Emperador Carlos Quinto,* Mejía must have used many written sources about the accounts of the time, such as the one Carriazo has himself uncovered and cites as an example: "Del desafío de los reyes de Francia e Inglaterra al Emperador y Rey nuestro señor, con sus respuestas" (Of the Challenge of the Kings of France and England to the Emperor and Our King, with His Answers), published in Burgos on 14 February 1528. The remarkable, lasting usefulness of Mejía's work is such that historian Manuel Fernández Álvarez often cites Mejía in his masterful study, *Carlos V, el César y el hombre* (1999 Charles V, the Caesar and the Man). Fernández Álvarez considers that Mejía flattered the court brilliantly but excessively with his writing, but he grants him unquestionable sincerity and even a certain independence of judgment. The historian draws attention to the relationship that Mejía established between the activities of the emperor and those of the conquistadores on the other side of the ocean.

As a humanist, Mejía's curiosity and talent were in total agreement with the passion for knowledge of his time. He helped greatly in disseminating knowledge drawn from antiquity. He found a way to use the rigor of his understanding of mathematics in the study of history. Marcel Bataillon's harsh judgment in his *Erasmo y España: Estudios sobre la historia espiritual del siglo XVI* (1950, Erasmus and Spain: Studies on the Spiritual History of the Sixteenth Century) does not appear justified since it is crucial to appreciate this author in the light of his century and of his endeavor. Mejía should be considered an historian who spread the knowledge of his time rather than as a creative literary author. The coherence of his works deserves to be pointed out, for each of his books announces or echoes the others. This organizing principle is to be interpreted as an effort to disseminate knowledge for the greater glory of Spain. He is indeed a representative figure of the small nobility within which the emperor usually recruited his officials. Pedro Mejía, an author of undeniable quality, is acknowledged as a reliable historical source and can still seduce with the liveliness of his style.

References:

Marcel Bataillon, *Erasmo y España: Estudios sobre la historia espiritual del siglo XVI,* 2 volumes (Mexico City: Fondo de Cultura Económica, 1950);

Antonio Castro Díaz, *Los "Coloquios" de Pedro Mexía* (Seville: Diputación Provincial, 1977);

Pierre Chaunu and Huguette Chaunu, *Sevilla y América siglos XVI y XVII,* translated by Rafael Sánchez Mantero (Seville: Publicaciones de la Universidad de Sevilla, 1983);

René Costes, "Pedro Mexía, chroniste de Charles Quint," *Bulletin hispanique,* 12 (1920): 1–36, 256–258;

Ángel Delgado Gómez, "Humanismo médico y humanismo erasmiano en España: dos visiones de la naturaleza y la providencia," in *El erasmismo en España,* edited by Manuel Revuelta Chaves and Ciríaco

Morón Arroyo (Santander: Sociedad Menéndez Pelayo, 1986), pp. 432–433;

J. Deloffre, "Note bibliographique sur Pero Mexía," *Revue Hispanique,* 44 (1918): 557–564;

Manuel Fernández Álvarez, *Carlos V, el Cesar y el hombre* (Madrid: Espasa-Calpe, 1999);

Jacqueline Ferreras, *Los Diálogos humanísticos del siglo XVI en lengua castellana* (Murcia: Universidad de Murcia, 2002);

Ferreras, "Géneros literarios en el siglo XV: el diálogo humanístico, crisol de experimentaciones literarias," in *Aspectos históricos y culturales bajo Carlos V,* edited by Christoph Strosetzki (Frankfurt am Main: Vervuert, 2000), pp. 288–308;

Ferreras, "Tratamiento y función de la mitología en la literatura castellana renacentista: algunos ejemplos," in *Europa y sus mitos,* edited by F. Carmona Fernández and José García Cano (Murcia: Universidad de Murcia, Servicio de Publicaciones, 2004), pp. 63–69;

Luis S. Granjel, "Las ideas antropológico-médicas del 'Magnífico Caballero' Pedro Mexía," *Humanismo y medicina* (1968): 75–99;

Willard F. King, *Prosa novelística y academias literarias en el siglo XVII,* volume 10 (Madrid: Real Academia Española, 1963), pp. 23–27, 86;

Fernando Lázaro Carreter, "Imitación compuesta y diseño retórico en la oda a Juan Grial," *Anuario de Estudios Filológicos,* 2 (1979): 89–119;

Isaías Lerner, "Acerca del texto de la primera edición de la Silva de Pedro Mexía," *Actas del VII Congreso de la Asociación Internacional de Hispanistas,* 2 (1982): 677–684;

Rafael Malparida Tirado, *Vario Lección de plática aurea* (Málaga: Analecta Malacitana, Universidad de Málaga, 2004), pp. 145–166;

José María López Piñero, *Ciencia y técnica en la sociedad española de los siglos XVI y XVII* (Barcelona: Labor Universitaria, 1979);

Ramón D. Perés, *Historia de la literatura española e hispano-americana* (Barcelona: Sopena, 1964);

Pedro Piñero Ramírez and Christian Wentzlaff-Eggebert, eds., *Sevilla en el imperio de Carlos V: Encrucijada entre dos mundos y dos épocas* (Seville: Universidad de Sevilla / Universidad de Colonia, 1991);

Alberto Porqueras Mayo and Joseph L. Laurenti, "Rarezas bibliográficas: La colección de ediciones y traducciones del sevillano Pedro Mexía (1496–1552) en la biblioteca de la Universidad de Illinois," *Archivo Hispalense,* 57, no. 175 (1974): 121–138;

Antonio Prieto, *La prosa española del siglo XVI,* volume 1 (Madrid: Cátedra, 1986), pp. 221–237;

Asunción Rallo Gruss, *Erasmo y la prosa renacentista española* (Madrid: Laberinto, 2003), pp. 73–80, 101–104;

Rallo Gruss, "El sevillano Pedro Mexía, historiador de Carlos V," in *Actas del I Congreso de Historia de Andalucía, diciembre de 1976,* volume 5 (Córdoba: Monte de Piedad y Caja de Ahorros de Córdoba, 1978), pp. 307–314;

José Luis Varela, "Pero Mexía: Límites de la Silva," in *Sevilla en el imperio de Carlos V: Encrucijada entre dos mundos y des épocas,* edited by Piñero Ramirez and Wentzlaff-Eggebert (Seville: Universidad de Sevilla / Universidad de Colonia, 1991), pp. 243–250.

Diego Hurtado de Mendoza

(1504 – 13 August 1575)

Eric W. Vogt
Seattle Pacific University

BOOKS: *Obras del insigne caballero don Diego de Mendoza,* edited by Juan Díaz Hidalgo (Madrid: Juan de la Cuesta, 1610);

Guerra de Granada, edited by Luis Tribaldos de Toledo (Lisbon: Giraldo de la Viña, 1627).

Modern Editions: "Obras del insigne caballero don Diego de Mendoza," in *Poetas líricos de los siglos XVI y XVII,* edited by Adolfo de Castro, Biblioteca de autores españoles, no. 32 (Madrid: Rivadeneyra, 1854), pp. 51–103;

Obras poéticas, edited by William I. Knapp (Madrid: Ginesta, 1877);

De la guerra de Granada, comentarios, edited by Manuel Gómez-Moreno (Madrid: Maestre, 1948);

"A tí, Doña Marina": The Poetry of Don Diego Hurtado de Mendoza, edited by C. Malcom Batchelor (Havana: Úcar-García, 1959);

Guerra de Granada, edited by Bernardo Blanco-González (Madrid: Castalia, 1970).

Edition in English: *The War in Granada,* translated, with an introduction, by Martin Shuttleworth (London: Folio Society, 1982).

ATTRIBUTED WORKS: *La vida de Lazarillo de Tormes, y de sus fortunas y adversidades* (Burgos: Juan de Junta, 1554);

"Conquista de Túnez y la Goleta por el emperador Carlos v. en 1535," *Colección de documentos inéditos para la Historia de España,* 1 (1842): 154–207;

"Diálogo entre Caronte y el ánima de Pedro Luis Farnesio" and "Carta de Don Diego de Mendoza al capitán Salazar," in *Curiosidades bibliográficas: Colección escogida de obras raras de amenidad y erudición, con apuntes biográficos de los diferentes autores,* edited by Adolfo de Castro, Biblioteca de autores españoles, no. 36 (Madrid: Rivadeneyra, 1855), pp. 1–7 and 547–550.

OTHER: *Mechánica de Aristóteles,* translated by Mendoza, edited by Raymond Foulché-Delbosc, *Revue Hispanique,* 5 (1898): 365–405.

Diego Hurtado de Mendoza (painting by Titian; Pitti Gallery, Florence, Italy; from Erika Spivakovsky, Son of the Alhambra: Don Diego Hurtado de Mendoza, *1970; Thomas Cooper Library, University of South Carolina)*

The importance of Diego Hurtado de Mendoza in Spanish literary and political history resulted from the opportunities at the highest levels of society to which his birth into a wealthy and noble family made him heir, as well as to his lifelong cultivation of his natural abilities, as the record of his life and works displays. By the time he entered the world, his branch of the Mendoza family was enjoying its second century of high-level involvement in the political, military, religious, and artistic life of Spain. Mendoza's life and works reflect the variety of cultural, religious, and literary heritages that define not only Spain but also sixteenth-century Europe. Although he is primarily remembered for his activities as a diplomat and courtier, his frank account of the Spanish conquest of Granada, in which his own family was intimately involved, and particularly his many letters have made a valuable contribution to modern understanding of the era.

Few details are known of the first twenty-five years of his life. What is known is derived from scant references to it in his own voluminous correspondence or that of others. Despite this biographical lacuna about his early years, the record that his copious epistolary efforts have left make his life the best known of all nonroyal Spaniards of his century and illuminate much of the background of the highest levels of the political events of that pivotal century. Don Diego's political career, from his maturity through his declining years, is best described collectively as a series of ambassadorships. Representing the interests of his monarch, Mendoza was a key figure, if not usually the principal one, in major negotiations or treaties that, during his life, defined the alternating fortunes and misfortunes arising from the competing interests of France and Spain, Spain and England, Venice and the Turks, and the Vatican and Italian city-states. As a military leader, Mendoza is known to have been present at major and minor clashes between Catholic and Protestant forces, papal armies and Italian city-states, as well as between Christendom and the Islamic powers of North Africa. A survey of his origins and his involvement in major events of his time is a primer for anyone interested in sixteenth-century Europe.

Mendoza was born in 1504 in the Alhambra to Francisca Pacheco, the second wife of Iñigo López de Mendoza, the second count of Tendilla. His great-great-grandfather, also named Diego de Mendoza, was a poet of the late fourteenth century, but he was not as well known as his son, Íñigo López de Mendoza, Marqués de Santillana, who is the most famous Spanish poet of the fifteenth century. The marqués was the father of seven sons, including Cardinal Pedro González de Mendoza, an archbishop of Toledo in 1482 who played a significant role in persuading the Catholic Monarchs to establish an Inquisition, and Íñigo López de Mendoza, a capable military leader and the first count of Tendilla, who

was the grandfather of Diego Hurtado de Mendoza. Mendoza's father was among the first to introduce Italian humanism into Spain. His involvement in the last wars of the Reconquista (Reconquest) in the area of Granada resulted in his becoming the commanding general of the Spanish troops in the south in 1492. After being named captain-general of Granada, Íñigo López de Mendoza spent the next twenty-three years there and converted his position into a hereditary post that his son and grandson later enjoyed.

Raised amid the material and intellectual opulence of the Alhambra, Mendoza, the fourth of at least eight children, learned Arabic in addition to Spanish during his childhood. From 1516 to 1517, Mendoza's studies in Salamanca brought him into contact with the formal studies of Latin and Greek. Mendoza also became fluent in Italian before studying in Rome from 1526 until 1529 and then for two more years in Siena. From 1529 until 1534 he traveled through the imperial possessions with King Charles V, after which, in 1535, he served in the Tunisian War.

His first international assignment required him to venture to his only post outside the Latin world. When Charles V heard of the death of his aunt Catherine of Aragon (the first wife of the English king Henry VIII), he saw a new opportunity to renew relations with England, hitherto interrupted because of Henry's divorce from Catherine. With an alliance secured by a successful dynastic marriage, Charles hoped to isolate France and ultimately defeat Protestant forces in the north of Europe. Mendoza served as ambassador to England from May 1537 until September 1538. His primary mission was to attempt to arrange a dynastic marriage between Mary, daughter of Henry VIII, and Charles V's brother-in-law, Luis of Portugal. Mendoza failed in this mission, and longing for Spain, he returned to Toledo in 1538.

His next imperial appointment was as ambassador to the doge of Venice. Mendoza promptly turned this position into an opportunity to reap huge profits from the starvation that resulted from persistent drought in the northeast of Italy. Parallel with his ambition, and fueling it, was his main diplomatic dilemma—how to keep the republic of Venice within the Holy League at a time when its people were hungry and the Turks possessed grain. Mendoza's plan, as revealed in his correspondence, was to buy wheat in Naples and sell it in Venice at exorbitant prices in order to reap huge profits. His plan failed, however, after he was unable to obtain the wheat in a timely manner.

In his letters from Venice it is also possible to observe Mendoza's human, weaker side. In these epistles, published in 1935 in *Algunas cartas de don Diego Hurtado de Mendoza escritas 1538–1552* (Some

Letters by Don Diego Hurtado de Mendoza Written 1538–1552), he reveals his temptations of the flesh and his willingness to joke about them and perhaps even revel in relating his exploits, or near exploits. Mendoza was struck by the beauty of a Jewish *putana* (prostitute), and in a jocular tone in one of his letters—written in August 1540 to Francisco de los Cobos, a royal secretary—he claims that she will not lie with him unless he is circumcised. The exaggerated tone of a letter a week later seems playful; yet, he writes that his plans to convert to Judaism are serious. By January 1541, however, Mendoza's tone changes. Having failed to win the woman's affection, he begins to lose interest. Moreover, he relates in his letters his disgust at her squalid living conditions in the Jewish Quarter, saying her house reeks like a slave ship. In the midst of this depiction of the dark side of humanity, Mendoza tells of how painful it had been to forego the circumcision and laments having thus lost the opportunity to enjoy her favors in a letter informed by a clearly perceptible amount of literary conceit based on the humorous paradox.

Though his affair with the Jewess had come to an end, his correspondence is spiced with references that attest to his continued illicit liaisons in Venetian brothels. Despite his obvious sexual interest in women, there is no record of his ever having had, or considered, a genuine relationship with a marriageable woman. In addition to his constant preoccupation with his own commercial and amorous intrigues, his Venetian correspondence also reveals the continual schemes of the French and the many attempts made on his life in this period, during which he was suspected of having murdered two French agents and found it necessary to employ bodyguards.

Mendoza's next appointment, one that occupied him off and on for two decades, was that of imperial delegate to the Council of Trent. During the early years of the council, Mendoza divided his time between Venice and Trent. He repeatedly proved his loyalty and zeal for the interests of Charles V during decades of political vicissitudes surrounding the various sessions of the council.

As an imperial delegate, Mendoza enjoyed both popularity and respect for his scholarly command of the issues. The planning sessions of the Council of Trent brought him into discussions with Nicholas Perrenot of Granvelle and his son, Antoine (who later succeeded Cobos as secretary to Charles V). Their discussions were supposed to be about reforming the clergy, but because of the Franco-Hispanic war, they were the only three participants. Soon after, Mendoza returned to Venice, but then he went back to Trent to take part in the debates. During the 1540s Mendoza

Mendoza's father, Íñigo López de Mendoza, whose exploits as commanding general of the Spanish troops in the 1492 conquest of Granada provided material for his son's Guerra de Granada, *published in 1627 (Patronato de la Alhambra y Generalife; from Erika Spivakovsky,* Son of the Alhambra: Don Diego Hurtado de Mendoza, *1970; Thomas Cooper Library, University of South Carolina)*

also shuttled for five years among Siena, of which Charles V appointed him governor in 1546, Rome, Florence, and Bologna. His travels resulted from the disputes between the interests of Cosimo I de' Medici of Florence and the Appiani family of the independent city-state of Piombino, as well as the affairs of the Council of Trent and those of the cities of Parma and Piacenza; he also traveled in his capacity as ambassador to two popes, Paul III and Julius III.

The conflicts between the ambitions of Charles V and Pope Paul III provide a good backdrop to examine Mendoza's diplomatic prowess and his proud, even haughtily displayed dedication to imperial interests. The background to Mendoza's role concerns the rule of Parma and Piacenza, pawns of Charles V since the sack of Rome in 1527 and the source of tension in imperial politics on the Italian peninsula. Pope Paul III, upon handing them over to his own profligate, perverted, and illegitimate son Pier Luigi Farnese, affronted the emperor. The gift was deemed a violation of papal statutes insofar as the Pope stood to gain personally from the donation. Charles V responded as a well-schooled Machiavellian. In 1546 the marqués de Vasto, governor of Milan, died, and the emperor appointed Ferrante Gonzaga as governor on the condition that he use his position to remove Farnese from Parma and Piacenza. On 10 September 1547, the day that a mob broke into the castle and murdered Farnese, Gonzaga's army marched into Piacenza and took control. To Mendoza, unaware that Farnese was murdered, nonetheless fell the duty of informing the Pope of the death of his illegitimate son. Being unaware of Charles's complicity (at least the fact that he had instigated Gonzaga to do as he saw fit), Mendoza was able to convey a convincing message to Paul III. Another son of the Pope, Ottavio Farnese, became ruler of Parma and Piacenza as an independent duchy, and by 1550 all seemed to be well.

When both Pope Julius III, the successor to Paul III, and Charles V had second thoughts about the appointment, Mendoza convinced both men to take back the cities. Farnese, in a resolute and cunning move, solicited the aid of Henry II of France, and in the course of a year in which no major battles were fought, Charles was worn down and withdrew; Julius III came to terms with Ottavio, and the French regained the foothold in Italy they had lost in the previous century.

The contests between Medici and the Appianis offered further scenes of intrigue in which Mendoza, who saw strategic importance in completing the chain of Spanish fortresses linked around the Mediterranean all the way to Naples, adroitly moved for his emperor. Mendoza's only diplomatic obstacle was the matriarch and ruler of the Appiani family, Elena Salvati. Upon hearing of her refusal to abandon Piombino, he removed her by physically carrying her away along with the chair in which she was sitting. In 1548 Medici, a colorful figure and a potential source of international conflict, was unwisely assigned as protector of Piombino, a position he eventually took advantage of by signing the city-state over to himself four years later. In the midst of the contentious atmosphere between all parties concerned in the Italian peninsula, the Council of Trent also demanded the attentions of pope, emperor, and Mendoza, the able diplomat, during the years from 1539 to 1552.

In October 1552, having spent ten years in the emperor's service without seeing him, Mendoza arrived in Germany, at Speier. His circuitous trip began after he slipped out of Rome, in the middle of the night, in the aftermath of a fistfight with a Roman police officer. Mendoza found the road to Siena blocked by French troops and went through Ortobello and then to Florence, where he stayed with Medici, who was basking in his political victory in the matter of Piombino. From there, Mendoza went to Genoa, Milan, Basel, and finally Speier. His twenty-two years of foreign service were rewarded parsimoniously with a small sum and membership in the esteemed order of Alcántara, the high-sounding title of comendador de las casas de Badajoz (commander of the houses of Badajoz), and free passage to Spain through Flanders and London. In reaction, in his letter to the future king Philip II of Spain, Mendoza unrestrainedly expressed his bitterness at being treated like a servant.

Upon returning to Spain, Mendoza's whereabouts for nearly three years after November 1553 are unknown, because of the fact that he ceased to correspond as he had when serving as ambassador. After reporting to the royal palace in Valladolid, as a knight of Alcántara, he likely spent at least one of these years in a monastery, as prescribed by the rules of the order. He did surface briefly in February 1554, possibly having completed the rituals necessary for his admission into that ancient military order, when his brother Bernardino requested his assistance to ready the ships about to convey Philip II to England, where the monarch to be was to wed Mary Tudor.

Named a supply officer for the king's armada in 1557, Mendoza served at Laredo in preparation for Philip II's planned invasion of France. It is not known whether Mendoza participated in this invasion or whether he was to be found among the victorious Spanish army at the famous battle of Saint-Quintin on 10 August 1557. That victory, in any case, symbolizes Mendoza's vindication as a diplomat, albeit partially, as it resulted in nearly a hundred years of peace with France and spelled the end of French ambitions in Italy. Siena passed to the duchy of Florence, however, and Piombino was returned to the Appianis.

In September 1557 Mendoza embarked for England, but perhaps his dislike of its weather is the reason he spent only days there before going to France to visit his king. After that, his whereabouts are unknown until he appears in a series of records of the Inquisition, in September 1559, November 1561, and June 1562. These documents were recorded in Madrid and deal with the case of the archbishop of Toledo, Bartolomé Carranza, who was incarcerated for seventeen years on charges of heresy, the exact nature of which remains unclear.

In 1561, Mendoza adopted his grandniece, Magdalena de Bobadilla, who shared his penchant for letter writing. Because of her epistolary efforts, a great deal is known about life in the Spanish capital among people of the economic and political status of the Mendozas.

The need to supply a third armada brought Mendoza back into public view. In 1567 he served as the commanding supply officer of a Spanish fleet intended to crush the Dutch rebellion in Flanders, a feat not accomplished until more than half a century later because Mendoza's fleet never left port. By July he was back in Madrid, at court, where he was involved in a briefly violent dispute with Diego de Leyva in the royal palace on 23 July 1568, outside the king's chambers. As a result, Mendoza was charged with lèse-majesté and banished to the castle of La Mota in Medina del Campo.

The quarrel was a consequence of a dispute over Mendoza's crude but literary reaction to a poem written by Leyva: "De don Diego de Leyva a don Diego de Mendoza, despidiéndose de Palacio" (1610, From Don Diego de Leyva to Don Diego de Mendoza, on the Latter's Taking Leave of the Court). Leyva's work seems innocuous when compared with Mendoza's vitriolic response, "Respuesta de don Diego de Mendoza" (Response by Don Diego de Mendoza). In Mendoza's response, he lambastes Leyva and insults his manhood from several perspectives. These two pieces are the sole documents, literary or otherwise, one has by which to judge this curious affair.

Despite Mendoza's perpetual banishment from court, however, one perceives no cessation in his sense of duty to his king. Indeed, at the end of his life in 1575, Mendoza magnanimously, and as a sign of his eternal loyalty, willed his vast library of manuscripts, bound works, and artifacts to the holdings of the Escorial, a project envisioned and financed by King Philip II.

Mendoza's poetic works include burlesques, satires, and frankly obscene, if not outright pornographic, verse. Often anthologized, these verses bestow on him much of his enduring fame, just as is the case for many of like spirit and content written by other major poets of the Golden Age, such as Francisco Gómez de Quevedo and Luis de Góngora. In addition, and in the typical Golden Age fashion of manifesting the full range of human virtues, vices, aspirations, and disappointments, Mendoza is the author of traditional courtly love poetry, epistolary poems, and works on classical themes, as well as Italianate poems and those of neo-Latin inspiration.

Mendoza's prose style is seminal for the Spanish language, and his treatment of the issues of the history of the conquest of Granada became a model for historiography. Mendoza's technique is most accessible in his *Guerra de Granada* (1627; translated as *The War in Granada,* 1982), published, as all his works were, in the centuries following his death. In this

Title page for a 1578 manuscript edition of Mendoza's history of the Spanish invasion of Granada (from De la guerra de Granada, *1948; Z. Smith Reynolds Library, Wake Forest University)*

work, the stylistic influences of the Roman historians he much admired, Livy and Tacitus, are evident. Mendoza's courage and frankness in criticizing even the actions of his close relatives in this war give him an air of credibility. In *Guerra de Granada* his tone is terse, sententious, and energetic, although at times his laconic style renders his meaning opaque. Mendoza's letters, often in epistolary verse—that is, composed of unrhymed hendecasyllables ending in a rhymed couplet—are a mine of biographical and historical data about him as well as many other prominent figures and events of the time, and they often include depictions of the darker side of human nature.

The enduring controversy over Mendoza's possible authorship of *La vida de Lazarillo de Tormes, y de sus fortunas y adversidades* (The Life of Lazarillo de Tormes, and His Fortunes and Adversities), published anonymously in three cities in 1554, is best described by Alberto Blecua, who in his introduction to the 1974 Castalia edition of the novel, asserts that

OBRAS
DEL INSIGNE
CAVALLERO DON
DIEGO DE MENDOZA, EMBAXA-
DOR DEL EMPERADOR CARLOS.
QVINTO EN ROMA.
RECOPILADAS POR FREI IVAN
Diaz Hidalgo, del Habito de San Iuan, Capellan, y Mu-
fico de Camara de fu Mageftad.
DIRIGIDAS A DON IÑIGO LOPEZ
de Mendoza, Marques de Mondejar, Conde de Tendilla,
Señor de la Prouincia de Almoguera,

Año   1610.

Con Priuilegios de Caftilla, y Portugal.
En Madrid, Por Iuan de la Cuefta.
Vendefe en cafa de Francifco de Robles, libiero del Rey nueftro feñor.

*Title page for the first edition of Mendoza's collected
works, published thirty-five years after his death
in 1575 (University of Illinois at
Urbana-Champaign Library)*

evince his capacity for voluminous labor and his efficacy in both secular and ecclesiastical arenas. The
record of his life and actions, not without scandals
and human foibles, testifies to his mastery of jurisprudence in Spain and abroad. Mendoza's contribution to Spanish Renaissance culture derives from his
works, including his prose, poetry, and correspondence, as well as his book collections and antiquarian
interests, all of which manifest his preeminence in
several areas of sixteenth-century humanistic learning.

Letters:

*Algunas cartas de don Diego Hurtado de Mendoza escritas
1538–1552,* edited by Alberto Vásquez and R.
Selden Rose (New Haven: Yale University Press,
1935).

References:

Fred Abrams, "Hurtado de Mendoza's Concealed Signatures in the *Lazarillo de Tormes,*" *Romance Notes,* 15
(1973–1974): 341–345;

Charles V. Aubrun, "El autor del *Lazarillo:* Un retrato
robot," *Cuadernos Hispanoamericanos,* 238–240
(1969): 543–555;

Alberto Blecua, introduction to *La vida de Lazarillo de
Tormes y de sus fortunas y adversidades,* edited by
Blecua (Madrid: Castalia, 1974);

Julio Caro-Baroja, *Los moriscos del Reino de Granada*
(Madrid: Instituto de Estudios Políticos, 1957);

José María de Cossío, *Fábulas mitológicas en España*
(Madrid: Espasa-Calpe, 1952);

J. P. W. Crawford, "Don Diego Hurtado de Mendoza
and Michele Marullo," *Hispanic Review,* 6 (1938):
346–348;

Crawford, "Notes of the Poetry of Diego Hurtado de
Mendoza," *Modern Language Review,* 23 (1928):
346–351;

David H. Darst, *Diego Hurtado de Mendoza* (Boston:
Twayne, 1987);

John Fesenmair, *Don Diego Hurtado de Mendoza: Ein spa-
nischer Humanist des XVI Jahrhunderst* (Munich:
Kutzner, 1882);

Raymond Foulché-Delbosc, "Etude sur la *Guerra de
Granada* de don Diego Hurtado de Mendoza,"
Revue Hispanique, 1 (1894): 101–161;

Foulché-Delbosc, "Les oeuvres attribuées a Mendoza,"
Revue Hispanique, 32 (1914): 1–86;

Foulché-Delbosc, "Un point contesté de la view de don
Diego Hurtado de Mendoza," *Revue Hispanique,* 2
(1895): 208–303;

Kenneth Garrad, "La Inquisición de los moriscos gra-
nadinos, 1526–1580," *Bulletin Hispanique,* 67
(1965): 63–77;

the various attributions of its authorship, whether to
Mendoza or others, depends on the manner in which
the work is interpreted. The issue is also treated in
every major work on Mendoza or *La vida de Lazarillo
de Tormes,* such as the studies by Erika Spivakovsky,
by David H. Darst, and by Angel González Palencia
and Eugenio Mele, to name some of the most accessible and best known.

In every sense a courtier, Diego Hurtado de
Mendoza epitomizes the image and personifies the
ideals of a Renaissance man. During his years in
Italy, he corresponded on a regular basis with the
leading humanists of the day, including Pietro Aretino, Benedetto Bembo, and Titian. These epistolary
exchanges represent a rarified intellectual atmosphere
that has since been revered by scholars. Mendoza's
diplomatic and military posts on behalf of the Holy
Roman Emperor Charles V of the Hapsburg dynasty

Angel González Palencia and Eugenio Mele, *Vida y obras de don Diego Hurtado de Mendoza,* 3 volumes (Madrid: Instituto de Valencia de don Juan Primero, 1941–1943);

Helen Nader, "Josephus and Diego Hurtado de Mendoza," *Romance Philology,* 26 (1972): 554–555;

Nader, *The Mendoza Family in the Spanish Renaissance 1350–1550* (New Brunswick, N.J.: Rutgers University Press, 1979);

Antonio Rodríguez Villa, *Noticia biográfica y documentos históricos relativos a don Diego Hurtado de Mendoza* (Madrid: Aribau, 1883);

Janie Oliva Scrouch, "El autor del Lazarillo sobre una reciente tesis," *Hispanófila,* 19 (1963): 11–23;

José Simón Díaz, "Hurtado de Mendoza (Diego)," in *Bibliografía de la literatura hispánica,* volume 11 (Madrid: CSIC, 1976), pp. 681–697;

Erika Spivakovsky, "Diego Hurtado de Mendoza and Averroism," *Journal of the History of Ideas,* 26 (1965): 307–326;

Spivakovsky, "The *Lazarillo de Tormes* and Mendoza," *Symposium,* 15 (1961): 271–285;

Spivakovsky, "Lo de *La Goleta y Túnez,* A Work of Diego Hurtado de Mendoza," *Hispania,* 23 (1963): 366–379;

Spivakovsky, "Mendoza's Renunciation of Fame as Revealed in his *Carta* VI from Alcántara," *Hispania,* 53 (1970): 220–224;

Spivakovsky, "New Arguments in Favor of Mendoza's Authorship of the *Lazarillo de Tormes,*" *Symposium,* 24 (1970): 67–80;

Spivakovsky, *Son of the Alhambra: Don Diego Hurtado de Mendoza* (Austin: University of Texas Press, 1970);

Spivakovsky, "¿Valdés o Mendoza?" *Hispanófila,* 12 (1961): 15–23;

Lucas de Torre y Franco-Romero, "Don Diego Hurtado de Mendoza no fue el autor de la *Guerra de Granada,*" *Boletín de la Real Academia de la Historia,* 64 (1914): 461–501, 557–596; 65 (1914): 28–47, 273–302, 369–415.

Jorge de Montemayor
(1521? – 1561?)

Elizabeth Rhodes
Boston College

BOOKS: *Exposición moral sobre el psalmo lxxxvi. del real propheta David* (Alcalá: Juan Brocar, 1548);

Las obras de George de Monte mayor, repartidas en dos libros, y dirigidas a los muy altos y muy poderosos señores don Juan, y doña Juana, principes de Portogal (Antwerp: Juan Steelsio, 1554);

Segundo cancionero (Antwerp: Juan Lacio, 1558);

Segundo cancionero spiritual (Antwerp: Juan Lacio, 1558);

Los siete libros de la Diana (Valencia: Joan Mey, 1559?);

Segunda edición de los siete libros de la Diana . . . agora de nuevo añadido el Triumpho de amor, de Petrarcha. Y la historia de Alcira [sic] *y Silvano. Con los amores de Abindarraez y otras cosas* (Valladolid: Francisco Fernández Córdoba, 1561);

Cancionero (Saragossa: Viuda de Bartolomé de Nagera, 1562).

Modern Editions: *El cancionero del poeta Jorge de Montemayor,* edited by Angel González Palencia (Madrid: Sociedad de Bibliófilos Españoles, 1932);

Exposición moral sobre el psalmo LXXXVI, edited by Francisco López Estrada, in *Revista de Bibliografía Nacional,* 5 (1944): 499–523;

Los siete libros de la Diana, edited by Enrique Moreno Báez (Madrid: Real Academia Española, 1955);

El Abencerraje pastoril: Estudio y edición, edited by Eugenia Fosalba (Barcelona: Universidad Autónoma de Barcelona, 1990);

La Diana, edited by Juan Montero, preliminary study by Juan Bautista de Avalle-Arce (Barcelona: Crítica, 1996);

Poesía completa, edited by Bautista de Avalle-Arce and Emilia Blanco (Madrid: Castro, 1996);

Los siete libros de la Diana, edited by Julián Arribas (London: Tamesis, 1996);

Diálogo spiritual, edited by María Dolores Estevà de Llobet (Kassel: Reichenberger, 1998).

Editions in English: *Diana of George of Montemayor Translated out of Spanish into English by Bartholomew Yong* (London: Edmund Bollifant, 1598);

A Critical Edition of Yong's Translation of George of Montemayor's Diana *and Gil Polo's* Enamoured Diana, edited by Judith M. Kennedy (Oxford: Clarendon Press, 1968);

The Diana, edited by RoseAnna M. Mueller (Lewiston, N.Y.: Edwin Mellen Press, 1989).

SELECTED BROADSIDES: *Cancionero de las obras de devoción* (N.p., 1552);

Diálogo spiritual (N.p., n.d.);

Glosa de diez coplas hecha por Jorge de Monte Moor [sic] *sobre la muerte de la princesa doña María* (N.p., n.d.).

OTHER: Ausiàs March, *Las obras de Ausias March traducidas por Jorge de Montemayor,* translated by Montemayor (Valencia: Joan Mey, 1560);

"A Carta ao senhor Francisco Sâ de Miranda," in *Poesias de Francisco de Sâ de Miranda,* edited by Carolina Michaëlis de Vasconcelos (Halle: Niemeyer, 1885), pp. 653–657;

"Epístola a Diego Ramírez Pagán," in Diego Ramírez Pagán, *Floresta de varia poesía,* volume 1, edited by Antonio Pérez Gómez (Barcelona: Selecciones Bibliófilas, 1950), pp. 122–137;

"Historia de los muy constantes y infelices amores de Píramo y Tisbe," in *Dos versiones de Píramo y Tisbe: Jorge de Montemayor y Pedro Sánchez de Viana,* edited by B. W. Ife (Exeter: University of Exeter, 1974), pp. 3–66;

"Glosa de diez coplas de Jorge Manrique hecha por Jorge de Montemayor," in *Pliegos poéticos españoles de la Biblioteca Nacional de Lisboa: Edición en facsímile precedida de un estudio,* 2 volumes, edited by María Cruz García de Enterría (Madrid: Joyas Bibliográficas, 1975), pp. 49–60;

"Historia de Alcida y Silvano," edited by Elizabeth Rhodes [Primavera], *Dicenda: Cuadernos de filología hispánica,* 2 (1983): 201–236.

In 1559 *Los siete libros de la Diana* (The Seven Books of the Diana), by the Portuguese musician and poet Jorge de Montemayor, was published in Valencia. The first edition was printed to be small enough to fit in the palm of one's hand. *La Diana* became a cultural phenomenon immediately in Spain and soon attained popularity throughout Europe; counting only the times it appeared in Spanish as a single work (as opposed to being included in collections), it was published thirty-two times during the sixteenth century alone and inspired a long list of imitations and continuations.

After the publication of *La Diana,* moralists complained about the pernicious effects the book was having on young ladies, who are described as its most avid readers in several documents of the period. Women are said to have hidden the book in their apron pockets, to the displeasure of those who were convinced that literature dealing exclusively and intensely with human passion would lead to the moral ruin of the public. Although highly conservative sixteenth-century readers censured *La Diana,* their protests stemmed not from any immoral behavior represented therein, for the characters and narrators alike in all of Montemayor's writings maintain a high fidelity to Christian moral and social virtue. What troubled some readers was the persistent scrutiny of human emotions in the book and its author's assessment of life in terms of love relationships, an attitude that challenged Aristotelian ideals of reason and balance.

In spite of the international fame attained by Montemayor's book, relatively little is known about Montemayor himself. In a 1552 verse epistle that he wrote to the Portuguese poet Francisco de Sâ de Miranda, published as "A Carta ao senhor Francisco Sâ de Miranda" (Letter to Mr. Francisco Sâ de Miranda) in 1885, Montemayor describes himself as having grown up along the banks of the Mondego River in Portugal, self-educated and lamenting his humble station in life. Nothing else is known about his youth. Had Montemayor been of noble extraction, biographical information would be readily available, and the fact that it is not suggests that he was either illegitimate or from a family whose members converted from Judaism to Catholicism, called *conversos.* The fact that Montemayor's last name is adapted from his birthplace, Montemôr-o-velho in Portugal, suggests the latter possibility, since it was common practice of *conversos* to adopt the names of towns as their last names upon conversion. Being a *converso* would have caused him particular strife, because Spanish society excluded all but Christians of untainted racial blood from civil and professional positions. Spaniards who could not prove the purity of their bloodline over several generations were also denied membership in religious orders and confraternities, and there was a dark stigma associated with Judaism during the period when Montemayor lived.

Title page for the first edition of Jorge de Montemayor's much-imitated pastoral novel (The Seven Books of Diana, 1559?; from Los siete libros de la Diana, 1955, *Thomas Cooper Library, University of South Carolina)*

In 1545, upon the death of the Portuguese princess María, Montemayor composed his first gloss of the famous medieval "Coplas que fizo a la muerte de su padre" (1492, Verses Written upon the Death of His Father) by Jorge Manrique. Therein, he expresses his predilection for lament and his fondness for meditation on the instability of human life, both features that remained constant throughout his writings. In his *Glosa de diez coplas hecha por Jorge de Monte Moor* [sic] *sobre la muerte de la princesa doña María* (Gloss of Ten Songs Made by Jorge de Montemayor on the Death of the Princess Doña María), the poet describes himself as intimate with the Portuguese royal family, and his choice to dedicate the work to Juan de Silva, alderman of Portugal, makes it likely that Montemayor was in Portugal when the princess died.

Sometime before 1548 Montemayor wrote his first known prose work, *Diálogo spiritual* (Spiritual Dialogue), extant in one manuscript, which is archived in the Biblioteca Publica in Evora it remained unpublished until the 1998 edition edited by María Dolores Estevà de Llobet. The author dedicated it to King João III of Portugal, who ruled from 1521 to 1557. The dialogue relates an exchange that takes place over two days between a courtier, Severo, and a hermit, Dileto, whose names suggest harshness and pleasure, respectively. From the ascetic point of view from which the dialogue is written, the courtly life, while full of earthly pleasures, exacts a severe accounting of the Christian soul because of its distractions from the truly important, whereas the hermit's life, removed from such temptations, permits greater proximity to God and thus greater pleasure. This conceptual antithesis, which juxtaposes that which seems good with that which is good, is a remnant of medieval Scholasticism and courtly love discourse and is typical of Montemayor's early works. The same contrast is manifest at the semantic level in his early secular love lyric as well, in the form of conflicts between the lover's *bien* (good), or the merits garnered by the practice of perfect love, and his *mal* (evil), meaning the pain and illness produced by that love. Thematic, semantic, and ideological parallels between Montemayor's religious and secular works sustain his entire artistic corpus, and there are close ties between the pastoral environment in which his most famous works are set and the isolated, contemplative life led by his idealized hermit.

The plot of the *Diálogo spiritual* is appropriately simple: Severo wishes to understand the intricacies of the Catholic faith and thereby improve his life. Enjoying a respite from courtly anxieties, he seeks out his former friend Dileto, who had renounced his courtly career to pursue spiritual perfection. Severo's questions range from inquiries into the nature of divinity to details of particular sins. The conversation between the two is purposefully stilted and artificial, since it is not meant to reflect a realistic conversation but rather an instructive exchange. The *Diálogo spiritual* thus follows the rhetorical tradition of Renaissance dialogue that employs the figure of a learner or innocent to query a learned individual about a specific topic. Montemayor's interlocutors review points of Catholic dogma in a pedantic fashion, relying heavily on the theology of Peter Lombard and St. John Climacus. In the process he renders delicate theological questions in a somewhat plodding fashion, resorting often to wordplay to explain subtleties whose more elegant exposition would have required rhetorical tools of greater sophistication. For example, Dileto makes the reformist distinction between Catholics who *saben de Dios* (know God superficially) and those who taste God, or *saben a Dios* (know God intimately). The *Diálogo spiritual* provides important testimony of Montemayor's deep interest in systems of ideological regulation and the nature of human desire, for a beloved person or for God, in contrast with the ideals of doctrine.

The dedications of these first works to royal personages indicate that Montemayor was a member of the Portuguese royal court during his early adulthood, a high social position that he earned by his merits rather than by noble blood. During these early years he was associated with important poets from Portugal, with whom he exchanged verse epistles and occasional poetry.

In 1548 Montemayor's prose and verse exposition of Psalm 86 was printed in an elegant parchment edition at Alcalá de Henares, the premier press of Spain, suggesting important connections and/or high esteem for the piece, titled *Exposición moral sobre el psalmo lxxxvi. del real propheta David* (Moral Exposition on Psalm 86 by the Royal Prophet David). The Psalms were a great source of inspiration to Montemayor, as they were for many reform-minded religious writers of this period. In their plaintive musicality he found a voice for his own disillusion and hope for a better future. True to the orthodox current of contemplative activity in Spain, *recogimiento* (withdrawal), Montemayor exercised his religious belief through careful, detailed meditation on biblical texts, notably the Psalms, several of which he wrote lengthy glosses in verse.

From 1548 through 1552 Montemayor's name appears on accounts as a salaried singer in the imperial chapel of the Spanish Hapsburgs, a family renowned as avid patrons of music. He was clearly a favored courtier in the imperial circle, for when Princess Juana left Madrid for Portugal in 1552 to marry the Portuguese prince João IV, Montemayor accompanied her to Lisbon as her chamberlain, a position of intimacy with the princess. Prince João died unexpectedly in 1554, and Juana returned shortly thereafter to Spain, to serve as regent of the Spanish Empire in the absence of her brother and father. Thereafter, no concrete information is available about Montemayor other than the publication of his writings.

Importantly, all of the author's known works from 1545 to 1552 are religious, and single religious poems of his were circulating in manuscript collections during the same years as well. In distinction to the more typical trajectory followed by poets from the secular to the divine, Montemayor's career began with several years of religious writing, at the conclusion of which he branched out into topics of human love, humor, and social critique, while briefly continuing to write about topics of morality and religion. His 1554 *Obras* (Works), published in Antwerp, is a volume of poetry in two parts, the first secular and the second religious, with the latter constituting about two-thirds of the book. Included in the religious poems are three *autos,* single-act religious dramas in verse celebrating the Nativity, which were performed for the young Philip II of Spain on an unspecified occasion. Also in the *Obras* is Montemayor's second gloss of Manrique's "Coplas que fizo a la muerte de su padre," a long poetic rendition of the Passion, two poems adapting works by the Catholic reformist Girolamo Savonarola (an exposition of Psalm 51 and another on the Lord's Prayer) and three religious sonnets, perhaps the first in Spanish literature devoted to sacred topics. All of Montemayor's religious writings before 1558 can best be described as doctrinal. His preference for explication and gloss, manifest already in the *Diálogo spiritual,* continues strong through this first publication of his poetry.

Because Montemayor is well known as an author of convincing female characters, his devotion to the Virgin Mary as represented in his religious writings is important. Already in 1554, Montemayor's fascination with the human woman who was able to reconcile the extremes of the Christian universe—the divinity and human flesh—is clear. Montemayor exalts Mary as a humble princess, the temple of the divinity itself, yet also a woman whose merit and suffering knew no measure. His verse rendition of the Passion celebrates Mary's compassionate suffering with her son in terms typical of the fascination of the period for the most terrible moments of Christ's life. Seeking to move his reader to reform, the narrator of the Passion poem describes Jesus' awareness of his mother's pain as yet another cross he had to bear: "mas la que a su madre pesa / le hace el peso doblado" (but the pain that weighs upon his mother / doubles the weight of his cross). Not exclusively focused on pain and suffering, Montemayor offers comic relief to his serious treatment of the Virgin in several poems, one of which, "Del infierno salío un moro" (A Moor Came out of Hell), describes how she beats Satan at a game of cards, the stakes of which are human salvation, by playing the hand of the Trinity: "Satanás toma entre dientes / sus tres cartas diferentes; / la Virgen tres de un metal: / del Padre el Hijo tomó, / y el 'Spríritu'" (Satan bites on / his three cards that are all different; / the Virgin takes three of a kind: / of the Father and Son she took two, / and of the Spirit another).

The secular verse in the 1554 volume displays the poet's taste for late-medieval love concepts and traditional Castilian poetic forms, typical of early-sixteenth-century Spanish lyrics. His first pastoral works appear in this 1554 collection: two eclogues and several popular *villancicos* (pastoral songs). The first eclogue, structured as a poetic dialogue between Lusitano and Tolomeo, evidences a quality that all of Montemayor's long prose works also display, a pedagogical objective to instruct the characters, and readers, in the nature of

Title page for an early edition (Saragossa, 1560) of Los siete libros de la Diana, *featuring an illustration of the eponymous shepherdess (from* Los siete libros de la Diana, *1996; Thomas Cooper Library, University of South Carolina)*

proper love. After Lusitano describes his beloved Vandalina in detail, using topoi of physical beauty inherited from the Petrarchan tradition, Tolomeo hastens to correct his friend's excessive focus on Vandalina's physical attributes, explaining that her beauty is indeed superlative, "mas no consiste en eso el pensamiento; / muy fuera va de ahí, que el amor fino / un solo efecto es del sentimiento" (but loving thoughts do not consist in that; / rather move in another direction, for pure love / is but an effect of feeling). In these early works Montemayor's lovers do not seek gratification or requital in their affections, rather perfection of form in love: selfless devotion to another, whose purpose is not to realize a mutually gratifying relationship but rather to display the lover's virtuosity of sentiment and intensity of expression.

The second eclogue has more narrative movement, and in it Montemayor's first female characters appear. The shepherdess Olinea and her friend Lusitano lament their separation from their lovers, the most exalted of situations according to Montemayor's scale of amorous merit. In contrast, their companion Solisa occupies the interesting position of a woman who espouses the Renaissance rendition of the classical carpe diem theme. In that trope as it appeared in sixteenth-century Europe, male anxiety about the passing of time is projected onto the body of a woman and rendered as a warning to her to take advantage of her youthful loveliness, which, when faded, will leave her unappealing to men and so, presumably, worthless. Solisa's complaint, while quite traditional ideologically, is a narrative innovation because it is in first person. As she competes with Olinea to determine which of them suffers most in love, Solisa protests to her friend, "¿No ves que pasa el tiempo y que me avisa? / Mas di, la frente lisa, / el rostro cristalino, / el cabello dorado / y el cuello delicado, / ¿no ves que pasa presto su camino?" (Don't you see that time is passing and is warning me? / Forsooth, the unwrinkled brow, / the crystalline face, / hair of gold / and delicate neck, / don't you see it all hastens to pass?). The nymph Belisa, to whom the case is presented for judgment, refuses to exalt Solisa's complaint over Olinea's overwhelming grief and concludes, with Lusitano, that the stability of life without human passion has less validity in the court of love than the tormented suffering of the lover separated from her or his beloved. This early eclogue introduces the fundamental problem of *La Diana* well before the book was published, since the unifying relationship of the plot of *La Diana*, that of Sireno and Diana, is undone because of the lovers' prolonged separation.

In 1558 Montemayor's second set of poems was published in two volumes, titled *Segundo cancionero* (Second Songbook) and *Segundo cancionero spiritual* (Second Spiritual Songbook). The fact that his second collection of poetry was published just one year before the first known edition of *La Diana* indicates that he was working on both of them at the same time. Much of his 1554 verse appears again in the 1558 volumes, and both collections are larger. The secular and religious poems alike in the 1558 set include more Italianate forms, particularly the eleven-syllable line, than his previous compilation. The poems in both volumes utilize less wordplay than the 1554 volume and express greater introspection. Two new eclogues appear with the original two, to which Montemayor made minor alterations. Also included is a long, narrative pastoral poem, "La historia de Alcida y Sylvano" (The History of Alcida and Sylvano), similar in style and tone to the eclogues and included in editions of *La Diana* after 1561. The third eclogue is of particular interest because it tells of the relationship between the primary characters of *La Diana*, Diana and Sireno, at a point immediately preceding the longer work. In the eclogue, Diana appears

immediately, lamenting the prolonged absence of Sireno and expressing fear not of his infidelity but of her own destiny: "mas temo a mi ventura, / que nunca en cosa mía está segura" (but I fear my fate, / which in my concerns is never secure). The loss of love for reasons completely out of the lovers' control is a repeated theme in Montemayor's works after 1554, and the extraordinary popularity of his writings indicates that it had particular resonance with his sixteenth-century public. This popularity is logical, given that at that time upper-class individuals were living in the age of transition between arranged, political marriage and matrimonial unions forged by couples who chose each other for sentimental reasons.

The religious verse of 1558 shows a marked development from Montemayor's earlier style of formulaic exposition and moves toward the manifestation of human desire for personal reform through the benefits of Jesus' sacrifice. The theme of exile, a hyperbolic version of the theme of separation that is frequent in his secular love poetry, dominates his mature religious verse and approaches essentially the same problem as the lover caught in circumstances that prohibit contact with the beloved. Montemayor devised a mode of expression, profoundly melancholy and acutely rendered in the *Segundo cancionero spiritual*, that articulates lament for that which cannot or should not be. The point of view expressed repeatedly in the 1554 *Obras* is that exalted adherence to high standards of perfection was an appropriate goal in itself, in human love and in devotion to God. Relinquishing not the idealism of this position but rather the hope that lovers of flesh and blood would ever attain its realization, Montemayor expressed his bitter yet resigned understanding that human beings are inherently flawed and exiled in a life that distances them from all ideals, no matter how desired or deserved. The anguish expressed by his poetic voice is hauntingly modern in its expression of a profound and irrevocable separation from home, whether represented by the presence of a beloved woman, a politically defined space, or a life of intimacy with God.

Among the works included in the *Segundo cancionero spiritual*, his paraphrase of Psalm 137, which begins "By the rivers of Babylon . . . ," is particularly moving. Therein, Montemayor adopts the voice of an exiled poet forced to sing in a foreign land. Defining his song as *lloro* (weeping), the narrator sings the remorse and resignation of a people whose infidelities to God resulted in their captivity: "en ver como tu pueblo va cautivo / y ver la ciudad santa despoblada / y destruido, el templo de Dios vivo" (upon seeing how your people are captive / and the holy city left with no one / and the temple of the living God destroyed). In his typical voice of the frustrated idealist, Montemayor employs the ancient psalm to represent the position of the victim unjustly suffering the consequences of others' misbehavior. The poem signifies via multiple allegories, all pertinent to the religious situation of sixteenth-century Iberia: of the converted Jews forced to practice Catholicism, of the exile of Catholic reformists from liberal Catholicism during the most repressive ecclesiastical regime of imperial Spain, of the righteous Christian whose attempts to practice his faith is frustrated yet also controlled by those less pure. In its multivalent expression, the poem renders with particular effectiveness the theme most prevalent in Montemayor's mature writings, religious and secular: the sad fate of the idealistic, self-righteous, and resigned lover who can never realize his ideal.

Montemayor's writings before 1559 manifest a clear preference for spiritual topics and an affinity for religious exposition. All but a few of his works in the corpus of his religious verse and prose are overtly didactic. Although his professional ambitions clearly included catechism, he lacked the training and church sanction to continue writing in the authoritative fashion characteristic of all his works. The career Montemayor sought as a representative of orthodox Catholicism was blocked abruptly by the Inquisition, whose officers took a keen interest in his works of devotion.

Montemayor's intensely dogmatic religious writings were published at a problematic moment. The Protestant revolution was well under way by the mid sixteenth century, and the political as well as religious distinctions between Protestantism and Catholicism ("heresy" and "orthodoxy" in Spain) were being drawn with increasing violence as the years progressed. The influence of Martin Luther himself was the product of a general Christian reform, begun in the late fifteenth century, in which Spain had played an important part, a reform that Spanish kings and queens cautiously supported. As Protestant believers began to claim geographical as well as ideological space in Europe, however, the ability of Catholic rulers to support reformist measures became increasingly compromised. Montemayor's patrons in Spain, the imperial family of Emperor Charles V, stood to lose valuable territories and resources if Spanish lands, which spanned the globe at the time, threatened the long-standing Catholic union of Europe by joining the political force of the Protestant wave, whose political implications were inseparable from its religious impetus. Spain would not tolerate Protestantism or any challenge to the hegemony of Catholicism over the Holy Roman Empire.

At precisely the time during which Montemayor was fashioning himself as a poetic spokesperson for Iberian Catholicism, ecclesiastical authorities were censor-

Title page for the first of at least eight editions of Montemayor's canciones (songbook) published under the title Cancionero after his death (from Bryant L. Creel, The Religious Poetry of Jorge de Montemayor, 1981; Thomas Cooper Library, University of South Carolina)

ing publications with increasing severity. The conservative inquisitor general at that time, Fernando de Valdés, is on record as having declared that there is no faith where there is no mystery, a statement that justified church control of those mysteries. Tenets of Catholicism such as the definition and function of the sacraments, the nature of the Trinity, the merits of Christ's Passion, and the Immaculate Conception were dangerous topics to treat in Spain during the middle of the sixteenth century. By that time, the Inquisition had long ferreted out false converts from Judaism and had turned its attention to Catholics whose ideas had become confused with those of the Protestants, the liberal Erasmists, or the Illuminists. Those three currents of faith, all of which were born of the Catholic reform of the fifteenth century, had tenets that celebrated individual immediacy with the divine. All three thereby reduced the significance of too many functions of the church hierarchy to be condoned in Spain. The fact that Montemayor, uneducated beyond the catechism offered all Catholics, raised his voice in defense of his faith reflects the reformist belief that all Christians should be able and willing to do exactly that. In a church determined to mediate all access to the secrets of that faith, such a voice had to be silenced.

Montemayor had long been associated with the liberal wing of Catholic Spain, particularly in his relationship with Princess Juana, who personally supported several Catholic reformers until she became regent of Spain. Around 1550, the tide of Spanish Catholicism turned against the reformers in favor of what was eventually called the Counter-Reformation. Montemayor was caught in the middle, between his patrons such as Juana and the conservative powers that were greater than any individual. Juana herself, whose secret vows as a Jesuit reveal her conservative yet energized Catholicism, compromised her reformist ideals under the pressure of the radical right wing and adapted her religious politics to conform to the political interests of her country, the most Catholic of all the early-modern European states. This compromise meant sacrificing the liberal notion that Christianity was a religion whose believers should all enjoy equal access to the Holy Writ, its meaning, and free experience of the mysteries of the faith. In this context, anyone lacking theological training or experience was not permitted to deal in matters of Christian theology.

In 1559, the first *Index Librorum Prohibitorum* (Index of Forbidden Books), including works in the vernacular, appeared under the name of Inquisitor General Valdés, who had no sympathy for inexactitude in doctrine. Montemayor's "obras en lo que toca a devoción y cosas cristianas" (works that deal with devotion and Christian things) appear in the index. Whether it was referring to the author's 1554 *Obras* or to his works in general is unknown. His religious writings may have been included in the index because they treated Catholic doctrine in a language other than Latin or because they were published outside of Spain, since all works that appeared under those conditions were prohibited on the same index.

Just as likely, however, Montemayor had made theological errors in one or several of his many expositional works, errors that could not be tolerated in a country anxious to distinguish itself from other nations by the purity of its Catholic faith. Although it was an exercise in mortification and was dangerous to have

one's writings included in the *Index Librorum Prohibitorum,* that Montemayor benefited from the notoriety it earned him is equally certain; Desiderius Erasmus and Luis de Granada, whom Montemayor admired greatly, were among the illustrious company also included on the list. No religious poems by Montemayor dated after his 1558 *Segundo cancionero spiritual* are known, and *Los siete libros de la Diana* was published the same year as the *Index Librorum Prohibitorum.*

Although Montemayor's poetry was extremely popular throughout the sixteenth century, he is remembered primarily as the author of *Los siete libros de la Diana.* The first of many *libros de pastores,* or fictional stories about pretend shepherds, *Los siete libros de la Diana* is a prose narration in seven chapters, each of which is itself called a "book." The most emotionally intense moments of each book are punctuated with poetry, which in the fictional context are sung.

The fact that the main characters of *La Diana* are shepherds and shepherdesses can be misleading; they are not sheepherders who worry about the weather or the well-being of their flocks. They are highly wrought, unrealistic characters of a long tradition. *La Diana* is Montemayor's contribution to the pastoral genre, a literary style originating in classical times and made popular in Spain by Garcilaso de la Vega's three eclogues, published in 1543, all of which are in verse. According to the pastoral norms followed by Garcilaso and Montemayor, sophisticated and literate characters appear as shepherds and wander about an idealized natural setting, the *locus amoenus* (pleasant place). In that setting, it is always spring and the weather is always fine.

This high-mimetic environment makes it possible for the characters to struggle with inner battles—in Montemayor's case, their problems with human love—rather than the mundane details of ordinary life or problems other than emotional ones. Thus, whereas a chivalric hero such as Amadís of Gaul is perpetually in motion and engages in fearless combat with ogres, enchanters, and evil knights, Montemayor's hero Sireno, whose name suggests a serene countenance, rarely moves at a pace more rapid than a stroll and struggles valiantly with his love problems and those of his friends. As José F. Montesinos observed in his essay "La Diana de Montemayor" (1997), "The pastoral costume is not a liberation, it is more a uniform that, like all uniforms, permits the enjoyment of certain privileges." Those privileges include leisure time for intense introspection and artistic expression, pleasures enjoyed only by the upper classes in early-modern Spain.

The purpose of pastoral poetry is to give voice to a lover's suffering, and although nothing appears to happen in the lovers' stories, in fact there is much going on. The characters examine the workings of love theory when put into practice in the imperfect human world. They are men and women who converse freely with each other in unsupervised, remote locations, cementing close social relationships based not on lineage, war activities, or social status but on quality of feeling.

Montemayor set the static lament of pastoral poetry in motion by casting *La Diana* in prose and moving his characters forward in narrative time and space. In so doing, he represented the invisible, emotional lives of literary characters as having a profound effect on their lives as a whole. This depiction was a novelty in the European narrative tradition, in which characters tended to be represented as motivated exclusively by forces external to their own psyches, such as honor, class, or political and social obligations. Sixteenth-century Europe, ripe with the effects of humanism and the exploration of the human psychological landscape, was receptive to Montemayor's representational formula, and its influence is apparent on most of the major literary figures of his day, such as Miguel de Cervantes and William Shakespeare.

La Diana is faithful to Montemayor's interest in the rules of behavior and how individual experience fails to realize idealized expectations. Montemayor's pastoral romance is structurally symmetrical, presenting three sets of love tangles in its first three books and bringing all the characters together at a magical palace in book 4. All of the lovers' tales resolve themselves in books 5 through 7, as the characters disperse from the narrative and geographic center of the book. In the crescendo, climax, and denouement of his plot, Montemayor includes a large variety of narrative and poetic styles, from pastoral lament to elevated courtly love conceits, to chivalric motifs and mythological characters. He was able to include much action in his book, without violating the pastoral mandate of inactivity, by filling with action the characters' autobiographical tales, recounted for the benefit of the pastoral company.

The three sets of characters, whose problems form the core of the book, are from three distinct social groups and geographic spaces. The first, the local folk, are represented as shepherds and shepherdesses who live along the banks of the Esla River in eastern Spain, in an area called Valencia de Don Juan near León. These three characters are Sireno, generally believed to represent Montemayor himself; Sireno's pastoral friend Sylvano; and Selvagia, a young woman sent to Sireno and Sylvano's village by her father. The book begins as Sireno arrives home to his native riverbanks after having been away for a year for unspecified but pressing reasons. He and Sylvano are both in love with Diana, in spite of the fact that this lovely shepherdess has recently married the wealthy shepherd Delio, and in

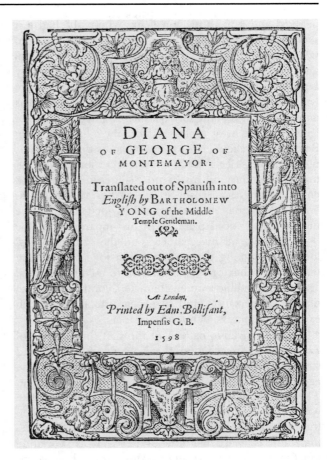

Title page for the first English-language edition of Los siete libros de la Diana *(from* A Critical Edition of Yong's Translation of George of Montemayor's Diana *and Gil Polo's* Enamoured Diana, *1968; Thomas Cooper Library, University of South Carolina)*

spite of the fact that she did so regardless of her supposed love for Sireno. After a long lyric interlude in which Montemayor sets the pastoral tone, Selvagia tells her story in book 1, a complicated tale of confused identities and inconstancy. She was left alone when her beloved, Alanio, wed another woman. Sireno, Selvagia, and Sylvano are thus confronted with an insurmountable problem in early-modern society: the marriage of those they love to someone else. This situation is quintessentially pastoral in that by the time the characters actually appear in the book, complaint is the only activity left to them, because any response to their failed love other than waiting for fortune to make its inevitable turn would compromise their status as perfect and faithful lovers.

Books 2 and 3 introduce Felismena and Belisa, whose stories constitute the two other narrative strands of Montemayor's book. Felismena is a courtly figure, a noblewoman dressed as a shepherdess to search for her beloved and unfaithful Don Félix, whom she had just served for months as a page (unbeknownst to him) while dressed as a man. Felismena, Sireno, Sylvano, and Selvagia save some nymphs from being ravaged by a pack of savages, for which the nymphs reward them with a visit to the palace of the wise Felicia, who, it is announced, will somehow be able to solve their problems. On the way to the palace, they happen upon Belisa, who believes her lover, Arsilio, is dead. Belisa is not as noble as Felismena, but she is a more urban figure than Sireno and his friends; she is in the pastoral environment because she is fleeing her sad reality at home. Montemayor thus presents a wide gamut of love interests and social patterns in his apparently simple book, uniting all his characters in the same physical locale and having them all suffer in love but varying their class, behaviors, and situations to hold his readers' attention. Credible women characters control almost all of the conversation and action in the book, which explains its success with female readers.

The narrative pattern of the first three books of *La Diana* is indirect action: the characters walk, talk and sing, and attempt to defend the nymphs from the savages, but there is relatively little physical movement. The love stories the characters tell, however, are replete with action and bring variety to the book. By the time the two men and three women reach Felicia's palace, the reader is aware that none of the lovers can continue indefinitely in their present circumstances. It is apparent that the notion of eternal, idealized love is untenable in human reality.

At Felicia's palace, the characters visit a gallery of heroes displaying images of prominent men whose deeds are briefly celebrated, after which they listen to a long song by the god Orpheus, who takes flesh to sing to them about the virtues of many real women in the Spanish royal and noble courts of Montemayor's day. These two narrative blocks provided Montemayor's first readers with information about political and domestic heroic figures of the day. The indirect presence of socially exalted individuals whose lives are celebrated at Felicia's materially splendid palace provides a narrative contrast to the more-humble characters who visit there, characters whose significance is sentimental rather than social.

Felicia's assembled company adjourns to a nearby field for a discussion of love theory, in a series of passages that Montemayor adapted from León Hebreo's Italian *Dialogui d'amore* (1535, Dialogues on Love). Whereas Hebreo was a devoted Neoplatonist and thus a defender of ideal and eternal love, Montemayor's characters are too experienced to share such idealism. In his translations from his source, the author subtly eliminated all of Hebreo's references to the eternal nature of human love, leaving the idealistic shell of the theory in place. Montemayor thus capitalized on Hebreo's popularity while undermining the essence of his source's philosophical doctrine. Much more intrigued by the power of time to transform desire and supportive of late-medieval notions of the irrevocable changes of fate, Montemayor uses this conversation about the nature and merit of love to prepare his characters to abandon their frustrated loves.

Felicia is a magical figure who puts Sireno, Sylvano, and Selvagia to sleep with a potion and then awakens them with a tap on the head with a book. This intervention is a thinly disguised symbol of the passage of time and has predictable consequences: Sireno reaches indifference to Diana's betrayal, and Sylvagia and Sylvano are completely in love with each other. Belisa's difficulties are solved by the revelation that Arsilio is not really dead, and the two are reunited in book 5. Book 6 follows Felismena to Portugal, where she is reunited with the wayward Félix, returned to his original affection for her with a draft of Felicia's magic potion.

Diana, previously beloved of Sireno and Sylvano, makes several appearances in the last two books of *La Diana*. Until then she had appeared only indirectly, as a lovely and flawed character talked about by others. When bringing Diana to the narrative present and allowing her to speak, Montemayor does something remarkable, given that his own sentimental interests are invested in the character of Sireno. He allows Diana to fully express her point of view, according to which her betrayal of Sireno was completely justified. In providing her version of the story, Diana insists not only that she was forced by her parents to marry Delio during Sireno's absence, but also that she is unhappy in her marriage. Montemayor thus provides readers with a realistic rendition of human experience, in which different people hold different opinions about the same events. This representation of one event from multiple points of view that cannot be reconciled was to be a cornerstone of Cervantes's representational technique in *Don Quixote* (1605, 1615).

By 1561 *Los siete libros de la Diana* was transformed into a showcase of its author's other works, and to it were appended several of his other writings. Among the additions were "La historia de Alcida y Sylvano," his poetic rendition of the Ovidian story of Piramus and Thisbe, and a Moorish romance, *El abencerraje*. Because the insertion of these texts into *Los siete libros de la Diana* is not known to have been Montemayor's idea, the authorship of these works was disputed until investigation of his other publications and his writing style provided evidence that they are all his. Verse elegies lamenting his death and praising his life were added as the years passed.

The date of Montemayor's death is unknown; several documents report that he died in a duel over the love of a woman in Italy, not long after the first publication of *La Diana*. In 1560 his Spanish translation of the *cants d'amor* (songs of love) by the medieval Catalan poet Ausiàs March was published in Valencia under the title *Las obras de Ausias March traducidas por Jorge de Montemayor* (The Works of Ausias March Translated by Jorge de Montemayor). The translation is important as testimony of Montemayor's enduring interest in medieval systems of devotion centered on the cult of innocent suffering.

Beginning in 1562, Jorge de Montemayor's poetry was republished at least eight times after his death under the title of *Cancionero* (Songbook), without the religious verse. The immense popularity of *Los siete libros de la Diana* influenced readers' interest in his poetry, but his success as a poet was well established before the publication of that book. The number of editions of Montemayor's *Cancionero* makes him one of the most published poets of his day, second only to Garcilaso. Readers seeking familiarity with the literary tastes of early-modern readers will find one of their most esteemed representatives in Montemayor.

References:

Juan Bautista de Avalle-Arce, *La novela pastoril española*, second edition (Madrid: Istmo, 1974): 101–140;

Bryant L. Creel, *The Religious Poetry of Jorge de Montemayor* (London: Tamesis, 1981);

Jean Dupont, "Un pliego suelto de 1552 intitulé: Cancionero de las obras de devociõ de Jorge de Montemayor," *Bulletin Hispanique,* 75 (1973): 40–72;

Ruth El Saffar, "Structural and Thematic Discontinuity in Montemayor's *Diana,*" *Modern Language Notes,* 86 (1971): 182–198;

Eugenia Fosalba, La Diana *en Europa: Ediciones, traducciones e influencias* (Barcelona: Seminari de Filologia i d'Informàtica, Departament de Filologia Espanyola, Universitat Autònoma de Barcelona, 1994);

Carrol B. Johnson, "Montemayor's *Diana:* A Novel Pastoral," *Bulletin of Hispanic Studies,* 48 (1971): 20–35;

José F. Montesinos, "La Diana de Montemayor," in *Entre renacimiento y barroco: Cuatro escritos inéditos,* edited by Pedro Álvarez de Miranda (Granada: Cátedra Federico García Lorca de la Universidad de Granada, Fundación Federico García Lorca, Editorial Comares, 1997), pp. 79–144;

Elizabeth Rhodes [Primavera], "Introducción a la *Historia de Alvida y Silvano* de Jorge de Montemayor," *Dicenda: Cuadernos de filología hispánica,* 2 (1983): 121–134;

Rhodes, "Montemayor's 'Diálogo spiritual,' Prologue to Pastoral," *Pacific Coast Philology,* 20 (1986): 39–46;

Rhodes, *The Unrecognized Precursors of Montemayor's* Diana (Columbia: University of Missouri Press, 1992);

Florence Whyte, "Three *Autos* of Jorge de Montemayor," *Publications of the Modern Language Association,* 43 (1928): 953–989.

Gonzalo Fernández de Oviedo

(August 1478 – 27 June 1557)

Federico A. Chalupa
Bowling Green State University

BOOKS: *Claribalte: Libro del muy esforçado y inuencible Cauallero dela Fortuna propiamete llamado don claribalte q segu su verdadera interpretaciõ quiere dezir don Felix o bienaventurado: Nuevamente escrito y venido a noticia dela lengua castellana por medio de gonçalo Fernandez de Ouiedo alias de sobrepeña* (Valencia: Juan Viñao, 1519);

Respuesta a la epístola moral del Almirante: Esta es una muy notable y moral Epístola que el muy ilustre señor Almirante de Castilla envió al autor de las sobredichas Quincuagenas, hablando de los males de España y de la causa dellos con la Respuesta del mismo autor (N.p., ca. 1524) [1 manuscript, Biblioteca Nacional, Madrid, Ms. 7.075];

Relación hecha por Gonzalo Fernández de Oviedo de los males causados en Tierra-Firme por el gobernador Pedrarias (N.p., ca. 1524) [2 manuscripts, Archivo General de Simancas and the Real Academia de la Historia, Colección Muñoz];

Relación de lo subcedido en la prisión del Rey Francisco de Francia desque fué traydo a España, y por todo el tiempo que estuvo en ella hasta que el Emperador le dio libertad y volvió a Francia, casado con Madama Leonor, hermana del Emperador Carlos V, Rey de España: Escrita por el capitán Gonzalo Fernández de Oviedo, alcayde de la fortaleza de la cibdad de Santo Domingo de la Isla Española, y Coronista de la Sacra Cesárea Magestad del Emperador Carlos V y de la Serenísima Reyna doéa Johana, su madre (N.p., ca. 1525) [1 manuscript, Biblioteca Nacional, Madrid, Ms. 8.756.156];

Sumario de la natural hystoria delas Indias. Con previlegio dela S.C.C.M. El psente tratado intitulado Ouiedo dela natural hystoria delas Indias se imprimio a costas del autor Gõçalo Fernãdez de Ouiedo al's de Valdes (Toledo: Ramón de Petras, 1526); translated by Richard Eden as "The hystorie of the Weste Indies," in *The Decades of the Newe World or West India*, edited by Eden (London: Guilhelmi & Powell, 1555);

La historia general de las Indias: Con priuelegio Imperial. Primera parte (Seville: Juan Cromberger, 1535); revised and enlarged as *Coronica de las Indias. La*

Hystoria general de las Indias, agora nuevamente impresa, corregida y emendada. Y con la conquista del Perú (Salamanca: Juan de Junta, 1547);

Cathalogo real de Castilla, y de todos los Reyes de las Españas e de Napoles y Çecilia, e de los Reyes y señores de las casas de Francia, Austria, Holanda y Borgoña: de donde proceden los cuatro abolorios de la Cesárea Magestad del Emperador don Carlos, nuestro señor: Con relación de todos los Emperadores y Summos Pontífices que han subcedido desde Julio Çesar, que fue el primero Emperador, y desde Apóstol Sanct Pedro, que fue el primero Papa, hasta este año de Christo de MDXXXII (N.p., 1535) [1 manuscript, Biblioteca del Escorial, Madrid, Ms. H-j-7, 451 ff.];

Libro de la camara real del principe don Juan e officios de su casa e seruicio ordinario, compuesto por Gonçalo Fernandez de Ouiedo (N.p., 1546) [1 autograph manuscript, Biblioteca del Escorial];

Batallas y quinquagenas, escriptas por el capitán Gonzalo Fernández de Oviedo, criado del príncipe don Johan, hijo de los Reyes Cathólicos, y coronista mayor de las Indias, del Emperador Carlos V (N.p., 1550) [3 manuscripts, Biblioteca Nacional, Madrid; Real Academia de la Historia, Madrid; and Biblioteca del Palacio, Madrid];

Libro del blasón: Tractado general de todas las armas e diferencia dellas, e de los escudos e diferencias que en ellas hay, e de la orden que se debe guardar en las dichas armas, para que sean ciertas no falsas, e de los colores e metales que hay en armería, e de las reglas e circunstancias a ese efecto convinientes (N.p., ca. 1551) [1 manuscript, Biblioteca de la Real Academia de la Historia, Madrid, Ms. 9-21-5-96, fols. 1–45];

Libro de linajes y armas que escribió el Capitán Gonzalo Fernández de Oviedo y Valdés, coronista del Emperador Carlos V y de las Indias (N.p., ca. 1552) [1 manuscript, Real Academia de la Historia, Madrid, Colección Salazar, C. 24];

Las quincuagenas de los generosos y no menos famosos reyes, príncipes, duques, marqueses, y condes e caballeros e personas notables de España, que escribió el capitán Gonzalo

Fernández de Oviedo y Valdés, alcaide de Sus Majestades en la fortaleza de la cibdad e puerto de Santo Domingo de la Isla Española, coronista de las Indias, isla e Tierra Firme del mar Océano, vecino y regidor desta cibdad e natural de la muy noble e leal villa de Madrid, 3 volumes (N.p., 1555) [1 manuscript, Biblioteca Nacional, Madrid, Mss 2.217 B 2.218 B 2.219];

Libro XX. Dela segunda parte dela general historia delas Indias. Escripta por el Capitan Gonzalo Fernandez de Ouiedo y Valdes, Alcayde de la fortaleza y Puerto de Sācto Domingo, d'la isla Española, Cronista de su Magestad. Que tratra del estrecho de Magallanes (Valladolid: Francisco Fernández de Córdoba, 1557).

Modern Editions: *Historia general y natural de las Indias, isles y tierra firme del mar Oceano, por el capitán Gonzalo Fernández de Oviedo y Valdés, primer cronista del Nuevo Mundo. Publícala la Real Academia de la Historia cotejada con el códice original, enriquecida con las enmiendas y adiciones del autor, e ilustrada con la vida y juicio de las obras del mismo por José Amador de los Ríos*, 4 volumes, edited by José Amador de los Ríos (Madrid: Imprenta de la Real Academia de la Historia, 1851–1855); translated by Sterling A. Stoudemire as *Natural History of the West Indies* (Chapel Hill: University of North Carolina Press, 1959);

Relación de lo sucedido en la prisión del Rey Francisco de Francia, in *Historia de la Villa y Corte de Madrid*, edited by Amador de los Ríos and Juan de Dios de la Rada y Delgado (Madrid: M. López de la Hoya, 1862);

Libro de la camara real del principe don Juan, edited by José María de la Peña (Madrid: Imprenta de la viuda e hijos de Galiano, 1870);

Las quincuagenas de los generosos y no menos famosos reyes, príncipes, duques, marqueses, y condes e caballeros e personas notables de España, que escribió el capitán Gonzalo Fernández de Oviedo y Valdés, alcaide de Sus Majestades en la fortaleza de la cibdad e puerto de Santo Domingo de la Isla Española, coronista de las Indias, isla e Tierra Firme del mar Océano, vecino y regidor desta cibdad e natural de la muy noble e leal villa de Madrid, edited by Vicente de la Fuente (Madrid: Imprenta y Fundición de Manuel Tello, 1880);

De la natural hystoria de las Indias (Chapel Hill: University of North Carolina Press, 1969);

Batallas y quinquagenas, transcribed by Amador de los Ríos, edited by Juan Pérez de Tudela y Buesa (Madrid: Real Academia de la Historia, 1983);

Claribalte, edited by María José Rodillo León (Mexico City: Universidad Autónoma Metropolitana – Unicac / Iztapalapa: Universidad Nacional Autónoma de México, 2002).

Editions in English: *The Journey of the Vaca Party: The Account of the Narváez Expedition, 1528–1536*, trans-

lated by Basil C. Hedrick and Carroll L. Riley (Carbondale: University Museum, Southern Illinois University, 1974);

The Conquest and Settlement of the Island of Boriquen or Puerto Rico, translated and edited by Daymond Turner (Avon, Conn.: Limited Editions Club, 1975).

OTHER: *Reglas de la vida espiritual y secreta theología*, translated by Oviedo (Seville: Domingo Robertis, 1548).

Gonzalo Fernández de Oviedo, royal page, quartermaster sergeant, notary for the Inquisition, deputy of Indian affairs, *veedor* (colonial inspector), *procurador* (agent) of colonial municipalities to the Spanish court, fortress commander, and the first *cronista real de las Indias* (royal chronicler of the West Indies), started writing at the age of thirty-nine, right after his first voyage to the New World. In the last forty years of his life, and in the midst of an active administrative and military career, he wrote fourteen works but lived to see only six of them published. The scope of his works is fairly wide and covers fiction, natural history, history of the Spanish Conquest, ethnological and geographical accounts, royal genealogy, heraldry treatises, morality, treatises on colonial administration, and politics. Oviedo intended in his most important work, *Historia general y natural de las Indias* (General and Natural History of the West Indies; the first part was published as *La historia general de las Indias: Con priuelegio Imperial. Primera parte* [The General History of the West Indies: With Imperial Privilege. First Part] in 1535), "hacer principal memoria de los secretos e cosas que la natura produce en nuestras Indias naturalmente, también consuena con el título de llamarla general historia recontar los méritos de los conquistadores de esas partes" (to write a principal memory of the secrets and things that nature produces in our Indies naturally and, as the title *general history* suggests, to retell the merit of the conquerors of those parts). His contemporaries, however, viewed his magnum opus as more than natural history or history of the conquest of the New World, as have modern readers. For many of his contemporaries, especially after the famous polemic between Bartolomé de Las Casas and Juan Ginés de Sepúlveda, *La historia general de las Indias* provided an account along the lines of Sepúlveda's view that the nature of the Indians was primitive savagery. Sepúlveda used this view to argue in favor of the legality of the Spanish Conquest via the use of force, as opposed to Las Casas's advocacy of pacifist colonization based on his view that the Indians were noble. Since the 1950s, Oviedo's name still is associated in opposition to de Las Casas's pro-Indigenous appeal and with Spanish imperialist discourses. On the

Title page for the first of Gonzalo Fernández de Oviedo's two works about the flora, fauna, and human inhabitants of the New World (1526, Summary of the Natural History of the Indies; from De la natural hystoria de las Indias, *1969; Thomas Cooper Library, University of South Carolina)*

At the age of eighteen he became *custodio de las llaves de cámara* (keeper of the chamber keys). He served the prince in this capacity for a year, until the heir suddenly died.

Those nine years of service, in particular the six years at the service of Prince John, had a profound impact on his future endeavors as a writer and as officer of the crown. His proximity to the prince, according to the customs of those days, allowed Oviedo to be present and participate when the heir received lessons in Latin, history, the classics, and music. By this means he obtained an education that otherwise would have been impossible for him to get. Probably during these initial formative years, Oviedo was introduced to the works of Pliny the Elder, the most important natural historian of the Old World. Pliny's *Historia naturalis* (Natural History) was the model that Oviedo, years later, followed to write his *La historia general de las Indias*. The years in the royal palace also provided Oviedo with inside knowledge of the court. This knowledge allowed him to write a treatise of heraldry, *Libro del blasón: Tractado general de todas las armas e diferencia dellas, e de los escudos e diferencias que en ellas hay, e de la orden que se debe guardar en las dichas armas, para que sean ciertas no falsas, e de los colores e metales que hay en armería, e de las reglas e circunstancias a ese efecto convinientes* (circa 1551, Book of the Coat of Arms: General Treatise of All the Arms and Their Differences, and of All the Shields and Their Differences, and of the Order That Such Arms Must Have to be True and Not False, and the Armory's Colors and Metals, and the Appropriate Rules and Circumstances); a ceremonial account, *Libro de la camara real del principe don Juan e officios de su casa e seruicio ordinario, compuesto por Gonçalo Fernandez de Ouiedo* (1546, Book of Prince John's Royal Chamber, the Trades and Ordinary Services of His House, Composed by Gonçalo Fernandez de Ouiedo); and a royal genealogical account, *Cathalogo real de Castilla, y de todos los Reyes de las Españas e de Napoles y Çecilia, e de los Reyes y señores de las casas de Francia, Austria, Holanda y Borgoña: de donde proceden los cuatro abolorios de la Cesárea Magestad del Emperador don Carlos, nuestro señor: Con relación de todos los Emperadores y Summos Pontífices que han subcedido desde Julio Çesar, que fue el primero Emperador, y desde Apóstol Sanct Pedro, que fue el primero Papa, hasta este año de Christo de MDXXXII* (1535, Royal Catalogue of Castilla, and of All the Kings of Spain, Naples and Sicily, and All Kings' and Lords' Houses in France, Austria, the Netherlands, and Burgundy: From Where Our Caesarean Lord Your Majesty the Emperor Don Charles' Four Ancestries Come: Naming All the Emperors and Supreme Pontiffs Who Have Succeeded from Julius Caesar, the First Emperor, and from Saint Paul the Apostle, the First Pope, to This Year of Christ, MDXXXII). These years in the service

other hand, *La historia general de las Indias* is read as the work that initiated the Europeans, in the words of Edmundo O'Gorman in his *Cuatro historiadores de Indias: Pedro Martín de Anglería, Gonzalo Fernández de Oviedo y Valdés, Fray Bartolomé de las Casas, Joseph de Acosta* (1972, Four Historians of the Indies: Pedro Martín de Anglería, Gonzalo Fernández de Oviedo y Valdés, Fray Bartolomé de las Casas, Joseph de Acosta), in "el gran proceso explicativo del Nuevo Mundo" (the great explicative process of the New World), what he, O'Gorman, called the invention of America.

Born in Madrid in August 1478, Gonzalo Fernández de Oviedo y Valdés spent the last three years of his childhood serving the duke of Villahermosa, a nephew of King Ferdinand. When Oviedo turned thirteen, he entered the service of Prince John, heir of the Spanish throne, as his personal *mozo de cámara* (chamber helper).

of the prince also gave Oviedo inside knowledge of the politics of the court. This knowledge helped him secure official positions in the future, such as *cronista real* of the West Indies and commander of Santo Domingo's fortress, and helped him write his political account, *Relación hecha por Gonzalo Fernández de Oviedo de los males causados en Tierra-Firme por el gobernador Pedrarias* (circa 1524, Account Related by Gonzalo Fernández de Oviedos of the Bad Deeds Caused by the Governor Pedrarias).

The death of Prince John prompted Oviedo's decision to leave Spain for Italy. He remained there from 1498 to 1502, serving different well-known personalities, such as the Borgias. Fifty-five years later he wrote about his time in Italy: "discurrí por toda Italia, donde me di todo lo que yo pude a saber e leer y entender de la lengua toscana y buscando libros en ella, de los quales tengo algunos que ha más de 55 años están en mi compañía" (I wandered around all Italy, where I did all that I could to know, read, and understand the language of Tuscany and looked for books written in it, some of which I have kept in my company for more than fifty-five years). Most likely, one of these books was the original, probably written by Fray Cherubino, that he translated into Spanish as *Reglas de la vida espiritual y secreta theología* (1548, Rules of Spiritual Life and Secret Theology).

Oviedo returned to Spain as a member of the royal retinue of Queen Juana of Naples, niece of Ferdinand, in 1502. From this year until 1512, King Ferdinand reassigned Oviedo to serve the duke of Calabria. While at his service, Oviedo was allowed to pursue other appointments, such as notary for the Inquisition and notary public. When Oviedo was in the service of the duke, Ferdinand suggested he write a genealogical account of the kings of Spain. Years later, following the king's suggestion, he wrote *Cathalogo real de Castilla*.

The divide between his formative years and the years when he wrote his works was marked by his first transatlantic voyage, in 1514. Thereafter he resided in the New World but traveled back to Spain for short stays to secure the continuation of the royal patronage he enjoyed and to publish six of his works. By the end of his life he had made a total of eleven transatlantic voyages. O'Gorman has suggested that Oviedo's early work developed in three progressive stages: fiction, moral literature, and *libros de verdad* (books of truth), or historiography. In terms of his complete oeuvre, it may be more appropriate to characterize this development as moving away from writing pure fictional literature to writing nonfictional literature.

Oviedo's first work was the novel *Claribalte: Libro del muy esforçado y inuencible Cauallero dela Fortuna propiamete llamado don claribalte q segu su verdadera interpretaciõ quiere dezir don Felix o bienaventurado: Nuevamente escrito y venido a noticia dela lengua castellana por medio de gonçalo Fernandez de Ouiedo alias de sobrepeña* (1519, Claribalte: Book of the Very Valiant and Invincible Knight of Fortune Appropriately Known as Don Claribalte Whose Name According to Its True Translation Means Don Felix or the Blessed and Again Written in Castilian Language by Gonçalo Fernandez de Ouiedo). This romance of chivalry also was his only work of fiction. In the foreword he states that he wrote this novel "estãdo yo en la India y postrera parte accidental que a presente se sabe" (when I was in the most western part of the West Indies known to this present day). It was published in Valencia under his personal supervision. The story features the adventures of Don Félix, or Claribalte (the names are used interchangeably throughout), and follows the literary conventions of the genre. One of the conventions is to demonstrate the nobility of the main character. According to the narrator, Don Félix is the son of Plonorio, the heir to the kingdom of Constantinople, and Princess Clariosa, sister to the king of Albania. Another convention is the declaration of the main character's intention to become a knight by assuming the name of one; in the novel Don Félix decides to name himself "Caballero de la Fortuna" (Knight of Fortune). A third convention is romantic in nature: the courtship of a lady to whom the knight-to-be dedicates his future quest and whose love is needed to fortify his valor. In the novel the woman who inspires Don Félix is the princess of England, Dorendayna. The last convention is when the knight-to-be undertakes the quests for knighthood. Under this convention the knight has to prove his valor in tournaments and then conquer a territory to reign over with his lady. The narrator sets Claribalte to participate in the Albanian tournaments. The novel concludes when he reconquers the territory of Constantinople, which used to belong to his family, and reigns over it with Dorendayna.

Claribalte is significant because it is Oviedo's sole work of fiction, but also because it is a chivalric novel. Tzvetan Todorov, in his *La conquête de l'Amérique: La question de l'autre* (1982; translated as *The Conquest of America: The Question of the Other,* 1984), has suggested that the novels of chivalry incited the imagination and were an important part of the drive behind the first wave of Spaniard commoners heading to conquer the New World. While these novels incited the dream of self-betterment, the New World provided to the commoners the possibility of materializing their dreams by ascending the social ladder and becoming landowners. As most of the land in Spain was already owned by the nobility and the Catholic Church, the New World, recently "discovered," made the materialization of the dream to own land possible to those brave enough to enlist. From this perspective fiction and reality converge in *Claribalte* at two different levels. At the fictional level,

Pages featuring a New World map and a depiction of a ceremonial dance from a manuscript copy of Oviedo's La Historia
general de las Indias *(General History of the Indies; © Patrimonio Nacional, Real Biblioteca, Palacio Real,
Madrid; from Chiyo Ishikawa, ed.,* Spain in the Age of Exploration: 1492–1819, *2004;
Thomas Cooper Library, University of South Carolina)*

the main character fulfills the quest for knighthood by conquering land and the love of a lady; at the level of reality, Oviedo, the author, headed back to his recently conquered possessions in the New World with his second wife and children.

In his later works, particularly in *Historia general y natural de las Indias,* Oviedo, according to O'Gorman, condemned the chivalric novels as "libros de mentiras" (books of lies) and those who read them as vain. According to O'Gorman, this condemnation indicates that "Oviedo ha recibido la influencia del erasmismo introducido en el mundo español con la corte flamenca de Carlos V" (Oviedo received the Erasmian influence introduced in the Spanish world by the Flemish court of Charles V). Desiderius Erasmus of Rotterdam emphasized the study of social and religious problems from a moralistic perspective in order to change wrong modes of conduct. This Erasmian perspective influenced Oviedo, as well as many of his European contemporaries, to write certain types of nonfictional texts, such as moralizing treatises and *libros de verdad,* and to avoid fictional writing. Oviedo's first moral treatise is *Respuesta a la epístola moral del Almirante: Esta es una muy notable y moral Epístola que el muy ilustre señor Almirante de Castilla envió al autor de las sobredichas Quincuagenas, hablando de los males de España y de la causa dellos con la Respuesta del mismo autor* (circa 1524, Response to the Admiral's Moral Epistle: This Is a Very Notable and Moral Epistle Which the Illustrious Admiral of Castile Sent to the Author of the Quincuagenas, Talking about the Maladies of Spain and Their Causes with the Response of the Same Author). Thereafter, Oviedo only wrote nonfiction works.

These works can be classified into two general categories, either as moralizing treatises or as *libros de verdad. Respuesta a la epístola moral del Almirante, Relación de los males causados en Tierra-Firme por el gobernador Pedrarias,* his translation *Reglas de la vida espiritual y secreta theología,* and *Las quincuagenas de los generosos y no menos famosos reyes, príncipes, duques, marqueses, y condes e caballeros e personas notables de España, que escribió el capitán Gonzalo Fernández de Oviedo y Valdés, alcaide de Sus Majestades en la fortaleza de la cibdad e puerto de Santo Domingo de la Isla Española, coronista de las Indias, isla e Tierra Firme del mar Océano, vecino y regidor desta cibdad e natural de la muy noble e leal villa de Madrid* (1555, The Quinquagenas of the Generous and Famous Kings, Princes, Dukes, Marquees, and Counts, and Knights and Notable Persons of Spain, Which Were Written by the Captain Gonzalo Fernández de Oviedo y Valdéz, Fortress Commander of Your Majesties in the City and Port of Santo Domingo on Hispaniola Island, Chronicler of the Indies, Island and Terra Firma of the Ocean, Neighbor and Alderman of This City, and Originally for the Noble and Loyal Village of Madrid) compose the former group.

Relación de lo subcedido en la prisión del Rey Francisco de Francia (circa 1525, Account of King Francis of France's Imprisonment) is the first *libro de verdad* written by Oviedo. His other works classified as such are *Sumario de la natural hystoria delas Indias* (1526, Summary of the Natural History of the Indies), *Historia general y natural de las Indias, Cathalogo real, Libro de la camara real del principe don Juan, Batallas y quinquagenas* (1550, Battles and Quinquagenas), *Libro del blasón, Libro de linajes y armas* (circa 1552, Book of Lineages and Arms), and *Libro XX. Dela segunda parte dela general historia delas Indias* (1557, Book Twenty of the Second Part of the General History of the Indies). Of this group, most are about the Spanish court and deal with topics such as genealogy, ceremonies, and events, though he is best known for two of his works about the New World, *Sumario de la natural hystoria delas Indias* and *Historia general y natural de las Indias.*

In 1524 Oviedo wrote *Respuesta a la epístola moral del Almirante* and *Relación de los males causados en Tierra-Firme por el gobernador Pedrarias* during his second stay in Spain, five years after the publication of *Claribalte.* In both of these works he displays an Erasmian moralistic perspective in order to denounce and change bad behavior. In *Respuesta a la epístola moral del Almirante* Oviedo pays attention to the social environment in Spain, while in *Relación de los males causados en Tierra-Firme por el gobernador Pedrarias* he writes about the political behavior of an official in the New World. As the full title of *Respuesta a la epístola moral del Almirante* points out, Oviedo wrote this treatise or epistle as a response to and in dialogue with a letter sent to him by Fadrique Enríquez, a nobleman, who was known as the "Admiral of Castile." The topic of their epistles is the corruption of the social customs in Spain. In *Relación de los males causados en Tierra-Firme por el gobernador Pedrarias,* as the title suggests, Oviedo wrote an account of the misadministration of governor Pedrarias Dávila, with whom he had had open and persistent disagreements since 1515. Oviedo's inside knowledge of the court and its bureaucracy allowed him to present his *Relación de los males causados en Tierra-Firme por el gobernador Pedrarias* to the Council of the Indies. He accuses Governor Dávila of violating the royal decree of 1519 that prohibited the maltreatment of the Indians and the misappropriation of royal funds and land. He recommends Dávila's removal as governor and that "hase de proveerqual que gobernara aquella tierra, sea hombre de buena sangre e que tenga çelo e fin prençipal de serviçio de Dios e del Rey, e que sea amigo de justicia e hombre de edad convenible para el rezo e para los trabajos" (whoever is assigned to govern that land must be a man of good blood and one who is fervid and whose principal goal is to serve God and the King, and must be a friend of justice and a man of the right age to pray and to work).

Oviedo was in Madrid in 1525 at the time of the victory of Charles V's Spanish army over that of Francis I of France in the battle of Pavía. In his *Relación de lo subcedido en la prisión del Rey Francisco de Francia* he wrote about how the court in Madrid took the news of the victory. He also wrote about King Francis I, his arrival to Madrid as prisoner, and his release from prison after he married Princess Leonor, sister of King Charles. According to Manuel Ballesteros Gaibrois in his *Vida del madrileño G. Fernández de Oviedo y Valdés* (1958, Life of the Madrilenian G. Fernández de Oviedo y Valdés), he additionally used the opportunity to inform readers about the important people in the court and his conversations with them, in which he was not a servant anymore but an equal nobleman. At the end of the same year he was able to obtain an official confirmation of his newly gained nobility when Charles emblazoned him by granting him an *escudo de armas* (armorial insignia or coat of arms) in Toledo.

According to Oviedo, he wrote *Sumario de la natural hystoria delas Indias* in 1526, prompted by the desire of the king to expand his royal knowledge about the Indies. Oviedo wrote the work from memory. He claimed he did not have with him his notes or his draft of a work in progress, assumed by critics to be *Historia general y natural de las Indias*. *Sumario de la natural hystoria delas Indias* is a brief description of what he considered the natural environment of the New World, that is, nature and the original peoples. He gives special attention to exotic descriptions of plants and animals as well as descriptions of the rites and customs of the Indians, emphasizing what he considers their natural condition of sin and savagery. These perceptions about the natural and human spaces of the New World transcended the immediacy of his declared intention to please the king. At the political level, this work influenced the debate on Indian policy brought to the court by Las Casas. At the epistemological level, it influenced the representation of the native peoples and nature of the Americas, in the words of O'Gorman, as objects of a "new philosophical consideration." This consideration informed his own *Historia general y natural de las Indias* in addition to the chronicles of Francisco López de Gómara and José de Acosta.

In 1535 Oviedo also oversaw the publication of the first part of *Historia general y natural de las Indias* as well as a revised edition of it in which he added information about the conquest of Peru. The full title of this edition is *Coronica de las Indias. La hystoria general de las Indias, agora nuevamente impresa, corregida y emendada. Y con la conquista del Perú* (1547, Chronicle of the Indies. The General History of the Indies, Once Again Printed, Revised and Amended. And with the Conquest of Peru). In *Historia general y natural de las Indias* he expanded the range of his descriptions about the New World by adding more

details to the accounts provided in *Sumario de la natural hystoria delas Indias* and by incorporating descriptions about regions recently "discovered." He also was charged by King Charles to add accounts about "las cosas que han sucedido en las nuestras Indias, desde el tiempo que así se descubrieron" (the things that have happened in our Indies since the time of their discovery). He did that by incorporating a history of the conquest as a significant thematic component.

Also in 1535 Oviedo finished *Cathalogo real* after three years of writing and thirty years after King Ferdinand recommended him to write such a work. The work consists of three parts. The first part shares the general title, and the second and third parts are titled "Epílogo real de Castilla" (Royal Recapitulation of Castile) and "Epílogo real y Pontificial" (Royal and Pontifical Recapitulation), respectively. His objective in this work was twofold. First, Oviedo records the genealogical connections between the Spanish royal families or Houses to other Houses in six European kingdoms, in particular, the genealogical background of King Charles V. Second, Oviedo describes the relations between those royal families and the popes.

Libro de la camara real del principe don Juan is another work that took him more than a decade to write. According to Oviedo, Count Manrique, who was tutoring young Prince Philip, urged him to write about the ceremonies at the House of Prince John, where he had served. After writing a brief recollection of some of the ceremonies and the organization of the House of Prince John in 1535, he decided in 1546 to write a more detailed account of the same, which he titled *Libro de la camara real del principe don Juan*. His account "Adiciones a los oficios de la Casa real de Castilla" (1547, Additions to the Services at the Royal House of Castile) completed the work and was included by José María de la Peña in his edition of *Libro de la camara real del principe don Juan*, published in 1870.

Two and a half decades passed before Oviedo decided to deal with moral issues again. However, in contrast to the social and political behaviors that he discussed in his previous moralizing treatises, his work of translation, *Reglas de la vida espiritual y secreta theología*, published in 1548, is, according to him, "[un] devoto libro" (a pious book), that is, a book that discussed the right modes of conduct in order to lead a Christian spiritual life. It is only known that the original was written in an Italian dialect spoken in the region of Tuscany. Daymond Turner speculates that the original was the *Regola della vita spirituale* written by Father Cherubino printed in Florence twice, in 1477 and 1487.

Oviedo was not able to complete any of the four volumes of his second genealogical work, *Batallas y quinquagenas*. Although Oviedo started this work in 1546 the

Drawing and description of a New World plant from a 1539–1548 manuscript copy of Oviedo's La historia
general y natural de las Indias *(HM 177 fol. 78r, Huntington Library, San Marino, California;
from Chiyo Ishikawa, ed.,* Spain in the Age of Exploration: 1492–1819, *2004;
Thomas Cooper Library, University of South Carolina)*

manuscript dates from 1550. Also, in contrast with his first genealogical work, Oviedo included genealogical accounts of other Spanish noble families and recorded court events that he witnessed during the reign of Ferdinand and Isabella. A third main difference with *Cathalogo real,* his first genealogical work, is that in *Batallas y quinquagenas* he displayed his account in the form of dialogues. The use of this form, according to O'Gorman, is another indication, this time at the stylistic level, of the influence of Erasmus on the work of Oviedo.

In 1551 and 1552 Oviedo wrote his last works about the Spanish court, *Libro del blasón,* also known as *Tractado general de todas las armas* (General Treatise of All the Arms) and its sequel *Libro de linajes y armas.* These works are written in the tradition of a heraldry account. In both of the works he traced and recorded genealogies of the noble Spaniards as well as the devising and granting of their respective armorial insignia or coats of arms.

Eight years later, after publishing *Reglas de la vida espiritual y secreta theología,* in January 1555, Oviedo presented to Prince Philip his last moralizing work, *Las quinquagenas,* which deals with the lives of noble Spanish men. His objective was to praise their virtues in order to help Christians achieve a life without vices. In the opinion of Juan Bautista Avalle-Arce, for the modern reader this work is valuable as a collection of memories about the renowned people Oviedo met and the events he witnessed. The work consists of a series of stanzas, each of them followed by a commentary on the moral lesson or virtues expressed in the preceding stanza. The number of verses in each stanza varies, but the verses are couplets, each of seven or eight syllables and in consonantal rhyme.

The second part of *Historia general y natural de las Indias* was in the process of being printed when Fernández de Oviedo died in 1557. The publisher printed only one section of this second part, *Libro XX.* The complete work, including all three parts, was edited and published by José Amador de los Ríos in four volumes titled *Historia general y natural de las Indias* (1851–1855).

The complete *Historia general y natural de las Indias* consists of three parts and fifty books; the first two parts have nineteen books in each and the last one contains twelve. In the first part Oviedo discusses the Caribbean, in the second the eastern region of the New World, and in the third the western region. However, Oviedo mainly deals with natural history in books 7 to 15 of the first part and only briefly in the second and third parts. In the last two parts, the main content is general history (history of the conquest). Oviedo uses narratives, dialogues, and drawings throughout the three parts of the work. In addition, he uses prologues to provide his reflections about the topics of his discussion in thirty-nine of the books. In these prologues the chronicler offered, according to Karl Kohut, his "philosophy of nature and history."

Critics continue to disagree about what this philosophical perspective is or if it is anchored in a medieval or modern epistemology. For instance, O'Gorman's opinion is that Oviedo is not a modern intellectual because he has a "messianic vision of history." On the other end of the spectrum, José Rabasa thinks his perspective is modern in that he has "a utopian vision of the New World." At the same time, there is a tacit agreement that the significance of Oviedo's perspective is twofold. In the first place, Oviedo initiated the validation and enforcement of European subjectivity as universal. Secondly, he drew the road map for the Western intellectual conquest of the New World.

Bibliography:

Daymond Turner, *Gonzalo Fernández de Oviedo y Valdés: An Annotated Bibliography* (Chapel Hill: University of North Carolina Press, 1966).

Biography:

Manuel Ballesteros Gaibrois, *Vida del madrileño G. Fernández de Oviedo y Valdés* (Madrid: Instituto de Estudios Madrileños, 1958).

References:

Manuel Ballesteros Gaibrois, *Gonzalo Fernández de Oviedo* (Madrid: Fundación Universitaria Española, 1981);

Juan Bautista Avalle-Arce, *Las memorias de Gonzalo Fernández de Oviedo* (Chapel Hill: North Carolina Studies in the Romance Languages and Literatures, 1974);

Chiyo Ishikawa, ed., *Spain in the Age of Exploration: 1482–1819* (Seattle: Seattle Art Museum, 2004);

Karl Kohut, "Fernández de Oviedo, historiador y literato: humanismo, cristianismo e hidalguía," in *Historia y ficción: Crónicas de América,* edited by Ysla Campbell (Ciudad Juarez: Universidad Autónoma de Ciudad Juárez, 1992), pp. 43–104;

Edmundo O'Gorman, *Cuatro historiadores de Indias: Pedro Martín de Anglería, Gonzalo Fernández de Oviedo y Valdés, Fray Bartolomé de las Casas, Joseph de Acosta* (Mexico City: Sep/Setentas, 1972);

José Rabasa, "Historiografía colonial y la episteme occidental moderna: Una aproximación a la etnografía franciscana, Oviedo y Las Casas," in *Historia y ficción: Crónicas de América,* edited by Campbell (Ciudad Juárez: Universidad Autónoma de Ciudad Juárez, 1992), pp. 105–139;

Tzvetan Todorov, *The Conquest of America: The Question of the Other,* translated by Richard Howard (New York: Harper & Row, 1984).

Juan Gutiérrez Rufo

(1547? – 1620?)

Kenneth Atwood
University of Tennessee, Knoxville

and

Adriano Duque
University of North Carolina, Chapel Hill

BOOKS: *La Austríada* (Madrid: Alonso Gómez, 1584);
Las seiscientas apotegmas y otras obras en verso (Toledo: Pedro Rodríguez, 1596).
Editions and Collections: *Poemas épicos,* edited by Cayetano Rosell y López (Madrid: Rivadeneyra, 1851);
"Poesía," in *Poetas líricos de los siglos XVI y XVII,* edited by Adolfo de Castro (Madrid: Rivadeneyra, 1857), pp. 417–420;
Las seiscientas apotegmas y otras obras en verso, edited by A. González de Amezúa (Madrid: Sociedad de bibliófilos españoles, 1923);
Las seiscientas apotegmas y otras obras en verso, edited by Alberto Blecua (Madrid: Espasa-Calpe, 1972).

The importance of Juan Gutiérrez Rufo as a significant figure of sixteenth-century Spanish literature is often overshadowed by the prominence of his contemporaries. Alongside names such as Luis de Góngora, Miguel de Cervantes, Francisco Quevedo, and Lope de Rueda, Rufo's is easily overlooked. In comparison to such figures, Rufo was not a prolific writer, producing only two major works in his lifetime: *La Austríada* (1584, The Austrian Poem) and *Las seiscientas apotegmas y otras obras en verso* (1596, Six Hundred Apothegms and Other Works in Verse). Nevertheless, these two works were enough to gain Rufo recognition among his peers and establish him as an important name in Spanish literature. In his 1584 laudatory poems *Demos gracias a Dios* (Let Us Thank God) and *Decid que es cosa* (Say How Great), Góngora praises the poetic achievements of *La Austríada*. In *Don Quixote* (1605, 1615), Cervantes refers to the work as one of the most valuable of Spanish literary treasures. Even Rufo's *Las seiscientas apotegmas,* considered by many as a minor work, influenced the prose style of writers after him, serving as an example of writing that emulated popular vernacular. More important to biographers,

Juan Gutiérrez Rufo (frontispiece for Las seiscientas apotegmas y otras obras en verso, *1923; Jean and Alexander Heard Library, Vanderbilt University)*

however, the work includes several autobiographical anecdotes that recount some of the personal episodes of Rufo's life. From these allusions and several other documents, biographers have pieced together a rather complete account of the author's life.

Juan Gutiérrez Rufo was born in Córdoba in 1547 in the sector of the city known as the Calle de Tinte (Dye

Street). He was the second son of Luis Rofos and María Núñez, both of whom were of modest backgrounds. Although little is known about Rufo's mother, Luis Rofos was a dyer by trade who inherited his father's business. He was the only child of four who adopted the surname Rofos; the other three children were all known as Gutiérrez, the last name of their paternal uncle. Though not of noble stock, Luis Rofos was an affluent man who ran a prosperous dyeing business, traded in building lumber, maintained at least one ranch on the outskirts of Córdoba where he raised sheep and cattle, and owned several properties around the city. Although he was not an overly rich man, he was part of the influential merchant class that was beginning to compete in importance and in wealth with the aristocracy by the end of the sixteenth century. Because of his father's prosperity, Rufo was able to afford a somewhat profligate lifestyle. Prone to gambling and spending more than he could pay, Rufo frequently found himself in debt and at the center of regretful incidents that his father was often left to settle. The first such incident occurred when he was only fourteen. He and his younger brother Tómas obtained a set of false keys to their father's coffer and took from it 500 ducats, gambling the money away the next day. Shortly after this *disparate gracioso* (embarrassing blunder), as Rufo's father referred to the incident, Luis Rofos decided to send his son to Salamanca, then a scholastic hub of Spain.

Presumably sent to a university to begin his academic career, Rufo is assumed to have been in Salamanca by 1561. The only indication that he spent time in Salamanca, however, is a reference in his father's last testament to 150,000 *maravedis* (about a thirteenth the value of a *real*) sent to Rufo for *gastos trasordinarios* (beyond ordinary expenses). There are no records of Rufo's ever having registered at the university, so it is unlikely that he attended classes. More likely, he spent his time and the 150,000 *maravedis* his father sent indulging two of his well-known diversions: gambling and carousing.

Although Rufo did not attend the university in Salamanca, he was formally educated. Receiving lessons in Latin and the classics at a young age, he mastered the language well enough to have read Virgil's *Georgics* and *Aeneid* in their original, both of which he cites extensively throughout *La Austríada*. His true talent, however, was his ease for verse. A gifted *vihuela* (a stringed instrument popular in sixteenth-century Spain) player, Rufo was able to improvise *cantares,* or short poems set to music, upon demand. Among his circle of friends, which included some of the more prominent writers and poets of his time, he was known for his ability to speak effortlessly in verse, matching wits on more than one occasion with Góngora during rhyming duels.

Famed for this uncanny ability, Rufo was frequently challenged to display his poetic genius. On one such occasion, a group of young poets entertaining the count of Palma challenged him to *glosar* (gloss), or to explain in verse, the second couplet of Jorge de Montemayor's first stanza regarding the fabled Píramo and Tisbe. Sure that the challenge was impossible, all were amazed when Rufo, without hesitation, improvised a perfect gloss in two stanzas.

After nearly four years in Salamanca, Rufo was back in Córdoba by 1565, in time to see Lope present several plays during his stay in Rufo's home city. Rufo wrote a short laudatory poem in honor of the playwright, which he included in his *Las Seiscientas apotegmas.* Now eighteen years old, Rufo had developed new interests. A tall and slender young man with a handsome face who possessed a flair for speaking, he began courting young ladies of good social standing in Córdoba. His first interest was the daughter of an unnamed but prominent lady of Córdoba whom he met shortly after his return from Salamanca. The affair was cut short when the young lady's mother discovered the couple alone in her house. Incensed that Rufo had denigrated her daughter's good name, she demanded that he marry her. When Rufo refused, the young lady's mother brought suit against him, charging that he had defamed her daughter. Rufo was saved from jail by the intervention of Fray Domingo Gutiérrez, presumably a relative, who paid 6,000 *maravedis* to the young lady's dowry in order to facilitate her marriage. Not long after this incident, Rufo found himself in a similar situation during a trip to the neighboring city of Jaez. While there, he seduced the daughter of Gaspar de Ayala, a well-known lawyer of the city. After only a few short weeks, the couple's secret affair was discovered when Ayala, returning home earlier than expected, found Rufo in bed with his daughter. Rufo again refused to marry and was charged with defaming the honor of the Ayala family. This time Rufo's father intervened, paying 8,000 *maravedis* to Ayala in order to keep his son out of jail.

In 1566 Luis Rofos bought a chair on the Council of Córdoba. A prosperous businessman, he now sought to establish his standing within the community by obtaining a title for himself. The council members, who were all of noble stock, refused to recognize Rofos on the basis that he was a merchant, blocking his appointment to the council. Over the next two years Rofos petitioned the council and the court of Philip II for his right to be recognized. After many letters and unsuccessful appeals, he ultimately had to admit that the council, a conservative aristocracy, would never admit a common merchant into their ranks. With no other alternative, he ceded the position to his son Juan, who was also eager to gain a worthy title for himself. At this time Rufo, who had been signing his name Juan Gutiérrez, modified his surname by adding to it *de Córdoba,* a nobler-sounding name worthy of his new title of councilman.

On 10 July 1568, Rufo presented himself before the Council of Córdoba, ready to take his oath of office. Before swearing him in, Pedro Fernández Monegro, the head of the council, excused Rufo so that he and the other members could discuss whether or not to admit the son of a merchant. There was no discussion, practically speaking, since the council's previous petition to Philip II asking to refuse Rufo's appointment had been denied. The members agreed, however, that they would send a new petition to the king in which they would outline specific prerequisites for councilmen to ensure that in the future commoners would not be able to obtain a seat. The council voted; Rufo was admitted; and the members agreed to not discuss the matter further.

During the assembly on 17 July, the first since Rufo's appointment, the topic of the new petition was raised. Fernández Monegro reminded the members that the matter was not to be discussed during session, but not before Juan de Velasco publicly denounced Rufo's appointment, vowing to take his objection to the king. Fernández Monegro called for order and suggested that the members take the matter up after session. Aciscío de Torreblanca then stood and commented that no mention need be made of Jews or Moors in the petition since, in Córdoba, everyone was of clean Christian blood. This remark was a thinly veiled accusation aimed at the Rofos family name.

Despite the tensions, Rufo was dutifully present at all of the assemblies called during the months of August, September, and October. Eager to prove himself worthy of his title, Rufo seemed to be carrying out the duties of his position to the fullest. The other council members recognized his commitment and soon named Rufo treasurer of the public grain deposit. The easy access to public money, however, proved too tempting for his covetous nature. During his first few months as treasurer, it was soon revealed, he had embezzled more than 600 *fanegas* (a *fanega* is equal to about 1.5 bushels) of wheat. By the time the accounting discrepancy was discovered, Rufo had already left for Portugal, where he sold the grain and gambled away the profits. Again, Rufo's father was left to settle his son's affairs, reimbursing the city of Córdoba for the lost grain.

The same year that Rufo took his seat on the Council of Córdoba, the Moriscos (Christianized Moors) revolted in Granada. They opposed Philip II's royal edict that banned the use of Arabic, forbade traditional *Moriscos* dress, and prohibited families from giving Muhammadan names to their children. The marquis of Mondejar, captain-general of Granada, who also strongly disagreed with the royal ordinance, was persuaded to present the objections of the *Moriscos* before the royal court. Indignant, King Philip refused to hear the protests, prompting the *Moriscos* to organize a general revolt. On Christmas Day 1568, the uprising was set in motion when Fernando de Valor was named as the sovereign of the *Moriscos* and given the title Mohammed Aben Humeya, king of Granada and Córdoba. From Granada, Ferag ben Ferag, a descendent of the royal house of Granada and one of the principal authors of the revolt, led his followers into the mountainous terrain of Las Alpujarras, where they could best make their stand against the royal forces. Poorly organized, underequipped, and taken by surprise, the local authorities were unable to put down the uprising promptly. The revolt quickly spread to the neighboring provinces of Málaga, Almería, and Murcia. With growing support from the surrounding *Morisco* populations and sustained by supplies coming from Algiers and the Berber Coast of Africa, the *Morisco* insurgents were able to maintain a successful guerrilla campaign in the Alpujarras for several months. Resolute in his desire to end the conflict, Philip dispatched his half brother, Prince John of Austria, to Granada to lead a campaign against the insurgents, demanding their total annihilation. John arrived in Granada and began organizing his crusade against the *Morisco* insurgence. In November, the Council of Córdoba was called on to provide Prince John two companies of four hundred men each. Having returned from Portugal weeks before, Rufo, as a member of the council, likely took part in the enlistment and arming of the men. Expected to participate in the campaign himself, Rufo paid Miguel de Torquemada to go in his stead, while he remained out of harm's way in Córdoba.

With the reinforcements sent from Córdoba, the last of the *Morisco* insurgents were subdued after nearly a year of conflict. To show his appreciation to the people of Córdoba, Philip II and his court paid a special visit to the city, arriving in February 1570. The king's arrival was met with all of the grandeur that the city could marshal. On the morning of his entrance, all of the high-ranking figures of Córdoba rode through the streets in a great procession toward the main gate of the city. Juan Pérez, the principal clerk of Córdoba, and Juan Ulloa de Toro, the inspector general, led the procession. Behind Pérez and Ulloa de Toro rode the members of the Council of Córdoba. Among them was Rufo, clad in royal velvet from head to toe. The procession ended at the Puerta de Placencia, where the city of Córdoba received the king upon his entrance. Pérez approached the king, kissed his hand, and welcomed him on behalf of the city. Then, by order of antiquity, Pérez called out each of the names of the council members as they approached, knelt, and kissed the king's hand.

Beyond his ceremonial duties as a member of the Council of Córdoba, it is doubtful that Rufo had any other occasion to address the king. The king's stay in Córdoba did provide him, however, with plenty of opportunity to mingle among the prominent members of his courtly entourage. Making himself present at all of the important social gatherings, Rufo met several influential people of the king's court, many of whom he names in his *Las seiscientas apotegmas*. Charming them with his spirited character and entertaining them with his gift for improvising verse, Rufo won the affection and patronage of several figures of noble standing. Encouraged to pursue his poetic talents, Rufo, eager to make a name for himself in the court of Philip II, resigned from his post on the council, passing his seat to Juan de Godoy. His resignation was denied, and over the next several months, Rufo made repeated attempts to resign his post, each time being refused. It was not until December of the same year that he was finally able to give up his seat, ceding it to his father, Luis Rofos, a decision that was later contested.

Rufo left for Madrid in January 1571 and, once there, took up residence at an inn on Calle del Baño (Bath Street), which has since been named Ventura de Vega. He began frequenting the *tertulias* (literary round tables) and the social gatherings at the homes of the prominent figures that he had met the year before. During one such occasion Rufo was presented to Prince John of Austria by his friend and benefactor Don Diego Fernández de Córdoba, the royal master of the king's stable. Charmed by Rufo's flair for speaking and lively character, the prince honored him with conversation. Their discussion soon turned to the fundamental nature of nobility when John commented on how, in the end, death makes equals of everyone. The prince, knowing of Rufo's gift for rhyme, challenged him to put his argument to verse, to which Rufo responded by improvising a short poem in eight verses. Impressed, Prince John lent Rufo his patronage, offering the poet his hospitality during his stay in Madrid.

During this time, Rufo must have proposed to write a poem that would eulogize the prince. His opportunity came on 20 May 1571, when Prince John was named supreme commander of the naval and land forces of the Santa Liga (Holy League), an alliance comprising Spain, Venice, and the Vatican. Prince John suggested that Rufo accompany him on his naval campaign against the forces of Selim II in the Tyrrhe-

Title page for an early edition of Rufo's 1584 epic (The Austrian Poem), which recounts the Spanish crusade against Muslim forces, culminating in the naval victory of the Christian forces over the Ottoman Turks in the battle of Lepanto in 1571 (University of Maryland Library)

nian Sea. Rufo enlisted in John's army and accompanied him to Italy in order to chronicle the battle in verse. They arrived in Messina on 23 June, where Prince John promptly assembled the Christian armada; among the fleet was the famed *Marquesa*, on which Cervantes sailed. The great naval battle of Lepanto took place nearly two months later, on 7 October. The clash between the Christian and Turkish armadas raged all day and into the night. By the morning of the following day, King Selim's fleet had been destroyed, temporarily pushing back the advance of the Turks. On 10 October, Prince John dispatched ten ships to Madrid to relate news of his victory to his half brother, Philip II. Rufo was among those sent.

From Madrid, Rufo returned to Córdoba where, after some controversy, he took back his seat on the council from his father and began a second term, signing in for the 21 July 1572 session. Not long after, restless and in need of money, he asked to recite a few untitled poems that he had composed during the battle of Lepanto–these poems were to become his famed *Austríada*. The council agreed to hear the poems and were sufficiently impressed to advance the aspiring poet 100 gold ducats for their publication. The money was to be repaid within eighteen months. In November 1573, Rufo left for Italy, leaving the poems unpublished and his father to settle his debt.

Rufo spent the next four years abroad, living for the most part in Naples, where he spent time interviewing the principal witnesses to the battle of Lepanto, verifying the events and reading his verses to anyone who would listen. After having read part of the poem to Andrea Doria and Juan de Soto, the prince's personal secretary, John of Austria offered Rufo a small pension and asked de Soto to stay behind and look after Rufo while he was away in Flanders. De Soto provided Rufo with details about the campaign against the Turks and was the one who suggested that Rufo expand his poem to include the events of the *Morisco* uprising.

Other than what Rufo mentions in *Las seiscientas apotegmas,* little else is known about his time in Italy. While there, he composed some minor poems in honor of important figures, which he later included in *Las seiscientas apotegmas:* "Elegía a la muerte de doña Ana de Toledo" (Eulogy for the Death of Lady Ana de Toledo) and "Soneto a don Alonso Idiaquez, general de la caballería de Milán" (Sonnet to Sir Alonso Idiaquez, General of the Calvary of Milan).

After the death of John of Austria in 1575 in Flanders, Rufo remained in Naples under the protection of the count of Sessa, returning with him to Spain in 1578. Deeply affected by the death of the prince, Rufo returned to Córdoba in August determined to finish his poems. He was soon distracted, however, when he met and fell in love with the young daughter of Hernando Ortiz, a court clerk in the city of Córdoba. After a short courtship, the two became lovers, meeting clandestinely on several occasions. Their love affair ended abruptly when the young lady's father discovered the couple together in bed. Rufo was thrown in jail, and Ortiz demanded nothing short of matrimony for his release. Writing of the incident in his *Las Seiscientos apotegmas,* Rufo claims that when he refused to marry Ortiz's daughter, she had the guards put a pair of shackles on his feet. She then asked Rufo if he wanted to marry her now, to which he replied: "Más vale grillos de hierro, que esposa con yerros" (Shackles of steel are worth more than a wife with flaws). Tired of Rufo's

careless behavior, Luis Rofos refused to pay for his son's release. Rufo was unable to convince his father to pay bail until Rofos finally agreed to visit his son some days later. The following day, Rofos made an appointment to speak with Ortiz. Ortiz was paid 28,000 *maravidis,* and Rufo was released from jail.

By December 1579, Rufo had completed *La Austríada,* a date that is confirmed by a letter written by Gómez del Castillo, Gómez Fernández de Córdoba, and Pedro de Hoces in which they beseech the king to approve the publication of *La Austríada.* The letter not only confirms the year by which Rufo had finished his poem, but also indicates that Rufo began signing his name as Juan Rufo at this time. Rafael Ramírez de Arellano, in his *Juan Rufo, jurado de Córdoba: Estudio biográfico y crítico* (1912, Juan Rugo, Councilman of Córdoba: Biographical and Critical Study), has suggested that the change more than likely came about after Rufo read Ambrosio de Morales's *Las antigüedades de las ciudades de España* (1577, The Antiquities of the Cities of Spain). In his history of ancient Spain, Morales tells of two Roman inscriptions that included the names of two Roman citizens by the name of Rufus, one of which was a citizen of Córdoba. Convinced that he was descended from this early Cordoban family, Rufo modified his father's surname and began signing the distinct last name immortalized by *La Austríada* and *Los seiscientos apotegmas.*

On 31 October 1581, Rufo resigned from his post on the Council of Córdoba for the last time, ceding his seat to Alonso Sánchez for 1,200 gold ducats. Two months later, he met and married María Carrillo, the daughter of Pedro Fernández de Villafranca and Inés de Aranda. In 1582 María bore Rufo his first son, Luis Rufo, who later became a reputed painter, defeating Michelangelo Caravaggio during a public painting contest. In January 1584 a second son, Juan Rufo, was born. In 1586 another son, José Gutiérrez, was born. Relying on the success of the recently published *La Austríada,* Rufo moved his family to Madrid in 1593, where they remained for the next four years. While in Madrid, he wrote several pieces of occasional poetry dedicated to the duke of Pastrana, the duke of Saboya, Martín de Córdoba, Cristóbal de Mora, Diego de Silva, and the duke of Alba. Seeking patronage, Rufo approached the duke of Alba, presenting him with his plan to compose a second part of *La Austríada* in which he intended to include the events of the campaign in Tunis, the uprisings at Geneva, and the campaign in Flanders, during which John of Austria became sick and died. When the duke refused to sponsor him, Rufo gave up his aspiration to write a second part.

After his father's death in 1595, Rufo returned with his family to Córdoba in 1597, where he stayed for the remainder of his life. He settled into life as a husband and father of three, moving into his father's house on La Calle de Tinte, signing his name Juan Gutiérrez again, and taking over the family business. Probably at this point in his life, Rufo decided to compile the six hundred apothegms and several poems that he had composed over the past several years. Not much more is known about him during this time of his life. He is assumed to have died sometime after 1620 and was buried, without fanfare, at the cathedral in Córdoba.

Although Rufo died before producing any other significant works, his contribution to the literary tradition of Spain has not gone unnoticed. During his lifetime, his works were well received by the general public and highly praised by his contemporaries. Although typically overshadowed by the major figures of the period, critics continue to revisit his writings, finding in them aspects that reveal much about the literary process in Spain during the sixteenth century. While both of Rufo's works offer insights into the Spanish literary tradition of the time, he is best known for his *La Austríada*.

La Austríada is written in the traditional *octavo real* (royal octave) meter, characteristic of Spanish epic verse. It consists of twenty-four cantos, divided into two main bodies. The first part of the poem—songs 1 through 10—recounts the revolt in the Alpujarras and John of Austria's campaign to put down the insurgency. The second half of the poem—songs 14 through 24—tells of the Santa Liga's victory over the Turks in the naval battle of Lepanto. The two main bodies are loosely tied together by a short transitional episode—songs 11 through 13—that briefly describes the island of Cyprus. Stylistically, the poem follows the classical traditions of Virgil, Diego Hurtado de Mendoza, and Juan de Mena. Because of the inherent poetic disjuncture that breaks with the classical precept of the three unities, however, and because *La Austríada* lacks a clear religious motif, many critics have characterized it less as an epic poem in the classical sense and more as an historical poem or rhymed chronicle that emulates classical style.

There is no doubt that with *La Austríada* Rufo intended to eulogize Prince John and to extol the role of Spain in the Catholic crusade against the Muhammadans. Rufo clearly saw peace and the rule of God as the ultimate purpose of war. Nevertheless, behind the patriotic tone of the laudatory songs, the poem reveals a critical undertone. Although Rufo praises the Christians for their bravery during battle throughout the poem, he also reveals their propensity to looting and enslaving their captives, conveying on more than one occasion a sympathetic attitude toward the non-Christian enemies. War, although celebrated in the poem as a glorious act

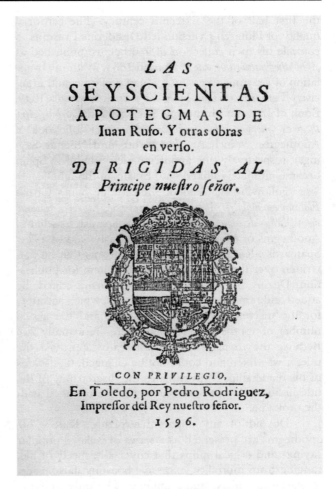

Title page of Rufo's miscellanea (Six Hundred Apothegms and Other Works in Verse) in which he included autobiographical anecdotes and poems of tribute to various figures in the Spanish royal court (from Las seiscientas apotegmas y otras obras en verso, 1923; Jean and Alexander Heard Library, Vanderbilt University)

when conducted in the name of God, is also depicted as confusion wrought with injustices and errors. Greed and material pursuit appear in combination with attitudes that are unacceptable for an honorable soldier, such as cowardice, disobedience, and disorder; the Christians in the poem are portrayed as often being motivated by greed rather than by God.

Rufo's other significant work, *Los seiscientos apotegmas*, derives its name from Plutarch's *Apophthegmata*, translated into Spanish by Diego Gracián de Alderete in 1533 under the title *Apothegmas, que son los dichos notables y breves de los Emperadores* (Apothegms, Which Are Notable and Brief Sayings of the Emperors). The original Greek version consisted of a series of short moral quips of a censorial tone that became widely popular during the first half of the sixteenth century. The censorial quality of Plutarch's version led Desiderius Erasmus to compile his own collection of apothegms, published as *Apophthegmatum sive scite dictorum* in 1531. With the translation of Erasmus's version by Juan de Jarava and Francisco Támara—as *Libro de vidas y dichos graciosos* (1549, Book of Life and Humorous Sayings) and *Libro de Apothegmas, que son dichos grasiosos y notables* (1549, Book of Apothegms, Which Are Humorous and Notable Sayings), respectively—the apothegmatic tradition in Spain became intimately linked with Erasmian thought.

Following the lead of Melchor de Santa Cruz's *Floresta española de Apothegmas o sentencias sabias y graciosamente dichas de algunos españoles* (1574, Spanish Garden of Apothegms or Maxims and Humorously Said of a Few Spaniards), Rufo compiled the apothegms that he had written over the years and submitted them for publication. During the time the book was being edited, he added and removed several apothegms, which accounts for the discrepancy between the title and the actual number of apothegms included—there are actually 707. Because the royal printer had already approved the title, it was fixed and could not be changed. Conscious of his readership, Rufo explains the discrepancy of the title in an apology to the reader that he included with the prologue.

Devoid of any apparent structure, Rufo's 707 apothegms are presented as a series of isolated popular sayings and critical quips that cover all aspects of life, ranging from mortality, excessive boasting, false pride, monastic life, piety, and gambling. The only unifying aspect of the work is the autobiographical nature of the apothegms, most having originated from Rufo's own life experiences. This aspect of the work sets it apart from the others of the same tradition. In the work, Rufo adopts an individualistic and personal tone, taking his lessons not from the courtly tradition, as was common

to the apothegmatic genre, but rather from the daily life of common occurrences. The conceptual wordplay of the work, the cynical tone of the humorous slights, and the repeated theme of the brevity of life anticipate themes characteristic of the canonical Golden Age literature of Spain.

Overshadowed by the prominent figures of the time, the literary contributions of Juan Gutiérrez Rufo are often overlooked. Writing during a time when traditional Spanish verse was giving way to the influence of imported Italian meter and the *tradición de caballería* (tradition of chivalry) was yielding to the cynical tones of mannerist and baroque tendencies, Rufo's work is often characterized by its affinity with the classical tradition. Both of his works stem from classical traditions: the apothegm and epic poetry. Such a designation, however, fails to recognize the works of Rufo as transitory pieces that employ classic models while expressing themes and tendencies advanced by canonical writers such as Góngora, Cervantes, and Quevedo. Although a minor figure in comparison to such names, Rufo deserved the recognition that his contemporaries paid him, and his contributions to the literary culture in Spain merit further examination by modern scholars.

References:

Georges Cirot, "A La Guerra de Granada y la Austríada," *Bulletin Hispanique,* 22 (1920): 149–159;

Elizabeth B. Davis, *Myth and Identity in the Epic of Imperial Spain* (Columbia: University of Missouri Press, 2000), pp. 61–97;

Raymond Foulché-Delbosc, "Authenticité de la Guerra de Granada," *Révue Hispanique,* 35 (1915): 476–538;

Rafael Ramírez de Arellano, *Juan Rufo, jurado de Córdoba: Estudio biográfico y crítico* (Madrid: Hijos de Reus, 1912).

Diego Sánchez de Badajoz

(? – 1552?)

Moses E. Panford Jr.
Virginia Polytechnic Institute and State University

BOOKS: *Farsa sobre el matrimonio, es para representar en bodas* (Medina del Campo: Juan Godinez de Millis, 1530);

Recopilación en metro del Bachiller en la qual por gracioso, cortesano y pastoril estilo se cuentan y de claran muchas figuras y autoridades de la Sagrada Escritura: Ahora nuevamente impreso y dirigido al ilustrísimo Señor Don Gómez Suárez de Figueroa. Con privilegio (Seville: Junto al mesón de la castaña, 1554).

Modern Editions: *Recopilación en metro del bachiller Diego Sánchez de Badajoz*, 2 volumes, edited by Vicente Barrantes (Madrid: Fé, 1882, 1886);

Farsa sobre el matrimonio, in *Obras dramaticas del siglo XVI*, edited by Gabriel Ochoa (Madrid: Clásica español, 1914);

Recopilación en metro del bachiller Diego Sánchez de Badajoz (Sevilla, 1554), edited by the Real Academia Española (Madrid: Tipografía de Archivos, 1929);

Recopilación en metro del bachiller Diego Sánchez de Badajoz, edited by José López Prudencio (Badajoz: Centro de Estudios Extremeños, 1941);

Recopilación en metro (Sevilla, 1554), edited by Frida Weber de Kurlat (Buenos Aires: Universidad de Buenos Aires, Facultad de Filosofía y Letras, 1968);

Farsas, edited by José María Díez Borque (Madrid: Cátedra, 1978);

Farsas, edited by Miguel Angel Pérez Priego (Madrid: Cátedra, 1985).

Edition in English: "Theological Farce," translated by Willis Knapp Jones, in his *Spanish One Act Plays in English: A Comprehensive Anthology of Spanish Drama from the 12th Century to the Present* (Dallas: Tardy, 1934), pp. 31–48.

Diego Sánchez de Badajoz is one of the prominent literary figures of the Spanish Renaissance. He is credited with the most influential contributions to the development of Spanish religious drama in general, and especially to such one-act dramatic genres as the *entremés* (interlude) and the *auto sacramental* (Eucharistic play). He put to various uses the conventional shepherd-clown who functioned as exegete, wise fool, and the channel for social criticism, paving the way for the eventual development of the buffoon. He also contributed to the evolution of ethnic characters such as blacks. His chronologically flexible presentation and "secularization" of Orthodox dogma, the use of prefiguration, allegory, satire, and humorous language, generated interest in theology in his audiences. Although he was not a trained playwright, his natural talent, together with his *converso* (convert from Judaism to Catholicism) or new Christian origin, occupation as clergyman, and pragmatic style, informed his aesthetic and ultimately defined his role in Spanish literary history. His works were habitually staged in Badajoz during Corpus Christi and Christmas festivities.

Little is known about Diego Sánchez's life prior to 1533. He was born toward the end of the fifteenth century, and internal evidence from his works suggests Talavera as his hometown. He signed his *Farsa de la muerte* (Farce of Death) as Diego Sánchez de Talavera, and his *Farsa del Santísimo Sacramento* (Farce of the Holy Sacrament) and *Introito de pescadores* (Introit of Fishermen) evidence great familiarity with the vicinity, where he had relatives. He was neither a relative of the poet Garcí Sánchez de Badajoz nor a member of the noble Sánchez de Badajoz clan.

Like many other literary figures, Sánchez was educated in the Renaissance cultural center of Salamanca as a student of Cardinal Juan Martínez Siliceo, under whom he earned his *bachiller* (bachelor or holder of the general certificate of education). He served as parish priest of Talavera la Real (in the province of Badajoz) from 1533–the year in which his signature first appears in the parish records as "bachiller Diego Sánchez, clérigo" (bachelor Diego Sánchéz, priest)–until 1549, after which there are no records of his signature in the archives. In 1552 he was mentioned as deceased, both in his nephew's letter to Gómez Suárez

First page of Diego Sánchez de Badajoz's 1530 play (Farce about Matrimony), in which a corrupt friar mediates a debate about whether the husband or wife is the superior marriage partner (from Obras dramaticas del siglo XVI, *1914; Thomas Cooper Library, University of South Carolina)*

de Figueroa, the Count of Feria, and in the *privilegio* (copyright) for the original collection of his works.

As was common with many of the writers of the period, the works of Sánchez were published posthumously. In 1552 his nephew Juan de Figueroa obtained the required permission for the publication of the original volume, *Recopilación de farsas y sermones con un confisionario* (Compilation of Farces and Sermons, with a Confessional), which Sánchez had supposedly prepared. The definitive collection of his plays, without the sermons and confessional, was published in Seville in 1554 in the print shop of Juan Canalla, under the title *Recopilación en metro del Bachiller en la qual por gracioso, Cortesano y Pastoril estilo se cuentan y de claran muchas figuras y autoridades de la Sagrada Escritura: Ahora nuevamente impreso y dirigido al ilustrísimo Señor Don Gómez Suárez de Figueroa.*

Con privilegio (Compilation in Verse Form by the "Bachiller," which Narrates and Explains Many Figures and Authorities of the Holy Scriptures in an Amusing, Courtly, and Pastoral Style. Newly Published and Dedicated to His Excellency Sir Gómez Suárez de Figueroa. With Copyright). Figueroa must have deliberately omitted the sermons and confessional because he did not consider them appropriate for inclusion in the extant edition, although he claimed that he published the works that he had been able to find. The rubric *nuevamente impresa* (reprinted) appended to the titles of some of the pieces, suggests that these had been originally published, or had circulated as *sueltas* (individual pieces) even after the publication of *Recopilación en metro* in 1554: *Farsa del rey David* (circa 1560?, Farce of King David), *Farsa sobre el matrimonio* (1530?, 1603?, Farce of Matrimony), and *Farsa del molinero* (1603, Farce of the Miller) are the only extant *sueltas*.

The possibility of tampering by Figueroa has generated considerable debate on the order and chronology of the individual pieces in the *Recopilación en metro*. Sánchez's most productive writing period was between 1525 and 1547. Critics have managed to determine the dates of some individual plays, and the general consensus is that they are chronologically arranged in *Recopilación en metro* and reflect the author's gradual evolution and experience as a playwright. *Recopilación en metro* is mainly known for the twenty-seven plays known as *farsas*. They are variously categorized according to their most prominent themes: for example, *officium pastorum* (pastoral) plays, biblical plays, symbolic and prefigurative (prefiguration of the Eucharist) plays, allegorical plays, hagiographic plays, guild plays, and wedding plays. The hybrid nature of some of them defies categorization, however. For example, *Farsa de la Iglesia* (Farce of the Church) can be classified as either an allegorical or prefigurative play that was most probably presented at Corpus Christi.

For many talented *conversos*, especially those who could not escape to the New World nor join the Church, writing was the refuge of choice. Such writers usually manifested their conformity with the established order by chastising religious minorities and defending the hegemonic ideology. Sánchez's anti-Semitic tendencies are displayed in pieces such as *Farsa de la Iglesia, Farsa de los doctores* (Farce of the Doctors), *Farsa de Salomón* (Farce of Solomon), and *Farsa de Tamar* (Farce of Tamar). *Farsa de la Iglesia* is perhaps the most profound display of Sánchez's anti-Semitism. In it, an old woman dressed in mourning clothes represents the Synagogue (Judaism), while the Church (Christianity) is represented by a beautiful, nicely dressed woman. Synagogue is bitter that Church has usurped her power, while the latter characterizes the former as intransigent. The author highlights the triumph of Christianity over Judaism and Islam, further substantiated through the baptism of the Moor and the shepherd in the play. A final *villancico* (Christmas carol) and *copla* (couplet) also celebrate the triumph of the Holy Scriptures.

Farsa de Salomón is a Christmas play that stages the biblical story of Solomon's Wisdom (1 Kings 3:16–28); a good mother and a bad one represent the Church and the Synagogue, respectively, with the former triumphing over the latter. *Farsa de Tamar,* which was staged at the Feria palace in Zafra, is a dramatization of the biblical story of Judah and Tamar (Genesis 38), in which Tamar is successively married to two of Judah's sons and is widowed without children. Judah does not fulfill his promise to marry her to his third son. She therefore seduces Judah as a prostitute and bears his twin sons. He decides to burn her alive; but after she provides proof of his guilt, he decides to undergo the punishment himself. Unlike the biblical story, Sánchez pardons everybody because Jesus is born. The play ends with a poetic composition in honor of the count of Feria. The author also displays his anti-Semitic tendencies through his condemnation of Tamar's disguise, because it leads to sinful adulterous acts by men who cannot discern the true identity of such women who contravened dress codes. *Farsa de los doctores* is a dramatization of Jesus' appearance at the temple among the doctors (Luke 2:41–52). Although the biblical account does not specify the topics of discussion and names of the doctors, Sánchez incorporates three named doctors and specific Old Testament prophecies regarding the Messiah, whom they all conclude is the boy Jesus, who symbolizes the triumph of Christianity. The devil's appearance onstage reinforces Jesus' power over evil.

In other works, however, Sánchez advocates reconciliation between Christians and Jews. Thus, *Farsa de Tamar* is peculiar because the authorial anti-Semitism is extenuated by the foregrounding of a harmonious coexistence between Old and New Christians, through the birth of Jesus Christ, who will pardon everyone. A similar case is *Farsa de Isaac* (Farce of Isaac), a prefigurative play in which a shepherd serves as commentator. It dramatizes the Old Testament story (Gen. 27:1–40) of how Jacob deceived his father, Isaac, into blessing him instead of his twin brother, Esau. Part of Esau's consolation blessing is that "By your sword you shall live, and you shall serve your brother; but when you break loose, you shall break his yoke from your neck" (Gen. 27:40). The shepherd claims that these words have been fulfilled because Judaism is no longer the dominant religion, and that Jesus' birth ushers in prosperity as reward for good acts and offers reconciliation

between old and new Christians. He also exhorts the audience to accept God through the Scriptures as they hear them because hearing is the only dependable sense.

Farsa de San Pedro (Farce of St. Peter) is a medieval-style debate on the merits of shepherds and fishermen. The author presents the solution through the shepherd: God used the old shepherds (who symbolize the Old Testament) to safeguard the Old Law but used the new fishermen (who symbolize the New Testament) to obtain the Church. Thus, there is interdependence between the two occupations, a relation that points to the authorial reconciliation between Old Christians (Christians of "pure," or non-Jewish, ancestry) and New Christians. This reconciliation is reinforced through the presence of the tax collector, followed by Christ's sending Peter to fish and to use the proceeds to pay taxes. The shepherd exhorts everybody to change his or her ways because of the infernal fire.

Sánchez was overtly critical of dishonest clergymen, in an attempt to negotiate the discomfort associated with New Christians in the ecclesiastical echelons. Such criticism is manifested through the sometimes unfavorable representation of the friars in his plays. The friar in *Farsa de Salomón,* for example, is dishonest and unworthy of his role. He teams up with the shepherd to deceive a prostitute, who plays the role of an innkeeper. The figure of the dishonest friar is also present in *Farsa del colmenero* (Farce of the Beekeeper), *Farsa sobre el matrimonio,* and *Farsa militar* (Military Farce). The first is a Corpus Christi guild/allegorical play in honor of beekeepers. It dramatizes a dispute between a peasant and a shepherd with regard to the merits of their occupations. An apparently dishonest friar settles the dispute by highlighting the virtues of both, especially the beekeeper's work. The shepherd's characteristic clownishness and vulgar language add a touch of entertaining humor to the play. *Farsa sobre el matrimonio* is a wedding play originally published as an individual piece, under the title *Farsa sobre el matrimonio, es para representar en bodas* (Farce of Matrimony, to Be Staged at Weddings), in Medina del Campo in 1530. It is a debate on the superiority of one spouse over the other. By virtue of his religious role, an ultimately corrupt friar manages to settle the dispute through claims that matrimony unites the two spouses into one, with complementary roles. He covets Mencía, who is to be betrothed to his servant Martín. The playwright's criticism against dishonest clergy becomes apparent as the friar's sexual overtures—as in the play on words "para que se la freylemos" (so that we make her a "mother" friar)—become public. In the allegorical Christmas play *Farsa militar,* which was staged at the Feria palace in Zafra, a shepherd plays the double role of presenting the introit and later entering the play proper. The play dramatizes the battle of the flesh, the world, and the devil against spiritual people, who are represented by a friar. Unlike his counterparts in other plays, he is a relatively strong, spiritual person. Although he ultimately succumbs to the devil's temptations, he repents, and his contrition is cause for the Christmas Eve rejoicing with which the play ends.

The author's disrespect toward the clergy was not always kindly received. As indicated in *Farsa de la muerte,* he composed the play in an attempt to appease the clergy of Badajoz, who had been infuriated by his use of the denigrating phrase "Dios mantenga" (literally, "May God maintain you"). The play reinforces the basic Christian tenet that "blessed are the poor, for theirs shall be the kingdom of heaven." After the shepherd's explanation that it is better to be guided by the hand of God, the Christian idea of suffering as an inherent virtue is dramatized through a wretched old man, a boastful, rich, and handsome young man, and Death. Although the old man triumphs over Death, which he prefers to suffering, Death strikes down the young man for his boastful attitude. The farce also honors bricklayers for their useful, hard work, which serves to maintain the world.

The shepherd is a constant figure in the works of Sánchez de Badajoz. His multiple roles vary from deliverer of the prologue, to actor in the body of the play, to foil, trickster, exegete, and inquisitor. His role as exegete is exemplified in *Farsa de la muerte.* In prologues, he usually presents the introits. He often enters the main body of the play in different roles, including that of commentator, such as in *Farsa de Santa Bárbara* (Farce of Saint Barbara), which advocates the emulation of the eponymous saint, who disobeyed her pagan parents and converted to Christianity, thereby gaining the kingdom of God. Contrary to expectation, but in resonance with the authorial ideological objective of championing conversion to Christianity, without harsh consequences, the play does not conform to the hagiography of St. Barbara. The author excludes parts of the legend in which her own father handed her over to a tribunal, ordered her beheaded, and shortly thereafter was struck dead by lightning.

Sánchez often turned the shepherd into the inquisitor of religious minorities. His character denigrates the Moor in *Farsa de la Iglesia.* His questioning of the Christian honesty of the baptized black figure contributed to the eventual representation of the latter as a false Christian and the devil's counterpart in the pre-Lopean theater. This portrayal is most prevalent in Sánchez's *Farsa theologal* (Theological Farce). Although the main themes of the play are the nativity and incarnation of Jesus Christ, the shepherd from the prologue later returns in the body of the play to condemn false Christianity strongly. He questions the faith of Magdalena, a black servant, whose name (together with that of her husband, Francisco) suggests that she had been baptized previously. She is consequently silenced, and both she and her Moorish master are subjected to catechismal instruction. This mode of representation of the black figure is also discernible, to varying degrees, in *Farsa de Moysén* (Farce of Moses), *Farsa de la hechicera* (Farce of the Sorceress), *Farsa de la ventera* (Farce of the Innkeeper), and *Farsa de la fortuna o hado* (Farce of Destiny). Their common denominator is the shepherd's denigration of blacks.

Farsa de Moysén is another Corpus Christi prefigurative play that makes use of both Old and New Testament authority figures to elucidate challenging questions about Christ and the Holy Sacrament. The initial explanations offered are subsequently substantiated through the miraculous resuscitation of a black man as soon as he is given bread and wine. *Farsa de la hechicera* is a wedding play that parodies courtly love by presenting a suicidal courtier. He faints in his attempt to commit suicide, and the shepherd brings a sorceress to attend to him. The devil she invokes scares the shepherd, whose shouts attract the bailiff. The sorceress falsely accuses the shepherd of attempted rape, and he is arrested. Notably, the rejected courtier in turn rejects a black female who attempts to console him. *Farsa de la ventera,* which was staged as part of an unidentified nuptial celebration, censures dishonesty and social evils and warns against their consequences. The innkeeper is a dishonest woman who victimizes people because of their own greed and dishonest intentions. She ignores her black maid's warnings and is consequently swept away by the devil. *Farsa de la fortuna o hado* constitutes a discussion of the injustices of destiny and the justification for the dichotomy between the rich and the poor. The play urges the various classes and social levels to be content with their destiny in order for society to function harmoniously. Their ultimate goal should be to embrace Christianity. Thus, the play also exemplifies Sánchez's defense of the hegemonic ideology that discourages the crossing of social boundaries.

Of the remaining plays, *Farsa de la Natividad* (Farce of the Nativity) dramatizes a rhetorical debate on whether the Holy Conception or Birth (argued by a priest and a friar, respectively) was more joyous to the Virgin Mary. Juan (a shepherd) tricks them into the debate, and Science (the allegorical figure) settles the dispute. The audience is exhorted to refrain from useless conversation and to pursue science–that is, enlightenment.

Farsa moral (Moral Farce) is an allegorical play that dramatizes how the four cardinal virtues rectify human shortcomings. Evil is represented as arrogant and is defeated by all the virtues. As in the biblical account, Job's fortune is restored to him for not succumbing to Evil's enticement. Nebuchadnezzar, on the other hand, is an arrogant king who falls for Evil's malice and loses his wealth until he repents. The Virgin Mary and the infant Jesus appear on stage, with Jesus embodying the Word. All four virtues honor him with offerings in the form of the instruments with which they appeared on stage. Evil is banished, thus illustrating the moral thematic content of the play: the rewards of humility and obedience and the harsh consequences of disobedience.

Farsa racional del libre albedrío (Rational Farce of the Free Will) is an allegorical Christmas farce that dramatizes the battle between the spirit and the flesh, to underline Matt. 26:41: "Stay awake and pray that you may not come into the time of trial; the spirit indeed is willing, but the flesh is weak." Flesh, represented as the Body and second only to God in power, succumbs to the persistent temptations of sensuality. As in other farces, a shepherd offers the prologue and appears in the main play, joining two colleagues, Body and Carefree. The ultimate repentance of Body leads to the Christmas jubilation at the end of the play.

In *Farsa del Santísimo Sacramento* a friar explicates the symbolism in the Holy Sacrament, as well as the symbolic pieces of a priest's robe that endow him with special spiritual powers. At the end of this prefigurative play, Juan, a shepherd-clown, and his companion break into a Christmas song of praise. *Farsa del molinero* is a Corpus Christi prefigurative guild play that serves to explicate certain doubts that a shepherd presents about the Holy Sacrament. His image as a wise fool is evidenced by the apparently silly yet confounding questions he puts to a friar. The latter is able to satisfy the shepherd's infantile curiosity, and therefore, as is typical of Sánchez, the play ends in singing.

Farsa de Santa Susaña (Farce of St. Susanna) is a Corpus Christi prefigurative play staged on a cart in the form of a garden. The first part of the play constitutes a long introit in which a shepherd and a gardener discuss the virtues of good work. It is followed by Susanna's rejection of the sexual advances of two old men, who attempt to rape her. Infuriated by their failure, they proceed to accuse her of illicit sexual relations with a young lad. The prophet David, through his wisdom, is able to detect their false testimony and consequently sentence them to death by stoning. The play ends in joyous singing.

Farsa del rey David is a biblical play for Christmas celebration. It dramatizes the story of David and Goliath and reinforces the Christian teaching of humility. The five stones used by David prefigure Jesus' five wounds. The pastor's sermonic introduction is exempli-

Title page for the standard sixteenth-century edition of Sánchez's theatrical works (Compilation in Verse Form by the Bachiller), published in 1554 (Thomas Cooper Library, University of South Carolina)

fied through David's triumph. The pastor also serves as an observer and commentator in the play; in contrast with the religious theme, his subsequent use of foul language underlines contemporary usage, which in turn indicates the sociocultural makeup of the participatory audience of the festival, the target of the technique that was later formulated as *enseñar deleitando* (playful instruction). The presence of a Portuguese character and the use of Portuguese terms are other demographic indicators of the sociocultural fiber of the province.

Farsa de Abraham (Farce of Abraham) is a Corpus Christi prefigurative play that focuses on the Holy Trinity and the Holy Sacrament, particularly the importance of the solemn preparation for the latter. A shepherd acts as a commentator on Abraham and Sarah's service to three angels. *Farsa del herrero* (Farce of the Blacksmith) is a Corpus Christi prefigurative guild play that honors and explains the inclusion of blacksmiths in the festive procession. Their occupation is described as one of the most important because all manual labor depends on their products. The feeding of a hungry pilgrim underscores the kindness supposedly associated with the occupation. *Farsa de la salutación* (Farce of the Salutation) is a staging of the biblical salutation of the Virgin Mary, which a shepherd uses as a pretext to preach on humility.

Farsa en que se representa un juego de cañas espiritual de virtudes contra vicios (A Farce Which Dramatizes a Spiritual Reed-Spear Tournament between Virtues and Vices), popularly known as *Farsa del juego de cañas* (Farce of the Reed-Spear Tournament), is a Christmas play in which the author adapts the *juego de las cañas* (a game in which opposing teams throw reed spears at each other) into a spiritual game in which St. John the Baptist preaches the good news and the seven virtues triumph over the seven deadly sins, thus highlighting the virtue of Christian life.

Recopilación en metro comprises more than the twenty-seven farces with which it is usually associated. *Danza de los pecados* (Dance of Sins) is the only play in the collection that is not specifically titled a *farsa*. Inserted after *Farsa del juego de cañas,* with which it shares a common theme, it is a dramatization of how the seven deadly sins dominate mankind. In the end all the allegoric figures of the seven sins flee from a remorseful Adam, the protagonist. The concluding remark from a shepherd is that divine clemency helps repentance turn the *vencido* (defeated) into a *vencedor* (victor). The use of dramatic poetry in this play and its later chronological appearance in the collection signal Sánchez's gradual evolution as a playwright, just as the relatively simple plots, props, and stage directions of the earlier pieces are indicators of his lack of professional training. The dramatist Lope de Vega's generation, in the latter half of the sixteenth century, finally made dramatic poetry the norm in the Spanish theater of the era.

There are also twelve other poetic compositions with varied themes in *Recopilación en metro*. Of these lyrical pieces, "Montería espiritual" (Spiritual Hunt) is an allegorical representation that advocates the use of reason to dominate the will or carnal desires, while "Matraca de jugadores" (Players' Tricks) criticizes the "plague," or addiction to games, with (Spanish) cards and dice as examples. Each of the four suits of Spanish cards, golden coins, swords, goblets, and clubs, are personified as agents of avarice, destruction of lives, vanity, and wretchedness, respectively. In "Romance sobre la sarna" (Romance of Scabies), Sánchez likens scabies to the Trojan War and ultimately characterizes the Greeks as political and religious enemies who wage war and turn life on Earth into "un purgatorio en la tierra / de gran llanto" (a purgatory on Earth / of great lamentation). The titles of "Romance de nuestra Señora" (Romance of Our Lady) and "Romance de la Pasión" (Romance of the Passion) are suggestive of their content. *Introito de pescadores, Introito de los siete pecados* (Introit

of the Seven Sins), and *Introito de herradores* (Introit of Blacksmiths) were probably meant to be staged at the beginning of other pieces with which they share thematic similarity: *Farsa de San Pedro, Danza de los pecados* or *Farsa del juego de cañas,* and *Farsa del herrero,* respectively.

The remaining pieces in *Recopilacion en metro* are works composed to be sung. "Un invitatorio" (An Invitational), which advocates eternal worship of the Lord, and "Otro cantar" (Another Song) were supposed to be sung by the acolytes or children's choir during Corpus Christi to underscore the Holy Trinity and the Holy Sacrament. "Coplas a San Juan Baptista" (Couplets to St. John the Baptist) is a six-stanza ballad in honor of the saint. "Coplas a una monja . . . nombrada Santi Spiritus" (Couplets to a Nun . . . Called Holy Spirit) stresses virginal purity and "pobreza de corazón" (poverty of heart) as the two most fundamental advantages of religious over secular misery. Its last stanza advocates religious good works as the justification for equality among all Christians. Thus, the title caption, which indicates the nun's senior standing in religion, becomes suggestive: Old Christians are implicitly compared to New Christians, with regard to the "purity of blood" that preoccupied the author.

As one of the most prominent dramatists of his time, Diego Sánchez de Badajoz is often mentioned in the same breath as other early Spanish Renaissance playwrights such as Juan del Encina, Bartolomé Torres Naharro, and Lucas Fernández. Despite his misleading adopted last name, de Badajoz, it is known that he hailed from Talavera and was a New Christian. His Renaissance education in Salamanca shines through his dramatic aesthetic. The precarious publication practices of his time and the posthumous publication of his works make it difficult to establish the exact dates of his individual pieces. Nonetheless, the literary qualities of his production, his pragmatism, his religious ideology, and his contribution to the evolution of Spanish religious drama stand out. On one front, he modified the liturgical drama, adapting it to the outdoor processional Corpus Christi staging and including the vulgate and the common person as his target audience. On the other, he upheld certain traditional Christian tenets such as the Holy Trinity and the Holy Sacrament, while advocating reconciliation between Old and New Christians. As was prevalent with other new Christian writers, Sánchez negotiated his "tainted blood" origin through the adoption of dominant religious ideology, the defense of the hierarchical structuring of society, and the display of anti-Semitic tendencies, as evidenced in plays such as *Farsa theologal, Farsa de la Iglesia,* and *Farsa de la fortuna o hado.* Perhaps his most important contribution to the development of Spanish drama in general was the conversion of the traditional shepherd into an exegete whom he used not only as advocate but also as the channel of attack on various sectors of society. Thus, he paved the way for the buffoon figure and the later development of one-act genres such as the *entremés* and the *auto sacramental*.

References:

John Brotherton, *The Pastor-Bobo in the Spanish Theatre before the Time of Lope de Vega* (London: Tamesis, 1975);

James P. Wickersham Crawford, "Early Spanish Wedding Plays," *Romanic Review*, 12 (1921): 370–384;

Crawford, "The Pastor and the *Bobo* in Spanish Religious Drama of the XVI Century," *Romanic Review*, 2 (1911): 376–401;

Patrick Gallagher, *The Life and Works of Garci Sánchez de Badajoz* (London: Tamesis, 1968);

Edward Glaser, "Referencias antisemitas en la literature peninsular de la Edad de Oro," *Nueva Revista de Filología Hispánica*, 8 (1954): 39–62;

Fernando González Ollé, "*La farsa del Santísimo Sacramento* y su significado en el desarrollo del Auto Sacramental," *Revista de Literatura*, 35 (1969): 127–165;

Donna Gustafson, "The Role of the Shepherd in the Pre-Lopean Drama of Diego Sánchez de Badajoz," *Bulletin of the Comediantes*, 22 (1973): 5–13;

Gustafson, "Towards the *Auto Sacramental:* Eucharistic Prefiguration in the *farsas* of Diego Sánchez de Badajoz," *Hispanófila*, 2 (1975): 79–94;

Elena Hueber, "Rasgos estilísticos significativos en la *Farsa de la muerte* de Diego Sánchez de Badajoz," in *Homenaje al Instituto de Filología y Literaturas Hispánicas "Dr. Amado Alonso" en su cincuentenario (1923–1973)* (Buenos Aires: Instituto de Filología, 1975), pp. 122–129;

William Shaffer Jack, *The Early Entremés in Spain: The Rise of a Dramatic Form* (Philadelphia: University of Pennsylvania, 1923);

José López Prudencio, *Diego Sánchez de Badajoz: Estudio crítico, biográfico y bibliográfico* (Madrid: Tipografía de la Revista de Archivos, 1915);

Raquel Minian de Alfie, "Algunas versiones del tema bíblico de Susana en el teatro de los siglos XVI y XVII," *Filología*, 15 (1971): 183–204;

Moses E. Panford Jr., "Diego Sánchez de Badajoz: El discurso religioso hegemónico y la marginación de los negros," *Revista de Estudios Hispánicos*, 32 (1998): 57–73;

Miguel Angel Pérez Priego, *El teatro de Diego Sánchez de Badajoz* (Cáceres: Universidad de Extremadura, 1982);

Celina Sabor de Cortázar, "*La Farsa de la fortuna o hado* de Diego Sánchez de Badajoz y su sentido trascendente," *Filología*, 13 (1968–1969): 329–347;

Sabor de Cortázar, "Un tema teológico en Diego Sánchez de Badajoz: Las potencias del alma y su acción recíproca," in *Studia Hispanica in honorem R. Lapesa*, 3 volumes, edited by Eugenio de Bustos and others (Madrid: Cátedra-Seminario Menéndez Pidal/Gredos, 1972–1975), II: 564–572;

Bruce W. Wardropper, *Introducción al teatro religioso del Siglo de Oro: Evolución del Auto Sacramental antes de Calderón* (Salamanca: Anaya, 1967);

Frida Weber de Kurlat, "Gil Vicente y Diego Sánchez de Badajoz: A propósito del *Auto da sebila Casandra* y de la *Farsa del juego de cañas*," *Filología*, 9 (1963): 119–162;

Elaine C. Wertheimer, "Sánchez de Badajoz and the Reconciliation of the Two Testaments," *Romanische Forschungen*, 91 (1979): 24–42;

Ann E. Wiltrout, "Antisemitism and Christian Reconciliation in the Theater of Diego Sánchez de Badajoz," *American Hispanist*, 3, no. 20 (1977): 11–13;

Wiltrout, *A Patron and a Playwright in Renaissance Spain: The House of Feria and Diego Sánchez de Badajoz* (London: Tamesis / Wolfeboro, N.H.: Longwood, 1987).

St. Teresa of Ávila

(28 March 1515 – 4 October 1582)

Susan M. Smith
Hampden-Sydney College

BOOKS: *Regla primitiva y constituciones de las monjas descalças de la Orden de Nuestra Señora la virgen María del Monte Carmelo* (Salamanca: Herederos de Mathías Gast, 1581);

Tratado que escribió la Madre Teresa de Jesús a las hermanas religiosas (Evora: Viuda de Andrés de Burgos, 1583)–comprises *Camino de perfección* and *Avisos espirituales;*

Libro llamado castillo interior, o las moradas que escribió la Madre Teresa de Jesús, fundadora de las descalças carmelitas para ellas, por mandado de su superior y confesor, compiled by Fray Luis de León (Salamanca: Foquel, 1588)–comprises *Castillo interior* and *Exclamaciones;*

Los libros de la Madre Teresa de Jesús, fundadora de los monasterios de monjas y frayles Carmelitas descalços de la primera regla, 3 volumes, compiled by León (Salamanca: Foquel, 1588)–comprises volume 1, *Libro de la vida* and *Relaciones espirituales;* volume 2, *Camino de perfeccón* and *Avisos;* and volume 3, *Castillo interior* and *Exclamaciones o meditaciones del alma a su Dios;*

Libro primero de la Madre Teresa de Jesús con un tratado de su vida (Saragossa: Tabano, 1591); translated by William Malone, S.J., as *The lyf of the Mother Teresa of Jesus, foundresse of the monasteries of the descalced or bare-footed Carmelite nunnes and fryers, of the first rule* (Antwerp: Jaye, 1611);

Libro de las fundaciones de las hermanas Descalças Carmelitas, que escribió la Madre Fundadora Teresa de Jesús, edited by Fray Gerónimo Gracián (Brussels: Velpio, 1610);

Conceptos del amor de Dios escritos por la Beata Madre Theresa de Jesús, sobre algunas palabras de los Cantares de Salomón, annotated by Gracián (Brussels: Velpio & Antonio, 1611);

Obras de la gloriosa Madre Santa Teresa de Jesús, fundadora de la reforma de la Orden de Nuestra Señora del Carmen (Madrid: Joseph Doblado, 1778).

Modern Editions: *Poesías de Santa Teresa de Jesús entresca-das de las diversas ediciones de sus obras,* edited by R. P. Francisco Jiménez Campaña, Flores de la mística

St. Teresa of Ávila (portrait by Fray Juan de la Miserias; from Bradley Smith, Spain: A History in Art, *1966; Thomas Cooper Library, University of South Carolina)*

española (Madrid: Librería de Gregorio del Amo, 1913);

Obras de Sta. Teresa de Jesús, 9 volumes, edited by R. P. Silverio de Santa Teresa, C.D. (Burgos, Spain: El Monte Carmelo, 1915–1924);

Obras completas de Santa Teresa de Jesús, 3 volumes, edited by Fray Efrén de la Madre de Dios, O.C.D., and Fray Otilio del Niño Jesús, O.C.D. (Madrid: Biblioteca de Autores Católicos, 1951–1959).

Editions in English: *The Way of Perfection and Conceptions of Divine Love,* translated by John Dalton (London: Dolman, 1852; New York: Dunigan, 1852);

The Interior Castle; or, The Mansions, translated by Dalton (London: Jones, 1852);

Book of the Foundations, translated by Dalton (London: Jones, 1853);

The Book of Foundations of St. Teresa of Jesus, with the Visitation of Nunneries, the Rule and Constitutions, translated by David Lewis (London: Baker, 1913; New York: Benziger, 1913);

Minor Works of St. Teresa: Conceptions of the Love of God, Exclamations, Maxims and Poems of St. Teresa of Jesus, translated by the Benedictines of Stanbrook (London: Baker, 1913; New York: Benziger, 1913);

The Complete Works of Saint Teresa of Jesus, 3 volumes, edited by E. Allison Peers (London & New York: Sheed & Ward, 1944–1946);

Way of Perfection by St. Teresa of Jesus, translated by Alice Alexander (Westminster, Md.: Newman, 1946; Cork, Ireland: Mercier, 1946);

The Life of Teresa of Jesus, edited and translated by Peers (Garden City, N.Y.: Doubleday, 1960);

Interior Castle, translated by Peers (Garden City, N.Y.: Doubleday, 1961);

The Collected Works of St. Teresa of Ávila, 3 volumes, edited by Kieran Kavanaugh and Otilio Rodríguez (Washington, D.C.: Institute of Carmelite Studies, 1976–1985).

The Catholic Church of sixteenth-century Spain restricted women to roles of subservience and obedience to male authorities. Therefore, for a nun to rise to a position of power and influence would be highly unlikely. St. Teresa of Ávila, however, was an exceptional woman, a religious reformer and a writer. Twenty-five years after taking her vows, she began to write at the request of her confessors and spiritual advisers. She wrote in an effort to explain her practice of mental prayer and her visions. Later, she continued to write to guide other nuns in their spiritual journeys. Her works include her autobiography and many manuscripts on mysticism, biblical interpretation, and mental prayer. She wrote major theological treatises that continue to be required reading for students of theology and Counter Reformation history. Not only a writer, she was also a woman of action as leader of the reform movement of the Carmelite Order. The new order became known as the Discalced, or Barefoot, Carmelites because they wore no shoes, or only *alpargatas* (hemp sandals), as an outward sign of their ascetic rule. They lived in strict enclosure and practiced rigorous obedience to the vows of poverty and humility. St. Teresa established eighteen convents and monasteries throughout Spain for the Discalced Order. She was beatified in 1614, just thirty-two years after her death, and was canonized in 1622 with the name of St. Teresa

of Ávila. In 1970 Pope Paul VI named her a doctor of the church, the first woman to receive the title. Her remarkable life of extensive writing, travel, and political and religious influence is all the more remarkable for a woman in sixteenth-century Spain.

Teresa de Ahumada y Cepada was born into a family of the minor nobility in Ávila, Spain, early in the sixteenth century. Her social standing, however, was compromised by religious tensions of the period. Those who passed the test of *limpieza de sangre* (pure blood), that is, old Christians of long standing without the taint of Jewish or Moorish blood, were perceived as superior to the new Christian, or *converso,* who had converted from Judaism or Islam or descended from such converts. Elite families of means guarded the secret of any unorthodox ancestors within the family, both for their protection and to forestall obstacles to their receiving promotions in social position, making good marriage matches, and holding important offices in the government of the town or region.

Teresa's grandfather Juan Sánchez of Toledo was Jewish by birth but converted to Christianity. Sánchez de Toledo, nevertheless, was later punished by the Inquisition as a *judaizante,* or follower of Jewish practices. His punishment was to march through the streets of Toledo with his family every Friday for seven weeks dressed in robes of shame. Teresa's father, Alonso Sánchez de Cepada, suffered from such a public penance and decided to move from Toledo and start over in a new town. He chose Ávila, where he soon prospered in the wool and silk trade. He further pursued ties to prestigious old Christian families through marriage, and his past was soon obliterated. In fact, it was not until the 1940s that the Jewish roots of St. Teresa came to light.

Teresa was born on 28 March 1515 to Alonso de Cepeda and Doña Beatriz de Ahumada, Alonso's second wife. She was one of twelve children; the two oldest were from Alonso's first marriage, which ended with the early death of his wife. From her childhood, Teresa possessed a zeal for adventure, having inherited her mother's interest in romantic chivalric tales combined with the reading of saints' lives. The oft-told tale of her intent to run away with her brother Rodrigo on a personal crusade to convert the Moors, or die in the attempt, sets the tone for her life—spirited, deeply religious, and daring to go beyond the traditional confines of her sixteenth-century woman's world.

With the death of her mother in 1528, when Teresa was thirteen years old, she was left under her father's care and guidance. All biographers agree that by her teens Teresa was attractive and lively, involved in parties and social functions, and interested in beautiful clothes. When she was sixteen, rumors began to cir-

Anonymous seventeenth-century painting of Teresa at age seven, along with her eleven-year-old brother Rodrigo, whom she convinced to run away with her on a mission to convert the Moors (from Cathleen Medwick, Teresa of Ávila: The Progress of a Soul, *1999; Thomas Cooper Library, University of South Carolina)*

culate about her flirtatious behavior, alarming her father with the potential for scandal. In Teresa's autobiography, which skips quickly over her early years, she remarks only that when she was young, she almost lost her honor. The Spanish word for honor, *honra,* has many connotations, including family pride, nobility, or public reputation. For a beautiful, teenage girl, loss of honor could also suggest loss of chastity. There is much disagreement on exactly what Teresa meant by her comment regarding her honor, since she does not explain further. Over the centuries, the different intents of her biographers have influenced the interpretations of this remark. Her contemporary hagiographers, who concentrated on relating early signs of saintliness, passed over this minor aspect of her life. More recent feminists have searched for the flesh-and-blood woman behind the mystical saint, and a few have declared a

clear case for a sexual affair. Whatever the real story, this brush with dishonor caused sufficient anxiety for her father to result in sending her off in 1531 to a convent school to be under the protection and watchful eyes of the Augustinian nuns.

This period was a decisive one in the life of sixteen-year-old Teresa. At first, she was strongly against becoming a nun. Although impressed by the austere practices followed by the fourteen nuns of her small convent of Our Lady of Grace, she thought it too strict. The next year she became ill and was sent to the house of a devout uncle, Don Pedro, to recuperate. His large library offered her spiritual readings, and in conversations with her uncle about her reading she came to see her world of wealth and privilege as vanity. Although she still resisted becoming a nun, she convinced herself to enter the Carmelite Order at the Convent of the Incarnation in Ávila in 1535, more out of fear for her soul than love for God, as she says in her autobiography. She was twenty years old.

The Convent of the Incarnation differed greatly from the strict convent of Our Lady of Grace. It had a more relaxed atmosphere where many aristocratic daughters found a home. In fact, several friends and acquaintances of Teresa already lived there. Since the modification of the original Carmelite rule of poverty in 1432, the nuns were no longer required to renounce worldly possessions. Aristocratic social codes were observed, and the higher-born women continued to be addressed by title and live in private quarters rather than the dormitories of the lower-born women. Teresa was addressed as Doña Teresa rather than Sister Teresa, for example. Jodi Bilinkoff, in *The Ávila of Saint Teresa: Religious Reform in a Sixteenth-century City* (1989), provides an extensive description of Teresa's life at the Convent of the Incarnation. Bilinkoff writes that she enjoyed all the comforts her family wealth could afford. Her father had provided a generous annual donation in addition to a considerable dowry when she entered. She had a private apartment of two floors that included facilities for cooking. Other female relatives lived with her, and her parlor became the meeting place for a large circle of friends and relatives. Since her early years at the Convent of the Incarnation were prior to the edict of enclosure issued by the Council of Trent, which required all nuns to be cloistered, it was not unusual during the early sixteenth century for the Carmelite nuns to spend time living with family or with wealthy women requesting visits of extended periods of time to provide spiritual guidance or consolation. The nuns always answered their calls for assistance, as these wealthy aristocrats might well become benefactors of the convent.

In 1538 Teresa again fell ill and was sent to her uncle to recuperate. During this second sojourn, she read Francisco de Osuna's *Tercera parte del libro llamado abecedario espiritual* (1527, Third Part of the Book Called Spiritual Alphabet), an introduction to spiritual devotion. This work includes a description of the mystical prayer of recollection, that is, a quietness or emptying of the mind awaiting God's will. Over the next two decades this concept of mental prayer transformed Teresa from a relaxed nun into the reformed practitioner of mysticism, leading to raptures and trances that changed the course of her life. While living with her uncle for a second time Teresa's physical condition worsened, and she returned to her father's house in Ávila, where she lapsed into a coma for three days. After awakening, she continued to suffer almost complete paralysis for the next three years. During this trauma she gave up mental prayer, returned to the Convent of the Incarnation in 1540, and slipped back into the relaxed order and her former social life. She continued to read works such as the *Confessiones* (397–401, Confessions) of St. Augustine and increasingly became dissatisfied with the Carmelite Order. By 1544 she again took up prayer, and, as she would relate in her autobiography, she continued to search for guidance from a confessor or spiritual director but could not find anyone who understood her.

Sometime in the mid 1540s Teresa experienced her first divine revelation. She saw Jesus Christ watching her with disapproval, and she began to see her attachment to worldly things as a hindrance to complete devotion to God. During the next ten years, her visions became more frequent as she devoted more time to mental prayer, listening for the will of God. Still fearing, however, that her visions might be more diabolical than divine, a common accusation against women mystics at the time because of several famous cases of fraud, she sought reassurance. Prevailing belief was that supernatural phenomena should be dismissed as delusions or other mental illnesses. This belief applied especially to women, who were considered weak, lacking in intelligence, and easy prey for satanic forces. One of Teresa's acquaintances, a respected preacher of Ávila, referred her to the fathers of the newly formed Society of Jesus, who were familiar with the concept of mental prayer and noted for spiritual discernment; they provided the knowledgeable and sympathetic confessors Teresa needed. Father Diego de Cetina, the first of many confessors during her life, determined her visions were from God and not the devil and encouraged her to continue praying.

There is some disagreement about the exact date, but most scholars give 1554 as the year Teresa experienced a profound conversion, sometimes referred to as her second conversion. Standing before an *Ecce Homo,* a sculpture of Christ as the wounded and suffer-

ing Man of Sorrows, she felt a strong connection to the humanity of Jesus. Thinking that Christ, in his most vulnerable moment, might accept her, she felt an intense need to offer comfort. This conversion marks the beginning of her mystical life and an increase in the frequency of the episodes of visions and voices. Falling ill once again, she convalesced this time at the home of a rich young widow, Doña Guiomar de Ulloa, sister of a nun at the Convent of the Incarnation. The friendship begun during her illness continued throughout their lives, as evidenced by the many letters exchanged between them. During three years at Guiomar's house, Teresa was able to practice prayer and contemplation in more-effective seclusion than in her rooms at the convent. With the help of Baltazar Alvarez, a young Jesuit assigned as her spiritual director, she further developed her ideas about mental prayer. In her autobiography she reports that while she was in a state of rapture God commanded her ("No longer do I want you to converse with men, but with angels") and that these words gave her the freedom and strength to do what she could not have done alone. Shortly thereafter she returned to the Convent of the Incarnation, where she continued to experience raptures, trances, and levitations.

This time was a difficult one for Teresa, since the many mystical texts available in the vernacular in the first half of the sixteenth century were taken out of circulation. With the publication of the first *Index Librorum Prohibitor* (Index of Prohibited Books) in 1559, and subsequent censorship by the Inquisition of many books published after that date, works on mental prayer were scarce, those written in Spanish rarer still, and books by women disappeared completely. The Inquisition strongly discouraged the reading of vernacular literature by women and laymen and punished severely those found practicing mental prayer. At this time, in 1560, Teresa had her most profound mystical experience, called the Transverberation or Transfixion. The experience has also become the most famous of her raptures since it is depicted in Gian Lorenzo Bernini's statue called *L'estasi di Santa Teresa* (1647–1652, The Ecstasy of St. Teresa) in the Church of Santa María della Vittoria in Rome. An angel appeared with a fiery arrow and pierced Teresa's heart. As the arrow was withdrawn she felt an intense burning desire for God. From that time on she devoted herself to serving God and saving souls. During the next twenty years, Teresa wrote her entire body of work while simultaneously heading the reform of the Carmelite Order and founding eighteen convents for Discalced Carmelites.

Teresa solidified her ideas for reform during her stay at the home of Guiomar. She was convinced that it was essential to return to a life of poverty and austerity, as was the original rule of the Carmelite Order. She

Statue by Gian Lorenzo Bernini depicting Teresa's 1560 mystical experience, in which an angel pierced her heart with a fiery arrow, instilling in her an intense desire for God (Church of Santa María della Vittoria, Rome; from Robert T. Petersson, The Art of Ecstasy: Teresa, Bernini and Crashaw, *1970; Thomas Cooper Library, University of South Carolina)*

believed that silence and solitude were crucial for progress in prayer and that the social life of the Convent of the Incarnation limited spiritual growth. As Gillian T. W. Ahlgren writes in her *Teresa of Ávila and the Politics of Sanctity* (1996), Teresa felt called "to reformulate religious life so that it would support the nun's contemplative vocation." Furthermore, she felt that she had a divine charge, that both the reform and the founding of new convents were undertaken at God's command. She argued before church authorities that reform could instill a stronger discipline among nuns as well as greater devotion to the will of God. Such reform could, therefore, strengthen the Catholic Church against the heresy of the Protestant Reformation.

Teresa's proposal to found a convent with the intention of embracing poverty and refusing endowments by benefactors caused considerable problems with civic and religious authorities. Town leaders feared the new convent would become a financial bur-

den if it did not have an endowment. The Carmelites at the Convent of the Incarnation anticipated a reduction in alms given to them and were also hostile to Teresa's austerity as reflecting badly on their relatively easy life. Teresa had the support, however, of her new confessor, the Dominican Fray Pedro Ibáñez, and used as a model the recent reforms of the Franciscan Order begun in 1540 by the ascetic Pedro de Alcántara. The process for receiving a permit and license dragged on, and when Teresa was about to compromise with the city fathers and accept a private endowment to get started, Alcántara appeared to her in a vision and insisted she not do so. She continued to press for permission to establish the convent without an endowment, and in August 1562 she won her case in the courts. She received authorization from Rome to found the Convent of St. Joseph. In order to avoid the class distinctions that so disrupted the spiritual order at the Convent of the Incarnation, as Bilinkoff argues, Teresa accepted nuns for their moral virtue, not their dowries; no preference was given to those who claimed special privilege because of their lineage. Teresa remained at the Convent of the Incarnation for a short time while petitioning to be allowed to join the four nuns at the Convent of St. Joseph. She and two other nuns from the Convent of the Incarnation ultimately received permission, and with the move to the Convent of St. Joseph, Teresa, who was given the name Teresa of Jesus, began a new phase in her religious life.

In 1562 Teresa completed the first draft of her autobiography—first published in 1591 under the title *Libro primero de la Madre Teresa de Jesús con un tratado de su vida* (translated as *The lyf of the Mother Teresa of Jesus, foundresse of the monasteries of the descalced or bare-footed Carmelite nunnes and fryers, of the first rule,* 1611)—which she had begun the previous year at the request of an old friend, Fray García de Toledo, to whom she addressed the text. García de Toledo had encouraged Teresa to record her experiences and her methods of prayer. She sent him the first draft, to which he proposed some changes and asked her to expand on her visions and other communications from God. In this regard, Teresa had to maintain a delicate balance, describing God's words as directives to her to be carried out through the mediation of the church. In other words, she received locutions (messages from God) but would only act on them after being given clerical authority. Teresa repeatedly convinced the ecclesiastical authorities to permit her continued activities of writing and reform by the sincerity and humility with which she described God's communications with her.

In her autobiography, as in her other major works, Teresa employs a conversational tone, expressing her self-doubts and chronicling her failures. For example, she calls herself a *mujercilla,* a mere woman, without special talent or learning. In the prologue to *Libro primero de la Madre Teresa de Jesús con un tratado de su vida* Teresa speaks of obedience and makes clear that she writes because she was ordered to so do by superiors. The text can be divided into three parts. The first ten chapters cover the period from birth to age thirty-nine. She briefly describes her childhood and adolescence and, in more depth, her early years as a nun. She looks back on her struggles to commit herself completely to God, to be accepted by God, and yet to be accepted still in the world of her aristocratic connections. Patterned after Augustine's *Confessiones,* Teresa emphasizes her weakness, vanity, and pride. She credits God with providing good companions such as her uncle Don Pedro, and a particular nun at the Augustinian Convent school for her eventual deliverance from a sinful life.

The middle chapters provide a digression into mystical theology. This segment is an addition requested by Fray García, who wanted more detail about Teresa's experiences in prayer. As she wrote about prayer, especially mental prayer, the pressure exerted by inquisitorial censorship obligated her to take great care. Ahlgren concludes that Teresa's influence and authority often escaped censure through her insistence on obedience and humility and her proclamations of unworthiness. Despite the prohibition in the 1559 *Index Librorum Prohibitor* against writing about mystical theology, Teresa was able to discuss the subject in this section of her work. She describes the stages of prayer through water imagery, as Mary E. Giles explains in her article on Teresa for *Great Thinkers of the Western World* (1992), by "making the valuable distinction between watering the garden of the soul by one's own effort, which is mental prayer or meditation, and having the garden watered by the Holy Spirit, which is contemplation."

The manuscript ends with a return to Teresa's life in chapters 23 through 40, including the difficulties encountered in the foundation of the Convent of St. Joseph. These last chapters bring the reader full circle. Rowan Williams, in *Teresa of Ávila* (1991), connects the opening and closing sections in this way: "If chapters 1 to 10 describe God's victory over Teresa's weakness, 23 to 40 describe God's victory *through* Teresa's weakness over the skepticism and hostility of the religious establishment." Teresa began writing her autobiography before the Convent of St. Joseph was approved. She completed revisions and additions after the resolution of litigation and controversy between herself and civic and church leaders. Her manuscript was circulated among several advisers in 1565 and approved to be copied, but not for wider circulation. Teresa had hoped, at least, to offer her own experience as a text for the reformed Carmelites, even though the spiritual litera-

ture that had provided guidance for her was now banned by inquisitorial censorship. Her superiors, however, felt that other nuns should not read Teresa's autobiography because of the personal details of her experiences.

With the founding of the Convent of St. Joseph, a new set of operating procedures was required, and in 1562 Teresa was authorized to draw up the documents for Discalced Carmelites. To this end, in 1563 she completed work on *Regla primitiva y constituciones de las monjas descalças de la Orden de Nuestra Señora la virgen María del Monte Carmelo* (Primitive Rule and Constitutions of the Discalced Nuns of the Order of Our Lady the Virgin Mother of Mount Carmel, 1581; translated as "Rule and Constitutions" in *The Book of Foundations of St. Teresa of Jesus, with the Visitation of Nunneries, the Rule and Constitutions,* 1913), in which she reverts to the stricter, primitive Carmelite rule by adding elements from edicts by the Council of Trent and introducing her own beliefs about the contemplative life. The Discalced Carmelites were to observe enclosure, cut ties with their families, ignore class status, and live by alms alone. Through poverty they would gain autonomy not possible when receiving payments from the elite, who expected, in reciprocity, special favors such as prayers and a privileged place for their daughters.

According to this book, the nuns' day was divided between prayer and work. Teresa believed that idleness was sinful, and even during the recreation hour everyone was required to be sewing or weaving while they talked. During disciplinary meetings once a week offenses were read aloud and penalties assigned. More than one-third of the book deals with transgressions and the penance required. Teresa distinguishes misdemeanors from more-serious faults. For example, less-serious offenses include arriving late for meals or prayers, making a mistake in reading or singing, or making noise in the dormitory, while more-grievous errors include refusing to do a penance, acquiring personal possessions, or spreading malicious gossip.

Teresa had been greatly saddened, as she writes in her autobiography, with the loss of books on meditation, contemplation, and mental prayer as a result of inquisitorial censorship. Only those texts written in Latin, and therefore accessible to learned men, had been allowed since 1559. One of Teresa's purposes in founding the new convent and reforming the rules and constitutions was to allow for women to seek spiritual perfection. She knew from her own struggles during her first twenty years as a nun the value of guiding texts, and so she began to prepare treatises to help her sisters. In this spirit, between 1565 and 1567 she wrote *Tratado que escribió la Madre Teresa de Jesús a las hermanas religiosas* (Treatise Written by Mother Teresa of Jesus to Her

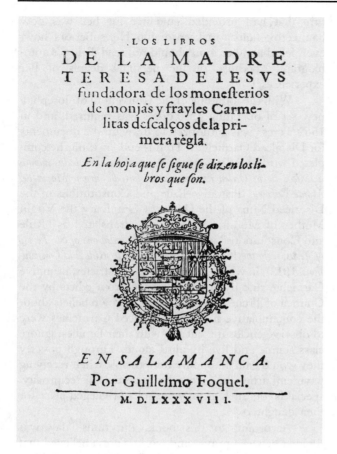

Title page for the first posthumous edition of Teresa's works (from Emmanuel Renault, Ste Thérèse d'Ávila et l'experience mystique, *1970; Thomas Cooper Library, University of South Carolina)*

Religious Sisters, 1583; translated as "The Way of Perfection" in *The Way of Perfection and Conceptions of Divine Love,* 1852), a work commonly referred to as *Camino de perfección* (Way of Perfection), and *Conceptos del amor de Dios escritos por la Beata Madre Theresa de Jesús, sobre algunas palabras de los Cantares de Salomón* (1611; translated as "Conceptions of Divine Love" in *The Way of Perfection and Conceptions of Divine Love).*

The dating of *Camino de perfección* is uncertain with regard to the two extant manuscripts of this text (the Escorial manuscript and the Valladolid manuscript). General consensus suggests that the first version, the Escorial manuscript, probably dates from 1565 or 1566; the second, the Valladolid manuscript, from 1566 or 1567. According to E. Allison Peers, a scholar, translator, and editor of Teresa's work, the Valladolid manuscript, edited by Teresa herself, is the version that she wished to be the definitive one since she had many copies made for friends and spiritual daughters. Peers also observes that the editing done by Teresa greatly improves the clarity and precision of the work. Most

printings of *Camino de perfección,* beginning with the first in 1583, follow the Valladolid manuscript.

Camino de perfección is probably the most easily understood of Teresa's works and can be read with profit not only by those in the cloister; it also has served as a guide on prayer to millions of lay readers. Except for a few sections, there is little mystical description or vocabulary. The book was written at the request of Teresa's sisters in the Convent of St. Joseph, who knew she had discussed prayer in her autobiography. Since the Carmelite superiors did not believe it suitable for other nuns to read Teresa's autobiography, Father Domingo Báñez, one of her confessors, asked her to write another book dealing only with the life of prayer. Therefore, in this work the language is simple and familiar and directed to the specific audience of women she knew well and with whom she had lived for several years.

Aware, as always, of inquisitorial censorship, Teresa makes clear in the preface her unconditional obedience to the Roman Catholic Church and the orthodoxy of her faith. She insists that she will address only elementary matters appropriate for women, thus anticipating possible objections to a woman teaching about prayer. Knowing her own weaknesses and being concerned for the spiritual health of her sisters, she states that she simply wishes to share some of her experiences. In the forty-two chapters of this book, Teresa distinguishes mental from vocal prayer (recitation of set prayers); she offers a concrete example of how to practice the former based on meditation on the Lord's Prayer, an example of the latter.

The first fifteen chapters of *Camino de perfección* explain Teresa's reasons for founding reformed convents and further expound on some parts of *Regla primitiva y constituciones de las monjas descalças de la Orden de Nuestra Señora la virgen María del Monte Carmelo.* She also stresses the importance of the vows of poverty and humility, the need for equal love among the sisters without "special friends," and the requirement for detachment from the world and its beliefs about social position, lineage, and honor. Following these precepts leads one along the way of perfection. Chapters 16 through 26 discuss prayer and contemplation. Teresa teaches the best kind of prayer according to her experience, defends women's right to mental prayer, and provides guidance to achieve union with God for those so gifted. Chapters 27 through 42 offer a concrete example of the synthesis of vocal and mental prayer in a meditation on the seven petitions of the Lord's Prayer.

In *Camino de perfección* Teresa writes to her sisters and daughters in religious spheres and to women who have been told they are incapable of intellectual prayer and should stick to sewing and leave meditation and contemplation to educated male theologians. She includes a list of the arguments against women, such as their susceptibility to illusion and misunderstanding. Church authorities, she writes, say it is better that the women restrict themselves to the Our Father and the Hail Mary. She then provides the answer to their arguments: all prayer–vocal or mental–requires the nun praying to be attentive in heart and mind to what she is saying; therefore, recitation of set prayers is also mental prayer. Using the seven petitions of the Lord's Prayer as a concrete example, Teresa shows the impossibility of praying without focusing the mind on one's relationship to God. For each phrase of the prayer she stresses the unity between vocal, memorized recitation, and the application of the mind to understanding what is meant by the words.

The date is also uncertain for Teresa's *Conceptos del amor de Dios escritos por la Beata Madre Theresa de Jesús, sobre algunas palabras de los Cantares de Salomón*. The first, untitled draft appears to have been written in 1566 or 1567 and the final version in 1570. The work is a commentary on the Old Testament book called the Song of Solomon or Song of Songs, which fascinated many mystics because of its erotic imagery. The Song of Solomon, a love poem, is traditionally understood to be an allegory of God's love for the soul. To explain the sexual images, however, was an extraordinary undertaking for a woman. It was dangerous not only because of the nature of the images but also because it might be interpreted as assuming authority to teach about Scripture, something specifically forbidden for women since the Council of Trent. Teresa defends her right to comment by suggesting that one can picture to oneself events recorded in the Bible as long as there is no contradiction with the teachings of the church.

In 1567 the prior general of the Carmelite Order, Father Rossi (called Rubeo in Spain), arrived from Rome to visit the Convents of the Incarnation and St. Joseph. He was sent to see that the decrees of the Council of Trent were enforced, and he was so impressed with Teresa's restoration of original austerity at St. Joseph that he gave her permission to found more convents under the same rule and constitutions. By August of the same year, a new foundation was completed at Medina del Campo with the help of a former confessor, Baltazar Álvarez, who was at Medina as the rector of a Jesuit house. A convent was established by two nuns from the Convent of St. Joseph, two others (Teresa's cousins) from the Convent of the Incarnation, and thirteen novices waiting for them at Medina.

Teresa's twenty-year career as reformer and founder of convents had begun. In 1568 she established a house at Malagón and another in Valladolid, where she met a young friar who would become her spiritual

son and the mystical poet Juan de la Cruz. She taught him her way of life, and they became close friends and coworkers in the reform movement. Later the same year, they established the first foundation of friars at Duruelo. During the next three years, Teresa established a house at Toledo, two at Pastrana (one for nuns and one for friars), and one each at Salamanca and Alba de Tormes. By 1571 she had established ten houses–eight for nuns and two for friars. Bilinkoff writes that with each foundation Teresa believed she was striking a blow against the heresies of the Reformation churches by increasing the number of nuns and friars praying for the salvation of the Protestant souls.

During these early years of foundations, Teresa also wrote *Exclamaciones* (Exclamations), which was never published separately. The original was lost, but copies had been made and were later found bound with the manuscript of *Libro llamado castillo interior, o las moradas que escribió la Madre Teresa de Jesús, fundadora de las descalças carmelitas para ellas, por mandado de su superior y confesor* (Book Called Interior Castle, or the Mansions, by Mother Teresa of Jesus, Founder of the Discalced Carmelites, Written for Them by Order of Her Superior and Confessor, 1588; translated as *The Interior Castle; or, The Mansions,* 1852). The combination of manuscripts makes sense insofar as *Exclamaciones* features a similar theme, that is, love for Jesus and an intense desire for the union of her soul with God. *Exclamaciones* appeared in the first posthumous publication of Teresa's works in 1588 and in later revisions and translations of her complete works. The first editor of the work, Fray Luis de León, presents *Exclamaciones* as having been written in 1569 on different days after Communion to express Teresa's sentiments on favors received from God.

The last eleven years of Teresa's life (1571 to 1582) were filled with turmoil, although she established eight more convents in Castile and Andalusia. Following Teresa's greatest period of activity, the conflict between the reformed Discalced Carmelites and the unreformed, also known as the Calced branch, understandably increased. Arguments among Carmelite leaders in Spain and Italy who were trying to keep both branches under the same authority led to an order in 1571 to send Teresa back to the Convent of the Incarnation in Ávila. Although she had not been elected by the nuns at the Convent of the Incarnation, Teresa was sent to be their prioress in an effort to calm tensions and stop the founding of more reformed convents. Juan de la Cruz accompanied her as chaplain of the convent and as Teresa's confessor. The nuns were at first hostile to Teresa, but her humility won them over. While at the Convent of the Incarnation from 1571 to 1574, she began writing *Libro de las fundaciones de las hermanas Des-*

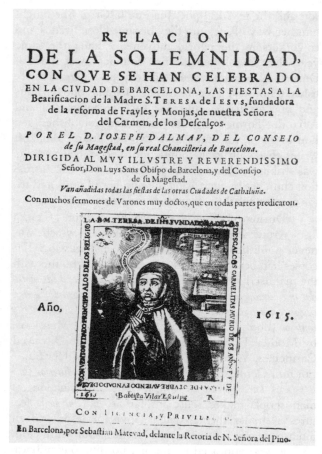

RELACION
DE LA SOLEMNIDAD,
CON QVE SE HAN CELEBRADO
EN LA CIVDAD DE BARCELONA, LAS FIESTAS A LA
Beatificacion de la Madre S. Teresa de Iesvs, fundadora
de la reforma de Frayles y Monjas, de nueſtra Señora
del Carmen, de los Deſcalços.
POR EL D. IOSEPH DALMAV, DEL CONSEIO
de ſu Mageſtad, en ſu real Chancilleria de Barcelona.
DIRIGIDA AL MVY ILLVSTRE Y REVERENDISSIMO
Señor, Don Luys Sans Obiſpo de Barcelona, y del Conſejo
de ſu Mageſtad.
Van añadidas todas las fieſtas de las otras Ciudades de Cathaluña.
Con muchos ſermones de Varones muy doctos, que en todas partes predicaron.

Año, 1615.

En Barcelona, por Sebaſtian Matevad, delante la Rectoria de N. Señora del Pino.

Title page for a 1615 announcement celebrating the beatification of Teresa the previous year (Report of the Solemnity, Whereupon Has Been Celebrated, in the City of Barcelona, the Festivals of the Beatification of the Mother St. Teresa of Jesus; from Emmanuel Renault, Ste Thérèse d'Ávila et l'experience mystique, 1970; Thomas Cooper Library, University of South Carolina)

calças Carmelitas, que escribió la Madre Fundadora Teresa de Jesús (Book of the Foundations of the Discalced Carmelite Sisters Written by the Founding Mother, Teresa of Jesus, 1610; translated as Book of the Foundations, 1853).

Probably the least-known of Teresa's major works, the narrative Libro de las fundaciones de las hermanas Descalças Carmelitas builds on the description of the founding of the Convent of St. Joseph in Libro primero de la Madre Teresa de Jesús con un tratado de su vida. Teresa begins by lamenting her bad memory, writing that she will probably leave out important things and put in unimportant things since she lacks talent for writing well. This humility, however, is a tactic evident in her earlier works, and her self-professed lack of talent clearly does not prevent her from continuing to write. Having faced criticism from church authorities for her travels, and often having to resort to less than honest

behavior in accomplishing her foundations, she presents this defense in chapter 5: "Sería recia cosa que nos estuviese claramente diciendo Dios que fésemos a alguna cosa que le importa y no quisiésemos sino estarle mirando, porque estamos más a nuestro placer" (It would be a distressing thing if God were clearly telling us to go after something that matters to him and we would not want to do so but want to remain looking at Him because that is more pleasing to us). Locutions and visions as well as directives from her spiritual leaders guide Teresa. It has often been suggested that, until she vowed obedience to Father Gerónimo Gracián in 1575, she regularly consulted with several advisers and confessors so that at least one would direct her to do what she wanted to do.

No foundation was without its difficulties, which Teresa accepted, writing that God told her she would suffer great trials. The narrative recounts various forms of opposition from civic leaders, townspeople, and/or religious authorities, often with ironic humor. She describes heroic stamina in her extensive travel by mules or wagons, over rough roads, in extreme heat and cold, only to be met with legal and financial obstacles on arrival at each place. Carole Slade, in her St. Teresa of Ávila: Author of a Heroic Life (1995), sees Teresa's evangelism in Libro de las fundaciones de las hermanas Descalças Carmelitas as parallel to the empire building described in the chronicles of the conquistadores of the New World. In the first chapter, in fact, Teresa notes how the tales that she had heard from a visiting missionary from the New World affected her, and how she envied the missionaries who were saving lost souls.

The reader finds in this work themes already presented in Teresa's earlier writings: the assumed inferiority of women, undue regard for honor based on lineage, the power of material wealth rather than virtue, and the importance in society of old Christian limpieza de sangre. In this book she emphasizes repeatedly the major roles played by women in each foundation while cleaning, repairing, and restoring the houses. Novices for the convents were accepted for their virtues of humility and obedience, whether they could provide a rich dowry or not, and financial assistance from conversos was as gratefully received as donations from the aristocratic old Christians. All of these issues brought Teresa civic and religious criticism as well as acclaim.

Critics note that in Libro de las fundaciones de las hermanas Descalças Carmelitas the reader also becomes aware of some personal traits not seen in Teresa's earlier works. With evangelistic zeal and the belief that she was following God's will, she relegates to second place concern for honesty. In many cases she resorts to deceptions, half-truths, and coercion to outwit superiors who block her way. Alison Weber, in Teresa of Ávila and the Rhetoric of Femininity (1990), describes her as a *pícaro* (rogue), a figure popular at that time as the protagonist in a genre of episodic novels. While some might describe the *pícaro* as dishonest, others saw him as shrewd, only doing what was necessary to survive. Similarly, Teresa rejected the world to become a nun, but to serve God she had to be much involved in worldly affairs. The establishment of each convent required permissions, licenses, and the resolution of financial matters between her and civic and church leaders.

Teresa was not shy about cutting corners or playing one official against another to reach her goal. For example, while founding the Convent of St. Joseph in Ávila she arranged to renovate a house given to her by her brother Lorenzo, who was in Ecuador. To avoid arousing suspicions before she was ready to move nuns into the house, she let it be known that the renovations were being made in anticipation of Lorenzo's return home. In the case of Toledo, as in other instances, Teresa knew she would face opposition from city officials, so she moved the nuns into the house in the middle of the night and arranged for an early morning mass, which consecrated possession of the house before anyone knew they were in town. The successful ploy of taking possession in the wee hours of the morning was repeated in several foundations.

Chapters 5 through 9 digress from the foundation narratives to advise prioresses on how to handle the nuns in their charge. The importance of strict observance of the rules in *Regla primitiva y constituciones de las monjas descalças de la Orden de Nuestra Señora la virgen María del Monte Carmelo,* especially as regard obedience, is repeated and amplified. The prioress must be severe, Teresa writes, but supportive in maintaining discipline. In these chapters the reader also finds more on Teresa's treatment of what was called "melancholy." The religious life for some nuns provided free rein with regard to mental or emotional problems disguised as spirituality. Teresa knew well the disruptiveness of such problems on the prayer life of the community and insisted that prioresses guard against such difficulties by watching for excessive behavior. She warns that they must discipline any nun who spends long hours alone, deliberately seeks physical pain through self-flagellation, or neglects the body by starvation. While one should not be anxious about one's health, she says, inflicting suffering beyond the prescribed exercises is self-indulgent and dangerous.

From the same period, 1571 to 1574, comes a brief work titled "Desafío espiritual" (Spiritual Challenge). Carmelite communities were accustomed to sending each other spiritual challenges as a mental activity for recreation, and the challenge Teresa answers in "Desafío espiritual" is believed to have been sent by the friars at Pastrana. Another brief text, probably from 1576, also involves a spiritual challenge. Titled "Vejamen sobre las palabras 'Búscate en mí'" (Judgment on the Words "See Thyself in Me"), it comprises Teresa's humorous response to a question she posed. During prayer, she had heard the locution: "See thyself in me." Unclear about its meaning, Teresa sent the phrase as a challenge for interpretation to her brother Lorenzo, her friend Juan de la Cruz, Bishop Julián of Ávila, and Francisco de Salcedo, a lay religious scholar. Each responded with a possible explanation for the meaning of the phrase, which elicited Teresa's critical judgment on their interpretations. Neither "Desafío espiritual" nor "Vejamen sobre las palabras 'Búscate en mí'" was ever published separately, and they are printed only in later collections of her work.

After three years of relatively quiet enclosure at the Convent of the Incarnation in Ávila, Teresa received permission in 1574 to continue her foundations and began to travel again. During the next eight years, she founded one more convent in Castile, at Segovia, and then moved into Andalusia to found convents in Beas, Seville, Caravaca, Villanueva, Palencia, Soria, and Granada, whereupon she returned to Castile for the last foundation at Burgos. She continued to add to her *Libro de las fundaciones de las hermanas Descalças Carmelitas* with a personal, detailed record of each of these foundations, completing the manuscript just a few months before her death. From this work the reader learns about Teresa's renewed personal problems. The princess of Eboli, a former supporter, denounced her to the Inquisition at Valladolid in 1574, charging that her autobiography was a book of visions. The princess had become Teresa's enemy for several reasons. As a strong-willed young aristocrat, she was accustomed to having her own way, and she had often wanted Teresa to comply with her wishes. At the founding of the Convent of St. Joseph, for example, she wished to be patroness of the convent, but Teresa was adamant about not accepting the restrictions patronage demanded. The whims of the princess, somewhat moderated while her husband was alive, did not diminish. By 1574, now a widow, she had entered the recently founded convent at Pastrana, even though she was five months pregnant. She declared herself ready for the life of a nun, but she insisted that the other nuns serve her and bow before her, which caused great problems for the prioress in trying to maintain discipline. The emotional instability of the princess caused such disturbances that Teresa was forced to close the convent, sending the Pastrana nuns (except for the princess) to the convent at Segovia. At this time the princess filed her denunciation, and the inquisitors asked for the manuscript of Teresa's autobiography. The manuscript was sent to Teresa's former confessor, Father Domingo

Title page for an edition of Teresa's collected works, published eight years after her canonization (from Emmanel Renault, Ste Thérèse d'Ávila et l'experience mystique, *1970; Thomas Cooper Library, University of South Carolina)*

Báñez, for an evaluation. Báñez supported the reforms but concluded that the manuscript should not circulate in convents and that Teresa should not teach other women who might be more susceptible than she to diabolical deception in prayer. The manuscript remained in the hands of the inquisitors and, fearing that it might be burned, the Carmelites made additional copies that circulated in secret.

From accounts in *Libro de las fundaciones de las hermanas Descalças Carmelitas,* the reader also learns of Teresa's meeting in 1575 with Father Gracián, who became her last confessor, cofounder, and best friend. Teresa writes that she discovered in Gracián a soul mate, even though at thirty years old he was about half her age. Information in this book and their correspondence reveals that the relationship between Teresa and Gracián was one of mutual admiration. New problems with the Inquisition erupted in 1576, in part because the tensions between the reform movement and the unreformed branch of the order had reawakened with Teresa's efforts to found more convents. While Teresa

was at Seville, some sisters of the unreformed Carmelites in the city began to spread scandalous stories about her. María del Corro, a novice who had left the convent, denounced the reformed Carmelite practices as heterodoxy and accused Gracián of having affairs with the nuns when he visited the convent, as well as having a sexual relationship with Teresa. Ahlgren writes that it was common in the last half of the sixteenth century to charge sexual misconduct against spiritual women, and some of Teresa's detractors even accused her of running a house of prostitution. Suspicions of mystical experiences were added to the accusations because of the ten hours of required prayer in the reformed convent. Teresa had to write two accounts of her life and visions for the inquisitorial tribunal at Seville in order to present her defense. She was persuasive, insisting that as always she was subject to the Catholic faith and that her spiritual gifts were given by God and never sought by her. The tribunal investigated and decreed the charges unfounded. Her two accounts were later collected with others and published posthumously as "Relaciones" (Reports) in her collected works.

Father Gracián at this time held the designation of provincial and visitor, responsible for oversight of the convents of both the Calced and Discalced Carmelites. This responsibility required regular visits to assess the correct observation of the rules of the order and to address any problems in the administration of the convent. Gracián requested that Teresa write *Tratado del modo de visitar los conventos* (1588, Treatise on the Method for the Visitation of Convents) as a guide for him in visiting the new Discalced houses. He wanted direction on how the visits could be of the greatest possible profit to the religious communities.

Unknown to Teresa, Father Rossi, who originally gave permission for the reform movement, had called a Chapter of the Order (official meeting) in Italy in 1575 to discuss the situation in Spain. He was losing patience with the arguments between the two Carmelite branches over the question of authority for the Discalced nuns and friars. The question remained a source of considerable tension. Rossi, as prior general of the order, sought to bring peace. This time he did not decide in Teresa's favor; rather, he ordered all Discalced friars to leave their houses and return to the Calced houses. He also ordered no more foundations of reformed convents and renewed the edict of the Council of Trent that all nuns be enclosed in their convents. Teresa was named specifically, declared an apostate and excommunicated, and ordered to return to the Toledo convent. It took more than a year, however, for her to receive the news, and, in the meantime, she completed the Seville foundation before returning to Toledo in 1576.

Between 1576 and 1580 the struggle continued between the Carmelite branches and between the authorities in Italy and King Philip II of Spain. Teresa's follower in founding reformed houses for friars, Juan de la Cruz, was kidnapped by unreformed Carmelites in 1577 and imprisoned for nine months. In 1580 the king's council called in consultants to settle the matter. The consultants recommended separating the two branches, allowing the Discalced to form an independent order. This compromise was accepted by Rome, and Father Gracián became the provincial leader, much to Teresa's delight. In the meantime, Teresa had remained enclosed in Toledo for a year and then returned to the Convent of the Incarnation at the request of the nuns, where she remained until 1579. With a respite from traveling, she decided that it was time to add new ideas on prayer to her autobiography. Gracián, however, convinced her to write a new book, and between June and November 1577 Teresa wrote her masterpiece, *Libro llamado castillo interior, o las moradas que escribió la Madre Teresa de Jesús, fundadora de las descalças carmelitas para ellas, por mandado de su superior y confesor.*

In this book Teresa describes prayer as a process by which her soul approaches God, who dwells in the innermost part of her. The goal is not just union with God, but with the will of God shown in obedience and service. Teresa visualizes the soul as a crystal castle of seven concentric mansions. Each mansion has many rooms. As she navigates through these rooms, she passes along the mystical way, which consists of three phases—purgative, illuminative, and unitive. In the first phase (comprising the first three mansions) the soul must purge itself of imperfections and build virtues in imitation of Christ. The illuminative way is the second phase (the fourth and fifth mansions), in which the soul experiences passive contemplation as the senses and faculties are quieted. In the unitive phase (the sixth and seventh mansions), the soul moves from spiritual betrothal to mystical marriage. Each movement inward becomes a more intense and more intimate relationship with God.

The door to the castle is prayer. In the first three mansions, which represent the active stage, the soul tries to please God by doing good works, practicing virtue, and engaging in mental prayer and through devotional reading. The soul enjoys these activities and reaches the point of passive recollection in which the senses and faculties are no longer disturbances. This state is a gift, not reached by activity, and marks the transition to the illuminative way. The next four mansions deepen the recollection until the soul feels peace, quiet, and humility. The senses and faculties progres-

sively reach a point at which raptures, visions, and flights of spirit may come, but they are not necessary. The soul must continue to trust God and do works of charity. At the deepest point of recollection, the highs and lows of rapture and its restlessness cease. The soul harmoniously combines the active Martha and the contemplative Mary resting in God's presence. The will of the soul is conformed to the will of God.

Throughout the book the reader encounters advice and warnings to test the certainty of what is being experienced. Not all locutions are from God. Giles summarizes Teresa's two criteria to determine if such phenomena come from God: "If the vision or locution occurs unexpectedly and if the effects are positive in the sense that the soul is at peace, joyous, and humble, they are from God." Early in her religious life, Teresa lacked adequate spiritual guides and often doubted herself and her visions, especially when her confessors began to suggest that they might be diabolical rather than heavenly. She was sensitive, then, to the need of others for guidance and wrote with familiar images and without theological language. Some images, however, become mixed as her improvisational style allows her to become distracted by new ideas. She then returns to the original image and tries to combine unlikely pairs. In this work, the castle simile meets the water simile from Teresa's autobiography, and the soul is described variously as a worm-turned-butterfly, a stray sheep, soft wax, and a victorious soldier. Each image takes on several metaphors, and the reader can get lost in the complexity.

Libro llamado castillo interior, however, is considered by most critics to be Teresa's most systematic work, moving from oral prayer to mystical union. It provides a synthesis of mystical themes developed over twenty years and reflects her personal experience in seeking perfection in the religious life. This work guides the soul along the mystical way, warning against false interior spirituality and celebrating the joy and peace of finding unity with the will of God. In this work Teresa devotes herself to the role of visions, the discernment of spirits, the spiritual and moral weakness of women, and the importance of allegiance to the orthodox church. Teresa finished the book in only five months while at the Convent of the Incarnation in 1577. Father Gracián reviewed the manuscript, censored a few passages, and returned it to her, and a copy was also submitted to the Inquisition, who kept the manuscript, along with her autobiography and *Camino de perfección,* until after her death.

During the same twenty years, Teresa had been regularly challenged by inquisitional tribunals, spiritual advisers, and confessors to explain her mystical experiences in writing for their examination. The many accounts that she wrote of her life and visions, such as

Teresa's burial site in the Convent of the Incarnation in Ávila, where she spent much of her life as a nun (from Juan Chabás, Santa Teresa, 1954; Thomas Cooper Library, University of South Carolina)

those prepared in her defense for the tribunal in Seville, describe her struggles to understand the visions and voices and to authenticate her experience. In them she defends her orthodoxy and insists she is subject always to the Catholic faith. She separates herself from the visionaries of her time, some of whom were proven to be frauds, and aligns herself with the Augustinian interpretation of visions. These writings were completed and collected in 1579. The texts have been arranged by different editors and given a variety of titles, including "Relaciones espirituales" (Spiritual Reports), "Testimonios espirituales" (Spiritual Testimonies), "Cuentas de consciencia" (Accounts of Conscience), or simply "Escritos sueltos" (Loose Writings). The earliest surviving text, from about 1560, was written for her confessor, Pedro Ibáñez; other texts followed in 1562, 1563, and 1564. After the completion of her autobiography in 1565, which treated her spiritual experiences in the eleven middle chapters, she produced no more such texts until 1571. Many more of these texts were written during the 1570s at the height of the conflict between Calced and Discalced Carmelites, as Teresa suffered accusations and denunciations from many quarters. The last text, in which she declares her soul to be completely secure in God's hands, was written in Palencia in May 1581. In all, sixty-seven authenticated texts, gathered from various manuscripts and notebooks, survive.

Early in 1580 Teresa established a new convent at Villanueva, after which she traveled to Toledo, where she contracted influenza, a serious illness for her at sixty-five years old. After she recovered, she continued her work with the help of a lay sister, Ana de San Bartolomé, and founded a convent at Palencia in December and one at Soria the following year. This same year, 1581, *Regla primitiva y constituciones de las monjas descalças de la Orden de Nuestra Señora la virgen María del Monte Carmelo* was finally confirmed and printed as the official rule for the newly independent Order of the Discalced Carmelites. Her last foundation was completed in Burgos in April 1582, although she was suffering from another serious illness. Modern medical opinion, based on the description of her symptoms, suggests that she probably had an internal cancer. From Burgos she returned to Alba de Tormes, where she finished her manuscript of *Libro de las fundaciones de las hermanas Descalças Carmelitas,* just months before her death, on 4 October 1582. Teresa was buried in the convent chapel at Alba.

Nine months later, Father Gracián had her body exhumed from the tomb, which was emitting a mysterious fragrance (referred to by the religious as the "odor of sanctity"), and he found her body whole and uncorrupt. Several miracles and visionary appearances had been reported by the nuns of Alba as well. Three years later, her body was exhumed again and secretly transferred to Ávila for final burial. The body was still in good condition, although with each disinterment various body parts had been cut off as holy relics. Teresa's body was exhumed five times in all, the last time for public display in the middle of the eighteenth century; it was still intact although badly mutilated, missing a hand, an arm, and even her heart. Pope Gregory XV canonized Teresa in 1622.

Other than *Regla primitiva y constituciones de las monjas descalças de la Orden de Nuestra Señora la virgen María del Monte Carmelo,* none of Teresa's work was published during her life. Copies of all her major writings, however, circulated in manuscript form in the convents. The inquisitors scrutinized her work, given the subject of mental prayer and spiritual visions, and after careful examination and censorship, permission was granted to publish her writings shortly after her death. The first print copy of *Camino de perfección* was published as *Tratado que escribió la Madre Teresa de Jesús a las hermanas religiosas* in Burgos in 1583. *Avisos espirituales* (Spiritual Counsels) was included in this edition and those that followed. "Avisos espirituales" consists of sixty-nine brief items, which offer her nuns spiritual counsel with regard to humility, detachment, mortification, and obedience. Teresa's disciple, Ana de Jesús, was successful in retrieving her autobiography and *Libro llamado castillo interior* from the files of the Inquisition in 1586 and with Fray Luis de León prepared them for publication in Salamanca in 1588. *Avisos espirituales* was also published in this 1588 edition under the title "Sentencias" (Sayings). Some later translations of Teresa's collected works also include the counsels under the title "Maxims." These sayings are believed to have been collected and written down by Father Gracián, Teresa's last confessor.

Although some of Teresa's correspondence was published in *Cartas de la gloriosa Madre Santa Teresa de Jesús* (1658, Letters by the Glorious Mother St. Teresa of Jesus), a complete edition of her 468 letters was not published until the twentieth century, when they were printed in volume three of *Obras completas de Santa Teresa de Jesús* (1951–1959, The Complete Works of St. Teresa of Jesus). The first complete English edition of her letters was translated by the Benedictines of Stanbrook and was published several decades before the Spanish edition under the title *The Letters of Saint Teresa* (1916–1924). Teresa's first letter is dated 1541 and the last, 15 September 1582, less than three weeks before her death; many were written during her twenty years of travel to found new convents. Her letters highlight aspects of her personality that are not as readily seen in her more polished manuscripts. The reader of these letters forgets that she is a mystic and a saint. Teresa wrote to family members, friends (inside and outside religious life), convent administrators, merchants and other businessmen, benefactors, archbishops, and kings. The tone of the letters demonstrates the entire range of her humanity: teasing and angry, saddened and joyous, pleading and exhorting. The reader can sense both sincerity and false flattery. One learns that she liked good food and disliked physicians and that she felt offended when her letters did not receive a timely response. Teresa treats most of her correspondents with love and charity, although she can also be indignant and blunt. Her letters help to complete the picture of her as a woman living with the same range of human emotions as others.

Teresa's thirty-one poems were also written at various times throughout her life and are published in modern editions of her works. Unlike other mystical poets, who wrote to express the inexpressible in the language of poetry, Teresa wrote her poems as relaxation. It was not uncommon in the convent, at the hour of recreation or on special occasions, for the nuns to entertain themselves by making up verses. Some of Teresa's poetry is humorous, as she makes light of the difficulties of the austere rules of the order. Such a case is the poem whose chorus repeats the wish that the coarse cloth of their habits does not contain vermin. Written as songs, many poems were composed for Christmas or other holy days, to be sung by the nuns in processionals. Teresa's Christmas story in verse reveals another manner by which she blends humor with edification by using popular dialect rather than biblical language. For other celebrations at the convent, such as a novice's taking of the veil, Teresa wrote poems of sacred humor with wordplay or expressions of double meaning. These occasional poems clearly demonstrate her playfulness, even while teaching or reinforcing an important theological precept.

Teresa's more serious mystical poetry also has its playful aspect in the intellectual games employed. She uses complex verse to explore theological paradoxes such as the wish to die in order to live. One such poem, "Vivo sin vivir en mí" (I Am Living without Life in Me), is written in a common verse form of the time, which begins with a few lines of poetry, or "head," on which the poet expands, or glosses, the idea through a series of stanzas. The trick was that the stanzas had to conform to the rhyme pattern of the lines being explained, and all the stanzas had to end with the same last line as that employed in the first few verses. Teresa wrote seven stanzas on this theme. A variation of this glossed poem is one in which each stanza, expanding on the theme of the "head," must end sequentially with the verses of it. Her poem "Nada te turbe" (May Nothing Disturb You) begins with a nine-line poem. The nine stanzas that follow must expand on the general idea while ending each stanza with a line, in order, from the beginning poem. Both of these poems illustrate a kind of poetic word game at which Teresa excelled. Her poetry, however, is generally considered inferior to other mystical poets, especially Juan de la Cruz. The reader can appreciate in Teresa's poems, nevertheless, a wide range of meters, verse forms, and poetic tropes and the cleverness of wordplay in these hastily composed lines.

St. Teresa of Ávila holds an important place in the history of Spanish letters and in the history of the Catholic Church. She wrote more than one thousand pages on her experiences with God, her practice of meditation, contemplation, and mental prayer. The first publication of her major works in 1588 in Salamanca had an immediate impact insofar as she was the only woman to have theological works published between 1550 and 1600. By her canonization in 1622, her works had been translated into Italian, Flemish, Portuguese, French, and German. Other reformed orders for years thereafter based their constitutions on Teresa's model. For four centuries, as a regular part of the recreation hour and mealtime devotions at convents and monasteries of many different orders, selections from Teresa's works have been read. All Spanish-literature anthologies include readings from St. Teresa, usually the only woman writer represented before the nineteenth century. Modern universities offer courses in theology, Counter Reformation history, and women's studies based on her writings, and nowhere can there be a discussion of mysticism without reference to her work.

Letters:

Cartas de la gloriosa Madre Santa Teresa de Jesús, 2 volumes, edited by Juan de Palafox y Mendoza (Saragossa: Diego Dormer, 1658);

The Letters of Saint Teresa, translated by John Dalton (London: Baker, 1853);

The Letters of Saint Teresa, 4 volumes, translated by the Benedictines of Stanbrook (London: Baker, 1916–1924).

Bibliography:

María Jiménez Salas, *Santa Teresa de Jesús: Bibliografía fundamental* (Madrid: Consejo Superior de Investigaciones Científicas, 1962).

Biographies:

Francisco de Ribera, *Vida de Santa Teresa de Jesús,* edited by Jaime Pons (Barcelona: Gili, 1908);

E. Allison Peers, *Mother of Carmel: A Portrait of St. Teresa of Jesus* (London: SCM, 1945; New York: Morehouse-Gorham, 1946);

Efrén de la Madre de Dios and Otger Steggink, *Tiempo y vida de Santa Teresa,* second edition (Madrid: Editorial Católica, 1977);

Victoria Lincoln, *Teresa, a Woman: A Biography of Teresa de Ávila,* edited by Elias Rivers and Antonio T. de Nicolás (Albany: State University of New York Press, 1984).

References:

Gillian T. W. Ahlgren, *Teresa of Ávila and the Politics of Sanctity* (Ithaca, N.Y.: Cornell University Press, 1996);

Alberto Barrientos and others, eds., *Introducción a la lectura de Santa Teresa* (Madrid: Editorial de Espiritualidad, 1978);

Tessa Bielecki, *Teresa of Ávila: An Introduction to Her Life and Writings* (Tunbridge Wells, U.K.: Burns & Oates, 1994);

Jodi Bilinkoff, *The Ávila of Saint Teresa: Religious Reform in a Sixteenth-century City* (Ithaca, N.Y. & London: Cornell University Press, 1989);

Américo Castro, *Teresa la santa y otros ensayos* (Madrid: Alianza, 1982);

Juan Chabás, *Santa Teresa,* fourth edition (Barcelona: Seix Barral, 1954);

Stephen Clissold, *St. Teresa of Ávila* (London: Sheldon, 1979; New York: Seabury, 1982);

Mary E. Giles, "Teresa of Ávila," in *Great Thinkers of the Western World,* edited by Ian P. McGreal (New York: HarperCollins, 1992), pp. 159–163;

Deirdre Green, *Gold in the Crucible: Teresa of Ávila and the Western Mystical Tradition* (Shaftesbury, U.K.: Element Books, 1989);

Helmut Hatzfeld, *Santa Teresa de Ávila* (New York: Twayne, 1969);

Cathleen Medwick, *Teresa of Ávila: The Progress of a Soul* (New York: Knopf, 1999);

Robert T. Petersson, *The Art of Ecstasy: Teresa, Bernini and Crashaw* (New York: Atheneum, 1970);

Margaret A. Rees, ed., *Teresa de Jesús and Her World: Papers of a Conference Held at Trinity and All Saints' College on October 24th and 25th 1981 in Preparation for Commemoration of the Quartercentenary of the Death of Saint Teresa of Ávila (1515–1582)* (Leeds: Trinity and All Saints' College, 1981);

Emmanuel Renault, *Ste Thérèse d'Ávila et l'experience mystique* (Paris: Seuil, 1970);

Isaías Rodríguez, *Santa Teresa de Jesús y la espiritualidad española: Presencia de Santa Teresa de Jesús en autores espirituales españoles de los siglos XVII y XVIII* (Madrid: Consejo Superior de Investigaciones Científicas, Instituto Francisco Suárez, 1972);

Carole Slade, *St. Teresa of Ávila: Author of a Heroic Life* (Berkeley: University of California Press, 1995);

Bradley Smith, *Spain: A History in Art* (New York: Doubleday, 1966);

Alison Weber, *Teresa of Ávila and the Rhetoric of Femininity* (Princeton: Princeton University Press, 1990);

Rowan Williams, *Teresa of Ávila* (London: Chapman, 1991);

Women and Spirituality II: Homage to Teresa of Ávila, 1582–1982 (Sacramento: California State University, 1982).

Francisco de la Torre

(fl. late sixteenth century)

J. Michael Fulton
Wake Forest University

BOOKS: *Obras del bachiller Francisco de la Torre,* edited by Francisco de Quevedo (Madrid: Printed for R. de Guzmán and sold by D. Gonçález, 1631);

Poesías, que publicó D. Francisco de Quevedo Villegas, Cavallero del Orden de Santiago, Señor de la Torre de Juan Abad, con el nombre del bachillèr Francisco de la Torre, edited by Luis Joseph Velázquez (Madrid: Printed by E. Bieco, 1753).

Modern Editions: *Obras del bachiller Francisco de la Torre,* facsimile edition, edited by Archer M. Huntington (New York: De Vinne, 1903);

Francisco de la Torre: Poesías, edited by Alonso Zamora Vicente (Madrid: Espasa-Calpe, 1956);

Francisco de la Torre: Poesía completa, second edition, edited by María Luisa Cerrón Puga (Madrid: Cátedra, 1984; revised, 1993).

The details of Francisco de la Torre's life remain as enigmatic as they were when his works were published in 1631. Despite many attempts to discover the identity of this sixteenth-century pastoral poet, knowledge of him is limited to the deduction that he lived and composed poetry early in the reign of Philip II, who ruled Spain from 1556 through 1598. Torre is considered significant because of his connection with the group of poets known as the Salmantine school, which included Fray Luis de León, Francisco Sánchez de las Brozas (El Brocense), and Benito Arias Montano. He is considered a follower of Garcilaso de la Vega and Juan Boscán, though he was not a mere imitator. Torre is an intermediary figure between Garcilaso and later poets such as Francisco de Quevedo and Luis de Góngora: in tone and style, his works demonstrate the transition from the delicate melancholy of Renaissance love poetry to baroque hyperornamentation and *desengaño* (disillusionment).

The first collection of Torre's works, *Obras del bachiller Francisco de la Torre* (Works of the Bachelor Francisco de la Torre), edited by Quevedo, was published in 1631, the same year in which Quevedo published the poems of Fray Luis de León. In a letter to

Ramiro Felipe Guzmán, Quevedo claims that he purchased the original manuscript of Torre's poetry from a street vendor, who was glad to be rid of it. He then goes on to identify the author of the manuscript as a *bachiller* (university graduate) who lived prior to Boscán and Garcilaso. Critics have considered it incomprehensible that a poet of Quevedo's stature should so confuse the era in which the poems were composed; María Luisa Cerrón Puga, in the introduction to her 1993 edition of Torre's poems, even suggests that it was a deliberate effort on his part to obscure the real source of the manuscript.

Since the publication of Torre's poetry, many critics have advanced theories as to the true author's identity. Luis Joseph Velázquez, who published the second edition of Torre's works in 1753, was the first to do so. He flatly asserts on the title page that Quevedo himself composed the poems. This hypothesis, however, has been rejected. Subsequent efforts to uncover details about Torre's background have either argued that the name is a pseudonym or tried to connect the poems with known figures of the same or a similar name. The theories claiming different identities hiding behind a pseudonym have generally lacked sufficient evidence to be convincing, while studies in the latter vein have been complicated by the fact that there were several individuals named Francisco de la Torre who lived during the period when the poems are believed to have been composed. The 1860 essay "Discurso de Recepción en la Real Academia de la Lengua de don Aureliano Fernández-Guerra," includes Aureliano Fernández-Guerra's deductions concerning one such person who attended the University of Salamanca. His comments, however, are based heavily on conjecture: Gregorio Torres Nebrera, in his *Antología lírica renacentista* (1983, Anthology of Renaissance Poetry), asserts that Fernández-Guerra "imaginó" (imagined) his study, while Gethin Hughes, in *The Poetry of Francisco de la Torre* (1982), calls it a "fabrication." Adolphe Coster, in his 1925 study "Sur Francisco de la Torre" (On Francisco de la Torre), also rejects Fernández-Guerra's conclusions and argues

Title page for the first collection of Francisco de la Torre's poetry (Works of the Bachelor; from Obras del bachiller Francisco de la Torre, *1903; Starr Library, Middlebury College)*

instead that Francisco de la Torre is a pseudonym for Juan de Almeida. J. P. W. Crawford, in his essay "Francisco de la Torre and Juan de Almeida" (1927), rejects Coster's finding, however, as do other critics. In "Algunos datos sobre Hernando de Acuña y Francisco de la Torre" (1941, Some Data on Hernando de Acuña and Francisco de la Torre), Narciso Alonso Cortés suggests that a Francisco de la Torre mentioned in a Valladolid court document dated 1551 was the author of the poetry: the only evidence he offers is a reference to the Duero River in one poem, but this isolated allusion seems scant evidence in light of the abundant references to other rivers, especially the Tagus. Jorge de Sena's 1974 investigation, *Francisco de la Torre e D. João de Almeida* (Francisco de la Torre and Don Juan de Almeida), posits that Torre is really Miguel de Termón, but this theory has been discarded like others before it. *Entre Fray Luis y Quevedo: En busca de Francisco de la Torre* (Between Fray Luis and Quevedo: In Search of Francisco de la Torre), the 1982 monograph by Antonio Blanco Sánchez, offers superabundant historical and genealogical data on a student who attended the University of Salamanca during the approximate time

when Torre is believed to have lived but fails to provide convincing proof that it is the same Francisco de la Torre whose works Quevedo discovered. The various hypotheses that have been adduced concerning the identity of Torre have failed to produce any consensus among critics.

Modern editions of Torre's poetry duplicate the division, made by Quevedo in *Obras del bachiller Francisco de la Torre*, into four sections, or books. The first book, subtitled *Libro primero de los versos líricos* (First Book of Lyric Verses), includes thirty-two sonnets, with six odes and two *canciones* (songs) interspersed among them. The *Libro segundo de los versos líricos* (Second Book of Lyric Verses) is similar: the same number of sonnets is included, along with five odes and four *canciones*. The *Libro tercero de los versos adónicos* (Third Book of Adonic Verses) comprises ten *endechas* (dirges or lamentations). The last book, *La bucólica del Tajo* (The Bucolic of the Tagus), consists of eight eclogues.

The chief influences on Torre's poetry include classical and contemporary sources that affected other Spanish pastoral poetry of that period. Naturally, Virgil's evocation of the *locus amoenus*–a pleasing depiction of nature in harmony–should be noted. Horace's *beatus ille* motif, the praise of simple rural life, was also influential, particularly in the odes. Torre also drew many mythological references from Ovid's *Metamorphoses* and imitated or translated poems of Renaissance Italian poets, including Francesco Petrarch, Bernardo Tasso, Andrea Navagero, and Benedetto Varchi. The sonnets and eclogues of Garcilaso were also an important influence on Torre. Torre's poetry consists almost entirely of amorous lamentation: only seven of his ninety-one poems–sonnet 13, sonnet 26, ode 1, and ode 3 in book 1; sonnet 3, sonnet 6, and ode 3 in book 2–fall outside this category. The rest of his works follow the Petrarchan model of courtly love poetry that Garcilaso and Boscán exemplify.

Torre's poems typically focus on the separation between the speaker and his beloved, who is often referred to as Filis. The shepherd who speaks in sonnet 10 of book 2 complains, "ella cruel huyendo / desamparado monte y valle umbrío, / huyó de mí, y el viento socorrióla" (she, cruelly fleeing / the lonely mountain and the shadowy valley, / abandoned me, / and the wind aided her). *Canción* 1 in book 2 compares the speaker's pain to that of the ivy, which has been cruelly torn from the oak tree. Similarly, *endecha* 1 concludes, "Mas el cielo ordena / que apartado viva, / el alma cautiva, / y el cuerpo en cadena" (But fate ordains / that I live apart, / my soul captive, / and my body in chains).

The anguish caused by this separation is conveyed through several images that correspond to the Petrarchan/Garcilasan model. One such topos is the contrast between the speaker's ardent affection and his beloved's icy indifference. Often these elements are combined. For example, the speaker of sonnet 3 in book 1 complains, "Siento luego abrasarme en vivo yelo, / y siento luego helarme en fuego vivo" (First I feel myself burn in living ice, / and then I feel myself freeze in living fire). Likewise, sonnet 14 in the same book describes an "ardiente yelo" (burning ice) that "yela el alma con su fuego" (freezes the soul with its fire).

The beloved's disdain is also characterized as being harder than rocks. *Endecha* 8, for example, describes a lovely shepherdess as "más endurecida / que montaña herida / de alterado viento" (more hardened / than the mountain split / by an angry wind), which echoes the shepherd Palemón's statement in the first eclogue: "más que roca del viento sacudida / respondes a mis quejas despiadada" (harder than the rock buffeted by the wind / you respond mercilessly to my pleas). She is also characterized as being the enemy of the speaker in many poems, or even as a victorious conqueror. For instance, she is the "enemigo vencedor amado" (beloved triumphant enemy) of sonnet 10 in book 1, the "tirano crudo tan violento" (harsh, violent tyrant) in sonnet 12, also from book 1, the "tirano tierno" (tender tyrant) in sonnet 25 of the same book, and the plunderer of the speaker's heart in many poems.

Although specific descriptions of Filis's appearance are rare, her beauty is described as being overwhelming, which is typical of pastoral literature. The poet lauds her "beldad divina" (divine beauty) in sonnet 2 of book 1, and she is his "visión divina y rara" (rare and divine beauty) in sonnet 11 of the same book. Other evocations of her appearance demonstrate the influence of Renaissance Neoplatonism, which viewed feminine beauty as a reflection of divine glory. Thus, for example, the speaker of sonnet 11 of the first book refers to her as "El ídolo purísimo que adoro, / deidad al mundo y en el cielo diosa" (The purest idol, whom I adore, / deity to the world and goddess in the heavens), while sonnet 24 of the same book calls her the "divina idea" (divine idea). The speaker of sonnet 28 of the first book identifies himself as a "templo a su simulacro consagrado" (temple consecrated to her image). In sonnet 23 of book 2, the speaker extols "la hermosura donde yo dicierno, / que está escondida más divina cosa" (the beauty where I discern / that a more divine thing is hidden). The first interlocutor of eclogue 6, Florelo, bemoans the cruelty of the "más que divina Galatea" (more-than-divine Galatea).

The lady's affections are often described as the speaker's light and guide, while her aloofness is compared to clouds and tempests. In sonnet 2 of the second book, for instance, the beloved's eyes are the speaker's guiding stars, which have been obscured by "la escura nube del desdén altivo" (the dark cloud of arrogant disdain). Likewise, Filis is portrayed in sonnet 8 of book 2 as "más resplandeciente / que el claro cielo" (more resplendent than the clear sky). In the sixteenth sonnet of the same book, the speaker contrasts Títiro, who has a guiding star clearly in view, with his own lack of any such illumination. The two shepherds of the first eclogue, Títiro and Palemón, also claim that their ladies outshine the sun and the stars. For that reason, the shepherdesses' disfavor is utterly disorienting.

Torre's poetry conveys a level of despair that exceeds the gentle melancholy typical of Boscán and Garcilaso. While they both express the sadness of rejection, Torre's sonnets in particular communicate deeper anguish: the Petrarchan theme of sweet suffering that Boscán and Garcilaso pick up becomes in Torre's poetry simply suffering. Sonnet 9 of book 1, for example, expresses the speaker's complete hopelessness thus: "Yo, de llorar contentos y memorias / de pasados placeres, de livianas / firmezas, muero como al cielo agrada" (I, from crying over joys and memories / of past pleasures, of / fickle faith, die as fate decrees). The pessimism Torre expresses in this passage and others is more fully developed in the works of such baroque authors as Quevedo and Góngora, particularly in their sonnets.

Nocturnal allusions are a second major motif found in Torre's poetry and are connected to the first: dusk or midnight are often the setting in which the pains of unrequited love and descriptions of the beloved's beauty are expressed. Moreover, in many poems the night is not merely a suitable venue for a lover's complaint, but is also a sympathetic listener that commiserates with the speaker. One of the most cited examples of this type of apostrophe is found in sonnet 7 of book 1, wherein the speaker, Damón, addresses the "amiga y esperada Noche" (friendly and longed-for Night). The relationship between the forlorn lover and the night sky is nowhere more elegantly described than in sonnet 20 from the same book: "¡Cuántas veces te me has engalanado, / clara y amiga Noche! ¡Cuántas llena / de escuridad y espanto la serena / mansedumbre del cielo me has turbado!" (How many times you have adorned me in yourself, / friendly and clear Night! How many times, full / of darkness and wonder, the placid / serenity of the skies you have disturbed!). The fifteenth sonnet of the second book is of similar content; two *endechas,* the second and the ninth, likewise present the night sky as a lovesick soul's lone companion, and the evening or deep night is the setting for four of the eight eclogues as well.

A third central theme in Torre's verse is the instability of circumstances, which is often coupled with the conviction that fate conspires to ensure the speaker's misfortune. Sonnet 1 of book 1 includes one such

POESIAS,

QUE PUBLICÒ D. FRANCISCO de Quevedo Villegas, Cavallero del Orden de Santiago, Señor de la Torre de Juan Abad,

Con el nombre del Bachillèr Francifco de la Torre.

AÑADESE EN ESTA SEGUNDA EDICION

UN DISCURSO,

EN QUE SE DESCUBRE SER el verdadero Autor el mifmo Don Francifco de Quevedo:

POR DON LUIS JOSEPH Velazquez, Cavallero del Orden de Santiago, de la Academia Real de la Hiftoria.

CON PRIVILEGIO: EN MADRID, en la Imprenta de Mufica de D. Eugenio Bieco, Calle del Defengaño. Año de 1753.

Title page for the second edition of Francisco de la Torre's poems. The publisher, Luis Joseph Velázquez, asserts incorrectly on the title page that the author of the collection is Don Francisco de Quevedo (Olin Library, Wesleyan University).

phrase: "Yo, para lamentar y arder nacido, / la vida esquivo y aborrezco el hado" (Born to lament and to burn with love, / I shun life and abhor my destiny). The hostility of fate is also evoked in the following poems: sonnet 9 from book 1 and sonnets 14, 15, 26, and 29 from book 2; odes 2 and 4 from book 1 and ode 2 from book 2; *canción* 1 from book 1; *endechas* 3 and 7; and the sixth eclogue. Jordi Gracia García's study "La retórica del destino en Francisco de la Torre" (1989) provides detailed analysis of this leitmotiv.

The extensive descriptions of nature that abound in Torre's poems are a fourth important motif. He evokes babbling streams surrounded by verdant flora in vibrant spring or, in some cases, in full summer. Where space permits, such as in the eclogues and *endechas,* the cataloguing of botanical detail is more extensive than in such early Renaissance works as Garcilaso's first eclogue. This increasing ornamentation demonstrates the gradual transition toward the baroque, which reached full flower in such later poems

as Góngora's "Soledades" (1613, Solitudes), which opens with an elaborate landscape description.

Torre used certain other topoi with less frequency. The leitmotivs of a dove that has lost its mate and a wounded stag, for example, reflect the speaker's own trials. Other themes include the *naufragio* (shipwreck) motif, references to the poisoned arrows of love that enter the speaker's eyes and proceed to his heart, and the many *contrarios* (competitors) who vie for Filis's attention.

In terms of poetic style, Torre utilized the sonnet, which consists of fourteen lines of eleven syllables each, more than any other lyric form. He also used the *estancia* in all six *canciones* and in eclogues 2, 4, 6, 7, and 8. This metric form consists of alternating heptasyllabic and hendecasyllabic verses: each stanza in a given *estancia* follows the same pattern and rhyme sequence, but there is variation from one *estancia* to the next. The eclogues that were not written as *estancias* consist of either the *octava real*—hendecasyllabic verse, with the rhyme scheme *abababcc*—or in one case of stanzas of free hendecasyllables. Torre also employed the *redondilla*—heptasyllabic quatrains with an *abba* rhyme scheme—in all the *endechas* except the second, which consists of a series of nonrhyming six-syllable verses. The odes are where Torre's poetry is the most varied. In three of the odes he utilizes the Horacian *lira*—five-verse stanzas of alternating heptasyllable and hendecasyllable—which was a favorite of Fray Luis de León. In four others he uses a distinctive quatrain—which has come to be known as the *estrofa de la Torre* (Torre stanza)—which consists of an unrhymed combination of three hendecasyllables and a heptasyllable. In two odes he uses another distinctive quatrain of alternating hendecasyllable and heptasyllable, with an *abab* rhyme scheme.

In general terms, Torre's poetry is characterized by an unadorned elegance that contrasts with the elaborate, even pompous style of some later authors. Quevedo praises him for this reason, as does Lorenço Vander Hammen y León, one of the inquisitorial censors who authorized the publication of Torre's works. The simplicity to which they refer is relative, however: the erudite syntax and many mythological references do present some obstacles to modern readers. Nonetheless, Torre's style is nowhere as complex as that of Góngora, whose poem "Soledades," for example, is so complex as to be nearly incomprehensible to readers unfamiliar with his lyric technique.

Among the rhetorical devices that typify Torre's style, parallelism—the creation of parallel structures within a verse or within a stanza—is one that has received perhaps the most attention by critics. This emphasis is not without merit, since Torre's poems are replete with such passages: "crece mi miedo, y mi tormento crece" (my fear grows, and my torment grows) from sonnet 27 in book 1; "que adoro ardiendo, y reverencio amando" (which, burning, I adore, and, loving, I worship) from sonnet 1 of book 2; "Huyen las nubes, resplandece el cielo" (The clouds flee, the heavens shine) in the fifth eclogue; and "Llorando me dejas, / hállasme llorando" (You leave me crying, crying you find me) in the ninth *endecha*. Repetition is another discursive tool common in Torre's poems. Both the first and the third eclogues include clear examples, such as "Solo, por la ribera sola, llega, / de su dolor acompañado sólo" (Alone, by the lonely river bank, he arrives, accompanied only by his pain) from the former poem, and from the latter "Solo se va buscando sus becerros, / y a la cabaña sola se va solo" (Alone he wanders away seeking his livestock, / and goes alone to his solitary cabin). Without doubt, the most commonly cited example of repetition is in sonnet 23 of book 1, in which the adjective *bella* (lovely) is repeated nine times.

Some of these verses also demonstrate Torre's use of *epanalepsis*–a lyric device in which the first word of a line is also the last word of either that line or the following one. The function of *epanalepsis* is to give rhythmic emphasis to a concept the poet wishes to underline, as seen, for example in the seventh eclogue: "Desengañado de mi bien agora, / agora de mi bien desengañado" (Disillusioned now from my good, / now from my good disillusioned). Obviously, this example features parallelism and repetition as well. This sort of accumulation of rhetorical devices is common in Torre's poetry and anticipates the even more complex compositions that abound in later Baroque verse.

While virtually nothing is known about Francisco de la Torre's life, his works constitute an important part of Spanish lyric poetry in the mid to late sixteenth century. His poetry, which is of a pastoral and amatory nature, was influenced by Virgil, Horace, Ovid, Petrarch, several sixteenth-century Italian poets, Boscán, and Garcilaso. The presence of these influences, however, should not be construed as ruling out any originality on Torre's part. Indeed, his poetry, while affected by his literary milieu, anticipates subsequent authors in several ways. By the more exaggerated melancholy of his laments, and in the complexity of his style, Torre exemplifies the transition from Renaissance to baroque poetry in Spain.

References:

Dámaso Alonso, "Manierismos por reiteración, en Francisco de la Torre," in *Strenae: Estudios de filología e historia dedicados al profesor Manuel García Blanco* (Salamanca: Universidad de Salamanca, 1962), pp. 31–36;

Narciso Alonso Cortés, "Algunos datos sobre Hernando de Acuña y Francisco de la Torre," *Hispanic Review,* 9 (1941): 41–47;

Antonio Blanco Sánchez, *Entre Fray Luis y Quevedo: En busca de Francisco de la Torre* (Salamanca: Gráficas Cervantes, 1982);

Agustín del Campo, "Plurimembración y correlación en Francisco de la Torre," *Revista de filología española,* 30 (1946): 385–392;

María Luisa Cerrón Puga, *El poeta perdido: Aproximación a Francisco de la Torre* (Pisa: Giardini, 1984);

Adolphe Coster, "Sur Francisco de la Torre," *Revue Hispanique,* 45 (1925): 74–132;

J. P. W. Crawford, "Francisco de la Torre and Juan de Almeida," *Modern Language Notes,* 42 (1927): 365–371;

Aureliano Fernández Guerra, "Discurso de Recepción en la Real Academia de la Lengua de don Aureliano Fernández-Guerra," in *Discursos leídos en las recepciones públicas que ha celebrado desde 1847 la Real Academia Española* (Madrid: Imprenta Nacional, 1860), pp. 79–104;

Amelia Fernández Rodríguez, "Sobre la construcción temática en los sonetos amorosos de Francisco de la Torre," *Castilla,* 14 (1989): 57–74;

Jordi Gracia García, "La retórica del destino en Francisco de la Torre," *Boletín de la biblioteca de Menéndez y Pelayo,* 65 (1989): 71–96;

Gethin Hughes, *The Poetry of Francisco de la Torre* (Toronto & Buffalo, N.Y.: University of Toronto Press, 1982);

Hughes, "Versos bimembres and Parallelism in the Poetry of Francisco de la Torre," *Hispanic Review,* 43 (1975): 381–392;

Peter M. Komanecky, "Quevedo's Notes on Herrera: The Involvement of Francisco de la Torre in the Controversy over Góngora," *Bulletin of Hispanic Studies,* 52 (1975): 123–133;

Fray Luis de León, *Fray Luis y la escuela Salmantina,* edited by Cristóbal Cuevas (Madrid: Taurus, 1982);

Soledad Pérez-Abadín Barro, "La influencia de Bernardo Tasso en Francisco de la Torre," *Bulletin of Hispanic Studies,* 63 (1996): 13–18;

Pérez-Abadín Barro, "La oda en Francisco de la Torre, fray Luis de León y Francisco de Medrano," in *La oda,* edited by Begoña López Bueno (Seville: Universidad de Sevilla / Córdoba: Universidad de Cordóba, 1993), pp. 249–275;

Jorge de Sena, *Francisco de la Torre e D. João de Almeida* (Paris: Fundação Calouste Gulbenkian, Centro Cultural Português, 1974);

Gregorio Torres Nebrera, *Antología lírica renacentista* (Madrid: Narcea, 1983).

Bartolomé de Torres Naharro

(1485? – 1523?)

Alexander J. McNair
University of Wisconsin–Parkside

BOOKS: *Psalmo en la gloriosa victoria que los Españoles ouieron contra Venecianos* (N.p., ca. 1514);

Concilio de los galanes y cortesanas de Roma inuocado por Cupido (N.p., ca. 1516);

Comedia Tinellaria (Rome?, ca. 1516);

Propalladia (Naples: Jean Pasquet de Sallo, 1517; enlarged edition, Seville: Jacob Cromberger, 1520; enlarged again, Seville, 1533–1534); expurgated edition published as *Propaladia de Bartolomé de Torres Naharro, y Lazarillo de Tormes: Todo corregido y emendado, por mandado del consejo de la santa, y general inquisicion* (Madrid: Pierres Cosín, 1573);

Comedia Aquilana (Naples, ca. 1523–1524?).

Modern Editions: *Propaladia*, 2 volumes, volume 1 edited by Manuel Cañete, volume 2 edited by Marcelino Menéndez y Pelayo, Libros de Antaño, nos. 9–10 (Madrid: Librería de los Bibliófilos, 1880, 1900);

Propaladia de Bartolomé de Torres Naharro (Naples, 1517), facsimile edition (Madrid: Real Academia Española, 1936);

Propalladia and Other Works of Bartolomé de Torres Naharro, 4 volumes, edited by Joseph Gillet (Bryn Mawr, Pa. & Menasha, Wis.: Banta, 1943–1961);

Tres comedias: Soldadesca, Ymenea y Aquilana, edited by Humberto López Morales (New York: Las Américas, 1965);

Teatro selecto de Torres Naharro, edited by Humberto López Morales (Madrid: Escelicer, 1970);

Comedias: Soldadesca, Tinelaria, Himenea, edited by D. W. McPheeters (Madrid: Castalia, 1973);

Obras completas, edited by Miguel Ángel Pérez Priego (Madrid: Turner-Biblioteca Castro, 1994).

Edition in English: *Hymen,* translated by W. H. H. Chamber, in *The Drama,* volume 6, edited by Alfred Bates (London: Athenian Society, 1903), pp. 253–280.

Bartolomé de Torres Naharro had a short but significant literary career. With a modest output of nine plays and a handful of lyrics he managed to contribute a great deal to succeeding generations of dramatists. His first theatrical work, *Diálogo del nascimiento* (circa 1505, Nativity Dialogue), appears to imitate the short religious pageants of Juan del Encina and Lucas Fernández, though even in this first play Torres Naharro began to differentiate himself from his late-fifteenth-century predecessors. He abandoned religious drama immediately thereafter and began writing full-length secular plays. He singlehandedly developed the genre of romantic comedy in the Spanish language. Torres Naharro was, moreover, the first Spanish playwright to stage an honor play in the *capa y espada* (cape and sword) style that later became a commonplace in the popular theater of seventeenth-century writers such as Lope de Vega and Pedro Calderón de la Barca. Torres Naharro is also the first modern dramatist to set down practical and theoretical observations on dramatic writing, almost a century before the publication of Lope's *Arte nuevo de hacer comedias* (1609, New Art of Writing Plays). Although he demonstrated knowledge of classical precepts, citing Cicero and Horace, Torres Naharro (like Lope after him) found it convenient to ignore them and prioritize what actually worked on the stage.

Scholars generally agree that Torres Naharro was born around 1485, though perhaps as early as 1480. Little is known of his life, and almost all of what is known has been culled from the author's *Propalladia*, a collection of works initially published in 1517. A letter in Latin by I. Barberius Mesinierus included in the 1517 edition (translated into Spanish as a biographical notice in the expurgated edition of 1573) notes that the playwright was from the Badajoz area of Extremadura, a region of western Spain near the Portuguese border.

The letter also claims he was a native of the village of Torre de Miguel Sexmero, about twenty miles southwest of the city of Badajoz, and of the Naharro family. The papal privilege on the 1517 edition refers to Torres Naharro as a "clericus Pacensis diocesis" (a cleric of the Badajoz diocese), which means that he must have had university studies and took orders at some point, though it is unclear exactly when. Research has not uncovered any further documentation, and many assumptions have been made about his early years. Most of these assumptions are based on the writer's own works, which suggest familiarity with the life of a soldier, extensive travel, and extended residence in Seville, Valencia, and Rome. Some scholars speculate that he was a student-servant at the University of Salamanca or that he was a professional actor there in the service of Encina and/or Fernández. The only thing that is certain—attested to in the Mesinierus letter—is that he sailed for Italy sometime shortly after 1500 (his early knowledge of the Valencian dialect of Catalan would seem to suggest he sailed from that port). Torres Naharro was, like many Spaniards, perhaps encouraged to go to Rome by the facts that Pope Alexander VI was a Borgia from Spain and that the Spanish colony in Rome was a growing one. Before reaching Italian soil, however, his ship was attacked by pirates of North African or Turkish origin. Torres Naharro was taken captive and ransomed soon afterward, arriving in Rome probably around 1503.

Scholars conjecture a great deal about Torres Naharro's early years in Italy. Between 1503 and 1505 he was possibly soldiering in the service either of the "Gran Capitán" (Great Captain), Gonzalo Fernández de Córdoba, or of Cesare Borgia, both of whom prosecuted the Italian campaigns of Ferdinand of Aragon and Alexander VI. He may, however, have come to Rome as a cleric, servant, man of letters, or courtier seeking the patronage of the Spanish cardinal Bernardino de Carvajal or of Giulio de' Medici. No matter the patron, Torres Naharro wrote mostly in Spanish during his decade-long residence in Rome, indicating that he probably split time between writing for the Spanish colony there and writing for a multilingual aristocratic audience that must have had more than a passing familiarity with his mother tongue. *Diálogo del nascimiento,* Torres Naharro's first work, was probably composed between 1505 and 1507. It is a Christmas play similar to the dramatic eclogues written and performed by Encina in Spain in the early 1490s. Encina is, by virtue of these dramatic eclogues, considered the father of Spanish drama. In his more-primitive nativity plays a contemporary shepherd comes before the audience, speaking in rustic dialect, to introduce the main action of the play. Encina's play proper transports the spectator to the bib-

Title page for the first collected edition of Bartolomé de Torres Naharro's plays and other writings. The author claims in the introduction that he arranged the works as if they were courses at a banquet, with his comedies as the entrées (*from* Propaladia de Bartolomé de Torres Naharro, *1936; Perry-Castañeda Library, University of Texas at Austin).*

lical eve of Christ's birth, where all (actors and audience) can witness the miracle and rejoice in the message of hope. Torres Naharro departs from this model in several ways. First, the rustic who introduces the play cannot help but digress from his purpose, commenting on his own sexual exploits (or blunders) and making a brutally anticlerical observation about his fiancée and the local sacristan before introducing the subject of the ensuing dialogue. Torres Naharro uses this dramatic formula, perhaps influenced by classical Roman comedy, repeatedly to introduce his plays. His rustics are not the simpletons so often portrayed by Encina and Fernández; they are frequently cruder—certainly more sexually explicit—but far from naive, anticipating in many ways the rogues of Spanish picaresque novels such as the anonymous *La vida de Lazarillo de Tormes y de sus fortunas y aduersidades* (1554) or Mateo Alemán's *Guzmán de Alfarache* (1599). Some critics also see in Torres Naharro's rustic prologuists the prototype for the *gracioso,* or comic figure, so popular in the Spanish

Golden Age theater of Lope. They base this theory on the fact that Torres Naharro's dramatic prologues are longer. Unlike Encina, whose rustic introductions are brief and only meant to capture the audience's attention, Torres Naharro makes use of a more developed introductory scene divided into two parts: first the *introito* (or entrance) with the rustic's satirical digressions, then the detailed *argumento* (or plot summary) to prepare the spectator for the characters and scenes to follow.

Though ostensibly a nativity play, *Diálogo del nascimiento* seems to be less about Christmas than about human depravity. The two pilgrims whose conversation makes up the dialogue comment on the constant wars among French, Italian, and Spanish leaders. The social and political landscape of Europe in the first decade of the sixteenth century contrasts directly with the manger scene and angelic apparitions that the spectator is told must have taken place those many years ago. The pilgrims' dialogue ends with the singing of the first *romance* (ballad) to be incorporated into a Spanish play; the ballad verse form later became a staple in the repertoire of Spanish dramatists. This particular ballad, "Triste estaua el padre Adán" (Sad Was Father Adam), was itself reprinted in lyric collections many times over, a testament to Torres Naharro's potential as a lyric poet. The ballad is followed by a conversation between the two pilgrims and two rustics. This closing conversation is riddled with sexual innuendo and lewd remarks, including a bawdy vernacular send-up of a Latin carol. Torres Naharro, writing in the Rome of Popes Julius II and Leo X, is much more irreverent than Encina or Fernández could have been in the Spain of the Inquisition (established there on the request of the Catholic Monarchs Ferdinand and Isabel in 1480). *Diálogo del nascimiento* marks a definite shift away from what would have been interpreted as empty or hypocritical religious pageantry toward a more purely secular drama. The debauchery and hypocrisy of the Church of Rome probably turned Torres Naharro away from religious drama, in the same way that Martin Luther's experience with Rome and the church hierarchy turned him away from the sacraments and rituals of Roman Catholicism just a few years later. Throughout his literary career Torres Naharro continued to satirize the abuses of the clergy, the corruption of Roman society, and the lack of moral direction from the leadership of the church. In the mouths of the rustics that satire was direct and uncouth, though in other contexts it could be subtler (as would befit a courtier seeking patronage from Italian nobility), yet just as effective.

Over the course of the decade following *Diálogo del nascimiento,* Torres Naharro wrote eight more plays, all introduced by the same rustic *introito-argumento* for-

mat. Most of these plays were written in Rome, and all of them have five acts, though varying in total length from about 1,300 to 3,100 lines per play. No one is certain how he hit upon the idea of dividing his plays into five acts (or *jornadas* as he called them, perhaps from the Italian *giornata*), but in the *Prohemio* (preface) to his 1517 collection he wrote that this division "not only seems nice, but is very necessary" because it gives the audience a break to absorb everything they have witnessed. Torres Naharro's prefatory remarks continue with practical observations about dramaturgy. He claims, for example, that the number of characters will vary depending on the play: "there should not be so few as to render the party dull, but not so many as to create confusion." Between six and twelve characters is about right, according to Torres Naharro, but he admits he is perfectly willing to exceed this number if the subject of the play calls for it. This flexibility demonstrates practical knowledge of the use of theatrical space and of the dynamics between a play and its audience. In addition to his more practical observations, Torres Naharro is believed to be the first European writer since antiquity to theorize about comedy. He divides his comedies into two subgenres: *comedia a noticia,* variously translated as history play, comedy of observation, or comedy of manners (the latter two being the most accurate), and *comedia a fantasía,* usually rendered as fictional or romantic comedy. The first two plays that Torres Naharro wrote after his *Diálogo del nascimiento* provide examples of these subgenres.

Comedia Seraphina (Seraphina's Comedy or Seraphic Comedy) was probably written in 1508 or 1509, which would make it the first full-length romantic comedy written mostly in the Spanish language. Seraphina and her maid actually speak in the Valencian dialect of Catalan; the friar and his servant speak Latin (after a fashion); and the Roman Orphea and her maid speak Italian; while the rest of the cast speaks Castilian Spanish. Miraculously, the characters have little trouble making themselves understood or understanding others. *Comedia Seraphina* is a love-triangle comedy: Floristán, the gallant, is in love with Seraphina, but his father has already arranged his marriage by proxy to Orphea. The fortunate return of Floristán's brother, Poliziano, and the subsequent revelation that Orphea is Poliziano's long-lost love help to resolve the conflict but not before the exaggerated Floristán considers both suicide and murder, heightening the comic effect. The play ends happily with the promise of multiple weddings, as do many romantic comedies written in Spain after Torres Naharro. The influence of Roman comedy, especially Plautus, is evident throughout, and the multilingualism adds to the generic Mediterranean ambience. Yet, there is something unmistakably Spanish, specifically Castilian, about the play that comes through in Torres Naharro's use of the traditional Spanish *octosílabos* (eight-syllable verses) for all his characters, regardless of the language they speak. In both plot and lyric form, this play literally sets the stage for the countless romantic comedies to come in the flowering of Spain's Golden Age theater a century later.

Torres Naharro's *Comedia Soldadesca* (Soldier's Comedy), written around 1510, is by contrast a *comedia a noticias,* a comedy of manners. The distinction between the two subgenres has nothing to do with the difference between fiction and history, as early critics believed. Indeed, both romantic comedies and comedies of manners, as Torres Naharro conceived of them, were works of fiction; the distinction is one of degree. *Comedia Soldadesca* is clearly fictional, but the playwright meant to portray scenes realistically as they might occur in the day-to-day lives of idle soldiers; it was thus conceived differently from the farfetched *comedia a fantasía* with its impossible (though entertaining) plot twists. Torres Naharro's other widely known *comedia a noticia* is the *Comedia Tinellaria* (1516, Kitchen Comedy), which provides a scathing portrait of servant life in a Roman cardinal's household. The *comedia a noticia* is also translated as "documentary comedy," and traditionally these two plays have been understood as collections of unrelated scenes that give lighthearted glimpses of life and customs in the lower classes. Scholarly reappraisals, however, have found that the apparently disconnected scenes are unified by an underlying satirical intent. The satire is directed only partially at the lower classes and their customs; the cumulative effect of so many scenes is in fact a satire of the ruling class, whose poor moral standards and lack of leadership reinforce the more unfortunate manners of their subordinates.

In the half decade following his composition of *Comedia Soldadesca,* Torres Naharro wrote several pieces for specific occasions. The *Psalmo en la gloriosa victoria que los Españoles ouieron contra Venecianos* (Psalm on the Glorious Victory the Spanish Had over the Venetians), written and published around 1514, is a 254-verse panegyric poem in celebration of the Spaniards' decisive victory over the Venetians in 1513. Of similar celebratory tone is *Comedia Trophea* (Triumph Comedy), written in praise of King Manuel I of Portugal on the occasion of his ambassador's 1514 visit to Rome. The ambassador presented the Pope with news of and presents from Portuguese conquests in Asia. Torres Naharro presented the ambassador and his entourage with what appears to be a highly flattering portrayal of Portuguese royalty, though not exempt from Torres Naharro's accustomed satirical touches.

Later that same year or early in 1515 the playwright composed *Comedia Jacinta* (Jacinto's Comedy).

Painting by Leonardo da Vinci of Isabella d'Este, the Marquesa de Mantua, whose visit to Rome in 1514–1515 was likely the occasion for Torres Naharro's play Comedia Jacinta *(1515, Jacinto's Comedy; Musée de Louvre, Paris; from* Comedias: Soldadesca, Tinelaria, Himenea, *1973; Thomas Cooper Library, University of South Carolina)*

Scholars consider this play an occasional piece as well, reasoning that it was probably written to honor Isabella d'Este, whose 1514–1515 visit to Rome was cause for much festivity. Divina, the leading lady of this play, whose name indicates she is the idealized Renaissance woman, could have been written with d'Este in mind. Divina is the lady of a castle and has her servant detain three men traveling on the road outside. Each male character in turn narrates his story; the title character, Jacinto, ends up marrying Divina. *Comedia Jacinta* is a strange play for the modern reader as it is largely allegorical. Much of its strangeness, moreover, is exacerbated because the exact nature of the allegory is unclear. Divina, for example, has been seen as a metaphor for Rome, the church, religion, and womankind. The male characters of the play and their difficulties may portray different facets of Torres Naharro's own life. Allusions to the problems faced by Spanish *conversos* (converts to Christianity) lead some to infer that the

Title page for the 1533–1534 edition of Torres Naharro's
Propalladia, *one of the first to include all nine of his*
extant plays (from Teatro selecto de Torres
Naharro, *1970; Thomas Cooper Library,*
University of South Carolina)

is the only one of Torres Naharro's plays to be translated into English (as *Hymen,* 1903), and it walks a fine line between tragedy and comedy, like many Shakespearean dramas. The hero, Hymen, is in love with Phebea, who is jealously guarded by her brother, the Marquis. The Marquis himself is not unfamiliar with those amorous adventures that begin under cover of night and through windows and balconies, so when he detects an evening visitor at Phebea's window he fears the worst. The universal double standard (men are encouraged to seduce while women are expected to remain chaste) is employed to advantage by Torres Naharro, who further complicates the issue with the theme of honor. *Comedia Ymenea* is the first Spanish play in which the audience witnesses the dramatic honor code that was omnipresent in the Spanish theater for more than a century and a half. According to this code, any male relative can avenge an affront to his family's honor by killing the woman whose indiscretion brings shame on the household. If Phebea gives in to Hymen's advances, she dishonors the family; and a stain on the family honor can only be washed away with blood. It does not matter whether the illicit relationship is actually consummated; if rumor should spread of Phebea's possible affair the noble family would be disgraced. Even the slightest suspicion of sexual impropriety on his sister's part would justify the Marquis's vendetta. Attempting to catch the presumed lovers in the act, the Marquis finds Phebea alone and threatens to kill her even though she insists on her innocence and he can find no proof of wrongdoing. Her submission to the will of her brother (her only regret being that she will go to the grave without having been with the man she loves) is a moving demonstration of loyalty and dignity. Tragedy is narrowly averted when Hymen comes on the scene to defend Phebea. He proclaims her virtue and offers himself as her husband. Satisfied with Hymen's nobility, the Marquis acquiesces, and the play ends happily.

In late 1516 or early 1517 Torres Naharro left Rome for Naples, seeking the patronage of Fabrizio Colonna, his daughter Victoria (herself an accomplished poet), and son-in-law Fernando de Ávalos, Marquis of Pescara. Torres Naharro published his *Propalladia* in Naples in the spring of 1517 (Mesinierus's letter is dated in March and the papal privilege in April), dedicating it to the marquis. The author states in his *prohemio* that the collection was carefully arranged like the courses of a banquet, with some brief lyric poems to start off, followed by the main course or the "works of substance" (that is, the *comedias*), and closing with some more lyric poetry (including three sonnets in Italian, along with poems in traditional Spanish verse). Torres Naharro named his collection *Propalladia,* he

author was himself a convert from Judaism or Islam. If Torres Naharro were indeed a *converso,* it definitely would have complicated his life in a Spain newly obsessed with blood purity and may provide another explanation for his departure to Italy a decade after the conquest of Granada and the Edict of Expulsion. Nevertheless, judging from the satirical verses on Roman society that Torres Naharro felt compelled to include in so many of his works, Italy was apparently not the answer to all of his problems.

The final play he wrote in Rome was *Comedia Ymenea* (Hymen's Comedy) of 1516. It is the first romantic comedy to make use of the *capa y espada* intrigue that became popular in Spain a century later. In *Comedia Ymenea* can also be found the seed of the type of conjugal-honor revenge tragedy cultivated successfully by Spanish playwrights from Lope on. *Comedia Ymenea* tells readers, because it is meant as "a first offering to Pallas Athena," the goddess of wisdom. Torres Naharro's activity after 1517 is unknown, but it is assumed that he returned to Spain, probably Seville, where his *Propalladia* was published again in 1520 with the addition of the *Comedia Calamita* (Calamita's Comedy). This 2,796-line play follows the model of Roman and Italian comedy and features a somewhat more evolved *gracioso* character, Jusquino, similar to those of Spanish Golden Age theater. Torres Naharro's longest play, *Comedia Aquilana* (Aquilano's Comedy), written in the early 1520s, was another *capa y espada* intrigue published separately in Naples in 1523 or 1524, then again as an addition to the *Propalladia* in 1524 in Naples. The separate publication of *Comedia Aquilana* is important because it concludes with Fernando de Merino's verses announcing his friend Torres Naharro's death, presumably in the months prior to publication. This announcement is strong evidence for a date of death in 1523 (but no later than 1524). The *Propalladia* included both the *Comedia Calamita* and the *Comedia Aquilana* together for the first time in the Seville editions of 1526 and 1533–1534; all subsequent editions in the sixteenth century derived from them and follow the Sevillian editions in printing all nine of Torres Naharro's known dramatic works.

Bartolomé de Torres Naharro continued to influence the Spanish theater for more than half a century after his death because of the popularity of his *Propalladia*, which was reprinted in Toledo, Seville, Antwerp, and Madrid. Even the often critical Juan de Valdés had words of praise for Torres Naharro in his *Diálogo de la lengua* (circa 1535, Dialogue on the Spanish Language). In 1573 *Propalladia* was published in an expurgated edition in Madrid, which surprisingly (given the virulence of Torres Naharro's satire) meant only slight changes and deletions. This edition, published together with the picaresque novel *La vida de Lazarillo de Tormes, y de sus fortunas y adversidades,* was probably the one that a youthful Lope and the dramatists of his generation knew. With his work continuously in print for half a century after his death, Torres Naharro influenced the evolution of Spanish secular theater as much as, if not more than, any other early-sixteenth-century writer. Although Encina is considered by modern critics as the father of Spanish drama, he was known mostly as a poet of ribald verse in the late sixteenth century. Torres Naharro's theatrical sense and comic intrigues had a more lasting impact on dramaturgy in Spain. The seeds of the honor play, the *capa y espada* drama, and the *gracioso* may all be found in Torres Naharro's work.

References:

Américo Castro, "Algunas observaciones acerca del concepto del honor en los siglos XVI y XVII," *Revista de Filología Española,* 3 (1916): 1–50, 357–386;

J. P. Wickersham Crawford, *Spanish Drama before Lope de Vega,* revised and edited by Warren T. McCready (Philadelphia: University of Pennsylvania Press, 1967), pp. 57–58, 81–100;

Nina Cox Davis, "Torres Naharro's Comic Speakers: Tinellaria and Serafina," *Hispanic Review,* 56 (1988): 139–155;

Albert M. Forcadas, "El carácter subversivo del eroticismo y jocosidad de la 'inocua' *Comedia Serafina* de Torres Naharro," *Monographic Review/Revista Monográfica,* 7 (1991): 38–57;

Forcadas, "El entretejido de la *Propalladia* de Torres Naharro en el Prólogo y Tratado I del *Lazarillo de Tormes,*" *Revista de Literatura,* 56 (1994): 309–348;

Stephen Gilman, "Retratos de conversos en la *Comedia Jacinta* de Torres Naharro," *Nueva Revista de Filología Hispánica,* 17 (1963–1964): 20–39;

John Lihani, *Bartolomé de Torres Naharro* (Boston: Twayne, 1979);

Lihani, "New Biographical Ideas on Bartolomé de Torres Naharro," *Hispania,* 54 (1971): 828–835;

Lihani, "Play-Audience Relationship in Bartolomé de Torres Naharro," *Bulletin of the Comediantes,* 31 (1979): 95–102;

Francisco Ruiz Ramón, "Torres Naharro," in his *Desde sus orígenes hasta 1900,* volume 1 of *Historia del teatro español,* second edition (Madrid: Alianza, 1971), pp. 78–85;

Charlotte Stern, "The Early Spanish Drama: From Medieval Ritual to Renaissance Art," *Renaissance Drama,* new series 6 (1974): 177–201;

Ronald E. Surtz, *The Birth of a Theater: Dramatic Convention in the Spanish Theater from Juan del Encina to Lope* (Princeton: Princeton University, Department of Romance Languages and Literatures / Madrid: Castalia, 1979), pp. 61–191;

Stanislav Zimic, *El pensamiento humanístico y satírico de Torres Naharro,* 2 volumes (Santander: Sociedad Menéndez Pelayo, 1978).

Alfonso de Valdés
(circa 1490? – October 1532)

Juan Carlos Conde
Indiana University

BOOKS: *Diálogo en que particularmente se tratan las cosas acaecidas en Roma* (N.p., ca. 1529); translated as *The Sacke of Roome, Exsequuted by the Emperour Charles Armie Even at the Nativitie of This Spanish Kinge Philip: Notablie Described in a Spanish Dialogue, with All the Horrible Accidents of This Sacke, and Abhominable Sinnes, Superstitions & Diseases of That Cittie, Which Provoked These iust iudgements of God* (London: Abell Ieffes, 1590);
Diálogo de Mercurio y Carón (N.p., ca. 1529).

Modern Editions: *Diálogo de Mercurio y Carón*, edited by José F. Montesinos (Madrid: "La Lectura," 1929);
Diálogo de las cosas acaecidas en Roma, edited by Rosa Navarro Durán (Madrid: Cátedra, 1993);
Diálogo de Mercurio y Carón, edited by Joseph V. Ricapito (Madrid: Castalia, 1993);
Obra completa, edited by Ángel Alcalá (Madrid: Fundación de José Antonio de Castro, 1996);
Diálogo de Mercurio y Carón, edited by Navarro Durán (Madrid: Cátedra, 1999).

Editions in English: *Alfonso de Valdés and the Sack of Rome: Dialogue of Lactancio and an Archdeacon*, translated by John E. Longhurst, with the collaboration of Raymond R. MacCurdy (Albuquerque: University of New Mexico Press, 1952);
Dialogue of Mercury and Charon, translated, with an introduction and notes, by Joseph V. Ricapito (Bloomington: Indiana University Press, 1986).

Alfonso de Valdés's short life appears tied, in one way or another, to many of the people, places, and events that mark in a decisive way the trajectory of the first third of the sixteenth century, precisely the part that is most associated with movements of political change and spiritual reform in Spain and Europe. Valdés's closeness to great personages of sixteenth-century European life such as Desiderius Erasmus of Rotterdam or the Emperor Charles I enlists him as a protagonist of the political, literary, and spiritual life of the period. His literary production consists of two works: *Diálogo en que particularmente se tratan las cosas acae-*

cidas en Roma (Dialogue Dealing Especially with the Events which Happened in Rome), which is better known by its modern title, *Diálogo de las cosas ocurridas en Roma* (Dialogue on the Events which Happened in Rome), and sometimes called *Diálogo de Lactancio y un arcediano* (circa 1529?; translated as *The Sacke of Roome, Exsequuted by the Emperour Charles Armie Even at the Nativitie of This Spanish Kinge Philip: Notablie Described in a Spanish Dialogue, with All the Horrible Accidents of This Sacke, and Abhominable Sinnes, Superstitions & Diseases of That Cittie, Which Provoked These iust iudgements of God*, 1590); and *Diálogo de Mercurio y Carón* (circa 1529?; translated as *Dialogue of Mercury and Charon*, 1986).

The exact date of birth of Alfonso de Valdés is unknown. It is known that he was born in Cuenca; that his parents were Fernando de Valdés, a businessman and governor of Cuenca between 1482 and 1520, and María de la Barrera (who probably died before 1530); and that Alfonso had six brothers and five sisters. Various historians have sustained the idea that Alfonso was the twin brother of Juan de Valdés, also an important figure in Spanish literature and thought during the first third of the sixteenth century. The defenders of this supposition situate the date of birth for both brothers around 1490. Other scholars, on the other hand, consider Alfonso and Juan not to have been twins and believe that the latter was born after the former. If this hypothesis is true, the date of birth of Alfonso must have been around 1490, while Juan must have been born no later than 1500 or 1502.

Both the father and mother of Alfonso de Valdés were descended from families of *conversos* (converts from Judaism to Catholicism). One of Valdés's maternal uncles, Fernando de la Barrera, a priest of the church of El Salvador de Cuenca, was accused of being a *judaizante* (one who keeps secretly practicing the Jewish religion in spite of one's public conversion to Christianity) and condemned by the Inquisition to be burned alive; the sentence was carried out in December 1491.

Not much is known about the education of Valdés. Indeed, almost nothing is known about him during the first thirty years of his life, and no document attests to his status as a student at any university. In spite of a lack of documented evidence, various scholars have asserted that Valdés was a disciple of the Italian humanist Pietro Martir d'Anghiera, who was active in Spain between 1490 and 1525 and with whom he forged a firm, lifelong friendship. In any case, Valdés's writings can only be explained as a product of a vast and deep humanistic culture and of a perfect mastery of Latin, undoubtedly a result of an excellent higher education. It seems appropriate to think that the quality of his education, his intellectual brilliance, and his personal talent were the factors that permitted Valdés to become, around 1520, part of the chancellery of Emperor Charles I. A person of the greatest importance in Valdés's political career was Mercurio Gattinara, who was named imperial chancellor by the emperor in 1521 and who was the true director of the politics of the empire until his death in 1530. Valdés's success and progress in the imperial chancellery were undoubtedly because of Gattinara's approval.

As a member of the imperial chancellery Valdés witnessed many of the historical events of the time. His presence in the imperial court in Flanders and Lower Germany in 1520 and 1521 is documented in his correspondence. In 1524 Valdés was the editor of the Ordinances of the Imperial Chancellery, which promulgated under his name and that of Gattinara in Valladolid. During the following year he served as compiler and editor of an important letter, which he also probably wrote, known as "Carta-relación de la Batalla de Pavía" (Letter-Report of the Battle of Pavía), which officially records the highly important victory of the troops of Charles I over the French in Pavía. The final part of this letter focuses on future expansion of a Christian monarchy headed by Charles I, a notion whose conception and elaboration has been attributed to Valdés by scholars.

In 1526 Valdés was recognized for his excellence in the Latin language and named secretary of Latin letters by the emperor, one of the most important posts in the imperial chancellery, which put him in closer and more frequent contact with Charles I himself. While serving in this capacity Valdés became an active participant in the conceptual and textual formalization of the political aims of Charles I. This fact is evident in Valdés's literary works, which are for the most part the products of a literary formulation of his political theories.

Among the letters written by Valdés as imperial secretary, those directed to Erasmus or that pertain to Erasmus, his doctrines, or his thought, are of special interest. Besides the intrinsic interest of this correspondence between Valdés and one of the most prestigious

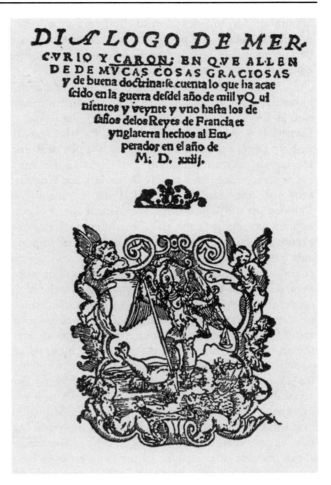

Title page for Valdés's circa 1529 work (translated in 1986 as Dialogue of Mercury and Charon), in which the eponymous mythic figures discuss the political rivalries between Emperor Charles V and the kings of France and England (from Ramón D. Perés, Historia de la literature española e hispanoamericana, 1964; Thomas Cooper Library, University of South Carolina)

and influential intellectuals of the Renaissance, the pro-Erasmian position expressed throughout all these letters, many of which are preserved in Valdes's own hand, is especially interesting. Erasmus was the public and intellectual figure whom Valdés admired most, and Erasmus's ideology and literary practice are both constant presences in Valdés's literary works. Moreover, the imperial letters signed by Valdés, those written by him, and in many cases those conceived by him, were undoubtedly an extremely important factor in the acceptance, recognition, and diffusion of the Erasmian texts and doctrines in Spain. Valdés was one of the most important defenders of Erasmus in Spain, and he knew how to utilize his high place in the imperial administration in order to support Erasmus's cause. His admiration for and devotion to the figure of Erasmus prompted Valdés's friend Pedro Juan Olivar to describe him explicitly in a letter to Erasmus as "erasmicior Erasmo" (more Erasmian than Erasmus).

In May 1527 there took place an event of extreme importance for sixteenth-century European history as well as for Valdés personally. On 5 May the troops of Charles I, which had roamed through Italy for months without being paid, stormed and took the city of Rome. During the following months, the city and the Papal States were sacked and largely destroyed, the churches profaned and plundered, and Pope Clement VII rounded up and imprisoned. The sack of Rome, a consequence of the pretensions of the kings of Spain and France over the dominion of Italy and the anti-imperial and pro-French policy of the papacy, caused a true commotion: for some it was a moment of unprecedented crisis and a blasphemous contempt for the highest representation of Christianity on earth; for others, on the other hand, it was a necessary and consequent step of imperial policy and an act resulting more from the will of God than from the actions of men, which opened expectations of a renewed Christianity, free from venality and corruption. The sack of Rome was certainly a controversial event, and one to which it was impossible to stay indifferent. Valdés responded to the event during the summer of 1527, when he wrote *Diálogo en que particularmente se tratan las cosas acaecidas en Roma,* his particular analysis of the facts from an Erasmian perspective and completely faithful to the policies of Charles I. The important position of Valdés in the imperial court assured the resonance and the influence of the text and the version of the facts that it presented.

The political uneasiness in Europe became grave in January 1528 when Francis I of France and Henry VIII of England issued a letter of defiance (a surprising reminder of one of the most characteristic practices of medieval chivalry) to Charles I. As an outgrowth of this event, Valdés wrote *Diálogo de Mercurio y Carón,* which manifests his capacity for reflecting upon the state of European politics. In the summer of 1529 Valdés traveled to Italy to accompany Charles I. This voyage was the start of a long period of traveling and political and diplomatic activity, which ended only with Valdés's own death. Valdés was present during the interviews in 1529 between Charles I and Pope Clement VII in Bologna and at the subsequent formal coronation of Charles as Holy Roman Emperor by the Pope. Valdés also participated in the Diet of Ratisbona, and most certainly was not far away from the negotiations that led to the peace of Cambray. During his travels, he surely would have received news of the controversial reception granted to his *Diálogo de las cosas ocurridas en Roma.* One of the strongest critics of this text was the papal nuncio

in Spain, Baldassare Castiglione, who accused Valdés before Charles I and the general inquisitor of acts contrary to the Christian religion and the papacy.

The year 1530 was a difficult one for Valdés. On 5 June, Chancellor Gattinara, his great protector in the court, died. During the same year Valdés's father also died. It was also a year of frenetic political and diplomatic activity for him in the emperor's service, including various missions in Italy (among them the second and third formal imperial coronations of Charles I) and participation in the Diet of Augsburg. During the course of this assembly, whose frustrated aim was to reach the long-sought-after agreement between Lutherans and Catholics, Valdés personally interviewed with Philipp Melanchthon, leader of the Lutheran legation, in an attempt to reconcile the different postures between the two. The fact that such delicate matters were put in Valdés's hands is proof of the preeminent position that he occupied in the court and of the prestige that he enjoyed.

Valdés also engaged in intense political activity in 1531–1532: his stays in Ghent, Brussels, and Ratisbona are documented. He had bitter news during these years, however, namely, that the Inquisition was carefully examining his literary works in search of material contrary to the Catholic faith. The possibility of imprisonment by the Inquisition must have played an important role in Valdés's decision never to return again to Spain. In September 1532 the court of Charles I, including Valdés, arrived in Vienna. The emperor and his retinue hastily left the city at the beginning of October because of an outbreak of the plague. One of its victims was Valdés himself, who died, most likely in Vienna, between 5 and 20 October. On 5 October he dictated his will, and on 20 October he is mentioned as having died in a letter sent by the English diplomat Thomas Cranmer to Henry VIII.

The literary texts of Valdés, *Diálogo de las cosas ocurridas en Roma* and *Diálogo de Mercurio y Carón,* are, as their titles reveal, conspicuous examples of the popularity and the importance that the dialogue had as a literary genre in Renaissance literature, both in Spain and in the rest of Europe. The classic prestige of the dialogue as a genre, from Plato to Lucian, passing through Cicero, made it an exceptional vehicle for the expression of the mixture of literature and pedagogy so characteristic of humanism, the tradition in which Valdés willingly places himself behind his admired model, Erasmus. The illusion of orality created by the dialogue allows Valdés to attain the stylistic ideal of the Renaissance reflected in the paradigmatic phrase by his brother Juan: "Escribo como hablo" (I write as I speak).

Diálogo de las cosas ocurridas en Roma was written to provide a vision, an explanation, and a reason for the

Painting by Maarten van Heemskerck of the siege of Pope Clement VII in the Castel Sant'Angelo during the sack of Rome in 1528,
which inspired Valdés's Diálogo en que particularmente se tratan las cosas acaecidas en Roma *(1529,*
Dialogue That Particularly Treats the Things That Happened in Rome) (Getty/Hulton Archive;
from E. R. Chamberlain, The Sack of Rome, *1979; Thomas Cooper*
Library, University of South Carolina)

terrible events associated with the entrance of the imperial army in Rome in 1527, as well as to aid the cause of
Charles I's foreign policy and the plan for the regeneration of the Catholic Church vigorously advocated by
Erasmus. The imperial army, badly paid and poorly
governed, burst into Rome in May 1527 with unusual
violence and carried out a terrible sacking in which
death, rape, robbery, torture, and desecration occurred.
While the act in itself was terrible and ostentatious
(recalling the fall of Rome at the hands of the Vandals
of Alaric), the fact that the churches of Rome and all the
possessions and papal palaces in that city were sacked,
desecrated, and destroyed could not leave anyone indifferent during a time in which multiple voices called for
a radical reform of the church that would end the corruption of the clergy and the scandalous participation of
the papacy in political matters. Valdés wrote his *Diálogo
de las cosas ocurridas en Roma* during the summer of 1527
in order to explain what happened from a perspective
that was absolutely pro-imperial (as would be expected
from a person with high responsibilities in the court of
Charles I) and passionately pro-Erasmian. Perhaps the
fact that the text does not hide Valdés's preference for

Erasmus and aversion toward the papacy explains why
the work appeared without the name of the author,
even though the notoriety of its authorship was displayed both in the angry response to the work by Castiglione and in the attempts of some anti-Erasmian
circles to submit Valdés to the pressure and judicial process of the Inquisition by accusing him of being a Lutheran.

Diálogo de las cosas ocurridas en Roma recounts a conversation that takes place in the Castilian city of Valladolid between Lactancio, "un caballero mancebo de la
corte del Emperadour" (a young cavalier of the court of
the Emperor), and an unnamed archdeacon "que venía
de Roma en hábito de soldado" (returning from Rome
in a soldier's dress), as they are introduced in the
"Argument" that opens the text. The clergyman disguised himself as a soldier in order to flee from the
armies of the emperor. The two characters engage in a
dialogue about what had happened in Rome: the archdeacon recounts the atrocities committed against the
Catholic Church by the troops, and Lactancio comments on the events with a highly precise intention,
according to the "Argument": "in the first part [. . . he]

explains why the Emperor is not to blame for the affair; in the second part he shows that God permitted the whole thing for the good of Christianity." The dialogue thus employs a recurring pattern: the archdeacon narrates and expounds some detail relative to the sack of Rome and its consequences, which Lactancio interprets and explains in light of his ideological and political position.

In the first part of *Diálogo de las cosas ocurridas en Roma,* Charles I is absolved of ultimate responsibility for the barbarities committed in Rome. The archdeacon thinks that Charles's culpability is clear: he claims that desire for vengeance against the Pope is the reason why the emperor decided to send his army to ransack Rome. According to the archdeacon's version, this desire for vengeance, generated by the political rivalries between Spain and the Holy See, is the cause for the destruction of Rome and the affront against the Catholic Church. Lactancio opposes this position by firmly exonerating Charles and by accusing the papacy of treachery and inconsistency in political matters. Throughout this first part of *Diálogo de las cosas ocurridas en Roma,* Lactancio—in whom it is easy to see an alter ego of Valdés himself—constantly blames Pope Clement VII for going back on his word, for creating or inducing political and military alliances against the Spanish interests, and for interfering more than necessary in earthly matters, thus putting aside his responsibilities as a servant of Christ and head of the church. In the end, Lactancio blames the destruction of Rome on the Pope: "If you will look at this matter fairly, no one was to blame but the Pope himself. He could have lived in peace; he chose war." This first part of *Diálogo de la cosas ocurridas en Roma* presents a vision of European politics of the first quarter of the sixteenth century in complete alignment with the cause of Charles I, a vision centered especially in the relations between Spain and the territories of Italy.

The second part of *Diálogo de las cosas ocurridas en Roma* is without a doubt the more interesting. Through Lactancio, Valdés effects an interpretation of the sack and destruction of Rome as a divine punishment against the corrupt and immoral ecclesiastic hierarchy. Even the archdeacon himself recognizes without hesitation the lamentable moral state of the Roman church. In the end, Lactancio proves that this degeneration of the church was the ultimate origin of its destruction, by divine will, and a necessary step toward its future regeneration.

The commentaries of Lactancio are the epitome of the ideas sustained by Erasmus concerning the situation of the church. Valdés, a devotee of Erasmus and his writings, has Lactancio offer the following assessment of Erasmus, who is presented as having been sent

from God: "Besides the many good teachers and preachers He had sent in the past, He now sent that excellent man Erasmus of Rotterdam. And Erasmus, writing with eloquence, prudence, and modesty, exposed the vices and deceptions not only of the Roman court but of all ecclesiastics in general." Valdés infuses the most important points of the Erasmian doctrine into his corrective and exemplifying interpretation of the incidents in Rome. In this spirit he criticizes the venality of the church; the clerical practice of keeping concubines; the corruption of the clergy—the ultimate cause for the Lutheran schism; the superstition manifested by the idolatrous worship of relics and images in detriment to the proper and sincere adoration of Christ; and the lack of sincere piety and evangelistic charity in the ecclesiastic hierarchy. The final conclusion is that the death, destruction, and sacrileges suffered by Rome and by the church resulting from the sack by imperial troops were consequences of God's desire to punish all those vices and defects of the church so that it would rethink its state and undertake the necessary rehabilitation and correction that would return it to the spirit of the message of the gospel.

Valdés's other literary work, *Diálogo de Mercurio y Carón,* equally presents a vision of European politics in line with imperial policy, in this case with respect to Spanish relations with France and England. Valdés probably wrote *Diálogo de Mercurio y Carón* between 1528 and 1529. The work is a defense and justification of the policies of Charles I to the detriment of his political rivals and enemies, and the formulation and development of a series of ideals of moral, social, and religious behavior from unequivocally Erasmian roots. Like *Diálogo de las cosas ocurridas en Roma, Diálogo de Mercurio y Carón* was originally published without the name of the author. This fact, the cause in the past for the mistaken attribution of the text to Juan de Valdés, is without a doubt related to the controversies that the work must have provoked in the Spain of the time, of which Valdés must have been well aware.

Diálogo de Mercurio y Carón is preceded by a prologue in which the author clearly explains his purposes. The most outstanding traits of this prologue are the tone of self-justification and self-defense that runs through it and the pronouncement that the work presented within does not correspond with the original draft, which was much sharper in its social and religious criticism (and which the author claims to have corrected after being advised by a theologian). The author also states his literary models, Lucian, Pontanus, and Erasmus, to which he declares openly and proudly his ties with a literary, religious, and ethic ideology clearly in line with Christian humanism.

Painting by Giorgio Vasari of Pope Clement VII (left) and Holy Roman Emperor Charles V. Valdés's Diálogo en
que particularmente se tratan las cosas acaecidas en Roma, *in which he supports the emperor and criticizes
Clement VII, earned Valdés the enmity of the papacy (Hall of Clement VII, Palazzo Vecchio, Florence;
from André Chastel,* The Sack of Rome, 1527, *1983; Thomas Cooper
Library, University of South Carolina).*

Diálogo de Mercurio y Carón is presented as a dialogue whose point of departure is an encounter between Mercury, the messenger god of Roman mythology, and Charon, the boatman in charge of transporting to Hades the souls of the dead. Mercury, true to his role as messenger, wakes up Charon in order to make him aware of an important event: the formal challenge issued to Charles I by Francis I of France and Henry VIII of England. This historic act gives rise to an inspection by Mercury of the most relevant events in European history, always from a perspective undoubtedly favorable to Charles I and bitterly critical of Francis I, Henry VIII, and Clement VII. The point of departure for the historiographic account elaborated by Mercury is the ascension to the Spanish throne by Charles I in 1516 and his election in 1519 as emperor of the Germanic Holy Roman Empire. This last act led to the eruption of a long enmity with Francis I (the other candidate to the imperial throne), which brought about the complicated European history of the first half of the sixteenth century narrated in *Diálogo de Mercurio y Carón*.

As would be expected from an author who was not only Spanish but also an integral part of the court of Charles I and a fervent supporter of his policies, the presentation by Valdés of the events of European politics (including a retelling of the sack of Rome) is totally favorable to Charles and extremely critical of Francis I and his allies. Charles is presented as a Christian ruler, always attentive to achieving peace and unity in Christianity, always clement, virtuous, and generous. On the other hand, Francis is presented as ambitious, a liar, a traitor, and a coward, which is similar to the depictions of Clement VII and Henry VIII.

The most interesting parts of *Diálogo de Mercurio y Carón*, both from a literary as well as an ideological point of view, are those that deal with the parade of the various souls that, on their way to the Great Beyond, interrupt the discourse of Mercury and speak with Charon about their behavior on earth in a manner that recalls the dances with death of medieval Europe. Following the examination of the vices and immoralities of said souls, a large number of strongly critical considerations toward behaviors and practices habitual to the times are made. In the first part of the dialogue various figures related to the church (a preaching friar, a bishop, a cardinal, a priest, a theologian, and a Carthusian friar) parade before Charon, all of them presented in terms fully consistent with the Erasmian critique of a merely external and insincere religiosity and of a church more preoccupied with the accumulation of goods and promoting wars and dissensions than with the salvation of its faithful and with peace and unity within Christianity. This gallery of religious figures, corrupt and without faith, embodies in the text the vision, expressed by Mercury, of a church completely foreign to the evangelical message. As a whole, this critique derives to a large extent from a markedly Erasmian orthodoxy and was responsible for the profound aversion that both the Spanish church and the representatives of the papacy felt toward Valdés.

The rest of the souls that parade before Charon—with one exception—pertain to the sphere of political power. All of them (a member of the government, a duke, an adviser to the king of England, a king, a secretary to the king of France) give testimony of a behavior guided by ambition, the longing for power and wealth, the lack of integrity and the ability to keep one's word, and the absolute ignorance about those they governed. Especially interesting is the testimony provided by the soul of the king, clearly identifiable as an alter ego of Francis I, who is presented as tyrannical, immoral, womanizing, selfish, irresponsible, warmongering, and un-Christian. Also noteworthy is the testimony of the councillor of the king of England, who blames Cardinal Thomas Wolsey for a great part of the iniquities committed by King Henry VIII. The only exception to this general scene of immorality, corruption, and lack of Christian charity is the soul of a married man who embodies modestly and sincerely the ideal of piety, interior Christianity, and laical sanctity that is derived from a life in accordance with the evangelic message. This last positive figure of the first part of *Diálogo de Mercurio y Carón* represents a positive Christian model and possibly a civic and moral regeneration based on an Erasmian ethic.

As the prologue states, all of the second part of *Diálogo de Mercurio y Carón* is an addition suggested by "one of the most renowned theologians" in Spain. Its objective is to attenuate the negativity of the critique presented in the first part of the work. This part includes Mercury's account of the final outcome of the challenge issued by the king of France to Charles I, but there is a substantial difference regarding the souls who appear on the scene: they correspond not to sinners who represent authentic antimodels of virtue but to the

souls of extremely virtuous people, who are presented as models of perfection in customs and behavior.

Diálogo de Mercurio y Carón and *Diálogo de las cosas ocurridas en Roma* are lively testimonies to the intellectual and aesthetic restlessness of a minority who, in the context of a Europe shaken by wars and uncertainty and divided spiritually by the tensions surrounding the Protestant Reformation, tried to find in the political scheme of Charles I and in the spiritual proposal of Erasmus of Rotterdam a path for an evangelical and united Europe that never came to be, the greatest and most lamented of the Renaissance utopias. Although this imperial plan was never realized, Alfonso de Valdés is remembered as one of the preeminent statesmen of the Spanish Renaissance. Because of his literary output, Valdés has achieved renown among scholars and readers for his contributions to the evolution of Spanish humanism.

References:

Giuseppe Bagnatori, "Cartas inéditas de Alfonso de Valdés sobre la Dieta de Augsburgo," *Bulletin Hispanique,* 57 (1955): 353–374;

Marcel Bataillon, "Alonso de Valdés, auteur du Diálogo de Mercurio y Carón," in *Homenaje ofrecido a Menéndez Pidal: Miscelánea de estudios lingüísticos, literarios y históricos,* volume 1 (Madrid: Hernando, 1925), pp. 403–415;

Bataillon, *Erasme et l'Espagne,* 3 volumes, edited by Charles Amiel (Geneva: Droz, 1991);

Eduard Boehmer, "A. Valdesii Litterae XL," in *Homenaje a Menéndez Pelayo en el año vigésimo de su profesorado: Estudios de erudición española,* volume 1 (Madrid: Suárez, 1899), pp. 385–412;

Fermín Caballero, *Alfonso y Juan de Valdés,* volume 4 of his *Conquenses ilustres* (Madrid: Oficina tipográfica del hospicio, 1875);

E. R. Chamberlain, *The Sack of Rome* (London: Batsford, 1979);

Dorothy Donald and Elena Lázaro, *Alfonso de Valdés y su época* (Cuenca: Diputación Provincial de Cuenca, 1983);

Mar Martínez-Góngora, *Discursos sobre la mujer en el humanismo renacentista español: Los casos de Antonio de Guevara, Alfonso y Juan de Valdés y Luis de León* (York, S.C.: Spanish Literature Publications, 1999);

Miguel Martínez Millán, *Los hermanos conquenses Alfonso y Juan de Valdés: Su ambiente familiar y la clasificación social de su familia* (Cuenca, 1976);

José F. Montesinos, "Algunas notas sobre el *Diálogo de Mercurio y Carón,*" *Revista de Filología Española,* 16 (1929): 225–266;

Margherita Morreale, "Comentario a una página de Alfonso de Valdés sobre la veneración de los santos," in *Doce consideraciones sobre el mundo hispano-italiano en tiempos de Alfonso y Juan de Valdés: Bolonia, abril de 1976,* edited by Francisco Ramos Ortega (Rome: Publicaciones del Instituto Español de lengua y Literatura de Roma, 1979), pp. 265–280;

Morreale, "Comentario de una página de Alfonso de Valdés: el tema de las reliquias," *Revista de Literatura,* 21 (1962): 67–77;

Morreale, "¿Devoción o piedad? Apuntaciones sobre el léxico religioso de Alfonso y Juan de Valdés," *Revista Portuguesa de Filología,* 7 (1956): 365–388;

Morreale, "*El Diálogo de las cosas ocurridas en Roma* de Alfonso de Valdés. Apostillas formales," *Boletín de la Real Academia Española,* 37 (1957): 395–417;

Morreale, "Juan y Alfonso de Valdés: de la letra al espíritu," in *El erasmismo en España: Ponencias del coloquio celebrado en la Biblioteca de Menéndez Pelayo del 10 al 14 de junio de 1985,* edited by Manuel Revuelta Sañudo and Ciriaco Morón Arroyo (Santander: Sociedad Menéndez Pelayo, 1986), pp. 417–427;

Morreale, "Para una lectura de la diatriba entre Castiglione y Alfonso de Valdés sobre el saco de Roma," in *Nebrija y la introducción del Renacimiento en España,* edited by Víctor García de la Concha (Salamanca: Universidad de Salamanca, 1983), pp. 65–103;

Morreale, "Sentencias y refranes en los Diálogos de Alfonso de Valdés," *Revista de Literatura,* 12 (1957): 3–14;

Rosa Navarro Durán, *Alfonso de Valdés, autor del* Lazarillo de Tormes (Madrid: Gredos, 2003);

Navarro Durán, *Lazarillo de Tormes de Alfonso Valdés* (Salamanca: SEMYR, 2002);

Ramón D. Perés, *Historia de la literatura española e hispano-americana* (Barcelona: Sopena, 1964);

Asunción Rallo Gruss, *El "Mercurio y Carón" de Alfonso de Valdés: Construcción y sentido de un diálogo renacentista* (Rome: Bulzoni, 1989);

Joseph V. Ricapito, "De los Coloquios de Erasmo al Mercurio de Valdés," in *El erasmismo en España,* edited by Revuelta Sañudo and Morón Arroyo, pp. 501–507;

Ana Vián Herrero, *El "Diálogo de Lactancio y un arcidiano" de Alfonso de Valdés: Obra de circunstancias y diálogo literario; Roma en el banquillo de Dios* (Toulouse: Presses Universitaires du Mirail, 1994).

Juan de Valdés

(circa 1508 – 1541)

María Soledad Salazar

BOOKS: *Diálogo de doctrina christiana, nuevamente compuesto por un religioso, dirigido al muy ilustre señor don Diego López Pacheco, marqués de Villena,* anonymous (Alcalá de Henares: Miguel de Eguía, 1529);

Alphabeto Christiano, che insegna la uera uia dácquistare il lume dello Spirito Santo (Segue, del medesimo autore): In che maniera il Christiano ha da studiare nel suo libro, et che fruto ha da trahere dallo studio, et como la santa scrittura gli serve come interprete, o comentario (Vinegia, 1545); translated by Benjamin B. Wiffen as *Alfabeto Christiano: Which Teaches the True Way to Acquire the Light of the Holy Spirit* (London: Bosworth & Harrison, 1861);

Le cento e dieci dieci diuine considerationi del S. Giovanni Valdesso: Nelle quali si ragiona delle cose più utili, più necessarie, e più perfette della christiana profesione (Basilea, 1550); translated by Nicholas Ferrar as *The Hundred and Ten Considerations of Signior Iohn Valdesso: Treating of Those Things Which Are Most Profitable, Most Necessary, and Most Perfect in Our Christian Profession,* with notes by George Herbert (Oxford: Printed by Leonard Lichfield, 1638);

Diálogo de las lenguas, anonymous, in *Origenes de la lengua española, compuestos por varios autores, recogidos por don Gregorio Mayáns i Siscár, bibliothecario del rei nuestro señor* (Madrid: Juan de Zúñiga, 1737).

Modern Editions: *Diálogo de la lengua,* edited by José F. Montesinos (Madrid: Espasa-Calpe, 1926);

Diálogo de doctrina christiana y El salterio traducido del hebreo en romance castellano, translated, with an introduction and notes, by Domingo Ricart (Mexico City: Universidad Nacional Autónoma de México, 1964);

Diálogo de la lengua, edited by Juan M. Lope Blanch (Madrid: Castalia, 1983);

Diálogo de la lengua, sixth edition, edited by Cristina Barbolani (Madrid: Cátedra, 1998).

TRANSLATIONS: *Comentario o declaración breve y compendiosa sobre la epístola de San Paulo Apóstol a los Romanos, muy saludable para todo Christiano* (Venice:

Philadelpho [Geneva: Crispin], 1556); translated by John T. Betts as *Juan de Valdés' Commentary upon St. Paul's Epistle to the Romans* (London: Trübner, 1883);

Comentario o declaración familiar y compendiosa sobre la primera epístola de San Paulo Apóstol a los Corinthios, muy útil para todos los amadores de la piedad Christiana (Venice: Philadelpho [Geneva: Crispin], 1557); translated by Betts as *Juan de Valdés' Commentary upon St. Paul's First Epistle to the Church at Corinth* (London: Trübner, 1883);

El Saltiero: Trauduzio del hebreo en romance castellano, edited by Edward Boehmer (Bonn: Georgi, 1880);

El Evangelio según San Mateo declarado por Juan de Valdés, edited by Edward Boehmer (Madrid: Librería Nacional y Extranjera, 1880); translated by Betts as *Juan Valdés' Commentary upon the Gospel of St. Matthew: Now for the First Time Translated from the Spanish and Never Before Published in English* (London: Trübner, 1882);

Comentario a los Salmos, escrito por Juan de Valdés en el siglo XVI, y ahora impreso por primera vez, edited by Manuel Carrasco (Madrid: Librería Nacional y Extranjera, 1885).

The life of Juan de Valdés coincided with one of the most pivotal moments in Spanish history, and in order to understand his personality it is necessary to comprehend the contemporary sociopolitical atmosphere in Spain. Spain, with Charles V as its monarch, was at its height as an imperial power. Naples and Sicily were Spanish viceroyalties, which ensured a cultural exchange of ideas between Spain and Italy during the Renaissance. Ideologically, Spain was experiencing an intellectual and religious renovation in part because of the influence of Desiderius Erasmus of Rotterdam, who inspired new ways of thinking and encouraged the return of the Catholic Church to its evangelical origins in order to end the corruption of the clergy.

Valdés's work, a product of this humanist environment, was openly diffused in Spain at the beginning of the sixteenth century, during a time when new religious approaches (such as the project, promoted by Cardinal Francisco Jiménez de Cisneros in Alcalá de Henares, to create a polyglot Bible) could be expressed more openly—that is, prior to the Counter-Reformation. The early decades of the 1500s gave rise to a burgeoning Renaissance culture in which flourished the study of Latin and Hebrew and the translation of religious texts into Romance languages, as well as the new artistic tendencies that arrived from Italy. This culture began to lose momentum toward the middle of the century after the Lutheran reform, with which many of the new Renaissance ideas were associated, spread throughout Europe and was closely scrutinized by the Inquisition. Within this complex political and cultural milieu, Valdés became one of the most renowned humanist thinkers and writers of the Spanish Renaissance.

Valdés was born in Cuenca, during the first decade of the sixteenth century, into a family headed by Fernando or Hernando Valdés. As *regidor de Cuenca* (the governor of Cuenca), the elder Valdés was in charge of the economic administration of the city. Of the five sons born to Fernando Valdés, two—Alfonso, who became known for his erudition and served as secretary to Charles V, and Juan—achieved significant success. During the early years of his life, Juan de Valdés served at the court of the marquis of Villena. Valdés's mother, María de la Barrera, may have been a *conversa* (convert from Judaism to Catholicism), and one of his uncles was condemned by the Inquisition to die at the stake. Around 1523 Valdés established contact with Pedro Ruiz de Alcalá, a lay preacher who had formed a small community of followers. The religious ideas Valdés acquired during the time, such as his critical attitude toward institutional Christianity, remained with him for the rest of his life.

The following years marked Valdés's intellectual formation. Between 1526 and 1529, after leaving the service of the marquis of Villena, he was a university student at Alcalá, where he probably studied Latin, Greek, and Hebrew, as suggested by his knowledge of these languages. During these years he also likely read Antonio de Nebrija's monumental study of Spanish, *Gramática de la lengua castellana* (1492, Grammar of the Castilian Language), a work that influenced Valdés's writings on the same subject. In 1528 he also maintained a correspondence with Erasmus. In 1531 Valdés went to Rome, where he was "gentilhombre de capa y espada" (gentleman of the cape and sword), an honorific charge at the papal court of Clement VII for several years, but when he arrived in Italy is unknown. The year after he entered the court, 1532, was a significant one in Valdés's life because of the sudden death from a

Title page for Juan de Valdés's first book (1529, Dialogue of Christian Doctrine, Newly Composed by a Devout Individual), in which a young man and a priest receive religious instruction from the archbishop of Granada (from Diálogo de doctrina christiana y El salterio traducido del hebreo en romance castellano, *1964; Thomas Cooper Library, University of South Carolina)*

contagious disease of his brother Alfonso, with whom Juan had maintained a close relationship. After Alfonso's death, Valdés hoped to be named archivist in Naples, but he occupied this post only for a short period of time and was removed because of unknown reasons. Valdés then returned to Rome, where he stayed until 1534, when Pope Clement VII died. In 1535 he went again to Naples, although his occupation there is unknown.

Most of Valdés's works are on Christian topics, and in addition to his original books he also translated sacred texts from Hebrew and Greek. Of his Greek translations only one part of St. Matthew's Gospel remains; his translation from Hebrew of the Book of Psalms is, according to Marcelino Menéndez Pelayo, the best translation of the Psalms ever written in Castilian. Only one of Valdés's works was published (anonymously) during his lifetime, and his complete literary output is unknown. Although he wrote in Castilian, his supporters published his works in Italian in order to disseminate his ideas in Italy. Some of these supporters were also his friends, such as Mario Galeota (humanist and Garcilaso de la Vega's colleague while he stayed in Naples), who diffused his works clandestinely; Marcantonio Flaminio, who was an important poet of the time and specialist in Latin; Pietro Carnesecchi, who was accused of and condemned for heresy; and Giulia Gonzaga, Valdés's best pupil, to whom he directed and dedicated some of his works.

Valdés's first written and published work, *Diálogo de doctrina christiana, nuevamente compuesto por un religioso, dirigido al muy ilustre señor don Diego López Pacheco, marqués de Villena* (Dialogue of Christian Doctrine, Newly Composed by a Devout Individual, Dedicated to the Very Illustrious Mr. Diego López Pacheco, Marquis of Villena), was published anonymously in 1529. In this doctrinal dialogue, which demonstrates the influence of the ideas of Erasmus, the author speaks to several individuals, including the marquis of Villena, who recounts the story of Eusebio, a young man who seeks religious instruction in a small church, where he establishes contact with a priest named Antronio. Both Eusebio and the priest are invited to visit Pedro de Alba, the archbishop of Granada, to receive religious instruction. The archbishop greets them kindly, and they spend time together analyzing various aspects of Christian doctrine and discussing aspects of religious practice that might be improved. They start with the Credo, then continue with the Ten Commandments and chapters 5, 6, and 7 of the Gospel of St. Matthew, as they believe these texts to summarize the essence of Christian thought. In order to be able to practice this doctrine, man should count on virtues, on the gifts of the soul, and on the commandments of the church, but most of all on prayer. They also talk about an intimate way of praying and stress the importance of internalizing religious principles. This way of thinking shows Erasmus's influence but also caused Valdés problems with the Inquisition.

The publication of *Diálogo de doctrina christiana* met with scrutiny, and the work was denounced before the Inquisition because of its religious ideas. At that time Erasmus's influence had already given rise to Lutheranism, and the Inquisition was watching carefully so that reformist positions were not diffused. At last, the situation was resolved after the intervention of a theological commission from Alcalá, which included some of Valdés's friends. Other works by Valdés also indirectly had problems with the Inquisition, but after Valdés's first confrontation with the institution he decided to leave Castile and to spend his remaining years abroad in Italy.

He expected that in Rome his ideas would find more support.

Valdés was at the center of one of the most important intellectual and religious circles in Naples between 1537 and 1541, when he died, a few months before the instauration in Rome of the Inquisition. According to testimonies and affirmations from Iacopo Bonfadio and Galeota, within this setting Valdés displayed many of the characteristics that corresponded to the humanistic ideal of the moment: he was cultivated, possessed vast knowledge, was a good conversationalist, and was loyal to his friends. According to the opinion of Counter-Reformation historians, who considered him a fanatic, Valdés could also be violent and intransigent when his ideas were not accepted, which caused him to have some enemies within the group of reactionary Catholics.

Several years after his death, his next work, *Alphabeto Christiano, che insegna la uera uia dácquistare il lume dello Spirito Santo (Segue, del medesimo autore): In che maniera il Christiano ha da studiare nel suo libro, et che fruto ha da trahere dallo studio, et como la santa scrittura gli serue come interprete, o comentario* (1545, Christian Alphabet, Which Teaches the True Way to Acquire the Essence of the Holy Spirit [Followed by, from the Same Author]: The Manner by Which the Christian Should Study the Book, and the Benefit That Should Be Derived from Such Study, and How the Holy Scripture Serves as an Interpretation, or Commentary), was first published in Italian, though it was not published in Castilian until the nineteenth century. The book is a dialogue between Valdés and his pupil, Gonzaga, conceived as a work of devotion, that is, a work that searches to promote spiritual life. It is an intimate communication between teacher and pupil in which they discuss ideological issues associated with the Reformation, the use of holy books, and the notions of faith, charity, and salvation in order to advocate the practice of orthodox Christian doctrines. The work was dedicated to his pupil, with whom he shared a spiritual relationship based on religion and on sharing the discussion of these new ideas.

Another work by Valdés in Italian, *Le cento e dieci diuine considerationi del S. Giovanni Valdesso: Nelle quali si ragiona delle cose più utili, più necessarie, e più perfette della christiana profesione* (1550; translated as *The Hundred and Ten Considerations of Signior Iohn Valdesso: Treating of Those Things Which Are Most Profitable, Most Necessary, and Most Perfect in Our Christian Profession*, 1638), is based on an original Castilian version that was not published. The book underscores the importance of devotion to Christ as a means of uniting with God and of turning away from worldly things, especially those that give pleasure. The most important activity for believers, once they realize their miserable condition, is prayer and contemplation, which leads to divine illumination. As a result of this illumination and divine love, the soul can achieve a kind of union with God, although according to the text this union does not exist in this life. In this work Valdés also offers advice concerning conduct dangerous to believers, including different types of sins. Some of the ideas expressed by Valdés in *Le cento e dieci dieci diuine considerationi del S. Giovanni Valdesso* reverberated in works of Spanish mysticism, for example, those of St. Teresa of Ávila.

The work for which Valdés is most known, *Diálogo de la lengua* (Dialogue of the Language), was at first diffused only as a manuscript, and it sank into oblivion for centuries until it was published anonymously in 1737 (under the title *Diálogo de las lenguas*). Valdés's authorship of *Diálogo de la lengua* was established near the end of the nineteenth century, and it is believed that he originally composed the work in 1535. *Diálogo de la lengua* is the only profane work written by Valdés, and it is the work that enlists him as one of the most important Spanish humanists.

Valdés probably began to study Castilian grammar, the focus of *Dialogo de la lengua,* while a student at Alcalá, and during the years he spent in Italy he broadened his views on these topics. The four interlocutors that appear in this complex dialogue, a frequently cultivated literary form during the Renaissance, display different attitudes with respect to the Castilian language. Two of the characters, the Spaniards, know Castilian well, while the others, Italians, possess a superficial and imperfect knowledge. Valdés, included as one of the Spanish characters, endeavors to enliven communication in Castilian. To this end, the author employs colloquial language and documents fragments of contemporary discussions, which lend his ideas a conversational character. *Dialogo de la lengua* treats a variety of themes dealing with Castilian grammar and discourse, including the origin of the language, pronunciation, orthography, use of language, and style, as well as comparisons between Spanish, Italian, and Latin.

Diálogo de la lengua begins with a discussion of the Latin origins of Castilian, a language that also includes words from Arabic and Greek. According to Valdés, most of the words that come from Latin refer to common aspects of life; those that come from Arabic refer to extraordinary things; and words from Greek refer to religious doctrine. Valdés is fond of word games and of using words with double meanings, and his comments regarding the incorporation of words into the Castilian vocabulary, which caused controversy among his contemporaries, are especially interesting. He is careful to point out that the Basque language existed prior to the introduction of Latin, although his focus is on the Latin tradition, which has its roots, as the work underscores, in

ORIGENES
DE LA LENGUA ESPAÑOLA,
COMPUESTOS
POR VARIOS AUTORES,
RECOGIDOS
POR DON GREGORIO
MAYÁNS I SISCÁR,
Bibliothecario del Rei
Nueftro Señor.

TOMO I

CON LICENCIA:
En Madrid, por Juan de Zuñiga,
Año 1737.

Title page for the collection (Origins of the Spanish Language, Comprising Various Authors) in which Valdés's best-known work, Diálogo de la lengua *(circa 1535, Dialogue of the Language) was first published (from* Diálogo de la lengua, *1983; Thomas Cooper Library, University of South Carolina)*

the Greek language. With respect to Castilian grammatical topics, Valdés's main concerns are those that had been considered by Renaissance grammarians such as Nebrija: prepositions and articles, for example, and uses of the verbs. According to Valdés, the Castilian language is similar to Greek in the use of articles.

Perhaps the most interesting feature of *Diálogo de la lengua* is Valdés's preference for the use of Castilian rather than Latin. To validate this attitude, he gives two explanations. First, he considers Latin a corrupted language, as it was mixed first with Greek and then with the language of the Visigoths. He also points out the fact that in Latin two negatives make an affirmation, while in Castilian two negatives negate each other, as in Greek and in Hebrew. The longest section of the work is dedicated to lexical items such as the origin of particular words, recommendations with regard to their usage, and the importance of neologisms in order to further the enrichment of the Castilian vocabulary.

One of Valdés's greatest concerns in *Diálogo de la lengua* is the perfection of Castilian as a literary language, which he approaches in a simple manner. Valdés begins by considering his own use of Castilian and determines that his style is natural and thus appropriate for written discourse. In other words, he writes as he speaks, being careful not to alter his terms as he writes them down. In this light he rejects the use of affectations, as such echoing one of the most important principles of Renaissance discourse. While the Italian language possesses two models, Petrarch for poetry and Boccacio for prose, Valdés struggles to find similar models for Castilian. He rejects medieval Spanish writers, whose style is too Latinate, fantastic, or verbose, and prefers instead to be as succinct as possible, so that the elimination of any word from a sentence would result in a reduction in its elegance or a change in its meaning.

Diálogo de la lengua, a product of the humanistic interest in the study of language, is the first extensive study of Spanish and a precursor of modern linguistic analysis. The influence of Erasmus on *Diálogo de la lengua* testifies to the impact of that thinker on Juan de Valdés, who never saw his book published and who lived for much of his adult life in a type of unofficial exile as the Inquisition increased its scrutiny of *erasmistas* (followers of Erasmus). For this work, and in particular for his unaffected and succinct style that influenced subsequent authors, Valdés is commonly considered one of the most important writers of prose of the Spanish Renaissance.

Letters:

Letter from Valdés to Dantisco, edited by Edward Boehmer, *Rivista cristiana,* 10 (1882): 93–96;

Letter from Valdés to Cardinal Scipione Gonzaga, edited by Boehmer, *Rivista cristiana,* new series 2 (1900): 87–89;

José F. Montesinos, "Cartas inéditas de Juan de Valdés al Cardenal Gonzaga," *Anejos de la Revista de Filología Española,* 14 (1931): 183–191.

References:

Eugenio Asensio, "Juan de Valdés contra Delicado. Fondo de una polémica," in *Studia philologica: Homenaje ofrecido a Dámaso Alonso por sus amigos y discípulos con ocasión de su 60. aniversario,* volume 1 (Madrid: Gredos, 1960), pp. 101–103;

Julio Calvo-Pérez, *Juan de Valdés y la fuerza de la contradicción,* Tres biografías lingüísticas en torno a Cuenca, no. 1 (Cuenca: Diputación Provincial de Cuenca, 1991);

Edmondo Cione, *Juan de Valdés, la sua vita e il suo pensiero religioso* (Bari, Italy: Laterza, 1938);

Rita Hamilton, "Juan de Valdés and Some Renaissance Theories of Language," *Bulletin of Hispanic Studies,* 30 (1953): 125–133;

Pasquale Lopez, *Il movimento valdesiano a Napoli: Mario Galeota e le sue vicende col Sant'Uffizio* (Naples: Fiorentino, 1976);

Margherita Morreale, "La antítesis paulina entre la letra y el espíritu en la traducción y comentario de Juan de Valdés (Rom. 2, 29 y 7, 6)," *Estudios bíblicos,* 13 (1954): 167–183;

José C. Nieto, *Juan de Valdés and the Origins of the Spanish and Italian Reformation* (Geneva: Droz, 1970);

A. Percauti, "Giulia Gonzaga e il movimento valdesiano in Italia nel Sec. XVI," *Studium,* 39 (1953): 169–179;

Domingo Ricart, *Juan de Valdés y el pensamiento religioso europeo en los siglos XVI y XVII* (Durango: Colegio de México / Lawrence: University of Kansas, 1958);

Fray Domingo de Santa Teresa, *Juan de Valdés, 1498(?)–1541: Su pensamiento religioso y las corrientes espirituales de su tiempo* (Rome: Universitatus Gregorianae, 1957).

Gil Vicente

(1465 – 1536/1540?)

Stanislav Zimic
University of Texas at Austin

See also the Vicente entry in *DLB 287: Portuguese Writers*.

BOOK: *Copilaçam de todalas obras de Gil Vicente,* edited by Luis Vicente (Coimbra & Lisbon: Printed by João Álvares, 1562).

Modern Editions: *Obras completas de Gil Vicente,* third edition, 6 volumes, edited by P. Marques Braga (Lisbon: Sá da Costa, 1958);

Obras completas, revised edition, edited, with an introduction, by A. J. da Costa Pimpão (Porto: Livraria Civilização, 1962);

Obras dramáticas castellanas, edited by Thomas R. Hart, Clásicos Castellanos, no. 156 (Madrid: Espasa-Calpe, 1962);

Copilaçam de todalas obras de Gil Vicente, 2 volumes, edited by Maria Leonor Carvalhão Buescu (Lisbon: Imprensa Nacional/Casa da Moeda, 1984);

Teatro castellano, edited by Manuel Calderón, introductory study by Stephen Reckert (Barcelona: Crítica, 1996);

Las obras de Gil Vicente, 5 volumes, edited by José Camões (Lisbon: Imprensa Nacional/Casa da Moeda, 2002).

Editions in English: *Lyrics of Gil Vicente,* translated by Aubrey F. G. Bell (Oxford: Blackwell, 1914);

Four Plays of Gil Vicente, translated by Bell (Cambridge: Cambridge University Press, 1920);

The Ship of Hell by Gil Vicente, translated by Bell (Watford, U.K.: Voss & Michael, 1929);

A Critical Edition with Introduction and Notes of Gil Vicente's Floresta de enganos, edited by Constantine C. Stathatos (Chapel Hill: University of North Carolina Press, 1972);

The Play of Rubena, translated by Jack E. Tomlins, edited by René P. Garay and José I. Suárez (New York: National Hispanic Foundation for the Humanities, 1993);

The Boat Plays, translated and adapted by David Johnston (London: Absolute, 1997);

Three Discovery Plays: Auto da Barca do Inferno, Exortação da guerra, Auto da Índia, translated by Anthony Lappin (Warminster, U.K.: Aris & Phillips, 1997);

Gil Vicente (frontispiece to Obras completas, *1958; Thomas Cooper Library, University of South Carolina)*

The Sibyl Cassandra: A Christmas Play with the Insanity and Sanctity of Five Centuries Past, translated by Cheryl Folkins McGinniss (Lanham, Md.: University Press of America, 2000).

Little is known about the life of Gil Vicente, one of the greatest Portuguese playwrights and poets. Because

Title page for the collection of fifty-four of Vicente's plays compiled by his son Luis (from Copilaçam de todalas Obras de Gil Vicente, *1984; William T. Young Library, University of Kentucky)*

although the dramatic and theatrical devices by which it is represented are, logically, different from those utilized to portray historical, realistic, quotidian life. Be they *a noticia* (based on fact) or *a fantasía* (invented)—to use the terms of Bartolomé de Torres Naharro, a contemporary Spanish playwright—Vicente's imaginative plots, articulated by original dramatic techniques, reveal themselves always and foremost as coherent, ingenious, and meaningful metaphors of human and poetic truth.

Vicente was born in 1465 and died between 1536 and 1540. Between 1502, when he staged his first work, *Auto de uma visitaçam* (Play of the Visitation), frequently called the *Monólogo do vaqueiro* (The Herdsman's Monologue), and 1536, the date of his last known play, *A comédia chamada floresta de enganos* (The Play of the Forest of Deceits), he composed forty-seven theatrical works of varying lengths, some only a few pages long, others exceeding fifty. Forty-four of these plays, composed in Portuguese and Spanish, were published in the 1562 *Copilaçam de todalas obras de Gil Vicente* (Compilation of All the Works of Gil Vicente) by Luis Vicente, the author's son. Fifteen plays in the *Copilaçam* are written in Portuguese, and eleven are written in Spanish (despite their Portuguese titles). The other plays are written in both Castilian and Portuguese in varying proportions.

Three of Vicente's plays have been lost, while two extant ones attributed to him lack sufficiently convincing evidence to ascertain their authorship. The last part of *Copilaçam de todalas obras* is a collection of all the *trovas* and *coisas miudas* (miscellaneous writings) that Luis (probably collaborating with his sister Paula) could recover after his father's death. Apparently, many other compositions of this kind have been lost. The extant ones reveal Vicente's participation also in nonliterary pursuits and, above all, his ever-vigilant and critical spirit concerning crucial social, religious, and political events. Some of these miscellaneous works, thus, are most valuable as authentic, illuminating, historical documents. For instance, in his "Romance . . . que fez quando foi levantado por Rei el-Rei Dom João" (1521, Romance . . . Written for the Coronation of John III), Vicente addresses the king regarding the 1531 earthquake that devastated part of the country, which some ignorant friars attributed to the presence of Jews in Portugal. Here he reveals his lucidly rational mind as well as his socially noble spirit. His judicious, persuasive arguments saved the Jewish population from the bloody persecution that the friars contemplated. The "Sermão de Abrantes" (The Sermon of Abrantes) likewise is fascinating for its well-reasoned suggestions for delivering an ideal religious sermon, in contrast to the usual ones, which bulged with sophistic, esoteric theological questions and speculations while lacking any genuine Christian spirit. Vicente manifests an essentially Eras-

of the linguistic peculiarities of some of his fictional characters, as well as because of the frequency with which he alludes in his works to people, places, and customs of Beira, it is believed that he was born in this region. Some scholars, however, hypothesize that Barcelós, Guimarães, Lisbon, or one of various other cities or towns may have been his birthplace. Because the exact location of his birth seems lost to history, people all over Portugal regard him as their favorite son. Vicente's plays have broad appeal because of their fundamental themes, particularly the existential quest of humankind. The Portuguese, Castilian, or any other fictional setting of his plays is ultimately significant only as a variation on the universal human comedy, or rather tragicomedy, which always transcends the limits of narrow parochialism. Part of this same universe is also the mythological, fabulous, and flagrantly fantastic world of many of Vicente's plays, mian spirit in even his earliest works, which does not, however, imply necessarily a direct relationship between the playwright and Desiderius Erasmus. Their moral and spiritual kinship is based on the fact that the corrupt, degenerate society in which they both lived was the common source for many of their works.

Some scholars believe that Vicente started his service at the royal court as a goldsmith and that he performed important commissions in this position. Possibly, he made the famous Belem monstrance, with the gold that Vasco da Gama had brought back from his second trip to India as a gift from the king of Quiloa to the Portuguese monarch. When Vicente staged his first play at court, however, at the request of the royal family, he must have been known already, above all, as "autor e actor" (playwright and performer), in the expression of the poet García de Resende, his contemporary. Probably, Vicente drew the attention of the court early on as an energetic, imaginative actor and organizer of the frequent religious and secular festivities at the royal palace. From the beginning the royal family favored him, especially Leonor, the queen dowager, who admired his artistic talents and constantly encouraged his theatrical and poetic creativity. Predictably, this privileged status provoked the envy and resentment of the *rascones* (villainous courtiers or rapscallions). Because of their moral corruption, treachery, vainglory, and incompetence, they often figured as the butt of Vicente's satire. The Portuguese secular theater, indeed, begins with the *Monólogo do vaqueiro,* which dramatizes precisely this enmity between the malevolent, scheming *rascones* and Vicente. The latter identifies himself with the Herdsman, who brings his grievances to the monarchs. Vicente resorted on several other occasions to this theatrical strategy, with similar intent, notably in *A comédia chamada floresta de enganos,* in the role of a philosopher, and in *Auto da festa* (The Festival Play), in the personage of Truth. In this play he also humorously refers to his supposedly failed amorous pursuit of an old lady, while in *Tragicomédia chamada templo d'Apolo* (1526, The Play of the Temple of Apollo) he pokes fun at his own rotund body. Some other references to himself are grave and somber, as, for instance, the foreboding of his impending death, in a letter to King John III he composed in January 1531. Some of his plays suggest clearly autobiographical sources. For instance, in *A Comédia do viúvo* (1521 or later, The Play of the Widower), its protagonist deeply mourns his wife's death, yet eventually finds consolation and spiritual serenity through his paternal love. Vicente was widowed twice and left to care for five children. Luis and Paula, born from his second marriage, repaid him with their love, respect and, evidently, also with a profound admiration for his genius. After Vicente's death, Luis and Paula fulfilled their father's express desire to see his work in print.

Their editorial labor with *Copilaçam de todalas obras* is often criticized for its many inadequacies. The deep filial affection that spurred them to undertake such a formidable task is not to be discounted, however.

Nothing is certain about Vicente's formal education. Perhaps he learned to read from religious texts as an altar boy for some rural priest. This hypothesis gains credibility when one considers his extensive knowledge of ecclesiastical Latin and the detailed information that he possesses about the condition and habits of the provincial clergy. One also can imagine the intellectual eagerness with which he would take advantage of the abundant educational and cultural resources that he found during his lifelong service at court. Partly because of the scarce references to classical literature in his works, and because of his apparent indifference to European Renaissance culture—supposedly demonstrated even in his humorous reactions to Sá de Miranda, who had introduced the sonnet and other Italianate poetic forms to Portugal, in his *Farsa do clérigo da Beira* (1529, The Priest of Beira)—Vicente often is considered as still a medieval man, not affected by contemporary humanistic ideas. If humanism is understood, however, in a more essential and profound sense, as an intellectual, spiritual, social, and moral interest in all that pertains to the human being, as a commitment to one's complete personal fulfillment, and, above all, as a fervent defense and exaltation of one's dignity, then Vicente should be considered as one of the most prominent European humanists of the early sixteenth century. More precisely, he is a Christian humanist, which already is evident in his extensive knowledge of biblical and patristic literature and, of course, in his sincere and intense devotion to the simple Christian message of love and charity, free of any theological sophistry. While he does not possess the classical, philosophical, literary, and theological erudition of Erasmus, his humanistic spirituality is akin to that of this great thinker. Just as Erasmus and other famous, contemporary European moralists did—but not necessarily because of their influence on him—Vicente criticized severely and continually the moral corruption and hypocrisy of those who boasted of being Christians yet behaved more like grotesque infidels. With deep moral and civic concern and utter indignation he observed the monstrous degeneration of the political, social, and religious institutions and the destructive consequences for the whole of society. It is, thus, erroneous to consider Vicente's earnest satire as simply a part of the traditional, good-humored, medieval anticlerical jest, so often devoid of any moral transcendence. Vicente was clearly a Renaissance man, with a keenly open, curious, intelligent mind and a sincere, amiable, and generous soul.

In his letter to King John III, Vicente classified all his theatrical production as "moralidades, farsas e comé-

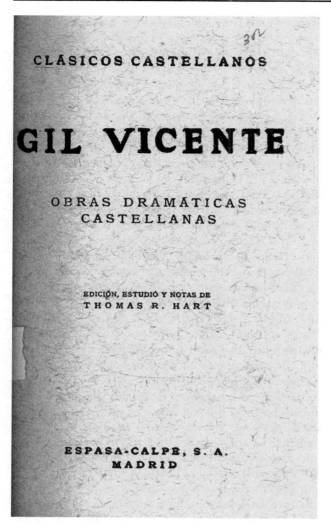

CLÁSICOS CASTELLANOS

GIL VICENTE

OBRAS DRAMÁTICAS
CASTELLANAS

EDICIÓN, ESTUDIÓ Y NOTAS DE
THOMAS R. HART

ESPASA-CALPE, S. A.
MADRID

*Title page for the 1962 collection of Vicente's plays
written in Castilian (Thomas Cooper Library,
University of South Carolina)*

dias" (morality plays, farces, and comedies), without offering definitions of these genres. In *Copilaçam de todalas obras,* Luis Vicente distributed the plays among four categories: "Obras de devoção" (Works of Religious Devotion), "Comédias" (Comedies), "Farsas" (Farces), and "Tragicomédias" (Tragicomedies). The younger Vicente, likewise, did not explain his criteria for classifying the plays, although the modern reader can understand the placement of the plays in the first group. A possible exception is the *Monólogo do vaqueiro,* the primary preoccupation of which is secular. Also, the grouping of the *farsas* is defensible generally, although some of these works include weighty implications that seem to overwhelm conventional notions of the farcical. Other *farsas* display elaborate dramatic structures and perhaps should be classified more properly as *comédias.* On the other hand, it is not clear precisely why some of the *comédias* are classified

as such. The most perplexing are the plays in the fourth group, the *tragicomédias,* especially considering that other plays with analogous constitutive elements are categorized differently. One should note, however, that Vicente's vision of human existence was essentially tragicomic. Thus, from this perspective, the label *tragicomédia* could apply to many of his plays.

Dissatisfied with Luis's groupings, critics across the centuries have proposed several other ways of classifying Vicente's plays. Although intelligent and interesting, these efforts, in fact, have complicated and obscured the problem even further. Some plays seem to defy all the proposed definitions offered so far, while others lend themselves to so many terms that, ultimately, their true nature remains perplexing for the reader. A thematic approach based on the plays' conceptual matter is perhaps the most apt, logical, and promising one. Of course, the crucial step in this categorization is identifying precisely the most important theme in each case, distinct from the secondary ones, which Vicente usually deploys to complement or contrast with the primary one. Contrary to some older views, still echoed in much of modern criticism, Vicente's plays display an impressive dramatic unity, and their artistic success is revealed by the harmony among all their parts. Using the conceptual theme as the organizing factor—without excluding other possible approaches or different criteria—Vicente's theater may be classified in four broad groups: plays on the theme of religious devotion; plays on the theme of social and religious criticism; plays on the theme of love; and plays dramatizing celebratory occasions.

Vicente composed and staged all of his plays to celebrate religious holidays or important political and social events for the nation or the royal family. In the plays of the fourth group, however, the occasion that inspires them, and even the organizational and artistic preparations for its celebration, are the focus of the dramatization. For instance, the *Tragicomédia chamada cortes de Júpiter* (1521, The Courts of Jupiter) bids farewell to the Princess Beatriz, who is departing for her marriage to the duke of Savoy. The play represents with anticipation the many forms of farewell and good wishes that the people of Lisbon will bestow on their princess as she departs on her sea voyage to Savoy. Some plays in this group also assume the function of conveying to the monarchs the preoccupations, frustrations, complaints, and hopes of the common people. For example, in *Tragicomédia chamada templo d'Apolo* and *Tragicomédia pastoril da serra da Estrêla* (1527, The Pastoral Tragedy of the Estrela Mountain Range), Vicente subtly makes the king aware of problems affecting the nation that require urgent attention.

Even before Vicente started serving at the royal court, a tradition of theatrical representations, secular and religious, already existed there. These plays were probably rudimentary in every aspect, however, because in 1502 Vicente's *Monólogo do vaqueiro* evidently impressed the public as an extraordinarily successful theatrical novelty. The work of the Spaniard Juan de Encina, whose *eglogas* (theatrical pieces) Vicente knew well, was a decisive influence for him. Encina's influence, as well as that of other Spanish playwrights, notably Lucas Fernández and Torres Naharro, are evident in the themes, in the rustic characters who speak in their folksy *sayagués* dialect, and in the dramatic structure and technique—in short, in several fundamental aspects of Vicente's early religious plays: *Auto pastoril castelhano* (1502, The Castilian Pastoral Play), *Auto de los reis magos* (1503, The Play of the Magi), and *Auto de S. Martinho* (1504, The Play of Saint Martin). Vicente's spiritual complexity and artistic subtlety make even these first creations highly original. His later religious plays reach such a high level of sophistication, both in ideology and dramatic craft, that they no longer recall the Spanish masters but readily surpass them. Some of Vicente's most extraordinary dramatic and theatrical achievements among these religious plays figure in the *Auto dos quatro tempos* (1511, The Play of the Four Seasons). In this play the whole universe seems to surge across the stage: angels, archangels, stars, planets and comets, nature, the four seasons, mythological as well as legendary figures, and solemn biblical prophets. All created beings, great and small, appear to worship joyfully the Baby Jesus and his Mother. The four seasons of the year also represent the ages of man and, more significantly yet, a divine macrocosm. All the seasons flow toward the time of Jesus' birth and—simultaneously, in a reverse sense—toward the primordial time of eternal God, finding mutual justification in their divine atemporality, by which past, present, and future coexist inextricably and harmoniously. Before the spectators' eyes, through some of Vicente's most charming poetry, the seasons reveal a cornucopia of fauna and flora, prodigious in their variety of forms, sizes, and colors, which bear exotic and melodious names, some coined by the popular imagination and others by the author himself. Through it all breathes an affectionate, loving Franciscan spirit. The performances of the seasons convey a marvelous sensation of the plenitude of life, of Creation, of divine immanence even in the smallest, most insignificant elements. Because of the melodious quality and great metrical and rhythmic variety of the verses, as well as because, in a representation, several parts are sung with musical accompaniment, *Auto dos quatro tempos* is indeed opera-like. Even discounting the songs and music, however, the poetry alone, with its charming onomatopoeic effects, has a musical quality. The play thus in some senses seems to anticipate Antonio Vivaldi's *The Four Seasons* (1725).

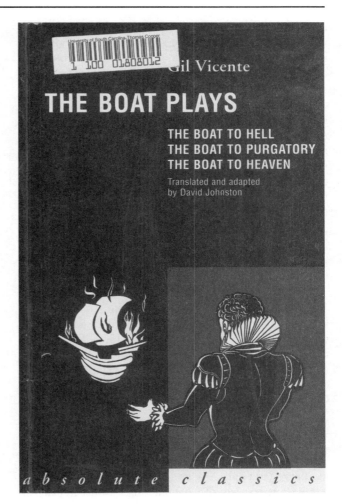

Cover for the 1997 English-language edition of three allegorical plays by Vicente (Thomas Cooper Library, University of South Carolina)

In other plays, such as *A comédia do viúvo* and *Auto da barca do purgatório* (1518, Play of the Ship of Purgatory), Vicente ponders the idea that the world is the creation of a perfect craftsman but, nevertheless, is subject to the ravages of death and a wide range of inequities. Ultimately, the belief prevails that man must act with virtue, discretion, and dignity when facing both prosperity and adversity. Providence always offers opportunities for the triumph of the human spirit. To attribute to God's will the suffering and injustices that human wickedness causes is sacrilegious. In *Romagem de tragicomédia dos agravados* (1533, Tragicomedy of the Aggrieved) such blasphemous attributions are spread among the naive, ignorant populace by a hypocritical clergy, intent on diverting attention from their own transgressions and on promoting their materialistic ambition and profit. The clergy's gross abuse of their professional and spiritual obligations and their many misdeeds are often satirized in Vicente's plays, although in some cases only in passing. His frequent, burlesque references to merely external religious practices reflect the serious preoccupation that he shared with many other moralists and theologians about the extreme discrepancy between word or religious rite and genuine sentiment, because of ignorance or, worse, hypocrisy. From this perspective, armed with a keen intelligence, sound rationality, discretion, and an unconditional commitment to truth, Vicente confronts all the critical problems affecting the religious profession. He tackles themes ranging from the clergy's spiritual and educational mission to its irregular marital arrangements, from its frequently improper use of Latin to spread the Christian message to, most significantly, any questionable interpretations concerning the divine mystery. For instance, in *Auto pastoril em Português* (1523, The Portuguese Pastoral Play) he even examines the possible opposing perspectives concerning an alleged miracle.

Instead of censoring the grave trespasses of their subordinates, the high religious authorities tolerated and, by their own examples, even encouraged the local clergy to stray. In the *Auto da barca da glória* (1519, The Play of the Ship of Heaven), the Devil accuses the Pope of lust, simony, and pride, among many other capital failings. In the *Auto da sibila Cassandra* (1513, The Play of the Sybil Cassandra) he satirizes the religious attitudes of the contemporary church hierarchy by ironically comparing them to the ideal love between the church and God, according to the conventional allegorical reading of the Song of Songs. Cassandra, who personifies the church, has perverted God's love and abandoned him to become a grotesque travesty of what she ought to be. In *Auto da feira* (1526, The Play of the Fair), Vicente even justifies the 1527 sack of Rome by Charles V's army as a punishment for severe ecclesiastical failings. In the beautiful *Auto da alma* (1518, Play of the Soul's Journey), Vicente renders his perhaps definitive statement on what he identifies as the only true religion: genuine love for one's fellow man.

Quite significantly, Vicente shows the vices and transgressions of both low and high clergy as major contributing causes of all the worst ills besetting society: greed, corruption, parasitism, thievery, exploitation, poverty, fornication, adultery, violence, sloth, pride, vainglory, superstition, foolishness, and ignorance. He also identifies the entrenched accomplices of the immoral clergy in victimizing the nation. Incompetent and corrupt bureaucrats at all levels of government are indicted in *Tragicomédia do inverno e verão* (1529, The Play of Winter and Summer), *Farsa do clérigo da Beira,* and *Farsa do juíz da Beira* (1525, The Farce of the Judge of Beira), and false professionals are the target in *Auto dos físicos* (1524, The Play of the Doctors). Particularly—in, for example, *Farsa do clérigo da Beira, Romagem de tragicomédia do agravados,* and *Farsa de "Quem tem farelos?"* (The Play of "Who Has the Bran?")—he attacks the rapacious, arrogant *rascones cortesanos,* parasitic courtiers, whose sole aim is to enrich themselves and advance their personal ambition by the most unscrupulous means, at the expense not only of the common people but of the royal family itself. Even the highest nobility often is guilty of the greatest transgressions. In *A comédia Chamada floresta de enganos,* classical myths—which are transparent satirical disguises—represent the scheming political opportunism of the nobility. The satirically subtle ending of the *Auto da barca da glória* suggests that hell is the inexorable destiny of the monarch and his whole court, although, of course, there is no overt identification of individuals. The characters who inhabit the plays of social and religious criticism parade across a vast, encompassing panorama of contemporary society. Although from a dramatic, literary standpoint they often are regarded only as "types," plays such as the *A farsa de Inês Pereira* (1523, The Farce of Inês Pereira) forcefully show that Vicente also created well-rounded individuals.

Like most Renaissance writers, Vicente is profoundly interested in the multifaceted expressions and effects of love on life. In his works he examines love from seemingly all conceivable perspectives. In *Tragicomédia da frágua* (1525, The Play of the Forge), love can transform the world. With its magical power, it fills the hearts of humankind with hope and illusions, at times despite the most unyielding realities. In *Nau de amores* (1527, Ship of Love), all the passengers of the titular ship are frustrated, disillusioned lovers, whose pursuits are absurdly impossible. Nevertheless, none among them hesitates to continue the trip because, despite the likelihood of new disappointments, everyone maintains the hope of ultimately finding that elusive happiness. Among Vicente's plays on the theme of love, one finds some of his greatest dramatic achievements: *A comédia do viúvo, Auto farsa do velho da horta* (1512, The Old Man of the Orchard), *Comédia de Rubena* (1521, The Play of Rubena), and *A farsa de Inês Pereira.* No matter what the subject, theatrical genre, or tone, in each case the author's conviction that even a little bit of true love performs miracles and improves humankind is conveyed with his customary artistic subtlety. Human dignity itself is asserted by the expression of true love. This thought is expressed with poetic beauty in *Tragicomédia de Dom Duardos* (1522?, Tragicomedy of Don Duardos). In a mythical time, Don Duardos, prince of England, falls in love with Flérida, princess of Constantinople. Eager to win her love, he wonders whether she could ever love him for his intrinsic personal worth and not solely for his renowned royal status. To ascertain the truth, he disguises himself as a gardener tending Flérida's garden, thus enabling him to converse frequently with her. Gradually, Flérida recognizes Don Duardos's refined, noble spirit and his pro-

The Teatro Nacional Dona Maria II in Lisbon, Portugal. The statue sitting on top of the colonnade is of
Vicente (from Giovanna Magi, Lisbon: Sintra-Queluz-Cascais-Estoril, 1991;
Thomas Cooper Library, University of South Carolina).

found love for her. She falls in love with him, but, due to deeply rooted class prejudices in her society, she experiences great anxiety and uncertainty when she weighs her lover's supposedly humble status. Finally, the power of her genuine love enables her to express it with joy and dignity.

In addition to the Spanish, Portuguese, and Castilian that Vicente uses in his plays, in some, such as *A farsa chamada auto da fama* (1510, The Play of Fame), he also sporadically uses other languages: Italian, French, and "African." At times, the author's fertile imagination suggestively approximates forms of these languages or dialects. With such linguistic manipulations, he increases their theatrical efficacy without sacrificing clarity and meaning. The nationality of the character who speaks usually determines the use of Spanish or Portuguese. The Castilian dramatic tradition is another decisive reason that Vicente employs Spanish, particularly in the early plays on the theme of religious devotion. He probably utilizes Spanish in some plays (for instance, *Tragicomédia de Dom Duardos* and *Tragicomédia de Amadís*) because the original sources for them were in Spanish. Another consideration for Vicente was the fact that two successive

wives of King Manuel I, who reigned in Portugal from 1495 until 1521, were daughters of Isabel I and Ferdinand V, while his third wife was Charles V's sister. Another of the emperor's sisters was the wife of Manuel I's successor, King John II. Although the Portuguese court was bilingual, Vicente understandably would have wanted to make the cordial gesture of acknowledging these ladies by having them hear their native language whenever theatrically appropriate.

Vicente wrote in *Tragicomédia do inverno e verão* that "quem quiser fingir / na castelhana linguagem achará quanto pedir" (he who wants to write fiction, / will find in the Castilian language / whatever he may seek). This statement represents the extent of his regard for the Spanish language. He was not, however, implicitly criticizing some supposed shortcomings of the Portuguese language. Indeed, Vicente's work proves the contrary. With the use of the various languages in his plays, he wanted to share extraordinary human experiences with all the world as eloquently and effectively as possible.

Not all critics believe that Gil Vicente the author can be identified convincingly with the goldsmith of the same name, arguing that this name was not uncommon then and, more significantly, that had he been a goldsmith, more information certainly would have survived. Although it is strange that Vicente should refer repeatedly to himself as "el que faz os Autos a el Rei" (the one who makes the plays for the King) and never as a goldsmith, without further documented evidence this question remains open. Without a doubt, however, Vicente approached his theatrical work as a craftsman, deploying the poetic forms and meters from a variety of written and oral traditions, Portuguese and Castilian, often modified and enriched by a new turn, tone, hue, or rhythm. The densely lyrical verse, always present to some degree in his theater, makes the latter an important precursor of modern poetic drama. Some of Vicente's daring dramatic and theatrical conceptions (in, for instance, *Comédia de Rubena*) are likewise precocious forerunners of modern experiments in the theater. The interplay of dramatic action, dynamic characters, stagecraft, poetry, song, and music that he often achieves reminds playgoers of Pedro Calderón de la Barca's lavish palace plays or Richard Wagner's mythical operas, among other extraordinary forms of theatrical spectacle. In reference to Vicente's theater, some of the most illustrious authors of all times are often evoked, including Plautus, Lope de Vega, Miguel de Cervantes, William Shakespeare, Calderón, Molière, and Johann Wolfgang von Goethe.

Bibliographies:

Constantine C. Stathatos, *A Gil Vicente Bibliography (1940–1975)* (London: Grant & Cutler, 1980);

Stathatos, *A Gil Vicente Bibliography, 1975–1995: With a Supplement for 1940–1975* (Bethlehem, Pa.: Lehigh University Press, 1997);

Stathatos, *A Gil Vicente Bibliography, 1995–2000* (Kassel: Reichenberger, 2001).

Biographies:

Anselmo Braamcamp Freire, *Vida e obras de Gil Vicente: "Trovador, Mestre da Balança,"* second edition (Lisbon: Revista de Ocidente, 1944);

Jack Horace Parker, *Gil Vicente* (Boston: Twayne, 1967).

References:

Aubrey F. G. Bell, *Gil Vicente* (Oxford: Oxford University Press, 1921);

José Augusto Cardoso Bernardes, *Sátira e Lirismo: Modelos de síntese no teatro de Gil Vicente* (Coimbra, Portugal: Por Ordem da Universidade, 1996);

Reis Brasil, *Gil Vicente e o teatro moderno: Tentativa de esquematização de obra vicentina* (Lisbon: Minerva, 1965);

D. L. Pereira da Costa, *Gil Vicente e sua época* (Lisbon: Guimarães, 1989);

René Pedro Garay, *Gil Vicente and the Development of the Comedia* (Chapel Hill: University of North Carolina Department of Romance Languages, 1988);

M. L. García da Cruz, *Gil Vicente e a Sociedade Portuguesa de Quinhentos: Leitura crítica num mundo de "Cara Atrás": As personagens e o Palco da sua Acção* (Lisbon: Gradiva, 1990);

Hope Hamilton-Faria, *The Farces of Gil Vicente: A Study in the Stylistics of Satire* (Madrid: Playor, 1976);

Thomas R. Hart, *Gil Vicente: Casandra and Don Duardos,* Critical Guides to Spanish Texts, no. 29 (London: Grant & Cutler, 1981);

Laurence L. Keates, *The Court Theatre of Gil Vicente* (Lisbon: Livraria Escolar Editora, 1962);

Celso Láfer, *O judeu em Gil Vicente* (São Paulo: Conselho Estadual de Cultura, Comissão de Literatura, 1963);

Marcelino Menéndez y Pelayo, "Gil Vicente," in his *Antología de poetas líricos castellanos,* volume 3 (Santander: Aldus, 1944), pp. 347–395;

Neil T. Miller, *O elemento pastoril no teatro de Gil Vicente* (Porto: Inova, 1970);

Stephen Reckert, *Gil Vicente: Espíritu y letra* (Madrid: Gredos, 1977);

I. S. Révah, *Recherches sur les oeuvres de Gil Vicente* (Lisbon: Institut Français au Portugal, 1951);

Leif Sletsjøe, *O elemento cénico em Gil Vicente* (Lisbon: Casa Portuguêsa, 1965);

Luciana Stegagno Picchio, *Storia del teatro portoghese* (Rome: Ateneo, 1964);

José I. Suárez, *The Carnival Stage: Vicentine Comedy within the Serio-Comic Mode* (Rutherford, N.J.: Fairleigh Dickinson University Press / London: Associated University Presses, 1993);

Ronald E. Surtz, *The Birth of a Theater: Dramatic Convention in the Spanish Theater from Juan del Encina to Lope de Vega* (Princeton: Princeton University, Department of Romance Languages and Literatures, 1979);

María José Teles, María Leonor Cruz, and S. Marta Pinheiro, *O discurso carnavalesco em Gil Vicente no âmbito de uma História das Mentalidades* (Lisbon: GEC Publicações, 1984);

Paul Teyssier, *Gil Vicente: O Autor e a Sua Obra,* translated by Alvaro Salema (Lisbon: Instituto de Cultura e Língua Portuguesa, 1982);

R. A. Young, "Gil Vicente's Castilian Debut," *Segismundo* (1972–1973): 25–50;

Stanislav Zimic, *Ensayos y notas sobre el teatro de Gil Vicente* (Madrid: Iberoamericana / Frankfurt am Main: Vervuert, 2003).

Antonio de Villegas

(fl. 1560s)

J. Ignacio Díez Fernández

Universidad Complutense (Madrid)

BOOK: *Inventario de Antonio de Villegas, dirigido a la Magestad Real del Rey Don Phelippe, nuestro señor* (Medina del Campo: Francisco del Canto, 1565; enlarged, 1577).

Modern Editions: *Inventario,* 2 volumes, edited by Francisco López Estrada (Madrid: Tipografía Madrileña de Cándido Bermejo, 1955, 1956);

Antonio de Villegas' "El Abencerraje," bilingual edition, edited and translated by López Estrada and John Esten Keller (Chapel Hill: University of North Carolina Press, 1964);

La historia de Píramo y Thisbe, in Pedro Correa Rodríguez, *La historia de Píramo y Thisbe de Antonio de Villegas* (Granada: Universidad de Granada, 2000), pp. 127–159.

Antonio de Villegas is a Golden Age Spanish writer about whom little is known. Based on what he wrote in his only work, *Inventario de Antonio de Villegas, dirigido a la Magestad Real del Rey Don Phelippe, nuestro señor* (1565, Inventory of Antonio de Villegas, Directed to His Royal Majesty King don Philip, Our Sovereign), he most probably spent his life in the Castilian town of Medina del Campo. Composed of diverse compositions in prose and verse, *Inventario de Antonio de Villegas* is an interesting miscellany that was published in two editions in the sixteenth century (in 1565 and, with some additions, in 1577). Villegas is undoubtedly better known for his connection with what is considered the first Moorish novel, *El Abencerraje y la hermosa Jarifa* (1565, The Abencerraje and the Beautiful Jarifa); although one of the first appearances of that work was in *Inventario de Antonio de Villegas,* its authorship is still under scholarly examination. Villegas's authorship of one of the earliest pastoral novels, *Ausencia y soledad de amor* (Absence and Solitude of Love), also included in his miscellany, is unquestioned, however. Owing to certain features of *Inventario de Antonio de Villegas,* some scholars have suggested the possible *converso* (a term designating Jewish converts to Catholicism) origin of Villegas, although this theory has yet to be proven.

Because of a lack of documentary information, Villegas's biography is almost unknown. The place and date of both his birth and death remain mysteries, although from the transactions leading to the publication of his only book it is evident that he was still alive in 1574 and 1576. In fact, as Francisco López Estrada points out in his introduction to the 1955–1956 edition of the *Inventario,* "cuanto se sabe de él es lo que puede deducirse del contenido de su obra" (everything we know about him is deduced from the content of his work). Hence, the first reference to Villegas is found in his application for a license to print a work already written in 1551 (when he requested the license), even though this work, for reasons unknown, was not published then. His application to publish *Inventario de Antonio de Villegas* in 1565, the date of the first edition, indicates that he resided in Medina del Campo. Villegas again requested a privilege for ten years, in 1574, before the expiration of the previous one, and in his application he declares himself once again to be a resident of Medina del Campo. It seems that he wrote an extensive poem afterward, "Cuestión y disputa entre Ayax Telamón y Ulises sobre las armas de Aquiles" (Question and Dispute between Ajax Telamon and Ulysses over Achilles' Arms), which received approbation in October 1576. At that time Villegas asked for a new license for printing, which was granted on 25 October 1576.

One handwritten document concerning Villegas was found during the twentieth century in the Fernán Núñez Collection at the Bancroft Library, University of California at Berkeley. Among assorted documents in volume 183 of this collection, there appears a "Carta escripta a Antonio de Billegas sobre un libro que queria imprimir por un çierto autor" (Letter Written to Antonio de Villegas Regarding a Book That He Wanted to Print by a Certain Author). This letter was composed by Damasio de Frías in the sixteenth century, as Juan Montero explains in his "Noticia de un texto recuperado: La invectiva de Damasio de Frías contra Antonio de Villegas y su *Inventario*" (2003, Notice of a Recov-

Title page for Antonio de Villegas's collection (Inventory of Antonio de Villegas, Directed to His Majesty King don Philip, Our Sovereign), one of the earliest books in which the first Moorish novel, the anonymous El Abencerraje y la hermosa Jarifa *(1559?, The Abencerraje and the Beautiful Jarifa), appears (from Francisco López Estrada, ed.,* El Abencerraje y la hermosa Jarifa: Cuatro textos y su estudio, *1957; Thomas Cooper Library, University of South Carolina)*

was granted in order to publish the first edition of *Inventario de Antonio de Villegas* in 1565. He may have decided to publish a second edition in 1577 because of the unlikely success of the first one, or perhaps because his literary ambitions were fostered by the rich editorial life in the small town where he was living. During the sixteenth century, Medina del Campo was, in López Estrada's words in his introduction to the *Inventario,* "rica y turbulenta, estaba concurrida de gran número de gente que, sobre todo en las ferias, acudían a tratar sus mercaderías" (rich and turbulent, frequented by a great number of people who, especially at the time of the fairs, went to buy and sell their goods). The book trade was important in Medina del Campo, as is evident from the 248 books printed there throughout the sixteenth century, as Pérez Pastor's bibliography makes clear.

In *Inventario de Antonio de Villegas* Castilian and Italian forms are employed, although the license for its printing lists the work as "un libro de ciertas obras en metro castellano" (a book of certain works in Castilian verse). The combination of Castilian and Italian meters is typical of the period, and Villagas alternates between the two, as do many other poets of the Renaissance. *Inventario de Antonio de Villegas* is dedicated to King Philip II; Villegas is stereotypical in seeking protection for his book, which, as he writes, "huido y amenazado de la murmuración, señora de la gente" (escaped and menaced by gossip, lady of the people), takes refuge in the king "como a lugar sagrado donde no puede prender" (as a sanctuary where it cannot be caught). The book seems to be clearly arranged in two parts, although the texts are not explicitly grouped in their wider categories: octosyllabic verses first and hendecasyllabic verses later. There are also preliminary pieces, including an exhortation to the book and some texts about the death of illustrious celebrities, as well as a general, positive reflection on death. *Ausencia y soledad de amor* and *El Abencerraje y la hermosa Jarifa* seem to frame the work, with *Ausencia y soledad de amor* placed immediately after the poetic preliminaries and *El Abencerraje y la hermosa Jarifa* at the close of the collection.

The exhortatory prologue to *Inventario de Antonio de Villegas,* in five-line stanzas, begins: "Ve con Dios, hijo querido, / cargado de mis hazañas, / con mil dolores parido, / salido de mis entrañas, / engendrado en mi sentido" (Go with God, dear son, / carrying my achievements, / given birth to with a thousand aches, / coming from my innermost parts, / engendered in my sense). Among the supposed complaints the book may give rise to, one is particularly significant: "otros te pondrán un ceño / diciendo que eres amargo / como libro, en fin, sin dueño" (others will frown at you / saying you are bitter / as a book, finally, with no owner), which

ered Text: the Invective of Damasio de Frías against Antonio de Villegas and His *Inventario*), and it is an invective against Villegas and his book. Frías makes fun of the long time (fifteen years) Villegas spent preparing *Inventario de Antonio de Villegas* and asserts that the final product did not meet with the expectations of his reading public.

From a bibliographical viewpoint, the second edition of *Inventario de Antonio de Villegas* is considered a "libro bastante raro" (quite rare book), as Cristóbal Pérez Pastor states in his *La imprenta en Medina del Campo* (1895, The Press in Medina del Campo). One gap in scholarly knowledge of the work is what led Villegas to wait fifteen years from the time he requested permission to print, in 1551, until the time he used the license he appears to create a negative tone even though in the whole introduction there is clearly an amorous leitmotiv. This introductory nucleus closes with the poem "A la muerte" (To Death). This poem expresses at times rather macabre praise—"¿Qué puede temer el hombre / metido en un ataúd?" (What can man fear / inside a coffin?)—and includes many references to the soul and body and allusions to the "ley cristiana" (Christian law) "porque en esta ley cristiana, / cuanto emponzoña la vida, / la muerte después lo sana" (because by this Christian law, / what life poisons, / death later cures).

Many octosyllabic poems in *Inventario de Antonio de Villegas* deal with figures such as Dido and Aeneas, the Princess Juana, and the duke of Sessa. These poems involve themes such as love or circumstantial matters and develop glosses based on works composed by Villegas and other poets. Villegas's hendecasyllabic poems commence with a mythological fable, *La historia de Píramo y Thisbe* (Story of Pyramus and Thisbe), a work modeled on Ovid that comprises more than 1,300 lines and is composed in Italian meter. After this long poem, *Inventario de Antonio de Villegas* continues with eleven sonnets and one Petrarchan song, before closing with *El Abencerraje y la hermosa Jarifa*. The second edition of Villegas's book adds various poems, all of which are in traditional octosyllabic verse: "Cuestión y disputa entre Ayax Telamón y Ulises sobre las armas de Aquiles," "Llanto de Pílades por la muerte de Orestes, su gran amigo" (Pilades's Lament for the Death of Orestes, His Great Friend), and some circumstantial compositions, of which "A una dama, enviándola un espejo" (To a Lady, Sending Her a Mirror) and "A un ventalle que envió a una dama" (To a Fan He Sent a Lady) are representative.

As with all of Villegas's work, the date of composition of the two prose novels he includes is not known. Both novels are customarily associated with another work of the time, Jorge de Montemayor's *Los siete libros de Diana* (1559, The Seven Books of Diana), a text that has traditionally been recognized as the first milestone of the pastoral novel. The story in *Ausencia y soledad de amor* is told by an individual afflicted with suffering, who introduces the reader to two couples. The text alternates prose and verse, as would thereafter be customary in the genre.

When critics speak of Villegas, it is almost always in connection with *El Abencerraje y la hermosa Jarifa*, which is, as López Estrada writes in the introduction to *Antonio de Villegas' "El Abencerraje"* (1964), "the most important and outstanding example of the genre we know as the Moorish novel, and is also one of the literary masterpieces of the Spanish Renaissance." The novel has been preserved in different versions, although the editors tend to prefer the version included

in *Inventario de Antonio de Villegas*. *El Abencerraje y la hermosa Jarifa* appeared, almost at the same time, in very different works during the middle of the sixteenth century. It is included in the 1561 edition of *Los siete libros de Diana*, which was published by Francisco Fernández de Córdoba in Valladolid. The text can be found at the end of the fourth book of that collection, under the title *Historia de Abindarráez y la hermosa Xarifa* (Story of Abindarraez and the beautiful Xarifa). Also in 1561, in Toledo, Miguel Ferrer included *El Abencerraje y la hermosa Jarifa* in his *Chrónica* (Chronicle), which has been preserved without preliminaries, the first page, or information on the place and year of printing (although it is usually thought to have appeared in Saragossa). Finally, a shorter manuscript text, the *Historia del moro* (Story of the Moor), also includes *El Abencerraje y la hermosa Jarifa*. The extent to which the different versions of *El Abencerraje y la hermosa Jarifa* were revised by the authors of the books in which they appear is not clear.

Whether Villegas wrote *El Abencerraje y la hermosa Jarifa* is unknown. The issue is clouded by the general title of the collection, which may indicate that the book is actually a compilation, as López Estrada notes: "por de pronto, el mismo título de *Inventario,* tomado del léxico de las leyes, puede aludir a este carácter complejo, de un conjunto de obras reunidas a lo largo de una vida y que se recoge para asegurar su persistencia, pues de otro modo se perdería cada pieza por su parte" (at first glance, the title of *Inventory,* taken from legal language, may allude to this complex character of a collection of works brought together over a whole life and united in order to assure their survival, because otherwise each part in isolation might be lost). Moreover, even though the novel has usually been placed in bibliographies under Villegas's name, this convention does not always imply a declaration in favor of his authorship but rather simply the scholarly preference for the version of the novel published in *Inventario de Antonio de Villegas*.

Modern scholars have not endorsed the theory that Villegas wrote *El Abencerraje y la hermosa Jarifa*. The degree of Villegas's participation in the composition of the work remains unclear, with scholarly opinions ranging between both extremes, that is, from those that support his authorship to those that envision him solely as a compiler. Marcel Bataillon, in his essay "¿Melancolía renacentista o melancolía judía?" (1952, Renaissance Melancholy or Jewish Melancholy?), argues that for stylistic reasons—that is, because of the difference between the "elegancia" (elegance) of the novel and the "pesadez" (tediousness) of Villegas's prologue—he does not believe that Villegas wrote the novel. José Navarro Gómez argues in his essay "El autor de la versión del *Abencerraje* contenida en la Diana ¿era Montemayor?"

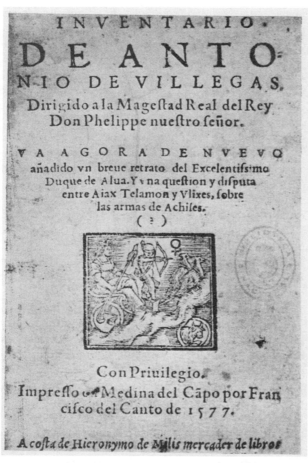

Title page for the enlarged edition of Villegas's only published work (from Francisco López Estrada, ed., El Abencerraje y la hermosa Jarifa: Cuatro textos y su estudio, *1957; Thomas Cooper Library, University of South Carolina)*

question as being sufficient to prove the author's *converso* identity. The establishment of Villegas's authorship of *El Abencerraje y la hermosa Jarifa* might potentially resolve the question insofar as several critics support the hypothesis that the author of that work was a *converso*. This hypothesis is based on a variety of evidence, such as the fact that one of the versions of *El Abencerraje y la hermosa Jarifa* is dedicated to Jerónimo Jiménez de Embún—"whose mother and wife were conversas," as Samuel G. Armistead observes in his 1995 essay *"El Abencerraje* as a Converso Text"—or the critical consensus regarding the message of the novel (the peaceful coexistence of the members of different religions).

As a whole, *Inventario de Antonio de Villegas* has been received positively by modern scholars. The almost total ignorance of Antonio de Villegas's biography is only partly offset by the little information that can be gleaned from the preliminary sections of the collection and by the hypotheses that can be formulated from readings of the work. The discovery of the handwritten text in which an anonymous author makes fun of several details of Villegas's work, such as the lapse of time invested in publishing the book, perhaps adds to what is known about him. Whether Villegas actually wrote *El Abencerraje y la hermosa Jarifa,* his name is permanently linked to the text. For his role as either author or editor of *El Abencerraje y la hermosa Jarifa*—a work described by María Soledad Carrasco Urgoiti in her essay "Las cortes señoriales del Aragón mudéjar y *El Abencerraje*" (1972, The Noble Courts of the Mudejar Aragon and *El Abencerraje*) as "one of the finest examples of that frequent encounter in Spanish Golden Age literature of themes rooted in the traditions of the past with artistic and ethical concepts of the present"—as well as for the other texts included in *Inventario de Antonio de Villegas,* Villegas has gained a place within the panorama of Spanish Golden Age literature.

(1978, The Author of the Version Contained in *Diana* was Montemayor) that Montemayor wrote *El Abencerraje y la hermosa Jarifa* and adds to well-known arguments and hypotheses his comparison of a paragraph in the final pages of *Los siete libros de Diana* with another one in the 1561 Toledo edition of *El Abencerraje y la hermosa Jarifa.*

Another unresolved issue regarding Villegas's work and life is the possibility that he descended from *conversos*. Given the lack of information about Villegas's biography, it is not possible to solve the question by referring to documents about his family and friends, as has been done, for instance, in the case of the sixteenth-century poet Gutierre de Cetina. In the case of Villegas, the hypothesis of his *converso* origin is based only on some aspects of his work, such as his use of references to the Old Testament, which scholars such as Bataillon

References:

Samuel G. Armistead, *"El Abencerraje* as a Converso Text," in *Apples of Gold in Filigrees of Silver: Jewish Writing in the Eyes of the Spanish Inquisition,* edited by Colbert I. Nepaulsingh (New York: Holmes & Meier, 1995), pp. 83–101;

Marcel Bataillon, "¿Melancolía renacentista o melancolía judía?" in *Estudios hispánicos: Homenaje a Archer M. Huntington* (Wellesley, Mass.: Wellesley College, 1952), pp. 39–50;

Bataillon, "Salmacis y Trocho en *El Abencerraje,*" in *Hommage à Ernest Martinenche: Etudes hispaniques et américaines* (Paris: Editions d'Artrey, 1939), pp. 355–363;

María Soledad Carrasco Urgoiti, "Las cortes señoriales del Aragón mudéjar y *El Abencerraje,*" in *Homenaje a Casalduero,* edited by Rizel Pincus Sigele and Gonzalo Sobejano (Madrid: Gredos, 1972), pp. 115–128;

Carrasco Urgoiti, *The Moorish Novel: "El Abencerraje" and Pérez de Hita* (Boston: Twayne, 1976);

Carrasco Urgoiti, "La novela morisca," in *La novela española en el siglo XVI* (Madrid: Iberoamericana / Frankfurt am Main: Vervuert, 2001), pp. 51–87;

José María de Cossío, *Fábulas mitológicas en España* (Madrid: Espasa-Calpe, 1952), pp. 163–167;

J. P. W. Crawford, "Un episodio de *El Abencerraje* y una 'Novella' de Ser Giovanni," *Revista de Filología Española,* 10 (1923): 281–287;

George Irving Dale, "The Date of Antonio de Villegas' Death," *Modern Language Notes,* 36 (1921): 334–337;

José Ignacio Díez Fernández, "Textos literarios españoles en la Fernán Núñez Collection (Bancroft Library, Berkeley)," *Dicenda: Cuadernos de Filología Hispánica,* 15 (1997): 139–182;

Joaquín Gimeno Casalduero, "*El Abencerraje y la hermosa Jarifa:* Composición y significado," *Nueva Revista de Filología Hispánica,* 21 (1972): 1–22;

Richard F. Glenn, "The Moral Implications of *El Abencerraje,*" *Modern Language Notes,* 80 (1965): 202–209;

Claudio Guillén, "Individuo y ejemplaridad en *El Abencerraje,*" in *Collected Studies in Honour of Américo Castro's Eightieth Year,* edited by M. P. Hornik (Oxford: Lincombe Lodge Research Library, 1965), pp. 2–23;

Francisco López Estrada, "El Abencerraje de Toledo, 1561: Edición crítica y comentarios," *Anales de la Universidad Hispalense,* 20 (1959): 1–60;

López Estrada, "Estudio y texto de la narración pastoril *Ausencia y soledad de amor,* del *Inventario* de Villegas," *Boletín de la Real Academia Española,* 29 (1949): 99–133;

López Estrada, ed., *El Abencerraje y la hermosa Jarifa: Cuatro textos y su estudio* (Madrid: Revista de Archivos, Bibliotecas y Museos, 1957);

Juan Montero, "Noticia de un texto recuperado: La invectiva de Damasio de Frías contra Antonio de Villegas y su *Inventario,*" *Voz y letra,* 14, no. 2 (2003): 79–98;

José Navarro Gómez, "El autor de la versión del *Abencerraje* contenida en la *Diana* ¿era Montemayor?" *Revista de Literatura,* 39 (1978): 101–104;

Cristóbal Pérez Pastor, *La imprenta en Medina del Campo* (Madrid: Rivadeneyra, 1895);

Aristide Rumeau, "*L'Abencérage,* un texte retrouvé," *Bulletin Hispanique,* 59 (1957): 369–395;

George A. Shipley, "La obra literaria como monumento histórico: El caso del *Abencerraje,*" *Journal of Hispanic Philology,* 2 (1978): 103–120;

Keith Whinnom, "The Relationship of the Three Texts of *El Abencerraje,*" *Modern Language Review,* 54 (1959): 507–517.

Juan Luis Vives
(1493 – 6 May 1540)

Montserrat Piera
Temple University

BOOKS: *Christi Jesu Triumphus* (Paris, 1514);

Ovatio Virginis Dei Parentis (Paris, 1514);

Veritas Fucata (Paris, 1514);

Libri quatuor Hyginii historiographi (Paris, 1514);

Meditationes in septem psalmos quos vocant poenitentiae (Louvain, 1518);

Anima senis (Louvain, 1518);

Fabula de homine (Louvain, 1518);

De tempore quo natus est Christus (Louvain, 1518);

Genethliacon Jesu Christi (Louvain, 1518);

De initiis, sectis et laudibus philosophiae (Louvain, 1518);

Praelectio in Georgica Publii Vergili Maronis (Louvain, 1518);

Aedes legum (Louvain, 1519);

Somnium et vigilia in Somnium Scipionis (Basel, 1519);

Adversus pseudodialecticos (Sélestat, 1519/Louvain, 1520);

Praefatio in Leges Ciceronis (Louvain, 1520);

Declamationes quinque Syllanae (Antwerp: Hillenius, 1520);

Declamatio qua Quintiliano respondetur (Louvain, 1521);

De ratione studii puerilis (Strasbourg, 1521);

Commentarii in XXII libris De Civitate Dei, divi Aurelii Agustini (Basel: Frobenium, 1522); translated by John Healey as *St. Augustine of the Citie of God: with the learned comments of Io. Lod. Vives* (London, 1610);

De consultatione (Oxford & London, 1523);

De institutione feminae christianae (Antwerp: Hillenius, 1524); translated by Richard Hyrde as *A Very Frutefull and Pleasant Boke Called the Instruction of a Christen Woman* (London: Printed by Thomas Berthelet, 1529);

Introductio ad sapientiam (Strasbourg, 1524); translated by R. Morysone as *An Introduction to Wysedom* (London: Printed by Thomas Berthelet, 1540); republished by Marian Leona Tobriner as *Vives' Introduction to Wisdom: A Renaissance Textbook* (New York: Teachers College Press, 1968);

De pacificatione (Basel, 1529);

De Europae dissidiis et bello Turcico (Basel, 1525 or 1526);

De subventione pauperum (Bruges: Hubert de Crouck, 1526);

Juan Luis Vives (Academia de Ballas Artes de San Fernando; from J. A. Fernández-Santamaría, The Theater of Man: J. L. Vives on Society, *1998; Thomas Cooper Library, University of South Carolina)*

De conditione vitae christianorum sub Turca (Ypres, 1526/Antwerp, 1529);

De officio mariti (Bruges, 1528); translated by Thomas Paynell as *The Office and Duetie of a Husband, made by the excellent philosopher Ludovicus Vives* (London: Printed by J. Cawood, 1550);

De concordia et discordia in humano genere (Antwerp, 1529);

Diurnum sacrum de sudore domini nostri Jesu Christi (Bruges, 1529);

De disciplinis: I. De causis corruptarum artium, II. De tradendis disciplinis, III. De artibus (Antwerp, 1531); second

part, *De tradendis disciplinis,* translated by Foster
Watson as *On Education* (Cambridge: Cambridge
University Press, 1913);
De ratione dicendi (Louvain, 1533);
Excitationes ad animi in Deum (Antwerp, 1535);
De communione rerum (Bruges, 1535);
De conscribendis epistolis (Leipzig, 1536);
Bucolicarum Vergilii interpretatio allegorica (Breda, 1537);
De anima et vita (Basel, 1538);
Censura de Aristotelis operibus (Basel, 1538); translated as *A
    Short Summary of Aristotle's Philosophy* (London,
    1540);
Linguae latinae exercitatio (Breda, 1538);
De veritate fidei christianae (Basel: Printed by Oporinus,
    1543);
Joannis Ludovici Vivis, Valentini, Opera Omnia, 2 volumes,
    edited by H. Coccius (Basel: Printed by Nicolas
    l'Evesque le Jeune, 1555).

Modern Editions: *Opera Omnia,* 8 volumes, edited by
    Gregorio Mayans y Siscar (Valencia: Benito
    Monfort, 1782–1790; facsimile edition, London:
    Gregg, 1964);
*Vives: On Education: A Translation of the "De Tradendis Dis-
    ciplinis" of Juan Luis Vives,* translated by Foster
    Watson (Cambridge: Cambridge University
    Press, 1913; reprinted, Totowa, N.J.: Rowman &
    Littlefield, 1971);
Literae virorum eruditorum ad Franciscum Craneveldium,
    edited by H. de Vocht (Louvain: Libraire Univer-
    sitaire, 1928);
Obras completas (1493–1540), 2 volumes, edited by L. Riber
    (Madrid: Aguilar, 1947, 1948);
In Pseudo-Dialecticos: A Critical Edition, edited and trans-
    lated by Charles Fantazzi (Leiden: Brill, 1979);
Selected Works of J. L. Vives, 7 volumes, edited by
    C. Matheeussen, C. Fantazzi, E. George, and J.
    Ijsewijn (Leiden: Brill, 1987–2002)–comprises vol-
    ume 1, *Early Writings* (1987); volume 2, *Declamationes
    Sullanae, I* (1989); volume 3, *De conscribendis epistolis*
    (1989); volume 4, *De Subventione Pauperam* (2002);
    volume 5, *Early Writings 2* (1991); volume 6, *De Insti-
    tutione Feminae Christianae. Liber Primus* (1996); and
    volume 7, *De Institutione Feminae Christianae. Liber
    Secundus* (1998);
Ioannis Lodovici Vivis, Valentini, Opera Omnia, 3 volumes,
    edited by Antonio Mestre (Valencia: Edicions
    Alfons el Magnànim, Generalitat Valenciana,
    Instituto de Cultura Juan Gil-Albert, Universitat
    de Valencia, 1992–1993)–comprises volume 1,
    Volumen Introductorio (1992); volume 2, *Philologica 1.
    Comentarii ad divi Avrelii Avgustini De Civitate Dei.
    Libri I–V* (1993); and volume 3, *Philologica 2.
    Comentarii ad divi Avrelii Avgustini De Civitate Dei.
    Libri VI–XIII* (1992);

De arte dicendi. El arte retórica, edited and translated by
    Ana Isabel Camacho (Barcelona: Anthropos,
    1998).
Edition in English: *Somnium et vigilia in Somnium Scipio-
    nis: Commentary on the Dream of Scipio,* edited and
    translated by Edward V. George (Greenwood,
    S.C.: Attic Press, 1989);
The Instruction of a Christen Woman, edited, with an intro-
    duction, by V. Walcott Beauchamp, E. H. Hage-
    man, and Margaret Mikesell (Urbana & Chicago:
    University of Illinois Press, 2002).

Juan Luis (or Joan Lluis in Catalan, his native
tongue) Vives was a humanist philosopher, scholar,
and educational reformer. Although born in Spain, he
spent most of his adult life in northern Europe; he
attended university in Paris and later lived in Bruges,
Louvain, Oxford, and London, where he became Mary
Tudor's preceptor. He is, therefore, considered a member of the group of northern humanists that includes
Desiderius Erasmus of Rotterdam, Thomas More, and
Guillaume Budé. Vives is best known for his pioneering work in psychology and educational reform, but he
also wrote prolifically on philosophy, religion, international politics, morality, and the relief of the poor. The
originality of his contributions rests on his empirical
approach to the sciences and the observation of nature
and his interest in the practical arts and inventions.

Vives lived during the Reformation, and like
Erasmus, one of the most visible thinkers of the times,
he was a devout Christian who was, however, critical
of the corruption of the Catholic Church and its
emphasis on superficial and ostentatious religious rituals. He believed instead in the value of intrinsic virtue.
He lived during a turbulent period in European history,
and his works indicate how deeply troubled he was by
the religious conflicts of the time and the constant warfare they provoked. He often attempted to effect social
change and to promote international peace by addressing not only the common public but also kings and religious dignitaries.

Vives was born in 1493–not in 1492, as previously believed–in Valencia, Spain, the son of Luis
Vives Valeriola and Blanquina March Maçana. His
parents were Jewish *conversos* (converts to Catholicism)
from prosperous and well-established families, a group
that suffered greatly at the hands of the Tribunal of the
Inquisition, established in 1480. Vives's cousin, Miquel
Vives, was executed by the Inquisition, together with a
large group of converted Jews from Valencia, after a
clandestine synagogue was discovered in his house in
1500. In 1505 Vives's great-grandfather, Manuel Vives,
was burned at the stake and his ashes scattered in a
public dump.

Vives's father had clashes with the authorities in 1479 and 1500. Then, in 1524, when his son was already teaching at Oxford, he was also burned at the stake. Vives's mother, who had died from the plague in 1508, was tried post mortem by the Inquisition and found guilty of following Jewish rites. Her remains were exhumed by the authorities and burned. Vives, fearing for his own safety, never returned to Spain, even when he was offered, in 1522, the chair in rhetoric that the famous grammarian Antonio de Nebrija had occupied at the University of Alcalá.

Apart from some brief sketches from his writings, most of the biographical information about Vives has been obtained from his copious correspondence, especially those letters addressed to his friend Frans von Craneveldt from 1522 to 1528. Vives's correspondence makes clear that he was afraid of the power of the Inquisition and was always wary about a possible return to Spain. His connection to his native city remained strong, however, to the extent that he always appended *Valentinus* (of Valencia) to his name, kept well informed about the social and political developments taking place in Spain, and seemed inclined to interact and to live among people from the Iberian Peninsula. Nevertheless, he was predominantly trained as a humanist and scholar in the northern European tradition, and his writings attest to that influence.

His national affiliation has been, however, ardently debated. On one hand, as Luis E. Rodríguez states in his essay "Juan Luis Vives: Horizonte de España" (1995, Juan Luis Vives: Horizon of Spain), "la historiografía hispana [ha] tendido a apropiarse desde un punto de vista nacionalista la figura de Vives" (Spanish historiography has had the tendency of appropriating Vives from a nationalistic standpoint). For example, José Jiménez Delgado, in his edition of *Epistolario de Juan Luis Vives* (1978, Letters of Juan Luis Vives), calls him "the greatest Spanish humanist of the sixteenth century." There are scholars, on the other hand, especially from outside Spain (such as Marcel Bataillon), who regard Vives not as a Spanish thinker but as a European thinker.

After a brief period of schooling in Valencia, Vives was sent to Paris to study at the age of sixteen in 1509. He studied Scholastic logic and medieval physics at the College of Montaigu in Paris. His disappointment with his professors and the methods of the medieval Scholastic philosophy that they followed prompted him to produce his first influential text, *Adversus pseudodialecticos* (Against the Pseudo-Dialecticians), which was published in 1520. Much to Vives's surprise, this book, which harshly criticized the academic milieu in Paris, was well received and not only established him as a leading voice in the debate with the Scholastic dialecti-

cians but also contributed to changing the nature of nonlogical discussions at the university. Before the publication of this polemical pamphlet, Vives had also written several religious works published in Paris in 1514, such as *Christi Jesu Triumphus* (The Triumph of Jesus Christ) and *Ovatio Virginis Dei Parentis* (Praise of Mary, Mother of God), which, as the titles indicate, were devoted to discussing various aspects of the nature of Jesus and his mother, Mary.

Vives left Paris in 1514 and settled in Bruges, where he found a thriving and welcoming community of Spanish Jews who had chosen to leave Spain after the Edict of Expulsion of 1492. Among them were Bernat Valdaura and Clara Cervent, who hired Vives to tutor their three children and whose daughter Margaret became Vives's wife in 1524. In 1517 he became the tutor of the nineteen-year-old William of Croy (Guillaume de Croy), who was not only already bishop of Cambrai and a cardinal but also the most likely successor to Francisco Jiménez de Cisneros, cardinal of Toledo and inquisitor general of Spain. This appointment granted Vives not only financial security but also the protection of an influential man who could ensure the safety of Vives's family.

This new and prestigious position forced Vives to move to Louvain, where he worked from 1517 to 1523, teaching privately and at the university, despite the fact that he never obtained a formal university degree from the schools where he studied. Jozef Ijsewijn, in his *Humanisme i literatura neollatina* (1996, Humanism and Neo-Latin Literature), believes that his lack of a degree would explain why the name of Vives was never included in the official lists of professors at the University of Louvain. Notwithstanding, Vives must have been well received among the professors of the university, and he must have enjoyed the possibilities for intellectual exchange, because during this period he was extremely productive. He wrote thirteen works in the first three years. The untimely death of his employer and patron, William of Croy, from a fall from a horse, brought his professional prospects to an abrupt end, however.

While in Louvain he undertook his own commentary on Erasmus's edition of Augustine's *De civitate Dei* (The City of God), which he completed in 1522 and dedicated to Henry VIII of England. Vives's painstaking edition of the text (a task that he claimed was not enjoyable for him) and his extensive commentaries demonstrate the philosopher's thorough knowledge of classical, Christian, and contemporary texts and his excellent mastery of Latin. This work was omitted from Vives's *Opera Omnia* (Complete Works) of 1555 because the church listed it in the *Index Librorum Prohibitorum* (Index of Prohibited Books) because of its praise of

Erasmus, who was by then beleaguered, and the alleged heterodoxy of some of Vives's comments. This omission is repeated in the next two editions of the *Opera Omnia,* in 1782–1790 in Valencia and in 1964 in London.

During this period Vives also wrote *Somnium et vigilia in Somnium Scipionis* (1519, Dream and Vigil in the Dream of Scipio), a commentary on Cicero's *Somnium Scipiones* (52 C.E., Scipio's Dream), and *De ratione studii puerilis* (1521, Children's Pedagogy) where, presumably inspired by his experiences with his new charge, William of Croy, he methodically presents his pedagogical strategies on how to educate children effectively. This text became quite influential and often was reprinted (in the original Latin as well as in the translations) together with two other later treatises that Vives devoted to the topic of education: *De institutione feminae christianae* (1524; translated as *A Very Frutefull and Pleasant Boke Called the Instruction of a Christen Woman,* 1529) and *De officio mariti* (1528; translated as *The Office and Duetie of a Husband,* 1550).

Then, in August 1522 an unexpected proposal offered Vives the possibility of returning to Spain and ending his economic problems. Don Fadrique of Toledo, second duke of Alba, aware of Vives's growing reputation, chose him as the tutor to his two grandchildren. Vives, however, never found out about the offer because the friar sent by the duke did not relay the message to the Valencian philosopher. Thus, Vives lost what should have been another prestigious and well-remunerated position. In his letters to his friend and fellow humanist Erasmus, Vives expresses his bitterness at this turn of events.

A year later, however, in 1523 he was invited by Cardinal Thomas Wolsey to teach at Oxford. He became a professor of Latin, Greek, and rhetoric at Corpus Christi College, recently founded by the cardinal. At Oxford, Vives was able to experiment with his educational reforms and brought about several changes in the curriculum that were eagerly adopted by his colleagues. The next year he published one of his most famous works, *De institutione feminae christianae,* a moral treatise in which he offers his ideas on marriage and on the education of women. This book has aroused interest among contemporary feminist critics and scholars of early-modern intellectual history. The most remarkable aspect of the treatise is the fact that in it Vives ardently advocates the education of women. He considered that education was the key to becoming a good Christian, and consequently, women could not become good Christians unless they were educated. Although the notion might seem revolutionary and profeminist, it should be noted that the educational program presented by Vives in *De institutione feminae christianae* was

Title page for an early edition (Antwerp: Gorneensis, 1520) of Vives's Somnium et vigilia in Somnium Scipionis *(1519, Dream and Vigil in the Dream of Scipio; from* Somnium et vigilia in Somnium Scipionis, *1989; Thomas Cooper Library, University of South Carolina)*

fully in accord with the prevailing views about the role and position of women during the sixteenth century. Thus, Vives states that the activities of women, which he considered of crucial importance for a harmonious society, should be limited to the rearing of children and household chores such as spinning and weaving. As for their intellectual formation, Vives asserts that women must learn to read but that the reading material permitted to women should only be of a pious or religious nature, such as the lives of saints. Vives, like many other Christian humanists of the period, abhorred profane literature, especially chivalric novels, and considered it especially harmful to young maidens. In *De institutione feminae christianae,* which was widely read and frequently translated, Vives offers an extensive list of suitable as well as unsuitable readings for the education of women. Many of these ideas are repeated in *De officio mariti,* a manual addressed to prospective husbands with advice on how to find a suitable bride and how to achieve a successful marriage.

Vives returned to Bruges in 1524 for a short period. In May he married Margaret Valdaura, the daughter of Vives's friend and former protector. One of Vives's most widely read books, *Introductio ad sapientiam* (translated as *An Introduction to Wysedom,* 1540), was published that year and translated into German, English, Spanish, and French in the first half of the sixteenth century. This work, written for Princess Mary Tudor, is a good example of Vives's interest in practical philosophy; it is a little handbook of morals and manners that uses short sentences and aphorisms to teach Christians their obligations toward God and their fellow citizens.

By October of the same year Vives was back in England, but he did not start teaching again until January 1525. In spite of his editorial success, this period was a difficult one for Vives. On one hand he received news of his father's death at the stake in Valencia; on the other his own health began to deteriorate considerably. He began to suffer from gout and other illnesses.

His *De subventione pauperum* (Concerning the Relief of the Poor) was published in 1526. This work was one of the first that studies solutions to eradicate poverty. Vives believed that the first step was the creation of a social order that favored the poor. He urged the participation of the magistrates in a more egalitarian distribution of resources and their intervention through charity organizations. His proposal was profoundly revolutionary because it challenged the accepted view of the time, which claimed that the existence of the poor was necessary in the cities in order to stimulate the virtue of charity among the rich. Vives insisted that it was the duty of the magistrates to ensure that justice prevailed and that charity reached everyone. This work became so influential that the Lawyers' Guild in Bruges not only granted Vives the prize of a silver vase for it but also requested that the city fund its publication. Others expressed their dissatisfaction with the work. An Agustinian friar, Lorenzo de Villavicencio, wrote *De oeconomia sacra circa pauperum curam* (1564, On the Sacred Order of the Treatment of Poverty) as a response to Vives's proposals, which he claimed were pernicious and greatly imperiled the sanctity of the church.

In February 1526 Vives returned to England but no longer held his position at Oxford. He began a period of constant travel between London and Bruges that lasted until October 1527, when he was appointed preceptor to Princess Mary. This advantageous position did not last long, however, and in February of the following year Vives was placed under house arrest for more than a month. As he said in one of his letters to Erasmus: "Tempora habemus difficilia, in quibus nec loqui nec tacere possumus sine periculo" (We live in difficult times, where one can neither talk nor be silent without danger). In this tumultuous period England had solidified its alliance with France against Holy Roman Emperor Charles V (also Charles I of Spain); furthermore, Henry VIII had started his divorce proceedings against Catherine of Aragon, Mary's mother

and aunt of Charles. Therefore, the powerful Wolsey was increasingly suspicious of the Valencian philosopher and his possible connections to his natural lord, the Emperor Charles V, through his ambassador in London.

In 1528, fearing for his safety, Vives left England but was called back in November of that year to counsel Catherine of Aragon's lawyers during the examination of the royal marriage conducted by the papal legate, Lorenzo Cardinal Campeggio. He incurred Catherine's wrath by advising the queen not to take part in a trial that he viewed as unlawful. Catherine dismissed him, and Vives left England once more, never to return. Impoverished and disillusioned, he took refuge in Bruges. Since King Henry VIII decided to discontinue Vives's royal pension, the philosopher found himself again in a strained financial situation. For a few years he traveled to various places (Paris, Brussels, and Louvain) in search of teaching or tutoring positions. In addition to his economic problems, his father-in-law's long illness almost ruined the Valdaura family. From 1528 to 1531 Vives lived in poverty. The only influx of money during these years was the generous sum sent in 1531 to him by the king of Portugal, João III, as payment for the first two books of *De disciplinis* (On Instruction): *De causis corruptarum artium* (On the Causes of the Corruption of the Arts) and *De tradendis disciplinis* (On the Transmission of the Arts; translated as *On Education,* 1913).

In the late 1520s and 1530s Vives wrote his most influential works. *De concordia et discordia in humano genere* (Accord and Discord among Humans) was published in 1529. Vives's intention in this work, according to Carlos Noreña in his *Juan Luis Vives and the Emotions* (1989), was to use his humanistic training to bring together divergent positions such as Augustinian religious views on one hand and Stoic metaphysical and ethical conceptions on the other. He also makes a plea to Charles V to consider an ecumenical council to resolve the theological differences within Christianity. Increasingly, in those years, Vives made use of his writings to make various exhortations to the authorities in reference to diverse social and political concerns of his. Thus, in 1529 he wrote *De pacificatione* (On Pacification), dedicated to Alfonso Manrique, archbishop of Seville and grand inquisitor of Spain, and in it he appeals to Manrique to use his authority in the service of peace, to curtail the excessive authority of the Holy Tribunal, and to reject the concept of nobility based on blood rather than on the nobility of the spirit, a proposition frequently invoked by *conversos* or their descendants during the sixteenth century.

De disciplinis is Vives's most comprehensive work on education. The humanistic premise that he seconds in this work is that education means bringing out the abilities of each individual, and that the goal of education is to make men into virtuous and useful citizens and not just elegant scholars. Vives expresses his respect for the models of classic antiquity and the need to study them, but he also emphasizes that erudition for purely aesthetic purposes is not desirable. The importance of the practical and ethical aspects of education for Vives aligns him again with the northern humanists such as Erasmus, who expressed similar viewpoints, and contrasts him to Italian humanists. *De disciplinis* is considered a pioneering work in the pedagogical field because it presents many concepts that have validity in the modern world. Strongly supported is the idea of the secularization of public education, the need to teach in the vernacular languages and not just in Latin, the education of women, the active participation of the student in his own education, the necessity of physical exercise and games to stimulate intellectual activity, and the creation of schools for the adequate training of prospective teachers.

In 1532 Vives began receiving a modest pension from Emperor Charles V, and in 1537 he became preceptor to Doña Mencía de Mendoza, wife of the duke of Nassau in Breda. At this time she requested that he write an allegorical interpretation of Virgil's *Bucolics*. Vives's chief essay on rhetoric, *De ratione dicendi* (The Art of Rhetoric) was published during these years, in 1533. In this essay he further develops the ideas he had already expressed in his *Adversus pseudodialecticos*. He breaks away from the rhetoric of the Scholastics. Vives regarded words and language as practical tools that belong to the people and not as a monopoly of the realms of rhetoric, dialectics, and grammar. Vives also insists that there must be a correlation between *verbum* (the word) and *res* (the concept) and attacks the Scholastics' preference for abstract language that dissociated the *verbum* from the *res*. Vives's concept of the use of the Latin language in daily life, that is, as a spoken and lively language adapted to the needs of its users, also stems from his formulation of the preeminence of the *sermo communis* (common discourse) above other types of discourses, expressed in *De ratione dicendi*.

In the theory of language defined in this text Vives achieves two of the goals of the humanists: first, he combines rhetoric and morality by insisting on the necessity of an elegant but unadorned and pure language that is intelligible to all; and second, he pays homage to his classical models by setting them as examples to emulate in order to accomplish the first goal. The following passage exemplifies it clearly:

Privata et familiaris collocutio simplex debet esse, recta, naturalis, plana, nuda prorsum, modo ne sordida, aut spurca; deforme est enim quicquid in plano tumet, cura in ea et cultus ambitiosi sunt, aut arrogantis animi, nec gratiam conciliat, sed vanitatem arguit. Optimum quotidiani sermonis exemplum dedero epistolas Ciceronis ad Atticum, vel Terentii fabulas.

(Private and familiar conversation must be simple, straight, natural, plain, totally naked, without being ignoble or dishonest, because stuffiness deforms simple language. Adornment in it is typical of an ambitious and arrogant spirit and it does not engender favor but demonstrates vanity instead. The best examples of familiar language are Cicero's letters to Attic or Terence's comedies.)

In 1538 one of Vives's last works, *De anima et vita* (On the Soul and Life), was published in Basel. Noreña defines it as "the culmination of Vives's constant effort to understand human nature not as a metaphysician but as a moralist and a pedagogue." The book deals with the study of all emotions. Vives defines the different emotions, describes how they are interconnected, what causes them, how they can be controlled, and how they relate to sensation, memory, and intellect. For the depth of his insights in this work, Vives has been considered the father of modern psychology.

During this period he also produced the most popular of his educational books, *Linguae latinae exercitatio* (1538, Use of the Latin Language). Following a model based on the Socratic dialogue and favored by other humanists such as Erasmus, this book consists of twenty-five amusing short dialogues in which Latin words and expressions are displayed in the context of daily activities and familiar settings and situations. This short manual was published in different countries with the dialogue in Latin on one side and their corresponding translation to the vernacular on the other side of the page. There were about 320 editions of this book, and there is ample evidence that many schools used it for Latin instruction for many years. Miquel Batllori, in his 1986 essay "Las obras de Vives en los colegios jesuíticos del siglo XVI" (The Works of Vives in the Jesuit Colleges of the Sixteenth Century), explains that the schools created by the Jesuits in Spain and Spanish territories recommended the use of *Linguae latinae exercitatio* for instruction, at least until 1552, when both Erasmus and Vives fell out of favor among the Jesuits. Also, Alois Bömer researched the curriculum of several German schools and found that many of them specified that one or more hours of the day should be devoted to the study of Vives's dialogues.

The last few years in the philosopher's life were filled with sorrow and bitterness. Vives complained in his correspondence about his gout, which had taken over his whole body. In addition, he expressed his sad-

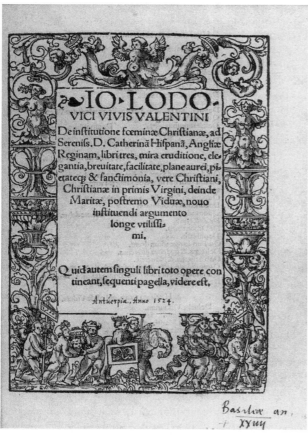

Title page for Vives's De institutione feminae christianae, *translated in 1529 as* A Very Frutefull and Pleasant Boke Called the Instruction of a Christen Woman *(from* The Instruction of a Christen Woman, *2002; Thomas Cooper Library, University of South Carolina)*

and religion and the figure of Jesus. Books 3 and 4 are, respectively, an attack against the Jewish faith and an attack against Islam. The final book is devoted to discussing the superiority of the Christian faith. Surprisingly, Vives's last work does not deal at all with the theological matters that were hotly debated during the period of the Reformation and concentrates instead on undermining Islam and Jewish rabbinic theology. Given his ancestry and his awareness of the problems Erasmus and others had encountered for expressing views that were considered unorthodox, Vives likely decided to avoid the presentation of polemical views in his final work.

Vives's legacy manifested itself in various ways. Even though he was a loyal Catholic, some of his prayers from his *Excitationes ad animi in Deum* (1535, Stimuli to Awaken the Soul to God) were readily adopted by the Church of England; they were used by Edward VI (1549) and Elizabeth I (1559), and they figure prominently in the *Book of Common Prayer* (1578). His influence in England is also evident in the writings of Thomas Elyot and John Milton. His educational theories seem to have influenced François Rabelais, and some scholars believe that René Descartes was familiar with Vives's theory of the emotions. Furthermore, his belief in the progress of science combined with his skepticism about the possibility of obtaining complete knowledge also attracted Michel de Montaigne.

As for Spain, even though Vives complained in a letter to Juan Maldonado in 1538 that he had no detractors in Spain because few read his works, the fact is that he was admired by many humanists in his native country. His ideas about rhetoric influenced Francisco Sánchez de las Brozas (El Brocense), Juan Lorenzo Palmireno, and Alfonso García Matamoros. Vives's theological works were discussed and debated by famous theologians such as Bartolomé de Las Casas, Melchor Cano, and Juan de Mariana, while his ideas on education in general and on the education of women in particular found their way into the academic curriculum and into the works of several prominent writers of the sixteenth century, notably Fray Luis de León and his *La perfecta casada* (1583; translated as *The Perfect Wife*, 1943). In addition, especially after 1537, when Vives's works were widely disseminated in Italy, there was a remarkable increase of his books in Spanish libraries, as Juan F. Alcina documents in his 1995 essay "Notas sobre la pervivencia de Vives en España (s. XVI)." His reputation in Spain had grown so much that in 1547 Francisco Decio wrote a poem in praise of the city of Valencia in which its native and illustrious son is described as a genius that has made the city famous all over the world. Despite his supposed fame, however,

ness at the loss of so many of his friends. More had been arrested and executed in 1535. In Spain his close friends and correspondents, Juan de Vergara and Alonso de Virués, were processed by the Inquisition. Catherine of Aragon and Erasmus died in 1536, and Manrique, one of the few remaining supporters of Erasmian views in Spain, died in 1538. On 6 May 1540 Vives died in Bruges at the age of forty-seven, possibly of a kidney stone. The city where he felt most at home mourned his death and proudly paid for his funeral.

Vives's last literary contribution, *De veritate fidei christianae* (On the Verity of the Christian Faith), was edited after his death by his wife, Margarita, and his friend Cranevelt and published in Basel in 1543 with a letter addressed to Pope Paul III. It is a volume on the defense of Christianity, divided into five books. The first two books describe the foundations of true piety

Vives did not really inaugurate a new school of thought and had few followers.

Juan Luis Vives's writings cover a wide array of subjects, from social welfare and educational reform to the nature of moral wisdom and the relation between reason and faith. In spite of all his intellectual achievements and the influence of his thought during the sixteenth century, Vives's contributions have not endured through the centuries as much as those of his friends and contemporaries Erasmus and More. Nevertheless, his text allows the reader a comprehensive glimpse at the complexity of issues that fascinated thinkers and readers of the century in which he lived.

Letters:

Desiderius Erasmus, *Opus Epistolarum Des,* 12 volumes, edited by P. S. Allen and H. M. Allen (Oxford: Clarendon Press, 1906–1959);

Epistolario de Juan Luis Vives, edited by José Jiménez Delgado (Madrid: Editora Nacional, 1978).

Bibliography:

Dionisia Empaytaz, *Juan Luis Vives: Un intento de bibliografía* (Barcelona: Ediciones Singulares, 1989).

References:

Juan F. Alcina, "Notas sobre la pervivencia de Vives en España (s. XVI)," in *Juan Luis Vives: Sein Werk und seine Bedeutung für Spanien und Deutschland. Akten der internationalen Tagung vom 14–15. Dezember 1992 in Münster,* edited by Christoph Strosetzki (Frankfurt am Main: Vervuert, 1995), pp. 213–228;

Marcel Bataillon, *Erasmo y España* (Mexico City: Fondo de Cultura Económica, 1950);

Miquel Batllori, "Las obras de Vives en los colegios jesuíticos del siglo XVI," in *Erasmus in Hispania, Vives in Belgio: Acta colloquii Brugensis 23–26 IX 1985,* edited by Jozef Ijsewijn and Angel Losada (Louvain: Peeters, 1986), pp. 121–146;

Alois Bömer, *Die lateinischen Schülergespräche der Humanisten,* 2 volumes (Berlin: Harrwitz, 1897, 1899);

Frans von Craneveldt, *Litterae virorum eruditorum ad Franciscum Craneveldium, 1522–1528: A Collection of Original Letters,* edited by Henry de Vocht (Louvain: Libraire Universitaire, 1928);

J. A. Fernández-Santamaría, *The Theater of Man: J. L. Vives on Society* (Philadelphia: American Philosophical Society, 1998);

Angelina García, *Els Vives: Una familia de jueus valencians* (Valencia: Tres i Quatre, 1987);

Jozef Ijsewijn, *Humanisme i literatura neollatina: Escrits seleccionats,* edited by Josep Lluís Barona (Valencia: Universitat de Valencia, 1996);

Carlos Noreña, *Juan Luis Vives and the Emotions* (Carbondale: Southern Illinois University, 1989);

Manuel de la Pinta Llorente, O.S.A., and José María de Palacio, *Procesos inquisitoriales contra la familia judía de Juan Luis Vives* (Madrid: Instituto Arias Montano, 1964);

Luis E. Rodríguez, "Juan Luis Vives: Horizonte de España," in *Juan Luis Vives: Sein Werk und seine Bedeutung für Spanien und Deutschland. Akten der internationalen Tagung vom 14–15. Dezember 1992 in Münster,* edited by Christoph Strosetzki (Frankfurt am Main: Vervuert, 1995), pp. 187–212.

Topical Essays

The Spanish Byzantine Novel

Matthew G. C. Tornatore
Truman State University

SELECTED MAJOR FIGURES: Alonso Núñez de Reinoso (1492? – 1552?);

Jerónimo de Contreras (circa 1520 – circa 1585);

Miguel de Cervantes Saavedra (29 September 1547 – 1616);

Lope Félix de Vega Carpio (Lope de Vega) (1562 – 1635).

SELECTED BOOKS: Alonso Núñez de Reinoso, *Historia de los amores de Clareo y Florisea y de los trabajos y de los trabajos de Ysea: Con otras obras en verso, parte al estilo Español, y parte al Italiano* (Venice: G. Giolito de Ferrari, 1552);

Jerónimo de Contreras, *Selva de aventuras* (Barcelona: Alonso de la Barrera, 1565);

Bartolomé Villalba y Estaña, *El pelegrino curioso y grandezas de España* (Madrid, 1577?);

Alonso López Pinciano, *Filosofia antigua poética* (Madrid: Thomas Iunti, 1596);

Lope de Vega, *El peregrino en su patria* (Seville: Clemente Hidalgo, 1604); translated anonymously as *The Pilgrime of Casteele* (London: E. All-de, 1621);

Miguel de Cervantes Saavedra, *Novelas ejemplares* (Madrid: Iuana de la Cuesta, 1613); translated by James Mabbe as *Dilight in severall shapes, dravvne to the life in six pleasant histories* (London: William Sheares, 1654);

Cervantes, *Trabajos de Persiles y Sigismunda, historia setentrional* (Madrid: Iuana de la Cuesta, 1617); translated anonymously as *The Trials of Persiles and Sigismunda, A Northern Story, amongst the Variable Fortunes of the Prince of Thule, and This Princesse of Frisland, Are Interlaced Many Witty Discourses, Morall, Politicall, and Delightfull* (London: H.L., 1619).

Modern Editions: Miguel de Cervantes Saavedra, *Trabajos de Persiles y Sigismunda: Historia sententrional,* 2 volumes, edited by Juan Antonio Pellicer y Pilares (New York: Laruza, Mendia, 1827);

Bartolomé Villalba y Estaña, *El pelegrino curioso y grandezas de España,* 2 volumes, edited by Pascual de Gayangos (Madrid: Ginesta, 1886, 1889);

Bonaventura Carles Aribau, *Novelistas anteriores á Cervantes* (Madrid: Atlas, 1944), pp. 431–506;

Cervantes, *Los Trabajos de Persiles y Sigismunda,* edited by Juan Bautista Avalle-Arce (Madrid: Castalia, 1969);

Lope de Vega, *El peregrino en su patria,* edited by Myron A. Peyton (Chapel Hill: University of North Carolina Press, 1971);

Lope, *El peregrino en su patria* (Madrid: Clásico Castalia, 1973);

Alonso López Pinciano, *Philosophia antigua poetica,* edited by Alfredo Carballo Picazo (Madrid: Instituto "Miguel de Cervantes," 1973);

Cervantes, *Novelas Ejemplares* (Madrid: Castalia, 1987);

Jéronimo de Contreras, *Selva de aventuras, 1565–1583,* edited by Miguel A. Teijeiro Fuentes (Saragossa: Institución "Fernando el Católico" / Cárceres: Departamento de Filología Hispánica de la Universidad de Extremadura, 1991);

Alonso Núñez de Reinoso, *Historia de los amores de Clareo y Florisea y de los trabajos de Isea,* edited by José Jiménez Ruiz (Málaga: Universidad de Málaga, 1997);

Pinciano, *Philosophía antigua poética,* edited by José Rico Verdú (Madrid: Fundación José Antonio de Castro, 1998).

Editions in English: Miguel de Cervantes Saavedra, *The Trials of Persiles and Sigismunda: A Northern Story,* translated by Celia Richmond Weller and Clark A. Colahan (Berkeley & London: University of California Press, 1989);

Cervantes, *Exemplary Novels,* 4 volumes, translated by B. W. Ife (Warminster, U.K.: Aris & Phillips, 1992).

The Byzantine novel in many respects represents a clearly unified set of writings in sixteenth-century Spain. Like many of the products of the Renaissance, they derive their form from works of ancient Greece. Given that plagiarism, or the "ownership" of intellectual property, is a modern concept, the Renaissance European writer, in fact, garnered prestige by modeling his works on those of celebrated figures that preceded

273

Title page for the first Spanish Byzantine novel (History of the Loves of Clareo and Florisea, and of the Woes of Isea), written by Alonso Núñez de Reinoso (University of California, Berkeley, Library)

audience for these works was the aristocracy, who could appreciate the classical references and would be familiar with the historical or foreign scenarios implied. These novels, while possessing certain artistic dimensions and modeling flawless moral behavior, were intended as diversions for those who enjoyed abundant leisure time, as evidenced by their length and interminable plots. They were directed toward, or at least appealed to, a female audience. Women are usually the main protagonists in the Byzantine novel, and love is portrayed in the most noble of terms; through ideal love the enamored adventurers attain the wisdom and inspiration that repeatedly delivers them from nefarious forces. In this context love is not only a right but an obligation on the part of all humanity.

The Byzantine novel might be seen as an intermediate stage in the evolution of the Spanish novel. Its predecessor is the chivalric romance, which reflects the imagination of medieval man imbued with fantasies and the supernatural, while its successor is the picaresque novel, which offers a critical analysis of Spanish society of the time, with an antihero protagonist who represents both the struggle of the masses as well as the decadent state of affairs of that age. The Byzantine novel is found between both of these literary designs, diverging from the books of chivalry because of its moral didacticism and greater contextual plausibility, without aiming toward the derision and vilification of society that is boldly manifested in the picaresque novel. Also, both the Byzantine and picaresque novels include an underlying recognition, which is implicit in the actions of the protagonists, of the brevity of earthly existence. The former, however, subscribes to a distinct approach to the many issues; the Byzantine protagonist is a refined intellectual whose role is to extol humankind and its virtues. The Byzantine novel parts company with the chivalric novel in that the latter apotheosizes the knight, singing the praises of his often superhuman victories, while the Greek-influenced protagonist of the former deplores vainglory, assuming a humble stance before a more realistic world. The Byzantine novel seeks to teach by example. What it shares with chivalric books are its many accounts of adventures and the love for a lady that guides the plot. Yet, these Greek imitations also recognize the need to redress, in subtle fashion, the immorality that was thought to pervade society. Observed from a distinct viewpoint, the Byzantine novel is the offspring of various prior subgenres of novel—the sentimental novel, the adventure novel, and the book of chivalry—but combined with a new twist that respected the evolved audience of the 1500s and 1600s. These novels, as Marcelino Menéndez y Pelayo notes in his *Orígenes de la novela* (1943, Origins of the Novel), are classic examples

him, in particular by drawing from the ancients. The author of Spanish Byzantine novels often informed his reader of his classical references, not out of critical exigencies to cite sources but to enhance the perceived value of his own work by association. Spanish Byzantine novels typically describe a series of voyages to exotic lands, some identifiable (such as Sicily, the Nile, and Morocco) and others apparently fantastical. In general, the plots are rather tortuous and forced. Characters commonly assume new identities to abscond from others, for example, and dress as members of the opposite sex in order to preclude the possibility of recognition by an enemy or even by loved ones. The primary of the Spanish Renaissance, whereby the Greco-Roman tradition was combined with the Christian spirit to create works that are idealistic in a Neoplatonic sense but also relatively realistic.

While the so-called Byzantine novel in Spain dates from the middle of the sixteenth century, one must reach further back in time to find its original inspiration. The designation *Byzantine* suggests that the place of origin of these romances was Byzantium. While this supposition is now known to be inaccurate, it was the assumption of Erwin Rohde, who claimed that the initial exemplars of this genre hailed from the rhetorical schools of the Second Sophistry during the Byzantine Empire. He based his conclusions on romances and many précis belonging to Photius, the patriarch of Constantinople between 858 and 886. In the Spanish Byzantine novels some or all of a variety of Greek devices are found: prophecy, oaths, dialogues and rhetorical speeches, epiphanies, dreams, soliloquies, and contemplations of suicide.

The first so-called Byzantine writers sought inspiration in the works of Aristides of Miletus, an author of the second century B.C. who composed erotic short stories. His stories were meant for pleasure reading and were later defamed by the Romans. In the second and third centuries A.D. they were revived and combined with many other literary components, which resulted in texts of much greater style and appeal. This new genre erroneously became dubbed the Byzantine novel. Early representative works are *Ephesiaca, Habrocomes and Anthia* by Xenophon of Ephesus; *A True History and Lucius or the Ass* by Lucian of Samosata; *Chaereas and Callirhoe* by Chariton of Aphrodisias; *Daphnis and Chloe* by Longus; *Aristander and Callithea* by Constantine Manasses; *Dosicles and Rhodanthe* by Theodorus Prodromus; *Hysmine and Hysminias* by Eustathius; *Charicles and Drusilla* by Nicetas Eugenianus; *Babyloniaca, Rhodanes and Sinonis* by Iamblichus, a Syrian; and *The Wonderful Things beyond Thule* by Antonius Diogenes inter alia. Two main works were particularly influential on the Spanish Byzantine novel: *Leucippe and Cleitophon* by Achilles Tatius from Alexandria, who wrote in the second century, and Heliodorus's *Aethiopica, Theagenes and Chariclea* from the third century.

Aethiopica, Theagenes and Chariclea became popular in Italy shortly following its 1534 publication. The first translation into Italian by Lodovico Dolce was in 1546 under the title *Amorosi ragionamenti* (Love Discourse). The Castilian version did not appear until 1554 in Amberes by an anonymous translator. This translation was later surpassed in both quality and celebrity by that of Fernando de Mena in 1587. Some of the features of Heliodorus's *Aethiopica, Theagenes and Chariclea* that are paralleled in Spanish Byzantine novels include inaccu-

rate descriptions of geography and historical events and chapters full of fabulous environs designed to captivate the imagination of the sophisticated Greek public. In *Aethiopica, Theagenes and Chariclea,* victories and glory derive from superior Greek prowess. Sixteenth-century Spanish Byzantine novels rendered this tendency in the devout Christian who does not succumb to concupiscence and always prevails over the barbarian. Examination of the characters in *Aethiopica, Theagenes and Chariclea* reveals equivalents in the Spanish novels, though there may be a distinction in the ulterior motives. For instance, Heliodorus's Theagenes is prepossessing, robust, and valiant; yet, he is ultimately dependent on Chariclea, the resourceful better half, who preserves her chastity and who intelligently devises escapes from the perilous situations in which they repeatedly find themselves. In the Spanish versions this dynamic is sometimes reversed, not only to provide a laudable example to the Renaissance audience (which was reputed for its decadence), but also to entice a female readership that would be taken by the professions of selfless, if not platonic, love on the part of a handsome young adventurer.

The first Spanish Byzantine novel was Alonso Núñez de Reinoso's *Historia de los amores de Clareo y Florisea y de los trabajos de Isea* (1552, History of the Love between Clareo and Florisea and of the Woes of Isea), which is mostly a translation of many volumes of *Leucippe and Cleitophon,* which was translated and published in Italian and Spanish during the Renaissance. The first English translation of *The Adventures of Leucippe and Clitophon,* by William Burton, dates from 1597. Chariton's *Chaereas and Callirhoe* is customarily employed as the perfect foil to *Leucippe and Cleitophon* to aid in the appreciation of the stylistic and thematic evolution of the Greek romances. While Chariton's work is marked by simplicity and sincerity, the writing of Tatius is wrought with complexity, hyperbole, and occasionally with irony. They both, however, exalt the virtuous life, underscoring pure love and marital bliss. This emphasis in part explains the popularity of these romances in Erasmian Spain. The second Spanish Byzantine novel, *Selva de aventuras* (Jungle of Adventures), was published in Barcelona in 1565 by Jerónimo de Contreras. Both *Selva de aventuras* and *La historia de los amores de Clareo y Florisea y de los trabajos de la sin ventura Isea* enjoyed popularity and were reprinted many times during the decades after their respective publications.

Little has been verified about the private life of Núñez de Reinoso. From his writings it has been inferred that he was born in Alcarria in the province of Guadalajara in the early 1490s. In one of his poems he informs that he pursued coursework in jurisprudence at Salamanca only to please his parents, although he never

*Title page for Jerónimo de Contreras's popular Byzantine novel
(Jungle of Adventures). In another edition, published in 1582,
Contreras added material to placate the Spanish Inquisition,
which had censured the first edition of the work (from
Contreras,* Selva de aventuras, 1565–1583,
*1991; Thomas Cooper Library, University
of South Carolina).*

practiced law and may not even have completed his degree. From Salamanca he probably moved on to Portugal, where he resided from approximately 1530 until 1540. He is thought to have been received on the estate of António and Nunálveres Pereira in the province of Entre Minho e Douro. This country villa was a haven for freethinking intellectuals.

The few who have researched Núñez de Reinoso postulate that he may have been a *converso* (convert from Judaism to Catholicism) fleeing the strong arm of the Inquisition. Núñez de Reinoso never shares any personal information that might reveal his family identity, which could be a result of his need to abscond from the authorities, as his association with certain groups suggests. Constance Hubbard Rose, the authority on Núñez de Reinoso, admits in her *Alonso Núñez de Reinoso: The Lament of a Sixteenth-Century Exile* (1971) that "the conflicting versions of the various genealogies preclude any definitive conclusion as to the *converso* origins

of the Reinosos." In line with this theory, however, is his unexplained departure from Portugal somewhere between 1530 and 1547, a period that corresponds to Portugal's purge of heretics. The first edict by the Spanish Inquisition was read in Lisbon in 1530 but was repealed on several occasions by the Portuguese. The Spanish made their will known by holding an auto-da-fé in the capital city in 1540, which spurred many *conversos,* including many who had continued to practice Judaism in secret after conversion, to search for new homes. Núñez de Reinoso may have taken his leave in response to these activities of the Inquisition. By 1547 the Inquisition was fully authorized to exercise its prerogative in Portugal; if Núñez de Reinoso was a *converso* who had reason to fear inquisitorial persecution, he would have had his final opportunity to emigrate that year.

During this time Núñez de Reinoso undertook a voyage to Italy, where he arrived around 1550 and secured the patronage of the Nasis, a renowned *converso* family in Ferrara. The family was surnamed Miquez in Portugal but, believing to be out of peril in Italy, took on the Jewish name Nasi. Núñez de Reinoso may have spent the years unaccounted for, between 1547 and 1550, in Flanders alongside the wealthy Miquez clan, which, fleeing Portugal, first went to Flanders and later landed in Ferrara. There, it appears, Núñez de Reinoso was the children's tutor. The question still remains, however, whether Núñez de Reinoso shared a common ethnoreligious bond with the Miquez/Nasi family or if he was merely a neutral beneficiary of their privileged social position. In any case, after the publication of Núñez de Reinoso's novel nothing else is known of him. He may have moved on to Turkey with the Nasi family, which, in conjunction with the Grand Turk, was to settle a Jewish enclave. In fact, Gracia Nasi is documented as having been received in Constantinople with ample ceremony. Joseph Nasi soon became a powerful figure in the sultan's court and was appointed duke of Naxos. Whether or not Núñez de Reinoso accompanied the Nasis to Turkey, however, has not been determined. Furthermore, taking into consideration that the dukedom of Ferrara was an open city that allowed the development of Jewish communities and was lavished with praise by Núñez de Reinoso himself, it is equally possible that he remained there the rest of his life.

Núñez de Reinoso's Byzantine novel, *La historia de los amores de Clareo y Florisea y de los trabajos de la sin ventura Isea,* is based on classical sources as well as those of the Renaissance, in particular Petrarch and Giovanni Boccaccio. The underlying theme of the work, which narrates the desolation of Troy and the subsequent need to found a new homeland, is human suffering, and as such is said to reflect Núñez de Reinoso's *converso* condition. For example, many of the characters in the novel are fatalistic; like the *conversos,* they are not masters of their own destiny. In this light, many scenes in the work are open to several interpretations. Such a scene is the one in which Isea tries to persuade Clareo to cast aside his moral restraint while they are together on the high seas and consummate their love. He resists. Rose explains this moment as one when the gods do not smile upon Isea, as is the case in many other episodes. The sea, according to Rose, is symbolic of the turbulence of life. In another sense, however, the scene reflects the value placed on virtue and honor in sixteenth-century society. This constant struggle with Fortune, the irrational behavior of the gods at whose mercy the pilgrims find themselves, might have been part of the allure of the Byzantine novel to Spanish Erasmian followers. This disquiet could be likened to the desperation experienced in Spain not only by *conversos* with respect to the Inquisition but also by the discerning Christians petitioning for religious reform. Adding further credence to this interpretation is Núñez de Reinoso's heroine, who never achieves victory. She endures a nomadic life in search of peace, compelled to forge onward with adversity ever at her heels.

Núñez de Reinoso's stated purpose for writing his novel is that he is a friend of the Muses and that he attains a certain tranquillity, if not catharsis, by practicing his art. This claim is repeated by Isea, who, according to critics, represents the author. An additional motivation may have been to honor his host family, the Nasis, to whose generous and learned household he alludes in the novel. Núñez de Reinoso's sentiments, regardless of the hypothesized particulars of his life, are for the most part consistent with the age and genre of which he partakes. The pastoral aspects lend serenity to a tumultuous world, and the rudimentary Byzantine features provide solace and a distraction from exasperating daily tribulations. Núñez de Reinoso's novel possesses no literary originality, nor is it especially artful. His work was not printed in Spain until 1846, when the Spanish Royal Academy included the novel in a collection of incunabula that were being catalogued in the Biblioteca de Autores Españoles (Library of Spanish Authors) series.

Little is known about Contreras, who lived from approximately 1520 to around 1585. His native city may have been Saragossa, but in any case authorities feel relatively sure that he was from Aragon, as all of his professional associations and his time in Italy, a focus of Aragonese enterprise, would suggest. Contreras may have served the Portuguese monarchy and may have lived in Portugal through the early 1540s. In 1560 he received a government post in Toledo, and

some time after that he might have traveled to Naples, where, it is speculated, he may have begun his life as a writer. Contreras referred to himself as a royal chronicler, though that title is yet to be substantiated by historical archives. He could possibly have earned the title of imperial chronicler if he rendered services to the king or if in his publication he addressed the deeds of his monarch. Contreras's *Dechado de varios subjetos* (1572, A Paragon of Many Characters) indubitably would have met such a requirement with its panegyrical passages regarding Phillip II's irreproachable conduct and political achievements. Despite the fact that Contreras published two later works—*Dechado de varios subjetos* and *Historia y libro primero del ynvencible esforçado caballero don Polismán* (The Story and First Book of the Insuperable and Refined Knight Lord Polisman), which remained unpublished but in 1573 was copied in Saragossa—he is best known for *Selva de aventuras.*

Dechado de varios subjetos is a poetic work that has two purposes: moral didacticism and heartfelt patriotism. It is essentially a *libro de la fama* (book of fame), a genre in Spain dedicated to singing the glories of contemporary celebrities. *Dechado de varios subjetos* is supposed to have been composed in Italy, where Contreras was pensioned by the Royal Palace; thus, no small number of pages is wrought with encomia for King Philip II. Petrarch's *I trionfi* (Triumphs) may have been a model for the basic structure of *Dechado de varios subjetos,* as Contreras himself intimates. Possible sources of inspiration closer to the author in both space and time would have been the Iñigo López de Mendoza, marqués de Santillana's *Triumphete de amor* (1437, Minor Triumphs in Love) and Juan de Mena's *El laberinto de fortuna* (1444, The Labyrinth of Fortune).

Contreras's *Historia y libro primero del ynvencible esforçado caballero don Polismán* is another *libro de caballerías* (novel of chivalry). The knights-errant are unfaltering in their courage and steadfast in their love for their lady. The publication of chivalric novels persisted on the Iberian Peninsula into the sixteenth century, at least in part due to Spanish court life, which by now was more opulent and imposing than ever and as such was inclined to greater ceremony, whence evolved new heights of chivalric customs. Thus, interest in the *libros de caballerías,* which might have otherwise become a moribund genre, was reinforced.

The first publication of *Selva de aventuras* in 1565 consisted of seven books; the 1582 edition published in Alcalá de Henares comprised nine books. *Selva de aventuras* is modeled after Heliodorus's work and includes all the elements of a true Byzantine novel. The suitor, Luzmán, because of unrequited love from the virtuous object of his affections, Arbolea, embarks on a voyage that lasts a decade. After adventures and misfortunes he

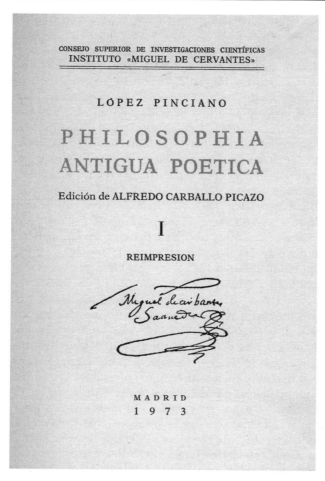

CONSEJO SUPERIOR DE INVESTIGACIONES CIENTÍFICAS
INSTITUTO «MIGUEL DE CERVANTES»

LÓPEZ PINCIANO

PHILOSOPHIA
ANTIGUA POETICA

Edición de ALFREDO CARBALLO PICAZO

I

REIMPRESION

MADRID
1973

*Cover for a twentieth-century edition of the 1596 work of poetic
theory by Alonso López Pinciano, whose writings on the
relationship between the realistic and the fantastic in
verse were influential on contemporary authors of
Byzantine novels (from López Pinciano,*
Philosophia antigua poetica, *1973;*
*Thomas Cooper Library, University
of South Carolina)*

is taken captive by Moroccan corsairs and ends up in Valencia, where he finds spiritual fulfillment in humble but creative work. *Selva de aventuras,* however, unlike some other Byzantine novels, is highly plausible; the geographical trajectory is accurate enough, and the stories recounted by the characters, although fantastic, are well woven into the plot. These secondary characters usually provide an experience for the protagonist that contributes to his self-consciousness, and the ascetic notion of purification of the soul through deprivation and suffering informs this work with a Counter-Reformation ideology.

It has been suggested that the nine-book version of Contreras's *Selva de aventuras* was a response to the fact that the original was included in the 1581 edition of the *Index Librorum Prohibitorum* (Index of Forbidden Books) compiled by the Inquisition. Consequently, the two additional books printed in 1582 would have constituted a "correction" to the original, which apparently spared this edition the disapprobation of the church. Inexplicably, it appears that both versions enjoyed reprints throughout the following decades despite the official church interdiction. The last edition of *Selva de aventuras* dates from 1615, and the work was not again printed in Spain until 1849 when the Spanish Royal Academy included it in its Biblioteca de Autores Españoles series. The editor of the 1849 edition, Bonaventura Carles Aribau, based it on the Barcelona edition.

Contreras has often been seen as a precursor to Lope Félix de Vega Carpio (known generally as Lope de Vega) and Cervantes. In *Selva de aventuras* the Byzantine schema is fundamental but does not exclude other genres, such as the chivalric, pastoral, sentimental, and picaresque novels. Perhaps the most distinctive trait adopted is an ascetic orientation in the person of Luzmán and the various mysticism markers, such as deep and intimate spirituality attained through sincere conversion by means of discipline, meditation, and examination of the consciousness. The work is, therefore, to some degree a renunciation of the Renaissance tendency toward glory and aggrandizement of the individual in that it emphasizes the more medieval values of life dedicated to meditation on the divine, symbolized by Luzmán's beloved Arbolea, and to the spiritual realization through self-abnegation that Luzmán's journey entails. It is, therefore, generally concluded that *Selva de aventuras* is a piece of Counter Reformation literature.

Byzantine novels are said to partake of the Counter-Reformation in Spain. The essence of the Catholic Counter-Reformation was otherworldliness and contempt for the flesh as inferior to the spirit. *Selva de aventuras* denounces man's proclivity to ephemeral gratification by devoting one complete book and various passages in others to the topic. This attitude is reflected in the work when Luzmán becomes distraught by Arbolea's rejection of his honorable marriage proposal. Arbolea, as her name (which derives from *arbol,* meaning *tree*) implies, is strong and constant and elects instead to serve the Lord. Luzmán in turn endures the many life lessons proffered him along his way, emerges conscious of the folly of his ingenuous earlier quests, and redirects his energies to God alone. At this point he is prepared to be united with his true love.

The indelible mark of Erasmus permeates the Spanish Byzantine novel, but perhaps the influence of this adamant advocate of Catholic reformation is most evident on the topic of marriage. Erasmus is not simply interested in the preservation of virginity; he is clear on his acceptance of the healthy exercise of natural desires within the confines of matrimony. He upholds this principle in part because it is necessary to secure social order, but also he sees the bonds between man and woman as essential to a well-evolved life. Within such a bond develops a mutually enriching friendship; moreover, in this way a man (he is mainly concerned with male extramarital dalliances) can learn to love by caring for and nurturing a family. By extension such a man would gain keener awareness of good citizenship, whereby he would be more civic-minded, reliable, compassionate, and active in charitable works. The unmarried man is otherwise doomed to a life turned inward, which can only lead to degeneration and dissatisfaction. This philosophy may explain why the ending of *Selva de aventuras* was changed in the second edition, thus removing it from the *Index Librorum Prohibitorum*. In the second edition of *Selva de aventuras,* rather than the protagonist's resigning the rest of his life to a hermitage in lieu of marital bliss, he is allowed to wed and live out a devout life within a couple and thus delight in a fulfilling existence. The spiritual significance of marriage was not a solitary fixation of the Dutch theologian, but rather a much debated issue of an age plagued by materialism, concubinage, and the general secularization of European society. Marsilio Ficino's *Matrimonii Laus* (1518, In Praise of Marriage), Giovanni Campano's *Libellus de Dignitate Matrimonii* (1532, Pamphlet on the Dignity of Marriage), Leon Battista Alberti's *I libri della famiglia* (1433, The Books of the Family), and Torquato Tasso's *Il padre di famiglia* (1583, Family Father) are all devoted to the correction of the same dilemma treated by Erasmus in his controversial *Encomium Matrimonii* (1518, A Commendation of Marriage) as well as in his explosive *Institutio Christani Matrimonii* (1526, The Christian Institution of Matrimony).

The voyages present in the Spanish Byzantine novel are part of a long tradition with rich significance. Such travels are not only in imitation of its pagan literary predecessors but also parallel the Old Testament "journey" leitmotiv. In other words, converging in this new literary configuration is the search for love, for a series of adventures, and for Platonic idealism that ultimately hark back to the biblical concept of life as a journey. This journey theme is developed in *Selva de aventuras,* and Contreras is the first to designate his hero as a *peregrino* (pilgrim). Adventure is, therefore, the purveyor of experience, and love is no longer a sensual endeavor but an enterprise of soulful transcendence. This idea is in conformity with Christian doctrine that human affection is to be subordinate to the constancy of God's love. Hence, in each episode Luzmán is able to teach based on his experiences and to acquire a deeper understanding of the human condition drawing from

Prolific playwright and novelist Lope de Vega, author of the 1604 Byzantine novel El peregrino en su patria *(translated as* The Pilgrime of Casteele, *1621; from Miguel Romera-Navarro,* Historia de la literatura española, *1928; Thomas Cooper Library, University of South Carolina)*

his current encounters. As true Catholics, the pilgrims are driven onward by a call to take account of the many divine wonders of creation, and the adversities and suffering they endure along the way are cherished as opportunities to purify themselves further in order finally to attain distance from worldliness.

The popularity of these works is related to the sixteenth-century cultural environment in which they were produced. This period was one in which modern science took root and the public became more discriminating, demanding more-feasible plots that simultaneously responded to the curiosities of the age. Consequently, at this time novels of chivalry were under assault by the intelligentsia as well as by the clergy. The valiant knights and fair damsels were condemned as not only frivolous, fallacious, implausible, and devoid of educative content but also as contributing to the corruption of the moral fiber of contemporary society. In this vein the Byzantine novels are an attempt to compensate for these "defects" by projecting images of upstanding comportment: the maidens are chaste, and their suitors are vigilant of their ladies' honor.

Title page for Lope de Vega's Byzantine novel, in which two lovers must overcome a series of misfortunes, including abduction by Moorish pirates, before they are reunited (from El peregrino en su patria, *1973; Thomas Cooper Library, University of South Carolina)*

These novels comprise an imposing number of adventures that exhibit some or all of the typical features of this class of novel. The adventures take place in alien lands, often on uncharted islands where the characters have been shipwrecked or have taken refuge while fleeing an enemy vessel on the high seas. First among the motives for placing these adventures in foreign countries is the attraction for an educated reader of the time who would be familiar with the references to parts of the Mediterranean or at least interested in learning about them. At other times, the scene of a Byzantine novel is an unrecognizable territory that draws the audience in with its new places and people. Such settings were intended to satisfy readers' fascination with the discoveries occurring in the New World, the many reports of which intrigued with their never-before-seen civilizations, flora, and fauna. Men from all

over Spain were departing for America in search of fame and fortune, as conquistadores, entrepreneurs, administrators, and colonizers. Unfamiliar scenarios also enhanced the credibility of the story. Unlike novels of chivalry, with their blatant falsehoods and hyperbolic deeds, the Byzantine novels, which are no less fictitious, take full advantage of distant locations in order to cloak their many unfounded pretensions.

Significant to the development of the Byzantine novel were two powerful factions in sixteenth-century Spain—the Erasmian enthusiasts and the preceptists. The regime of Aristotelian preceptists condemned not only the chivalric novels but also ascetic writings, unwavering in their demand for both plausibility and *el enseñar deleitando* (to teach while amusing), a phrase describing the harmonic pairing of didacticism with entertainment. This principle obeys the parameters established by Tasso, an ardent advocate of Counter-Reformation thought. The preceptist position reverts back to Horace, who maintains that the best strategy for successful fiction is that the author, while seeking to provide enjoyment, should take heed never to stray too far from truth. The plot must remain credible.

In 1604 Lope de Vega published his Byzantine novel, *El peregrino en su patria* (translated as *The Pilgrime of Casteele,* 1621), dedicated to the marquis of Priego. Contreras has often been seen as a precursor to Lope and Cervantes, and *Selva de aventuras,* with its *peregrino* protagonist, may well have been the model for Lope's *El peregrino en su patria.* As a result of Lope's ample understanding of foreign affairs, other cultures, and the human condition in general, his texts are frequently rich and able to withstand the test of time. From his oeuvre, two epic poems, as well as *El peregrino en su patria,* evidence the religious preoccupations of the era. References to official church positions are identifiable in *El peregrino en su patria,* which includes four well-known *autos sacramentales* (allegorical religious plays): *El viaje del alma* (The Voyage of the Soul), *Las bodas del alma y el amor divino* (The Marriage of the Soul and Divine Love), *La maya* (The Mayan), and *El hijo pródigo* (The Prodigal Son). Within these writings are many of the major constituents that distinguish *El peregrino en su patria* as a Byzantine novel. The plot is complicated with many adventures and astonishing incidents and has a happy ending. Unlike most Byzantine novels, Lope does not take recourse to foreign lands for exoticism. Almost the entirety of the novel takes place on the Iberian Peninsula, especially in the regions of Valencia, Saragossa, Barcelona, and Toledo. Lope draws from his personal experiences in Valencia for much of the action there. This autobiographical element perhaps explains why the scenes here and in Monserrate in the first and second book are considered to be the most realistic.

This story involves two lovers on a journey, which because of many unexpected turns takes them through many parts of Portugal and Spain. They are carried into captivity by Moors but manage to escape and make their way homeward by traversing Italy as pilgrims. In Spain they are shipwrecked in Barcelona, but all ends well, with the two marrying in the city of Toledo. It should be noted that this story of true love is set in 1598–1599, which corresponds to the marriage of Philip III. In celebration of the wedding, reportedly, for eight consecutive evenings Lope's dramas were performed, among which were also *El Perseguido* (The Pursued One) and *El Galán Agradecido* (The Thankful Gentleman). At the end of *El peregrino en su patria,* Lope includes a list of all of his comedies published, which numbered 219 at the point of its first printing. With the many reprints of *El peregrino en su patria,* this number was regularly updated.

The unforeseen success of *El ingenioso hidalgo don Quijote de la Mancha* (1605; translated as *The history of the valorous and wittie knight-errant don Quixote of the Mancha,* 1612) paved the way for Cervantes's Byzantine-fashioned *Novelas ejemplares* (Exemplary Novels) in 1613. This book comprises twelve short novels, each distinct, falling into clear categories. For example, *La española inglesa* (The English Spanish Girl), *Las dos doncellas* (The Two Maidens), *El amante liberal* (The Liberal Lover), and *La señora Cornelia* (Mrs. Cornelia) seem to evidence an Italianate novella style, which contrasts with the realistic *El casamiento engañoso* (The Deceptive Wedding), *El celoso extremeño* (The Jealous Man from Extremadura), and *La ilustre fregona* (The Illustrious Scouring Maid). Ruthless realism is identifiable in the picaresque *Rinconete y Cortadillo* (Rinconete and Cortadillo) as well as in the social satires *El licenciado Vidriera* (The Bachelor Vidriera) and *El coloquio de los perros* (A Discussion with Dogs). In 1617 Cervantes published his Byzantine novel *Trabajos de Persiles y Sigismunda, historia setentrional* (The Trials of Persiles and Sigismunda, a Northern Story). The first translation of *Trabajos de Persiles y Sigismunda* in English was by an anonymous author in 1619; the defects of this translation resulted from the fact that it was not translated directly from Spanish but from a French translation. In 1741 another anonymous English translation was published that evidences many characteristics of the era, that is, great liberties are taken in the interpretation of the original text, including the alteration of plots and names. Later, in 1854, Margaret Stanley translated a version of Cervantes's last great work. This attempt is riddled, however, with misinterpretations and reductions of the original. A more accurate translation by Celia Richmond Weller and Clark A. Colahan was published in 1989.

The two main characters of this novel are Persiles, the prince of Thule, and Sigismunda, the daughter of the king of Friesland, who are in love. Throughout their adventures they claim to be siblings under the pseudonyms Periandro and Auristela. Only at the end of the novel are their true aristocratic identities revealed, even to the reader. They traverse both sea and land, migrating from the frigid and inhospitable shores of the North Pole toward the blazing Mediterranean sun of the south. As they set out on the high seas, they are taken captive by corsairs. Sigismunda is overtaken and enslaved in Denmark, where the prince of this nation becomes enamored of her. She cleverly manages to flee the grip of her suitor, as she does from many others along the way, and escapes bondage only to land on an island inhabited by barbarians. Here she finds Persiles. Descriptions of the northern countries are astonishingly accurate given that Cervantes never toured this part of Europe; hence, all of his knowledge of the geographic points mentioned derived from books.

In contrast, the second half of the novel (books 3 and 4) begins with the couple's arrival in the Mediterranean area, and Cervantes's stories, based on his personal experiences as a soldier, sailor, and traveler, become more detailed and animated. Many scenes are veritable samples of *costumbrismo* (a form of literature and painting, especially popular in the nineteenth century, that describes traditions and cultural behavior in the daily life of a region or country). In these countries the reader sees the starving poet, the street performers, the conniving mayor, the picaresque vagabonds, and the frightened Moriscos (Moorish converts to Christianity who remained in Spain after the Reconquista). The two cross through France, Portugal, and Italy on their way to their final destination, Rome, where they seek a papal blessing of their love. They share a bond that has been nurtured and strengthened through the many hardships they endured together. The love that unites them is chaste and profound. They receive the pontifical benediction and then marry and live to see their great-grandchildren. The narrative is a complicated one, as it is frequently interrupted by external forces that echo the fickle and enigmatic confluences that pervade life in general and particularly impede the young lovers from realizing their happiness. Cervantes, as he did in *Don Quixote,* creates an atmosphere in which reality is questioned. Dreams and facts are difficult to differentiate. At times it is not clear whether Periandro, for example, is narrating what he actually sees or what he is dreaming.

In *Trabajos de Persiles y Sigismunda,* Cervantes coins the phrase *peregrino andante* (the itinerant/wandering pilgrim), a figure reminiscent of the *caballero andante* (itiner-

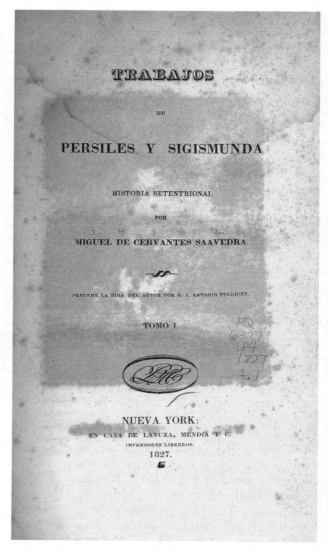

Frontispiece and title page for volume one of the 1827 edition of Miguel de Cervantes Saavedra's 1617 Byzantine novel (translated as The Trials of Persiles and Sigismunda, *1619), in which the travels of two noble lovers take them from the North Pole to the Mediterranean (Thomas Cooper Library, University of South Carolina)*

ant knight) in the chivalric novel. The obvious redundancy, if not duplicity (that is, a pilgrim without a destination), typical of Cervantes's subtle tongue-in-cheek approach to the universal questions of existence further nuances *Novelas ejemplares* and *Trabajos de Persiles y Sigismunda* while remaining faithful to the age. Cervantes is said to have taken his lead from Contreras, whose pilgrim seems to wander aimlessly, but this interpretation is a superficial one, since Luzmán's real journey, like Persiles and Sigismunda's, is one of religious growth, from terrestrial ambitions to celestial enlightenment. Cervantes's other inspiration for this novel was Heliodorus's *Aethiopica, Theagenes and Chariclea,* according to Schevill and Bonilla, while Menéndez y Pelayo also perceives Tatius's *Leucippe and Cleitophon* as a major

influence. Both Menéndez y Pelayo and Palomo Roberto agree that foremost is the model provided by Núñez de Reinoso's *La historia de los amores de Clareo y Florisea y de los trabajos de la sin ventura Isea.*

Other Spanish works from the sixteenth and seventeenth centuries manifest characteristics typical of the Byzantine novel. These works include *Philosofía antigua poética* (1596, Ancient Poetic Philosophy), by Alonso López Pinciano; *El pelegrino curioso y grandezas de España* (1577?, The Curious Pilgrim and the Marvels of Spain), by Bartolomé y Villalba y Estaña; *Teatro popular* (1622, Folk Theater), by Francisco de Lugo y Dávila; *Historias panegíricas y exemplares* (1623, Laudatory and Model Stories) and *Historia de Hipólito y Aminta* (1627?, The Story of Hypolitus and Aminta), by Francisco de Quintana;

Eustorgio y Clorilene "historia moscovita" (1629, Eustorgio and Clorilene, a Muscovite Story), by Enrique Suárez de Mendoza; *Fiestas en Lima* (1632, Holidays in Lima), by Rodrigo de Carvajal y Robles; *Historia de las fortunas de Semprilis y Geronodano* (1629, Semprilis and Geronodano's Tale of Fortune), by Enrique de Zúñiga; *Novelas de varios sucesos, en ocho discursos morales* (1635, Novels on Many Events in Eight Moral Speeches), by Ginés Carrillo Cerón; *Los hijos de la fortuna. Teágenes y Cariclea* (1664, Children of Fortune: Theagenes and Chariclea), by Pedro Calderón de la Barca; and *Arte de ingenio: Tratado de agudeza* (1642, The Exercise of Wit: A Book on Shrewdness) and *Criticón* (1651, Critical), by Baltasar Gracián.

Three fundamental themes of the Byzantine novel are love, adventure, and religion. Secondly, all begin in media res, with the reader given the necessary information piece by piece as the plot unfolds. Not infrequently one will encounter revealing dreams, humor, and a happy ending. The felicitous conclusion would be peace, which is the reward for having overcome so many *trabajos* (tribulations). Lastly, a moral foundation is made explicit by pronouncements with unmistakable religious overtones. Hence, in the Byzantine novel two major currents converge: the Renaissance proclivity for the retrieval of the literature of antiquity and the spiritual zeal of the Counter-Reformation.

As for the major exemplars of the Spanish Byzantine novel, while the "late-comers" in this genre, Cervantes and Lope de Vega, are the best known and most researched, the earliest specimens in Castilian are those of Núñez de Reinoso and Contreras. Despite the similarities, these distinct Spanish novels differ from their classical Byzantine models in several ways. In the Greek renditions characters are kidnapped by their own, whereas in the Spanish novels characters are captured by Moors or Turks. Their presence not only adds to the exotic milieu but also reflects actual events of the age; often Christians were held by Muslims for ransom. Unlike the works of antiquity, these Renaissance novels are concerned with expanding the protagonists' comprehension of Catholicism. Such a concern was also projected onto the "infidels" who are moved to conversion in several of the novels. In addition, the outcome in the Hellenic world was dependent on destiny, the will of the gods. In sixteenth-century writings the final effects are consequent to the individual's conduct and spiritual fortitude, all at his disposition because of the Christian concept of free will.

Biography:

Constance Hubbard Rose, *Alonso Núñez de Reinoso: The Lament of a Sixteenth-Century Exile* (Rutherford, N.J.: Fairleigh Dickinson University Press, 1971).

References:

Damaso Alonso, *De los siglos oscuros al de oro: Notas y artículos a través de 700 años de letras españolas* (Madrid: Gredo, 1958):, pp. 210–217;

Marcel Bataillon, *Erasmo y España: Estudios sobre la historia espiritual del siglo XVI* (Mexico City & Buenos Aires: Fondo de Cultura Económica, 1950);

Bataillon, *Varia lección de clásicos españoles* (Madrid: Gredos, 1964);

Emilio Carilla, "La novela bizantina española," *Revista de filología española,* 46 (1968): 275–287;

Armando Durán, *Estructura y técnicas de la novela sentimental y caballeresca* (Madrid: Gredos, 1973);

Manuel Durán, *Cervantes* (Boston: Twayne, 1974);

Ruth El Saffar, *Beyond Fiction: The Recovery of the Feminine in the Novels of Cervantes* (Berkeley: University of California Press, 1984);

Alban K. Forcione, *Cervantes and the Humanist Vision: A Study of Four Exemplary Novels* (Princeton: Princeton University Press, 1982);

Forcione, *Cervantes, Aristotle, and the Persiles* (Princeton: Princeton University Press, 1970);

Javier González Roviro, *La novela bizantina de la Edad de Oro* (Madrid: Gredos, 1996);

Juergen Hahn, *The Origins of the Baroque Concept of Peregrinatio* (Chapel Hill: University of North Carolina Press, 1973);

Elizabeth Hazelton Haight, *Essays on the Greek Romances* (New York: Longmans, Green, 1943);

Marcelino Menéndez y Pelayo, *Orígenes de la novela,* 4 volumes (Madrid: Consejo Superior de Investigaciones Científicas, 1943), IV, pp. 153–156;

John C. Olin, *The Catholic Reformation: Savonarola to Ignatius Loyola* (New York: Harper & Row, 1969);

Erwin Rohde, *Der griechische roman und seine vorläufer* (Leipzig: Breitkopf & Härtel, 1876);

Miguel Romera-Navarro, *Historia de la literatura española* (Boston: Heath, 1928);

Miguel Angel Teijeiro Fuentes, *La novela bizantina española: Apuntes para una revisión del género* (Cáceres: Ediciones Universidad de Extremadura, 1988);

Antonio Vilanova, *Erasmo y Cervantes* (Barcelona: Lumen, 1989);

Stanislav Zimic, "Alonso Núñez de Reinoso, Traductor de *Leucipe y Clitofonte,*" *Symposium,* 21 (1967): 166–175.

The Sixteenth-Century Spanish Epic

Jesús Rodríguez-Velasco
University of California, Berkeley

BOOKS: Francisco de Jerez, *Libro primo de la conquista del Peru & provincia del Cuzco de le indie occidentali* (Vinegia: Maestro Stephano da Sabio, 1535);

Juan de Quirós, *Cristo Pathia* (Toledo: Juan Ferrer, 1552);

Nicolás Espinosa, *La segunda parte de Orlando* (Saragossa: Pedro Bernuz, 1555);

Francisco Garrido de Villena, *El verdadero suceso de la famosa batalla de Roncesualles* (Valencia: Juan de Meyr, 1555);

Jerónimo Sempere, *Primera y segunda parte de la Carolea: Trata las victorias del Emperador Carlo V, Rey de España* (Valencia: Juan de Arcos, 1560);

Alonso Girón y de Rebolledo, *La pasión de nuestro señor Jesu Christo según san Juan* (Valencia: Juan de Meyr, 1563);

Diego Ramírez Pagán, *Historia de la sagrada pasión de nuestro redemptor Jesu Christo* (Valencia: Juan de Meyr, 1564);

Jerónimo de Arbolanche, *Las Abidas* (Saragossa: Juan Millán, 1566);

Luis de Zapata, *Carlo famoso* (Valencia: Juan de Meyr, 1566);

Diego Jiménez de Ayllón, *Los famosos, y heroicos hechos del invencible y esforzado Cavallero, onrra y flor de las Españas, el Cid Ruydíaz de Bivar* (Antwerp: Viuda de Juan Lacio, 1568);

Baltasar de Vargas, *Breve relación en octava rima de la jornada que ha hecho el señor duque de Alva desde España hasta Flandes* (Antwerp: Amato Taverniero, 1568);

Alonso de Ercilla y Zúñiga, *La Araucana* (Madrid: Cossin, 1569);

Juan Coloma, *Década de la pasión de nuestro redentor Jesu Christo, con otra obra intitulada Cántico de su Gloriosa Resurrección* (Caller: Vincenzo Sembenino, 1576);

Benito Sánchez Galindo, *Primera y segunda parte de la Christi Victoria* (Barcelona: Sansón Arbus, 1576);

Martín Abarca de Bolea, *Libro de Orlando determinado* (Lérida: Miguel Prats, 1578);

Jerónimo Corte Real, *Felicísima victoria en el golfo de Lepanto* (Lisbon: Antonio Ribero, 1578);

Andrés de la Losa, *Batalla y triunfo del hombre contra los vicios* (Seville: Bartolomé González, 1580);

Diego de Oseguera, *Libro intitulado estaciones del christiano* (Valladolid: Diego Fernández de Córdoba, 1580);

Francisco Balbi de Correggio, *Vida del ilustrísimo señor Octavio Gonzaga* (Barcelona: Hubert Gotard, 1581);

Hipólito Sans, *La Maltea* (Valencia: Juan Navarro, 1582);

Gonzalo Gómez de Luque, *Los famosos hechos del príncipe Celidón de Iberia* (Alcalá de Henares: Juan Iñiguez de Lequerica, 1583);

Francisco Hernández Blasco, *Universal redención, pasión, muerte y ressurrección de nuestro señor Jesuchristo* (Alcalá de Henares: Juan Gracián, 1584);

De la Losa, *Verdadero entretenimiento del christiano* (Seville: Alonso de la Barrera, 1584);

Luis Martí, *Historia del bienaventurado padre fray Luis Bertrán* (Valencia: Juan Navarro, 1584);

Juan Rufo, *La Austríada* (Madrid: Alonso Gómez, 1584);

Cristóbal Tamariz, *Martirio de los sanctos mártires de Cartuja que padescieron en Londres* (Seville: Alonso de la Barrera, 1584);

Jerónimo de Urrea, *El victorioso Carlos V*, Biblioteca Nacional de Madrid ms. 1469 (1584);

Gaspar García de Alarcón, *La victoriosa conquista de don Álvaro de Bazán* (Valencia: Herederos de Juan Navarro, 1585);

Agustín Alonso, *Historia de las hazañas y hechos del invencible caballero Bernardo del Carpio* (Toledo: Juan Boyer, 1585);

Pedro de la Vezilla Castellanos, *El león de España* (Salamanca: Juan Fernández, 1586);

Luis Barahona de Soto, *Las lágrimas de Angélica* (Granada: Hugo de Mena, 1586);

Miguel Giner, *El sitio y toma de Anvers* (Milan: Pacífico Poncio, 1587);

Pedro de Padilla, *Grandezas y excelencias de la Virgen Señora Nuestra* (Madrid: Pedro Madrigal, 1587);

Pedro de Escobar Cabeza de Vaca, *Luzero de la tierra sancta y grandezas de Egipto y Monte Sinay* (Valladolid: Bernardino de Santodomingo, 1587);

Esteban de Villalobos, comp., *Thesoro de la divina poesía* (Toledo: Juan Rodríguez, 1587);

Cristóbal de Virués, *El Monserrate* (Madrid: Querino Gerardo, 1587);

Gabriel de Mata, *Primera, segunda y tercera parte del Cavallero Asisio en el nacimiento vida y muerte del seraphico padre sanct Francisco en octava rima compuesto* (Bilbao: Matías Mares, 1587);

Pedro Alonso Pimentel, *Guerras civiles de Flandes,* manuscript (ca. 1587–1588);

Balbi de Correggio, *Pasada del serenísimo Vicenzo Gonzaga y Austria por el Estado de Milán* (Mantua: Giacomo Ruffinello, 1588);

Jerónimo de Huerta, *Florando de Castilla* (Alcalá de Henares: Juan Gracián, 1588);

Gabriel Lasso de la Vega, *Cortés valeroso y Mexicana* (Madrid: Pedro Madrigal, 1588);

Juan de Castellanos, *Elegías de varones ilustres de Indias* (Madrid: Viuda de Alonso Gómez, 1589);

Diego Sánchez de la Cámara, *Pasión de Nuestro Señor en versos castellanos* (Madrid: Querino Gerardo, 1589);

Lorenzo de Zamora, *Historia de Sagunto, Numancia y Cartago* (Alcalá de Henares: Juan Iñiguez de Lequerica, 1589);

Duarte Díaz, *La conquista que hizieron los poderosos y catholicos reyes don Fernando, y doña Ysabel, en el reyno de Granada* (Madrid: Viuda de Alonso Gómez, 1590);

Francisco de Aldana, *El parto de la Virgen* (Madrid: Pedro Madrigal, 1591);

Eugenio Martínez, *Libro de la vida y martirio de la divina virgen y mártir santa Inés* (Alcalá de Henares: Hernán Ramírez, 1592);

Balbi de Correggio, *Historia de los amores del valeroso moro Abinde-Arráez y de la hermosa Xarifa* (Milan: Pacífico Poncio, 1593);

Cristóbal de Mesa, *Las Navas de Tolosa* (N.p., 1594);

Gaspar de los Reyes, *Obra de la redención* (Seville: Alonso de la Barrera, 1595);

Pedro de Oña, *Arauco domado* (Ciudad de los Reyes: Antonio Ricardo de Turín, 1596);

Diego de Santisteban, *La Araucana* (Salamanca: Juan y Andrés Renaut, 1597);

Mata, *Vida, muerte y milagros de S. Diego de Alcalá* (Alcalá de Henares: Juan Gracián, 1598);

Luis Hurtado de Toledo, *Vida de Sant Joseph* (Toledo: Pedro Rodríguez, 1598);

Félix Lope de Vega, *La Dragontea* (Valencia: Pedro Patricio, 1598);

Lope de Vega, *Isidro* (Madrid: Juan de Montoya, 1599);

Antonio de Saavedra Guzmán, *El peregrino indiano* (Madrid: Pedro Madrigal, 1599);

De Santisteban, *Guerras de Malta y toma de Rodas* (Madrid: Licenciado Várez de Castro, 1599);

Bartolomé de Segura, *Del nacimiento, vida y muerte del glorioso confesor san Julián* (Cuenca: Miguel Serrano de Vargas, 1599).

Modern Editions: Cristóbal de Virués, *El Monserrate,* in *Poemas Épicos,* edited by Cayetano Rosell, volume 1, Biblioteca de Autores Españoles, no. 17 (Madrid: Rivadeneyra, 1864);

Luis Hurtado de Toledo, *Historia de s. Joseph,* in *Poemas épicos,* edited by Rosell, volume 2, Biblioteca de Autores Españoles, no. 29 (Madrid: Rivadeneyra, 1866);

Juan Rufo, *La Austríada,* in *Poemas épicos,* edited by Rosell, volume 2, Biblioteca de Autores Españoles, no. 29 (Madrid: Rivadeneyra, 1866);

Juan de Castellanos, *Elegías de varones ilustres de Indias,* edited by Bonaventura Carles Aribau, Biblioteca de Autores Españoles, no. 4 (Madrid: Rivadeneyra, 1874);

Pedro de Oña, *Arauco domado,* edited by José Toribio Medina (Santiago, Chile: Imprenta universitaria, 1917);

Diego Ramírez Pagán, *Historia de la sagrada pasión de nuestro redemptor Jesu Christo,* edited by Antonio Pérez Gómez (Valencia: Duque & Marqués, 1950);

Baltasar de Vargas, *Breve relación de la jornada que ha hecho el señor duque de Alva desde España hasta Flandes,* edited by Jacobo Stuart Fitz-James y Faló, Duque de Alba, and J. López de Toro (Madrid: Arcadia, 1952);

Benito Sánchez Galindo, *Christi Victoria,* edited by Pérez Gómez (Valencia: Duque & Marqués, 1954);

Juan de Quirós, *Cristo Pathia,* edited by Pérez Gómez (Valencia: Duque & Marqués, 1955);

Pedro Alonso Pimentel, *Guerras civiles de Flandes,* edited by Fernando González Ollé, *Boletín de la Real Academia Española,* 45 (1965): 141–184;

Jerónimo de Arbolanche, *Las Abidas,* facsimile edition, notes by González Ollé (Madrid: Consejo Superior de Investigaciones Científicas, 1972);

Luis Barahona de Soto, *Las lágrimas de Angélica,* edited by José Lara Garrido (Madrid: Cátedra, 1981);

Luis Zapata, *Carlo Famoso,* edited by Winston A. Reynolds (Madrid: Porrúa, 1984);

Alonso de Ercilla y Zúñiga, *La Araucana,* edited by Marcos A. Morínigo and Isaías Lerner (Madrid: Castalia, 1990);

Francisco de Jerez, *La Conquista del Perú: Poema heroico de 1537,* edited by M. Nieto Nuño (Cáceres: Institución Cultural "El Brocense" de la Excma. Diputación Provincial de Cáceres, 1992);

Alonso Girón y de Rebolledo, *La pasión de nuestro señor Jesu Christo según san Juan* (Valencia: Universidad de Valencia, 1995);

Félix Lope de Vega, *La Dragontea,* in his *Poesía,* edited by Antonio Carreño, volume 1 (Madrid: Fundación José Antonio de Castro, 2002);

Vega, *Isidro,* in his *Poesía,* edited by Carreño, volume 1 (Madrid: Fundación José Antonio de Castro, 2002).

In Spain, the years between 1549 and 1599 mark the initial appearance, development, and adaptation of an important current of literary epic characterized by steady growth and increasing levels of achievement, one that stretches well into the end of the eighteenth century. Yet, only a small number of the many works produced during this period attracted a broad readership or have received the critical attention they deserve. The vast majority of these compositions remain, when not completely unknown, mostly unread. The development of the literary and learned epic (those written by humanist scholars with a background in Latin) in early-modern Spain may be traced to a confluence of several traditions, both classical and modern, that sought to represent themes and situations that emerged from the Spanish imperial experience as it spread across the globe during the sixteenth century. The literary epic became both a medium for justifying the conquest and the cultural and religious hegemony of the Spanish kingdoms as well as a means for constructing, sustaining, and propagating the image of a triumphant imperial Spain.

The foundational tradition upon which the Spanish literary epic rests remains the Italian epic romance, or the *romanzi cavallereschi* (chivalric romance), usually composed in the Tuscan language. The latter's beginnings may be traced to the early sixteenth century, when Andrea da Barberino first rewrote the legends of the medieval Carolingian epic tradition in his long poem *La Spagna* (Spain). The crucial texts that serve as the center of gravity for all Renaissance literary epic reflect two reinterpretations of material from the same Carolingian cycle upon which Barberino drew, namely Mateo Maria Boiardo's *Orlando Innamorato* (1483, Orlando in Love) and Ludovico Ariosto's *Orlando Furioso* (1516, Orlando the Mad). To these must be added yet another important work in the same vein, written almost a century before—Torquato Tasso's *Gerusalemme Liberata* (1581, Jerusalem Liberated), which may be considered yet another touchstone in the Renaissance epic tradition in addition to Boiardo's and Ariosto's poems.

A second tradition that figures in the origins of the Spanish literary epic is derived from the epic models taken from classical antiquity, principally Virgil's *Aeneid.* The introduction of Virgil's poems into Castile occurred during the first quarter of the fifteenth century, thanks in large part to a translation and gloss of the *Aeneid* prepared by Enrique de Villena (also known as Enrique de Aragón). During the decades following the appearance of Villena's work there was an increasing interest in epic literature, which made possible the reading, abridgments, and translations of the Homeric *Ilias latina* (a medieval digest of Homer's Greek epic) and Lucan's *Pharsalia.* To be sure, Lucan's poem should be regarded as a critical point of reference in the emergence of the Hispanic epic, not only because of Lucan's Hispano-Roman origins (he was born at Corduba, modern-day Córdoba), often invoked by Spaniards during the period leading to the consolidation of the cultural and literary traditions of the formative period of the Hispanic epic from the fifteenth to the nineteenth centuries, but also as a source of metaphors, images, and epic formulas. This subject has yet to receive careful attention from critics and scholars.

Additionally, and partially derived from the late-medieval interest in the classical epic, there is yet one more important source that is often ignored by literary historians in tracing the origins of the Spanish learned epic: the modest, but native, tradition of Castilian vernacular literary epic of the fifteenth century. The latter was composed in sonorous eight-line stanzas called *coplas de arte mayor castellano* (stanzas of lines of more than eight syllables). Its main cultivators were authors such as Juan de Mena; Iñigo López de Mendoza, Marqués de Santillana; and Juan Barba. These authors not only exploit the heroic images and patterns of ancient epic known at the time but also imitate within their larger frames the exegetical commentaries that are historically associated with the heroic and elevated styles and frequently found in manuscripts with translations of Virgil, Homer, and Lucan.

There is a third touchstone for understanding the foundations of the Spanish literary epic, a theoretical one that traces its origin to the intensive commentaries of Aristotle's *Poetics* and Horace's *Epistula ad Pisones* (Letter to the Pisones) during the Renaissance. Given its broad humanistic roots, this tradition is essentially an Italian import and closely related to the *romanzi cavallereschi* and, more generally, the epic writings in Tuscan and in ottava rima (octave rhyme, also known as epic meter). As those kinds of compositions emerged to assert their primacy, several learned theorists attempted to describe and prescribe the nature of the *romanzo* (romance) in terms of Aristotle's and Horace's works. One of the results of this effort was a fairly new literary product that sought to actualize the ideas about epic and tragedy expressed by both Greek and Roman authors. It is noteworthy that not all of those theorists were eager to advocate such an adaptation: while there are some treatises that seek to dignify the *romanzi,* others exclude them from any comparison to the classical notions of the sublime styles of literature (classical literary theory considered both epic and tragedy as forms of the sublime). The impact of this current of neoclassical commentary on Spanish and Italian, and on the literary production of the Spanish Golden Age in particular, especially on epic poetry composed in Spain, has been studied by such scholars as Frank Pierce, Antonio García Berrio, and José Lara Garrido.

Finally, the ample and long popularity of the Spanish *libros de caballerías* (books of chivalry) also played an important role in the emergence of literary epic in Spain. Chivalric narrative was a literary and commercial editorial genre comprising extensive prose fictions centering on the life and deeds of a knightly hero, whose tremendous popularity in Spain during the sixteenth century would be difficult to exaggerate. The catalogue of native Spanish chivalric romances is led both chronologically and editorially by *Amadís de Gaula* (Amadís of Gaul). Many more works competed with *Amadís de Gaula* for preeminence, however, and won the allegiance of a broad readership. Among these works there were translations of the Italian *romanzi cavallereschi,* originally composed in epic meter but rendered in prose when translated into Spanish.

The learned literary epic of the Spanish Renaissance deals with heroic themes in an elevated style. In order to narrate the deeds that it chronicles, it adopts a specific verse form, namely the *octava real* with hendecasyllabic lines, which resonates with a hexametric echo; calqued clearly upon the Italian ottava rima, it nevertheless preserves its prosodic bond to the rhythmic cadences and pronunciation of the Spanish *copla de arte mayor* from the fifteenth century. The *octava real* is, thus, a Spanish version of the Tuscan ottava rima. It is composed of eight eleven-syllable lines that rhyme *abababcc.* Conforming to the formal patterns of its Italian models, literary epic in Spain generally divides itself into cantos, each one constituting a single chapter or narrative unit; the number of cantos per poem varies. While divisions of twelve cantos, following Virgil's *Aeneid,* or twenty-four in imitation of Homer, carried with them an inevitable prestige, there is a tendency in the Spanish epic to enlarge the poem into as many as fifty, which approximates the forty-six into which Ariosto had divided his *Orlando Furioso.* At the same time, the learned, literary epic in Spain explores many rhetorical and poetical devices discussed in the prescriptive and theoretical treatises on poetic commentary of the Renaissance through the process called *imitatio auctorum* (imitation of authors). As a result, it is possible to find epics that use either an *ordo artificialis* (artificial order), beginning the

Italian poet Ludovico Ariosto, whose epic Orlando Furioso *(1516, Orlando the Mad) was influential on Spanish practitioners of the chilvaric epic (frontispiece for Edmund G. Gardner,* The King of Court Poets, *1906; Thomas Cooper Library, University of South Carolina)*

narration at a midpoint in the events, or an *ordo naturalis* (natural order) that starts the narrative at the beginning of the story. In addition, throughout Spanish literary epics there is an exploration of some of the characteristic features of epic narratives, as in the case of the dual, or coupled, protagonists, where a hero is accompanied by a friend who serves as his foil; the hyperbolic portrayal of the antagonist's forces; descriptive or "ecphrastic," pictorial interludes; and the use of epic formulaic diction.

Translations of epic poems play a major role in the history and development of the genre, since a crucial component in the adaptation and development of the epic in Spain may be traced back to the translation of one particular *romanzo cavallerescho* couched in epic form, which provided the standard for all subsequent manifestations of the genre in the Iberian Peninsula: the Spanish-language edition of Ariosto's *Orlando Furioso* completed by Jerónimo Jiménez de Urrea. First published in 1549, it represents the direct accommodation into Castilian of the *octava real* stanza for epic narrative, that is, the first adaptation of the ottava rima. Jiménez de Urrea's translation was printed several times, and it was probably reviewed and corrected in 1588. Its impact in Spanish literary circles composed of both learned readers and a public avid for chivalric narrative was significant, provoking several erudite polemics on literature in general and poetry in particular. One of these debates dealt with the legitimacy of adapting Italian verse into Spanish, which some authors perceived as an unjustified substitution of native Spanish metric procedures with an Italian import. Jiménez de Urrea's translation does indeed exhibit a certain Tuscanized style, at times giving the impression of the direct transposition of many Italian words rather than their translation. Notwithstanding some resistance to it in Spain, Jiménez de Urrea's translation of Ariosto was not unique; one year later, in 1550, Hernando Alcocer completed his own *de verbo ad verbum* (word-by-word—that is, prose) translation of Ariosto. A third translation of *Orlando Furioso,* also in prose, was published in Madrid in 1585 by Diego Vázquez de Contreras. It is significant to note that even if Ariosto's literary themes remained among the most compelling ones in the Spanish epic cycles (as shown by Maxime Chevalier in his *Ariosto en España* [1969, Ariosto in Spain]), no one, after Jiménez de Urrea, dared to translate the Tuscan work into Spanish verse.

From this introduction of Ariosto's work to Spain, the learned epic in *octava real* as previously defined took on new ways of expression, mostly in a religious vein. Although religious themes are commonplace in the Italian epic starting with Giacoppo Sannazaro's *De Partu Virginis* (On the Virgin's Labor), translated into Spanish twice (first in 1554 by Licenciado Gregorio Hernández de Velasco), the importance of religion in the development of an epic literature in Spanish cannot be stressed enough. Several works stand out in this vein, the most important of which is *Sanazaro Español: Los tres libros del parto de la Virgen* (1620, Spanish Sannazaro: The Three Books on the Virgin's Labor), by Francisco Herrera y Maldonado, which was composed in *octavas reales* and reprinted four times during the seventeenth century.

Jean Frappier, in volume one of his *Les Chansons de Geste du Cycle de Guillaume d'Orange* (1955, The Epic Songs of the Cycle of Gillaume d'Orange), explains the construction and rise of epic cycles, noting that with respect to the epic children beget their parents, meaning that the epic narratives of the ancestors come only after their descendants have achieved a level of success. Something similar can be said about the order of trans-

lations: although Boiardo's poem precedes Ariosto's, the translation of Ariosto's text into Spanish led to the rendering of Boiardo's poem into the same language. The *Orlando Innamorato* was, in fact, only translated into Spanish after Ariosto's work had achieved widespread popularity, and it served also as a crucial point of reference in the debate among the antagonists to Jiménez de Urrea's translation of Ariosto. The translator, Francisco Garrido de Villena, decided to translate in a verse form but sought to avoid the use of Italian metric structures. Instead, he composed his work using a variety of Castilian polymetric verses. Some years later, in 1591, Hernando de Acuña—the staunchest critic of Jiménez de Urrea and, in general, of all who favored Italian meters—prepared and published his own translation of Boiardo's *Orlando Innamorato* in *octava real.*

Other Italian and Portuguese poems were translated into Spanish during the sixteenth century, including epics by Tasso, Luigi Tansillo, and Luís de Camões. Tasso's *Gerusalemme Liberata* is a poem based on the Crusades and the epic hero Geoffrey of Bouillon, who loomed large in the French Crusade cycle of narratives during the Middle Ages and in the late-thirteenth-century Spanish *Gran Conquista de Ultramar* (The Great Overseas Conquest). *Gerusalemme Liberata* served as a point of reference for several imitations that, in fact, may be considered wholly original works, like the one by Félix Lope de Vega, already published in the sixteenth century. Around 1585, according to Pierce in his *La poesía épica del Siglo de Oro,* Bartolomé Cayrasco finished his translation of Tasso's poem, but it remained in manuscript and was never printed. Two years later, in 1587, the first widely circulated, printed version of the *Gerusalemme Liberata* appeared, signed by the humanist Juan Sedeño. *Gerusalemme Liberata* serves as the epicenter of a renewal of Renaissance epic as it entwines the Crusades with the mythical world of courtly chivalry. In part, the younger Tasso had learned the possibilities of this twofold combination from his father, Bernardo Tasso, himself author of a chivalric epic in Tuscan titled *Amadigi* (Amadis), which was never translated into Spanish although it was dedicated to Philip II, king of Spain. When Torquato composed *Gerusalemme Liberata* at the court of the Della Rovere family, the theme of crusade and the sentiments underpinning the Counter Reformation were already circulating in both Italy and Spain.

While it remains true that the Spanish epic exploits most of the well-established European epic cycles—that is, those mostly derived from the tradition of medieval epic song and the cycles that deal with the translations of Ariosto, Boiardo, and Tasso—some are additionally based, either all or in part, on historiography. The exploration of new epic themes can be grouped in two sets. The first has a spiritual dimension and is manifested most commonly in the themes of Christ's Passion and the life of the Virgin, hagiography, and biography of religious persons, all of which exhibit strong doctrinal underpinnings and allegorical content. The second set is composed of poems more closely linked to historical accounts of both ancient and modern historical provenance, especially from the reign of the Catholic Monarchs forward. In this second set there is yet another small number of compositions that can be deemed actual *romanzi cavallereschi* but may also be read as allegorical renderings of recent history.

The first manifestation of epic poetry, Juan de Quirós's *Cristo Pathia* (1552, Christ's Passion), is a narrative poem that is composed in octaves and divided into songs. Quirós's poem is closely related to medieval Passion poetry, an important subject that remained strong in all the literary genres. One of the most important points underscored by Pedro M. Cátedra's research on this topic in his *Poesía de Pasión en la Edad Media: El "Cancionero"* (2001, Poetry of Passion in the Middle Ages) is how the theme of the Passion, frequently linked to prayer, meditation, and contemplation, looks toward different textual and generic traditions and manages to infiltrate nearly all forms of literary production. The same may be said about Passion epics, especially the *Cristo Pathia,* which opened the door to a whole gamut of generic possibilities and transformations. Additionally, the work must be examined in light of the spiritual reforms that took place during the Renaissance. Not by chance did Quirós's poem appear almost exactly at the height of the Council of Trent, which convened from 1545 to 1563. From the twelfth century on, Passion poetry had served as a point of reference for meditation and Christian devotion and thus as a means for the introduction of new Christian doctrines and ideologies especially because of its allegorical and hermeneutical bent. How the long tradition of Passion poetry from the Middle Ages forward aimed to transmit and implement doctrinal and spiritual reform related to the Reformation and Counter Reformation is a study that has yet to be undertaken.

Quirós's poem is the first in a long series of similar works, of which the most canonical example, *Christiada,* by the Dominican (the Catholic order most closely associated with the Inquisition) Diego de Hojeda, was written in the second half of the sixteenth century and published in Seville in 1611. During these years Alonso Girón y Rebolledo published in Valencia a work, *La pasión de nuestro señor Jesu Christo según san Juan* (1563, The Passion of Jesus Christ According to Saint John), oddly written in *quintillas,* a five-line stanza of short syllabic quantity. This metrical structure is the

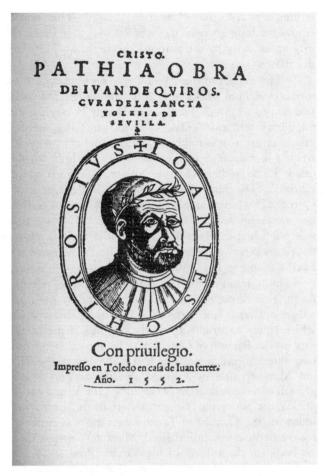

Title page for Juan de Quirós's 1552 poetic rendering of the Passion story (Christ's Passion), the first epic poem written in Spain (from Quirós, Cristo Pathia, *1955; Mervyn H. Sterne Library, University of Alabama, Birmingham)*

same chosen by Diego Ramírez Pagán to compose his *Historia de la sagrada pasión de nuestro redemptor Jesu Christo* (1564, A History of the Sacred Passion of Our Redeemer Jesus Christ), published as well in Valencia. In 1576, an anthology of similar poetry was published by Juan Coloma. The first part of Coloma's volume, *Década de la pasión de nuestro redentor Jesu Christo* (Decade of the Passion of Our Redeemer Jesus Christ), is written, like Dante Alighieri's *La divina commedia* (circa 1310–1314, The Divine Comedy) in tercets; the second part takes a more heroic direction and narrates Christ's triumph. Composed in octaves, the latter is titled *Cántico de su Gloriosa Resurrección* (Canticle of His Glorious Resurrection). That same year Benito Sánchez Galindo published *Christi Victoria* (Christ's Victory), a short text in octaves composed of two songs. Several years later, *Universal redención, pasión, muerte y ressurrección de nuestro señor Jesuchristo* (1584, Universal Redemption, Passion, Death, and Resurrection of Our Lord Jesus Christ) was written by Francisco Hernández Blasco. This poem enjoyed a long success and was revised four times in fifty years, once by the author's brother, Luis Hernández Blasco.

The impact of the Passion epic on popular literature is evident in works such as the anthology *Thesoro de la divina poesía* (1587, Treasure of Divine Poetry), compiled by Esteban de Villalobos, which includes, among other literary works linked to the spiritual epic, a poem written in *redondillas* (quatrains) signed by Juan Micón titled "La Sagrada Passión de Nuestro Redemptor Jesu Christo" (The Holy Passion of Our Redeemer Jesus Christ). The last example of the Passion poems in this era was composed by Diego Sánchez de la Cámara and was published in Madrid in 1589 under the title *Pasión de Nuestro Señor en versos castellanos* (The Passion of Our Lord Composed in Castilian Verses).

In addition to the role played by Passion poetry, the origins of the epic are also tied to the tradition of *compassio Virginis* (the Virgin's compassion). This vein, which traces its origins to the beginnings of the literature on the Passion of Christ, may be approached from two different directions. The first is the epic of the Virgin Mary written in Tuscan, and the second is the growth and consolidation of the cult of the Virgin Mary during the sixteenth century, especially in the period following the Council of Trent, when the prayer of the rosary became institutionalized. Marina Warner's classic book on the subject of the Virgin, *Alone of All Her Sex: The Myth and Cult of the Virgin Mary* (1976), provides many useful insights on how to approach and understand the small but substantial number of poems related to the Sorrows of the Virgin Mary. The first poem to be published on the Sorrows of the Virgin was written by Pedro de Padilla. Composed in *octavas*, his *Grandezas y excelencias de la Virgen Señora Nuestra* (1587, Excellencies of the Virgin Our Lady) is divided into nine songs. More significant, however, is the poem composed by the Neoplatonist humanist Francisco de Aldana, whose *El parto de la Virgen* (The Virgin's Labor) was published in Madrid in 1591.

The poetry related to the lives of saints and devout religious persons is also of interest when chronicling the rise of the epic mode in Renaissance Spain. To be sure, the alliance between the saintly and the heroic belongs to the most-ancient epic traditions. Nevertheless, the Spanish Renaissance hagiographic epic, the first example of which—Luis Martí's *Historia del bienaventurado padre fray Luis Bertrán* (1584, History of the Blessed Father Luis Bertrán)—appeared rather late, can also be located within the sphere of Counter Reformation ideology. One of the consequences of the Council of Trent and the effects of its edicts, supported staunchly by Philip II, was the consolidation of certain notions about piety, devotion, and beatitude. These ideas became morally centered in everyday life rather than linked theologically to the sacred history of the saints. In this milieu, with its emphasis on the need to pursue saintliness in the world, new church institutions closely tied to Spain, like the Jesuit order, arose. There was thus a need to celebrate a new form of sainthood and to identify new saints for the Christian pantheon. During the period immediately after the Council of Trent, a group of newly beatified and canonized men and women appeared, whose purpose was to spur a renewed piety centered on new attitudes, ideas, and ways of life that had come to displace many of the ancient notions of saintliness. Within this sphere of spiritual action, the hagiographic epic played an extremely important role. At the same time, there are some saintly epic poems that deal with the most widely known ancient saints, although they are of interest mostly to the particular locale in which they are set. These works deal either with the patron saint of a city, or they are linked to another particular saint. An example is Lope de Vega's *Isidro,* a poem centering on the patron of Madrid and published there in 1599.

On other occasions, the saintly epic takes as its subject the *laus urbis,* or praise of a particular city, often from an apologetic point of view and seeking to exhort feelings of crusade aimed at animating the citizens of imperial Spain. Among the works written in this vein, Pedro de Escobar Cabeza de Vaca's *Luzero de la tierra sancta y grandezas de Egipto y Monte Sinay* (1587, Shining Star of the Holy Land and Grandeur of Egypt and Mount Sinai), stands out. There are at least eleven surviving poems that can be identified within this tradition. The first is Martí's *Historia del bienaventurado padre fray Luis Bertrán.* The same year Martí's work appeared, Licenciado Cristóbal Tamariz published his *Martirio de los santos mártires de Cartuja que padescieron en Londres* (The Martyrdom of the Saint Martyrs from Cartuja Who Suffered in London), composed in octaves and comprising six songs. Tamariz's poem is closely linked to Philip II's political program and propaganda aimed at England, eventually doomed to failure in 1588 with the defeat of the Spanish Armada. Also in 1587, Gabriel de Mata wrote and published his epic *Primera, segunda y tercera parte del Cavallero Asisio en el nacimiento vida y muerte del seraphico padre sanct Francisco en octava rima compuesto* (First, Second and Third Parts of the Knight of Assisi, on birth, life and death of the Seraphic Father Saint Francis, composed in octava rima), about St. Francis of Assisi, in which he is portrayed according to Franciscan tradition as well as a hero with chivalric attributes. Mata's work enjoyed a certain success and was revised two years later. *El Monserrate* (The Montserrat), by Cristóbal de Virués, was published in 1587. This work is about the Virgin of Montserrat and the foundation of her sanctuary on the mountain that bears her name near Barcelona; almost all of it is narrated in a prophetic tone by a hermit (often a key figure in chivalric narrative). Virués claims the absolute veracity of his narrative despite the use of clear literary devices derived from the chivalric traditions. In 1589 Mata published yet another hagiographic epic, *Vida, muerte y milagros de S. Diego de Alcalá* (Life, Death, and Miracles of St. Diego de Alcalá). Additionally, a life of St. Agnes, *Libro de la vida y martirio de la divina virgen y mártir santa Inés* (Book of the Life of the Martyr of the Divine Virgin and Martyr St. Inés), was composed by Eugenio Martínez and published in 1592. Several years later Luis Hurtado de Toledo published *Vida de Sant Joseph* (1598, Life of St. Joseph). The last two works in the procession of saintly epic are Bartolomé de Segura's *Del nacimiento, vida y muerte del glorioso confesor san Iulián* (1599, On the Birth, Life, and Death of the Glorious Confessor St. Julian), which tells of the life of one of the bishops of Cuenca, and Lope de Vega's *Isidro*.

The epic genre has always been marked by allegory, and, therefore, it is often read from a figural perspective using exegetical methods of long tradition. To be sure, many commentaries literally "surround" certain epic narratives since they are marginal glosses that envelop entire stanzas and represent centuries of accretion. This way of reading finds its origins in the most ancient epics, such as Virgil's *Aeneid,* and has contributed as much as the text itself to the prestige of the epic, endowing it with a great deal of didactic and doctrinal capacity. Many authors of Renaissance epic willingly wrote poems that lent themselves to allegory, portraying the struggle of vices and virtues through the persons of their protagonists and antagonists. Three Spanish poems fall clearly into this category. The first is Andrés de la Losa's *Batalla y triunfo del hombre contra los vicios* (1580, Battle and Triumph of Man against His Vices), which is composed of octaves and organized into sixteen cantos. The same year that this work was published, Diego de Oseguera completed his *Libro intitulado estaciones del christiano* (Book Titled Stations of the Christian), followed four years later by another poem by de la Losa, his *Verdadero entretenimiento del christiano* (True Care of the Christian).

Every epic narrative that deals with a given set of recurring themes and situations that refer to other epic songs and poems can be acknowledged to belong to an established tradition and to form part of an epic cycle. In large part, the Spanish Renaissance epic locates itself mostly in the Carolingian cycle of medieval French provenance. Several notable cycles deal with El Cid, the exotic lyric, and the romantic world of the Abencerrajes of Granada. The most important and widespread of

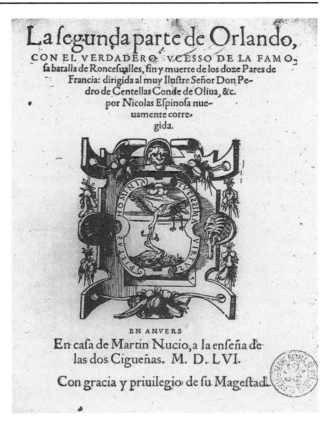

Title page for an early edition of Nicolás Espinosa's 1555 epic poem, a sequel to Ariosto's Orlando Furioso *(Orlando the Mad), which introduces the heroic Spanish knight Bernardo del Carpio (Kansas State University Library)*

these cycles, however, remains the Carolingian one. As old as the origins of the medieval European epic and manifested in all the Romance languages, the Germanic languages, and in Latin, it serves as a fundamental thematic touchstone for understanding all Renaissance epics. Ariosto's and Boiardo's works, which belong to the Carolingian cycle, mark a new point of departure for exploring a range of subjects and characters from new perspectives and, at the same time, constitute a large web of narrative plots that often serve as the origin for additional subcycles. For example, female characters such as Bradamante or Angelica or even central events, such as the battle of Roncevaux, or an historical one, such as the youth of Roland, may become points of departure for entirely new epics. Since the epic normally leaves the plot open at both the beginning and at the end of a narrative, cyclic texts usually go on to attempt to complete one or the other by creating a beginning or crafting an ending, seeking to address entirely new things left out of Boiardo's and Ariosto's works.

The first poem in the Spanish Carolingian cycle is Nicolás Espinosa's *La segunda parte de Orlando* (1555,

The Second Part of Orlando). Both Espinosa and Garrido de Villena, in his *El verdadero suceso de la famosa batalla de Roncesualles* (1555, The Actual Facts of the Famous Battle of Roncevaux) introduce the Spanish hero Bernardo del Carpio as a foil to the French in their Carolingian tales. According to the legend of Bernardo del Carpio, he was the actual slayer of Roland at Roncevaux, where he enveloped Roland in his arms and squeezed him to death, evoking the death of Anthaeus by Hercules. The political strategies underpinning the myth of Bernardo and his reputed place in the genealogy of several noble Spanish families has been studied by Lara Garrido in his *Los Mejores Plectros: Teoría y práctica de la épica culta en el siglo de oro* (1999, The Best Plettri: Theory and Practice of the Learned Epic in the Golden Age). A similar kind of accommodation of the Roland cycle to a Tuscan setting was carried out by Martín Abarca de Bolea in his *Libro de Orlando determinado* (1578, Book on the Determined Orlando).

Other remarkable examples of epic belonging to this group are Luis Barahona de Soto's *Las lágrimas de Angélica* (1586, The Angelica's Tears) and Lope de Vega's *La Dragontea* (The Green Dragon) first published by itself in 1598. Both poems develop a subcycle derived from the Roland tradition, expanding the love plot between Angelica and Medoro, characters who originally appeared in Ariosto's *Orlando Furioso*. Both works also include, like the previous ones, the Bernardo del Carpio legend from the beginning, so that readers can be sure that they are not in unknown literary territory. Barahona de Soto's work mixes verse octaves with several kinds of prose, above all, in the summaries at the beginning of each song, which is reminiscent of the *ordinatio* (book organization) that later impressed Miguel de Cervantes. The second level of prose comprises a series of *advertimientos* (counsels) that constitute an exegesis of the verse text. Barahona de Soto's work was one of the most successful epic poems and remains a text of great interest thanks to the interesting scholarly work on it carried out by Lara Garrido.

The fusion of the Roland and Bernardo cycles, in addition to the renown acquired by Bernardo in the *romancero* (ballad) tradition after 1570, inspired several authors to return directly to the story of Bernardo del Carpio, including Agustín Alonso, whose *Historia de las hazañas y hechos del invencible cavallero Bernardo del Carpio* (A History of the Facts and Deeds of the Invincible Knight Bernardo del Carpio) was published in 1585. While a mix of the Roland and Bernardo cycles seems to be the core of this epic cycle, there are also other interests that are woven into it. At the same time, it is interesting to note that other Spanish epic cycles, like the one on El Cid, were only rarely developed in the literary epic of the Renaissance, although they were popular in the the-

ater, in poetry, and in historiography. In the sixteenth century, the only example of such a text is Diego Jiménez de Ayllón's *Los famosos, y heroicos hechos del invencible y esforzado Cavallero, onrra y flor de las Españas, el Cid Ruy Díaz de Bivar* (1568, The Renown and Heroic Deeds of the Invincible and Strong Knight Cid Ruydíaz of Bivar). The Abencerraje cycle, whose blend of lyric, romance, epic, and exoticism is well known, was also the object of an epic poem by Francisco Balbi de Correggio, *Historia de los amores del valeroso moro Abinde-Arráez y de la hermosa Xarifa* (1593, The History of Love between the Valiant Moor Abindarraez and the Beautiful Jarifa). Two poems inspired by the Roland model but with autonomous themes and development— or, more aptly, two books of chivalry composed as if they were epic poems—deserve final mention. The first is Gonzalo Gómez de Luque's *Los famosos hechos del príncipe Celidón de Iberia* (1583, The Famous Deeds of Prince Celidon of Iberia); the second is *Florando de Castilla* (1588, Florando of Castile), by Jerónimo de Huerta.

The literary epic in Spain also developed as a narration of events dealing with the near past and the present, as well as centering on the distant past. As noted, epic poetry as a genre establishes a close relationship with history, and, at the same time, it opens the door to the use of fiction in a controlled, strategic way to embellish and explain history. An entire current of scholarly research on the Spanish epic, as exemplified by the work of Ramón Menéndez Pidal and Pierce, considers Spanish Renaissance epic a form of historical verisimilitude, while another critical tradition is clearly at odds with the latter. Lara Garrido has pursued research that shows that the point of departure for many epic poems is the desire to achieve not historicity or truthfulness but a high form of poetry or the construction of a poetic discourse that is dialectically opposed to historiographical discourse.

Epic narratives on America, called colonial epics, occupy a significant place in the catalogue of Spanish Renaissance epics. Among them are poems that deal with varying versions of the conquest of Chile, Mexico, and Peru. Other such works focus on a history laden with crusading ideology. This current of historical epic centers on the conquest of Granada by the Catholic Monarchs, a major point of inflection in the history of the Reconquista (Reconquest), and continues to deal with events up through the reign of Philip II, focusing on the king's political and military program against the Turkish Ottoman Empire, the way in which Spain confronted the religious conflicts in the rest of Europe, and the wars in Flanders. Indeed, this type of epic narrative finds its greatest expression during the reign of Philip II and stands as proof of how a need to consolidate a Spanish cultural image arose amid the myriad social and political tensions stemming from the involvement of Spain in both Europe and America. Additionally, this current of epic may touch upon the conflicts with France and England, just as it deals with Philip II's religious politics after the Council of Trent, whose consequences culminated in the radicalization of the relationship between church and state.

The first poem in this cluster of epic works is Jerónimo Sempere's *La Carolea* (1560, The Charliad), which was followed six years later by another poem on the same subject, Luis de Zapata's *Carlo famoso* (Charles the Famous). The wars in Flanders, a burning political issue during the reign of Philip II, and especially the embassy undertaken by the duke of Alba to the Low Countries, is the subject of Baltasar de Vargas's *Breve relación de la jornada que ha hecho el señor duque de Alva desde España hasta Flandes* (1568, A Brief Report on the Journey that the Lord Duke of Alba Made from Spain to Flanders).

The battle of Lepanto, in which the forces of Philip II and the Holy League defeated the Ottoman army, is narrated by Jerónimo Corte Real in his *Felicísima victoria en el golfo de Lepanto* (1578, The Very Felicitous Victory of the Gulf of Lepanto). Balbi de Correggio employed the motif of the journey to relate the settlement in Montferrato of Octavio Gonzaga, Duke of Mantua, in *Vida del ilustrísimo señor Octavio Gonzaga* (1581, Life of the Illustrious Lord Octavio Gonzaga). The campaigns in Malta were the subject of Hipólito Sans's *La Maltea* (1582, The Maltese Campaigns). In 1584 Jerónimo de Urrea published the poem *El victorioso Carlos V* (The Victorious Charles V), in which he portrays the Holy Roman Emperor in a heroic light. One of the most successful and well-constructed poems in this series is one by the humanist Juan Rufo, *La Austríada* (1584, The Austrian Campaign). Rufo narrates the deeds of Philip II's half brother, Don Juan de Austria, and his campaigns in the Mediterranean, putting special emphasis on the battle of Lepanto. Rufo's poem is one of the most powerful assertions of the righteousness of Philip II's religious and defensive politics. The work deals with the most complicated relationships between Spain and Portugal, and its understanding may be complemented by Gaspar García de Alarcón's text concerning conquest of the Azores Islands by the marquis of Santa Cruz in 1583, *La victoriosa conquista de don Álvaro de Bazán* (Victorious Conquest by Don Álvaro de Bazán), published two years after the events, in 1585. *El león de España* (The Spanish Lion), by Pedro de la Vezilla Castellanos, first printed in 1586, relates the deeds of the victorious, almost mythical character Don Juan de Austria, admiral of the Spanish armada of the Mediterranean and leader of the Spanish troops in Flanders. Miguel Giner's poem *El sitio y toma de Anvers* (The Siege

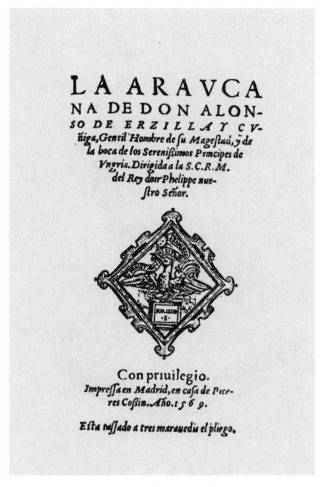

Title page for Alonso de Ercilla y Zúñiga's account of the Spanish conquest of Chile (The Conquest of Arauco; from Alonso de Ercilla y Zúñiga, La Araucana, 1945; Thomas Cooper Library, University of South Carolina)

and Taking of Antwerp), published in Milan in 1587, deals with the wars in Flanders.

The foundation and progress of the House of Austria through Don Juan de Austria is the subject of a subcycle, one of whose parts centers on the life of the duke of Mantua, Vincenzo Gonzaga, a cousin of Don Juan, whose entry into Milan is related in grand fashion by Balbi de Correggio in his *Pasada del serenísimo Vicenzo Gonzaga y Austria por el Estado de Milán* (1588, Trip of His Excellence Vicenzo Gonzaga y Austria through the State of Milano). That same year Gabriel Lasso de la Vega published his epic on the conquest of Mexico and the figure of Hernán Cortés, *Cortés valeroso y Mexicana* (The Valiant Cortés and the Mexican Conquest). The topic of America is developed in classical form by Juan de Castellanos in his *Elegías de varones ilustres de Indias* (1589, Elegies of Illustrious Men of the Indies). Lorenzo de Zamora, meanwhile, reaches back in time to portray

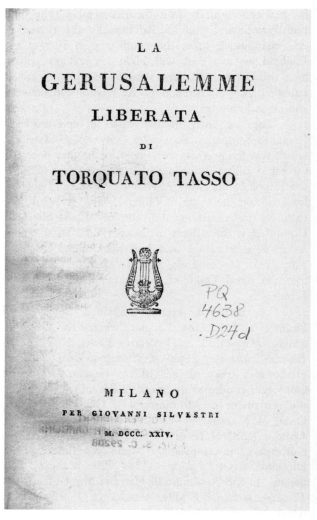

Frontispiece and title page for an 1824 edition of Italian poet Torquato Tasso's 1581 account of the capture of Jerusalem during the First Crusade; the work was first translated into Spanish in 1585 and inspired many imitations among Spanish poets (from Tasso, La Gerusalemma Liberata *[Milan: Giocanni Silvestri, 1824]; Thomas Cooper Library, University of South Carolina)*

the sieges of the Roman cities of Sagunto and Numancia, one of the founding myths of Spanish sovereignty and independence, in *Historia de Sagunto, Numancia y Cartago* (1589, History of Sagunto, Numancia, and Carthage). In 1590 Duarte Díaz published *La conquista que hizieron los poderosos y catholicos reyes don Fernando, y doña Ysabel, en el reyno de Granada* (The Conquest Made by Don Fernando and Doña Isabel of the Kingdom of Granada), which serves not only as an historical reference to this culminating point of the Reconquista but also as a touchstone for understanding the politics crafted to deal with the many Morisco rebellions during and after the reign of Philip II. Perhaps the most important and typical work in this vein is the great epic narrative *La Araucana* (1569, The Con-

quest of Arauco), by the Spanish soldier Alonso de Ercilla y Zúñiga. Ercilla's poem relates the conquest of Chile. One of his most interesting literary devices involves the depiction of the strength and virtue of the Araucanian Indians and the leadership of their chieftain, Caupolican. By exalting the dignity and power of the antagonists, Ercilla redoubles the perception of the courage and strength of the Spanish troops.

During the second half of the sixteenth century, poets were inclined to retell certain episodes from the Reconquista, as illustrated by Cristóbal de Mesa's poem on the important battle of Las Navas de Tolosa in 1212, *Las Navas de Tolosa* (1594). Ercilla's theme of the conquest of Chile found a new voice in Pedro de Oña, who crafted the first sequel to *La Araucana,* his *Arauco domado* (1596, Araucao Tamed). The second continuation of Ercilla's work was composed by Diego de Santisteban, who published his own *La Araucana* in 1597. Antonio de Saavedra Guzmán published an interesting poem, *El peregrino indiano* (The Indian Pilgrim), in 1599, while the campaigns in Malta and in Rhodes were given epic treatment, along with several additional chapters of Philip II's Mediterranean politics, by Santisteban in *Guerras de Malta y toma de Rodas* (1599, The Wars of Malta and Taking of Rhodes).

Many of the major cultural, political, and historical issues of sixteenth-century Spain are clearly recorded in the literary epic. From both spiritual and historical perspectives, the literary activity of epic narrative poetry may be linked to the tensions of the Reformation and Counter Reformation and their political consequences in Europe. At the same time, however, the Renaissance epic also proposes ways to value the social and existential universe of Europe in early modernity. In his essay "La épica culta" (1976, The learned epic), Chevalier wonders what kind of audience these poems had. Chevalier points out that in all these works there appears a reorganization of Spanish aristocratic and political society, that is to say, a sort of a sharing of power and a process of historical legitimization among several families and genealogies. It certainly seems that the most interested readers of the genre also formed part of the emerging families of Spanish society during these times. Perhaps this audience might explain why the epic poems of the sixteenth and seventeenth centuries enjoyed such incredible success in their time, and why subsequently they were seldom read. Pierce's analysis and readings of these works show that the entire genre fell almost into scorn, if not into oblivion, by the time of the rise of the bourgeoisie in the eighteenth and nineteenth centuries. The literary epic in Renaissance Spain emerged from the confluence of several traditions and represents an attempt to create an aesthetically legitimate current of heroic narrative that could replace the French epic tradition of the Middle Ages. From this point on, the Spanish epic explores the topics and issues directly related to the invention, construction, and maintenance of Spanish power, from both historical and spiritual perspectives, which led to an affirmation of Spanish claims to preeminence in the Americas, Europe, and in the religious politics and the cultural formations of the reign of Philip II.

References:

Juan Bautista Avalle-Arce, *La épica colonial* (Pamplona: Universidad de Navarra, 2000);

Giovanni Caravaggi, *Studi sull'epica ispanica del Rinascimento* (Pisa: Università, 1974);

Pedro M. Cátedra, *Poesía de Pasión en la Edad Media: El "Cancionero"* (Salamanca: Seminario de Estudios Medievales y Renacentistas, 2001);

Maxime Chevalier, *Ariosto en España* (Madrid: Castalia, 1969);

Chevalier, "La épica culta," in *Lectura y Lectores en la España de los siglos XVI y XVII* (Madrid: Turner, 1976), pp. 104–137;

Elizabeth B. Davis, *Myth and Identity in the Epic of Imperial Spain* (Columbia: University of Missouri Press, 2000);

Jean Frappier, *Les Chansons de Geste du Cycle de Guillaume d'Orange,* volume 1 (Paris: Société d'édition d'enseignement supérieur, 1955);

Antonio García Berrio, *Formación de la teoría literaria moderna,* 2 volumes (Murcia: Universidad de Murcia, 1977, 1978);

Cedomil Goić, "Alonso de Ercilla y la poesía épica," in *Época colonial,* volume 1 of *Historia y Crítica de la Literatura Hispanoamericana,* edited by Goić (Barcelona: Crítica, 1988), pp. 196–215;

Javier Gómez-Montero, *Literatura caballeresca en España e Italia (1483–1542): El Espejo de cavallerías (Deconstrucción textual y creación literaria)* (Tübingen: Niemeyer, 1992);

Jules Horrent, *Historia y poesía en torno al "Cantar del Cid"* (Barcelona: Ariel, 1973);

José Lara Garrido, *Los Mejores Plectros: Teoría y práctica de la épica culta en el siglo de oro* (Málaga, Spain: Analecta Malacitana, 1999);

Isaías Lerner, "América y la poesía épica áurea: la versión de Ercilla," *Edad de Oro,* 10 (1991): 125–140;

Francisco López Estrada, *La conquista de Antequera en el romancero y en la épica de los siglos de oro: Discurso de ingreso en la Real academia de buenas letras* (Seville: Escuela de Estudios Hispano-Americanos, 1956);

Ramón Menéndez Pidal, *La épica medieval española: Desde sus orígenes hasta su disolución en el romancero,* edited by Diego Catalán and María del Mar de Bustos (Madrid: Espasa-Calpe, 1992);

Félix Merino, *Poesía épica de la Edad de Oro: Ercilla, Balbuena, Hojeda* (Saragossa: Ebro, 1955);

Frank Pierce, *La poesía épica del Siglo de Oro,* revised and enlarged edition (Madrid: Gredos, 1968);

Pierce, "La poesía épica española de la Edad de Oro," *Edad de Oro,* 4 (1985): 87–105;

Marina Warner, *Alone of All Her Sex: The Myth and Cult of the Virgin Mary* (New York: Knopf, 1976).

Sixteenth-Century Spanish Humanism

Dana C. Bultman
University of Georgia

SELECTED BOOKS: Antonio de Nebrija, *Introductiones latinae* (Salamanca, 1481);

Nebrija, *Gramática castellana* (Salamanca, 1492);

Biblia polyglotta, 6 volumes, edited by Nebrija (Alcalá de Henares: Arnaldi Guillelmi de Brocario, 1514–1517);

Homer, *Esta es la Iliada de Homero en romance traducida por Juan de Mena,* translated by Juan de Mena (Valladolid: Arnaldí Guillelmi de Brocario, 1519);

Juan Luis Vives, *Aduersus pseudodialecticos* (Sélestat: Apud Lazarum Schurerium, 1520);

Vives, *De institutione feminae Christianae* (Antwerp: Byrckman, 1524); translated by Charles Fantazzi as *Education of a Christian Woman: A Sixteenth-Century Manual* (Chicago: University of Chicago Press, 2000);

Juan de Valdés, *Diálogo de doctrina christiana, nuevamente compuesto por un Religioso, Dirigido al muy ilustre señor don Diego López Pacheco, marqués de Villena* (Alcalá de Henares: Miguel de Eguía, 1529);

Baldassare Castiglione, *Los quatro libros del cortesano, agora nuevamente traduzidos en lengua castellana por Boscan,* translated by Juan Boscán (Barcelona: Pedro Montpezat, 1534);

Boscán and Garcilaso de la Vega, *Las obras de Boscán y algunas de Garcilasso de la Vega repartidas en quatro libros* (Barcelona: Carlos Amarós, 1543);

Benito Arias Montano, ed., *Biblia Sacra Hebraice, Chaldaice, Graece, & Latine* (Antwerp: Platinus, 1569–1572);

Luis de León, *Exposición del Libro de Job,* edited by Diego Tadeo González (Madrid: Pedro Marin, 1779);

Nebrija, *La educación de los hijos* (Valencia: Universidad de Valencia, 1981);

Valdés, *Diálogo de la lengua,* edited by Cristina Barbolani (Madrid: Cátedra, 1998);

Alfonso de Valdés, *Diálogo de Mercurio y Carón,* edited by Rosa Navarro (Madrid: Cátedra, 1999).

Edition in English: Alfonso de Valdés, *Dialogue of Mercury and Charon,* translated by Joseph V. Ricapito (Bloomington: Indiana University Press, 1986).

The Latin term *humanista* became commonly used in sixteenth-century Europe to describe a specialist in the humanities, that is, someone who studied the disciplines of grammar, rhetoric, history, poetry, and moral philosophy. Jeremy N. H. Lawrance, in his essay "Humanism in the Iberian Peninsula" (1990), writes that the word *humanist* was first coined in the 1490s in Italy to refer to this new group of Renaissance scholars, "a witty cross-formation of the term studia humanitatis and the titles of the humanist arch-rivals, the canonists, jurists, and legists." The first recorded reference in Spain, cites Ottavio Di Camillo, was in 1552, but by then, "the impact of humanism, as it manifested itself in Spain, had been felt in all aspects of cultural life." Humanists, who typically were either employed as teachers at universities and secondary schools or as secretaries to nobility, initiated the rigorous study of classical languages and the modern vernaculars. Their rise was instrumental in the rise of literature and the revolution in the interpretation of Scripture of the Renaissance.

The term *humanism,* on the other hand, was not used in the Renaissance to describe a discipline or ideology, appearing for the first time only in the nineteenth century. Paul Oskar Kristeller, the highly influential twentieth-century scholar of Renaissance humanism, uses this term in his *Studies in Renaissance Thought: The Classic, Scholastic, and Humanist Strains* (1961) to mean "merely the general tendency of the age to attach the greatest importance to classical studies, and to consider classical antiquity as the common standard and model by which to guide all cultural activities." Since the eighteenth century, the word *humanism* has taken on an additional connotation used to refer to a human ideal within some modern philosophies. This meaning would be anachronistic if applied to the activities of sixteenth-century Spanish humanists, whose arguments, concerns, and religious doctrines are diverse enough to dissuade most scholars from attempting to identify a cohesive system of beliefs that unites them all.

The texts produced by Spanish humanists have often been studied against the backdrop of Spain's historical competition with the superior culture of Renaissance Italy. The Castilian and Aragonese courts of Isabel and Ferdinand, as well as the court of their grandson Charles V, strove to accompany their political ascendancy with a matching cultural ascendancy. Di Camillo has rightly described early Spanish humanists as being in the service of imperial glory. They admired their Italian precursors and professors for a few generations before learning to consider Italian eminence a thing of the past and Castilian destiny the result of a deserved *translatio imperii*, or transmission of empire to a more virtuous nation. Lawrance explains that rivalry with Italy skewed perceptions of the value of native Spanish humanists' contributions: "The pride and confidence of the native tradition was to shape the destiny of humanism in Iberia."

The indebtedness of Spain to Italian humanism was, however, never forgotten by writers of the age, and adherence to the ideals of empire does not fully account for developments in Spanish humanism after Antonio de Nebrija. An alternative focus and account of the development of humanism in Spain is offered by scholars who are more inclined to admire sixteenth-century humanists as specialists in languages and literatures, highlighting their moments of resistance to the glory-seeking programs of rulers. Di Camillo explains that the Flemish court of Charles V brought with it northern ideas and inaugurated a more international generation of humanists. In Spain, the careers of sharp-witted humanists, sometimes of exemplary courage, are directly related to the dissemination of the texts of the most famous humanist and Catholic reformer in Europe, Desiderius Erasmus of Rotterdam. Marcel Bataillon's monumental study *Erasme et l'Espagne: Recherches sur l'histoire spirituelle du XVIe siècle* (1936, Erasmus and Spain: Research in the Spiritual History of the Sixteenth Century), which describes the initial triumph of Erasmism in Spain and its eventual suppression with the prohibition of his texts because of their association with heretical Protestant ideas, inaugurated an important new way of comprehending the period. Bataillon's work was criticized by some for blurring the distinction between humanism and Erasmism as well as including within his definition of Erasmism all liberal or reform-minded humanist thought. In his prologue to the 1950 Spanish edition of his work, Bataillon responds frankly to this criticism that he is clearly more sympathetic to the Christian humanist perspectives of Erasmus and related writers than to the theocratic tendencies of their adversaries, Protestant or Catholic.

The humanists who served empire, religion, or more personal causes naturally met strong resistance of various kinds from those they challenged. Although humanists were involved in battles over intellectual authority and institutional power, it is a mistake to conclude that their many opponents were always on an identifiably different side with regard to knowledge of classical materials, belief in particular religious doctrines, or adherence to personal virtue. The Renaissance period, Kristeller argues, is mainly characterized by a radical broadening and deepening of the knowledge of Latin and Greek texts

Desiderius Erasmus of Rotterdam, the Dutch reformist Christian writer whose works were influential among Spanish humanists until the Inquisition suppressed his ideas as heretical (from José García López, Historia de la literatura española, *1962; Thomas Cooper Library, University of South Carolina)*

as well as the methods for studying them. Within this period Aristotelian, Platonic, and humanist doctrines and methodologies were constantly intersecting, and these intersections were complicated by regional and personal tensions. The sum effect of many different humanist efforts was the discovery and collection of classical texts, the publication of new editions of these texts, the translation or retranslation of these texts into Latin as well as the vernacular languages, and their dissemination, sometimes with learned commentary as a guide, for a widening spectrum of readers.

In Spain the particular trajectory of humanism begins with an importation of the Latin eloquence and knowledge of Greek achieved in Renaissance Italy to Iberian courts. It develops into a battle over orthodoxy and authority in the field of theology when humanist philology is applied to sacred texts and culminates with a growing appreciation of the importance of literature as a vehicle for humanist endeavors and a prevalent admiration for the values of neo-Stoicism as expounded in the texts of Justus Lipsius. Spanish humanists of the sixteenth century inherited from the fifteenth century the political ascendancy of Castile and Aragón and their rivalry with Italy, as well as their pride in native traditions. A renewed interest in Seneca, Lucan, and other Latin authors from the Iberian Peninsula was encouraged by Alfonso de Santa María de Cartagena, bishop of Burgos, whose Episcopal Palace was a center of learning. Vernacular humanism, the translation and adaptation of classical works for the instruction and entertainment of nobles and others unable to read Latin well, had been exemplified by activity at the court of Juan II of Aragón and Navarre. A notable example was *Esta es la Ilíada de Homero en romance traducida,* published in Valladolid in 1519, Cordoban poet and prose writer Juan de Mena's translation of the *Iliad* from a Latin version. Di Camillo views vernacular humanism to be a key trait of the continuing humanist activity in Spain.

This activity was accompanied by an awareness of a more profound cultural renewal coming from the east. Iñigo López de Mendoza, Marqués de Santillana, whose famous collection of Florentine manuscripts is now at the Biblioteca Nacional in Madrid, commissioned translations of classical works in Tuscan since he could not read Latin. As an imitator of Petrarch's sonnets and promoter of Italian learning, Santillana is often cited as the figure who opened Spain to the practices of humanist philology. The Italians who taught and tutored Spaniards had benefited from the knowledge of Greek scholars who, in the fifteenth century, had taken refuge in Italy after the fall of Constantinople and brought with them a fresh understanding of Aristotle. Kristeller writes, "Western scholars learned from their Byzantine teachers to study the works of Aristotle in the Greek original." The Byzantine tradition, with its knowledge of Neoplatonism and literature, was quite different from the Western Latin tradition or the Arabic tradition. The introduction of Byzantine scholarship in Italy brought many aspects of modern philology into the universities of western Europe.

The second wave of Spanish humanism, that of the sixteenth century, is marked by the brilliant career of Elio Antonio Martínez de Cala de Nebrija. Born in Seville, Nebrija is considered the greatest of all Spanish Renaissance humanists. His contributions to the systematic study of both Latin and Castilian were highly influential, and he sought to base biblical scholarship on philological inquiry instead of traditional authoritative interpretations. Dissatisfied with the state of classical scholarship at the University of Salamanca, as a young man he traveled to Bologna to study theology, law, medicine, and classical philology, after which he returned to Salamanca to teach grammar

and rhetoric from 1486 to 1505, also holding the post of royal chronicler in 1508–1509. His most celebrated work was *Introductiones latinae* (Introduction to Latin), published in 1481. It was the first skillful Latin grammar written in Spain and was based on the teaching method of the Italian humanist Lorenzo Valla, who greatly influenced Nebrija's textual criticism. Nebrija, like Juan Luis Vives after him, was also concerned with the education of the young. As his *De liberis educandis* (written in 1509 but not published until 1903; On Liberal Education) demonstrates, Spanish humanism was characteristically interested in improving pedagogy.

He also published *Gramática castellana* (1492, Grammar of the Castilian Language), the first grammar of a Romance language of its kind, which begins with his well-known dedication to Queen Isabel, "Cuando bien conmigo pienso muy esclarecida Reina, y pongo delante los ojos el antiguedad de todas las cosas que para nuestra recordación y memoria quedaron escritas, una cosa hallo y saco por conclusión muy cierta: que siempre la lengua fue compañera del imperio, y de tal manera lo siguió que juntamente comenzaron, crecieron y florecieron y después junta fue la caida entrambos" (When I ponder, most illustrious Queen, and I place before my eyes the antiquity of all those things that for our recollection and memory have been written, one thing I find and conclude for certain: that language always was the companion of empire, and so closely did the one follow the other that they began together, grew, flowered and afterward both fell together). Nebrija's considerations of the cultural place of language resonated through the literature of the sixteenth century and beyond as they proved Castilian to be a suitable vehicle for grand political and literary ambitions.

Nebrija left Salamanca in 1513 after not being appointed to the chair of grammar and was invited by Cardinal Francisco Jiménez de Cisneros (1436–1517) to the recently founded University of Alcalá (1508) to oversee the production of the Biblia Políglota Complutense (1514–1517, Complutensian Polyglot Bible), named after Complutum, the Latin name for Alcalá de Henares. Nebrija possessed both a notoriously contentious temperament and rigorous philological expectations; scholars provide various reasons for his withdrawal from the project after arriving at Alcalá. José C. Nieto writes, "He was not officially a collaborator because he wanted to emend the texts and purify them instead of editing them as was Cisneros's plan. Cisneros and he disagreed on the matter, but Nebrija enjoyed his confidence and never was brought by Cisneros under any charges of heresy although many others tried hard to do so." Nieto's mention of the inquisition refers specifically to the Inquisitor general of Spain before Cisneros, Diego de Deza, who confiscated some of Nebrija's papers in order to stall his philological analyses of the Bible, according to Jerry H. Bentley. Bentley observes that Nebrija insisted upon "the right of grammarians and philologists to treat scriptural problems having to do with language, words, and their meanings," a polemical stance contested by theologians who preferred to accept the authority of traditional interpretations.

Cisneros, a Castilian from a hidalgo family who rose to wealth and power during the reign of the Catholic Monarchs, was grand inquisitor and civil administrator of Spain under Fernando II and also a member of the Franciscan reform movement. Nieto writes, "The University of Alcalá is the most concrete expression of Cisneros' desire to reform the Church, and as such is to be considered as the magnificent manifestation, in cultural form, of Cisnero's Evangelical-Franciscan Spirit." Cisneros was arguably the most powerful promoter of humanism in sixteenth-century Spain. He was also known for his brutality in carrying out his programs for reform and his violent repression of the Moors of Granada, and is considered to have been influential in Isabel and Fernando's decision to expel the Jews from Spain in 1492. Cisneros, the founder of the university in Spain most closely associated with humanism and later with Erasmian thought, as well as the mysticism of Teresa de Jesús, which is traceable back to the Franciscan Francisco de Osuna, was characterized by intolerance and Christian arrogance.

The date of the beginnings of the Complutensian Polyglot Bible is uncertain. Scholars have long thought it began in 1502, but Bentley convincingly argues that the text, "a work magnificent to behold," was probably begun in 1510 by the group of Greek, Hebrew, and Latin scholars brought to Alcalá by Cisneros. The extant evidence as to who participated in the Complutensian Polyglot Bible, and in what capacity, does not provide a clear picture. Among the circle of humanists associated with the text and the early years of the University of Alcalá was the priest and theologian Juan de Vergara (1492–1557), who did translations of Aristotle commissioned by Cisneros. He was a friend of Erasmus and corresponded with him frequently, although his arrest by the Inquisition and imprisonment between 1533 and 1537, Lu Ann Homza explains, was not caused by this association, as was once thought. Hernán Núñez de Toledo y Guzmán (1475–1553), "El Comendador Griego" (The Greek Commander), was an eminent Greek scholar who had been a tutor to the Mendoza family and published critical editions of Seneca and Pliny. He eventually took the chair of Greek left open at Salamanca upon the death of Nebrija.

Printing of the text was started in 1513 and the New Testament volume was finished in 1514, but the whole of the work was not published until 1520. In its entirety it includes six volumes: the Old Testament in the original Hebrew as well as Aramaic, Greek, and

Antonio de Nebrija, known as the greatest of Spanish Renaissance humanists for his contributions to grammar, philology, and biblical scholarship (from El siglo de frai Luis de León: Salamanca y el Renacimiento, *1991; Thomas Cooper Library, University of South Carolina)*

Latin versions in four volumes; the New Testament; and a sixth volume containing a Hebrew-Aramaic-Latin lexicon and a Hebrew grammar. The intention of Cisneros was to provide an authoritative Bible that would encourage adherence to a unified Christianity. Bentley writes, "Though eclipsed by the fame of Erasmus' work, the world's first printed Greek New Testament must obviously figure significantly in any study of early modern scholarship." What should have been the crowning achievement of Spanish humanism and the culmination of Nebrija's career instead was already viewed as a conservative and outdated text upon publication.

Erasmus had a philological freedom Nebrija did not enjoy, but to be a humanist in early-sixteenth-century Spain could as easily make a scholar suspect of heresy as it could require him to have an enthusiastic attitude toward imperial expansion. To the example of Cisneros, one can add the case of Juan Ginés de Sepúlveda (1490–1573), who translated Aristotle's *Politics* and used it as evidence in his self-serving polemic against Bartolomé de Las Casas's defense of Indian rights, *Destrucción de las Indias* (1552, Destruction of the Indies). Another scholar, Francisco de Vitoria (1486–1546), more a Scholastic than a humanist, had, like Las Casas, written in favor of the political sovereignty of the American Indians in *Relectio de Indiis* (On the Indians) in 1537. Sepúlveda, on the other hand, in his *Democrates alter; sive, de justi belli causis* (1541, Second Democrates; or, on the Just Conquest of the Indians), justified the enslavement of the Indians with references to classical authority. Lawrance writes, "His pamphlet, from its hyperbolical rhetorical style to the jaunty dialogue format in which Democrates, the author's alter ego, is given all the good arguments against the villainous Lutheran stooge Leopoldo, was thoroughly humanist."

While humanist expertise clearly was used to gain favor in the service of empire, not all strains of humanist thought that remained loyal to monarchical aggrandizement and expansion were as equally reprehensible as that of Sepúlveda. The admirable work of Alfonso de Valdés, born in Cuenca, is a case in point. Joseph V. Ricapito, in the introduction to his translation, describes Valdés's reputation for embodying the values of the Renaissance—"he has come to represent the Renaissance in Spain, especially for his role in promulgating the thought of Erasmus,"—as well as his dedication to Charles V for whom he served as secretary: "his first loyalty was to the Emperor and his cause." Considered by Ricapito and others as the possible author of *Lazarillo de Tormes* (1554), Valdés has been identified as such in a 2003 book by Rosa Navarro Durán.

Valdés's *Diálogo de Mercurio y Carón* (translated as *Dialogue of Mercury and Charon,* 1986), probably written between 1528 and 1530, sets out to defend Charles V from the criticism he received from France and England after the siege and sack of Rome by his troops in 1527, as Valdés explains in his preface. The text also describes the conversion of an ambitious prince into an ideal ruler through the figure of Polydorus, who is among the souls who speak with Mercury and Charon on their way toward heaven or hell. A king in life, Polydorus recounts how he came to understand that he was responsible for his subjects: "Luego se me representó cuánta multitud dellas había perdido después que comencé a reinar, cuán poco cuidado había tenido de apascentarlas y gobernarlas y cómo las había tratado, no como padre a sus hijos, no pastor a las ovejas de su amo, mas como señor a sus esclavos . . . y todo esto ¡con tanto daño, con tanta infamia y afrenta del nombre cristiano!" (I recalled how many of them I had lost after I came to rule and what little interest I had in nourishing and governing them and how I had treated them, not like a father with his children nor a shepherd with his master's sheep but rather like a master to his slaves . . . and all this with such great harm, with such infamy and affront to the name "Christian!"). He then describes his forceful spiritual change of heart and gives a lengthy and enthusiastic account of the reforms he made to create an ideal kingdom. Its satirical

wit and radical insights make Valdés's beautifully written dialogue a text comparable to Thomas More's *Utopia* (1516), but more accessible to readers for having been written in Castilian, not Latin.

Alfonso de Valdés's brother, Juan de Valdés, applied his humanist background to the development of linguistic and theological knowledge rather than social reform. Juan de Valdés studied at the University of Alcalá but moved to Italy to avoid the Inquisition after the publication of his *Diálogo de doctrina cristiana* (Dialogue on Christian Doctrine) in 1529, eventually settling in Naples in 1535, where he led a circle of followers. Juan de Valdés did translations and commentaries on Old and New Testament texts and stands out among Spanish humanists for his *Diálogo de la lengua,* written around 1535 but not published until 1737. In it he scoffs at Nebrija's linguistic authority, to whom he consistently refers to as "Lebrija," evidently out of a prejudice against Andalusians, but also because of the differences he cites between Nebrija's understanding of language and his own. Several times in the text Valdés opposes the absolute authority accorded to Nebrija's texts. Among his complaints he says, "Mas quiero que sepáis que aún ay otra cosa por qué no estoy bien con Librixa en aquel Vocabulario, y es ésta: que parece que no tuvo intento a poner todos los vocablos españoles, como fuera razón que hiziera, sino solamente aquéllos para los quales hallava vocablos latinos o griegos que los declarassen" (And there is another reason why I am not in accord with what Lebrija says in that Vocabulary that I want you to know, which is this: that it seems like he did not intend to include all Spanish words, as it would be reasonable for him to do, but just those for which he could find Latin or Greek words that would explain them).

For his part Valdés considers the influences upon Castilian of Basque, Arabic, and Hebrew in addition to those of Latin, Greek, and the modern languages. The characters within *Diálogo de la lengua* are surprised to hear that words grow old with the passage of time and through use, thus the choice of the best word changes over time. He also discusses the question of whether Basque or a variation of Greek was the original language of the peninsula.

When Valdés challenges his reader metaphorically at the end of his text to overtake him in his intellectual trajectory, he opens a door to a rethinking of Castilian as an object of study: "Camine quien más pudiere, que yo ni estorvaré al que me fuere adelante, ni esperaré al que se quedare atrás" (Let him move forward who is most able, for I will not hinder he who goes ahead of me, nor will I wait for he who lags behind). The fact that his dialogue circulated, as Cristina Barbolani writes in her introduction to the text, through clandestine channels that were among restricted cultural circles in contact with the

Frontispiece for a 1488 edition of Nebrija's 1481 work Introductiones latinae *(Introduction to Latin), one of the earliest Latin grammars published in Spain (Biblioteca Nacional, Madrid; from* El siglo de frai Luis de León: Salamanca y el Renacimiento, *1991; Thomas Cooper Library, University of South Carolina)*

Reformation, does not cancel out the fact that the opinions of Valdés reflected a current of thought regarding Castilian that continued throughout the sixteenth century and into the seventeenth: a concept of a living language flexible enough to accept the growth and change that comes with the addition of foreign words and influences. As Valdés explains, " . . . yo no compongo vocablos nuevos, sino me quiero aprovechar de los que hallo en las otras lenguas" (. . . I do not invent new words, I just want to take advantage of those that I find in other languages). While Nebrija makes Castilian into a valid object of study, Valdés emphasizes the fluidity of a language that is not made to be eternal, but rather is defined by common usage, historically composed of a confluence of multiple languages, and is constantly in contact with new influences.

The great humanist Vives, arguably the most internationally influential Spanish thinker of the sixteenth century, was like the Valdés brothers of *converso* (as Jews converted to Christianity were known) ancestry. Vives was a Valencian who left Spain for Paris at the age of seventeen. His family was persecuted by the Inquisition for cryptojudaism, the continued hidden observance of Jewish traditions after conversion to Christianity, after Vives's departure. His father was executed by burning in 1525, and his mother's remains were exhumed and burned as well in 1528 after her posthumous condemnation. Although invited to the University of Salamanca to replace Nebrija after his death, Vives refused, never returning to the Iberian Peninsula, having chosen in 1523 to accept Cardinal Thomas Wolsey's invitation to take a lectureship at Oxford College, where he instituted curricular reforms. A friend and correspondent of Erasmus, More, and Guillaume Budé, Vives's publication in 1520 of *Aduersus pseudodialecticos* (Against the Pseudodialecticans), a harsh critique of the Scholastic methods he was subjected to as a student at the University of Paris, launched his reputation. At the request of Erasmus, Vives wrote a commentary on Augustine's City of God that, Kristeller comments, "was said in true humanist fashion to have restored St. Augustine to his ancient integrity."

The massive bibliography of Vives's contributions to pedagogy, psychology, and social reform should not be underestimated, for his influence in Europe was broad and lasting. Carlos G. Noreña, in his *Juan Luis Vives* (1970), writes, "In the short period of two years (1538–1540) there were more than one hundred different editions of his books." One of the most popular of those was *De institutione feminae Christianae* (1524, The Education of a Christian Woman). The work was originally written in 1523 for the education of Princess Mary, daughter of Catherine of Aragon and Henry VIII. Charles Fantazzi writes that the treatise's central theme that a healthy state

requires the education of women "laid the groundwork for the Elizabethan age of the cultured woman." Although Vives insists obsessively in the work on chastity, his positive evaluations of women's natural intelligence and chief merit as companions in marriage, rather than vehicles of procreation, filtered humanist advances into women's lives.

Despite the fact that Vives's treatise on the education of women was published in a Spanish translation in 1528, in Spain women's participation in education in capacities other than patron and passive student was harshly repressed. The lost writings of María de Cazalla, known for her erudite letters and knowledge of Erasmus, are an example of the cultural loss caused by this repression. Cazalla was associated with the Spanish *alumbrados* (illuminists), a group Juan de Valdés also had connections with before his departure for Italy. The *alumbrados* were suspected of adhering to many of the forty-eight unorthodox doctrines outlined in the 1525 Edict of Toledo. Among them was the assertion that hell did not exist and that it was used to frighten the faithful like one would frighten children, that God could be found within the individual soul sooner than in the bread of communion, and that worshiping images of the Virgin was idolatry and, as one man put it, he needed no image since merely by gazing at a woman he would be reminded of "Our Lady." These practices were effectively wiped out by the Inquisition by 1540, before they could develop into a cohesive movement, with Cazalla being one of the most well-known defendants.

The issue of whether Cazalla assumed the position of teacher, impermissible for a woman, is one that is insisted upon by the inquisitors. Cazalla's letters, which according to Milagros Ortega Costa were collected by a professor of logic and metaphysics at the University of Alcalá who planned to publish them, would have been a key source for truly understanding both Cazalla and the *alumbrado* beliefs had they survived. In the spirit of humanism she was offering an education to those without access, while challenging church doctrine on the status of women. Cazalla spent thirty-two months in prison and underwent torture before she was released, having been found not guilty of the charges. Since after her trial nothing else is known of Cazalla, not even the date of her death, one can assume that the Inquisition effectively destroyed her involvement in public life.

Local power struggles, as well as those within the universities and at court, went hand in hand with a distrust of the new philological learning that overturned established authority and complicated obedience to a shared Christian identity and national unity. Humanism and Catholic orthodoxy were not closely associated. For example, Sepúlveda's youthful repudiation of Lutheranism is placed by Luis Gil Fernández in the context of the growing link seen to exist between Greek studies and Protestantism. This association provoked a shift in the sixteenth century that resulted in frequent reaffirmations of orthodoxy by authors wishing to defend their humanist tendencies.

Meanwhile, the court of Charles V was the site of increased activity in the development of Italianate culture. The Catalonian poet Juan Boscán translated Baldassare Castiglione's highly influential book *Il cortegiano* (1527) as *Los quatro libros del cortesano, agora nuevamente traduzidos en lengua castellana por Boscan* (1534, The Four Books of the Courtier, Newly Translated in the Castilian Tongue by Boscán). Boscán's name is forever linked to that of his friend, Garcilaso de la Vega, because their poetry, published together after Boscán's death by his widow Ana Girón de Rebolledo in 1543 as *Las obras de Boscán y algunas de Garcilasso de la Vega repartidas en cuatro libros* (The Works of Boscán and Some by Garcilaso de la Vega, Divided into Four Books), initiated the rise of Italianate lyric in Spain. The degree to which the new poetry was associated with the ideals of empire is a difficult question to answer because Garcilaso, and court poets in his wake, conceded their personal independence to an increasingly powerful king. As Lawrance explains, "After the drama of the comunero [as the defenders of local Castilian interests were known] revolts, brutally put down in 1520–1523, many brilliant minds went abroad, or compromised themselves deeply with the imperial machine." The grandson of Santillana, Diego Hurtado de Mendoza (1503–1575), historian and diplomat, is an example of a noble humanist poet whose support of imperialism is deceptive. Hurtado de Mendoza spent fifteen years in Italy, was fluent in Latin, Greek, and Arabic, and translated Aristotle's *Mechanics* from Greek into Spanish. Helen Nader writes, "His aesthetic values, with their emphasis on the Romans, were superficially compatible with the heady dreams of imperialism at the court of Charles V, but Diego's supposed imperialism was in fact based on traditions that had little connection with Charles's empire." Hurtado de Mendoza, Nader argues, was deeply critical of the Crown, his first loyalty being to the values and family ambitions of his noble father and grandfather.

In the second half of the sixteenth century, the golden age of Spanish poetry initiated by Boscán and Garcilaso was accompanied by an ongoing bitter fight to remove humanist scholarship from theology. These two developments in humanism intersected brilliantly in the career of Fray Luis de León, a philologist, theologian, and professor at the University of Salamanca. León inherited the poetry of Garcilaso, the mystical methods of the Franciscans around Alcalá, and Nebrija's linguistic revolution. In *Studies in Spanish Renaissance Thought* (1975) Noreña writes that Fray Luis synthesized scholastic and

Title page for Juan Luis Vives's 1520 attack on the Scholastic methods practiced at the University of Paris (Juan Luis Vives, Valentinus, against the Pseudodialecticians), where he spent time as a student (from Rita Guerlac, Juan Luis Vives against the Pseudodialecticians, 1978; Thomas Cooper Library, University of South Carolina)

humanist traditions: "Fray Luis represents first of all an eclectic and compromising position in the sixteenth century conflict between grammar and speculation, rhetoric and dialectics, Erasmian philology and scholastic metaphysics, positive and rational theology. . . . Fray Luis's massive Latin works nullify any project to leave out of consideration the scholastic origins of his thinking. On the other hand it is true that if Fray Luis's scholastic teaching reveals to us the most conservative aspect of his personality, his linguistic concerns betray him as the 'novelty seeker' (amigo de novedades) the Inquisition persecuted." León's most influential humanist legacy was his championing of the dissemination of theological works in the vernacular, exemplified by his widely read *De los nombres de Cristo* (1583, The Names of Christ).

Benito Arias Montano (1527–1598), born the same year as his friend León, was a professor of oriental languages at the Escorial. Also a theologian and a poet, Arias Montano supervised the production of the Antwerp Polyglot Bible of 1569–1572, collected books in Flanders for Phillip II's library at the Escorial, and like León was fascinated by the Song of Songs, of which he wrote a version, *Parafrasis del Cantare de cantares de Salomón* (Paraphrase of the Song of Songs of Solomon). Francisco Sánchez de las Brozas, known as "el Brocense" after his place of birth, Las Brozas, Cáceres, developed the linguistic theory Nebrija had initiated. The premier humanist colleague and friend of León's at the University of Salamanca, Sánchez de las Brozas is lauded by Menéndez y Pelayo as the father of general grammar and the philosophy of language. He translated Ovid and Virgil, wrote his own poetry in Latin, and commented upon the works of Juan de Mena and Garcilaso. He also wrote philosophical and scientific treatises.

León's eventual release in 1576 after his long imprisonment by the Inquisition for criticizing the authority of the text of Jerome's Latin Bible (the Vulgate) is viewed by Colin P. Thompson as a victory for those who supported philological advances in biblical scholarship in Spain. After León's death in 1591, however, a conservative group within Spanish theology continued to resist humanism, as the late publication date of León's most radical biblical commentary, *Exposición del Libro de Job* (1779, Commentary on the Book of Job), attests. Arias Montano also had a brush with the Inquisition, and subsequently in 1601 Sánchez de las Brozas died before receiving a verdict from the Inquisition on charges similar to those brought against León.

In spite of these battles, the phenomenon of humanism dramatically changed the texts inherited by the Renaissance from medieval theology. In the sixteenth century, Kristeller explains, "the pope appointed a special committee of scholars for the purpose of publishing the writings of the Fathers in new critical editions." By the end of the sixteenth century, humanism's influence had been assimilated into theology and, at least superficially, into literature and political thought. Di Camillo remarks that "while the role of the humanist remained unchanged, the term *humanista* had become so popular that treatises had to be written to distinguish the real from the false *humanista*."

Perhaps the most deeply embedded cultural legacy of humanism in sixteenth-century Spain was its challenge to theological authority and the contact it created between literature and theology because of the application of similar methods of interpretation to both fields.

References:

Marcel Bataillon, *Erasmo y España: Estudios sobre la historia espiritual del siglo XVI,* translated by Antonio Alatorre (Mexico City & Buenos Aires: Fondo de Cultura Económica, 1950);

Jerry H. Bentley, *Humanists and the Holy Writ: New Testament Scholarship in the Renaissance* (Princeton: Princeton University Press, 1983);

Ottavio Di Camillo, "Humanism in Spain," in *Renaissance Humanism: Foundations, Forms, and Legacy,* 3 volumes, edited by Albert Rabil Jr. (Philadelphia: University of Pennsylvania Press, 1988), II: 55–108;

José García López, *Historia de la literatura española* (Barcelona: Vicens-Vives, 1962);

José García Oro, *Cisneros, el cardenal de España* (Barcelona: Ariel, 2002);

Luis Gil Fernández, *Panorama social del humanismo español (1500–1800)* (Madrid: Alhambra, 1981);

María Laura Giordano, *María de Cazalla* (Madrid: Ediciones del Orto, 2000);

Rita Guerlac, *Juan Luis Vives against the Pseudodialecticians: A Humanist Attack on Medieval Logic* (Dordrecht & Boston: Reidel, 1978);

Lu Ann Homza, *Religious Authority in the Spanish Renaissance* (Baltimore: Johns Hopkins University Press, 2000);

Paul Oskar Kristeller, *Studies in Renaissance Thought: The Classic, Scholastic, and Humanist Strains* (New York & London: Harper & Row, 1961);

Jeremy N. H. Lawrance, "Humanism in the Iberian Peninsula," in *The Impact of Humanism on Western Europe,* edited by Anthony Goodman and Angus MacKay (London & New York: Longman, 1990);

Alfonso Martín Jiménez, *Retórica y literatura en el siglo XVI: El Brocense* (Valladolid: Secretariado de Publicaciones e Intercambio Científico, Universidad de Valladolid, 1997);

Helen Nader, *The Mendoza Family in the Spanish Renaissance, 1350 to 1550* (New Brunswick, N.J.: Rutgers University Press, 1979);

Rosa Navarro Durán, *Alfonso de Valdés, autor de Lazarillo de Tormes* (Madrid: Gredos, 2003);

José C. Nieto, *Juan de Valdés and the Origins of the Spanish and Italian Reformation* (Geneva: Droz, 1970);

Carlos G. Noreña, *Juan Luis Vives* (The Hague: Nijhoff, 1970);

Noreña, *Studies in Spanish Renaissance Thought* (The Hague: Nijhoff, 1975);

Milagros Ortega Costa, *Proceso de la Inquisición contra María de Cazalla* (Madrid: Fundación Universitaria Española, 1978);

El siglo de frai Luis de León: Salamanca y el Renacimiento: Colegio del Arzobispo Fonseca, Escuelas Menores, Antigua Universidad, Salamanca, octubre–diciembre 1991 (Salamanca: Centro Nacional de Exposiciones, Ministerio de Cultura, Dirección General de Bellas Artes y Archivos, Universidad de Salamanca / León: Junta de Castilla y León, 1991);

Colin P. Thompson, *The Strife of Tongues: Fray Luis de León and the Golden Age of Spain* (Cambridge: Cambridge University Press, 1988).

The Moorish Novel of the Sixteenth Century

Michael J. McGrath
Georgia Southern University

BOOKS: *El Abencerraje y la hermosa Jarifa*, anonymous, in *Los siete libros de la Diana*, by Jorge de Montemayor (Barcelona: Jayme Cortey, 1561);

El Abencerraje y la hermosa Jarifa, anonymous, in *Inventario de Antonio de Villegas, dirigido a la Magestad Real del Rey Don Phelippe, nuestro señor* (Medina del Campo: Francisco del Canto, 1565);

Ginés Pérez de Hita, *Historia de los vandos de los Zegries y Abencerrajes Cavalleros Moros de Granada, de las Civiles guerras que huvo en ella, y batallas particulares que huvo en la Vega entre Moros y Christianos, hasta que el Rey Don Fernando Quinto la ganó* (Saragossa: Miguel Jimeno Sánchez, 1595);

Mateo Alemán, *Historia de los dos enamorados Ozmín y Daraja*, in his *Primera parte de Guzmán de Alfarache* (Madrid: Varez de Castro, 1599);

Pérez de Hita, *Segunda parte de las Guerras Civiles de Granada, y de los crueles vandos, entre los convertidos Moros y vezinos Ch[r]istianos: Con el levantamiento de todo el Reyno y ultima revelion, sucedida en el año de 1568* (Cuenca: Domingo de la Iglesia, 1619).

Modern Editions: Ginés Peréz de Hita, *Guerra civiles de Granada*, 2 volumes, edited by Paula Blanchard-Demouge (Madrid: Bailly-Baillière, 1913, 1915);

El Abencerraje y la hermosa Jarifa: Cuatro textos y su estudio, edited by Francisco López Estrada (Madrid: Revista de Archivos, Bibliotecas y Museos, 1957);

Aristide Rumean, "*L'Abencérage*, un texte retrouvé," *Bulletin Hispanique*, 59 (1958): 369–395—includes the Corónica version of *El Abencerraje y la hermosa Jarifa*;

Pérez de Hita, *Guerras civiles de Granada, Primera parte*, edited by Shasta M. Bryant (Newark, Del.: Juan de la Cuesta Hispanic Monographs, 1982);

Mateo Alemán, *La historia de los dos enamorados Ozmín y Daraja* (Seville: Alfar, 1988).

Edition in English: Gines Peréz de Hita, *The Civil Wars of Granada*, translated by Thomas Rodd (London: Thomas Rodd, 1803).

The invasion of a Muhammadan army from the north of Africa in 711 signified the beginning of nearly eight centuries of bloodshed as Christians fought to reclaim the Iberian Peninsula from its Muslim invaders. Christian poets immortalized this period in Spanish history, known as the Reconquista (Reconquest), in poems that described the conflicts between the Christians and Moors. *Romances fronterizos,* or frontier ballads, so named because they were composed in the regions bordering Moorish kingdoms, are from the fourteenth and fifteenth centuries and relate the heroic and amorous adventures of both Christian and Moorish knights. The Christians' fascination with the Moors' exotic culture and civilization contributed to the popularity of these poems. The *romances fronterizos* communicated to the people events that interested them and, for this reason, were not fictional in nature. The earliest example of this genre is from the fourteenth century and describes how in 1368 Christian soldiers successfully defended the village of Baeza in Andalusia from an attack led by the Moorish king of Granada. Sixteenth-century Spaniards, however, employed the novel to create a new genre of Moorish literature. The Moorish novels of the sixteenth century—*El Abencerraje y la hermosa Jarifa* (The Abencerraje and the Beautiful Jarifa), Ginés Pérez de Hita's *Guerras civiles de Granada* (1595; translated as *The Civil Wars of Granada,* 1803), and Mateo Alemán's *Historia de los dos enamorados Ozmín y Daraja* (1599, Story of the Two Lovers Osmin and Daraja)—idealize Moorish-Christian encounters and describe the Moors with both sympathy and admiration.

The plot of *El Abencerraje y la hermosa Jarifa* centers around Rodrigo de Narváez, a Christian who conquered and later became governor of the towns of Antequera and Álora, and Abindarráez, a young Moorish knight whom the author of the novel depicts as a formidable yet sympathetic warrior. Five of the ten squires directly under Narváez's command do battle with the young Moor. Abindarráez surrenders only after Narváez intervenes and defeats the weary Moor in one-on-one combat. Narváez learns that his prisoner is a member of the Abencerrajes, a once-powerful clan that lost its prestige because of a rumor of treason.

Title page for an early edition of Jorge de Montemayor's Los siete libros de la Diana (1559?, The Seven Books of Diana), *which includes the Moorish novel* El Abencerraje y la hermosa Jarifa (The Abencerraje and the Beautiful Jarifa). *Montemayor is one of several writers scholars have proposed as the author of the anonymous work (from José García López,* Historia de la literatura española, *1962; Thomas Cooper Library, University of South Carolina).*

Abindarráez informs his Christian captor that he grew up under the care of the governor of Cártama, who had a daughter named Jarifa of the same age. Jarifa and Abindarráez fell in love with one another but, thinking they were brother and sister, were unable to love freely. Shortly after each learned that they were not related by blood, Jarifa's father was transferred to another town. Jarifa, however, informed Abindarráez that she would send for him as soon as she could. The young Moor describes to Narváez in lyrical and highly emotional language how his surroundings constantly remind him of his love for Jarifa, whom he was to reunite with before the encounter with Narváez and his squires. Sympathetic to the young Moor's plight, Narváez

grants his captive a three-day leave in order that he might see Jarifa, with the stipulation that he return. The young lovers exchange vows, but their bliss turns to sadness when Abindarráez informs his new bride of his agreement with Narváez. The honorable Moor insists that he must fulfill his promise and return to Álora. The inhabitants of the town receive the newlyweds with respect and courtesy, as they are friends of Governor Narváez. Abindarráez asks Narváez to intercede on his behalf to seek the pardon of Jarifa's father. The Christian governor agrees to grant the young Moor's freedom in exchange for the Moorish king's pardon of Abindarráez and Jarifa. The king accepts the proposal, and the governor returns home with his daughter and new son-in-law. The story concludes with the exchange of letters and gifts between Narváez and the Moors.

There are three different versions of *El Abencerraje y la hermosa Jarifa,* known by scholars as the Corónica, Diana, and Inventario versions. While it is common to find multiple versions of ballads, short stories, and contemporary historical accounts, novels normally have a single version. In addition to the ambiguity created by the different versions, all three texts are for the most part anonymous. Printed in 1561 in Toledo and later published in 1958, the Corónica version has neither a title nor preliminary material that would provide important bibliographical data. The Diana version appeared in the Valladolid edition of Jorge de Montemayor's *Los siete libros de la Diana* (1561, The Seven Books of Diana). The Inventario version appeared as part of a miscellaneous collection of literary compositions titled *Inventario de Antonio de Villegas* (Inventory of Antonio de Villegas). The book, published in Medina del Campo in 1565, includes several poems and a pastoral novelette titled *Ausencia y soledad de amor* (Absence and Solitude of Love). It is not known if Villegas wrote the text of *El Abencerraje y la hermosa Jarifa* that he published in his collection.

Literary critics throughout the years have debated the relationship between Montemayor's *Los siete libros de la Diana* and the different versions of *El Abencerraje y la hermosa Jarifa.* Francisco López Estrada, in his *El Abencerraje y la hermosa Jarifa: Cuatro textos y su estudio* (1957, The Abencerraje and the Beautiful Jarifa: Four Texts and Their Studies), believes that the author of the Diana version incorporated into this version elements of both the Corónica and Inventario texts. Keith Whinnom, in his essay "The Relationship of the Three Texts of *El Abencerraje*" (1959), contends that the Diana followed the Corónica and that the two combined formed the basis of the Inventario version. The Diana version was the most widely read of the three versions of *El Abencerraje y la hermosa Jarifa* and provided a model for later versions, notably an abridged version by early American author Washington Irving.

A possible source of *El Abencerraje y la hermosa Jarifa* is a story titled "Historia del moro y Narváez" (The Story of the Moor and Narváez), which is part of a manuscript from the sixteenth or early seventeenth century that includes a miscellany of texts from the Middle Ages and the Renaissance. Both the story and the novel feature colorful descriptions of Abindarráez's dress, and in both versions Narváez allows the Moor to see Jarifa after listening to Abindarráez's story about their separation. Further parallels include the noble behavior of Abindarráez and Jarifa, as well as Narváez's request that the young Moor relate to him the source of his sadness. Two major differences between the story and the novel, however, cast doubt upon the belief that the story is a source of the novel. The short narrative has the young Moor surrendering without a fight to the five squires who attack him. More significantly, Abindarráez's character in the story does not have a name. This omission convinces some critics that the plot of the story was not a source of the novel. Citing as evidence the widely known details about the legend of the Abencerrajes, María Soledad Carrasco Urgoiti, in her study *The Moorish Novel: El Abencerraje and Pérez de Hita* (1976), comments: "It is more believable that the story represents an early casting in literary form of an anecdote that may have occurred in real life, since noble acts of Moors or of Christians found their way easily into one form or another of historical writing." While the plot and stylistic similarities may suggest a relationship between the two, the degree of that relationship is debatable.

While there is no doubt surrounding the authorship of *Las guerras civiles de Granada*, little is known about its author, Pérez de Hita. Born sometime in the 1540s in Murcia, Pérez de Hita was an artisan by trade who enjoyed reading books of chivalry and composing poetry and folk plays. Actors performed his plays at religious and civic celebrations. Pérez de Hita had intimate knowledge of the Moorish culture. He fought against the Moriscos, Moors who falsely converted to Christianity, in 1569 and 1570. On his way to Madrid in 1585, Pérez de Hita stopped in the village of Villanueva de Alcardete, where a group of Moriscos lived after deportation there, and interviewed several of them about their war experiences. In addition to his battle experiences, Pérez de Hita lived among people of Moorish ancestry who were artisans and farmers in and around Murcia. As an artisan of leather goods, Pérez de Hita's style showed a Moorish influence, no doubt a result of his close ties to this community.

Part 1 of *Las guerras civiles de Granada* appeared in 1595 under the title *Historia de los vandos de los Zegries y*

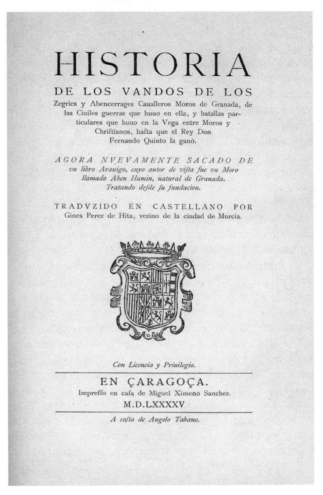

Title page for Ginés Pérez de Hita's 1595 work (History of the Factions of the Zegries and Abencerrajes, Moorish Horsemen of Granada), which the author claimed to have translated from the writings of a fictitious Arab, Aben Hamin (from Ginés Pérez de Hita, Guerra civiles de Granada, 1913, 1915; Thomas Cooper Library, University of South Carolina)

Abencerrajes Cavalleros Moros de Granada, de las Civiles guerras que huvo en ella, y batallas particulares que huvo en la Vega entre Moros y Christianos, hasta que el Rey Don Fernando Quinto la ganó (A History of the Factions of the Zegris and the Abencerrajes, the Gentleman Moors from Granada, of the Civil Wars That Took Place There, and Specific Battles That Occurred in Vega between the Moors and the Christians, until King Fernando V Conquered Granada). The title page informs the reader that Pérez de Hita translated the novel from an Arab book by an author named Aben Hamin. While the Arab author is a literary invention by Pérez de Hita to explain dubious legendary material, Pérez de Hita did find inspiration for *Las guerras civiles de Granada* in other publications about Moorish Granada, namely historian

Estaban de Garibay's *Compendio historial de todos los reinos de España* (1571, Historical Compendium of All the Kings of Spain). Part 1 begins with a brief account of the origin of Granada. In his discussion of the Muslim conquest, Pérez de Hita writes about the Moors with compassion and describes their surroundings with ornate language. Since there is no single character that is the protagonist, much of the action takes place in outdoor settings that enable Pérez de Hita to write about many different characters. The first conflict that the author writes about is the battle of Alporchones in Murcia. As he does throughout both parts of the novel, Pérez de Hita quotes from frontier ballads, which provided him with much inspiration in his discussion of the preparations and the actual fighting that occurred in the battle of Alporchones.

Perhaps the most significant scene of part 1 is a description of festivals and pageantry that took place in Granada at the time when Boabdil replaced his father as king. Pérez de Hita explains and exalts different aspects of Moorish culture through his descriptions of their celebrations and festivities. He provides elaborate accounts of their jewelry, their clothes, and their emblems. The celebration of Boabdil's coronation included a joust between a Christian knight and a Moor. Later in part 1, Pérez de Hita discusses the rivalry between the Abencerrajes and the Zegrís against the background of a bullfight and a *juego de cañas* (game of canes; a simulated combat with much pageantry).

Pérez de Hita fictionalizes historical events throughout the novel. The fictional action of the novel consists of interlaced subplots with different themes and settings. One such event is the joust between the Christian and the Moor. Pérez de Hita invents a scene that involves Muza, the Moorish knight who participates in the joust, the woman with whom he is in love, and the woman who loves him. In spite of the fictional characters and scenes, however, part 1 reads like an historical narrative. The minute details with which Pérez de Hita describes both the geographic settings and the many characters create the appearance of a chronicle.

Part 2, published in 1619, is titled *Segunda parte de las Guerras Civiles de Granada, y de los crueles vandos, entre los convertidos Moros y vezinos Ch[r]istianos: Con el levantamiento de todo el Reyno y ultima revelion, sucedida en el año de 1568* (The Second Part of the Civil Wars of Granada and of the Cruel Factions, between the Converted Moors and Their Christian Neighbors: With the Entire Kingdom's Unprising and Last Rebellion, Which Occurred in 1568). It is a narration of Pérez de Hita's own memories of an unsuccessful Morisco revolt in the Alpujarras (a region of mountain villages in Granada) and begins with a somewhat angry tone, as the author narrates the hardships endured by the descendants of the Moors of

Granada until 1566, the year in which Philip II decreed an end to the practice of Muslim religion and customs in Spain. As Pérez de Hita narrates the Morisco revolt, he interjects detailed descriptions of both Christian and Morisco soldiers and embellishes the story with long speeches.

Since part 2 is more history than novel, the author writes with greater detail about those episodes he witnessed and personages that he knew firsthand, especially descriptions of celebrations. While the Morisco king Aben Humeya waits for reinforcements to arrive from Africa, he decrees a series of festivities that include races, hand-to-hand fights, and contests of strength, followed by singing and dancing that allude to the Moriscos' revolt. Following the pattern established by the frontier ballads, Pérez de Hita narrates in more detail battle scenes and events that lead to the death of important Christians and Moriscos. For example, he highlights the ambush of a Christian captain and his men in a Morisco leader's hometown, as well as the defeat of a black Moorish leader, who escaped in spite of hostile enemy fire.

Pérez de Hita introduces the theme of love in part 2 in his descriptions of the death of Aben Humeya, who holds captive a woman whose lover plots with the king's Turkish allies to kill him. Subsequently, Pérez de Hita describes the escalation of the battle, as both the Christian and the Morisco forces grow in number. As the conflict becomes a full-blown war, the author describes in elegant yet somber detail the ambushes, looting, marches, and battles for small towns. He then narrates the siege and seizure of Galera, a village near Granada, by Don Juan de Austria, the half brother of King Philip II. This narration, however, is from a chronicle kept by a Christian officer; Pérez de Hita inserts many details he claims he learned from talking to Moriscos. The author writes with both shock and amazement how women fought and how men killed their wives and children before dying in battle themselves. Pérez de Hita concludes the novel with a melancholy account of the Moriscos' deportation from Granada.

Since Pérez de Hita rarely cites dates and often dedicates many pages to small incidents, part 2, while more fact than fiction, cannot be considered a reliable account of what actually happened. Pérez de Hita elaborates more upon those episodes that he witnessed and in which he often participated. For this reason, part 2 is considered a valuable source of information about the common man who participated in the battles; not only does Pérez de Hita describe both Christian and Morisco soldiers, but he also complements the information by discussing how the soldiers felt about him. The author praises the courage and solidarity of the common people and condemns the disheartened attitude of the upper-class Moriscos who did not participate in the revolt by choice. It is equally difficult to know which details cited by the author are his own invention and which are based on information the Morisco soldiers told to him.

The last sixteenth-century Moorish novel, *Historia de los dos enamorados Ozmín y Daraja* (Story of the Two Lovers Osmin and Daraja), resembles both *El Abencerraje y la hermosa Jarifa* and *Las guerras civiles de Granada*. It appears in *Guzmán de Alfarache* (1599), a picaresque novel by Mateo Alemán, and the action takes place at the same time as the conquest of Baeza, in 1489. Alemán presents an idealized portrayal of the Moorish lovers and utilizes flowery language to describe their characteristics and attire. In addition, the length and single-plot structure of *Historia de los dos enamorados Ozmín y Daraja* parallel *El Abencerraje y la hermosa Jarifa*. James Fitzmaurice-Kelly, in his introduction to a 1967 English-language edition of *Guzmán de Alfarache*, believes Alemán's Moorish story may have influenced the intercalated stories of Miguel de Cervantes's *Don Quixote* (1605, 1615).

The Moorish novel of the sixteenth century appealed to Spaniards who no longer felt as threatened by the Moors and who enjoyed tales of Christian-Moor confrontations that included amorous adventures. The Moorish novel was not only popular during the sixteenth century, but until the twentieth century, as evidenced by the number of authors who wrote poetry, prose, and drama that deal with Muslim culture and civilization. A genre of the Spanish *comedia*, the *comedia de moros y cristianos* (comedy of Moors and Christians), was popular among seventeenth-century Spaniards, who attended plays in the playhouses throughout Spain. *Comedias de moros y cristianos* typically included a fierce Moor, who seized every opportunity to confront Christians, and a virtuous Moorish knight, who practices Christian virtues and becomes a convert. The colorful portrayal of the Moorish-Christian confrontation and the chivalric qualities embodied by both Moorish and Christian knights made this dramatic genre a favorite of seventeenth-century Spaniards. Lope de Vega wrote several plays that included as characters both Moors and Christians. In addition, some of Lope's *comedias de moros y cristianos* evolved from his own Moorish ballads. Part 2 of Pérez de Hita's novel inspired Calderón de la Barca to write *Amar después de la muerte o El Tuzaní de la Alpujarra* (1633, Love after Death or El Tuzaní from Alpujarra). Calderón's play renewed interest both in the frontier ballads and the Moorish novels.

Interest in Moorish civilization, however, was not restricted to Spain. In the novel *Almahide ou l'Esclave reine* (1660–1663, Almahida or the Slave Queen) French

Title page for Mateo Alemán's 1599 picaresque novel, which includes his tale of Moorish lovers, Historia de los dos enamorados Ozmín y Daraja (Story of the Two Lovers Ozmín and Daraja; from Thomas Hanrahan, La mujer en la novela picaresca de Mateo Alemán, 1964; Thomas Cooper Library, University of South Carolina)

author Madeleine de Scudéry describes Moorish Granada as a refined European court. The English poet John Dryden modeled the Moorish court in his heroic play *Almanzor and Almahide* or *The Conquest of Granada by the Spaniards* (1672) after the equestrian festivals described in Pérez de Hita's Nasrid Granada. Neoclassic poet Nicolás Fernández de Moratín's eighteenth-century poem "Fiesta de toros en Madrid" (Festival of the Bulls in Madrid) describes a picturesque bullfight in a Madrid modeled after Moorish Granada. The popularity of Moorish literature, and in particular Pérez de Hita's *Las guerras civiles de Granada*, was especially strong during the Romantic period. In 1803 Thomas Rodd translated part 1 of *Las guerras civiles de Granada* into English. Many Romantic authors combined personal memories of Granada with legendary or fictional motifs. The Frenchman François-René de Chateaubriand, Irving, and the Spaniard José Zorrilla are three Romantic authors who wrote about their fascination with their experiences in Granada. In *Les Aventures du dernier Abencérage* (1826; translated as *The Last of the Abencerages,* 1850), Chateaubriand incorporates his impressions of Granada into his own interpretation of the myth of the Abencerrajes. Irving's *Chronicle of the Conquest of Granada* (1829) is based upon firsthand documentation that the author uses to depict an accurate portrayal of the Christian conquest of the last Moorish kingdom. In his book *The Alhambra* (1800) he blends travel memories with picturesque descriptions and topics of orientalism. Zorrilla wrote poems called *leyendas* (legends), which he based on themes of the frontier and Moorish ballads. His book-length poem *Granada* (1852) was the result of extensive research and describes the early years of Nasrid history as well as the years leading up to the conquest of Granada.

The Moorish novel of the sixteenth century had a profound influence on Spanish literary culture, as it is generally considered a precursor to the modern historical novel. The long and varied tradition of Moorish literature, however, comes to an end in the twentieth century. With the exception of a few modernist authors, namely Francisco Villaespesa, Eduardo Marquina, and Enrique Larreta, Muslim culture and civilization did not inspire twentieth-century writers, who chose other literary trends to express their perceptions of the world in which they lived.

References:
Julio Caro Baroja, *Los moriscos del reino de Granada: Ensayo de historia social* (Madrid: Instituto de Estudios Políticos, 1957);

María Soledad Carrasco Urgoiti, *The Moorish Novel: El Abencerraje and Pérez de Hita* (Boston: Twayne, 1976);

Carrasco Urgoiti, *El moro de Granada en la literatura: Del siglo XV al XX* (Madrid: Revista de Occidente, 1956);

James Fitzmaurice-Kelly, introduction, in Mateo Alemán, *The Rogue; or The Life of Guzmán de Alfarache,* 4 volumes, translated by James Mabbe (New York: AMS, 1967);

José García López, *Historia de la literatura española,* seventh edition (Barcelona: Vicens-Vives, 1962);

Joaquín Gimeno Casalduero, "*El Abencerraje y la hermosa Jarifa:* Composición y significado," *Nueva Revista de Filología Hispánica,* 21 (1972): 1–22;

Richard F. Glenn, "The Moral Implications of *El Abencerraje,*" *Modern Language Notes,* 80 (1965): 202–209;

Thomas Hanrahan, *La mujer en la novela picaresca de Mateo Alemán* (Madrid: Porrúa Turanzas, 1964);

Francisco López Estrada, *El Abencerraje y la hermosa Jarifa: Cuatro textos y su estudio* (Madrid: Revista de Archivos, Bibliotecas y Museos, 1957);

Henri Mérimée, "*El Abencerrage* d'après diverses versions publiées au XVIme siècle," *Bulletin Hispanique,* 30 (1928): 147–181;

Luis Morales Oliver, *La novela morisca de tema granadino* (Madrid: Fundación Valdecilla, 1972);

Keith Whinnom, "The Relationship of the Three Texts of *El Abencerraje,*" *Modern Language Review,* 54 (1959): 507–517.

The Pastoral Novel of the Sixteenth Century

Benjamin J. Nelson
University of Chicago

and

Julio Vélez-Sainz
University of Massachusetts, Amherst

SELECTED BOOKS: Jorge de Montemayor, *Los siete libros de la Diana* (Valencia: Printed by Joan Mey, 1559?); translated by Bartholomew Yong as *Diana of George of Montemayor Translated out of Spanish into English* (London: Edmund Bollifant, 1598);

Alonso Pérez, *Segunda parte de la Diana de Jorje de Montemayor* (Valencia, 1563);

Gaspar Gil Polo, *Primera parte de la Diana enamorada* (Valencia: Printed by Joan Mey, 1564); translated by Yong as *Diana Enamoured* in *Diana;*

Miguel de Cervantes Saavedra, *Primera parte de la Galatea, dividida en seys libros* (Alcalá: Printed by Juan Gracián, 1585); translated by Gordon Willoughby James Gyll as *Galatea: A Pastoral Romance* (London: G. Bell, 1833);

Luis Gálvez de Montalvo, *El pastor de Fílida* (Lisbon: Printed by B. Rodrigues, 1589);

Lope de Vega, *Arcadia* (Madrid: Luis Sánchez, 1598);

Jerónimo de Tejeda, *La Diana de Montemayor* (Paris, 1627).

Modern Editions: Lope de Vega, *La Arcadia,* edited by Edwin S. Morby (Madrid: Castalia, 1975);

Gaspar Gil Polo, *Diana enamorada,* edited by Francisco López Estrada (Madrid: Castalia, 1987);

Miguel de Cervantes Saavedra, *La Galatea,* edited by Juan Bautista Avalle-Arce (Madrid: Espasa-Calpe, 1987);

Jorge de Montemayor, *Los siete libros de La Diana,* edited by Asunción Rallo (Madrid: Cátedra, 1999);

Cervantes, *La Galatea,* edited by Estrada and María López García-Berdoy (Madrid: Cátedra, 1999).

The pastoral novel (or romance) is a Renaissance narrative model that was born in sixteenth-century Spain. This narrative romance, involving prose and verse, was constructed upon the fiction of shepherds (hence its name) and their tales of love, deceit, and desire. Spanish pastoral novels stem from three main sources: the classical model

and its dramatic continuations in the later Middle Ages by Juan del Encina and Lúcas Fernández; the Italian Renaissance; and Garcilaso de la Vega's églogas (eclogues). During the Middle Ages pastoral poems also formed the foundation of dramatic pieces. The pastoral is highly literary, to the point that whenever the real shepherds are staged (as in the cases of Fernández or del Encina) they seem to parody their poetic avatars. The pastoral novel also intersects with reality, for it is usually a roman à clef, an idealized reconstruction of Renaissance court life. As a genre, the pastoral is extremely conventional: it requires a bucolic setting, idealistic characters, and a plot based on love and desire. The pastoral is intergeneric by nature, easily transformed into drama, prose, or verse, thus emphasizing the intertwining of the shepherds' songs and poems and their prose narrative frame. The action in the pastoral novel is dual: while their circular and convoluted prose extends and sometimes confuses the narrative plot, the intercalated poems develop psychological subtexts. The pastoral depends on both aspects to be fully developed.

Along with epic verse and drama, pastoral poetry, as illustrated by the works of Theocritus and Virgil, is one of the literary legacies of classical Greece and Rome. Theocritus was the first to write stories taken from shepherds in his poems, and he provided the idealized setting for them: they composed poetry under trees, on the grass, or by a spring. The shepherds typically use two instruments: the lyre or the pipe of seven reeds. Theocritus chose the character of the shepherd for several reasons: the shepherd has to spend time outdoors in the woods so he is connected with nature, he lives far from the wickedness of towns, and, most importantly, his profession allows him ample time for leisure and for composing poetry.

During the Roman period Virgil composed his eclogues and georgics, which became the standard model for the pastoral. The Virgilian pastoral is fairly simple: in it two shepherds exchange songs of love and vie in a con-

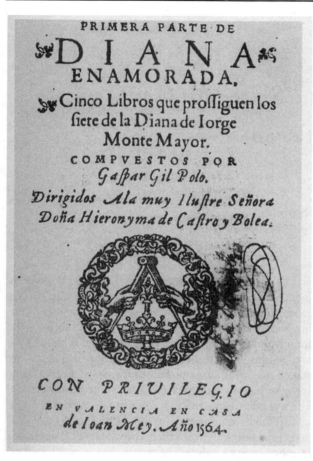

Title page for Gaspar Gil Polo's 1564 pastoral work (The First Part
of Diana Enamoured), one of several sixteenth-century sequels to
Jorge de Montemayor's Los siete libros de la Diana (1559?,
The Seven Books of Diana; from Gaspar Gil Polo, Diana
Enamorada, 1987; Thomas Cooper Library,
University of South Carolina)

test whose topic is their love for a shepherdess. According to the medieval rhetorician John of Garland in his *Poetria magistri Johannis anglici de arte prosaica métrica et rítmica* (Metric, Rhythmic, and Poetic Art of John of Garland, Master of Poetry), who comments on the Virgilian works and lists the necessary elements for a pastoral, the characters should be named Titirus or Melibeus; their flocks must consist of sheep (as opposed to oxen, typical of the farmers of the Georgics); the shepherds' preferred tool is the staff; and their tree is the beech tree. Garland considers the pastoral mode the ultimate example for the humble style of poetics. Moreover, since the shepherds are singers and poets, critics and commentators have accepted that Virgil used them as a means to present his ideas on poetry and self, which provides every pastoral with a metanarrative element. Virgil opens his eclogues by stating that Titirus is quietly sitting under a beech tree; medieval commentators transformed the resting

Titirus into an image of Virgil himself, that is, Titirus came to represent Virgil's alter ego. Virgil also converted the poetic contest into a real confrontation about whom will be granted love by his shepherdess; the poet Marron provided the perfect location for the poems, the fields of Arcadia, which symbolized an archetypical milieu of perfection and became the standard setting for the pastoral.

Writers of the Middle Ages continued to cultivate pastoral verse in Provençal *pastourelles,* which in turn influenced the genesis of some of the marqués de Santillana's pastoral lyric poems, or *serranillas* (circa 1429). The second source of sixteenth-century pastoral novels is the Italian Renaissance. Combining classical pastoral poetry with Renaissance pastoral prose, Giacomo Sannazaro wrote his *Arcadia* (1502) and added several of the indispensable features of the Renaissance pastoral. This Neapolitan emphasized the semi-autobiographical elements of the genre, and his pastoral became a roman à clef that represented the nobility of the Italian Renaissance. In philosophical terms Sannazaro is strongly dependent upon Marsilio Ficino's commentary on Plato's dialogues, which revived Plato's notion of the correspondence of the ideal and the physical realms. Sixteenth-century pastoral shepherd songs celebrate both the physical beauty and the spiritual reality of their beloved in a gallant game of courtesy that serves to integrate the notion of *otium* (leisure) and virtue.

The third clear source for the pastoral novel is the influential *Églogas* by Garcilaso de la Vega, in which Garcilaso surrounds different groupings of shepherds with an understanding Nature and nymphs. Garcilaso wrote three eclogues. In the first, which presents the shepherds Salicio and Nemoroso, he dedicates his poems to the viceroy of Sicily and equates him with Mars in an attempt to mimic Virgil. The viceroy should listen to his songs as well as fight in the Italian fields; a warrior must also be a courtier willing to listen to and compose elaborate verses; and arms must be accompanied by letters. In the second eclogue, in which Albanio and Camila join the shepherds of the first eclogue, Garcilaso intertwines the myth of Arcadia with the myth of Orpheus and his sympathetic beasts who listen to his laments. The Orphic voice of the shepherds is that of Garcilaso himself, and their complaints also have been connected with Garcilaso's love life. The third eclogue, which depicts the shepherds Tirreno and Alzino (or Alcino), adds more mythical subtexts (Apollo and Daphne, Adonis and Venus) through tapestries that nymphs weave throughout the poem. These tapestries explicate the contest between art and nature.

The inception of the pastoral novel in sixteenth-century Spain occurred after an established tradition of isolated pastoral episodes inserted into other prose genres—chivalric (as in the *pastourelle*), celestinesque (in the tradition of Fernando de Rojas's *Celestina,* 1499), Byzantine, and sentimental—and influenced by the circulation of Sannazaro's *Arcadia,* which was translated into Spanish around 1549. The first Spanish pastoral novel, Jorge de Montemayor's *Los siete libros de la Diana* (1559?; translated as *Diana of George of Montemayor Translated out of Spanish into English,* 1598), became a literary best-seller throughout Renaissance Europe during the sixteenth century, particularly in Spain. In a *locus amoenus* situated in León, the Renaissance themes of Neoplatonic love, reason, and fortune interplay as the refined Sireno, the rustic Sylvano, and their companions—Selvagia, Felismena, and Belisa—recount their amorous misadventures. Separated from his beloved Diana, Sireno returns to find that his absence has caused Diana to fall out of love with him and marry another shepherd. Sireno and his companions journey to the temple of the goddess Diana, in which resides the priestess Felicia, in hopes of receiving a magical cure to their amorous problems. As Luis Gálvez de Montalvo's *El pastor de Fílida* (1589, The Shepherd of Fílida) and Lope de Vega's *Arcadia* (1598) may be read as autobiographical reflections of their own lives, Montemayor, a courtier to both the Portuguese and Castilian courts, may have based his pastoral characters on real-life models. Book 1 hints at the double nature of this pastoral novel by asserting that the actions narrated are true "aunque van disfrazados debajo de nombres y estilo pastoril" (although they are disguised under names and pastoral style). In addition, Felismena is a courtier who escapes her palatine life, and book 4 presents the "Canto de Orfeo" (Song of Orpheus), which directly mentions the names of various noblewomen contemporary to Montemayor.

Book 4 of *Los siete libros de la Diana,* in which the reader encounters Felicia and her *agua encantada* (enchanted water), is of particular interest. Memory plays a predominant role in the loves of the various pastoral characters. The absence of Sireno causes Diana to forget her love for him and marry another (although Diana claims later that her parents forced her to marry). As the novel progresses, Sireno encounters other shepherds and shepherdesses who cannot forget their amorous *engaños* (deceits) and *desengaños* (disenchantments), as evidenced by their meticulous narrations. Although Diana forgets her love through Sireno's absence, the rest cannot mimic her act by physically separating themselves from their beloved. Sireno cannot forget, for he encounters Fonstant metonymic reminders of his love for Diana (a letter, a lock of her hair, the River Ezla). Therefore, Felicia's *agua encantada* resolves these conflicts. Sireno "forgets" his love for Diana, while Sylvano and Selvagia fall in love. Because of its fantastical aspects, this magical water may have been too controversial for a sixteenth-century reading audience overshadowed by the Counter-Reformation. In Miguel de Cervantes Saavedra's *Don Quixote* (1605, 1615), during

the Inquisition of Alonso Quexana's library, the town priest is willing to spare Montemayor's book from a fiery fate only if this pernicious section is removed. Although Sireno has forgotten Diana and she reacts with disdain upon discovering his new state, Montemayor's novel ends inconclusively in terms of their romance, for Diana regrets having married Delio and reveals that she is still in love with Sireno.

After its publication in 1559, Montemayor's novel was frequently translated and spread throughout Europe, where it might have influenced the appearance of later pastoral novels in Europe, particularly in France and England. The unresolved conclusion of *Los siete libros de la Diana* inspired the publication of at least two continuations: Alonso Pérez's *Segunda parte de la Diana de Jorge de Montemayor* (1563, Second Part of Jorge de Montemayor's Diana) and Gaspar Gil Polo's *Diana enamorada* (1564, Diana Enamored). Vying with the latter, Pérez might have sacrificed the overall pastoral harmony that Montemayor had achieved in order to publish his literary work first. While still borrowing from his predecessor's tradition, Pérez mixes in chivalric elements (such as the menacing attacks by the giant Gorforosto) that diminish the pastoral characteristics of the novel. What remains inconclusive in Montemayor's work, however, is nearly resolved in Pérez's book, for Pérez himself hints at the intended marriage between Sireno and Diana:

> Antes que d'España se fuese Montemayor, no se desdeñó comunicar conmigo el intento, que para hacer segunda parta a su Diana tenía: y entre otras cosas que me dijo fue, que había de casar a Sireno con Diana enviudando de Delio. Como yo le dijese, que casándola con Sireno con quien ella tanto deseaba, se había de guardar su honestidad, como había comenzado, era en algún modo cerrar las puertas para no poder más de ella escribir, y que mi parecer era, que la hiciese viuda, y requestada de algunos pastores juntamente con Sireno le agradó, y propuso hacerlo. De manera que el consejo que a él di, he yo tomado para mí.

> (Before Montemayor departed from Spain, he did not disdain from communicating with me the intent that he had to make a second part to his Diana: and among other matters that he told me was that one had to marry Sireno with Diana, widowing her from Delio. As I told him, that marrying her with Sireno whom she desired so much, one had to guard her honesty, as in the beginning, [for it] was a way to close the doors so that no one could write more of her, and that it was my understanding, that he would make her a widow, and having her pursued by several shepherds along with Sireno pleased him, and he proposed to do it. From the advice that I gave him, I have taken it for myself.)

Although Delio does indeed die in the eighth (and final) part, Pérez refrains from reconciling Sireno with

PRIMERA PARTE
DE LA GALATEA,
DIVIDIDA EN SEYS LIBROS.
Cópuesta por Miguel de Ceruantes.
Dirigida al Illustrissi. señor Ascanio. Colona Abad de
sancta Sofia.

CON PRIVILEGIO.
Impressa en Alcala por Iuan Gracian.
Año de 1585.
Acosta de Blas de Robles mercader de libros.

Title page for Miguel de Cervantes Saavedra's 1585 work (The First Part of the Galatea, Divided into Six Books), which deviates from the conventions of the pastoral novel by including mythic characters, real-world settings, and incidents of violence (from Miguel de Cervantes Saavedra, La Galatea, 1987; Thomas Cooper Library, University of South Carolina)

work. If Garcilaso and Montemayor believed that the high nobility would be the ideal recipient for their works, Gil Polo seems to be more interested in the high bureaucrats of King Philip II's empire. His audience also determines his style, which avoids Pérez's rhetorical and academic discourse and favors a relaxed and relatively uncomplicated plot. Since his intended audience is less interested in court gossip, Gil Polo moves away from the roman à clef structure of previous pastorals, stating in the introduction that his work is purely fictional.

Diana enamorada consists of five books that narrate the adventures of the main pastoral couple, Alcida and Marcelio, and the characters that join them in their pilgrimage to the temple of Diana. In the first book, Diana complains to Alcida and then to Marcelio about her love and her marriage. Marcelio in turn tells Diana of his love for Alcida. Both Diana and Marcelio decide to consult with Felicia concerning their amorous problems. In the second book, the two shepherds start their journey and find Ismenia during their pilgrimage. Ismenia joins them and recounts her love for Montano. In the third book, the group encounters Polidoro and Clenarda, Alcida's brothers. Polidoro sings of his own love issues. In the fourth book they to arrive at Felicia's palace. Felicia, just as she does in *La Diana,* resolves these problems. Gil Polo's narrative style owes much to Montemayor and to Sannazaro. The multileveled plot of *Diana enamorada* imitates Montemayor's work. Gil Polo unfolds a double narration: in the first layer the shepherds journey to Diana's temple, while in the second one they listen to one another's laments. The first level moves forward in the action and the second one backward into the characters' memory. In *Diana enamorada,* verse and prose are intended to complement one another. While the narrative unfolds in prose, Gil Polo's poems uncover the psychological situation of each character.

In addition to the works by Montemayor, Alonso Pérez, and Gil Polo, Gálvez de Montalvo's *El pastor de Fílida* is mentioned during the inquisition of Don Quixote's library and is spared from condemnation, partly because of the amity between Montalvo and Cervantes, since the former wrote a dedicatory sonnet for the latter's pastoral novel *La Galatea* (1585). Critics have pointed out that Gálvez de Montalvo used Sannazaro's *Arcadia* as his pastoral model, rather than Montemayor's work, insofar as *El pastor de Fílida* is a mixture of prose and verse and the poetry is written in the traditional Italian meter. (At the same time, however, Montalvo incorporates a temple of Diana, to which several of the shepherds sojourn. Inside this structure, which curiously lacks the presence of Felicia and her nymphs, the shepherds learn of the Seven Wonders of the World.) Siralvo's love for Fílida in *El pastor de Fílida* is interpreted by Juan Bautista Avalle-Arce, in his study

Diana and, in fact, complicates their relationship further by presenting for Diana two new suitors–Fausto and Firmio–providing the possibility of a third continuation. In the seventeenth century, Jerónimo de Tejeda composed *La Diana de Montemayor* (1627, Montemayor's Diana), which concludes what Pérez originally intended with the marriage between Sireno and Diana. Modern scholars, however, have not received *Segunda parte de la Diana* favorably, and in *Don Quixote* the book is condemned to be burned while Gil Polo's *Diana enamorada* is spared.

Like Garcilaso or Montemayor, Gil Polo was not a professional writer. Although there are hints in the preliminary sonnets of *Diana enamorada* to an epic poem (which points to the medieval tradition of composing an epic after a pastoral), his continuation of Montemayor's work is his only work of fiction. Gil Polo devoted his life to the study of law and was a notary of Valencia. He married and received several favors from the king, and his professional life defines the intended audience of his

La novela pastoril española (1974, The Spanish Pastoral Novel), as an autobiographical rendition of the author's love for Doña Magdalena Girón, sister of the duke of Osuna. With various amorous interludes, the inclusion of the magician Sincero (who sings of the death of the shepherdess Elisa) and the Cave of Erión (in which, as in the "Canto de Orfeo" in Montemayor's *Los siete libros de la Diana,* contemporary noblewomen are praised), the narrative concludes with festivities (in imitation of the courtly style) to celebrate the reconciliations between shepherds and shepherdesses, especially between the courtier-turned-shepherd, Alfeo, and Andria.

During the latter part of the sixteenth century pastoral novels were composed by two emerging Golden Age writers, Cervantes and Lope de Vega. Published in 1585, *Primera parte de la Galatea, dividida en seys libros* (translated as *Galatea: A Pastoral Romance,* 1833) as a whole follows the pastoral tradition established by Montemayor, but with several interesting deviations. Similar to *Los siete libros de la Diana,* Cervantes's *La Galatea* presents two shepherds—the rustic Erastro and the refined Elicio, who both are in love with the elusive Galatea—and follows their adventures as they encounter a multitude of others with their own amorous problems. Although following Montemayor's example, Cervantes early on in the narrative establishes a departure from *Los siete libros de la Diana.* Complaining about his inability to remove Galatea from his memory, Erastro tells Elicio: "si no he procurado mil veces quitarla de la memoria; y si otras tantas no he andado a los médicos y curas del lugar a que me diesen remedio para las ansias que por su causa padezco. Los unos me mandan que tome no sé qué bebedizos de paciencia; los otros dicen que me encomiende a Dios, que todo lo cura, o que todo es locura" (if I have not tried a thousand times to remove her from my memory; and if so many other times I have not walked to doctors and village priests to which they gave me remedy for the anguishes that from their cause I suffer. The doctors order me to take I don't know what potions of patience; the others say to entrust myself to God, that all will cure it, or that all is insanity). The ineffectiveness of these "potions of patience" shows how Felicia's *agua encantada* cannot remedy Cervantes's amorously suffering shepherds—suggesting that their problems are more severe than the ones Montemayor presents. As Felicia and her guests engage in academic discussions concerning love at the end of book 4 of *Los siete libros de la Diana,* book 4 of *La Galatea* includes a scholarly debate between Lenio, who condemns love, and Tirsi, who praises it (and apparently wins the debate, for later in the narrative Lenio himself falls victim to love).

Divided into six books, the work separates from the established tradition by presenting violent murders among shepherds and interaction with knights, who nar-

rate violent battles; book 6 includes the fantastical appearance of Calliope, the muse of epic (not pastoral) poetry, during a pastoral funeral. The knights, Timbrio and Silerio, relate to Elicio and Erastro their adventures, which include tales of Barcelona being invaded by Turks of the Ottoman Empire, the antagonists of the Hapsburg Dynasty. With this sense of geography, Cervantes's *locus amoenus* becomes restricted and isolated—unlike Montemayor's bucolic world, which is presented with less defined physical boundaries. In addition to these external concerns, the Neoplatonic love presented in the Spanish pastoral novel (especially in the earlier novels) becomes corrupted in *La Galatea* as amorous problems culminate. Finding herself promised by her father to marry a foreign shepherd, Galatea pleads to her friends, especially the disdained Elicio and Erastro, to help her out of this arranged marriage. Everyone agrees to aid her; the narrative ends inconclusively, however, with no mention of how they are going to resolve this problematic situation. Although Cervantes hinted at almost finishing a second part to his pastoral project in the prologues of later works, no continuation of the *Primera parte de la Galatea* has been found.

In the same year that King Philip II died and his son Philip III assumed the Spanish throne, 1598, Lope de Vega published the last pastoral novel of sixteenth-century Spain, *La Arcadia,* which has been read as an autobiographical reflection of the court of the duke of Alba. *La Arcadia* became one of the most circulated Spanish pastoral novels in its time, second only to *Los siete libros de la Diana.* One focus of modern scholars, however, has been Lope's lack of fidelity to the established structure of the pastoral genre. In book 1, the unidentified narrator transforms this bucolic setting into a theater, with the shepherds as actors: "Este es, pastores del dorado Tajo, el teatro de mi historia" (This is, shepherds of the golden [River] Tajo, the theatre of my history). Additionally, Lope distances himself from the typical Byzantine structure and transforms static shepherd characters into more dynamic ones, such as Anfriso, who becomes the first recognizable pastoral protagonist. As Barbara Mujica observes in her *Iberian Pastoral Characters* (1986), the sense of community, as portrayed in Montemayor's *La siete libros de la Diana,* diminishes gradually throughout the sixteenth century (perhaps because of the steady growth of capitalism) and develops into a focus on the individual in *La Arcadia.* As Montemayor has Felicia and her *agua encantada,* Lope presents to his reader the fantastical cave of Dardanio, both positioned in the middle of their respective narrative structures. As Sireno travels to Felicia's temple to forget his love for Diana, Anfriso enters Dardanio's cave either to remedy or dismiss his tumultuous relationship with Belisarda. In the final book of *La Arcadia,* Anfriso enters the Temple of Polinesta to forget his love

Luis Gálvez de Montalvo, whose 1589 work, El pastor de Fílida *(1589, The Shepherd of Fílida), combines autobiographical elements with conventions of the pastoral genre (from José M. Alonso Gamo,* Luis Gálvez de Montalvo: Vido y obra de ese Gran Ignorado, *1987; Thomas Cooper Library, University of South Carolina)*

for Belisarda, for he believes that any reconciliation is hopeless. After being educated in the seven liberal arts and poetry, Anfriso, who is not influenced by any magical elixir, forever parts ways from his beloved–suggesting that education (especially, as Frederick de Armas points out in his 1985 essay "Caves of Fame and Wisdom in the Spanish Pastoral Novel," the art of being a poet) is the true remedy to amorous problems, not magic.

As the Spanish Empire rose and fell during the sixteenth and seventeenth centuries, the pastoral genre did the same. Originally borrowing from classical poetical works and early Renaissance precursors to the novel, the pastoral novel established itself as a genre during the 1500s and continued to be cultivated through the first decades of the following century. At the same time, while writers idealized the pastoral setting and its inhabitants during the sixteenth century, those working in the seven-teenth century became disillusioned with this past. By the middle of the 1600s, the pastoral genre had fallen out of favor with its reading public, largely because of its overt artificiality and its irrelevance to reality. Although one can discern a pastoral influence in later Golden Age works and beyond the seventeenth century, the once great Spanish pastoral tradition had faded. The genre made a significant contribution to the evolution of Spanish literature, however, and its presence can be felt in the early development of the novel in Spain and throughout Europe.

References:

José M. Alonso Gamo, *Luis Gálvez de Montalvo: Vido y Obra de ese Gran Ignorado* (Guadalajara: Institución Provincial de Cultura, 1987);

Paul Alpers, *What Is Pastoral?* (Chicago: University of Chicago Press, 1996);

Juan Bautista de Avalle-Arce, *La novela pastoril española* (Madrid: Istmo, 1974);

Bryant L. Creel, "Aesthetics of Change in a Renaissance Pastoral: New Ideals of Moral and Culture in Montemayor's *Diana*," *Hispanófila*, 99 (1990): 1–27;

John T. Cull, "Androgyny in the Spanish Pastoral Novel," *Hispanic Review,* 59 (1989): 317–334;

Bruno M. Damiani, *"La Diana" of Montemayor as Social and Religious Teaching* (Lexington: University of Kentucky Press, 1983);

Damiani and Barbara Mujica, *Et in Arcadia ego: Essays on Death in the Pastoral Novel* (Lanham, Md.: University Press of America, 1990);

David H. Darst, "Renaissance Platonism and the Spanish Pastoral Novel," *Hispania,* 52 (1969): 384–392;

Frederick de Armas, "Caves of Fame and Wisdom in the Spanish Pastoral Novel," *Studies in Philology,* 82 (1985): 332–358;

Darío Fernández-Morera, *The Lyre and the Oaten Flute: Garcilaso and the Pastoral* (London: Tamesis, 1982);

Alban Forcione, "Cervantes en busca de una pastoral auténtica," *Nueva Revista de Filología Hispánica,* 36 (1988): 1011–1043;

Leonard W. Grant, *Neolatin Literature and the Pastoral* (Chapel Hill: University of North Carolina Press, 1965);

John of Garland, *Poetria magistri Johannis anglici de arte prosaica métrica et rítmica,* edited by Giovanni Mari, *Romanische Forschungen,* 13, no. 3 (1902): 883–965;

Mujica, *Iberian Pastoral Characters* (Washington, D.C.: Scripta Humanistica, 1986);

Renato Poggioli, *The Oaten Flute: Essays on Pastoral Poetry and the Pastoral Ideal* (Cambridge, Mass.: Harvard University Press, 1975);

Thomas G. Rosenmeyer, *The Green Cabinet: Theocritus and the European Pastoral Lyric* (Berkeley: University of California Press, 1969).

Sentimental Fiction of the Sixteenth Century

Antonio Cortijo
University of California, Santa Barbara

SELECTED BOOKS: Comendador Escrivá, *Quexa que da a su amiga ante el dios de amor, por modo de diálogo en prosa y verso,* in *Cancionero general,* compiled by Hernando del Castillo (Valencia, 1514);

Pedro Manuel Jiménez de Urrea, *Penitencia de amor* (Burgos: Printed by Fadrique Alemán de Basilea, 1514);

Qüestión de amor de dos enamorados, anonymous (Valencia: Printed by Diego de Gumiel, 1514)–includes *Égloga de Torino;*

Cartas y coplas para requerir nuevos amores, anonymous (Toledo: Printed by Juan de Vallaquirán, 1515?);

Naceo e Amperidónia, anonymous (circa 1517–1545) [manuscript, Biblioteca Nacional, Lisbon, ms. 11353];

Juan Sedeño de Arévalo, *Coloquios de amores y otro de bienaventuranza* (1536);

Ludovico Scrivá, *Veneris tribunal* (Venice: Printed by Aurelio Pincio, 1537);

Juan de Cardona, *Tratado llamado notable de amor* (1545–1547) [manuscript, Biblioteca Nacional, Madrid, ms. 8159];

Juan de Segura, *Proceso de cartas de amores* (Toledo: Printed by Fernando de Sancta Catalina y Diego Ferrer, 1548)–includes *Quexa y aviso de un caballero llamado Luzíndaro contra amor y una dama y sus casos, con deleitoso estilo de proceder hasta el fin de ambos, sacado del estilo griego en nuestro castellano;*

Bernadim Ribeiro, *Menina e moça* (Ferrara, 1554).

Editions: Pedro Manuel Jiménez de Urrea, *Penitencia de Amor,* edited by Raymond Foulché-Delbosc (Barcelona: Avenc, 1902);

Bernadim Ribeiro, *Menina e Moça,* edited by A. Braamcamp Freire and Carolina Michaëlis de Vasconcelos (Coimbra: Imprensa da Universidade, 1923);

Francisco López Estrada, ed., "Cartas y coplas para requerir nueuos amores," *Revista de Bibliografía Nacional,* 6 (1945): 227–239;

Juan de Segura, *Proceso de cartas de amores,* edited by Edwin D. Place (Evanston: Northwestern University Press, 1950);

Antonio Rodríguez Moñino, ed., *Cancionero general,* compiled by Hernando del Castillo (Madrid: Real Academia Española, 1958);

Rodríguez Moñino, ed., *Suplemento al Cancionero general de Hernando del Castillo (Valencia, 1511): Que contiene todas las poesías que no figuran en la primera edición y fueron añadidas desde 1514 hasta 1557* (Valencia: Castalia, 1959);

Segura, *Proceso de cartas de amores,* edited by Alonso Martín, Pedro Aullón de Haro, Pancracio Celdrán Gomariz, and Javier Huerta Calvo (Madrid: El Archipiélago, 1980);

Juan de Cardona, *Tratado llamado notable de amor,* edited by Juan Fernández Giménez (Madrid: Aula Magna, 1982);

Ludovico Scrivá, *Veneris tribunal,* edited by Regula Rohland de Langbehn (Exeter: University of Exeter, 1983);

David Hook, "Naceo e Amperidónia: A Sixteenth Century Portuguese Sentimental Romance," *Portuguese Studies,* 1 (1985): 11–46;

P. M. Cátedra, ed., *Coloquios de amor y bienaventuranza por Juan Sedeño* (Barcelona: Stelle dell'Orsa, 1986);

Luis Fagundes Duarte, ed., *Naceo e Amperidónia: Novela sentimental do século XVI* (Lisbon: Imprensa Nacional-Casa da Moeda, 1986);

Jiménez de Urrea, *Penitencia de Amor,* edited by Robert Hathaway (Exeter: University of Exeter Press, 1990);

Carla Perugini, ed., *Qüestión de amor* (Salamanca: Ediciones Universidad, 1995);

Jiménez de Urrea, *Penitencia de Amor,* edited by Domingo Ynduráin (Madrid: Akal, 1996).

The literary genre called "sentimental fiction" or "sentimental romance" comprises some thirty works written between around 1400 and around 1550. Although there is no complete agreement regarding the characteristics of works traditionally classified as sentimental fiction, critics have identified several widely accepted features of the genre. These works deal with the topic of love and narrate the unfortunate circum-

First page of Fernando de Rojas's La Celestina *(1499), a work that established many of the conventions of the sentimental romance in sixteenth-century Spain (Hispanic Society of America; from Miguel Romera-Navarro,* Historia de la literatura española, *1928; Thomas Cooper Library, University of South Carolina)*

stances of the relationship between two lovers who end their love affair in separation, death, or suicide because of honor or social constraints. Moreover, love is analyzed as a frustrating and frustrated passion and is usually envisioned within both a personal and social framework. The many references to love and its causes, its effects, and methods to pursue it and achieve satisfaction in it have prompted scholars to suggest that many sentimental romances are or include an *ars amoris* (love treatise) in the fashion of Ovid and Andreas Capellanus and similar to the Italian *trattati d'amore* (love treatises) by Marsilio Ficino and Pietro Bembo.

Many sentimental stories adopt the first person as the favorite narratological voice to explore the anguish of a tragic love journey. This pseudo-autobiographical nature of the genre seems to relate sentimental fictions to some Latin comedies from the twelfth century, Juan Ruiz's fourteenth-century *Libro de buen amor* (Book of Good Love), and late-medieval *cancionero* (songbook) poetry, which also focuses on the lover's feeling of

anguish, pain, and joy. In addition, pseudo-autobiography is also related to concepts such as verisimilitude, narrator's credibility, and narrator infidelity, features that are characteristic of sixteenth-century narratives and early novels. Many sentimental fictions include a lengthy exchange of letters between lovers; Juan de Segura's *Proceso de cartas de amores* (1548, Trial by Love Letters) is written entirely in this epistolary fashion. In general, the employment of letters in sentimental fictions fosters the adoption of several points of view, the disappearance of a narrator, and the exchange of pure dialogue between lovers. This use of letters has been linked to the development of the *ars dictandi* (epistolary technique), which was a popular contemporary subject at institutions of higher learning such as the University of Salamanca, which suggests a special relationship between the university and the bourgeois milieu that spawned sentimental fiction.

Most sentimental fictions include a lengthy and developed criticism of the behavioral code of courtly love, a type of love that is usually depicted as frustrating and unproductive. At the same time, although most sentimental fictions adopt courtly love as their point of departure, they adopt a tone of mockery or criticism toward it. In this regard, male lovers are usually in charge of defending their value as perfect, constant, and persevering, while female lovers ridicule the incoherencies of the male lover's discourse. Moreover, for the first time in literary history women attain important roles as readers in sentimental fictions and appear as characters with roles that are as significant as those of their male counterparts. As such, women figure prominently as addressees in many prologues to sentimental romances and within the works often point out the incoherence and inconsistency of the discourse of courtly love by frequently mocking and criticizing their male counterparts as fools.

In sentimental fictions, characters usually debate the essence of love, thus offering a multiplicity of voices and points of view regarding love as a personal and social phenomenon. Strikingly, the debate on love, together with the adoption of a multifaceted range of opinions on the subject, promotes in sentimental fiction the idea of love as a somewhat egalitarian force. All participants in the love game have an equal right to express their opinions about the game.

Although sentimental fictions originated among the fifteenth-century nobility, whose literary courts provided patronage for authors of these works, the presence of voices interspersed in the narratives (such as female voices, scholarly and university elements, and bourgeois characters), as well as the portrayal of personal and social crisis, point toward a milieu more complicated than that of the upper nobility. By extension, scholars have explained the presence of these voices within the context of new social relations at the end of the fifteenth century or against the backdrop of the emergence of new social classes, such as the bourgeoisie, during the late Middle Ages and early Renaissance. Moreover, critics such as Francisco Márquez Villanueva and Gregory B. Kaplan have seen in the crisis depicted in some sentimental texts a particular connection between this genre and the social predicament of the *conversos* (converts from Judaism and their descendants), who were treated as inferior Christians and subject to persecution by the Spanish Inquisition. As such, the crisis represented in some sentimental narratives, which impedes a union between the male and female protagonists, is understood to reflect the crisis endured by many *conversos* who were also prevented from achieving a union, that is, a seamless assimilation into Spanish Christian society.

The canonical list of sentimental romances written in the sixteenth century includes *Penitencia de amor* (1514, Love's Penance) by Pedro Manuel Jiménez de Urrea; *Quexa que da a su amiga ante el dios de amor, por modo de diálogo en prosa y verso* (1514, Complaint Addressed to His Lady before the God of Love) by the Comendador Escrivá; the anonymous *Cartas y coplas para requerir nuevos amores* (1515?, Letters and Poems to Request New Love); *Veneris tribunal* (1537, Venus's Tribunal) by Ludovico Scrivà; *Tratado llamado notable de amor* (1545–1547, Remarkable Love Treatise) by Juan de Cardona; and Juan de Segura's *Proceso de cartas de amores* and *Quexa y aviso de un caballero llamado Luzíndaro contra amor y sus casos, con deleitoso estilo de proceder hasta el fin de ambos, sacado del estilo griego en nuestro castellano* (1548, Complaint and Warning from a Gentleman called Luzíndaro against Love and Its Sufferings, with a Pleasing Manner of Proceeding toward Both Ends, in Our Castilian Language and Based on the Greek Style). Although scholars have long considered this genre as exclusively Castilian, subsequent criticism suggests that some Catalan and Portuguese works should be considered sentimental fictions as well. Thus, while the first canonical sentimental romance written in Castilian, *Siervo libre de amor* (Free Slave of Love, or Slave Free from Love) by Juan Rodríguez del Padrón, dates from around 1440, several critics have advanced the theory that *Frondino i Brisona* (Frondino and Brisona), a bilingual work written in Catalan and French around 1400, is already a developed sentimental fiction. Likewise, cases may be made that the Portuguese *Confissão do Amante* (circa 1430, Confessions of a Lover), Bernadim Ribeiro's *Menina e moça* (1554, Maiden and Young Girl), the anonymous *Naceo e Amperidónia* (circa 1517–1545, Naceo and Amperidónia), and the fifteenth-century Catalan *novelletes amoroses i senti-*

Title page for Pedro Manuel Jiménez de Urrea's 1514 romance (Love's Penance), in which a pair of lovers find happiness until the young woman's father imprisons them both in a tower for the rest of their lives (from Jordi de Sant Jordi, Obres poetiques, 1902; Jean and Alexander Heard Library, Vanderbilt University)

mentals (sentimental and love stories) should be included as part of the genre.

Among the main literary sources of sentimental fiction are the Arthurian novel, the French *voir-dit* (narrative poem), Giovanni Boccaccio's *novella* (short stories), medieval literature of *de regimine principum* (advice for princes), biblical texts, *cancionero* poetry, university treatises, homiletic literature, *relaciones* (descriptions of courtly events), and theatrical texts (such as eclogues and humanistic comedies). During the sixteenth century, there were some necessary overlaps between sentimental fiction and other literary genres, such as the chivalric novel, the pastoral romance, and the Byzantine novel. In addition, critics have usually ignored that sentimental fictions (or sentimental tones and motifs) continue well into the seventeenth century, for later adaptations of sentimental topics are found in works by authors such as Lope de Vega.

Critics have increasingly related sentimental fictions to Fernando de Rojas's *La Celestina* (1499), a novel in dialogue that deals with the theme of love, and many similar works written around 1490–1530. *La Celestina* has even been considered a sentimental fiction, and some critics have suggested that the work is a literary response to *Cárcel de Amor* (1492, Prison of Love), by Diego de San Pedro, one of the most popular sentimental fictions during the late fifteenth and early sixteenth centuries. In *La Celestina* the presence of dialogue, letters, and debates on love tends to overshadow the role of simple narrative in third person. At the same time, critics have also labeled *La Celestina* a theatrical piece or a romance. Regardless of the genre to which it belongs, *La Celestina* is an amalgam of literary love traditions, especially those associated with the sentimental fiction. By focusing on the urban milieu of Salamanca and (thematically) on the love sickness of the protagonists, Calisto and Melibea, *La Celestina* demonstrates the tendency, in works displaying features common to sentimental fictions, to deal with the contradictions resulting from the incorporation of courtly love rhetoric within the late-fifteenth-century urban social context that forms the backdrop of the work.

In Jiménez de Urrea's *Penitencia de amor,* Darino falls in love with a beautiful lady, Finoya. His love not being reciprocated at first, he seeks the help of two servants, Renedo and Angis. Through the diligence of his servants Darino obtains letters from Finoya and enters into a relationship with her, finally achieving the ultimate pleasure. Finoya's father discovers the lovers and imprisons them in a tower, where they do penance for the rest of their lives. This work is clearly related to *La Celestina* and has been considered among the sixteenth-century continuations of that work. In both works the prevalent tone throughout is ironic and burlesque.

Quexa que da a su amiga ante el dios de amor, by the Comendador Escrivá, is inspired by the medieval tradition of love visions. The work involves a narrator who is visited by the god of love, from whom he requests an interview with his lover. At first the female lover is reluctant, but the god decrees that she love the narrator. Nonetheless, the work ends with the female lover rejecting the narrator, who is expelled from love's paradise, putting an end to the vision. As in many other sentimental fictions, the female lover expresses her opinions and rejects the male lover.

The anonymous *Cartas y coplas para requerir nuevos amores* is a crucial text for the understanding of the development of sentimental fiction. The work includes exclusively letters between lovers, without any type of narrative frame or narrative intrusion, a feature that

links it to texts such as *Rota Veneris* (circa 1200, Love's Wheel) by Boncaompagno da Signa, as well as to rhetorical and compositional university manuals, which were in widespread use in Spain at institutions such as the University of Salamanca. The different letters in *Cartas y coplas para requerir nuevos amores* cover a broad spectrum of love situations, including acceptance, rejection, and sickness, and the work is also significant insofar as it demonstrates that sentimental topics can be dealt with in literary works composed outside of courtly circles, which in turn serves as an indication of the diffusion of sentimental literature among the bourgeois milieu.

Several decades later, Juan Sedeño de Arévalo published *Coloquios de amores y otro de bienaventuranza* (1536, Colloquies on Love and on Blessedness). In this work, Polinides and Leonida discuss their love, and the latter mocks Polinides' foolishness. In the second part of the work there is a curious denouement. Leonidas's mother is introduced into the dialogue to express clearly that the love relationship cannot be finalized satisfactorily unless Polinides entertains the possibility of matrimony. Courtly love rhetoric thus is annihilated in view of a more satisfactory social channeling of love (matrimony) in which the rhetoric of love pains is absolutely meaningless. *Coloquios de amores y otro de bienaventuranza* is an important work for its clear expression of a topic related to courtly love in sentimental fiction but ignored in other varieties of courtly literature: matrimony. By extension, the work allows for an appreciation of the social implications of the sentimental romance in postcourtly (postfeudal) society. The following year Ludovico Scrivá published *Veneris tribunal,* in which the narrator, who is studying law, tells of his unrequited love for a noble lady from Padua.

Cardona's *Tratado llamado notable de amor* deals with the love between two nobles, Cristerno and Ysiana, and the wars that occur during the early sixteenth century as their relationship evolves. In addition to its sentimental features, this work is important for its inclusion of a precise picture of contemporary European geography and politics, in particular the war between the rulers of France and Spain and between Europe and the Turks. *Tratado llamado notable de amor* also manifests the influence of another sixteenth-century literary genre, the Byzantine novel.

One of the most crtically studied sentimental fictions is Segura's *Proceso de cartas de amores*. Although scholars have treated this book as just one work, it may be understood to comprise two different novels: *Proceso de cartas de amores* and *Quexa y aviso de un caballero llamado Lucíndaro contra amor y casos*. The first part, which does not involve a narrator, consists of forty letters exchanged between two lovers. The male lover declares his love for his lady insistently until she reciprocates. Her brothers are opposed to this relationship and send her to the convent of San Clemente. The last five letters are written between the male lover and a friend of his, and between the male lover and Juliana, a nun who serves as go-between for the two lovers. The second part of the novel is, according to the text, a translation from an original written in Greek and displays a mix of Arthurian, Byzantine, and sentimental-romance traditions. After several incidents, the two lovers, Medusina and Lucindaro, rejoice in their love and consummate their union. Nonetheless, Medusina dies, and Lucindaro commits suicide in despair by eating the ashes of his lover's burned body. The extreme originality of this work resides in its combination of realistic and fantastic plots, thus combining the two main traditions present in the sentimental romance, that of the Arthurian-chivalric novel and that of works such as *La Celestina,* which involve more-realistic plots.

Sentimental fiction is neither a medieval nor a Renaissance genre. At the threshold of the Renaissance, sentimental romance is representative of the notion of crisis that defines this period. When talking about love affairs sentimental fictions tend to narrate love within a more developed (and realistic) social frame. In doing so, they differ from previous traditions, in particular the Arthurian novel and *cancionero* poetry, and place less emphasis on describing deeds and actions and more on analyzing the essence of the love crisis, both in individual and social terms.

Although sixteenth-century sentimental fiction is indebted to sentimental works from the 1400s (to the point that it is possible to talk about unity in this literary genre over the course of around 150 years), there are several tendencies in the sixteenth-century works that differentiate them from fifteenth-century texts. For example, there is a clear connection between eclogue and sentimental romance that has not been thoroughly explored by scholars. The issue is significant insofar as many eclogues composed between 1496 and 1550 are by authors of sentimental works. In addition, many eclogues include what are in essence sentimental plots, and some sentimental works such as *Égloga de Torino* (1514, Eclogue of Torino) even include eclogues as part of them. There is also a clear tendency toward realism in sixteenth-century sentimental fiction. In the depiction of courtly life, these sixteenth-century sentimental works tend to ignore the rather abstract and anachronistic portrayal of courtly life in the fashion of medieval chivalric literature. Instead, they include many references to contemporary politics, with frequent references to King Charles I, the Turks, and the Ottoman Empire. Unlike in many fifteenth-century sentimental fictions, sixteenth century plots do not always end with tragic

Title page for Ludovico Scrivà's Veneris tribunal *(1537, Venus's Tribunal), in which a law student pines for the love of a Paduan noblewoman (Center for Research Libraries, Chicago)*

deaths but with the refusal by the female lover's family (brothers, mother) to agree to the relationship between lovers unless there is matrimony. *Proceso de cartas de amores* signals clearly this tendency in its apparent division separating the work into two apparently independent and unconnected parts. Segura seems to have been conscious that there were by circa 1550 two distinct traditions within sentimental romance, that of abstract courtly atmosphere in the tradition of chivalric Arthurian romances and that of more-realistic plots that framed a love story within contemporary social structures and realities.

Although an enormously successful genre, sentimental fiction seems to have faded around 1550 after newer literary genres, such as the pastoral romance, the Byzantine novel, and the chivalric romance, became the fashionable genres of the Renaissance. At the same time, traces of the influence of sentimental fiction can be perceived in all of these Renaissance genres, and it can be justly said that sentimental fiction stands at the frontier of the creation of modern romance. By focusing

Title page for Juan de Segura's Proceso de cartas de amores *(1548, Trial by Love Letters), a romance written in epistolary form (from Juan de Segura,* Proceso de cartas de amores, *1980; Davis Library, University of North Carolina at Chapel Hill)*

on love both as a personal and social feeling and by mixing several narratological techniques (dialogue, debate, and letters), thus further complicating the status of the narrator and his position in the narrative, sentimental fictions gave birth to a new dialogical interest in the individual in communication with the society that fostered him or her. The social and personal features of the new Renaissance society described in sentimental fictions were later explored in novels that focused on the exoticism of travel, the material deeds of adventure, and/or the escape toward social utopia.

Scholars studying the sixteenth-century novel have pointed toward the partial sentimental-like characteristics of other distinct literary genres such as the chivalric novel, the Byzantine romance, and the pastoral romance. No attempt has been made to explain these genres in connection to the sentimental romance. Notably, these other genres developed precisely at a moment in which sentimental romance waned as a genre, which

may indicate that the new social conditions of sixteenth-century society made it difficult for readers to relate to the way sentimental romances contextualize love. As a result of these conditions, the developing genres offer different solutions to the love conflicts posed by sentimental narratives on love. For example, escapism and utopia are the focus of genres such as the chivalric novel, which tended to stress deeds over love rhetoric. The same can be said of the Byzantine novel, which focuses in turn more on exoticism and travel while maintaining a basic love plot. The Byzantine novel was also an answer to the new geography of sixteenth-century Europe in the age of exploration. Pastoral romance is more directly related to sentimental romances in that it suppresses action for the sake of discussions on love. It is also through the pastoral eclogue that a connection is revealed between sentimental and pastoral romances.

In spite of its decline in popularity during the middle of the sixteenth century, the enduring legacy of sentimental fiction is revealed in its contribution to the evolution of a variety of narrative techniques. Moreover, the genre was clearly experimental and receptive to narrative innovations and trials. For example, sentimental fictions stubbornly favor *prosimetra* (the combination of prose and verse), thus linking narrative and lyrical tones when dealing with love plots and marking the connection between *cancionero* poetry and the novel. Sentimental fiction also shows a reluctance to abandon the epistolary technique, a tendency that has been studied as a sign of the new times in which the genre evolved, that is, for the close relationship between sentimental fiction and the university and the courtly milieu of bureaucrats. In this light, the presence of scholars as characters in sentimental narratives also indicates a clear university connection. In addition, dialogue offered sentimental fictions an appropriate vehicle for exploring new manners of narration. If the epistolary technique is clearly a dialogic device, more so are the theatrical devices included in sentimental fictions. In this regard, it is clear that there is a connection in the fifteenth century between sentimental romance and the early evolution of Spanish theater, especially with regard to the depiction of plots and the employment of theatrical techniques.

During the approximately 150 years of its popularity, the genre known today as sentimental fiction came to occupy an important niche in the trajectory of late-medieval and early-Renaissance Spanish letters. In this regard, sentimental fiction must be studied as both a medieval and a Renaissance genre, spanning 150 years, whose success is demonstrated by its enormous popularity once the printing press distributed these works throughout Europe in massive numbers of copies, and by its influence on subsequent literature, which is evident from the Golden Age until modern times. Above all, the emergence of sentimental fiction signals the arrival of new times through the inclusion of innovative contexts and points of view. Sentimental narratives adopted many of the characteristics of medieval love literature and added more-realistic settings and plots that reflected the social tensions of sixteenth-century Spain (and Europe) and that contributed to the evolution of the Byzantine, pastoral, and chivalric romances of the sixteenth and seventeenth centuries, which assured the continuation of sentimental themes in Spanish Baroque literature.

Bibliography:

Keith Whinnom, *The Spanish Sentimental Romance 1440–1550: A Critical Bibliography,* Research Bibliographies and Checklists, no. 41 (London: Grant & Cutler, 1983).

References:

M. F. Aybar Ramírez, "La ficción sentimental del siglo XVI," dissertation, Universidad Complutense de Madrid, 1994;

Erasmo Buceta, "Algunas relaciones de *Menina e Moça* con la literatura española, especialmente con las novelas de Diego de San Pedro," *Revista de la Biblioteca, Archivo y Museo,* 10 (1933): 291–307;

J. L. Canet Vallés, *De la comedia humanística al teatro representable* (Valencia: UNED / Seville: Universidad de Sevilla, 1993);

Pedro M. Cátedra, *Amor y pedagogía en la Edad Media: Estudios de doctrina amorosa y práctica literaria* (Salamanca: Universidad de Salamanca, Secretariado de publicaciones, 1989);

Cátedra and others, eds., *Tratados de amor en el entorno de Celestina, siglos XV–XVI* (Madrid: Sociedad Estatal España Nuevo Milenio, 2001);

Antonio Cortijo Ocaña, *La evolución genérica de la ficción sentimental de los siglos XV y XVI. Género literario y contexto social* (London & Rochester, N.Y.: Tamesis, 2001);

Cortijo Ocaña, ed., "Critical Cluster (Sentimental Romance)," *La corónica,* 29, no. 1 (2000): 5–229;

Dinko Cvitanovic, *La novela sentimental española* (Madrid: Prensa Española, 1973);

Alan D. Deyermond, *Tradiciones y puntos de vista en la ficción sentimental,* Publicaciones Medievalia, no. 5 (Mexico: Universidad Autónoma de Mexico, 1993);

Armando Durán, *Estructura y técnicas de la novela sentimental y caballeresca* (Madrid: Gredos, 1973);

Juan Fernández Giménez, "Amor cortés en el Tratado notable de amor," *Explicación de Textos Literarios,* 10 (1981): 23–26;

Fernández Giménez, "Una versión inédita del discurso de Carlos V en Roma," *Hispania,* 56 (1982): 34–57;

F. Gómez Redondo, *Los orígenes del Humanismo: El marco cultural de Enrique III y Juan II,* volume 3 of *Historia de la prosa medieval castellana* (Madrid: Cátedra, 2002);

Joseph J. Gwara and E. Michael Gerli, eds., *Studies on the Spanish Sentimental Romance (1440–1550): Redefining a Genre* (London & Rochester, N.Y.: Tamesis, 1997);

Johan Huizinga, *Homo Ludens: A Study of the Play-Element in Culture,* translated by R. F. C. Hull (London & Boston: Routledge & Kegan Paul, 1949);

Gregory B. Kaplan, *The Evolution of* Converso *Literature: The Writings of the Converted Jews of Medieval Spain* (Gainesville: University Press of Florida, 2002);

Francisco Márquez Villanueva, "*Cárcel de amor,* novela política," *Revista de occidente,* 14 (1966): 185–200;

Arseni Pacheco, "L'anàlisi de la pació amorosa en alguns texts del segle XV: Anatomia dun gènere en embrio," in *Miscellània Pere Bohigas,* volume 3 (Montserrat: Publicacions de l'abadia de Montserrat, 1983), pp. 25–38;

Pacheco, ed., *Novelletes sentimentals del segles XIV i XV,* Antologia Catalana, no. 57 (Barcelona: Edicions 62, 1970);

Regula Rohland de Langbehn, *La unidad genérica de la novela sentimental española de los siglos XV y XVI,* Papers of the Medieval Hispanic Research Seminar, no. 17 (London: Department of Hispanic Studies, Queen Mary and Westfield College, 1999);

Manuel Romera-Navarro, *Historia de la literatura española* (Boston: Heath, 1928);

Jordi de Sant Jordi, *Obres poetiques de Jordi de Sant Jordi,* edited by J. Massó Torrente (Barcelona: "L'Avenç," 1902);

Isabel de Sena, "The Portuguese Sentimental Romance," dissertation, University of California, Santa Barbara, 1994.

La vida de Lazarillo de Tormes

Richard Terry Mount
University of North Carolina at Wilmington

BOOK: *La vida de Lazarillo de Tormes y de sus fortunas y adversidades* (Burgos: Printed by Juan de Junta, 1554); translated by David Rowland as *The Pleasaunt Historie of Lazarillo de Tormes a Spaniarde: Wherein is conteined his marueilous deedes and life* (London: Jeffes, 1586).

Modern Editions: *La vida del Lazarillo de Tormes, sus fortunas y adversidades,* unexpurgated edition (Gerona, Spain: Antonio Oliva, 1834);

La vida de Lazarillo de Tormes y de sus fortunas y adversidades, edited by Adolfo Bonilla y San Martín (Madrid: Ruiz, 1915);

Lazarillo de Tormes, preface by Gregorio Marañón (Madrid: Espasa-Calpe, 1940);

La vida de Lazarillo de Tormes y de sus fortunas y adversidades, edited by Julio Cejador y Frauca (Madrid: Espasa-Calpe, 1941);

La vida de Lazarillo de Tormes y de sus fortunas y adversidades, edited by Everett Hesse and Harry F. Williams (Madison: University of Wisconsin Press, 1948);

La vida de Lazarillo de Tormes y de sus fortunas y adversidades, edited by Alfredo Cavaliere (Naples: Giannini, 1955);

La vida de Lazarillo de Tormes y de sus fortunas y adversidades, edited by R. O. Jones (Manchester: Manchester University Press, 1963);

La vida de Lazarillo de Tormes y de sus fortunas y adversidades, in *La novela picaresca española,* edited by Angel Valbuena y Prat, fifth edition (Madrid: Aguilar, 1966), pp. 83–111;

La vida de Lazarillo de Tormes, y de sus fortunas y adversidades, edited, with prologue and notes, by José Caso González (Madrid: Aguirre, 1967);

La vida de Lazarillo de Tormes y de sus fortunas y adversidades, edited by Alberto Blecua (Madrid: Castalia, 1972);

Lazarillo de Tormes, edited by Francisco Rico, with bibliographical appendix by Bienvenido C. Morros (Madrid: Cátedra, 1987);

Lazarillo de Tormes: Medina del Campo, 1554, facsimile edition, introduction by Jesús Cañas Murillo (Mérida, Spain: Junta de Extremadura, 1996);

Lazarillo de Tormes, prologue by Rico (Madrid: Plaza & Janés, 1997);

La vida de Lazarillo de Tormes y de sus fortunas y adversidades, edited by José María Reyes Cano (Barcelona: Grupo Hermes Editora General, 1997);

La vida de Lazarillo de Tormes y de sus fortunas y adversidades, edited by Annette Grant Cash and James C. Murray (Newark, Del.: Cervantes, 2002).

Editions in English: *The Pleasaunt Historie of Lazarillo de Tormes,* facsimile edition, edited by J. E. V. Crofts (Oxford: Blackwell, 1924);

The Life of Lazarilllo de Tormes: His Fortunes and Adversities, translated by James Gerald Markley, introduction by Allan G. Holaday (New York: Liberal Arts Press, 1954);

Lazarillo de Tormes, translated by Michael Alpert, in *Two Spanish Picaresque Novels* (Harmondsworth, U.K.: Penguin, 1969), pp. 21–79;

The Life of Lazarillo de Tormes, His Fortunes and Misfortunes, translated, with an introduction, by Robert S. Rudder (New York: Ungar, 1973);

Lazarillo de Tormes, edited and translated by Stanley Appelbaum (Mineola, N.Y.: Dover, 2001).

La vida de Lazarillo de Tormes y de sus fortunas y adversidades (1554; translated as *The Pleasaunt Historie of Lazarillo de Tormes a Spaniarde: Wherein is conteined his marueilous deedes and life,* 1586) is generally considered the first picaresque novel or the prototype of the picaresque novel. The picaresque novel is a subgenre of the novel that enjoyed great vogue and was highly developed during the seventeenth century and afterward. It is characterized by its autobiographical form and episodic nature. The unifying element of the various episodes is the central figure, who is a *pícaro* (rogue), the Spanish term from which the name of the subgenre is derived. The *pícaro* narrates in first person his life experiences as he serves one master after another. He can be described as a petty thief of the lower classes who uses his cunning to save himself from starvation and in so doing comes across persons from all walks of life. This exposure to different elements of society allows the *pícaro* to meet, observe, and interact with a variety of people. By examining them with a critical eye and satirizing the corruption observed, he gives an overview of the hypocrisy of an entire society.

There remain unanswered questions as to authorship and date of composition of the anonymous *La vida de Lazarillo de Tormes*. The work first appeared in 1554 in four separate editions, the one printed in Burgos by Juan de Junta being considered the oldest. This edition was followed by one published in Antwerp (printed by Martín Nucio). A third, dated 26 February 1554, was printed with interpolations in Alcalá de Henares, Spain, by Salcedo; and a fourth, which was discovered in 1992, was printed by Francisco and Mateo del Canto in Medina del Campo, Spain, and is dated 1 March 1554. In 1555 a fifth edition of the novel was published with an anonymous sequel, *Segunda parte de Lazarillo de Tormes y de sus fortunas y adversidades* (Second Part of Lazarillo de Tormes and His Fortunes and Adversities), in Antwerp by Martín Nucio and Guillermo Simón.

It is generally accepted, though not proven, that there was a pre-1554 version of the work that either appeared in an edition now lost or circulated in manuscript form. Attempts to pinpoint the date of the lost original have proven inconclusive. Estimates place its composition as early as the mid 1520s, based on a reference in the last chapter of the work to the convocation of the parliament in Toledo by Charles V. There were two such meetings of parliament, one in 1525 and another in 1538–1539. Thus, 1525 may be considered the earliest possible date of composition. Any year between 1525 and 1553 cannot be ruled out, for it has not been established with certainty that the novel was completed at the time suggested by the narrator. Most critics believe, however, that the lost first edition was published near the time of the publication of the four 1554 editions, probably between 1550 and 1553.

That as many as five editions of *La vida de Lazarillo de Tormes* were published in 1554 and 1555 attests to its immediate popularity. The success of the original work was not sustained, however, for it was banned after being included in the Catholic *Index Librorum Prohibitorum* (Index of Prohibited Books) in 1559. The ban of *La vida de Lazarillo de Tormes* and other works was lifted in 1571 with the provision that certain passages be expurgated. Five censored editions—published in Madrid in 1573; Tarragona, Spain, in 1586; Milan in 1587; Antwerp in 1595; and Bergamo, Italy, in 1597—appeared in the dominions of Spain during the reign of Philip II (1556–1598), which was characterized by zealous suppression of criticism of the church. The fact that the first fully developed picaresque novel, Mateo Alemán's *Guzmán de Alfarache,* was published in 1599, the year following Philip's death, gives credence

Title page for the first picaresque novel (translated as The Pleasaunt Historie of Lazarillo de Tormes a Spaniarde, *1586; from Francisco Rico,* Problemas del Lazarillo, *1988; Thomas Cooper Library, University of South Carolina)*

to the supposition that *La vida de Lazarillo de Tormes* had no imitators during the half century following its appearance because of suppression of ideas critical of the establishment.

The first censored version, *Lazarillo de Tormes castigado* (Lazarillo de Tormes expurgated), omits the brief fourth chapter, in which the master is a *fraile de la Merced* (Mercedarian friar), and the fifth chapter, in which appears a *buldero* (pardoner), or seller of bulls of indulgences. Also suppressed are some sentences in the second chapter, in which Lazarillo serves a cruel priest from Maqueda. This expurgated version remained the only version printed in Spain until the Inquisition was officially abolished there in 1834. In that same year an unexpurgated edition was published in Barcelona.

The identity of the author of *La vida de Lazarillo de Tormes* is as elusive as its date of composition. Scholars have attributed the work to different sixteenth-century writers, such as Diego Hurtado de Mendoza, Sebastián de Horozco, Juan de Ortega, Juan de Valdés, Alfonso de Valdés, Hernán Núñez de Toledo, Cristóbal de Villalón, and Pedro de Rhúa. The anticlerical attitude of the narrator leads to the belief that the author was an Erasmist, but even this idea is inconclusive since criticism of the church and of clerics dates from the Middle Ages. Other theories propose that the author was a person of high social or ecclesiastical rank whose identity was protected through anonymous authorship, or that the author was a New Christian or *converso* (convert from Judaism to Catholicism) whose acerbic attitude was a product of a marginalized social status. Whatever the occupation, social rank, or philosophical bent the author held, it is clear that the writer was a learned person, a great observer of character, and one acutely aware of social conditions among the lower classes as well as of corruption within ecclesiastical institutions in the Spain of Charles V.

La vida de Lazarillo de Tormes consists of a prologue and seven chapters called *tratados*. It is told in autobiographical form and traces the early life of the narrator until the time of his marriage, when he considers himself prosperous and "en la cumbre de toda buena fortuna" (at the height of all good fortune). The chapters are uneven in length but relate significant episodes in Lázaro's life as he passes from childhood to adulthood. In the course of the novel he serves successively a blind man, a priest, a squire, a friar, a pardoner, a tambourine painter, a chaplain, and a constable. His association with the friar is only briefly and enigmatically described. With the tambourine painter and the chaplain, Lázaro holds his first jobs; he mixes paints for the former and works as a water vendor with the latter. Finally, he becomes town crier in Toledo and marries the servant of an archpriest.

At this stage in his life, Lázaro writes his fragmented story at the request of an unidentified person, whom he first addresses as "Vuestra Merced" (Your Grace) in the prologue. He does so to explain *el caso* (the matter of concern) to which he alludes. The full context of the request and the nature of the matter of concern are never revealed to the reader. The narrator states his rationale for beginning at the beginning rather than in the middle: first, it enables him to provide information for full understanding of his lot; second, it makes those born to high estate understand that fortune has blessed them. Further, the narrator states his belief that those who have prevailed over adverse fortune are the ones most to be admired, for they, by great effort and cunning, have brought themselves "a buen puerto" (to a good port, or admirable position in life). Thus is introduced the theme carried throughout the novel, that of rising in society from humble beginnings.

The first chapter gives the circumstances of Lázaro's birth and explains how he sets out on the path

that leads him through "fortunas y adversidades" and ultimately to apparent satisfaction with his professional and marital situation in the seventh chapter. He is the son of Tomé González and Antona Pérez, natives of Tejares in the province of Salamanca. The boy takes the surname "de Tormes" because, as he says, he was born on the Tormes River, a tributary of the Duero that flows through Salamanca. His father worked in a mill on the river, and Lázaro was born while his mother happened to be at the mill one night. When the boy is eight years old, the father is charged with stealing from the sacks of the mill clients. Tomé confesses and is punished. Exiled, the father serves and dies in an expedition against the Moors in North Africa. To support herself and her child, the widowed Antona Pérez goes to the city of Salamanca to ally herself with "good people" in order to become one of them; she rents a house where she cooks for university students and washes clothes for the stable hands of the commander of La Magdalena. Among the stable hands is a black man named Zayde, whom Lázaro's mother gets to know well. Zayde sometimes appears at the house at night and leaves the next morning. Other times he comes during the day, in order to buy eggs, and enters the house. At first, Lázaro is afraid of him because of his color, but as he begins to see that he eats better when Zayde visits, he comes to love him for the bread, meat, and firewood that he provides.

As this relationship continues, Lázaro's mother gives birth to a second child, the mulatto son of Zayde. Eventually, however, Zayde is caught stealing in order to provide for the family and is punished for theft and for the illicit relationship with Antona. In addition, Antona is given a hundred lashes and forbidden to go to the commander's house or to allow Zayde into her own. The mother moves with her two sons to work in an inn called La Solana. Thus, she is able to support her children. Lázaro helps out by running errands for the guests at the inn.

At this juncture, Lázaro meets the first of his masters. His mother turns the boy over to a blind beggar, assuring him that Lázaro is the son of a good man who in defense of the faith died in the battle of Los Gelves. Until now, Lázaro has been an innocent observer of those around him and dependent on his mother for basic necessities. With the blind man, his education and worldly experiences begin. The break with his home and family is symbolized by his crossing of the bridge as he leaves Salamanca. Lázaro learns his first lesson from the blind man precisely at the bridge; the blind man tricks the boy into placing his head next to the stone figure of a bull. When Lázaro draws close to the figure to hear a sound that the blind man says comes from inside it, the man knocks Lázaro's head against the stone with a painful blow. The man, laughing, tells Lázaro that a blind man's boy has to know a bit more than the devil. This cruel trick awakens the boy from his innocence; he now realizes that he is alone and must look out for himself. There follows a series of lessons, some of which the blind man teaches directly to Lázaro (for example, beggars' jargon) and others that Lázaro learns through his already keen gift of observation. He is impressed by the master's success at begging; the blind man is skilled in feigning a devout attitude when offering to say prayers in exchange for alms. Lázaro himself learns to steal a portion of the ill-gotten coins.

The most notable of Lázaro's experiences with the blind man deal with his efforts to avoid starvation by obtaining food and drink from his greedy and miserly master. He relates to Vuestra Merced only a few of the tricks that he must play on his master. In the first, he details his persistence in taking bread, bacon, and sausage from a locked sack by unstitching the seam and then sewing it back. Thus, he filches what he can, much like his father bled the sacks at the mill on the Tormes. As his tricks become more daring, the blind man's responses become more violent. Lázaro is severely injured when the blind man discovers him stealing wine; he breaks the wine jug against Lázaro's face, knocking out his teeth. To get even with his cruel master, Lázaro purposely leads him down rocky and muddy roads. He comments that although he himself does not remain dry at all, he is happy to put out one of his own eyes in order to put out two of someone who has none.

Other outstanding episodes in this chapter that show Lázaro matching wits with the blind man are those centering upon the grapes at Almorox and the sausage at Escalona. In the former, Lázaro and the blind man agree to share a bunch of overripe grapes, alternating so that each takes one grape at a time. When the blind man begins to take two and three, Lázaro says nothing; rather he simply follows suit. Shortly, the blind man accuses him of taking more than one grape at a time. Lázaro denies doing so but recognizes the astuteness of the master in deducing that he tolerated the man's cheating because he was acting dishonestly himself.

In the episode of the sausage, Lázaro substitutes a rotten turnip for a sausage being roasted on the end of a stick. After the blind man uses bread to remove the turnip from the stick, he bites into the bread and turnip at once. He accuses Lázaro of having taken the sausage and forces Lázaro's mouth open to smell the sausage on his breath. His long nose touches Lázaro's gullet, and the boy vomits the ill-gotten sausage into the blind man's face.

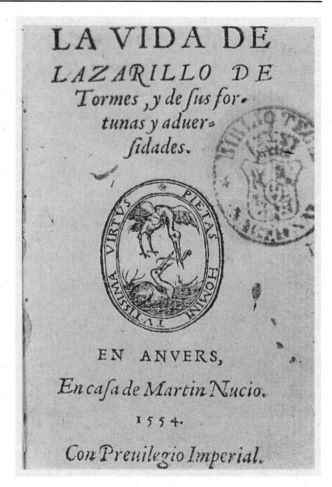

Title page for the second of four editions of La vida de Lazarillo de Tormes *published in 1554 (from Julio Neira,* Francisco de Aldana, *1990; Egbert Starr Library, Middlebury College)*

In the culminating episode of the chapter, Lázaro takes his long-awaited revenge. Seizing an opportune moment during a rainstorm, he leads the blind man to an inn for the night. To reach the inn, they must cross a water-swollen ditch at the edge of the street. Saying that he will lead his master to a place along the ditch where it will be easy for the blind man to jump across, Lázaro places him just opposite a pillar. The boy stands behind the pillar and has the man leap directly into it. Before abandoning the blind man, Lázaro taunts him: "¿Cómo, y oliste la longaniza y no el poste?" (What, you smelled the sausage and not the post?).

The second chapter relates Lázaro's experiences as the servant of a cleric. Having arrived at the town of Maqueda after leaving the blind man, Lázaro is begging in the streets when a cleric approaches and asks him if he knows how to assist at mass. Lázaro indicates that he is qualified and happily enters the service of the priest.

Although the cleric should be a charitable man, because of the nature of his religious calling, he soon begins to mistreat the unfortunate boy. Lázaro has gone from the frying pan into the fire or, as he puts it, "escapé del trueno y di en el relámpago" (I escaped the thunder to run into the lightning bolt). This plot development allows the author to express his criticism of corruption within the church and hypocrisy of the clergy.

The cleric stores bread left over from mass in a locked chest, the key to which he carefully keeps tied to his cassock. He himself eats meat regularly; yet, he shares with Lázaro only bread, some of the broth from the meat, and an onion every four days. When on Saturdays he enjoys a head of mutton, he turns the gnawed bones over to the starving boy in a great show of false generosity, declaring that Lázaro lives better than the Pope himself. After three weeks with the priest, Lázaro is so weak from hunger that he can barely stand.

Lázaro looks for opportunities to steal a coin or two, but he is unable to do so because his master is careful with the church offering and never entrusts Lázaro with errands that require money. Since the boy is able to eat his fill only at funeral feasts, he begins to pray that those to whom his master administers extreme unction will die; he curses the gravely ill whose condition improves and blesses those who do not survive. His desperation leads him to believe that death is the only way out of his miserable situation.

When a tinker appears at the door of the house, the Holy Spirit inspires Lázaro to buy a new key for the chest to "replace" one he purports to have lost. With the chest open, he sees "en figura de panes . . . la cara de Dios" (in the form of bread . . . the face of God). Lázaro has temporarily found a solution to his problem, but within three days the priest begins to keep a tally of the loaves.

Strangely, Lázaro begins to open the box just to adore the bread; he dares only to go so far as to look at it. After several days, another stratagem occurs to him. Since the chest is fraught with holes, Lázaro believes he can make the priest think that mice are nibbling away at the bread. The trick works until the priest boards up the holes. Seeing his efforts thwarted by this development, Lázaro decides that he can make the priest believe that a snake is the culprit. Taking a knife, he bores a small hole. When the priest discovers the hole and patches it, Lázaro simply makes another hole and resumes his pilfering. Neighbors convince the priest that there was at one time a snake in the house and that it must be the snake that is taking his bread. Thereafter, the alerted priest listens for the snake as he sleeps.

Meanwhile, at night, Lázaro keeps the key in his mouth for safekeeping. One night his mouth falls open, and he begins to make a whistling noise as his breath passes over the opening of the hollow key. The vigilant priest hears the noise and assumes it to be the hissing of the snake. In the darkness he beats at the source of the noise with a club and brains Lázaro. The priest then notices the key sticking out of his servant's mouth.

Three days later, Lázaro regains consciousness. He has apparently been attended by an old healer and some of the neighbors. After he recovers from his injuries, the priest leads him out of the house and tells him he is on his own, crossing himself as if it is he who needs divine protection from the likes of Lázaro.

Lázaro's first two masters have given him an opportunity to show the corruption of an unjust and hypocritical society in which things are not as they appear. The blind man, for example, pretends to be a devout beggar, but in reality he is a deceitful recipient of alms and a cruel master to his servant. He relies on the charity of others for a living but shows no real charity to Lázaro. The priest is even worse. He is a representative of God and the church at the most basic level of its ministry. Yet, as one anointed to fulfill the religious needs and satisfy the spiritual hunger of the faithful, symbolized in the bread of the Holy Eucharist, he lacks the Christian charity to alleviate Lázaro's physical hunger; he does not provide daily bread to the boy who is dependent on him for it.

Having established the theme of hunger in the first two chapters, the author continues it in the third to complete what some critics have called the trilogy of hunger within the novel. Still weak from the wounds received at the hands of the priest, Lázaro moves on to Toledo, the holiest city in Spain, and begins to beg on his own. Once he regains his strength, however, he is rebuked by the people he meets, who tell him he is nothing but a loafer and that he should look for a master to serve.

One morning, just when he has decided that charity is impossible to find in Toledo, he meets a well-dressed squire on the street who asks him if he is looking for a master. Lázaro, believing that his fortune has at long last changed, follows the gentleman and attends mass with him. Before and after mass, the gentleman passes up opportunities to buy bread and other food in the squares. Lázaro takes his new master's behavior as a sign that his pantry is well stocked and that a good meal is awaiting them once they reach his house. When they arrive there, however, it soon becomes clear that no meal is forthcoming. The gentleman claims that he ate a satisfying breakfast and that he will not need to eat again until suppertime. Lázaro, with death from starvation once again staring him in the face, feigns indifference, claiming to eat little himself.

When Lázaro takes out bread that he has tucked away in his clothing, the master admires the largest and best of the three pieces; on the pretense of sampling it, he gobbles the bread down and declares it delicious. The relationship between Lázaro and the squire is established in this first afternoon at the house. At first, each pretends to be something that he is not in order to gain benefit from the other. Lázaro has assured his new master that he requires little to eat and presents himself as a nondrinker. The pretentious squire maintains a refined facade, lecturing Lázaro on the vice of gluttony and the moderation befitting a gentleman.

Lázaro, having learned from experience to judge character, soon sees through the master's guise and finds himself feeling a curious mixture of scorn (evident in his asides) and pity for the man. This sense of pity leads him ultimately to exhibit the charity that he has looked for in others; he identifies with and becomes genuinely fond of the squire since he, like Lázaro, is penniless. Lázaro's pretending not to see what is going on enables the proud squire to preserve his social honor and dignity. Lázaro realizes that there are many petty noblemen in Spain whose social status and honor prevent them from working to earn a living and force them to keep up appearances. This circumstance, however, puts the burden on the boy, rather than on the master, to provide for them both. The silent agreement between master and servant is threatened when the town council, in reaction to a local crisis presented by a crop failure, orders that all beggars who have come from other towns leave. This order will prohibit Lázaro's continued begging and leave the squire without means. Four days after the decree, Lázaro sees a group of beggars being taken through the streets and whipped. After that, he dares to beg no more.

A pall settles over the already dark and gloomy house as days pass without any food. Neighbor women keep Lázaro alive by giving him a little of what they have. The compassion that Lázaro feels for his master is made evident when he says that he does not feel as sorry for himself as he does for the squire. He paints a poignant picture of the starving man going out into the streets, carrying himself straight and proud; although he is as skinny as a greyhound, he picks his teeth with a toothpick as if he has just eaten.

Near the end of the month, the master gives Lázaro a silver coin and directs him to go to the market to buy wine, bread, and meat. Happily making his way to the market, Lázaro meets a funeral procession with the corpse being carried down the street on a litter accompanied by clergy and other people. As the procession passes, he hears the widow crying and saying they are taking her husband to the poor, unhappy, dark, and gloomy house where no one ever eats or drinks. Since these are the terms that Lázaro and his master have used to describe their own house, the boy assumes that

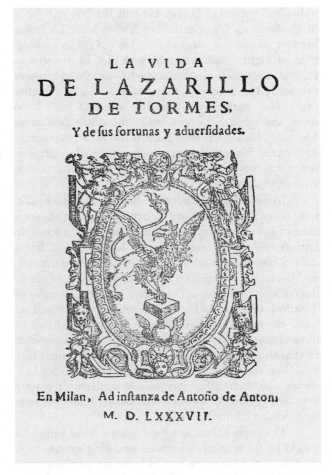

Title page for the first Italian edition of La vida de Lazarillo de Tormes *(from Salvador Aguado-Andreut,* Algunas observaciones sobre El Lazarillo de Tormes, *1965; Thomas Cooper Library, University of South Carolina)*

they are taking the dead man there. He hurriedly returns to the master's house, begs his master to help him bar the door, and relates what he heard the widow say. The master bursts into laughter. This episode is one of many borrowings from folklore that scholars have identified in the work. The author utilizes it in a way that affords comic relief to the desperate household situation. It has been suggested that this scene represents yet another example of Lázaro himself pretending—this time pretending to be afraid in order to give his master an opportunity to smile.

As the chapter approaches its conclusion, the author develops the character of the squire more fully as the gentleman tells Lázaro about his past. With this portrayal of himself, the squire reveals the nature of hierarchical Spanish society and the distortion of human values that it causes, especially as regards the individual's sense of honor. He tells the boy that he is originally from Old Castile but had to leave his home because he did not want to take his hat off to a nobleman of higher rank when he met him in the streets. Lázaro does not understand why he should resent extending this simple courtesy to a person of a higher rank. The master's reply is that it would have been more appropriate if occasionally the other gentleman had taken his hat off first. Lázaro still does not entirely understand his attitude and thinks that such a detail is not worth worrying about, especially with persons who are one's superiors.

Lázaro's lack of understanding irritates the squire, who takes the opportunity to explain how he thinks a man of his class should be treated by those inferior to him as well as by those who are his superiors. For a man of honor one's self-respect is of utmost importance, and the simplest exchange of courtesy must conform to the recognition of rank. The squire says that he came to Toledo hoping to find a good position but has had no luck. He mentions that officials of the church might have employed him but that he finds them impossibly tight with their money. Men of lesser rank would hire him, but they would expect him to be a jack-of-all-trades and then either pay him irregularly or simply give him his board and old articles of clothing as payment for his labors.

The master then imagines what a good squire he would be for a titled nobleman, knowing exactly how to make him happy. He would know how to lie to him and flatter him. He would laugh at his stories and jokes even if they were not funny. He would make it a point never to tell him anything unpleasant even if knowing it would be to his benefit. He would not make any extra effort unless his master were present to see it. He would only correct the servants when the master is around, and when the master himself scolds a servant he would appear to take the servant's side while making remarks that would serve to make the nobleman angrier. He would praise things that he knows the master likes but would also slander others. He would make a point to find out about other people's lives so he could tell his master about them. According to the squire, these sorts of things go on in palaces because the nobility is not interested in having men of good character in their homes.

While the squire is lecturing Lázaro on honor, a man and woman come to the house to collect rent, he for the house and she for the bed that she has rented to the squire. The squire courteously says that he will go to the town square to change his money and that they should come back in the afternoon. He leaves and never returns. Later, when questioned by the creditors, Lázaro tells them that he thinks his master has run off

from them as well as from him. The constable begins to question Lázaro under threat of arrest, but the neighbors convince him that Lázaro is innocent, having known his master only for a few days. As the chapter ends, Lázaro comments that things have turned upside down; normally he leaves his master, this time his master has left him.

The remaining four chapters of the novel are relatively brief. This brevity has led critics to comment upon the unbalanced structure of the novel. In the fourth chapter, which is the briefest of all, the narrator mentions his service to a friar of the Order of Mercy, called *pariente* (relative or "cousin") by the neighbor women of the preceding chapter. This master's primary characteristic is that he does not like convent life; as he dislikes chanting and eating in the monastery, he prefers to go around outside taking care of secular business and visiting. The friar runs around so much that he wears out more shoes than all the others in the monastery put together. Because of so much running around trying to keep up with him, and other things Lázaro prefers not to mention, the boy leaves this master. The fact that Lázaro chooses to give practically no details of his service to this second representative of the church invites the reader to speculate on exactly what the little unmentionable things might be and how they might point to corruption within the clergy. The juxtaposition of the terms *convento* (convent, monastery) and *trote* (trot) in the short, one-paragraph chapter suggests the Spanish *trota-conventos* (a procuress who serves monastic clients, among others) and that these things are sexual in nature.

In chapter 5 Lázaro has a new master, a pardoner or seller of indulgences, whom he serves for about four months. Again, the corruption within the institutions of the church is made evident as this pardoner is presented as the most dishonest one that Lázaro has ever seen. When the pardoner arrives in a town, he always goes first to the priest and other clergy in order to curry their favor by giving them gifts, generally of produce, that really are not worth much. With the inducement, however, they will be more inclined to support his efforts and encourage parishioners to buy the bulls of indulgence. Here, there is indirect critical commentary on the education of the clergy; Lázaro tells the reader that not all of them know Latin and neither does the pardoner. Therefore, the pardoner only pretends to speak Latin when certain that the cleric with whom he is dealing is an ignorant priest who has bought his position with the church. With the assurance that the priest does not know Latin, the pardoner begins to speak at length in a Latin of his own invention.

When the pardoner does not find ready purchasers of his indulgences, he resorts to underhanded

The Blinde Man.

Lazarillo.

Here i: *Lazarillo's* birth and life,
His wily feats and honeft wife,
With his feven mafters fhall you find,
Expreffing Spanyards in their kind

THE PLEASANT HISTORY OF

LAZARILLO de TORMES
a Spaniard, wherein is contained
his marvellous deeds and life.

With the ftrange adventures happened to him, in the fervice of fundry Mafters.

Drawne out of Spanifh by *David Rowland* of *Anglefey.*

The Third Edition, corrected and amended.

Accuerdo, Oluido.

LONDON,
Printed by *E.G.* for *William Leake*, and are
to be fold at his fhop in Chancery
Lane, neere the Rols. 1639.

Frontispiece and title page for an early English-language edition of La vida de Lazarillo de Tormes *(Newberry Library, Chicago; from Richard Bjornson,* The Picaresque Hero in European Fiction, *1977; Thomas Cooper Library, University of South Carolina)*

means of making their purchase attractive. He has an array of such means, but Lázaro chooses in this chapter to describe only one. He tells of the time in a village in the province of Toledo when the pardoner operates in collaboration with the local constable. Inside the church, the constable challenges the pardoner and the authenticity of the indulgences and is apparently struck down by divine intervention. This charade convinces the townspeople that God has performed a miracle as a sign that the indulgences are valid, and people for miles around clamor to buy the pardoner's indulgences. With this episode, the author addresses the contemporary problem of corruption within the church and among civil authorities, especially when representatives of the two groups join forces to take advantage of and deceive the people whom they are supposed to serve.

The sixth chapter is only slightly longer than the fourth. In it Lázaro summarizes his service to two masters: a tambourine painter and a chaplain. For the tambourine painter he mixes paints, and he alludes to some difficulties with the painter but gives no specifics. The chaplain gives him a job as a water seller in the city, supplying him with the necessary donkey, water jugs, and whip. Lázaro finds this employment significant as the first step toward success. He pays this master a fixed sum of the receipts on weekdays but is able to keep everything above that amount. On Saturdays he is allowed to keep all the profit. He works at this job for four years and saves enough to buy a used suit of gentleman's clothing, reminiscent of that worn by the squire. Fancying himself too good now to continue in this line of work, he returns the donkey to his master and leaves his employment.

In chapter 7 Lázaro arrives at what he deems to be the height of success. He first becomes a deputy to the constable but soon finds the job too dangerous and leaves it. Through connections of gentleman acquaintances and friends, he receives a civil-service appointment, which he says is the only kind of job that gets a man anywhere. He soon reveals, however, that this appointment is actually that of town crier and is not the lofty position that Lázaro believes (or would have the reader to believe that it is). Among his duties are announcing wines for sale in the town and assisting the hangman by calling out the crimes of the condemned person. This position is not a respected one; rather it is one scorned by the general populace. Lázaro's apparent good fortune increases when the archpriest of San Salvador, a friend of Vuestra Merced, takes an interest in him. Since Lázaro is so successful as town crier, the archpriest arranges for him to marry one of his servants. Lázaro does not regret marrying the servant, for she is good, hardworking, and helpful, and the archpriest provides help and favors to Lázaro. In fact, the benefit that he receives is not unlike that which he enjoyed through his mother's relationship with Zayde. The archpriest gives Lázaro's wife wheat regularly, meat on holidays, occasional loaves of bread, and articles of used clothing. The couple rents a house next door to the archpriest and takes meals with him on Sundays and feast days.

The archpriest's attentions are noticed by neighbors whose tongues begin to wag about Lázaro's wife's activities in the archpriest's quarters. As a consequence, the archpriest has a talk with Lázaro and tells him that no one ever gets ahead by paying attention to gossipmongers. He advises Lázaro that he should pay no mind to what they say and should focus on how he benefits from the relationship. Lázaro accepts this proposition, concluding, in words that he used in chapter 1 to describe his mother's intentions when she moved her family to Salamanca, that he has decided to remain in the company of those whom society considers "good men" and continue the arrangement without complaining or questioning his wife's virtue. Thus, the novel ends with its protagonist's considering himself to be in a position to live in peace and prosper and to remain at the "height of all good fortune."

In addition to the editions of the original *La vida de Lazarillo de Tormes*, there were also sequels, the first being the anonymous *Segunda parte de Lazarillo de Tormes*. Interpreted by critics as a social allegory, it was published in Antwerp in 1555 and reprinted in Milan in 1587 and 1615. It is a fanciful continuation of the life of the protagonist in which Lázaro joins the army, is shipwrecked, and falls into the sea. He does not drown because he is so full of wine that he cannot take in water. Amazingly, Lázaro is turned into a tuna and lives in the sea for many years, becoming an officer in the tuna army, marrying a tuna, and having three fish-children. Eventually, he is captured by Spanish fishermen, who discover that he is a man when they remove his fish skin.

In 1620, another "second part" was published in Paris by a Spaniard from Toledo, Juan de Luna. Like Miguel de Cervantes, who had written the second part of *Don Quixote* five years earlier, Luna's stated purpose is to give the lie to the previous continuation, which he says is filled with "disparates tan ridículos como mentirosos, y tan mal fundados como necios" (nonsense as ridiculous as it is untrue and as unfounded as it is foolish). Connecting his sequel to the original work as well as to events reported in the previous sequel, Luna has Lázaro leave his wife and a daughter to join an expedition against the Moors in Algiers. When he is shipwrecked off North Africa, fishermen catch him in their nets and, with the blessing of the Inquisition, reap a profit by exhibiting him throughout Spain as a monster: "un pez que tenía cara de hombre" (a fish with a man's face). Lázaro eventually arrives back in Toledo, where he finds that his wife is pregnant, and by all accounts the father of the unborn child is the archpriest, his former master. Lázaro brings a suit against his wife and the archpriest and wins the case. Within three weeks' time, however, the decision is reversed, thanks to false witnesses, and Lázaro is banned for life from Toledo. There ensue more picaresque adventures and, in the end of this sequel, Lázaro becomes a hermit.

The creator of *La vida de Lazarillo de Tormes* not only inspired others to continue the life of the title character in their own sequels but also provided the basic model for a myriad of creators of new *pícaros* and female *pícaras*. The picaresque genre found fertile ground in the hands of Spanish writers, who had their works printed in Spain as well as in other countries. Among the notable works by Spanish authors are *Guzmán de Alfarache; La pícara Justina* (1605, The *pícara* Justina), by Francisco López de Úbeda; *La hija de Celestina* (1612, Celestina's Daughter), by Alonso Jerónimo de Salas Barbadillo; *Marcos de Obregón* (1618), by Vicente Espinel; *Lazarillo de Manzanares* (1620), by Juan Cortés de Tolosa; *Vida del buscón, llamado don Pablos* (1626, Life of the Swindler Called Don Pablos), by Francisco Quevedo; *El diablo cojuelo* (1641, The Limping Devil), by Luis Vélez de Guevara y Dueñas; *Vida y hechos de Estebanillo González* (1646, Life and Deeds of Estebanillo González), by Estebanillo González; and *Vida de Torres Villarroel* (1742, Life of Torres Villarroel, 1742), by Diego de Torres Villarroel.

The first translations of *La vida de Lazarillo de Tormes* appeared in various European languages in the sixteenth and seventeenth centuries. While the genre developed in Spain and became more widely known, writers of other nationalities were producing notable picaresque works of their own. In England, Thomas Nashe wrote his *The Unfortunate Traveller; or, The Life of Jack Wilton* (1594) and Daniel Defoe wrote *The Fortunes* and *Misfortunes of the Famous Moll Flanders* (1721). In France, Alain-René Lesage wrote *Histoire de Gil Blas de Santillane* (1715–1735, History of Gil Blas of Santillane). The Russian novel *Mertvye dushi* (1842, Dead Souls) by Nikolai Gogol is in the picaresque vein. Strong picaresque elements are found in works produced in the Americas, notably the Mexican *El Periquillo Sarniento* (1816, The Itching Parakeet) by José Joaquín Fernández de Lizardi and *The Adventures of Huckleberry Finn* (1884) by Mark Twain.

Interest in a picaresque format and style continues in a variety of novels. Even if *La vida de Lazarillo de Tormes* had inspired no sequels, imitations, or translations, it would stand on its own as one of the major works of Spanish literature for its unforgettable characters (not the least of which is Lázaro himself); the humor, wit, and irony that pervades the author's language; and the sordid picture of Spanish society that it offers. The work is filled with characters who get by as best they know how but never grasp the circumstances of their own reality in a way that leads them to true prosperity and good fortune.

References:

Salvador Aguado-Andreut, *Algunas observaciones sobre* El Lazarillo de Tormes (Guatemala: Editorial Universitaria, Universidad de San Carlos de Guatemala, 1965);

Juan Luis Alborg, *Edad media y renacimiento,* volume 1 of *Historia de la literatura española,* second edition (Madrid: Gredos, 1970), pp. 746–796;

José Luis Álvarez Martínez, "La Biblioteca de Barcarrota: Fortuna del Lazarillo de Tormes," *Gazetilla de la U.B.Ex.,* no. 14 (1996) <http://www.unex.es/ubex/n14/pag7.htm>;

Marcel Bataillon, *Novedad y fecundidad del Lazarillo de Tormes* (Salamanca: Anaya, 1968);

Richard Bjornson, *The Picaresque Hero in European Fiction* (Madison: University of Wisconsin Press, 1977);

David H. Darst, *Diego Hurtado de Mendoza* (Boston: Twayne, 1987), pp. 95–99;

Robert L. Fiore, *Lazarillo de Tormes* (Boston: Twayne, 1984);

Víctor García de la Concha, *Nueva lectura del Lazarillo: El deleite de la perspectiva* (Madrid: Castalia, 1981);

R. O. Jones, *A Literary History of Spain: The Golden Age: Prose and Poetry: The Sixteenth and Seventeenth Centuries* (London: Benn / New York: Barnes & Noble, 1971), pp. 66–72;

Fernando Lázaro Carreter, *Lazarillo de Tormes en la picaresca* (Barcelona: Ariel, 1972);

Julio Neira, *Francisco de Aldana* (Merida, Spain: Editora Regional de Extremadura, 1990);

Alexander A. Parker, *Literature and the Delinquent: The Picaresque Novel in Spain and Europe, 1599–1753* (Edinburgh: Edinburgh University Press, 1967), pp. 1–52;

Francisco Rico, *La novela picaresca y el punto de vista,* second edition (Barcelona: Seix Barral, 1973), pp. 13–55;

Rico, *Problemas del Lazarillo* (Madrid: Cátedra, 1988);

Aldo Ruffinato, *Las dos caras del Lazarillo: Texto y mensaje* (Madrid: Castalia, 2001);

Harry Sieber, *Language and Society in La vida de Lazarillo de Tormes* (Baltimore: Johns Hopkins University Press, 1978);

Stanislav Zimic, *Apuntes sobre la estructura paródica y satírica del Lazarillo de Tormes* (Madrid: Iberoamericana, 2000).

Women Writers in Sixteenth-Century Spain

Lisa Vollendorf
Wayne State University

BOOKS: Beatriz Bernal, *Don Cristalián de España* (Alcalá de Henares: Juan Iñiguez de Lequerica, 1545);

Oliva Sabuco, *Nueva Filosofía de la Naturaleza del Hombre, no conocida ni alcanzada por los grandes Filósofos antiguos, la cual mejora la Vida y la Salud humana* (Madrid: P. Madrigal, 1587);

Valentina Pinelo, *Libro de las alabanças y excelencias de la Gloriosa Santa Anna* (Seville: Clemente Hidalgo, 1601);

María de San José, *Instrucción de novicias. Jesús María. Diálogo entre dos religiosas que Gracia y Justa se llaman sobre la oración y mortificación con que se deben criar las novicias* (N.p., 1602);

Isabel de Liaño, *Historia de la vida, muerte, y milagros de Santa Catalina de Siena, dividida e tres libros* (Valladolid: Luis Sánchez, 1604);

Luis Muñoz, *Vida de virtudes de la venerable virgin Doña Luisa Carvajal y Mendoza* (Madrid: Imprenta Real, 1632)—includes poems by Carvajal y Mendoza;

Ana de San Bartolomé, *Autobiografía y la narración de algunos milagros,* edited by Padre Elias von St. Teresa (Antwerp, 1632).

Modern Editions: Luisa de Carvajal y Mendoza, *Epistolario y poesías,* edited by Camilo María Abad and Jesús González Marañon (Madrid: Atlas, 1965);

Carvajal y Mendoza, *Escritos autobiográficos,* edited by Abad (Barcelona: Flors, 1966);

María de San José, *Instrucción de novicias. Jesús María. Diálogo entre dos religiosas que Gracia y Justa se llaman sobre la oración y mortificación con que se deben criar las novicias,* in *Escritos espirituales,* edited by Simeón de la Sagrada Familia, second edition (Rome: Postulación General, 1973);

Beatriz Bernal, "Don Cristalián de España. Edicion modernizada con introduccion crítica," edited by Sidney Stuart Park, dissertation, Temple University, 1981;

Ana de San Bartolomé, *Obras completas de la beata Ana de San Bartolomé,* 2 volumes, edited by Julián Urkiza (Rome: Teresanium, 1981, 1985);

Poesías completas, edited by María Luisa García-Nieto Onrubia (Badajoz: Diputación Provincial de Badajoz, 1990).

Editions in English: Luisa de Carvajal y Mendoza, *This Tight Embrace,* edited and translated by Elizabeth Rhodes (Milwaukee: Marquette University Press, 2000);

Carvajal y Mendoza, *The Writings of Doña Luisa de Carvajal y Mendoza, Catholic Missionary to James I's London,* edited and translated by Margaret A. Rees (Lewiston, N.Y.: Edwin Mellen Press, 2002).

Until the late twentieth century, scholars had not studied sixteenth-century women's writing in depth. In fact, many believed that few women wrote during this important period in Spanish history. Other than St. Teresa of Ávila, who was known widely, only a handful of women writers were known at all. As research on other European countries uncovered dozens of women's texts in the last two decades of the twentieth century, Spain still remained in the background. Spain was considered a frustrating, if not impossible, object of study for those seeking to recover Renaissance women's literary history. Viewed by non-Hispanists as a latecomer to the Renaissance and to women's incorporation into the public sphere, Spain was thought to have produced little writing by women before the 1800s. Even after Manuel Serrano y Sanz provided an indispensable reference tool that catalogues dozens of women writers' works—*Apuntes para una biblioteca de escritoras españolas desde el año 1401 al 1833* (1903, Notes for a Library of Spanish Women Writers from 1401 to 1833)—scholars simply had little information about and, often, little interest in women's writing.

At the end of the twentieth century, researchers of women's history turned to Spain's Renaissance and Baroque periods with renewed interest. The Baroque proved easier to investigate, as seventeenth-century Spain experienced what is now recognized as a flurry of women's literary activity. Among the texts still in existence, there is a plethora of documentation of women's lives and creative production from the Spanish

Painting by Víctor Villán de Ara of the death of St. Teresa of Ávila in 1582. Ana de San Bartolomé, whose 1632
Autobiografía y la narración de algunos milagros (Autobiography and a Narrative of Some Miracles)
recounts the early days of the Discalced Carmelite order, is at her side (courtesy of the Editorial de la
Espiritualidad; from Electa Arenal and Stacey Schlau, eds., Untold Sisters: Hispanic Nuns
in Their Own Works, *1989; Thomas Cooper Library, University of South Carolina).*

Baroque. Between 1600 and 1700, María de Zayas y Sotomayor and Mariana de Carvajal wrote prose fiction; Angela de Azevedo, Ana Caro, Leonor Cueva de Silva, and Feliciana Enríquez de Guzmán produced several dramas; and dozens more cultivated poetry and nonfiction both inside and outside of the convent.

The sociocultural factors that led to the notable increase in women's literary activity in the 1600s are important for understanding the contrast between the sixteenth and seventeenth centuries. By the 1600s, social and religious changes had contributed to an increase—albeit slight—in female literacy. The boom in convent foundations that resulted from the Council of Trent (1545–1563) and the ensuing reforms in the Catholic Church provided more women on the Iberian Peninsula with educational opportunities than ever before. Moreover, St. Teresa's

dogged dedication to writing had paved the way for legitimizing women's participation as writers.

Research on the existence of women who preceded or were contemporaries of St. Teresa began to intensify during the 1980s and 1990s, when continuing developments in feminist studies encouraged scholars to look again to the archives. The search for texts and biographical information was complicated by the political and social forces that had led to the destruction or loss of records, particularly those found in convents and other religious houses. In spite of these limitations, twenty-first-century scholars have at their disposal dozens of texts from Spanish women who lived during the period of intense nation building and imperialism that characterized Spain between 1500 and 1700. Many women are now known to have written during that

*Title page for Valentina Pinelo's 1601 work (A Book in Praise
of the Excellent Qualities of the Glorious St. Anne), in which
she advocates that all children be raised in the religious
environment of a convent (William T. Young Library,
University of Kentucky)*

time. The pool of writers is somewhat limited, as
women had access to education only if they were aristocrats or if they lived in convents. One group remains to
be studied more in depth: research has suggested that
families of Jewish descent educated their daughters
secretly as a way to pass on traditions in spite of religious persecution. Future research certainly will involve
amassing a body of texts to allow for more systematic
study of the written culture of *conversos,* those who converted from Judaism or who were descendants of such
converts. One of the best resources for women's writing
is the *Autoras españolas* (Spanish Women Writers) microfiche collection of women's writing housed at the Biblioteca nacional in Madrid. This microfiche collection
includes a wealth of evidence of women's literary activity during Spain's Renaissance and Baroque periods.
Now available at many North American university
libraries, the collection has aided greatly in filling in the
gaps of women's literary history for this important time

in Spanish history. Moreover, modern editions and
studies of women's writing have been published, helping to increase critical knowledge of a past that used to
be unknown.

Given women's limited access to education in the
Renaissance, their textual history is weighted heavily
toward texts produced in convents. It also weighs
heavily toward the upper classes and those of purportedly Old Christian ancestry. During the sixteenth century, purity-of-blood statutes were passed in Spain.
Aimed at rooting out those who had converted from
Judaism to Christianity during the Inquisition's first
wave of persecution, the statutes relegated to a secondary status people who could not prove their Old Christian lineage. Many religious orders required that
novices provide documentation of such lineage upon
entry into the convent. Indeed, St. Teresa's innovative
reform to the contrary—by which she refused to implement similar requirements for her order, the Discalced
Carmelites—flew in the face of this common discrimina-
tory practice. The unpopularity of St. Teresa's liberal
move is reflected in the policy change of 1597, when the
Discalced Carmelites adopted a statute that would have
prevented Teresa from joining her own order because
she was born a *conversa.*

The sociocultural landscape of sixteenth-century
Spain thus limited participation in institutionalized religion and political life to those of purportedly pure background. These limitations had significant repercussions
for women, who were excluded from the rights and
opportunities afforded upper-class men and clergy in
the period. Unless women joined convents or married,
little to no documentation about their lives exists. Aside
from what women authors recorded in their texts,
scholars have little firsthand information about women
in the period. Historians do not know even the most
basic information about women's literacy, for example,
although it is assumed that, like their male contemporaries, most women only heard texts read to them. For
the most part, women's life experiences remain outside
the written record. While St. Teresa's life has been
studied exhaustively, most other women remain relatively obscure. Their texts—and others such as letters,
legal documents, Inquisition cases, and biographies—
allow scholars to piece together a picture of women's
lives in the period.

A poetic biography of St. Catherine of Siena written by Isabel de Liaño provides textual evidence of
women's intellectual history. Liaño was born in Pala-
cios de Campos sometime in the second half of the sixteenth century. She does not seem to have come from
aristocratic stock. In *Historia de la vida, muerte, y milagros
de Santa Catalina de Siena, dividida e tres libros* (1604, The
History of the Life, Death, and Miracles of St. Cathe-

rine of Siena, Divided into Three Books), Liaño states that she has written for women only. Modern readers have inferred from her remarks the existence of women readers in the sixteenth century, as well as the fact that Liaño felt the need to address her position as a woman writer. Her anxiety toward her position as a writer presents itself in the tone of humility she uses to introduce herself. She refers to herself as a simple woman and attributes her literary abilities to God. Like many women writers throughout the centuries, Liaño's rhetoric is informed by humility in order to justify her text. She also undermines the inferiority that she imputes to women in the prologue by dedicating the book to Queen Margaret of Austria and by identifying women as her intended audience. In spite of many claims to the contrary, Liaño shows through her writing that she believed in women's intellectual abilities. Moreover, the complex poetic text she produced reveals that Liaño received a rigorous education that emphasized knowledge of classical literature. Liaño was unusual on two counts: she was a woman writer who neither lived in a convent nor belonged to the aristocratic class.

Another unusual figure emerged on the sixteenth-century literary scene when Beatriz Bernal published a chivalric novel, *Don Cristalián de España* (1545, Don Cristalián of Spain). Little is known about Bernal's life aside from the fact that she was born in Valladolid and that she lived in that city during the first half of the sixteenth century. She married Torres de Gatos and was survived by a daughter, Juana. In part because of the reprinting of *Don Cristalián de España* in 1587, some information about Bernal's artistic production remains. This edition includes a statement from King Philip II granting the widowed Juana Bernal de Gatos permission to reprint her mother's novel.

Bernal's unusual status as a writer of chivalric fiction deserves explanation. Novels of chivalry were extraordinarily popular during the period. Filled with adventures, romance, and elaborate plot structures, they were generally products of male authors' imaginations. Bernal is regarded as the first known woman writer of chivalric novels.

Don Cristalián de España does not appear to have been among the most popular chivalric novels of the day and was only printed on two occasions, unlike other works, which underwent many printings. Moreover, the second printing of *Don Cristalián de España* has been attributed to Bernal's widowed daughter's need for income and not to a public outcry for more copies of the book. *Don Cristalián de España* tells the story of the adventures of Cristalián and his brother, Lucescanio. It is a typical chivalric novel in many respects: it includes intricate plotlines and dozens of intertwined secondary stories, and it relies on magic and coincidence at every

turn. Some subtle differences in Bernal's text seem to distinguish it from male-authored novels of the same genre, however. Noting that Bernal included more than seventy female characters and that many of those characters experience problems common to women of their day, Judith Whitenack, in her essay "'Emphasis Added': An Introduction to Beatriz Bernal's *Don Cristalián de España*" (1997), suggests that Bernal injected a specifically female perspective into an otherwise entirely masculine genre.

Liaño and Bernal are exceptional examples of nonreligious women writers. In most cases, the extant texts from the period can be traced to convent production. In comparison to society at large, convent culture treated women's opinions, needs, and wishes as valid. Women usually were excluded from roles of power in the public sphere. One prominent example of this delegitimization occurred in the case of the Italian artist Sofinisba Anguissola. Anguissola gained sufficient fame as to be appointed court painter to Philip II of Spain. Yet, since her death her work often has been attributed to her famed contemporary, Alonso Sánchez Coello. The failure to acknowledge Anguissola's accomplishments exemplifies the degradation that traditionally has constituted one of the major stumbling blocks to women's incorporation into the public sphere.

In the early-modern period, the one place that provided women with opportunities for authority and legitimacy was the convent. Convents provided a nurturing environment for women throughout the early-modern period. Specifically, they offered the opportunity for education and for women to occupy positions of leadership and power. While convents were controlled by male clerics, the women were charged with the daily running of female religious houses. Across many orders, abbesses and other nuns dealt with convent finances, daily schedules, and interpersonal disputes. Women were often responsible for making decisions about such matters, thus leaving the oversight of the general spiritual welfare of the community to the confessors who worked therein.

While living in a convent, Valentina Pinelo, a nun in the convent of San Leandro in Seville, wrote *Libro de las alabanzas de las excelencias de la Gloriosa Santa Anna* (1601, A Book in Praise of the Excellent Qualities of Our Glorious St. Anne). While little is known of the author's life—her birth and death dates are unknown—in the prologue to *Libro de las alabanzas de las excelencias de la Gloriosa Santa Anna,* Pinelo mentions that she had lived in the convent almost since birth. This experience apparently impacted the author greatly, as she recommends in her book that parents should place their children in convents to be raised properly by religious women. Pinelo's deep commitment to convent life can be gleaned from her writing, as it is one of the major themes to emerge in her book on St. Anne.

As suggested by Bernal, Liaño, and Pinelo, women met the challenge of positioning themselves as legitimate artists, reformers, and leaders both inside and outside of convent walls. Given the contrast between the limited roles available to women in the public sphere and the legitimacy given to women in convents, it is not surprising to find religious women writers whose texts pay homage to other female religious figures.

María de San José provides an excellent example of the ways in which nuns positioned themselves as reformers and leaders in convents. Born María Salazar in Ciudad Imperial, as a child she lived in the palace of noblewoman Doña Luisa de la Cerda. During that time she had the opportunity to meet Teresa de Jesús, known to posterity as St. Teresa. Teresa de Jesús stayed with Luisa de la Cerda after the latter lost her husband. During that stay Teresa and Salazar spoke of the benefits of a religious life, which eventually led to Salazar's joining the Discalced Carmelite convent in Malagón on 9 May 1570, whereupon she changed her name to María de San José. A year later she took her final vows, and several years later was chosen to be the abbess of a new convent in Seville. During the next two decades María devoted herself to the religious order of St. Teresa. As a result of accusations brought before the Inquisition by a group of nuns and clerics, she was removed from office and imprisoned for more than six months in 1578. Later cleared of these charges and reinstated as mother superior, she was sent to Lisbon and elected prioress once again. Before the end of her life, María again was subjected to similar punishment as that suffered by other reformers, including St. Teresa, and she was placed under house arrest and in solitary confinement for one year in the Lisbon convent. The strife of the Carmelites owed much to the tension between the Calced and the Discalced orders. Through it all, María supported the reforms of Teresa de Jesús and remained true to the order until the end of her life in 1603.

María de San José's devotion to the order can be traced in the many texts she wrote during her tenure as a nun. Among her writings are dramatic dialogues, poetry, and a work titled *Carta que escribe una pobre y presa Descalza* (1593, Letter Written by a Poor and Imprisoned Discalced Nun). The themes of advice and tutelage run throughout her work. One particularly innovative text, *Instrucción de novicias. Jesús María. Diálogo entre dos religiosas que Gracia y Justa se llaman sobre la oración y mortificación con que se deben criar las novicias* (1602, Instruction of Novices. Jesus and Mary. Dialogue between Two Religious Women Named Gracia and

Justa about the Prayer and Mortification That Novices Should Be Taught), is structured around a series of dramatic dialogues among a group of nuns. In this work María portrays nuns instructing novices on the importance of prayer, self-control, and self-mortification (that is, physical punishment) within the Carmelite order. By highlighting the differences among the female characters and the intensity of their religious dedication, the text emphasizes that good intentions and true devotion are necessary to succeed as a Carmelite.

Like St. Teresa, María upheld a rigorous view of convent life in which individuals should sacrifice themselves fully to God and to the order. As suggested by the difficulties that led to her incarceration, she followed her own advice and remained devoted to the principles that guided her strict views toward Carmelite spirituality. At the request of the order, she traveled to Portugal to be abbess of the first Discalced convent there in 1584. While the period between 1584 and 1600 was relatively peaceful and resulted in many literary labors, in 1603 Madre María suffered the consequences of yet another changeover in leadership. At this point the nun was imprisoned once again, this time in an isolated house in Spain. She died shortly thereafter, in 1603.

Given the importance of St. Teresa in Catholic Europe of the time, it is not a coincidence that yet another important writer and reformer belonged to the Discalced Carmelites. Born in El Almendral in Castile in 1549, Ana de San Bartolomé learned basic reading skills as a child. In spite of her family's opposition to her leading a religious life, she entered the Discalced convent of San José of Ávila in 1570. San Bartolomé acted as secretary and, later, caretaker to Teresa de Jesús from 1577 to the end of Teresa's life. Extant writings include autobiographical texts, poetry, letters, and documents related to Carmelite reform.

Because of San Bartolomé's proximity to St. Teresa, the former's writings shed significant light on the turmoil that faced the Carmelite order. They also reveal the extraordinary importance of St. Teresa in the personal and spiritual lives of religious women in the sixteenth and seventeenth centuries in Spain. One of the most interesting aspects of San Bartolomé's writings lies in her reliance on St. Teresa as a guide, mentor, and authority figure who, at times, usurps the authority of the confessor in the nun's texts. Rather than demure to her confessor's mandates that she reveal all the details of her interior life, San Bartolomé mentions St. Teresa's dictate that the interior life should remain private.

Unlike most religious women writing in this time of fear of persecution by the Inquisition, San Bartolomé does not express great anxiety with regard to the possible heterodoxy of her spiritual experiences. Instead, she

Frontispiece and first page of Isabel de Liaño's Historia de la vida, muerte, y milagros de Santa Catalina
de Siena *(1604, History of the Life, Death, and Miracles of St. Catherine of Siena; Memorial Library,*
University of Wisconsin–Madison)

merely states on various occasions that St. Teresa had told her that the devil played no role in the experiences described. These examples point to a pattern in this work and those by other nuns: St. Teresa served as a role model and a source of authority for many women of her time and for many who lived after her. San Bartolomé's texts evoke an important aspect of Spanish and Latin American women's history. Hispanic women's literary history, and particularly the history of female religious figures, often must be understood in light of St. Teresa's enormous impact as reformer, writer, and authority figure. Indeed, with the exception of Queen Isabella of Castile in the fifteenth century, St. Teresa provided the most public and most persuasive example of a woman who occupied a position of authority in the public sphere. St. Teresa died in San Bartolomé's company in 1582. After working to extend the Discalced order in France and becoming adviser to such high-ranking individuals as the Princess Isabel Clara Eugenia, San Bartolomé died in 1626, at the age of seventy-seven.

Isabel Clara Eugenia and the Spanish nobility are connected to another important author of the period: Luisa de Carvajal y Mendoza. Born in Jaraicejo in 1566, Carvajal y Mendoza was a member of the famed Mendoza family. She lost her parents at a young age. Consequently, she spent the early years of her childhood at court in the care of her aunt, who also happened to be Isabel Clara Eugenia's governess. Upon her aunt's death, the young Carvajal y Mendoza was sent to live with her uncle, the diplomat Francisco de Hurtado y Mendoza in Pamplona in 1576. She later wrote of the harsh treatment she received at the hands of her governess, Isabel de Ayllon, and under her uncle's tutelage. She also wrote of Hurtado's interest in cultivating extremely harsh piety in his young niece. Through these two adult figures, a practice of severe self-mortification was encouraged in Carvajal y Mendoza during her formative years.

The austere environment in which Carvajal y Mendoza came of age laid the groundwork for her commitment to extreme piety as an adult. She followed an unusual route toward spiritual fulfillment. Rather than marry or join a convent, she wrote her own vows of poverty, obedience, chastity, and greater perfection. After devoting herself to helping the poor in Spain, she turned to missionary work abroad, seeking to fulfill a martyr's role in the complicated religious landscape of early-modern Europe. In 1605 she traveled to England, which was under the rule of King James I and extremely hostile toward Catholics and Catholic evangelism. Carvajal y Mendoza courted danger by spreading the word of Catholicism. She was arrested in England, where her presence created diplomatic problems for the Spanish as well. Eventually the Spanish Council of State ordered her departure from England in 1614, but she died shortly thereafter. Her remains were returned to Spain in 1615 and were sent by order of King Philip III to Madrid's Monasterio de la Encarnación. In spite of the desire of many to see Carvajal y Mendoza beatified, the church rejected her canonization hearings because she did not die a martyr's death. Carvajal wrote of her spiritual calling and her intense religiosity in beautifully rendered autobiographical writings and poetry. She has been called one of the best female poets of Spain's Golden Age.

While Spanish women are well represented among religious writers, one realm in which women are underrepresented in European history in general is that of science and philosophy. One of the few examples of a Renaissance female philosopher oriented toward science and medicine comes from Spain. Oliva Sabuco was the fifth of seven siblings. She was born in Alcaraz, Spain, in 1567 to a scientific family that included two druggists and a physician among its ranks. No record of Sabuco's education remains, but it seems clear that as a young woman she received rigorous training. In 1580 she married Acacio de Buedo. Years later she seems to have had a dispute with her father, possibly over his remarriage after her mother's death. Sabuco was thought to have died in 1522, but archival research has found a reference to her in 1529. A precise date of her death has yet to be determined.

Debate continues as to whether Sabuco actually wrote the text for which she has been known for several centuries. Her *Nueva Filosofía de la Naturaleza del Hombre, no conocida ni alcanzada por los grandes Filósofos antiguos, la cual mejora la Vida y la Salud humana* (1587, New Philosophy of Human Nature Not Known and Not Reached by the Ancient Philosophers That Improves Human Life and Health) provides an overview of human nature that emphasizes a holistic approach to health. The text urges that scientists take the view that people should be treated as complex beings whose emotional and physical health always are intertwined and interdependent. The seven-part treatise addresses such issues as self-knowledge, the art of true medicine, and philosophy of the nature of mankind. In 1903 the scholar José Marco e Hidalgo challenged Sabuco's claim to authorship of the work, publishing an article in which he attributed the text to her father, Miguel de Sabuco y Alvarez. Subsequent translators of the text into English have argued that textual evidence affirms Oliva Sabuco's role as principal author of the medical treatise. Regardless of whether the text was written by Sabuco herself, by her father, or as a collaborative endeavor between father and daughter, Sabuco received an education that seems to have included training in science and legal matters in a time when such training was anomalous for most citizens, let alone for women.

The debate that continues over the authorship of *Nueva Filosofía de la Naturaleza del Hombre* speaks to the increasing interest in women's literary history. Women's history can only be recovered and reinterpreted if researchers have sufficient documentation. Through the rigorous archival research such as that being done by specialists on Sabuco and others, scholars are learning more and more about Spanish women's past. While women previously were believed to have not participated at all in the foundations of Spanish literature, scholars now understand the necessity of looking to a wider range of sources and in a wider range of archives in order to find texts written by and about women. Religious documents, legal records, Inquisition trials, and self-consciously literary texts all provide insight into the lives and imaginations of women in sixteenth-century Spain. As researchers learn more about the lives of women and minorities, they continue to reexamine the traditional interpretations of Spanish culture, politics, and religion during the rise and fall of the Spanish Habsburg Empire. Since Spanish imperialism touched dozens of other cultures and countries during the sixteenth century, such analyses should disentangle and clarify the policies of colonialism that deeply affected the formation of modern-day Latin America. Research on women and other minorities will continue to help scholars understand the relationship of individuals to the state during the important time of national solidification and expansion that was the Spanish Renaissance. Such research also will shed light on the ways in which gender, race, class, and ethnicity have affected personal, group, and national identity throughout Western history.

References:

Electa Arenal and Stacey Schlau, eds., *Untold Sisters: Hispanic Nuns in Their Own Works,* translated by Amanda Powell (Albuquerque: University of New Mexico Press, 1989);

Anne J. Cruz, "Chains of Desire: Luisa de Carvajal y Mendoza's Poetics of Penance," in *Estudios sobre escritoras hispánicas en honor de Georgina Sabat de Rivers,* edited by Lou Charnon-Deutsch (Madrid: Castalia, 1992), pp. 97–112;

Cruz, "Gender and Class as Challenges for Feminist Biographies in Early Modern Spain," *Laberinto,* 3 (2000–2001) <http://www.gc.maricopa.edu/laberinto/2002/cruz.htm>;

Cruz, "Willing Desire: Luisa de Carvajal y Mendoza and Feminine Subjectivity," in *Power and Gender in Renaissance Spain: Eight Women of the Mendoza Family, 1450–1650,* edited by Helen Nader (Urbana: University of Illinois Press, 2004), pp. 177–194;

Renée Levine Melammed, *Heretics or Daughters of Israel? The Crypto-Jewish Women of Castile* (New York: Oxford University Press, 1999);

Julián Olivares and Elizabeth Boyce, eds., *Tras el espejo la musa escribe: Lírica femenina de los Siglos de Oro* (Madrid: Siglo Veintiuno, 1993);

Elizabeth Rhodes, "Luisa de Carvajal's Counter-Reformation Journey to Selfhood (1566–1614)," *Renaissance Quarterly,* 51, no. 3 (1998): 887–911;

Manuel Serrano y Sanz, *Apuntes para una biblioteca de escritoras españolas desde el año 1401 al 1833* (Madrid: Rivadeneyra, 1903);

María Vintro and Mary Ellen Waithe, *Oliva Sabuco Research and Translation Project* <http://www.sabuco.org/iresearch.html> [accessed 21 July 2005];

Lisa Vollendorf, *The Lives of Women: A New History of Inquisitional Spain* (Nashville: Vanderbilt University Press, 2005);

Alison Weber, "The Partial Feminism of Ana de San Bartolomé," in *Recovering Spain's Feminist Tradition,* edited by Vollendorf (New York: Modern Language Association of America, 2001), pp. 69–87;

Judith Whitenack, "'Emphasis Added': An Introduction to Beatriz Bernal's *Don Cristalián de España,*" *Monographic Review / Revista monográfica,* 13 (1997): 24–38.

Papers:

Collections of Luisa de Carvajal y Mendoza's manuscripts are held in the Convento de la Encarnación in Madrid.

Books for Further Reading

Abbott, Don Paul. *Rhetoric in the New World: Rhetorical Theory and Practice in Colonial Spanish America.* Columbia: University of South Carolina Press, 1996.

Abellán, José Luis. *Historia crítica del pensamiento, II: La edad de oro (siglo XVI).* Madrid: Espasa-Calpe, 1979.

Alsonso, Alvaro. *La poesía italianista.* Madrid: Laberinto, 2002.

Anderson Imbert, Enrique. *Historia de la literatura hispanoamericana,* sixth edition. Mexico City: Fondo de Cultura Hispanoamericana, 1974.

Arciniegas, Germán, ed. *Historiadores de Indias.* Mexico City: Conaculta-Océano, 1999.

Asensio, Eugenio. *Itinerario del entremés: Desde Lope de Rueda a Quiñones de Benavente.* Madrid: Gredos, 1965.

Avalle-Arce, Juan Bautista. *Dintorno de una época dorada.* Madrid: Porrúa, 1978.

Bataillon, Marcel. *Erasmo y España: Estudios sobre la historia espiritual del siglo XVI,* 2 volumes, translated by Antonio Alatorre. Mexico City: Fondo de Cultura Económica, 1950.

Blackmore, Josiah, and Gregory S. Hutcheson, eds. *Queer Iberia: Sexualities, Cultures, and Crossings from the Middle Ages to the Renaissance.* Durham, N.C. & London: Duke University Press, 1999.

Blecua, José Manuel, ed. *Poesía de la Edad de Oro I: Renacimiento,* third edition. Madrid: Castalia, 1984.

Brotherton, John. *The "Pastor-Bobo" in the Spanish Theatre before the Time of Lope de Vega,* Colección Támesis: serie A, monografías, no. 51. London: Tamesis, 1975.

Brown, Jonathan. *Painting in Spain: 1500–1700.* New Haven: Yale University Press, 1998.

Brownlee, Marina S., and Hans Ulrich Gumbrecht, eds. *Cultural Authority in Golden Age Spain.* Baltimore: Johns Hopkins University Press, 1995.

Cammarata, Joan F., ed. *Women in the Discourse of Early Modern Spain.* Gainesville: University Press of Florida, 2003.

Cascardi, Anthony J. *Ideologies of History in the Spanish Golden Age.* University Park: Pennsylvania State University Press, 1997.

Castro, Américo. *Aspectos del vivir hispánico: Espiritualismo, mesianismo, actitud personal en siglos XIV al XVI.* Santiago, Chile: Cruz del Sur, 1949.

Castro. *De la edad conflictiva.* Madrid: Taurus, 1961.

Castro. *Hacia Cervantes.* Madrid: Taurus, 1957.

Cohen, Walter. *Drama of a Nation: Public Theater in Renaissance England and Spain.* Ithaca, N.Y.: Cornell University Press, 1985.

Cortijo Ocaña, Antonio. *La evolución genérica de la ficción sentimental de los siglos XV y XVI: género literario y contexto social,* Colección Támesis: serie A, monografías, no. 184. London: Tamesis, 2001.

Crawford, J. P. Wickersham. *Spanish Drama before Lope de Vega,* second edition. Philadelphia: University of Pennsylvania Press, 1937; revised, 1967.

Damiani, Bruno M., and Ruth El Saffar. *Studies in Honor of Elias Rivers.* Potomac, Md.: Scripta Humanistica, 1989.

Domínguez Ortiz, Antonio. *Los judeoconversos en España y América*. Madrid: Istmo, 1971.

Dunn, Peter N. *Spanish Picaresque Fiction: A New Literary History*. Ithaca, N.Y.: Cornell University Press, 1993.

Elliot, John Huxtable. *Imperial Spain, 1469–1716*. London: Arnold, 1963.

Fernández Alvarez, Manuel. *La sociedad española del Renacimiento*. Salamanca: Anaya, 1970.

Fernández Alvarez. *La sociedad española en el Siglo de Oro*. Madrid: Gredos, 1989.

Fernández-Santamaría, J. A. *The State, War and Peace: Spanish Political Thought in the Renaissance, 1516–1559*. Cambridge & New York: Cambridge University Press, 1977.

Francis, Alan. *Picaresca, decadencia, historia: Aproximación a una realidad histórico-literaria*. Madrid: Gredos, 1978.

Fucilla, Joseph G. *Estudios sobre el petrarquismo en España*. Madrid: Consejo Superior de Investigaciones Científicas, 1960.

García Tapia, Nicolás. *Ingeniería y arquitectura en el Renacimiento español*. Valladolid: Secretariado de Publicaciones, Universidad de Valladolid, 1990.

Garin, Eugenio. *La revolución cultural del Renacimiento*, translated by Domènec Bergada. Barcelona: Crítica, 1981.

Gombrich, Ernst H. *Symbolic Images: Studies in the Art of the Renaissance*. London: Phaidon, 1972.

Green, Otis H. *The Literary Mind of Medieval and Renaissance Spain*, introduction by John E. Keller. Lexington: University Press of Kentucky, 1970.

Green. *Spain and the Western Tradition: The Castilian Mind in Literature from El Cid to Calderón*, 4 volumes. Madison: University of Wisconsin Press, 1963–1966.

Guijarro Ceballos, Javier, ed. *Humanismo y literatura en tiempos de Juan del Encina*. Salamanca: Universidad de Salamanca, 1999.

Guillén, Claudio. *El primer Siglo de Oro: Estudios sobre géneros y modelos*. Barcelona: Crítica, 1988.

Gwara, Joseph J., and Michael Gerli, eds. *Studies on the Spanish Sentimental Romance (1440–1550): Redefining a Genre*, Collección Támesis: serie A, monografías, no. 168. London: Tamesis, 1997.

Hatzfield, Helmut. *Estudios literarios sobre mística española*, second edition. Madrid: Gredos, 1976.

Hermenegildo, Alfredo. *La tragedia en el Renacimiento español*. Barcelona: Planeta, 1973.

Homza, Lu Ann. *Religious Authority in the Spanish Renaissance*. Baltimore: Johns Hopkins University Press, 2000.

Jones, Roysten. Oscar. *The Golden Age: Prose and Poetry, the Sixteenth and Seventeenth Centuries*. London: Benn / New York: Barnes & Noble, 1971.

Jones, ed. *Studies in Spanish Literature of the Golden Age Presented to Edward M. Wilson*, Collección Támesis: serie A, monografías, no. 30. London: Tamesis, 1973.

Kamen, Henry. *Inquisition and Society in Spain in the Sixteenth and Seventeenth Centuries*. London: Weidenfeld & Nicolson, 1985.

Kamen. *The Iron Century: Social Change in Europe, 1550–1660*. New York: Praeger, 1971.

Kamen. *The Spanish Inquisition: A Historical Revision*. New Haven: Yale University Press, 1998.

Keniston, Hayward. *Francisco de los Cobos: Secretary of the Emperor Charles V*. Pittsburgh: University of Pittsburgh Press, 1960.

King, Margaret T. *Women of the Renaissance*. Chicago: University of Chicago Press, 1991.

Kirkpatrick, F. A. *Los conquistadores españoles*, seventh edition. Buenos Aires: Austral, 1960.

Lapesa, Rafael. *De la Edad Media a nuestros días*. Madrid: Gredos, 1967.

Lapesa. *Historia de la lengua española*, eighth edition. Madrid: Gredos, 1980.

Loftis, John. *Renaissance Drama in England and Spain: Topical Allusion and History Plays.* Princeton: Princeton University Press, 1987.

López Estrada, Francisco, ed. *Siglos de Oro: Renacimiento.* Volume 2 of *Historia y crítica de la literatura española,* edited by Francisco Rico. Barcelona: Crítica, 1980.

López Piñero, José María. *El arte de navegar en la España del Renacimiento.* Barcelona: Labor, 1986.

Lucas, Henry S. *The Renaissance and the Reformation.* New York: Harper, 1934.

Márquez Villanueva, Francisco. *Espiritualidad y literatura en el siglo XVI.* Madrid: Alfaguara, 1968.

Menéndez Pidal, Ramón. *Romancero hispánico,* 2 volumes. Madrid: Espasa-Calpe, 1953.

Moseley, William W., Glenroy Emmons, and Marilyn C. Emmons, eds. *Spanish Literature, 1500–1700: A Bibliography of Golden Age Studies in Spanish and English, 1925–1980.* Westport, Conn.: Greenwood Press, 1984.

Mujica, Barbara. *Iberian Pastoral Characters.* Potomac, Md.: Scripta Humanistica, 1986.

Nader, Helen. *The Mendoza Family in the Spanish Renaissance, 1350–1550.* New Brunswick, N.J.: Rutgers University Press, 1979.

Navarrete, Ignacio. *Orphans of Petrarch: Poetry and Theory in the Spanish Renaissance.* Berkeley: University of California Press, 1994.

Nieto, José C. *El Renacimiento y la otra España: Visión cultural socioespiritual.* Geneva: Droz, 1997.

Noreña, Carlos G. *Studies in Spanish Renaissance Thought.* The Hague: Nijhoff, 1975.

Norton, F. J. *Printing in Spain (1501–1520).* Cambridge: Cambridge University Press, 1968.

Panofsky, Erwin. *Renaissance and Renascences in Western Art.* New York: Harper & Row, 1969.

Parker, Alexander. *The Philosophy of Love in Spanish Literature 1480–1680,* edited by Terence O'Reilly. Edinburgh: Edinburgh University Press, 1985.

Peers, E. A. *The Mystics of Spain.* London: Allen & Unwin, 1951.

Peers. *Studies of the Spanish Mystics,* 3 volumes. New York: Macmillan, 1951–1960.

Perry, Mary Elizabeth, and Anne J. Cruz, eds. *Cultural Encounters: The Impact of the Inquisition in Spain and the New World.* Berkeley: University of California Press, 1991.

Pierce, Frank. *La poesía épica del Siglo de Oro.* Madrid: Gredos, 1968.

Rabil, Albert, Jr., ed. *Renaissance Humanism: Foundations, Forms, and Legacy,* 3 volumes. Philadelphia: University of Pennsylvania Press, 1988.

Rennert, Hugo Albert. *The Spanish Stage in the Time of Lope de Vega.* New York: Dover, 1963.

Rico Verdú, José. *La retórica española de los siglos XVI y XVII.* Madrid: Consejo Superior de Investigaciones Científicas, 1973.

Rivers, Elias L., ed. *Renaissance and Baroque Poetry of Spain.* Prospect Heights, Ill.: Waveland, 1966.

Rodríguez-Moñino, Antonio. *Poesía y cancioneros (siglo XVI).* Madrid: Castalia, 1968.

Rohland de Langbehn, Regula. *La unidad genérica de la novela sentimental española de los siglos XV y XVI,* Papers of the Medieval Hispanic Research Seminar, no. 17. London: Department of Hispanic Studies, Queen Mary and Westfield College, 1999.

Shergold, N. D. *A History of the Spanish Stage from Medieval Times until the End of the Seventeenth Century.* Oxford: Clarendon Press, 1967.

Sicroff, Albert A. *Los estatutos de limpieza de sangre: Controversias entre los siglos XV y XVII,* translated by Mauro Armiño. Madrid: Taurus, 1985.

Sieber, Harry. *The Picaresque*. London: Eyre Methuen, 1977.

Smith, Paul Julian. *Writing in the Margin: Spanish Literature of the Golden Age*. Oxford: Clarendon Press, 1988.

Strosetzki, Christoph, ed. *Actas del V Congreso de la Asociación Internacional Siglo de Oro (Münster 1999)*. Madrid: Iberoamericana / Frankfurt am Main: Vervuet, 2001.

Surtz, Ronald E. *Writing Women in Late Medieval and Early Modern Spain: The Mothers of Saint Teresa of Ávila*. Philadelphia: University of Pennsylvania Press, 1995.

Todorov, Tzvetan. *The Conquest of America: The Question of the Other,* translated by Richard Howard. New York: Harper & Row, 1984.

Wardropper, Bruce W. *Historia de la poesía lírica a lo divino en la cristiandad occidental*. Madrid: Revista de Occidente, 1958.

Wardropper. *Introducción al teatro religioso del Siglo de Oro: Evolución del auto sacramental antes de Calderón*. Salamanca: Anaya, 1967.

Whinnom, Keith. *Medieval and Renaissance Spanish Literature: Selected Essays,* edited by Alan Deyermond, W. F. Hunter, and Joseph T. Snow. Exeter: University of Exeter Press, 1994.

Wilson, Edward M. *Spanish and English Literature of the Sixteenth and Seventeenth Centuries*. Cambridge: Cambridge University Press, 1980.

Wilson and Duncan W. Moir. *The Golden Age: Drama (1492–1700)*. London: Benn / New York: Barnes & Noble, 1971.

Contributors

Pepa Anastasio . . . . *Hofstra University*

Kenneth Atwood . . . . *University of Tennessee, Knoxville*

Mary Elizabeth Baldridge . . . . *Carson-Newman College*

Emilio Blanco . . . . *Universidade da Coruña*

Dana C. Bultman . . . . *University of Georgia*

Luis C. Cano . . . . *University of Tennessee, Knoxville*

Anthony J. Cárdenas-Rotunno . . . .

Federico A. Chalupa . . . . *Bowling Green State University*

Juan Carlos Conde . . . . *Indiana University*

Antonio Cortijo . . . . *University of California, Santa Barbara*

Bryant Creel . . . . *University of Tennessee, Knoxville*

E. Ernesto Delgado . . . . *Bowling Green State University*

J. Ignacio Díez Fernández . . . . *Universidad Complutense (Madrid)*

Denise M. DiPuccio . . . . *University of North Carolina at Wilmington*

Adriano Duque . . . . *University of North Carolina, Chapel Hill*

John Edwards . . . . *University of Oxford*

Jacqueline Ferreras . . . . *Université de Paris X-Nanterre*

J. Michael Fulton . . . . *Wake Forest University*

Millie Gimmel . . . . *University of Tennessee*

Robert A. Gorman . . . . *University of Tennessee*

Louis Imperiale . . . . *University of Missouri–Kansas City*

Elizabeth Franklin Lewis . . . . *Mary Washington College*

Michael J. McGrath . . . . *Georgia Southern University*

Alexander J. McNair . . . . *University of Wisconsin–Parkside*

Claudia Montoya . . . . *Midwestern State University*

Richard Terry Mount . . . . *University of North Carolina at Wilmington*

Benjamin J. Nelson . . . . *University of Chicago*

Moses E. Panford Jr. . . . . *Virginia Polytechnic Institute and State University*

Montserrat Piera . . . . *Temple University*

Roxana Recio . . . . *Creighton University*

Elizabeth Rhodes . . . . *Boston College*

Jesús Rodríguez-Velasco . . . . *University of California, Berkeley*

María Soledad Salazar . . . .

Susan M. Smith . . . . *Hampden-Sydney College*

Marilyn Stone . . . . *New York University*

Matthew G. C. Tornatore . . . . *Truman State University*

Laura Trujillo Mejía . . . . *University of Tennessee*

Julio Vélez-Sainz .... *University of Massachusetts, Amherst*
Eric W. Vogt .... *Seattle Pacific University*
Lisa Vollendorf .... *Wayne State University*
Stanislav Zimic .... *University of Texas at Austin*

Cumulative Index

Dictionary of Literary Biography, Volumes 1-318
Dictionary of Literary Biography Yearbook, 1980-2002
Dictionary of Literary Biography Documentary Series, Volumes 1-19
Concise Dictionary of American Literary Biography, Volumes 1-7
Concise Dictionary of British Literary Biography, Volumes 1-8
Concise Dictionary of World Literary Biography, Volumes 1-4

Cumulative Index

DLB before number: *Dictionary of Literary Biography*, Volumes 1-318
Y before number: *Dictionary of Literary Biography Yearbook*, 1980-2002
DS before number: *Dictionary of Literary Biography Documentary Series*, Volumes 1-19
CDALB before number: *Concise Dictionary of American Literary Biography*, Volumes 1-7
CDBLB before number: *Concise Dictionary of British Literary Biography*, Volumes 1-8
CDWLB before number: *Concise Dictionary of World Literary Biography*, Volumes 1-4

F

K

N

Cumulative Index

ISBN 0-7876-8136-9

90000

9 780787 681364